THE NEW INTERNATIONAL
WEBSTER'S
ENGLISH/SPANISH
DICTIONARY

TRIDENT
PRESS
INTERNATIONAL

Published by
Trident Press International
2002 Edition

ISBN 1582794391

Printed in USA

SPANISH PRONUNCIATION

The Spanish alphabet has twenty-eight letters. Note that ch, ll, and ñ are considered to be separate single letters and are so treated in the alphabetization of Spanish words. While rr is considered to be a distinct sign for a particular sound, it is not included in the alphabet and except in syllabification (notably for the division of words at the end of a line) is not treated as a separate letter, perhaps because words never begin with it.

Letter	Name	Sound
a	a	Like **a** in English **father**, e.g. **casa**, **fácil**.
b	be	When initial or preceded by **m**, like **b** in English **book**, e.g., **boca**, **combate**. When standing between two vowels and when preceded by a vowel and followed by **l** or **r**, like **b** in English **voodoo** except that it is formed with both lips, e.g., **saber**, **hablar**, **sobre**. It is generally silent before **s** plus a consonant and often dropped in spelling, e.g., **oscure** for **obscuro**.
c	ce	When followed by **e** or **i**, like **th** in English **think** in Castilian, and like **c** in English **cent** in American Spanish, e.g., **acento**, **cinco**. When followed by **a**, **o**, **u**, or a consonant, like c in English **come**, e.g., **cantar**, **como**, **cubo**, **acto**, **creer**.
ch	che	Like **ch** in English **much**, e.g., **escuchar**
d	de	Generally, like **d** in English **dog**, e.g., **diente**, **rendir**. When standing between two vowels, when preceded by a vowel and followed by **r**, and when final, like **th** in English **this**, e.g., **miedo**, **piedra**, **libertad**.
e	e	At the end of a syllable, like **a** in English **fate**, but without the glide the English sound sometimes has, e.g., **beso**, **menos**. When followed by a consonant in the same syllable, like **e** in English **met**, e.g., **perla**, **selva**.
f	efe	Like **f** in English **five**, e.g., **flor**, **efecto**.

Letter	Name	Sound
g	ge	When followed by **e** or **i**, like **h** in English home, e.g., **gente**, **giro**. When followed by **a**, **o**, **u**, or a consonant, like **g** in English **go**, e.g., **gato**, **gota**, **agudo**, **grande**.
h	hache	Always silent, e.g., **hombre**, **alcohol**.
i	i	Like **i** in English machine, e.g., **comain**, **ida**. When preceded or followed by another vowel, it has the sound of English **y**, e.g., **tierra**, **reina**.
j	jota	Like **h** in English **home**, e.g., **jardín**, **junto**.
k	ka	Like English **k**, e.g., **kilociclo**.
l	ele	Like **l** in English **laugh**, e.g., **lado**, **ala**.
ll	elle	Somewhat like **lli** in William in Castilian and like **y** in English **yes** in American Spanish, e.g., **silla**, **llamar**.
m	eme	Like **m** in English man, e.g. **mesa**, **amar**.
n	ene	Generally, like **n** in English **name**, e.g., **andar**, **nube**. Before **v**, like **m** in English **man**, e.g., **invierno**, **enviar**. Before **c** (k) and **g** (g), like **n** in English **drink**, e.g., **finca**, **manga**.
ñ	eñe	Somewhat like **ni** in English **onion**, e.g., **año**, **enseñar**.
o	o	At the end of a syllable, like **o** in English **note**, but without the glide the English sound sometimes has, e.g., **boca**, **como**. When followed by a consonant in the same syllable, like **o** in English **organ**, e.g., **poste**, **norte**.
p	pe	Like **p** in English **pen**, e.g., **poco**, **aplicar**. It is often silent in **septiembre** and **séptimo**.
q	cu	Like **c** in English **come**. It is always followed by **ue** or **ui**, in which the **u** is silent, e.g., **querer**, **quitar**. The sound of English **qu** is represented in Spanish by **cu**, e.g., **frecuente**.

Letter	Name	Sound
r	ere	Strongly trilled when initial and when preceded by **l**, **n**, or **s**, e.g., **rico**, **alrededor**, **honra**, **israelí**. Pronounced with a single tap of the tongue in all other positions, e.g., **caro**, **grande**, **amar**.
rr	erre	Strongly trilled, e.g., **carro**, **tierra**.
s	ese	Generally, like **s** in English **say**, e.g., **servir**, **casa**, **este**. Before a voiced consonant (**b**, **d**, **g** (g), **l**, **r**, **m**, **n**), like **z** in English **zero**, e.g., **esbelto**, **desde**, **rasgar**, **eslabón**, **mismo**, **asno**.
t	te	Like **t** in English **stamp**, e.g., **tiempo**, **matar**.
u	u	Like **u** in English **rude**, e.g., **mudo**, **puño**. It is silent in **gue**, **gui**, **que**, and **qui**, but not in **güe**, and **güi**, e.g., **guerra**, **guisa**, **querer**, **quitar**, but **agüero**, **lingüístico**. When preceded or followed by another vowel, it has the sound of English **w**, e.g., **fuego**, **dcuda**.
v	ve *or* uve	Like Spanish in all positions, e.g., **vengo**, **invierno**, **uva**, **huevo**.
x	equis	When followed by a consonant, like **s** in English **say**, e.g, **expresar**, **sexto**. Between two vowels, pronounced like **gs**, e.g., **examen**, **existencia**, **exótico**; and in some words, like **s** in **say**, e.g., **auxilio**, **exacto**. In **México** (for **Méjico**), like Spanish **j**.
y	ye *or* i griega	In the conjunction **y**, like **i** in English **machine**. When standing next to a vowel or between two vowels, like **y** in English **yes**, e.g., **yo**, **hoy**, **vaya**.
z	zeda *or* zeta	Like **th** in English **think** in Castilian and like **c** in English **cent** in American Spanish, e.g., **zapato**, **zona**.

Diphthong	Sound
ai, ay	Like **i** in English **might**, e.g., **baile**, **hay**
au	Like **ou** in English **pound**, e.g., **causa**
ei, ey	Like **ey** in English **they**, e.g., **reina**, **ley**
eu	Like **ayw** in English **hayward**, e.g., **deuda**
oi, oy	Like **oy** in English **boy**, e.g., **estoy**

SPANISH GRAMMAR

Stress, Punctuation, Capitalization

All Spanish words, except compound words and adverbs ending in **mente**, have only one stress. The position of this stress is always shown by the spelling in accordance with the following rules:

(a) Words ending in a vowel sound or in **n** or **s** are stressed on the syllable next to the last, e.g., **ca´sa**, **a´gua**, **se´rio**, **ha´blan**, **co´sas**.

(b) Words ending in a consonant except **n** or **s** are stressed on the last syllable, e.g., **se-ñor´**, **pa-pel´**, **fe-liz´**, **U-ra-guay´**, **es-toy´**.

(c) If the stress does not fall in accordance with either of the above rules, it is indicated by an acute accent placed above the stressed vowel, e.g., **ca-fé**, **a-pren-dí**, **na-ción**, **lá-piz**, **fá-cil**, **re-pú-bli-ca**. The acute accent is also used to distinguish between words spelled alike but having different meanings or parts of speech, e.g. **aun** (even) and **aún** (still, yet), **donde** (conj.) and **dónde** (adv.), **el** (def. art.) and **él** (pron.).

Question marks and exclamation points are placed both before and after a word or sentence, and the first is inverted, e.g. **¿Que tal?** (How's everything?), **¡Que lástima!** (What a pity!).

Capital letters are used less in Spanish than in English, e.g., **un inglés** (an Englishman), **el idioma español** (the Spanish language), **domingo** (Sunday), **enero** (January).

Gender of Nouns

A noun is either masculine or feminine. With few exceptions, nouns ending in **o** are masculine, e.g., **el libro** (the book); and nouns ending in **a**, **d**, and **ez** are feminine, e.g., **la ventana** (the window), **la ciudad** (the town), **la nuez** (the nut). There are no definitive rules for nouns that end in letters other than **o**, **a**, **d**, or **ez**.

iv

Plural of Nouns

The plural of a noun is formed by adding **s** to those ending in an unstressed vowel or a stressed **é**; and **es** to those ending in a consonant. Nouns that end in **es** or representing a family name remain unchanged from the singular.

Definite Articles

The definite article corresponds to the gender of the noun it specifies.

The singulars of the definite article are **el** (masculine) and **la** (feminine). Plurals are **los** (masculine) and **las** (feminine).

The definite article is omitted before nouns in apposition, e.g., **Madrid, capital de España** (Madrid, the capital of Spain), and in the numbered names of rulers and popes, e.g., **Luis catorce** (Louis the Fourteenth).

Indefinite Articles

The singulars of the indefinite article are **un** (masculine) and **una** (feminine); the plurals are **unos** (masculine) and **unas** (feminine), e.g. **un mes** (a month), **unos meses** (some months); **una calle** (a street), **unas calles** (some streets).

The form **un** is also commonly used before feminine singular nouns beginning with a stressed **a** or **ha**, e.g., **un arma** (a weapon).

The plural forms **unos** and **unas** when followed by a cardinal number, mean *about*, e.g., **unos cinco años** (about five years).

The indefinite article is not used before a noun of nationality, religion, occupation, and the like, e.g., **Mi amigo es abogado** (My friend is a lawyer). If the noun is modified, the indefinite article is generally used, e.g., **Mi hermano es un abogado excelente** (My brother is an excellent lawyer). The indefinite article is omitted before **otro**, which therefore means both *other* and *another*, e.g., **Quiero otro libro** (I want another book).

Gender of Adjectives

Adjectives agree in gender and number with the noun they modify.

Adjectives ending in **o** become feminine by changing **o** to **a**, e.g., **alto** and **alta** (high). Adjectives ending in any other letter have the same form in the masculine and the feminine, e.g., **constante** (constant), **fácil** (easy), **belga** (Belgian), except adjectives of nationality ending in **l**, **s**, or **z** and adjectives ending in **or**, **án** and **ón**, which add **a** to form the feminine, e.g.,

v

español and **española** (Spanish), **inglés** and **inglesa** (English), **conservador** and **conservadora** (preservative), **barrigón** and **barrigona** (big–bellied).

Comparatives ending in **or** have the same form in the masculine and the feminine, e.g., **mejor** (better), **superior** (upper, superior).

Plural of Adjectives

Adjectives ending in a vowel form their plurals by adding **s**, e.g., **alto** and **altos**, **alta** and **altas** (high), **constante** and **constantes** (constant).

Adjective ending in a consonant form their plurals by adding **es**, e.g., **fácil** and **fáciles** (easy), **barrigón** and **barrigones** (big–bellied). Those ending in **z** change the **z** to **c** and add **es**, e.g., **feliz** and **felices** (happy).

The acute accent found on the last syllable of the masculine singular of some adjectives ending in **n** and **s** is omitted in the feminine singular and in the plural, e.g., **inglés** and **inglesa**, *pl.* **ingleses** (English).

Position of Adjectives

Adjectives generally follow the nouns they modify, e.g., **vino italiano** (Italian wine). However, they precede the noun they modify when used in a figurative, derived or unemphatic sense, e.g., **pobre hombre** (poor or pitiable man), but **un hombre pobre** (a poor man), **cierta ciudad** (a certain city), but **cosa cierta** (sure thing).

Shortening of Adjectives

When **bueno** (good), **malo** (bad), **primero** (first), **tercero** (third), **alguno** (some, any), and **ninguno** (none, no) are used before a masculine singular noun, they drop their final **o**, e.g., **buen libro** (good book), **mal olor** (bad odor), **primer capítulo** (first chapter), **algun muchacho** (some boy), **ningun soldado** (no soldier).

When **grande** (large, great) is used before a masculine or feminine singular noun, it drops **de**, e.g., **gran nación** (great nation). If the noun begins with a vowel or **h**, either **gran** or **grande** may be used, e.g., **grande amigo** or **gran amigo** (great friend).

Ciento (hundred) drops **to** before a noun, e.g., **cien años** (a hundred years), **cien dólares** (a hundred dollars).

The masculine **santo** (saint) becomes **san** before all names of saints except **Domingo** and **Tomás**, e.g., **San Francisco** (Saint Francis). Before common nouns it is not shortened, e.g., **el santo papa** (the Holy Father).

Formation of Adverbs

Adverbs are formed from adjectives by adding **mente** to the feminine form, e.g., **perfecto** (perfect), **perfectamente** (perfectly); **fácil** (easy), **fácilmente** (easily); **constante** (constant), **constantemente** (constantly). With two or more such adverbs in a series, **mente** is added only to the last one, e.g., **Escribe clara y correctamente** (He writes clearly and correctly).

Comparison of Adverbs

As with adjectives, the comparative and superlative of an adverb is formed by placing **más** (more) or **menos** (less) before the adverb, e.g., **despacio** (slowly), **más despacio** (more slowly).

The following adverbs have irregular comparatives and superlatives:

Positive	Comparative and Superlative
bien (well)	**mejor** (better, best)
mal (bad, badly)	**peor** (worse, worst)
mucho (much)	**más** (more, most)
poco (little)	**menos** (less, least)

Subject Pronouns

	Singular	Plural
1st person	**yo** (I)	**nosotros, nosotras** (we)
2nd person (familiar)	**tu** (thou, you)	**vosotros, vosotras** (you)
2nd person (formal)	**usted** (you)	**ustedes** (you)
3rd person masculine	**él** (he, it)	**ellos** (they)
3rd person feminine	**ella** (she, it)	**ellas** (they)
3rd person neuter	**ello** (it)	

With the exception of **usted** and **ustedes**, which are regularly expressed, these pronouns are used only for emphasis, for contrast, or to avoid ambiguity, and when no verb is expressed, e.g., **Yo trabajo mucho** (*I* work hard), **Él es aplicado pero ella es perezosa** (He is diligent, but she is lazy), **¿Quién llama? Yo** (Who is calling? I or me).

When the 3rd person subject is not a person, it is rarely expressed by a pronoun, e.g., **es larga** ((it) is long) and it is never expressed with impersonal verbs, e.g., **llueve** ((it is) raining).

The adjective **mismo**, *fem.* **misma** (self) is used with the subject pronouns to form the intensive subject pronoun, e.g., **yo mismo**, **yo misma** (I myself); **tú** (or **usted**) **mismo**, **tú** (or **usted**) **misma** (you yourself); **él mismo** (he himself), **ella misma** (she herself), **nosotros mismos**, **nosotros mismas** (we ourselves), **vosotros mismos**, **vosotros mismas** (you yourselves), **ellos mismos**, *fem.* **ellas mismas** (they themselves), **ustedes mismos**, **ustedes mismas** (you yourselves).

Prepositional Pronouns

	Singular	Plural
1st person	**mí** (me)	**nosotros, nosotras** (us)
2nd person (familiar)	**ti** (thee, you)	**vosotros, vosotras** (you)
2nd person (formal)	**usted** (you)	**ustedes** (you)
3rd person masculine	**él** (him, it)	**ellos** (them)
3rd person feminine	**ella** (her, it)	**ellas** (them)
3rd person neuter	**ello** (it)	
3rd person reflexive	**sí** (himself, herself, itself)	**sí** (themselves, yourselves, yourself)

These pronouns are used as objects of prepositions, e.g., **Compró un libro para mi** (He bought a book for me), **Compró un libro para sí** (He bought a book for himself), **Vd. compró un libro para sí** (You bought a book for yourself).

Relative Pronouns

The form **que**, meaning *that, which, who, whom,* is the most frequent relative pronoun and is invariable. It is used as both subject and object of the verb and refers to persons and things. For example, **El hombre que me conoce**... (The man *who* knows me...), **El hombre que conozco**... (The man *whom* I know...), **El libro que lee**... (The book *that* he is reading...), **El trabajo a que dedico mi tiempo**... (The work to *which* I devote my time...).

The form **quien**, *pl.* **quenes** (who, whom) is inflected for number, refers only to persons, and takes the personal **a** as direct object, e.g. **El amigo con quien viajé por España**... (The friend with *whom* I traveled in Spain...), **La señora a quien ví en la estación**... (The lady *whom* I saw at the station), **Los señores para quienes he traido estos libros**... (The gentlemen for *whom* I brought these books...).

The forms **el que** (*fem.* **la que**, *pl.* **los que, las que**) and **el cual** (*fem.* **la cual**, *pl.* **los cuales, las cuales**), both meaning *who, which, that,* agree in gender and number with their antecedent and are therefore used to replace **que** where the reference might be ambiguous, e.g., **El hijo de aquella señora, el cual vive en Nueva York**... (the son of that lady who (i.e., the son) lives in New York).

The forms **lo que** and **lo cual**, both meaning *what, which,* are invariable and refer to a previous statement, e.g., **No entiendo lo que él dice** (I don't understand what he is saying), **Llegó a medianoche, lo que indicaba que habia trabajado mucho** (He arrived at midnight, which indicated that he had worked hard.

The form **cuanto** (*fem.* **cuanta**, *pl.* **cuantos**, **cuantas**) contains its own antecedent and it means *all that which, all those which, all those who* or *whom, as much as, as many as.* For example, **Eso es cuanto quiero decir** (This is all that I want to say), **Dijo algo a cuantas personas se hallaban alli** (He said something to all the people who were there).

Regular Verbs

Spanish verbs are classified into three conjugations: those ending in **ar**, those ending in **er**, and those ending in **ir**, e.g., **hablar, comer, vivir**

First Conjugation	Second Conjugation	Third Conjugation
	Infinitive:	
hablar to speak	**comer** to eat	**vivir** to live
	Gerund:	
hablando speaking	**comiendo** eating	**viviendo** living
	Past Participle:	
hablado spoken	**comido** eaten	**vivido** lived
	Indicative:	
Present:		
hablo I speak	**como** I eat	**vivo** I live
hablas	**comes**	**vives**
habla	**come**	**vive**
hablamos	**comemos**	**vivimos**
habláis	**coméis**	**vivís**
hablan	**comen**	**viven**

First Conjugation	Second Conjugation	Third Conjugation
Imperfect:		
hablaba I was speaking	**comía** I was eating	**vivía** I was living
hablabas	**comías**	**vivías**
hablaba	**comía**	**vivía**
hablábamos	**comíamos**	**vivíamos**
hablabals	**comíais**	**vivíais**
hablaban	**comian**	**vivían**
Preterit:		
hablé I spoke	**comí** I ate	**viví** I lived
hablaste	**comiste**	**viviste**
habló	**comió**	**vivió**
hablamos	**comimos**	**vivimos**
hablasteis	**comisteis**	**vivisteis**
hablaron	**comieron**	**vivieron**
Future:		
hablaré I shall speak	**comeré** I shall eat	**viviré** I shall live
hablarás	**comerás**	**vivirás**
hablará	**comerá**	**vivirá**
hablaremos	**comeremos**	**viviremos**
hablaréis	**comeréis**	**viviréis**
hablarán	**comerán**	**vivirán**
Conditional:		
hablaría I should speak	**comería** I should eat	**viviría** I should live
hablarías	**comerías**	**vivirías**
hablaría	**comería**	**viviría**
hablaríamos	**comeríamos**	**viviríamos**
hablaríais	**comeríais**	**viviríais**
hablarían	**comerían**	**vivirían**

Irregular Verbs

All simple tenses are shown in these tables if they contain one irregular form or more, except the conditional, and the imperfect and future subjunctive.

The letters (a) to (h) identify the tenses as follows:

(a) gerund	(e) present subjunctive
(b) past participle	(f) imperfect indicative
(c) imperative	(g) future indicative
(d) present indicative	(h) preterit indicative

abolir: defective verb used only in forms whose endings contain the vowel **i**.

acertar
- (c) **acierta**, acertad
- (d) **acierto**, **aciertas**, **acierta**, acertamos, acertáis, **aciertan**
- (e) **acierte**, **aciertes**, **acierte**, acertemos, acertéis, **acierten**

agorar
- (c) **agüera**, agorad
- (d) **agüero**, **agüeras**, **agüera**, agoramos, agoráis, **agüeran**
- (e) **agüere**, **agüeres**, **agüere**, agoremos, agoréis, **agüeren**

airar
- (c) **aíra**, airad
- (d) **aíro**, **aíras**, **aíra**, airamos, airáis, **aíran**
- (e) **aíre**, **aíres**, **aíre**, airemos, airéis, **aíren**

andar
- (h) **anduve, anduviste, anduvo, anduvimos, anduvisteis, anduvieron**

argüir
- (a) **arguyendo**
- (b) **argüido**
- (c) **arguye**, argüid
- (d) **arguyo**, **arguyes**, **arguye**, argüimos, argüis, **arguyen**
- (e) **arguya**, **arguyas**, **arguya**, arguyamos, arguyáis, **arguyan**
- (h) **argüí**, **argüiste**, **arguyó**, argüimos, argüisteis, **arguyeron**

asir
- (d) **asgo**, ases, ase, asimos, asis, asen
- (e) **asga**, **asgas**, **asga**, **asgamos**, **asgáis**, **asgan**

aunar
- (c) **aúna**, aunad
- (d) **aúno**, **aúnas**, aunamos, aunáis, **aúnan**
- (e) **aúne**, **aúnes**, aunemos, aunéis, **aúnen**

avongonzar
- (c) **avergüenza**, avergonzad
- (d) **avergüenzo, avergüenzas, avergüenza**, avergonzamos, avergonzáis, **avergüenzan**
- (e) **avergüence, avergüences, avergüence, avergoncemos, avergoncéis, avergüencen**
- (h) **avergonce**, avergonzaste, avergonzó, avergonzamos, avergonzasteis, avergonzaron

averiguar
- (e) **averigüe, averigües, averigüe, averigüeis, averigüen**
- (h) **averigüé**, averiguaste, averiguó, averiguamos, averiguasteis, averiguaron

bendecir
- (a) **bendiciendo**
- (c) **bendice**, bendecid
- (d) **bendigo, bendices, bendice**, bendecimos, bendecís, **bendicen**
- (e) **bendiga, bendigas, bendiga, bendigamos**, bendígáis, **bendigan**
- (h) **bendije, bendijiste, bendijo, bendijimos, bendijisteis, bendijeron**

bruñir
- (a) **bruñendo**
- (h) **bruñí, bruñiste, bruñó**, bruñimos, bruñisteis, **bruñeron**

bullir
- (a) **bullendo**
- (h) **bullí, bulliste, bulló**, bullimos, bullisteis, **bulleron**

caber
- (d) **quepo**, cabes, cabe, cabemos, cabéis, caben
- (e) **quepa, quepas, quepa, quepamos, quepáis, quepan**
- (g) **cabré, cabrás, cabrá, cabremos, cabréis, cabrán**
- (h) **cupe, cupiste, cupo, cupimos, cupisteis, cupieron**

caer
- (a) **cayendo**
- (b) **caido**
- (d) **caigo**, caes, cae, caemos, caéis, caen
- (e) **caiga, caigas, caiga, caigamos, caigáis, caigan**
- (h) caí, **caíste, cayó, caímos, caísteis, cayeron**

cocer
- (c) **cuece**, coced
- (d) **cuezo, cueces, cuece**, cocemos, cocéis, **cuecen**
- (e) **cueza, cuezas, cueza, cozamos, cozáis, cuezan**

coger
- (d) **cojo**, coges, coge, cogemos, cogéis, cogen
- (e) **coja, cojas, coja, cojamos, cojáis, cojan**

comenzar
- (c) **comienza**, comenzad
- (d) **comienzo, comienzas, comienza**, comenzamos, comenzáis, **comienzan**
- (e) **comience, comiences, comience, comencemos, comencéis, comiencen**
- (h) **comencé**, comenzaste, comenzó, comenzamos, comenzasteis, comenzaron

conducir
- (d) **conduzco**, conduces, conduce, conducimos, conducis, conducen
- (e) **conduzca, conduzcas, conduzca, conduzcamos, conduzcáis, conduzcan**
- (h) **conduje, condujiste, condujo, condujimos, condujisteis, condujeron**

construir
- (a) **construyendo**
- (b) **construído**
- (c) **construye**, construid
- (d) **construyo, construyes, construye**, construimos, construis, **construyen**
- (e) **construya, construyas, construya, construyamos, construyáis, construyan**
- (h) construi, construiste, **construyó**, construimos, construisteis, **construyeron**

continuar
- (c) **continúa**, continuad
- (d) **continúo, continúas, continúa**, continuamos, continuáis, **continúan**
- (e) **continúe, continúes, continúe**, continuemos, continuéis, **continúen**

crecer
- (d) **crezco**, creces, crece, crecemos, crecéis, crecen
- (e) **crezca, crezcas, crezca, crezcamos, crezcáis, crezcan**

dar
- (d) **doy**, das, da, damos, dais, dan
- (e) **dé**, des, **dé**, demos, deis, den
- (h) **dí, diste, dio, dimos, disteis, dieron**

decir
(a) **diciendo**
(b) **dicho**
(c) **di**, decid
(d) **digo, dices, dice,** decimos, decís, **dicen**
(e) **diga, digas, diga, digamos, digáis, digan**
(g) **diré, dirás, dirá, diremos, diréis, dirán**
(h) **dije, dijiste,dijo, dijimos, dijisteis, dijeron**

delinquir
(d) **delinco,** delinques, delinque, delinquimos, delinquis,
    delinquen
(e) **delinca, delincas, delinca, delincamos, delincáis,**
    delincan

desosar
(c) **deshuesa,** desosad
(d) **deshueso, deshuesas, deshuesa,** desosamos, desosáis,
    deshuesan
(e) **deshuese, deshueses, deshuese,** desosemos, desoséis,
    deshuesen

dirigir
(d) **dirijo,** diriges, dirige, dirigimos, dirigis, dirigen
(e) **dirija, dirijas, dirija, dirijamos, dirijáis, dirijan**

discernir
(c) **discierne,** discernid
(d) **discierno, disciernes, discierne,** discernimos, discernís,
    disciernen
(e) **discierna, disciernas, discierna, discernamos,**
    discernáis, distingan

distinguir
(d) **distingo,** distingues, distingue, distinguimos, distinguis,
    distinguen
(e) **distinga, distingas, distinga, distingamos, distingáis,**
    distingan

dormir
(a) **durmiendo**
(c) **duerme,** dormid
(d) **duermo, duermes, duerme,** dormimos, dormis, **duermen**
(e) **duerma, duermas, duerma, durmamos, durmáis,**
    duerman
(h) dormi, dormiste, **durmió,** dormimos, dormisteis,
durmieron

empeller
- (a) **empellendo**
- (h) empellí, empelliste, **empelló**, empellimos, empellisteis, **empelleron**

enraizar
- (c) **enraíza**, enraizad
- (d) **enraízo, enraízas, enraíza**, enraizamos, enraizáis, **enraízan**
- (e) **enraíce, enraíces, enraíce, enraicemos, enraicéis, enraícen**
- (h) **enraicé**, enraizaste, enraizó, enraizamos, enraizasteis, enraizaron

erguir
- (a) **irguiendo**
- (c) **irgue** or **yergue**, erguid
- (d) **irgo, irgues, irgue, yergo, hergues, yergue** } erguimos, erguis { **irguen yerguen**
- (e) **irga, irgas, irga, yerga, yergas, yerga,** } **erguimos, erguis** { **irgan yergan**
- (h) erguí, erguiste, **irguió**, erguimos, erguisteis, **irguieron**

errar
- (c) **yerra**, errad
- (d) **yerro, yerras, yerra**, erramos, erráis, **yerran**
- (e) **yerre, yerres, yerre**, erremos, erréis, **yerren**

esforzar
- (c) **esfuerza**, esforzad
- (d) **esfuerzo, esfuerzas, esfuerza**, esforzamos, esforzáis, **esfuerzan**
- (e) **esfuerce, esfuerces, esfuerce, esforcemos, esforcéis, esfuercen**
- (h) **esforcé**, esforzaste, esforzó, esforzamos, esforzasteis, esforzaron

esparcir
- (d) **esparzo**, esparces, esparce, esparcimos, esparcís, esparcen
- (e) **esparza, esparzas, esparza, esparzamos, esparzáis, esparzan**

estar
- (c) **está**, estad
- (d) **estoy, estás, está**, estamos, estáis, **están**
- (e) **esté, estés, esté**, estemos, estéis, **estén**
- (h) **estuve, estuviste, estuvo, estuvimos, estuvisteis, estuvieron**

haber
  (c) **hé,** habed
  (d) **he, has, ha, hemos,** habéis, **han** (v. impers.), **hay**
  (e) **haya, hayas, haya, hayamos, hayáis, hayan**
  (g) **habré, habrás, habrá, habremos, habréis, habrán**
  (h) **hube, hubiste, hubo, hubimos, hubisteis, hubieron**
hacer
  (b) **hecho**
  (c) **haz,** haced
  (d) **hago,** haces, hace, hacemos, hacéis, hacen
  (e) **haga, hagas, haga, hagamos, hagáis, hagan**
  (g) **haré, harás, hará, haremos, haréis, harán**
  (h) **hice, hiciste, hizo, hicimos, hicisteis, hicieron**
inquirir
  (c) **inquiere,** inquirid
  (d) **inquiero, inquieres, inquiere,** inquirimos, inquiris,
      inquieren
  (e) **inquiera, inquieras, inquiera,** inquiramos, inquiráis,
      inquieran
ir
  (a) **yendo**
  (c) **vé, vamos,** id
  (d) **voy, vas, va, vamos, vais, van**
  (e) **vaya, vayas, vaya, vayamos, vayáis, vayan**
  (f) **iba, ibas, iba, íbamos, ibais, iban**
  (h) **fui, fuiste, fue, fuimos, fuisteis, fueron**
jugar
  (c) **juega,** jugad
  (d) **juego, juegas, juega,** jugamos, jugáis **juegan**
  (e) **juegue, juegues, juegue, juguemos, juguéis, jueguen**
  (h) **jugué,** jugaste, jugó, jugamos, jugasteis, jugaron
leer
  (a) **leyendo**
  (b) **leído**
  (h) lei, **leíste, layó,** leímos, **leísteis, leyeron**
ligar
  (e) **ligue, ligues, ligue, liguemos, liguéis, liguen**
  (h) **ligué,** ligaste, ligó, ligamos, ligasteis, ligaron
lucir
  (d) **luzco,** luces, luce, lucimos, lucís, lucen
  (e) **luzca, luzcas, luzca, luzcamos, luzcáis, luzcan**

mecer
(d) **mezo**, meces, mece, mecemos, mecéis, mecen
(e) **meza, mezas, meza, mezamos, mezáix, mezan**

mover
(c) **mueve**, moved
(d) **muevo, mueves, mueve**, movemos, movéis, **mueven**
(e) **mueva, muevas, mueva**, movamos, mováis, **muevan**

oir
(a) **oyendo**
(b) **oído**
(c) **oye, oíd**
(d) **oigo, oyes, oye, oímos**, oís, **oyen**
(e) **oiga, oigas, oiga, oigamos, oigáis, oigan**
(h) oí, **oíste, oyó, oímos, oísteis, oyeron**

oler
(c) **huele**, oled
(d) **huelo, hueles, huele**, olemos, oléis, **huelen**
(e) **huela, huelas, huela**, olamos, oláis, **huelan**

pedir
(a) **pidiendo**
(c) **pide**, pedid
(d) **pido, pides, pide**, pedimos, pedís, **piden**
(e) **pida, pidas, pida, pidamos, pidáis, pidan**
(h) pedí, pediste, **pidió**, pedimos, pedisteis, **pedeiron**

perder
(c) **pierde**, perded
(d) **pierdo, pierdes, pierde**, perdemos, perdéis, **pierden**
(e) **pierda, pierdas, pierda**, perdamos, perdáis, **pierdan**

placer
(d) **plazco**, places, place, placemos, placeis, placen
(e) **plazca, plazcas, plazca, plazcamos, plazcáis, plazcan**
(h) plací, placiste, plació (or **plugo**), placimos, placisteis,
placieron

poder
(a) **pudiendo**
(c) (**puede**, poded)
(d) **puedo, puedes, puede**, podemos, podéis, **pueden**
(e) **pueda, puedas, pueda**, podamos, podáis, **puedan**
(g) **podré, podrás, podrá, podremos, podréis, podrán**
(h) **pude, pudiste, pudo, pudimos, pudisteis, pudieron**

poner
- (b) **puesto**
- (c) **pon**, poned
- (d) **pongo**, pones, pone, ponemos, ponéis, ponen
- (e) **ponga, pongas, ponga, pongamos, pongáis, pongan**
- (g) **pondré, pondrás, pondrá, pondremos, pondréis, pondrán**
- (h) **puse, pusiste, puso, pusimos, pusisteis, pusieron**

querer
- (c) **quiere**, quered
- (d) **quiero, quieres, quiere**, queremos, queréis, **quieren**
- (e) **quiera, quieras, quiera**, queramos, queráis, **quieran**
- (g) **querré, querrás, querrá, querremos, querréis, querrán**
- (h) **quise, quisiste, quiso, quisimos, quisisteis, quisieron**

raer
- (a) **rayendo**
- (b) **raído**
- (d) **raigo** (or **rayo**), raes, rae, raemos, raéis, raen
- (e) **raiga** (or **raya**), **raigas, raiga, raigamos, raigáis, raigan**
- (h) **raí, raíste, rayó, raímos, raísteis, rayeron**

regir
- (a) **rigiendo**
- (c) **rige**, regid
- (d) **rijo, riges, rige**, regimos, regís, **rigen**
- (e) **rija, rijas, rija, rijamos, rijáis, rijan**
- (h) regí, registe, **regió**, regimos, registeis, **rigieron**

reír
- (a) **riendo**
- (b) **reído**
- (c) **ríe, reíd**
- (d) **río, ríes, ríe, reímos**, reis, **ríen**
- (e) **ría, rías, ría, ríamos, riáis, rían**
- (h) reí, **reíste, rió, reímos, reísteis, rieron**

reunir
- (c) **reúne**, reunid
- (d) **reúno, reúnes, reúne**, reunimos, reunís, **reúnen**
- (e) **reúna, reúnas, reúna**, reunamos, reunáis, **reúnan**

rezar
- (e) **rece, reces, rece, recemos, recéis, recen**
- (h) **recé**, rezaste, rezó, rezamos, rezasteis, rezaron

rodar
- (c) **rueda**, rodad
- (d) **ruedo, ruedas, rueda**, rodamos, rodáis, **ruedan**
- (e) **ruede, ruedes, ruede**, rodemos, rodéis, **rueden**

roer
- (a) **royendo**
- (b) **roído**
- (d) **roo** (**roigo**, or **royo**), roes, roe, roemos, roéis, roen
- (e) **roa** (**roiga**, or **roya**), roas, roa, roamos, roáis, roan
- (h) roí, **roíste, royó, roímos, roísteis, royeron**

rogar
- (c) **ruega**, rogad
- (d) **ruego, ruegas, ruega**, rogamos, rogáis, **ruegan**
- (e) **ruegue, ruegues, ruegue, roguemos, roguéis, rueguen**
- (h) **rogué**, rogaste, rogó, rogamos, rogasteis, rogaron

saber
- (d) **sé**, sabes, sabe, sabemos, sabéis, saben
- (e) **sepa, sepas, sepa, sepamos, sepáis, sepan**
- (g) **sabré, sabrás, sabrá, sabremos, sabréis, sabrán**
- (h) **supe, supiste, supo, supimos, supisteis, supieron**

salir
- (c) **sal**, salid
- (d) **salgo**, sales, sale, salimos, salís, salen
- (e) **salga, salgas, salga, salgamos, salgáis, salgan**
- (g) **saldré, saldrás, saldrá, saldremos, saldréis, saldrán**

segar
- (c) **siega**, segad
- (d) **siego, siegas, siega**, segamos, segáis, **siegan**
- (e) **siegue, siegues, siegue, seguemos, seguéis, sieguen**
- (h) **segué**, segaste, segó, segamos, segasteis, segaron

seguir
- (a) **siguiendo**
- (c) **sigue**, seguid
- (d) **sigo, siegues, sigue**, seguimos, seguís, **siguen**
- (e) **siga, sigas, siga, sigamos, sigáis, sigan**
- (h) seguí, seguiste, **siguió**, seguimos, seguisteis, **siguieron**

sentir
- (a) **sintiendo**
- (c) **siente**, sentid
- (d) **siento, sientes, siente**, sentimos, sentís, **sienten**
- (e) **sienta, sientas, sienta**, sentamos, sentáis, **sientan**
- (h) sentí, sentiste, **sintió**, sentimos, sentisteis, **sintieron**

ser
    (c) **sé**, sed
    (d) **soy, eres, es, somos, sois, son**
    (e) **sea, seas, sea, seamos, seáis, sean**
    (f) **era, eras, era, éramos, erais, eran**
    (h) **fui, fuiste, fue, fuimos, fuisteis, fueron**

tañer
    (a) **tañendo**
    (h) tañí, tañiste, **tañó**, tañimos, tañisteis, **tañeron**

tener
    (c) **ten**, tened
    (d) **tengo, tienes, tiene**, tenemos, tenéis, **tienen**
    (e) **tenga, tengas, tenga, tengamos, tengáis, tengan**
    (g) **tendré, tendrás, tendrá, tendremos, tendréis, tendrán**
    (h) **tuve, tuviste, tuvo, tuvimos, tuvisteis, tuvieron**

teñir
    (a) **tiñendo**
    (c) **tiñe**, teñid
    (d) **tiño, tiñes, tiñe**, teñimos, teñis, **tiñen**
    (e) **tiña, tiñas, tiña, tiñamos, tiñáis, tiñan**
    (h) teñi, teñiste, **tiñó**, teñimos, teñisteis, **tiñeron**

tocar
    (e) **toque, toques, toque, toquemos, toquéis, toquen**
    (h) **toqué**, tocaste, tocó, tocamos, tocasteis, tocaron

torcer
    (c) **tuerce**, torced
    (d) **tuerzo, tuerces, tuerce**, torcemos, torcéis, **tuercen**
    (e) **tuerza, tuerzas, tuerza, torzamos, torzáis, tuerzan**

traer
    (a) **trayendo**
    (b) **traído**
    (d) **traigo**, traes, trae, traemos, traéis, traen
    (e) **traiga, traigas, traiga, traigamos, traigáis, traigan**
    (h) **traje, trajiste, trajo, trajimos, trajisteis, trajeron**

valer
    (d) **valgo**, vales, vale, valemos, valéis, valen
    (e) **valga, valgas, valga, valgamos, valgáis, valgan**
    (g) **valdré, valdrás, valdrá, valdremos, valdréis, valdrán**

variar
    (c) **varía**, variad
    (d) **varío, varías, varía**, variamos, variáis, **varían**
    (e) **varíe, varíes, varíe**, variemos, variéis, **varíen**

vencer
  (d) **venzo**, vences, vence, vencemos, vencéis, vencen
  (e) **venza, venzas, venza, venzamos, venzáis, venzan**
venir
  (a) **viniendo**
  (c) **ven**, venid
  (d) **vengo, vienes, viene**, venimos, venís, **vienen**
  (e) **venga, vengas, venga, vengamos, vengáis, vengan**
  (g) **vendré, vendrás, vendrá, vendremos, vendréis, vendrán**
  (h) **vine, viniste, vino, vinimos, vinisteis, vinieron**
ver
  (b) **visto**
  (d) **veo**, ves, ve, vemos, veis, ven
  (e) **vea, veas, vea, veamos, veáis, vean**
  (f) **veía, veías, veía, veíamos, veíais, veían**
volcar
  (c) **vuelca**, volcad
  (d) **vuelco, vuelcas, vuelca**, volcamos, volcáis, **vuelcan**
  (e) **vuelque, vuelques, vuelque, volquemos, volquéis, vuelquen**
  (h) **volqué**, volcaste, volcó, volcamos, volcasteis, volcaron
yacer
  (c) **yaz** (or yace), yaced
  (d) **yazco (yazgo**, or **yago**), yaces, yace, yacemos, yacéis, yacen
  (e) **yazca (yazga**, or **yaga**), **yazcas, yazca, yazcamos, yazcáis, yazcan**

The following verbs, some of which are included in the foregoing table, and their compounds have irregular past participles:

abrir	cubierto	proveer	puesto
cubrir	dicho	pudrir	provisto
decir	escrito	romper	podrido
escribir	frito	solver	roto
freír	hecho	ver	suelto
hacer	impreso	volver	visto
imprimir	morir	muerto	vuelto
abierto	poner		

xxi

Notes

A

a, *prep.* to, at
abadía, *f.* abbey; abbacy
abajo, *adv.* under, below; downstairs
abanderado, *m.* (mil.) ensign; standard bearer
abandonar, *va.* to abandon
abandono, *m.* abandonment; carelessness
abanicar, *va.* to fan
abanico, *m.* fan; derrick
abarcar, *va.* to comprise
abarrotes, *m. pl.* groceries
abastecer, *va.* to supply
abatimiento, *m.* low spirits, depression
abdicar, *va.* to abdicate
abdomen, *m.* abdomen
abecé, *m.* alphabet
abecedario, *m.* alphabet
abedul, *m.* birch tree
abeja, *f.* bee
abejarrón or **abejorro,** *m.* bumblebee
abejón, *m.* drone; hornet
abertura, *f.* cleft, opening
abierto, *adj.* open; sincere
abismo, *m.* chasm, abyss
ablandar, *va., vn.* to soften
abnegar, *va.* to renounce
abochornar, *va., vr.* to shame, be embarrassed
abofetear, *va.* to slap one's face
abogacía, *f.* profession of law
abogado, *m.* lawyer; advocate
abogar, *vn.* to advocate; intercede
abolengo, *m.* ancestry
abolir, *va. def.* to abolish
abominable, *adj.* abominable
abominar, *va.* to detest
abonar, *va.* to manure; to credit with; to pay on an account; **abonarse,** to subscribe to
abono, *m.* fertilizer; payment; season ticket
abordar, *va.* to board a ship; approach (a subject)
aborrecer, *va.* to hate, abhor
abortar, *vn.* to miscarry, abort
aborto, *m.* abortion; mon-strosity
abotonar, *va.* to button
abr., abreviatura, abbr, abbreviation
abrasar, *va.* to burn; to scorch
abrazar, *va.* to embrace
abrazo, *m.* embrace, hug
abrelatas, *m.* can opener
abreviar, *va.* to abbreviate
abrevistura, *f.* abbreviation
abridor, *m.* opener; **abridor de latas,** can opener
abrigar, *va.* to shelter; **abrigarse,** to wrap, cover up
abrigo, *m.* shelter; wrap, overcoat
abril, *m.* April
abrir, *va., vr.* to open
abrochar, *va.* to hook, clasp on
abrumar, *va.* to overwhelm
absceso, *m.* abscess
absorto, *adj.* absorbed; amazed
abstemio, *adj.* abstemious; *m.* teetotaler
abstenerse, *vr.* to abstain
abstinencia, *f.* abstinence
abstracto, *adj.* abstract
abstraer, *va.* to abstract; **abstraerse,** to be lost in thought
absuelto, *adj.* absolved, acquitted
absurdo, *adj.* absurd; *m.* absurdity
abuela, *f.* grandmother
abuelo, *m.* grandfather; **abuelos,** *pl.* ancestors
abundancia, *f.* abundance
abundar, *vn.* to abound
aburrido, *adj.* bored; boresome
aburrir, *va.* to bore; **aburrirse,** to be bored
abusar, *va., vn.* to abuse; to impose upon
abuso, *m.* abuse, misuse
a/c, a cuenta, on account, in part payment; **a cargo,** drawn on; in care of
A.C. or **A. de C., Anio de Cristo,** A.D. in the year of Our Lord
aca, *adv.* here, hither

acabar, *va., vn.* to finish, complete; to die
academia, *f.* academy
académico, *adj.* academic
acalorar, *va.* to heat; **acalorars,** to get excited, to become warm
acamper, *va.* to camp
acantonar, *va.* to quarter troops
acaparar, *va.* to monopolize
acariciar, *va.* to caress
acarrear, *va.* to transport; to occasion, cause
acarreo, *m.* cartage
acaso, *m.* chance, haphazard; **por si acaso,** just in case
acatar, *va.* to respect, obey (orders)
acatarrarse, *vr.* to catch cold
acaudalado, *adj.* rich, wealthy
acceder, *vn.* to accede, agree
accesible, *adj.* accessible
acceso, *m.* access, approach
accesorio, *adj.* accessory
accidental, *adj.* accidental
accidente *m.* accident
acción, *f.* act, action; share, stock
accionar, *vn.* to gesticulate
accionista, *m., f.* stockholder
aceitar, *va.* to oil
aceite, *m.* oil
aceituna, *f.* olive
acelerador, *m.* accelerator
acelerar, *va.* to accelerate
acento, *m.* accent
acentuar, *va.* to accentuate; to emphasize
acepción, *f.* meaning
aceptable, *adj.* acceptable
aceptación, *f.* acceptance
aceptar, *va.* to accept; to admit
acera, *f.* sidewalk
acerca de, *prep.* about
acercar, *va., vr.* to bring together; to approach
acérrimo, *adj.* very vigorous; **enemigo acérrimo,** bitter enemy
acertado, *adj.* accurate
acertar, *va.* to conjecture right
acertijo, *m.* riddle, conundrum

acicalarse, *vr.* to dress meticulously; to paint one's face
ácido, *m.* acid; *adj.* acid, sour
acierto, *m.* accuracy; ability
aclamación, acclamation
aclamar, *va.* to applaud
aclaración, *f.* explanation
aclarar, *va.* to clarify; **aclararse,** to clear up
aclimatar, *va.* to acclimatize
acne, *m.* (med.) acne
acogedor, *adj.* cozy, inviting
acoger, *va.* to receive; to protect; **acogerse,** to resort to
acogida, *f.* reception; welcome
acólito, *m.* acolyte; assistant
acometida, *f.* attack, assault
acomodado, *adj.* wealthy
acomodador, *m.* usher
acomodar, *va.* to accomodate, arrange; *vn.* to fit, suit
acompañamiento, *m.* accompaniment
acompañante, *m.* companion; accompanist
acompañar, *va.* to accompany
acongojarse, *vr.* to become sad
aconsejable, *adj.* advisable
aconsejar, *va.* to advise
acontecer, *vn. def.* to happen
acontecimiento, *m.* event, incident
acopiar, *va.* to gather, to store up
acorazado, *m.* battleship
acordar, *va.* to resolve; *vn.* to agree; **acordarse,** to remember
acorde, *m.* accord; chord
acortar, *va.* to abridge, shorten
acosar, *va.* to molest, harass
acostar, *va.* to put to bed; **acostarse,** to lie down; go to bed
acostumbrar, *va., vn.* to accustom; to be accustomed
acre, *adj.* acid; *m.* acre
acreditado, *adj.* accredited
acreditar, *va.* to assure, authorize; to credit; to accredit
acreedor, *m.* creditor; *adj.* worthy; **saldo acreedor,** credit balance

acrilico, *adj.* acrylic
acta, *f.* minutes of proceeding;
  acta de venta, bill of sale
ACTH, (med.) ACTH
actitud, *f.* attitude, posture
activar, *va.* to activate
actividad, *f.* activity; liveliness
activo *adj.* active, diligent; *m.*
  (com.) assets
acto, *m.* act; action
actuación, *f.* performance
actual, *adj.* actual, present
actualidad, actuality, current
  event
actuar, *vn.* to act
acuario, *m.* aquarium
acuático, *adj.* aquatic
acudir, *vn.* to assist, to be
  present; acudir a, to resort
  to
acueducto, *m.* aqueduct
acuerdo, *m.* agreement; resolution
acumulador, *m.* battery
acumular, *va.* to accumulate
acurrucarse, *vr.* to huddle
acusación, *f.* accusation
acusar, *va.* to accuse; to reproach; acusar recibo de,
  acknowledge receipt of
acusativo, *m.* accusative
acústica, *f.* acoustics
achacar, *va.* to impute, blame
achaque, *m.* ailment
achicar, *va.* to diminish; to
  bail a boat
adaptable, *adj.* adaptable
adaptar, *va.* to adapt
A. de J.C., antes de Jesucristo, B.C. Before Christ
adefesio, *m.* ridiculous attire
adelantado, *adj.* anticipated;
  por adelantadodo, in advance
adelantar, *va., vn.* to advance;
  adelantarse, to take the lead
adelanto, *m.* progress, advance
adelgazarse, *vr.* to lose weight
ademán, *m.* gesture; attitude
además, *adv.* moreover, also;
  además de, besides
adentro, *adv.* within; inwardly
adepto, *adj.* adept; *m.* follower
adeudar, *va.* to owe

adherencia, *f.* adhesion, adherence
adherir, *vn., vr.* to adhere
adhesión, *f.* adherence
adición, *f.* addition
adicto, *m.* addict; *adj.* addicted
adiós, *interj.* good-by, adieu
adivinanza, *f.* riddle
adivinar, *va.* to guess
adj., adjetivo, *adj.* adjective
adjetivo, *m.* adjective
adjuntar, *va.* to enclose, attach
administración, *f.* administration
administrar, *va.* to administer
admirable, *adj.* admirable
admiración, *f.* admiration;
  wonder; (gram.) exclamation
  point
admirar, *va.* to admire; admi-
  rarse, to be surprised
admisión, *f.* admission
admitir, *va.* to admit
adobar, *va.* to stew
adobo, *m.* stew
adolescencia, *f.* adolescence,
  youth
adolescente, *adj., m., f.* ado-
  lescent; bobby soxer
adonde, *adv.* whither, where
adopción, *f.* adoption
adoptar, *va.* to adopt
adoptivo, *adj.* adoptive;
  adopted
adormecer, *va.* to put to sleep
adornar, *va.* to embellish
adquirir, *va.* to acquire
adrede, *adv.* purposely
aduana, *f.* customhouse
adular, *va.* to flatter; to fawn
adulterar, *va.* to adulterate
adulto, *adj.* adult
adv., adverbio, *adv.* adverb
ad val., ad valórem, en proporción al valor, ad val. ad
  valorem, in proportion to the
  value
adverbio, *m.* adverb
adversario, *m.* adversary
adversidad, *f.* adversity
adverso, *adj.* adverse
advertencia, *f.* warning
advertir. *va.* to warn

aéreo, *adj.* air, aerial
aerógrafo, *m.* air brush
aeronáutica, *f.* aeronautics
aeroplano, *m.* airplane
aeropuerto, *m.* airport
afable, *adj.* affable
afamado, *adj.* famous
afán, *m.* anxiety, worry
afanarse, *vr.* to toil, labor
afección, *f.* disease
afectación, t. affectation
afectar, *va.* to affect
afectísimo, *adj.* devoted; yours truly
afecto, *m.* affection, love
afectuoso, *adj.* affectionate
afeitar, *va., vr.* to shave
afeminado, *adj.* effeminate
aferrado, *adj.* stubborn
afianzar, *va.* to bail, guarantee; to prop, fix
afición, *f.* preference; hobby
aficionado, aficionada, n. amateur
afilar, *va.* to sharpen
afiliado, *adj.* affiliated
afinar, *va.* to tune (musical instruments); to refine
afirmar, *va.* to secure, fasten; to affirm
afirmativo, *adj.* affirmative
aflicción, *f.* affliction, grief
afligirse, *vr.* to grieve
aflojar, *va.* to loosen
afmo. or **af.**^mo, **afectísimo,** idiomatic expression for "Cordially yours,' etc.
afortunadamente, *adv.* fortunately, luckily
afortunado, adj. fortunate
afrenta, *f.* outrage; insult
afro, *adj.* Afro
afrontar, *va.* to confront
aftosa, *adj.* (vet.) hoof-and-mouth disease
afuera, *adv.* out, outside
afueras, *f. pl.* outskirts
ágape, *m.* banquet; testimonial dinner
agarrar, *va.* to grasp
agasajar, *va.* to entertain
agente, *m.* agent
agitado, *adj.* excited
agitar, *va.* to shake; **agitarse,** to become excited

aglomerar, *va., vr.* to conglomerate
agobiar, *va., vr.* to oppress, burden
agonia, t. agony, anguish
agonizar, *vn.* to be dying
agosto, *m.* August (month); harvest time
agotado, *adj.* sold out; exhausted
agotar, *va.* to exhaust; **agotarse,** to run out of
agraciado, *adj.* graceful; gifted
agradable, *adj.* pleasant
agradar, *va.* to please, gratify
agradecer, *va.* to appreciate (a favor)
agradecido, *adj.* grateful
agradecimiento, *m.* gratitude, gratefulness
agrandar, *va.* to enlarge
agrario, *adj.* agrarian
agravar, *va.* to aggravate
agraviar, *va.* to wrong; **agraviarse,** to take offense
agregar, *va.* to add
agresión, *f.* aggression
agresivo, *adj.* aggressive
agriar, *va., vr.* to sour
agrícola, *adj.* agricultural
agricultor, *m.* agriculturist, farmer
agricultura, *f.* agriculture
agridulce, *adj.* bittersweet
agrietarse, *vr.* to crack
agrimensor, *m.* land surveyor
agrio, *adj.* sour; rude
agrónomo, *m.* agronomist
agrupar, *va., vr.* to group (in a picture); to crowd
agto. or **ag.**^to, **agosto,** Aug. August
agua, *f.* water, liquid; rain
aguacate, *m.* avocado, alligator pear
aguacerol, *m.* shower of rain
aguado, *adj.* watery
aguafuerte, *f.* etching
aguantar, *va.* to endure, bear
aguar, *va., vr.* to thin out with water; to spoil (a party, etc.)
aguardar, *va.* to expect, wait for
aguardiente, *m.* distilled liquor

aguarrás, *m.* turpentine
agudo, *adj.* acute; sharp-pointed
aguijón, *m.* sting of a bee, wasp, etc.; stimulation
águila, *f.* eagle
aguileño, *adj.* aquiline
aguinaldo, *m.* Christmas gift
aguja, *f.* needle; switch; **aguja de coser,** sewing needle
agujero, *m.* hole
aguzar, *va.* to whet; to stimulate
ahí, *adv.* there; **de ahí (que),** for this reason; **por ahí,** that way, more or less
ahijada, *f.* goddaughter
ahijado, *m.* godson
ahinco, *m.* zeal, earnestness
ahogar, *va., vr.* to drown; to suffocate
ahondar, *va.* to deepen; *vn.* to penetrate
ahora, *adv.* now, at present; *conj.* whether, or
ahorcar, *va., vr.* to kill by hanging
ahorita, *adv.* (Sp. Am.) just now, in just a minute
ahorrar, *va.* to save, economize
ahorro, *m.* saving, thrift
ahumar, *va.* to cure in smoke
ahuyentar, *va.* to put to flight
aire, *m.* air, wind
airear, *va.* to air, ventilate
airoso, *adj.* airy; graceful; successful
aislado, *adj.* insulated, isolated
aislador, *m.* (elec.) insulator
aislamiento, *m.* isolation; insulation; (fig.) solitude
aislar, *va.* to isolate; to insulate
ajar, *va.* to crumple
ajedrez, *m.* chess (game)
ajeno, *adj.* another's; contrary to
ají, *m.* chili pepper, chili
ajo, *m.* garlic; **¡ajo!** *interj.* darn!
ajustar, *va.* to regulate; to adjust; to tighten
ajuste, *m.* adjustment

al, contraction for **a el; al fin,** at last
ala, *f.* wing; brim of the hat
alabanza, *f.* praise, applause
alabar, *va.* to praise, extol
alabastro, *m.* alabaster; gypsum
alacena, *f.* cupboard
alacrán, *m.* scorpion
alambrado, *m.* wire fence
alambre, *m.* wire, copper wire; **alambre de púas,** barbed wire
alameda, *f.* poplar grove; tree-lined promenade
álamo, *m.* poplar, poplar tree; cottonwood tree
alarde, *m.* display; **hacer alarde,** to boast
alardear, *vn.* to brag, boast
alargar, *va.* to lengthen; to extend
alarido, *m.* outcry, howl
alarma, *f.* alarm
alarmante, *adj.* alarming
alarmar, *va., vr.* to alarm
a la v/, a la vista, (com.) at sight
alba, *f.* daybreak
albacea, *m.* executor; *f.* executrix
albañil, *m.* mason, bricklayer
albaricoque, *m.* apricot
albedrío, *m.* free will
alberca, *f.* reservoir; swimming pool
albergar, *va.* to lodge, house, harbor; **albergarse,** to take shelter
albergue, *m.* shelter
albóndiga, *f.* meat ball
alborada, *f.* early dawn; (mil.) morning watch
alborotar, *va.* to make a disturbance, stir
¡albricias! *interj.* good news!
álbum, *m.* album
albumen, *m.,* **albúmina,** *f.* albumen
alcachofa, *f.* artichoke
alcaide, *m.* jailer, warden
alcalde, *m.* mayor
alcaldía, *f.* mayor's office
alcance, *m.* reach, scope
alcancía, *f.* money box; sav-

ings bank
alcanfor, *m.* camphor
alcantarillado, *m.* sewage system
alcanzar, *va.* to overtake, to reach
alcaparra, *f.* caper
alcoba, *f.* alcove; bedroom
aldaba, *f.* knocker, door latch
aldea, *f.* village
aldeano, *m.* peasant
alegar, *va.* to allege, affirm
alegato, *m.* (law) allegation, pleading; (Sp. Am.) quarrel
alegrar, *va.* to gladden; **alegrarse,** to rejoice
alegría, *f.* mirth, cheer
alejamiento, *m.* distance, remoteness; aloofness
alejar, *va.* to remove to a greater distance; to separate; **alejarse,** to withdraw, move away
alemán, alemana, *adj., n.* German
Alemania, *f.* Germany
alentador, *adj.* encouraging
alentar, *va.* to animate; to cheer, encourage
alergeno, *m.* allergen
alergia, *f.* allergy
alerta, *adv.* vigilantly, **estar alerta,** to be alert
alerto, *adj.* alert, vigilant
aletear, *vn.* to flutter
alevosía, *f.* treachery
alfabético, *adj.* alphabetical
alfabeto, *m.* alphabet
alfiler, *m.* pin; **alfiler imperdible,** safety pin
alfiletero, *m.* pincushion
alfombra, *f.* carpet; rug
alfombrilla, (med.) measles
algarabía, *f.* clamor, din
álgebra, *f.* algebra
algo, *pron.* some, something; anything; *adv.* a little, rather
algodón, *m.* cotton
algodonero, *m.* cotton plant
alguno (algún), alguna, *pron.* somebody, someone, anyone; *adj.* some, any
alhaja, *f.* jewel, gem
aliado, *adj.* allied; *n.* ally
alianza, *f.* alliance, league

alias, *adv.* alias; otherwise
aliciente, *m.* attraction, incitement, inducement
aliento, *m.* breath; encouragement
aligerar, *va.* to lighten; to hasten
alimentación, *f.* food, nourishment, meals
alimentar, *va.* to feed, nourish
alimenticio, *adj.* nutritious
alimento, *m.* nourishment, food
alinear, *va.* to align
alistar, *va., vr.* to enlist; to get ready, make ready
aliviar, *va.* to lighten; to ease
alma, *f.* soul; heart
almacén, *m.* department store; warehouse
almacenar, *va.* to store, lay up
almanaque, *m.* almanac
almeja, *f.* clam
almendra, *f.* almond
almíbar, *m.* syrup
almidón, *m.* starch
almidonar, *va.* to starch
almirante, *m.* admiral
almohada, *f.* pillow
almohadón, *m.* large cushion
almorranas, *f. pl.* hemorrhoids, piles
almorzar, *vn.* to breakfast; to eat lunch
almuerzo, *m.* breakfast; lunch
alocado, *adj.* crack-brained
alojamiento, *m.* lodging accommodation
alojar, *va., vr.* to lodge
alondra, *f.* lark
Alpes, *m. pl.* Alps
alpiste, *m.* canary seed
alquilar, *va.* to let, hire, rent
alquiler, *m.* hire; house rent
alquitrán, *m.* tar
alrededor, *adv.* around
alrededores, *m. pl.* environs; neighborhood
alt., altitud, alt., altitude; **altura,** ht., height
alta, *f.* new member
altanero, *adj.* haughty
altar, *m.* altar
altavoz, *m.* loudspeaker
alterar, *va.* to alter, change; to

disturb; **alterarse,** to become angry

altercar, *va.* to dispute, quarrel

alternar, *va., vn.* to alternate

altiplano, *m.* high plateau

altísimo, *adj.* extremely high; **el Altísimo,** *m.* the Most High, God

altisonante, *adj.* high-sounding, pompous

altitud, *f.* altitude

altivo, *adj.* haughty, proud

alto, *adj.* high, elevated; loud; tall; *m.* height; story, floor; highland; (mil.) halt; (mus.) tenor

altoparlante, *m.* loudspeaker

altruismo, *m.* altruism

altura, *f.* height; highness; altitude; **alturas,** *pl.* the heavens

aludido, *adj.* referred to

aludir, *vn.* to allude, refer

alumbrado, *adj.* illuminated; *m.* lighting; **alumbrado fluorescente,** fluorescent lighting

alumbramiento, *m.* illumination; childbirth

alumbrar, *va.* to illuminate

alumbre, *m.* alum

aluminio, *m.* aluminum

alumno, disciple pupil

alusión, *f.* allusion, hint

alverjas, *f. pl.* peas

alza, *f.* advance in price; lift

alzar, *va.* to raise, lift up; to build; **alzarse,** to rise in rebellion

allá, *adv.* there; thither; **mas allá,** beyond

allanar, *va.* to level, flatten; to overcome (difficulties)

allegado, *adj.* near; related; *n.* follower, ally

allí, *adv.* there, in that place

A.M., antemeridiano, A.M. or a.m., before noon

ama *f.* mistress; **ama de casa,** housewife; **ama de llaves,** housekeeper

amable, *adj.* amiable, kind

amado, n. beloved, darling

amaestrar, *va.* to teach, to

train

amamantar, *va.* to suckle, nurse

amanecer, *m.* dawn, daybreak; *vn.* to dawn; to appear at daybreak

amanerado, *adj.* affected, overrefined

amansar, *va.* to tame, domesticate; to soften, pacify

amante, *m., f.* lover

amañarse, *vr.* to adapt oneself

amapola, *f.* (bot.) poppy

amar, *va.* to love

amargar, *va.* to make bitter; *vn., vr.* to be bitter

amargo, *adj.* bitter, acrid; painful

amargura, *f.* bitterness

amarillo, *adj.* yellow

amarrar, *va.* to tie, fasten

amasar, *va.* to knead

amatista, amethyst

amazona, amazon, masculine woman

ámbar, *m.* amber

Amberes, *f.* Antwerp

ambición, *f.* ambition

ambicioso, *adj.* ambitious

ambiental, *adj.* environmental; **contaminación ambiental,** environmental pollution

ambiente, *m.* environment

ambiguo, *adj.* ambiguous

ambos, *adj. pl.* both

ambulancia, *f.* ambulance

ambulante, *adj.* ambulatory; roving; **vendedor ambulante,** *adj.* peddler

amedrentar, *va.* to intimidate

amén, *m.* amen; acquiescence; **amén de,** besides; except.

amenaza, *f.* threat, menace

amenazar, *va.* to threaten

amenizar, *va.* to render pleasant; to adorn (a speech)

ameno, *adj.* pleasant, entertaining.

América del Norte, *f.* North America.

Amiérica del Sur, *f.* South America.

América Latina, *f.* Latin America.

americanismo, *m.* Americanism; an expression or word used in the Spanish of Spanish America

americano, americana, *n.,* *adj.* American

amiga, *f.* female friend

amigable, *adj.* friendly

amígdala, *f.* tonsil

amigo, amiga, n. friend.

aminoácido, *m.* amino acid.

amistad, *f.* friendship

amistoso, *adj.* friendly

amo, *m.* master, proprietor

amolar, *va.* to grind, sharpen

amoldar, *va., vr.* to mold; to adjust

amonestación, *f.* admonition; publication of marriage bans

amonestar, *va.* to admonish.

amontonar, *va.* to heap together; to accumulate

amor, *m.* love; the object of love; **por amor de,** for the sake of; **amor propio,** pride

amoroso, *adj.* affectionate

amortiguador, *m.* shock absorber

amortiguar, *va.* to mitigate; to deaden, absorb

amortizar, *va.* to amortize

amotinarse, *vr.* to mutiny

amparar, *va.* to shelter, favor, protect; **ampararse,** to claim protection

amparo, *m.* protection, help, support; refuge, asylum

amperio, *m.* (elec.) ampere

ampliación, *f.* amplification, enlargement

ampliar, *va.* to amplify; expand, increase

amplificador, *m.* amplifier

amplio, *adj.* ample

ampolla, *f.* blister; vial

amputar, *va.* to amputate

amueblar, *va.* to furnish

anales, *m. pl.* annals

analfabetismo, *m.* illiteracy

analfabeto, analfabeta, *n.* illiterate person

análisis, *m.* or *f.* analysis

analizar, *va.* to analyze

análogo, *adj.* analogous

anaquel, *m.* shelf in a bookcase

anaranjado, *adj.* orange colored

anatomía, *f.* anatomy

anatómico, *adj.* anatomical

anca, *f.* buttock; hindquarters (of a horse)

anciano, *adj.* aged, old; ancient.

ancla, *f.* anchor

anclar, *vn.* to anchor

ancho, *adj.* broad, wide; *m.* breadth, width

anchoa, *f.* anchovy

anchura, *f.* width, breadth

andamiaje, *m.* scaffolding

andamio, *m.* scaffold

andante, *adj.* walking, errant; (mus.) andante

andar, *vn.* to go, walk; to fare; to proceed; to function, (as a machine)

andén, *m.* (rail.) platform

andrajoso, *adj.* ragged

anécdota, *f.* anecdote

anegar, *va.* to inundate; **anegarse,** to be flooded

anémico, *adj.* anemic

anestesia, *f.* (med.) anesthesia

anestésico, *m., adj.* anesthetic

anexo, *adj.* annexed; *m.* attachment on a letter

anfitrión, *m.* host

ángel, *m.* angel

anglosajón, anglosajona, *n., adj.* Anglo-Saxon

angosto, *adj.* narrow, close

anguila, *f.* (zool.) eel

angular, *adj.* angular; **piedra angular,** cornerstone

angustia, *f.* anguish

anhelo, *m.* longing

anillo, *m.* ring, small circle

ánima, *f.* soul

animación, *f.* animation, liveliness

animado, *adj.* lively; animated

animal, *m., adj.* animal brute

animar, *va., vr.* to animate, enliven; to encourage

ánimo, *m.* soul, spirit; courage; mind; intention

animoso, *adj.* courageous, spirited

aniquilar, *va., vr.* to annihilate, destroy

aniversario, *m.* anniversary

ano, *m.* anus

anoche, *adv.* last night

anochecer, *vn.* to grow dark

anónimo, *adj.* anonymous

anormal, *adj.* abnormal

anotación, *f.* annotation, note

anotar, *va.* to comment, note

ansia, *f.* anxiety, eagerness, yearning; worry

ansiar, *va.* to long for

ansioso, *adj.* anxious eager

antagonista, *m., f.* antagonist

antaño, *adv.* long ago; yore

antártico, *adj.* Antarctic

anteayer, *adv.* day before yesterday

antecesor, antecesora, *n.* predecessor; forefather

antedicho, *adj.* aforesaid

antemano, de antemano, *adv.* beforehand, in advance

antemeridiano, *adj.* in the forenoon

antena, *f.* feeler; antenna, aerial

antenoche, *adv.* night before last

anteojo, *m.* spyglass, eyeglass; **anteojos,** *pl.* eyeglasses

antepasado, *adj.* elapsed; **semana antepasada,** week before last; **antepasados,** *m. pl.* ancestors

anterior, *adj.* anterior, fore; previous

anterioridad, *f.* priority; preference

antes, *adv.* first; formerly; before; rather

antibiótico, *m.* antibiotic

anticipación, *f.* anticipation; **con anticipación,** in advance

anticipado, *adj.* in advance

anticipar, *va.* to anticipate, to forestall

anticuado, *adj.* antiquated; obsolete

antidetonante, *m., adj.* antiknock

antídoto, *m.* antidote

antier, *adv.* (contraction) day before yesterday

antiguamente, *adv.* formerly

antigüedad, *f.* antiquity; ancient times; **antigüedades,** *f. pl.* antiques

antigum, *adj.* antique, old

antihigiénico, *adj.* unsanitary

antihistamina, *f.* antihistamine

antílope, *m.* antelope

antimateria, *f.* antimatter

antipatía, *f.* antipathy

antipático, *adj.* disagreeable, displeasing

antiséptico, *adj.* antiseptic

antojarse, *vr.* to have a yen for

antojo, *m.* whim; longing

antorcha, *f.* torch, taper

anual, *adj.* annual

anualidad, *f.* anuity

anuario, *m.* annual; yearbook.

anular, *va.* to annul; *adj.* anular; **dedo anular,** ring finger

anunciador, *m.* announcer

anunciante, *m.* advertiser

anunciar, *va.* to announce; to advertise

anzuelo, *m.* fishhook; allurement

añadir, *va.* to add; to join

añejo, *adj.* old, age(wines)

añicos, *m. pl.* bits; **hacer añicos,** to break into bits

añil, *m.* indigo; bluing

año, *m.* year; **año bisiesto,** leap year; **cumplir años,** to have a birthday; **tener . . . años,** to be . . . years old.

apaciguar, *va., vr.* to appease, pacify, calm down

apachurrar, *va.* to crush, flatten.

apagado, *adj.* low, muffled

apañar, *va.* to grasp; to catch

aparador, *m.* buffet, sideboard; window, showcase

aparato, *m.* apparatus, appliance; ostentation, show

aparatoso, *adj.* pompous, showy

aparecer, *vn.* to appear

aparentar, *va.* to pretend, deceive

aparente, *adj.* apparent; suitable; evident

apariencia, *f.* appearance,

looks
apartado, *m.* post-office box
apartamento, or **apartamiento,** *m.* apartment
apartar, *va.* to separate; to remove; **apartarse,** to withdraw
aparte, *m.* new paragraph; *adv.* apart, separately
apasionado, *adj.* passionate; impulsive; fond of
apasionarse, *vr.* to be prejudiced (about)
apatía, *f.* apathy, indifference
apego, *m.* attachment, fondness.
apelación, *f.* appeal; court appeal.
apellido, *m.* surname
apenarse, *vr.* to grieve; become embarrassed
apenas, *adv.* scarcely, hardly.
apéndice, *m.* appendix; supplement.
apendicitis, *f.* appendicitis
aperitivo, *m.* appetizer
apertura, *f.* opening, cleft
apestar, *vn.* to stink
apetito, *m.* appetite
apetitoso, *adj.* appetizing
ápice, *m.* summit point
apiñar, *va.* to press things close together; **apiñarse,** to clog, crowd
apisonadora, *f.* steam roller
aplacar, *va.* to placate
aplanar, *va.* to level, smooth
aplaudir, *va.* to applaud
aplauso, *m.* applause, praise
aplazar, *va.* to defer, postpone
aplicado, *adj.* studious, industrious
aplicar, *va.* to apply; to attribute
aplomo, *m.* poise, composure
apócope, *m.* shortening, cutting off
apoderado, *adj.* authorized, empowered; *m.* (law) proxy, attorney in fact
apoderar, *va.* to empower; to grant power of attorney; **apoderarse,** to take possession
apodo, *m.* nickname
apoplejía, *f.* apoplexy

aportar, *va.* to bring, contribute
aposento, *m.* room, abode
aposición, *f.* (gram.) apposition
apostar, *va.* to bet
apóstol, *m.* apostle
apoyar, *va.* to favor; to support; **apoyarse,** to lean upon
apoyo, *m.* prop, support; protection
apreciable, *adj.* appreciable, valuable, respectable; (com.) **su apreciable,** your favor (letter)
apreciar, *va.* to appreciate, value
aprecio, *m.* appreciation, esteem, regard
apremiar, *va.* to press, compel; to hurry
aprender, *va.* to learn
aprendiz, aprendiza, *n.* apprentice
aprensión, *f.* apprehension, fear, misgiving
apresurado, *adj.* hasty
apresurar, *va.* to accelerate, expedite; **apresurarse,** to hurry, hasten
apretado, *adj.* tight
apretar, *va.* to compress, tighten, squeeze; to pinch (of shoes)
apretón, *m.* sudden pressure; **apretón de manos** handshake.
aprieto, *m.* predicament
aprisa, *adv.* in a hurry
aprobación, *f.* approval
aprobar, *va.* to approve
apropiación, *f.* appropriation
apropiado, *adj.* appropriate, adequate
apropiar, *va.* to appropriate; **apropiarse,** take possession of
aprovechable, *adj.* available, usable
aprovechar, *va.* to avail, make use of; *vn.* to progress in studies, art, etc.; **aprovecharse de,** to take advantage of
aproximar, *va.,* *vr.* to approach; to move near, ap-

proximate
aptitud, *f.* aptitude, fitness, ability; talent
apto, *adj.* apt, fit, able
apuesta, *f.* bet, wager
apuesto, *adj.* elegant
apuntador, *m.* observer; prompter; (naut.) gunner
apuntar, *va.* to aim; to level, point out; to note; to write down; (theat.) to prompt
apunte, *m.* annotation; note, sketch
apurado, *adj.* poor, destitute; to be in a hurry
apurar, *va.* to rush, hurry; **apurarse**, to hurry; to worry
apuro, *m.* want, indigence; embarrassment; **salir de un apuro**, to get out of a difficulty.
aquel, aquella, *adj.* and **aquél, aquélla**, *pron.* that
aquello, *pron.* that, the former
aquí, *adv.* here, in this place
aquietar, *va.* to quiet, appease, lull; **aquietarse**, to become calm
árabe, n., *adj.* Arabic, the Arabic language; an Arab
arado, *m.* plow.
arancel, *m.* tariff
arañar, *va.* to scratch; to scrape.
arar, *va.* to plow the land
arbitraje, *m.* arbitration
arbitrar, *va.* to arbitrate
arbitrario, *adj.* arbitrary
árbol, *m.* tree; shaft; (naut.) mast
arca, *f.* chest, wooden box
arcángel, *m.* archangel
arce, *m.* maple tree
arcilla, *f.* argil, clay
arco, *m.* arc; arch; fiddle bow; hoop; **arco iris**, rainbow
arcón, *m.* large chest; bin
archipiélago, *m.* archipelago
archivar, *va.* to file, place in archives
archivo, *m.* archives, file
arder, *vn.* to burn, blaze
ardid, *m.* stratagem, trick
ardiente, *adj.* ardent, intense
ardilla, *f.* squirrel

ardor, *m.* great heat; fervor, zeal
arduo, *adj.* arduous
área, *f.* area
arenoso, *adj.* sandy
arenque, *m.* herring
aretes, *m. pl.* earrings
argentino, *adj.* silvery; Argentine
argolla, *f.* large iron ring
argüir, *vn.* to argue
argumento, *m.* argument; plot of a play
aria, *f.* (mus.) aria, air
árido, *adj.* arid; barren
arisco, *adj.* fierce, surly
aristocracia, *f.* aristocracy
aristócrata, *m., f.* aristocrat
aristocrático, *adj.* aristocratic
aritmética, *f.* arithmetic
arma, *f.* weapon, arm
armamento, *m.* armament
armar, *va.* to furnish with arms; to man; to arm, fit up; to assemble
armario, *m.* clothes closet; cupboard; bookcase
armazón, framework, skeleton; *m.* skeleton of the body.
armiño, *m.* ermine
armisticio, *m.* armistice
armonía, *f.* harmony
armonioso, *adj.* harmonious
armonizar, *va.* to harmonize
aro, *m.* hoop
aroma, *m.* aroma, fragrance
arpa, *f.* (mus.) harp
arqueado, *adj.* arched, bent
arqueología, *f.* archaeology
arquitecto, *m.* architect
arquitectura, *f.* architecture
arraigar *vn.* to take root; to become deep-seated
arrancar, *va.* to pull up by the roots; to wrest; *vn.* to start out
arranque, *m.* sudden start; extirpation; tantrum; (auto.) ignition, starter
arrasar *va.* to demolish, destroy
arrastrado, *adj.* dragged along; miserable, destitute.
arrear, *va.* to drive horses, mules, etc.; to urge on

arrebatado, *adj.* impetuous, rash, inconsiderate

arrebatar, *va.* to carry off, snatch; to enrapture

arrebato, *m.* sudden attack, rage, fit; rapture

arreciar, *vn.* to increase in intensity

arrecife, *m.* reef

arreglado, *adj.* moderate; neat

arreglar, *va.* to regulate; to adjust; to arrange; **arreglarse,** to dress; to manage

arreglo, *m.* arrangement, settlement

arrendamiento, *m.* leasing; rental

arrendar, *va.* to rent, lease

arreos, *m. pl.* appurtenances, accessories

arrepentimiento, *m.* remorse

arrepentirse, *vr.* to repent

arrestar, *va.* to arrest

arriba, *adv.* above, over, up, high, overhead, upstairs

arribo, *m.* arrival

arriendo, *m.* lease, farm rent

arriesgado, *adj.* risky, dangerous

arriesgar, *va., vr.* to risk, hazard.

arrimar, *va.* to approach, draw near; **arrimarse a,** to lean against, seek shelter under; to join

arroba, *f.* weight of twenty-five pounds; measure (thirty-two pints)

arrodillarse, *vr.* to kneel

arrogancia, *f.* arrogance

arrogante, *adj.* haughty, proud

arrojado, *adj.* rash, bold

arrojar, *va.* to dart, fling; to dash; to shed (a fragrance); to emit (light); to throw out; **arrojar un saldo,** to show a balance

arrojo, *m.* boldness; fearlessness

arrollar, *va.* to wind, coil

arropar, *va.* to clothe, dress; to cover (with blankets, etc.)

arroyo, *m.* gully, creek

arroz, *m.* rice

arruga, *f.* wrinkle; rumple

arrugar, *va.* to wrinkle; to rumple, fold; **arrugar el ceño,** to frown; **arrugarse,** to shrivel

arruinar, *va.* to demolish; to ruin; **arruinarse,** to lose one's fortune

arte, *m., f.* art; skill; **bellas artes,** fine arts

arteria, *f.* artery

arterial, *adj.* arterial; **tensión arterial,** blood pressure

artesano, *m.* artisan, workman.

ártico, *adj.* arctic

articular, *va.* to articulate.

artificial, *adj.* artificial

artillería, *f.* gunnery; artillery

artimaña, *f.* stratagem, deception

artista, *m.f.* artist

artisticó, *adj.* artistic

artritis, *f.* (med.) arthritis

arveja, *f.* (bot.) vetch; (Sp. Am.) green pea

arzobispo, *m.* archbishop

as, *m.* ace

asa, *f.* handle, haft, hold

asado, *adj.* roasted; *m.* roast

asaltar, *va.* to attack; to assail

asalto, *m.* assault

asamblea, *f.* assembly, meeting

asar, *va.* to roast

asbesto, *m.* asbestos

ascendencia, *f.* ancestry; line of ancestors

ascendente, *adj.* ascending

ascender, *va., vn.* to ascend, climb; to be promoted; to amount to

ascendiente, *m.* ascendant, forefather; influence

ascenso, *m.* ascent; promotion

ascensor, *m.* elevator, lift

asco, *m.* nausea; loathing

aseado, *adj.* clean, neat

asear, *va.* to clean, make neat

asediar, *va.* to besiege

asegurado, *adj.* assured, secured, insured; *n.* policyholder

asegurar, *va.* to secure, insure; to assure; to affirm

asemejarse, *vr.* to resemble
asentimiento, *m.* assent
asentir, *vn.* to acquiesce, concede
aseo, *m.* cleanliness
aserción, *f.* assertion
aserrar, *va.* to saw
asesinar, *va.* to assassinate
asesinato, *m.* assassination
asesino, *m.* assassin
asesorar, *va.* to give legal advice to; **asesorarse,** to employ counsel; to take advice
asfalto, *m.* asphalt
asfixiar, *va., vr.* to asphyxiate, suffocate
así, *adv.* so, thus, in this manner; therefore, so that
asiático, asiática, *n., adj.* Asiatic
asiento, *m.* chair, stool; seat; entry
asignar, *vt.* to allocate, apportion, assign
asignatura, *f.* subject of a school course
asilo, *m.* asylum, refuge
asimismo, *adv.* similarly; likewise
asistencia, *f.* actual presence; attendance; assistance; help
asistir, *vn.* to be present; to attend; *va.* assist
asma, *f.* asthma
asno, *m.* ass; stupid fellow
asociado, asociada, *n.* associate
asociar, *va., vr.* to associate
asolar, *va.* to destroy, devastate
asolear, *va., vr.* to expose to the sun
asomar, *vn.* to begin to appear; to peep; to show; **asomarse,** to lean out
asombrar, *va.* to frighten, amaze; to astonish
asombroso, *adj.* astonishing, marvelous
aspecto, *m.* appearance; aspect
áspero, *adj.* rough, rugged; austere, gruff
aspiración, *f.* aspiration; ambition

aspiradora, *f.* vacuum sweeper
aspirar, *va.* to inhale; to aspire
aspirina, *f.* aspirin
asqueroso, *adj.* loathsome; dirty
asta, *f.* staff, pole
asterisco, *m.* asterisk
astilla, *f.* chip; splinter
astillero, *m.* dockyard
astringente, *adj., m.* astringent
astro, *m.* star
astrólogo, *m.* astrologer
astronave, *f.* space ship
astronomía, *f.* astronomy
astrónomo, *m.* astronomer
asueto, *m.* holiday, vacation
asumir, *va.* to assume
asunto, *m.* subject; matter; affair, business
asustar, *va., vr.* to frighten
atacar, *va.* to attack, ram
atajo, *m.* by-path; short cut
ataque, *m.* attack
atar, *va.* to tie, fasten
atarantado, *adj.* dazed
atareado, *adj.* busy
atarearse, *vr.* to work hard on a task
atascarse, *vr.* to become bogged
ataúd, *m.* coffin
atavío, *m.* dress, ornament
Atenas, *f.* Athens
atender, *vn.* to be attentive; to heed; *va.* to look after
atenerse, *vr.* to depend or rely (on)
atentado, *m.* attempt, transgression; attack, assault
atentar, *va.* to try; to attempt crime
atento, *adj.* attentive; mindful; courteous
atenuar, *va.* to diminish
ateo, atea, *n., adj.* atheist, atheistic
aterrar, *va., vr.* to terrify
aterrizaje, *m.* (avi.) landing
aterrizar, *vn.* (avi.) to land
atesorar, *va.* to treasure or hoard up riches
atestar, *va.* to attest, witness; to cram, crowd; **atestarse de,** to stuff oneself with

atestiguar, *va.* to witness, attest

atinar, *va., vn.* to touch the mark; to conjecture rightly

atisbar, *va.* to pry

Atlántico, *n., adj.* Atlantic

atlas, *m.* atlas

atleta, *m., f.* athlete

atlético, *adj.* athletic

atmósfera, *f.* atmosphere

atmosférico, *adj.* atmospheric

atole, *m.* corn-flour gruel

atolondrar, *va., vr.* to stun, daze

atollar, *vn.* to fall in the mud

atómico, *adj.* atomic

atomo, *m.* atom

atónito, *adj.* astonish

atontar, *va., vr.* to stun, stupefy

atorar, *va.* to obstruct; **atorarse**, *vr.* to choke; to be stalled in the mud

atormentar, *va.* to torment

atornillar, *va.* to screw

atracar, *va.* to overhaul a ship; to glut; *vn.* (naut.) to make shore

atracción, *f.* attraction

atractivo, *adj.* attractive; *m.* charm, grace

atraer, *va.* to attract

atrapar, *va.* to trap; to overtake; to deceive

atrás, *adv.* backwards; behind; past

atrasado, *adj.* backward, behind the times; tardy; in arrears

atrasar, *va.* to postpone; to delay; **atrasarse**, to be in arrears

atraso, *m.* delay, backwardness; arrears

atravesar, *va.* to cross; to pass over; **atravesarse**, to get in the way; to thwart one's purpose

atreverse, *vr.* to dare, venture

atrevido, *adj.* bold, daring; impudent

atrevimiento, *m.* audacity

atribuir, *va.* to attribute, ascribe; to impute; **atribuirse**, to assume

atribular, *va.* to vex, afflict

atributo, *m.* attribute

atrio, *m.* porch; portico

atrocidad, *f.* atrocity

atropellar, *va.* to trample; to run over; **atropellarse**, to hurry, flurry

atropello, *m.* trampling; outrage, insult; **atropello de automóvil**, automobile collision

attmo. or **att.**^mo, **atentísimo**, very kind, very courteous

atto. or **att.°** **atento**, kind, courteous

atuendo, *m.* attire, garb; pomp, ostentation

atun, *m.* tunny fish, tuna

aturdir, *va.* to bewilder, confuse; to stupefy

audacia, *f.* audacity, boldness

audición, *f.* broadcasting; audition

audiencia, *f.* audience; hearing; a high court

audífono, *m.* earphone

audio-visual, *adj.* audio-visual

auditorio, *m.* assembly; audience.

auge, *m.* the pinnacle of power

augurar, *va.* to predict

aula, *f.* classroom

aullar, *vn.* to howl

aumentar, *va., vn.* to augment, increase

aumento, *m.* increase, growth

aun, *adv.* still, even; **aún**, *adv.* yet

aunque, *conj.* though, notwithstanding

aurora, *f.* first dawn of day

ausencia, *f.* absense

ausente, *adj.* absent

austero, *adj.* austere, severe

australiano, australiana, *n., adj.* Australian

austriaco, austriaca, *n., adj.* Austrian

autentico, *adj.* authentic

auto, *m.* judicial sentence; edict; auto, automobile

autobús, *m.* motorbus

autógrafo, *m.* autograph

autómata, *m.* automation; robot

automático, *adj.* automatic
automatización, *f.* automation
automatizar, *va.* to automate
automóvil, *m.* automobile
autonomía, *f.* autonomy
autónomo, *adj.* autonomous
autopista, *f.* expressway, superhighway
autor, *m.* author; maker
autoridad, *f.* authority
autorización, *f.* authorization
autorizado, *adj.* competent, reliable
autorizar, *va.* to authorize
auxiliar, *va.* to aid, help, assist; *adj.* auxiliary
auxilio, *m.* aid, help, assistance; **primeros auxilios**, first aid
a/v., a la vista, (com.) at sight
avaluar, *va.* to estimate, evaluate, appraise
avanzada, *f.* (mil.) vanguard
avanzar, *va., vn.* to advance
avaricia, *f.* avarice
avaro, *adj.* avaricious; *m.* miser
ave, *f.* bird; **ave de corral**, fowl
avellana, *f.* filbert, hazelnut
avemaría, *f.* Ave Maria, salutation to the Virgin Mary
avena, *f.* oats; oatmeal
avenida, *f.* avenue, boulevard
avenir, *va., vr.* to reconcile; to adapt (to circumstances)
aventajar, *va.* to have the advantage
aventar, *va.* to fan; to expel; to scatter; **aventarse**, to be puffed up
aventura, *f.* adventure
aventurar, *va.* to venture, risk
aventurero, *adj.* adventurous; *m.* adventurer
avergonzar, *va., vr.* to shame; be ashamed
aversion, *f.* aversion, dislike
avestruz, *m.* ostrich
aviación, *f.* aviation
aviador, *n.* aviator
aviar, *va.* to provision, equip
avión, *m.* airplane
avisar, *va.* to inform, give notice

aviso, *m.* information; notice; advertisement; warning
avispa, *f.* wasp
axila, *f.* armpit
¡ay! *interj.* alas!
aya, *f.* governess
ayer, *adv.* yesterday; lately
ayuda, *f.* help, aid
ayudante, *m.* assistant
ayudar, *va.* to help, assist
ayunar, *vn.* to fast
ayunas, en ayunas, *adv.* fasting, without food; ignorant (of an affair)
ayuntamiento, *m.* town council; city hall
azabache, *m.* jet
azada, *f.* spade, hoe
azadón, *m.* pickax; hoe
azafrán, *m.* saffron
azahar, *m.* orange blossom
azar, *m.* hazard; unforeseen disaster; **al azar**, at random
azogue, *m.* mercury
azorar, *va., vr.* to frighten, terrify
azote, *m.* whip, lash; scourge
azotea, *f.* roof garden
azteca, *n.* Aztec
azúcar, *m.* or *f.* sugar
azucarera, *f.* sugar bowl
azucena, *f.* white lily
azufre, *m.* sulphur, brimstone
azul, *adj.* blue
azulejo, *m.* tile; bluebird

B

baba, *f.* drivel; drool
babel, *m.* babel, confusion
babero, *m.* bib
baboso, *adj.* driveling, silly; *n.* (Sp. Am.) fool, idiot
bacalao, *m.* codfish
bacinica or **bacinilla**, *f.* chamber pot
bacteria, *f.* bacteria
bacteriólogo, *m.* bacteriologist
bachiller, *m.* bachelor (degree); a college graduate
bachillerato, *m.* bachelor's degree
bahía, *f.* bay
bailar, *vn.* to dance
bailarin, bailarina, *n.* dancer,

ballerina
baile, _m._ dance, ball
baja, _f._ fall, diminution; fall in prices; loss in membership
bajada, _f._ descent; downgrade
bajar, _va._ to lower; to decrease (the price); _vn._ to descend
bajeza, _f._ meanness; lowliness
bajo, _adj._ low; under; short; despicable; (mus.) bass
bala, _f._ bullet; bale of paper
balada, f. ballad
balance, _m._ fluctuation; rolling of a ship; balance; balance of accounts
balancear, _va., vn._ to balance; to roll; **balancearse,** to rock, to sway
balanza, _f._ scale; comparative estimate
balazo, _m._ shot; bullet wound
balboa, _m._ a coin of Panama
balbucear, _va., vn._ to stammer
balcón, _m._ balcony
baldar, _va._ to cripple
balde, _m._ bucket, pail; **de balde,** gratis; **en balde,** in vain
balístico, balística, _adj._ ballistic
balneario, _m._ bathing resort
balon, _m._ ball; bale
baloncesto, _m._ basketball
balonvolea, _m._ volleyball
balsa, _f._ raft, float; ferry
bálsamo, _m._ balsam, balm
ballena, _f._ whale; whalebone
bambolear, _vn., vr._ to reel, sway
bambú _m._ bamboo
banano, _m._ banana plant or fruit
bancario, _adj._ banking
bancarrota, _f._ bankruptcy
banco, _m._ bench; bank; **banco de sangre,** blood bank
banda, _f._ sash; band; gang; border
bandeja, _f._ tray
banderera, _f._ banner, flag
bandido, _m._ bandit, robber
bando, _m._ faction, team
banquero, banquera, _n._ banker
banqueta, _f._ sidewalk; three-legged stool

banquete, _m._ banquet; feast
bañar, _va._ to bathe; to water; to dip; **bañarse,** to take a bath.
bañera, _f._ bathtub
baño, _m._ bath; bathtub, bathroom; varnish; coat (of paint)
baraja, _f._ playing card; pack of cards; game of cards
baranda, _f._ banister, railing
barandal, _m._ railing
baratillo, _m._ bargain counter
barato, _adj._ cheap, lowpriced
barbacoa, _f._ barbecue
barbaridad, _f._ barbarity; rudeness; (coll.) ridiculous act; **una barbaridad,** a piece of nonsense; an "awful" lot; **¡que barbaridad!** how terrible!
bárbaro, _adj._ barbarous, savage; rash, daring; rude
barbería, _f._ barbershop
barbero, _m._ barber
barca, _f._ boat; barge
barítono, _m._ (mus.) baritone
barniz, _m._ varnish
barnizar, _va._ to varnish
barómetro, _m._ barometer
barón, _m._ baron
baronesa, _f._ baroness
barquillo, _m._ cone-shaped wafer
barra, _f._ crowbar, lever
barraca, _f._ barrack; hut
barranca, _f._ cliff; gorge
barranco, _m._ ravine; gorge
barrera, _f._ clay pit; barrier
barriga, _f._ abdomen, belly
barril, _m._ barrel; cask; jug
barrio, _m._ district or section of a town; quarter; **barrios bajos,** slums
basar, _va._ to base
báscula, _f._ platform scale
base, _f._ base, basis
básico, _adj._ basic
basílica, _f._ basilica (cathedral)
basketbol, _m._ basketball
basta, _f._ basting; **¡basta!** _interj._ enough!
bastante, _adj._ sufficient; quite, considerable; _adv._ enough; rather
bastar, _vn._ to suffice

bastardilla, *f.* italic
bastardo, *adj., m.* bastard
bastidor, *m.* embroidery frame; **bastidores,** *pl.* stage scenery; wings; **tras bastidores,** backstage
bastilla, *f.* hem
bastón, *m.* cane, stick
bastos, *m. pl.* clubs (suit in cards)
basura, *f.* sweepings; garbage
basurero, *n.* dustpan; dunghill
bata, *f.* dressing gown
batalla, *f.* battle, combat
batallar, *vn.* to battle, dispute
batallón, *m.* (mil.) battalion
batata, *f.* sweet potato
batea, *f.* round wooden tray
batería, *f.* battery; (mus.) percussion section
batidor, *m.* beater
batir, *va., vn.* to beat
batista, *f.* batiste, cambric
batuta, *f.* baton; **llevar la batuta,** to lead, to preside
baúl, *m.* trunk, chest
bautismo, *m.* baptism
bautizar, *va.* to baptize, christen
bautizo, *m.* baptism
baya, *f.* berry
bayo, *adj.* bay (of a horse)
bayoneta, *f.* bayonet
bazar, *m.* bazaar
beata, *f.* overly pious woman; hypocrite
beato, *adj.* devout
bebedor, bebedora, *n.* drunkard, drinker
beber, *va., vn.* to drink; *m.* drinking
bebida, *f.* drink, beverage; **bebida alcohólica,** intoxicant
beca, *f.* scholarship, fellowship
becerro, *m.* calf; calfskin
beldad, *f.* beauty
Belén, *m.* Bethlehem; **estar en Belén,** to be absentminded
belga, *adj., n.* Belgian.
Bélgica, *f.* Belgium
bélico, *adj.* warlike, martial
beligerante, *n., adj.* belligerent
belleza, *f.* beauty
bello, *adj.* beautiful, handsome; **bellas artes,** fine arts
bemol, *m.* (mus.) flat
bencina, *f.* (chem.) benzine
bendecir, *va.* to bless
bendición, *f.* benediction; blessing
bendito, *adj.* sainted, blessed; simple
benefactor, *m.* benefactor
beneficencia, *f.* beneficence, charity
beneficiado, beneficiada, *n.* beneficiary
beneficiar, *va.* to profit; to benefit
beneficiario, *m.* beneficiary
beneficio, *m.* benefit; profit
benemérito, *adj.* worthy
benévolo, *adj.* benevolent
berenjena, *f.* eggplant
berrear, *vn.* to low, bellow
berrinche, *m.* fit of anger; sulkiness
besar, *va.* to kiss
beso, *m.* kiss
bestia, *f.* beast; animal; dunce, idiot.
bestial, *adj.* bestial, brutal
betabel, *m.* (Mex.) beet
betarraga or **betarrata,** (bot.) beet
betatrón, *m.* betatron
bevatrón, *m.* bevatron
biberón, *m.* nursing bottle
Biblia, *f.* Bible
bíblico, *adj.* Biblical
bibliografía, *f.* bibliography
biblioteca, *f.* library
bibliotecario, bibliotecaria, *n.* librarian
bicarbonato, *m.* bicarbonate
bíceps, *m.* (anat.) biceps
bicicleta, *f.* bicycle
bicho, *m.* vermin; insect
bien, *m.* good; benefit;
bienes, *pl.* property, riches; land; *adv.* well; right; all right; **¡bienes!** *interj.* fine! all right!
bienal, *adj.* biennial
bienaventurado, *adj.* blessed, happy, fortunate
bienestar, *m.* well-being
bienhechor, *m.* benefactor
bienio, *m.* space of two years

bienvenida, *f.* welcome
bienvenido, *adj.* welcome
bifocal, *adj.* bifocal
biftec, *m.* beefsteak
bigamo, bigama, *n.* bigamist
bigote, *m.* mustache
bilingüe, *adj.* bilingual
bilis, *f.* bile
billar, *m.* billiards
billete, *m.* ticket; billet, label; note, short letter; love letter; banknote bill
billetera, *f.* billfold
billetero, billetera, *n.* (Sp. Am.) vendor of lottery tickets
billón, *m.* billion
billonario, billonaria, *n.* billionaire
bimestral, *adj.* bimonthly
bimestre, *m.* space of two months; bimonthly rent, salary, etc.
bimotor, *adj.* two-motored
binóculo, *m.* opera glass
bioastronáutica, *f.* bioastronautics
biografía, *f.* biography
biología, *f.* biology
biombo, *m.* screen
biopsia, *f.* biopsy
bioquímico, *adj.* biochemical; *m.* biochemist
biosfera, *f.* biosphere
bisabuela, *f.* great-grandmother
bisabuelo, *m.* great-grandfather.
bisagra, *f.* hinge
bisel, *m.* bevel
bisemanal, *adj.* semiweekly.
bisonte, *m.* bison
bisoño, *adj.* inexperienced; *n.* novice
bistec, *m.* beefsteak
bizcocho, *m.* cake, ladyfinger
biznieta, *f.* great-granddaughter
biznieto, *m.* great-grandson
blanco, *adj.* white, blank; *m.* blank; target
blancura, *f.* whiteness
blando, *adj.* soft, smooth; mellow; mild, gentle
blanquear, *va., vn.* to bleach; to whitewash

blasfemia, *f.* blasphemy; oath
bledo, *m.* (bot.) wild amaranth; **no me importa un bledo,** I don't give a rap, I don't care
bloc, *m.* bloc, political group; pad (of paper)
bloqueo, *m.* blockade
blusa, *f.* blouse
boa, *f.* (zool.) boa
bobería, *f.* folly, foolishness
bobina, *f.* bobbin; coil; spool; (elec.) coil; **bobina de reacción (nuclear),** reactor (nuclear)
bobo, boba, *n.* dunce, fool; *adj.* stupid; silly
boca, *f.* mouth; entrance, opening; mouth of a river
bocacalle, *f.* street intersection or opening
bocamanga, *f.* armhole
boceto, *m.* sketch
bocina, *f.* bugle horn; speaking trumpet; automobile horn
bocio, *m.* goiter
bochornoso, *adj.* shameful; sultry (weather)
boda, *f.* wedding; **bodas de plata** or **de oro,** silver or golden anniversary
bodega, *f.* wine cellar; warehouse
bofetada, *f.* slap on the face
bofetón, *m.* box on the ear
boga, *f.* vogue, fad, popularity
bogar, *vn.* to row, paddle
boicotear, *va., vn.* to boycott
boina, *f.* beret
bola, *f.* ball; globe; marble; (coll.) lie, fib; disturbance
bolear, *vn.* to knock the balls about (billiards); (Mex.) to shine shoes
bolero, *m.* Spanish dancer; Andalusian dance; (Mex.) top hat; bootblack
boletín, *m.* bulletin
boleto, *m.* ticket; **boletode ida y vuelta,** round-trip ticket; **boleto sencillo,** one-way ticket
boliche, *m.* bowling
bolillo, *m.* (Mex.) kind of bread roll

boliviano, boliviana, *adj., n.*
Bolivian; *m.* a Bolivian coin
bolo, *m.* bowling pin; bolo
(knife); **bolos,** *pl.* bowling
bolsa, *f.* purse, pouch; case;
money exchange; stock ex-
change
bolsillo, *m.* pocket
bomba, *f.* pump; bomb; **bomba atómica,** atomic bomb;
bomba de aerosol, aerosol
bomb; **bomba de hidrógeno,**
hydrogen bomb; **bomba de
neutrón,** neutron bomb
bombardeo, *m.* bombardment
bombear, *va.* to pump (water)
bombero, *m.* fireman
bombilla, *f.* light bulb; (Sp.
Am.) a tube to sip maté
bombón, *m.* bonbon, candy
bonanza, f. bonanza
bondad, *f.* kindness
bondadoso, *adj.* kind
bonito, *adj.* pretty
bono, *m.* (com.) bond, certificate
boquiabierto, *adj.* open-
mouthed
boquilla, *f.* mouthpiece
borbotón, *m.* bubbling, **hablar
a borbotones,** to speak in
torrents, babble
bordado, *m.* embroidery
bordar, *va.* to embroider
bordo, *m.* board; the side of a
ship; (naut.) **a bordo,** on
board; **franco a bordo,** free
on board (f.o.b.)
borinqueño, borinqueña, *n.,
adj.* Puerto Rican
borrachera, *f.* drunkenness
borracho, *adj.* intoxicated
borrador, *m.* eraser; rough
draft
borrar, *va.* to erase
borrasca, *f.* storm, squall
borrego, borrega, *n.* yearling
lamb
borrico, *m.* ass; blockhead
borrón, *m.* ink blot, splotch
borronear, *va.* to sketch,
scribble
borroso, *adj.* blurred
bosque, *m.* forest, woods
bosquejo, *m.* outline, sketch

bostezar, *vn.* to yawn; to gape
bostezo, *m.* yawn, yawning
bota, *f.* cask; boot
botánica, *f.* botany
botar, *va.* to cast, throw; to
launch
botarate, *m., f.* fool
bote, *m.* small boat, rowboat;
jar, bottle; **bote de salvamento,** lifeboat
botella, *f.* bottle, flask
botica, *f.* drugstore, pharmacy
boticario, *m.* druggist
botiquin, *m.* first-aid kit
botón, *m.* button; bud
bóveda, *f.* arch; vault
bovino, *adj.* bovine
boxeador, *m.* boxer, pugilist
boxear, *vn.* to box
boxeo, *m.* boxing, pugilism
boya, *f.* buoy
bozal, *m.* muzzle
bracero, *m.* day laborer
bragazas, *m.* milksop
bragueta, *f.* trousers fly
brama, *f.* rut, mating time
bramar, *vn.* to roar, bellow
brasa, *f.* live coal
brasero, *m.* brazier, hearth.
Brasil, *m.* Brazil
brasileño, brasileña, *n., adj.*
Brazilian
brasilero, *adj.* (Sp. Am.) Brazilian
bravío, *adj.* savage, wild
bravo, *adj.* brave, valiant;
fierce; excellent, fine; **¡bravo!**
interj. bravo!
bravura, *f.* bravery; courage;
bravado, boast
brazalete, *m.* bracelet
brazo, *m.* arm; **brazos,** *pl.*
hands, man power
brea, *f.* pitch, tar
brecha, *f.* breach; gap
bregar, *vn.* to contend, struggle
Bretaña, *f.* Brittany; **Gran Bretaña,** Great Britain
breve, *adj.* brief, short; **en
breve,** shortly
brevedad, *f.* brevity
bribón, bribóna, *adj.* rascally;
n. rogue
brida, *f.* bridle; check, curb

brigada, *f.* brigade
brillante, *adj.* bright, shining; *m.* brilliant, diamond
brincar, *vn.* to leap, jump
brinco, *m.* leap, jump, **dar brincos,** to leap
brindar, *vn.* to drink one's health, toast; *va.* to offer
brindis, *m.* health, toast
brío, *m.* strength, vigor
brioso, *adj.* vigorous, fiery
brisa, *f.* breeze
británico, británica, *adj., n.* British, Britisher
brocado, *m.* brocade
brocha, *f.* painter's brush
broche, *m.* clasp; brooch
broma, *f.* joke, jest
bromear, *vn.* to jest, joke
bromuro, *m.* bromide
bronce, *m.* bronze, brass
bronco, *adj.* rough, coarse
bronquio, *m.* bronchial tube
bronquitis, *f.* bronchitis
brotar, *vn.* to bud, germinate, to break out, appear (said of a disease)
bruja, *f.* witch, hag; *adj.* (coll.) broke, short of funds
brujo, *m.* sorcerer
brújula, *f.* compass; magnetic needle
bruma, *f.* mist, haze
brumoso, *adj.* misty, hazy
brusco, *adj.* rude, gruff
Bruselas, *f.* Brussels
brutal, *adj.* brutal, brutish
bruto, *m.* brute, blockhead; **bruto, bruta,** *adj.* brutal, stupid; crude (ore, oil, etc.); gross (profits, etc.); **en bruto,** in a raw (unmanufactured) state
bucear, *vn.* to dive
bucle, *m.* curl
buche, *m.* craw, crop; mouthful
buen, *adj.* good; **hacer buen tiempo,** to be good weather
buenaventura, *f.* fortune, good luck.
bueno, *adj.* good, perfect; proper; healthy; useful
buey, *m.* ox, bullock
búfalo, *m.* buffalo

bufanda, *f.* scarf
bufete, *m.* desk, lawyer's office
bufo, *m.* buffoon; **bufo, bufa,** *adj.* comic
bufón, *m.* buffoon; jester; *adj.* funny, comical
buho, *m.* owl
buitre, *m.* vulture
bujía, *f.* spark plug; candle
bulbo, *m.* (bot.) bulb
bulevar, *m.* boulevard
bulla, *f.* clatter; crowd
bullicio, *m.* bustle; uproar
buque, *m.* boat, ship, vessel
burdo, *adj.* coarse (of cloth); ordinary
burla, *f.* scoff, sneer; hoax
burlar, *va.* to mock, deceive; to frustrate; **burlar se de,** to make fun of
buró, *m.* bureau, chest of drawers
burocracia, *f.* bureaucracy
busca, *f.* search
busto, *m.* bust
buzo, *m.* diver
buzón, *m.* mailbox, letter drop

C

C., centigrado, C. Centigrade
c/, cargo, (com.) cargo, charge
C.A., corriente alterna, A.C. alternating current
cabal, *adj.* just, exact; complete, accomplished
caballería, *f.* cavalry; knighthood
caballeriza, *f.* stable
caballero, *m.* knight; gentleman
caballete, *m.* easel
caballo, *m.* horse; knight (in chess); **a caballo,** on horseback
cabaña, *f.* hut, shack; cottage, cabin; cabana
cabaret, *m.* cabaret, night club
cabecear, *vn.* to nod with sleep
cabecera, *f.* upper end; head (of a bed or a table); headwaters; **médico de cabecera,** attending physician

cabecilla, *m.* ringleader

cabellera, *f.* head of hair

cabello, *m.* hair of the head

cabelludo, *adj.* hairy; **cuero cabelludo**, scalp

caber, *va., vn.* to contain, include; to fit; to be possible

cabeza, *f.* head; top; leader

cabezudo, *adj.* headstrong, obstinate

cabida, *f.* content, capacity

cabildo, *m.* town council

cabina, *f.* (avi.) cockpit

cabizbajo, *adj.* pensive

cable, *m.* cable; rope

cablegrafiar, *va.* to cable

cablegráfico, *adj.* cable; **dirección cablegráfica**, cable address

cablegrama, *m.* cablegram

cabo, *m.* extremity cape, headland; end, tip; (mil.) corporal

Cabo de Buena Esperanza, Cape of Good Hope

Cabo de Hornos, Cape Horn

cabra, *f.* goat

cabria, *f.* hoist

cabritilla, *f.* kidskin

cabrito, *m.* kid

cacahuate or **cacahuete**, *m.* peanut

cacao, *m.* (bot.) cacao, cocoa seed

cacerola, *f.* casserole, pan

cacto, *m.* cactus

cacha, *f.* knife handle

cachete, *m.* cheek

cachorro, cachorra, *n.* cub (of any animal)

cachucha, *f.* man's cap

cada, *adj.* each, every;

cada uno, everyone; each

cadena, *f.* chain; series; network

cadencia, *f.* cadence

cadera, *f.* hip

cadete, *m.* (mil.) cadet

caducar, *vn.* to dote; to lapse (of a legacy, etc.)

C.A.E., **cóbrese al entregar**, C.O.D. or c.o.d. cash or collect on delivery

caer, *vn.* to fall; to befall, happen

café, *m.* coffee; café

cafetera, *f.* coffee pot; (Arg.) a noisy motorcycle; a jalopy

cafetería, *f.* coffee store; coffeehouse

cafeto, *m.* coffee tree

caída, *f.* fall, falling

caído, *adj.* fallen

caimán, *m.* caiman; (fig.) fox, sly individual

cajero, cajera, *n.* cashier

cajeta, *f.* (Mex.) confection made of goat's milk

cajón, *m.* drawer; locker; coffin; **ser de cajón**, (coll.) to be customary

cal, *f.* lime (mineral)

calabaza, *f.* pumpkin, gourd; **dar calabazas**, to jilt; to flunk.

calabozo, *m.* dungeon; jail

calamar, *m.* squid

calambre, *m.* cramp

calamidad, *f.* misfortune

calar, *va.* to penetrate, pierce

calavera, *f.* skull; madcap

calcetín, *m.* sock

calcio, *m.* calcium

calculador, *adj.* calculating; **calculador electrónico**, electronic computer

calculadora, *f.* adding machine

calcular, *va.* to calculate

cálculo, *m.* calculation; **cálculo biliario**, gallstone

caldera, *f.* caldron, kettle, boiler

calefacción, *f.* heating

calendario, *m.* almanac, calendar

calentador, *m.* heater

calentar, *va.* to warm, heat; **calentarse**, to grow hot; to dispute warmly

calentura, *f.* fever

calibre, *m.* caliber, gauge; (fig.) sort, kind

calicanto, *m.* stone masonry

cálido, *adj.* hot, warm

caliente, *adj.* hot; fiery

calificación, *f.* qualification; mark (in school)

calificar, *va.* to qualify; to rate

calisténica, *f.* calisthenics

cáliz, *m.* chalice; goblet

calma, *f.* calm; calmness
calmante, *m.* (med.) sedative
calmar, *va.,* *vr.* to calm, quiet, pacify
calor, *m.* heat, ardor; **hacer** or **tener calor,** to be warm
calorífero, *m.* heater; **calorífero de aire caliente,** hot air heater
calumnia, *f.* slander
caluroso, *adj.* warm, hot
calva, *f.* bald spot
calvo, *adj.* bald
calzada, *f.* roadway, street
calzado, *m.* footwear
calzar, *va.* to put on, to block with a wedge
calzoncillos, *m. pl.* shorts
calzones, *m. pl.* trousers
callado, *adj.* silent; quiet
callar, *vn.* to be silent; to hush
calle, *f.* street
callejero, *adj.* fond of loitering in streets
callejón, *m.* alley, narrow pass
callo, *m.* corn; callus
cama, *f.* bed, couch; litter
cámara, *f.* hall; chamber; camera; cockpit; chamber of a firearm
camarada, *n.* comrade, companion
camarera, *f.* waitress; chambermaid
camarero, *m.* waiter; steward
camarilla, *f.* clique
camarón, *m.* (zool.) shrimp
camarote, *m.* berth, cabin
cambiar, *va.* to barter, exchange; to change; to alter; to make change (money)
cambio, *m.* exchange, barter; change
camelia, *f.* camellia
camilla, *f.* pallet, stretcher
caminante, *m.* traveler, walker
caminar, *vn.* to walk; travel
camino, *m.* road, way
camión, *m.* truck, bus
camioneta, *f.* station wagon, small truck
camisa, *f.* shirt
camiseta, *f.* undershirt
camisón, *m.* nightgown
camote, *m.* (Sp. Am.) sweet potato
campamento, *m.* (mil.) encampment, camp
campana, *f.* bell
campanada, sound of a bell
campanario, *m.* belfry, steeple
campanilla, *f.* hand bell; (anat.) uvula
campaña, *f.* campaign, expedition
campechano, *adj.* frank; hearty
campeón, *m.* champion
campeonato, *m.* championship
campesino, *adj.* rural; *n.* peasant
campestre, *adj.* rural, rustic
campo, *m.* country; countryside; field; camp; ground
cana, *f.* gray hair
Canadá, *m.* Canada
canadiense, *n., adj.* Canadian
canal, *m.* channel, canal; gutter
Canal de la Mancha, *m.* English Channel
canalla, *f.* mob, rabble, populace; *m.* scoundrel
canallada, despicable act
canario, *m.* canary bird
canasta, *f.* basket, hamper; canasta (card game)
canastilla, *f.* small basket; layette
cancelar, *va.* to cancel, erase
cáncer, *m.* (med.) cancer
canceroso, *adj.* cancerous
canciller, *m.* chancellor; consular assistant
candado, *m.* padlock
candela, *f.* fire; light
candelabro, *m.* candelabrum
candelero, *m.* candlestick
candidato, candidata, *n.* candidate
cándido, *adj.* candid
candor, *m.* candor, frankness
cangrejo, *m.* crawfish, crab
canguro, *m.* kangaroo
caníbal, *m.* cannibal
canilla, *f.* shinbone
canjear, *va.* to exchange
cano, *adj.* gray-headed
canoa, *f.* canoe

canoso, *adj.* white-haired
cansado, *adj.* tired; tiresome
cansancio, *m.* weariness
cantaleta, *f.* singsong
cantante, *m., f.* singer
cantar, *va., vn.* to sing
cántaro, *m.* pitcher; **llover a cántaros,** to rain heavily
cantera, *f.* quarry
cantidad, *f.* quantity, number
cantina, *f.* canteen; barroom
cantinero, *m.* bartender
canto, *m.* song; singing; stone; edge
cantor, cantora, *n.* singer
caña, *f.* cane, reed; sugar cane; stalk
cáñamo, *m.* hemp; hempen cloth
cañaveral, *m.* sugar-cane field
cañería, *f.* pipe line
caño, *m.* tube; pipe line
cañón, *m.* pipe; canyon; cannon; gun barrel; **cañón antiaéreo,** antiaircraft gun; **cañón anticarro** or **antitanque,** antitank gun
caoba, *f.* mahogany
caos, *m.* chaos, confusion
capa, *f.* cloak; layer, coating
capacidad, *f.* capacity
capacitar, *va., vr.* to enable, qualify; to delegate
capataz, *m.* overseer; foreman
capellán, *m.* chaplain, minister
caperuza, *f.* hood; **Caperucita Roja,** Little Red Riding Hood
capilla, *f.* hood; chapel
capital, *m.* capital, stock; *f.* capital, metropolis; *adj.* capital; principal
capitalismo, *m.* capitalism
capitalista, *n., adj.* capitalist
capitán, *m.* captain
capitolio, *m.* capitol
capítulo, *m.* chapter (of a book)
caporal, *m.* chief, ringleader
capota, *f.* cape; top (of vehicles)
capote, *m.* cape, cloak; raincoat; **decir para su capote,** to say to oneself
capricho, *m.* caprice, whimsi-

cal; obstinate
capturer, *va.* to capture
capullo, *m.* pod of silkworm; bud
caqui, *m., adj.* khaki
cara, *f.* face, front; surface
carabina, *f.* carbine; **ser como la carabina de Ambrosio** to be good for nothing, to be worthless
¡caracoles! *interj.* Blazes! Confound it!
carácter, *m.* character, nature, disposition
característica, *f.* trait, characteristic
característico, *adj.* characteristic
¡caramba! *interj.* Heavens!
carambola, *f.* carom (in billiards); trick; **por carambola,** indirectly, by chance
carátula, *f.* mask; title page
caravana, *f.* caravan; (Mex.) bow, curtsy
carbónico, *adj.* carbonic
carbono, *m.* (chem.) carbon
carbunclo, *m.* carbuncle
carburador, *m.* carburetor
cárcel, *f.* prison; jail
carcomido, *adj.* wormeaten
cardán, *m.* universal joint
cardenal, *m.* cardinal
cardiaco, *m.* cardiac
cardinal, *adj.* cardinal (point); principal, fundamental
cardo, *m.* thistle
carecer, *vn.* to want, lack
carencia, *f.* lack; scarcity
carestía, *f.* scarcity, want; famine; high price
careta, *f.* mask
carey, *m.* tortoise, shell turtle; tortoise shell
carga, *f.* load, burden; freight; cargo; load (of a firearm)
cargado, *adj.* loaded, full
cargador, *m.* freighter; loader
cargamento, *m.* load, cargo
cargar, *va.* to load, carry; to freight; to attack; to load a gun; to charge (on account)
cargo, *m.* debit; office; charge; care; accusation
caribe, *adj.* Caribbean

caricia, *f.* caress
caridad, *f.* charity
caries, *f.* (med.) caries, decay
cariño, *m.* fondness, love
cariñoso, *adj.* affectionate
carmesí, *m.* crimson
carnada, *f.* bait, lure
carnal, *adj.* related by blood;
primo carnal, first cousin
carnaval, *m.* carnival
carne, *f.* flesh, meat; pulp of fruit
carnero, *m.* sheep, mutton
carnicería, *f.* meat market; slaughter
carnicero, *m.* butcher; *adj.* carnivorous
carnívoro, *adj.* carnivorous
caro, *adj.* expensive; dear
carpa, *f.* carp (fish); (Sp. Am.) a camping tent
carpeta, *f.* table cover; portfolio
carpintería, *f.* carpentry; carpenter's shop
carpintero, *m.* carpenter
carraspera, *f.* hoarseness
carrera, *f.* running; career; race; course, **carrera de relevos,** relay race; **carrera de vallas,** hurdles
carreta, *f.* cart; wagon
carretada, *f.* wagonload
carretaje, *m.* cartage
carretera, *f.* highway
carro, *m.* cart, freight car, car; wagon
carruaje, *m.* carriage, vehicle
carta, *f.* letter; charter
cartel, *m.* placard; handbill
cartera, *f.* brief case, letter case; pocketbook
cartero, postman
cartílago, *m.* cartilage
cartucho, *m.* cartridge
cartulina, *f.* Bristol board, fine cardboard
casa, *f.* house; concern; home
casamiento, *m.* marriage, wedding
casar, *va., vr.* to marry
cascabel, *m.* rattle; sleigh bell; (zool.) rattlesnake
cascajo, *m.* gravel
cascanueces, *m.* nutcracker

cascar, *va., vr.* to crack, break into pieces
cáscara, *f.* rind, peel, husk
casco, *m.* skull, cranium; helmet; hulk (of a ship); crown (of a hat); hoof
casero, casera, *n.* landlord or landlady; *adj.* domestic, familiar; homemade
casi, *adv.* almost, nearly
casilla, *f.* hut, booth, cabin; ticket office; **casilla de correos,** P.O. Box
casimir, *m.* cashmere
caso, *m.* case; event; occasion; (gram.) case
casta, *f.* caste, race, lineage; breed; kind, quality
castaña, *f.* chestnut
castaño, *m.* chestnut tree; *adj.* hazel; brown
castañuela, *f.* castanet
castellano, castellana, *n., adj.* Castilian; Spanish language
castidad, *f.* chastity
castigar, *va.* to punish
castigo, *m.* punishment
Castilla, *f.* Castile
castillo, *m.* castle; fortress
castizo, *adj.* pure, correct (as to language)
casto, *adj.* pure, chaste
castrar, *va.* to geld, castrate
casual, *adj.* casual, accidental
casualidad, *f.* casualty, accident; chance, coincidence; **por casualidad,** by chance
catalán, catalana, *n., adj.* Catalan, Catalonian
catálogo, *m.* catalogue; list
cataplasma, *f.* poultice, plaster
catar, *va.* to taste; to judge
catarata, *f.* cataract, waterfall; (med.) cataract
catarro, *m.* catarrh, cold
catástrofe, *f.* catastrophe, disaster
cátedra, *f.* professorship, subject taught by a professor
catedral, *adj., f.* cathedral
catedrático, *m.* professor of a university
categoría, *f.* category; rank
caterva, *f.* mob, throng

catolicismo, m. Catholicism
católico, adj., n. Catholic
catorce, m., adj. fourteen
catre, m. cot
cauce, m. trench, ditch, drain; bed of a river
caucho, m. rubber
caudal, m. property, wealth; abundance, plenty
caudaloso, adj. carrying much water (of rivers)
caudillo, m. chief, leader, dictator
causa, f. cause; occasion; motive, case, lawsuit; **a causa de,** on account of
causar, va. to cause, occasion
cautela, f. caution
cauterizar, va. to cauterize
cautivar, va. to captivate, charm, attract
cautivo, cautiva, n. captive, prisoner
caverna, f. cavern, cave
cavidad, f. cavity, hollow
cayo, m. cay, key
caza, f. game; hunting; m. (avi.) fighter plane
cazador, m. hunter, huntsman
cazar, va. to chase, hunt
cazuela, f. stewing pan; crock
C.C., corriente continua, D.C. or d.c., direct current
cebada, f. barley
cebo, m. food; bait, lure; priming
cebolla, f. onion
cebra, f. zebra
ceder, va. to grant, yield; vn. to submit, comply
cédula, f. charter, patent; ticket; permit, license; **cédulas hipotecarias,** mortgage, bank stock
céfiro, m. zephyr, breeze
cegar, vn. to become blind; va. to deprive of sight
ceguera, f. blindness
ceja, f. eyebrow
celda, f. cell
celebración, f. celebration
celebrar, va. to celebrate
celeste, adj. celestial, sky blue
celestial, adj. celestial; heavenly; perfect
célibe, m. unmarried person; bachelor
celo, m. zeal; rut (in animals); **celos,** pl. jealousy; **tener celos de,** to be jealous of
celosía, f. lattice of a window; Venetian blind
celoso, adj. jealous, zealous
célula, f. cell
cementar, va. to cement
cementerio, m. cemetery
cemento, m. cement; putty
cena, f. supper
cenagal, m. slough; swamp
cenar, vn. to have supper
cenicero, m. ash tray
ceniciento, adj. ash-colored; **Cenicienta,** f. Cinderella
cenit, m. zenith
censo, m. census
censor, m. censor, critic
censura, f. critical review censure, blame
censurar, va. to to censure, blame
centavo, m. a cent
centena, f. hundred
centenar, m. hundred
centenario, adj. centenary; m. centennial
centeno, m. (bot.) rye
centésimo, adj. centesimal, hundredth
centígrado, adj., m. centigrade
centigramo, m. centigram
centímetro, m. centimeter
céntimo, m. centime; cent
central, adj. central, centric; f. central or main station; powerhouse; (Sp. Am.) sugar mill
centralizar, va. to centralize
céntrico, adj. central
centro, m. center
Centroamérica, f. Central America
cénts., céntimos, ¢ or c., cents
ceño, m. frown
cepillo, m. brush; **cepillo de dientes,** toothbrush; **cepillo de carpintero,** plane
cera, f. wax; wax taper
cerámica, f. ceramics

cerca, *f.* enclosure, fence; *adv.* near, close by

cercanía, *f.* proximity

cercano, *adj., adv.* near, close by

cercar, *va.* to inclose; to fence

cerciorar, *va., vr.* to ascertain, affirm

cerdo, *m.* hog, pig

cereal, *m.* cereal; grain

cerebral, *adj.* cerebral

cerebro, *m.* brain

ceremonia, *f.* ceremony

cerezo, *m.* cherry tree

cerillo, *m.* (Mex.) wax match

cernir, *va.* to sift, strain

cero, *m.* zero

cerrado, *adj.* closed; stupid, dense

cerradura, *f.* lock

cerrajero, *m.* locksmith

cerrar, *va., vn.* to close, shut; to lock; **cerrarse,** to be obstinate

cerro, *m.* hill

cerrojo, *m.* latch (of a door)

certeza, *f.* certainty, assurance

certidumbre, *f.* certainty, conviction

certificado, *m.* certificate; *adj.* certified, registered (as a letter)

certificar, *va.* to certify, affirm; to register (a letter)

cerveza, *f.* beer, ale, lager

cesante, *adj.* jobless

cesáreo, *adj.* Caesarian

cesión, *f.* cession, transfer; concession

cesionario, cesionaria, *n.* assignee, indorsee (of negotiable instrument)

césped, *m.* sod, lawn

cesta, *f.* basket

cesto, *m.* hand basket

cetro, *m.* scepter

cf, costo de flete, freight cost; **caballo de fuerza,** h.p. horsepower; **confesor,** confessor

cg., centigramo, cg. centigram

cía, or **C.ia: Compañía,** Co. or co. Company; Soc., Society

cicatriz, *f.* scar

ciclista, *m., f.* cyclist

ciclo, *m.* cycle

cielón, *m.* cyclone

ciclotrón, *m.* cyclotron

cidra, *f.* citron

ciego, *adj.* blind; *n.* blind person

cielo, *m.* sky, heaven

ciempiés, *m.* centipede

cien, *adj.* one hundred (used before a noun)

ciencia, *f.* science

cieno, *m.* mud, mire

científico, *adj.* scientific

ciento, *adj.* one hundred; *m.* a hundred

cierto, *adj.* certain, true

ciervo, *m.* deer, hart, stag

c.i.f., costo, seguro y flete, c.i.f., (com.) cost, insurance and freight

cifra, *f.* cipher, number

cigarra, *f.* katydid, cricket

cigarrera, *f.* cigarette case

cigarrillo, *m.* cigarette

cigarro, *m.* cigar; cigarette

cigüeña, *f.* (orn.) stork; (mech.) crank

cigüeñal, *m.* crankshaft

cilíndrico, *adj.* cylindrical

cilindro, *m.* cylinder; barrel

cima, *f.* summit, peak

cimentar, *va.* to lay a foundation, to establish fundamental principles

cimiento, *m.* groundwork of a building; basis, origin

cinc, *m.* zinc

cincel, *m.* chisel

cincelar, *va.* to chisel, engrave

cinco, *adj., m.* five

cincuenta, *m., adj.* fifty

cincha, *f.* girth, cinch

cine, cinema, cinematógrafo, *m.* moving-picture play or show

cinta, *f.* ribbon, tape, band

cintura, *f.* waistline

cinturón, *m.* belt; **cinturón de asiento, cinturón de seguridad,** seat belt, safety belt; **cinturón salvavidas,** life belt

ciprés, *m.* cypress tree

circo, *m.* circus

circuito, *m.* circuit
circulación, *f.* circulation
circular, *adj.* circular; *vn.* to circulate
círculo, *m.* circle; circumference; district; orb; club
circundar, *va.* to surround, encircle
circunferencia, *f.* circumference
circunspecto, *adj.* circumspect, cautious
circunstancia, *f.* circumstance, incident
ciruela, *f.* plum; **ciruela pasa,** prune
ciruelo, *m.* plum tree
cirugía, *f.* surgery
cirujano, *m.* surgeon
cisne, *m.* swan
cisterna, *f.* cistern; reservoir.
cita, *f.* citation, quotation; appointment, date
citación, *f.* quotation; summons,
citar, *va.* to make an appointment to meet a person; to convoke; to cite; to quote; to summon
cítrico, *adj.* (chem.) citric
ciudad, *f.* city
ciudadanía, *f.* citizenship; citizens
ciudadano, ciudadana, *n.* citizen
cívico, *adj.* civic
civil *adj.* civil, polite
civilización, *f.* civilization culture
civilizar, *va.* to civilize
civismo, *m.* patriotism
cizalla, *f.* metal shears
clamor, *m.* clamor, outcry
clamoroso, *adj.* clamorous; **exito clamoroso,** howling success
clandestino, *adj.* clandestine
clara, *f.* egg white
claraboya, *f.* skylight
claridad, *f.* light, brightness, clearness
clarificar, *va.* to brighten; to clarify
clarín, *m.* horn, bugle; trumpet; trumpeter

clarinete, *m.* clarinet; clarinet player
claro, *adj.* clear, bright; intelligible; light, evident, manifest; ¡**claroro!** *interj.* of course!
clase, *f.* class, rank; kind
clásico, *adj.* classical, classic
clasificar, *va.* to classify, class
clausura, *f.* closing; ad- journment
clausurar, *va.* to close; to adjourn
clave, *f.* key, code; (mus.) clef; *m.* harpsichord, clavichord
clavel, *m.* (bot.) pink, carnation
clavícula, *f.* clavicle, collarbone
clavija, *f.* pin, peg; plug, key
clavo, *m.* nail; **clavo de especia,** clove; **clavo de rosca,** screw
clemencia, *f.* clemency, mercy
clérigo, *m.* clergyman
clero, *m.* clergy
clima, *m.* climate.
clínica, *f.* clinic.
clínico, *adj.* clinical
clisé, *m.* plate, mat, cut
cloaca, *f.* sewer
cloro, *m.* (chem.) chlorine
clorofila, *f.* chlorophyll
cloroformo, *m.* chloroform
cloruro, *m.* (chem.) chloride
club, *m.* club, association
clueca, *adj.* clucking (of a hen)
clueco, *adj.* decrepit; (Sp. Am.) presumptuous, vain
cm. or **c/m, centímetro,** cm., centimeter
Co., Compañía, Co., Company; Soc., Society
c/o, a cargo de, c/o or c.o., in care of
coagular, *va., vr.* to coagulate, curd
coartar, *va.* to limit, restrain
cobarde, *adj.* cowardly, timid; *m.* coward
cobardía, *f.* cowardice
cobertizo, *m.* small shed
cobija, *f.* bed cover, blanket
cobijar, *va.* to cover; to shelter
cobra, *f.* (zool.) cobra
cobrador, *m.* collector; street-

car or train conductor

cobrar, *va.* to collect; to recover; to receive; to charge (price, fee)

cobre, *m.* copper

cóbrese al entregar, cash on delivery, C.O.D.

cobro, *m.* collection; payment

cocaína, *f.* cocaine

cocer, *va.* to boil, cook; *vn.* to boil; to ferment

cocido, *adj.* cooked, boiled; *m.* kind of beef stew

cociente, *m.* quotient

cocina, *f.* kitchen, cuisine; **cocina económica,** cooking range

cocinar, *va., vn.* to cook

cocinero, cocinera, *n.* cook

coco, *m.* coconut, coconut tree; bogey, bugaboo

cocodrilo, *m.* crocodile; faithless person

cocuyo or **cucuyo,** *m.* firefly

coche, *m.* coach; carriage; car; **coche de alquiler,** cab

cochino, *adj.* dirty, nasty; *m.* pig

coctelera, *f.* cocktail shaker

codicia, *f.* lust, greed

codicioso, *adj.* covetous

código, *m.* code of laws

codorniz, *f.* (orn.) quail

coerción, *f.* coercion

cofre, *m.* trunk; box, chest; hood (of an automobile)

coger, *va.* to catch; to surprise

cohecho, *m.* bribery

coherente, *adj.* coherent, cohesive

cohesión, *f.* cohesion

cohete, *m.* skyrocket; **cohete especial de combustible sólido,** solid-fuel space rocket

cohibir, *va.* to restrain

coincidencia, *f.* coincidence

coincidir, *vn.* to coincide

cojear, *vn.* to limp, hobble

cojera, *f.* lameness, limp

cojín, *m.* cushion

cojinete, *m.* bearing (of an axle, etc.)

cojo, *adj.* lame, cripple

col, *f.* cabbage

cola, *f.* tail; train (of a gown);

line; glue; **hacer cola,** to stand in line

colaboración, *f.* collaboration

colaborar, *vn.* to collaborate

colador, *m.* colander, strainer

colapso, *m.* prostration, collapse

colar, *va., vn.* to strain, filter; **colarse,** (coll.) to squeeze (into a party) uninvited

colchón, *m.* mattress

colección, *f.* collection; set

colecta, *f.* collection of offerings

colectividad, *f.* collectivity; community

colectivización, *f.* collectivization

colectivizar, *va.* collectivize

colectivo, *adj.* collective; **contrato colectivo,** closed shop

colector, *m.* collector, gatherer

colegial, *m.* collegian; *adj.* collegiate

colegio, *m.* school; boarding school; college

cólera, *f.* anger, rage, fury; *m.* (med.) cholera

colérico, *adj.* enraged

colgante, *adj.* pendulous, hanging; **puente colgante,** suspension bridge

colgar, *va.* to hang; *vn.* to be suspended

colibrí, *m.* hummingbird

coliflor, *f.* cauliflower

colina, *f.* hill, hillock

colinabo, *m.* turnip

coliseo, *m.* opera house, theater

colmar, *va.* to heap up, fill up; **colmarse,** to reach the limit

colmena, *f.* hive, beehive

colmillo, *m.* eyetooth; long tusk

colmo, *m.* heap; completion; fill; limit

colocación, *f.* employment; situation, place; allocation

colocar, *va.* to arrange; to lay, place; to give employment to

colon, *m.* (anat.) colon

Colón, Columbus

colón, *m.* monetary unit of Costa Rica

colonia, *f.* colony; (Cuba) sugar-cane plantation; (Mex.) urban subdivision

colonial, *adj.* colonial

colonizar, *va.* to colonize

color, *m.* color, hue, dye; pretext

colorado, *adj.* ruddy, red

colorear, *va.* to color; to palliate, excuse; *vn.* to grow red

colorido, *m.* color; coloring

colorín, *m.* (orn.) linnet; vivid color; (Chile) a redheaded person

colosal, *adj.* colossal, great

coloso, *m.* colossus

columna, *f.* column; **columna vertebral,** spinal column

columpio, *m.* swing

collar, *m.* necklace

coma, *f.* comma (punctuation mark); (med.) coma

comadre, *f.* midwife; title given godmother of one's child; intimate woman friend, pal

comadrona, *f.* midwife

comandante, *m.* commander, chief; warden

comandita, *f.* (com.) silent partnership

comarca, *f.* territory, district; boundary, limit

combate, *m.* combat

combatiente, *m.* combatant

combatir, *va., vn.* to combat, fight; to attack; to contradict

combinar, *va., vr.* to combine

combustible, *adj.* combustible; *m.* fuel

comedia, *f.* comedy, play

comediante, *m., f.* actor, comedian

comedido, *adj.* eager to help

comedor, *m.* dining room

comején, *m.* white ant, termite

comentador, comentadora, *n.* commentator

comentar, *va.* to comment; to remark; to expound

comentario, *m.* comment, commentary

comer, *va.* to eat, chew; to dine; to take a piece in chess

comercial, *adj.* commercial

comerciante, *m.* trader, merchant, businessman

comerciar, *va.* to trade, have business intercourse with; **comerciar en,** to deal in

comercio, *m.* trade, commerce, business; communication, intercourse

comestable, *adj.* edible; **comestables,** *m. pl.* provisions, groceries

cometer, *va.* to commit

cometido, *m.* task, mission

comezón, *f.* itch

comicios, *m. pl.* elections; polls

cómico, *adj.* comic, comical; **cómico, cómica,** *n.* actor, actress

comida, *f.* food; dinner; meal

comienzo, *m.* beginning

comilón, comilona, *n., adj.* glutton

comillas, *f. pl.* quotation marks

comino, *m.* cumin (plant or seed); **no valer un comino,** to be worthless

comisario, *m.* commissary; deputy

comisión, *f.* trust, commission; committee

comisionado, *m.* commissioner

comisionar, *va.* to commission, depute

comité, *m.* committee

comitiva, *f.* retinue

como, *adv.* (interrogative, **cómo**) how, in what manner; as; like; **¿a cómo estamos?** what is the date?

cómoda, *f.* chest of drawers

comodidad, *f.* comfort; convenience

cómodo, *adj.* convenient, commodious; comfortable

compacto, *adj.* compact

compadecer, *va., vr.* to pity, sympathize with

compadre, *m.* godfather of one's child; friend, old pal

compañero, compañera, *n.* companion, comrade, friend, partner; pal

compañía, *f.* company, society; partnership

comparación, *f.* comparison

comparar, *va.* to compare

compartir, *va.* to share

compás, *m.* compass; (mus.) measure, time; beat

compasión, *f.* compassion, pity

compasivo, *adj.* compassionate

compatible, *adj.* compatible

compatriota, *m.,* *f.* countryman; countrywoman; fellow citizen

compeler, *va.* to compel, constrain

compendio, *m.* summary

compensación, *f.* compensation

compensar, *va.,* *vn.* to compensate

competencia, *f.* competition, rivalry; competence

competente, *adj.* competent

competidor, competidora, *n.* competitor

compilar, *va.* to compile

complacer, *va.* to please another; **complacerse,** to be pleased with

complaciente, *adj.* pleasing; accommodating

complejo, *m.* complex; **complejo, compleja,** *adj.* complex, intricate

complementario, *adj.* complementary

complemento, *m.* complement; (gram.) object

completar, *va.* to complete

completo, *adj.* complete

complexión, *f.* constitution, physique

complicación, *f.* complication

complicar, *va.* to complicate

cómplice, *m.,* *f.* accomplice

complot, *m.* plot, conspiracy

componer, *va.* to compose; to repair; to settle; **componerse,** to arrange one's hair, clothes, etc., **componerse**

de, to be composed of

comportarse, *vr.* to comport oneself

compositor, compositora, *n.* composer; compositor

compostura, *f.* composition; mending, repairing; composure

compota, *f.* preserves

compra, purchase

comprar, *va.* to buy, purchase

comprender, *va.* to include, comprise; to understand

comprensible, *adj.* comprehensible

comprensión, *f.* understanding

comprensivo, *adj.* understanding

compresión, *f.* compression

compresor, *m.* compressor

comprimir, *va.* to compress; to condense; to repress

comprobante, *m.* voucher

comprobar, *va.* to verify, check; to confirm

comprometer, *va.* to compromise; to put in danger; **comprometerse,** to commit oneself; to become engaged

comprometido, *adj.* betrothed

compromiso, *m.* compromise; commitment; engagement

compuerta, *f.* lock, floodgate

compuesto, *m.* compound; *adj.* composed; repaired

compulsorio, *adj.* compulsory

computar, *va.* to compute

cómputo, *m.* computation

comulgar, *vn.* to take communion

común, *adj.* common, usual; *m.* watercloset

comunicación, *f.* communication

comunicar, *va.* to communicate

comunidad, community

comunión, communion; fellowship; common possession

comunismo, *m.* communism

comunista, *m.,* *f.* communist

con, *prep.* with; by

conato, *m.* endeavor; crime attempted but not executed

concebir, *va., vn.* to conceive
conceder, *va.* to concede
concejal, *m.* councilman
concejo, *m.* town hall
concentración, *f.* concentration
concentrar, *va., vr.* to concentrate
concepción, *f.* conception
concepto, *m.* conception, concept; opinion
concerniente, *adj.* concerning
concernir, *v. imp.* to concern
concertar, *va.* to settle; *vn.* to agree, accord
concertista, *m., f.* concert performer or manager
concesión, *f.* concession, grant
conciencia, *f.* conscience
concienzudo, *adj.* conscientious
conciliación, *f.* conciliation
conciliar, *va.* to conciliate, reconcile
concilio, *m.* council
conciso, *adj.* concise, brief
conciudadano, conciudadana, *n* fellow citizen; countryman
concluir, *va.* to conclude, complete; to infer
conclusión, *f.* conclusion; consequence
concluyente, *adj.* conclusive
concordancia, *f.* concordance, concord; harmony
concordar, *va.* to accord; *vn.* to agree
concordia, *f.* conformity, union, harmony
concretar, *va.* to combine, unite; to limit; to sum up
concreto, *adj.* concrete
concubina, *f.* concubine, mistress
concurrencia, *f.* audience
concurrentes, *m. pl.* attendants, guests
concurrido, *adj.* crowded, well-attended
concurrir, *vn.* to concur, agree; to attend
concurso, *m.* competition, contest

concusión, *f.* concussion
concha, *f.* shell; tortoise shell
condado, *m.* county
conde, *m.* earl, count
condecorar, *va.* to confer a decoration on
condensación, *f.* condensation
condensar, *va., vr.* to condense
condesa, *f.* countess
condescendencia, *f.* condescension, compliance
condescender, *vn.* to condescend
condición, *f.* condition, quality; stipulation
condimentar, *va.* to season (food)
condimento, *m.* condiment
condiscípulo, condiscípula, *n.* fellow-student
condolerse, *vr.* to condole, to sympathize
cóndor, *m.* (orn.) condor
conducente, *adj.* conducive
conducta, *f.* conduct; behavior
conducto, *m.* conduit; channel; **por conducto de,** through (agent)
conductor, *m.* conductor, guide
conectar, *va.* to connect
conejo, coneja, *n.* rabbit
conejillo, *m.* small rabbit; **conejillo de Indias,** guinea pig
conexión, *f.* connection
confección, *f.* (med.) compound; confection
confeccionar, *va.* to make, put together
confederación, *f.* confederacy, confederation
confederado, confederada, *n.,* *adj.* confederate
conferenciante, *m., f.* public lecturer
conferenciar, *vn.* to hold a conference; to consult together
conferencista, *m., f.* lecturer, speaker
conferir, *va.* to confer, grant
confesar, *va.* to confess

confesión, f. confession

confesor, m. confessor

confiado, adj. confident; arrogant, forward

confianza, f. confidence, boldness; assurance; intimacy; trust; **digno de confianza,** reliable, trustworthy

confiar, va., vn. to confide, trust in; to hope, count on

confidencia, f. confidence

confidencial, adj. confidential

confidente, m., f. confidant

confín, m. limit, boundary

confinar, va., vn. to confine, limit; to border upon

confirmación, f. confirmation

confirmr, va. to confirm

confiscar, va. to confiscate

confite, m. candy, bonbon

conflicto, m. conflict

conformar, va. to conform; vn. to suit, fit; **conformarse,** to resign oneself

conforme, adj. conformable, suitable; **estar conforme,** to be in agreement; adv. according to

conformidad, f. conformity; patience, resignation

confort, m. comfort

confortante, adj. comforting; m. sedative

confortar, va. to comfort

confraternidad, f. confraternity, brotherhood

confrontar, va. to confront; to compare

confundir, va., vr. to confound; to perplex

confusión, f. confusion, disorder; perplexity

confuso, adj. confused; perplexed

conga, f. conga

congelación, f. freezing

congelador, m. freezer

congeladora, f. deep freezer

congelar, va., vr. to freeze, congeal

congeniar, vn. to be congenial

congénito, adj. congenital

conglomeración, f. conglomeration

congoja, f. anguish, grief

congratular, va. to congratulate

congregar, va. to assemble, meet

congreso, m. congress

congruencia, f. congruency

cónico, adj. conical

conjetura, f. conjecture

conjugar, va. to conjugate

conjunción, f. conjunction

conjunto, adj. united, conjunct; m. the whole, the ensemble

conjurar, va., vn. to conjure; to cospire

conmemoración, f. commemoration

conmemorar, va. to commemorate

conmemorativo, adj. memorial

conmigo, pron. with me, with myself

conmiseración, f. commiseration, pity

conmovedor, adj. affecting, moving, touching

conmover, va., vr. to disturb, move, stir

conmutador, m. electric switch

connivencia, f. connivance

conocedor, conocedora, n. expert; connoisseur

conocer, va. to know, to be acquainted; to understand

conocido, conocida, n. acquaintance

conocimiento, m. knowledge, understanding; consciousness; (com.) bill of lading; **poner en conocimiento,** to inform, to advise

conque, conj. so then

conquista, f. conquest

conquistador, m. conqueror

conquistar, va. to conquer

consagrar, va. to consecrate, dedicate

consciente, adj. conscious, aware

consecución, f. attainment

consecuencia, f. consequence; result

consecuente, adj. conse-

quent, logical
consecutivo, *adj.* consecutive
conseguir, *va.* to attain, get
consejero, *m.* counselor; councilor; advisor
consejo, *m.* counsel, advice; council; advisory board
consentido *adj.* pampered
consentimiento, *m.* consent, assent
consentir, *va.* to consent, to agree; to comply, acquiesce; to coddle
conserje, *m.* concierge, janitor
conserva, *f.* conserve, preserve; **conservas,** canned goods
conservador, *adj.* conservative
conservar, *va.* to conserve; to keep, maintain
couservatorio, *m.* conservatory
considerable, *adj.* considerable
consideración, *f.* consideration, regard
considerado, *adj.* prudent, considerate; esteemed
considerando, *conj.* whereas
considerar, *va.* to consider, think over; to respect
consigna, (mil.) watchword
consignación, *f.* consignation; consignment
consignar, *va.* to consign
consignatario, *m.* trustee; consignee
consigo, *pron.* with oneself
consiguiente, *adj.* consequent, consecutive; *m.* consequence, effect; **por consiguiente,** consequently
consistencia, *f.* consistence
consistente, *adj.* consistent; firm, solid
consistir, *vn.* to consist
consocio, *m.* partner, fellow member
consolación, *f.* consolation
consolar, *va.* to console, to cheer
consolidar, *va., vr.* to consolidate, strengthen
consorte, *m., f.* consort, companion

conspicuo, *adj.* conspicuous; prominent
conspiración, *f.* conspiracy, plot
conspirar, *vn.* to conspire, plot
constancia, *f.* constancy
constante, *adj.* constant, firm
constar, *v. imp.* to be evident or certain; to be composed of, consist of; **hacer constar,** to state; **me consta,** I know positively
constelación, *f.* constellation
consternar, *va.* to confound, dismay
constipación, *f.* cold; constipation
constipado, *m.* cold in the head
constitución, *f.* constitution
constitucional, *adj.* constitutional
constituir, *va., vr.* to constitute
construcción, *f.* construction
constructor, constructora, *n.* builder
construir, *va.* to build, construct; to construe
consuelo, *m.* consolation, comfort
cónsul, *m.* consul
consulado, *m.* consulate
consulta, *f.* consultation
consultar, *va.* to consult
consultivo, *adj.* advisory
consultor, consultora, *n.* adviser, counselor; *adj.* advisory, consulting
consultorio, *m.* doctor's office; clinic
consumar, *va.* to consummate, finish, perfect
consumidor, consumidora, *n.* consumer; *adj.* consuming
consumir, *va.* to consume; **consumirse,** to languish
consumo, *m.* consumption of provisions; demand (for merchandise)
consunción, (med.) consumption
contabilidad, *f.* accounting, bookkeeping

contacto, *m.* contact, touch
contado, *adj.* scarce, rare; **al contado,** cash, ready money
contador, *m.* accountant; counter; **contador de agua,** water meter; **contador Geiger,** Geiger counter
contagiar, *va.* to infect
contagio, *m.* contagion
contagioso, *adj.* contagious
contaminar, *va.* to contaminate
contante, *adj.* fit to be counted; **dinero contante y sonante,** ready cash
contar, *va.* to count, calculate; to relate.
contemplar, *va.* to contemplate, to coddle
contender, *vn.* to contend; to contest
contendiente, *m., f.* competitor; contender
contener, *va.* to contain, comprise; **contenerse,** to repress
contenido, *m.* contents
contentar, *va., vr.* to content
contento, *adj.* glad; pleased; content; *m.* contentment
conteo, *m.* countdown
contestación, *f.* answer, reply
contestar, *va.* to answer
contienda, *f.* contest, dispute
contigo, *pron.* with you (sing.)
continental, *adj.* continental
continente, *m.* continent, mainland
contingente, *adj.* accidental; *m.* contingent; share
continuación, *f.* continuation, continuance, continuity
continuamente, *adv.* continuously, continually
continuar, *va., vn.* to continue
continuidad, *f.* continuity
continuo, *adj.* continuous, continual
contorno, *m.* environs; contour, outline
contrabajo, *m.* bass viol
contrabandista, *m.* smuggler
contracción, *f.* contraction
contradecir, *va.* to contradict
contradicción, *f.* contradiction

contradictorio, *adj.* contradictory
contraer, *va., vn.* to contract; to reduce; **contraerse,** to shrink up
contrahecho, *adj.* deformed
contralor, *m.* controller
contralto, *m., f.* contralto
contraorden, *f.* countermand
contrapeso, *m.* counterweight; (Chile) uneasiness; **hacer contrapeso a,** to counterbalance
contrapunto, *m.* (mus.) counterpoint, harmony
contrariar, *va.* to contradict, oppose; to vex
contrarieded, *f.* opposition; disappointment
contrario, contraria, *n.* opponent, antagonist; *adj.* contrary, opposite; hostile; **al contrario,** on the contrary
contrarrestar, *va.* to counteract
contraseña, *f.* countersign; (mil.) watchword, password
contrastar, *va.* to contrast; to assay metals
contraste, *m.* contrast; opposition
contratar, *va.* to engage, hire; to contract
contratiempo, *m.* disappointment; mishap
contratista, *m.* contractor
contrato, *m.* contract, pact
contraveneno, *m.* antidote
contribuir, *va.* to contribute
contribuyente, *m., f.* contributor; taxpayer
contrincante, *m.* competitor
contrito, *adj.* contrite
control, *m.* control, check
contusión, *f.* contusion
convalecencia, *f.* convalescence
convalecer, *vn.* to convalesce
convencer, *va.* to convince
convencimiento, *m.* conviction
convención, *f.* convention
convencional, *adj.* conventional

convenido, *adj.* agreed
conveniencia, *f.* utility, profit; convenience; ease; desirability
conveniente, *adj.* convenient, advantageous; desirable
convenio, *m.* pact
convener, *vn.* to agree, coincide; to compromise; to fit, suit
convento, *m.* convent
conversación, *f.* conversation
conversar, *vn.* to converse, talk
converso, *m.* convert
convertir, *va.* to transform, convert; to reform; **convertirse,** to become
convicción, *f.* conviction
convidado, *adj.* invited; **convidado, convidada,** *n.* invited guest
convidar, *va.* to invite
convincente, *adj.* convincing
convocar, *va.* to convoke, assemble
convoy, *m.* convoy, escort
convulsión, *f.* convulsion
conyugal, *adj.* conjugal
cónyuges, *m. pl.* married couple, husband and wife
coñac, *m.* cognac, brandy
cooperación, *f.* cooperation
cooperar, *vn.* to cooperate
cooperativo, *adj.* cooperative; **cooperativa,** cooperative society
coordinación, *f.* coordination
coordinar, *va.* to coordinate
copa, *f.* cup; goblet; top of a tree; crown of a hat; **copas,** *pl.* hearts (at cards)
Copenhague, *f.* Copenhagen
copete, *m.* toupee; pompadour; top, summit
copia, *f.* copy, transcript; imitation
copiar, *va.* to copy; to imitate
copioso, *adj.* abundant
copla, *f.* couplet; popular ballad, folksong
coqueta, *f.* coquette, flirt
coquetear, *vn.* to flirt
coquetería, *f.* coquetry, flirtation

coquetón, coquetona, *adj.* flirtatious
coraje, *m.* anger
corajudo, *adj.* ill-tempered
coral, *m.* coral; *adj.* choral
coraza, *f.* cuirass; armor plate; shell of a turtle
corazón, *m.* heart; core; benevolence; center
corazonada, *f.* sudden inspiration; presentiment, hunch
corbata, *f.* necktie
corcovado, *adj.* humpbacked, crooked
corcho, *m.* cork
cordel, *m.* cord, rope
cordero, *m.* lamb; meek, gentle man
cordial, *adj.* cordial, affectionate; *m.* cordial
cordialidad, *f.* cordiality
cordillera, range of mountains
cordón, *m.* cord, string; military cordon
cordura, *f.* prudence, sanity, good judgment
corista, *m.* chorister; *f.* chorus girl
cornada, *f.* thrust with horns
córnea, cornea
corneta, *f.* cornet; *m.* bugler
coro, *m.* choir, chorus
corona, *f.* crown; coronet; top of the head; crown (English silver coin); monarchy; halo
coronar, *va.* to crown; to complete, perfect
coronel, *m.* (mil.) colonel
coronilla, *f.* crown of the head
corporación, *f.* corporation
corporal, *adj.* corporal, bodily
corpulento, *adj.* corpulent
Corpus, *m.* Corpus Christi (religious festival)
corral, *m.* poultry yard; **aves de corral,** poultry
correa, *f.* leather strap, belt; **tener correa,** to bear teasing good-humoredly
corrección, *f.* correction; proper demeanor
correcto, *adj.* correct
corredor, *m.* runner; corridor, broker
corregidor, *m.* corregidor

(Spanish magistrate)

corregir, *va.* to correct, amend; to reprehand

correo, *m.* mail; mailman; post office

correoso, *adj.* leathery

correr, *vn.* to run; to race; to flow; to blow (applied to the wind); to pass away (applied to time); *va.* to race (an animal); **correrse,** to become disconcerted

correría, *f.* excursion, incursion; **correrías,** youthful escapades

correspondencia, *f.* correspondence; proportion

corresponder, *va.* to reciprocate; to correspond; to agree

correspondiente, *adj.* corresponding; suitable

corresponsal *m.* correspondent

corretear, *vn.* to run around (as children)

corrida, *f.* course, race; **corrida de toros,** bullfight

corrido, *m.* (mus.) a special rhythm

corriente, *f.* current (of water, electricity, etc.); stream; **tener al corriente,** to keep advised; *adj.* current; ordinary

corromper, *va., vr.* to corrupt

corrupción, *f.* corruption

cortapapel, *m.* paper knife

cortaplumas, *m.* penknife

corte, *m.* cutting; cut; felling of trees; cut goods to make a garment; *f.* (royal) court, the court of chancery; retinue; courtship, flattery; **hacer la corte,** to woo; **Cortes,** *f. pl.* Cortes, Spanish Parliament

cortejar, *va.* to make love, court

cortejo, *m.* cortege, procession

cortés, *adj.* courteous, polite

cortesano, *m.* courtier; **cortesana,** *f.* courtesan

cortesía, *f.* courtesy

cortina, *f.* curtain

corto, *adj.* short; shy

cortocircuito, *m.* short circuit

corva, *f.* bend of the knee

cosa, *f.* thing; matter

cosecha, *f.* harvest; crop

cosechar, *va.* to crop, reap

coser, *va.* to sew; **máquina de coser,** sewing machine

cosmético, *m.* cosmetic

cosmopolita, *n., adj.* cosmopolite, cosmopolitan

cosquillas, *f. pl.* tickling; **hacer cosquillas,** to tickle

costa, *f.* cost, price; expense; coast, shore

costado, *m.* side; (mil.) flank

costal, *m.* sack, large bag

costar, *vn.* to cost

coste, *m.* cost, expense

costear, *va.* to pay the cost; *vn.* to sail along the coast

costero, *adj.* coastal

costilla, *f.* rib; (coll.) wife

costo, *m.* cost, price

costoso, *adj.* costly, expensive

costra, *f.* crust

costura, *f.* seam; needlework; sewing

costurera, *f.* seamstress

cotidiano, *adj.* daily

cotización, *f.* (com.) quotation

cotizar, *va.* to quote (a price)

coto, *m.* (med.) goiter

cotorra, *f.* magpie; (coll.) talkative woman

coyote, *m.* coyote

coyuntura, *f.* joint, articulation

C.P.T., Contador Público Titulado, C.P.A. Certified Public Accountant

cráneo, *m.* skull, cranium

cráter *m.* crater

creación, *f.* creation

Creador, *m.* the Creator, God

creador, *adj.* creative

crear, *va.* to create, make; to establish

crecer, *vn.* to grow; to increase; to swell

creces, *f. pl.* increase; **pagar con creces,** to pay back generously

creciente, *f.* swell; leaven; crescent (of the moon); (naut.) flood tide; *adj.* growing, increasing; crescent

(moon)
crecimiento, *m.* growth
credencial, *f.* credential
crédito, *m.* credit; reputation
crédulo, *adj.* credulous
creer, *va.* to believe; to think;
¡ya lo creo! you bet! of
course!
crema, *f.* cream
cremallera, *f.* (mech.) rack;
zipper
crepúsculo, *m.* twilight
crespo, *adj.* crisp; curly; *m.*
(Sp. Am.) a curl
crespón, *m.* crepe
cresta, *f.* cockscomb; crest of
some birds; top, summit of a
mountain; (Col.) a thing one
loves; love
cría, *f.* breed or brood of animals; hatch; (coll.) child
reared by a nurse
criada, *f.* maid servant
criadilla, *f.* testicle; small loaf;
truffle
criado, *m.* servant
criador, *m.* creator; breeder
crianza, *f.* breeding, education
criar, *va.* to create, produce,
to breed; to nurse; to suckle;
to bring up
crimen, *m.* crime
criminal, *adj., n.* criminal
crin, *f.* mane, horsehair
criollo, criolla, *n.* born in
Latin America of European
parents; peasant; *adj.* native,
typical of the region
crisis, *f.* crisis
crisma, *f.* (coll.) head
crisol, *m.* crucible; melting pot
cristal, *m.* crystal; crystal
glass; **cristal tallado,** cut
crystal
cristalería, *f.* glassware
cristalino, *adj.* crystalline,
clear
cristalizar, *va.* to crystallize
cristianismo, *m.* Christianism
cristiano, cristiana, *n., adj.*
Christian
Cristo, *m.* Christ
Cristóbal Colón, Christopher
Columbus
criterio *m.* criterion, judgment

crítica, *f.* criticism
criticar, *va.* to criticize
crítico, *m.* critic, censurer;
adj. critical
cromo, *m.* chromium, chrome
crónico, *adj.* chronic
cronista, *m., f.* chronicler; reporter
croqueta, *f.* croquette
cruce, *m.* crossing; crossroads
crucificar, *va.* to crucify; to
torment
crucifijo, *m.* crucifix
crucigrama, *m.* crossword
puzzle
crudo, *adj.* raw, crude; green
unripe; rude, cruel
cruel, *adj.* cruel
crueldad, *f.* cruelty
crujido, *m.* crack, creak
crujir, *vn.* to crackle, rustle;
crujir los dientes, to grind
the teeth
cruz, *f.* cross
cruzada, *f.* crusade
cruzado, *adj.* crossed; of
crossed breed, etc.
cruzar, *va.* to cross
c.s.f., costo, seguro y flete,
c.i.f.; cost, insurance, and
freight
cta. or **c.**ta , **cuenta,** (com.) a/c
or acc., account
cta., cte. or **cta., corr.**te ,
cuenta corriente, (com.)
current account
cte. or **corr.**te, **corriente,** current, usual, common
c/u, cada uno, each one,
every one
cuaderno, *m.* memorandum
book
cuadra, *f.* block of houses
cuadrado, *adj.* square; (Cuba)
rude and stupid; *m.* square
cuadragésimo, *adj.* fortieth
cuadrángulo, *m.* quadrangle
cuadrilátero, *adj.* quadrilat-
eral
cuadrilla, *f.* gang, crew, troop;
matador and his assistants
cuadro, *m.* square; picture;
picture frame
cuadrúpedo, *adj.* quadruped
cuajar, *va.* to coagulate; *vn.* to

succeed; to please; **cuajarse**, to coagulate

cual, *pron., adj.* which; such as; *adv.* as; how; like; ¿**cuál?** *interr.* which (one)?

cualidad *f.* quality

cualquiera, *adj., pron.* any; anyone, anybody, somebody

cuan, *adv.* how, as (used only before adj. or adv.); **cuán**, *adv.* how, what

cuando (*interr.* **cuándo**), *adv.* when; in case that; if; although; even; sometimes

cuanto, *adj.* as many as, as much as; ¿**cuánto?** how much?; ¿**cuántos?** how many?; *adv.* as; the more; **cuanto antes**, at once; **en cuanto a**, with regard to

cuarenta, *adj.* forty

cuarentena, *f.* quarantine

cuaresma, *f.* Lent

cuartel, *m.* barracks; **cuartel general**, headquarters

cuarteto, *m.* quartet

cuarto, *m.* fourth part, quarter; dwelling, room; *adj.* fourth

cuate, *m., adj.* (Mex.) twin; (coll.) pal

cuatro, *adj.* four; *m.* figure four; (mus.) quartet ; **las cuatro**, *f. pl.* four o'clock

cubano, cubana, *adj., n.* Cuban

cúbico, *adj.* cubic

cubierta, *f.* cover; envelope; wrapping; deck of a ship; (auto.) hood

cubierto, *m.* place for one at the table; regular dinner

cubil, *m.* lair of wild beasts

cubo, *m.* cube; pail; hub (of a wheel)

cubrir, *va.* to cover; to disguise; to cover a mare; **cubrirse**, to put on one's hat

cucaracha, *f.* cockroach

cucurucho, *m.* paper cone

cuchara, *f.* spoon

cucharada, *f.* spoonful

cucharita, *f.* teaspoon

cucharón, *m.* ladle, dipper, large spoon; scoop

cuchicheo, *m.* whispering, murmur

cuchillo, *m.* knife

cuello, *m.* neck; neck of a bottle; collar of a garment; **cuello de estrangulación**, bottleneck

cuenca, *f.* valley, basin of a river; (anat.) eye socket

cuento, *m.* story, tale, narrative; **cuento de hadas**, fairy tale

cuerda, *f.* cord; string for musical instruments; spring of a watch or clock; **bajo cuerda**, underhandedly; **dar cuerda**, to wind

cuerdo, *adj.* prudent, judicious; in his senses

cuerno, *m.* horn; corn, callosity; **cuerno de abundancia** horn of plenty

cuerpo, *m.* body; cadaver, corpse; staff, corps

cuervo, *m.* (orn.) crow, raven

cuesta, *f.* hill; **cuesta arriba**, uphill; with great trouble and difficulty

cuestión, *f.* question; dispute; problem; matter

cuestionario, *m.* questionnaire

cueva, *f.* cave, grotto, den

cuidado, *m.* care, attention; solicitude, anxiety; accuracy; **tener cuidado**, to be careful; ¡**cuidado!** *interj.* watch out!

cuidadoso, *adj.* careful

cuidar, *va.* to heed, care; to mind, look after; **cuidarse**, to be careful of one's health

cuita, *f.* grief, affliction

culata, *f.* breech of a gun; butt

culebra, *f.* snake; **culebra de cascabel**, rattlesnake

culo, *m.* breech, backside; anus; bottom

culpa, *f.* misdemeanor; sin; guilt; **tener la culpa**, to be at fault

culpable, *adj.* guilty

culpar, *va.* to accuse, blame

cultivar, *va.* to cultivate

cultivo, *m.* cultivation; farming; culture (of bacteria)

culto, *adj.* elegant, correct; polished; civilized; culture; worship, cult, religion; homage

cultura, *f.* culture

cumbre, *f.* top, summit

cumpleaños, *m.* birthday

cumplido, *adj.* polished, polite; *m.* compliment

cumplimiento, *m.* compliment; accomplishment; fulfillment; expiration (of credit, etc.)

cumplir, *va.* to execute, carry out; to fulfil; **cumplir años,** to have a birthday; *vn.* to fall due

cúmulo, *m.* heap, pile

cuna, *f.* cradle; native country; lineage; origin

cuñado, cuñada, *n.* brother- or sister-in-law

cuociente, *m.* quotient

cuota, *f.* quota, fixed share; fee

cupé, *m.* coupé; cab

cupo, *m.* quota, share

cupón, *m.* coupon

cúpula, *f.* cupola, dome

cura, *m.* priest, parson; *f.* healing, cure, remedy

curandero, *m.* quack, medicaster

curar, *va.* to cure, heal

curiosidad, *f.* curiosity; neatness; rarity

curioso, *adj.* curious, strange; neat; diligent

cursar, *va.* to study (a course)

curtir, *va.* to tan leather; to sunburn; to inure to hardships

curva, *f.* curve, bend, curved line; **curva cerrada,** sharp bend; **curva doble,** s-curve

curvo, *adj.* curved, bent

cúspide, *f.* apex, peak

custodia, *f.* custody, keeping, hold; guard, escort; (rel.) monstrance

custodiar, *va.* to guard, watch

cutícula, *f.* cuticle

cuyo, cuya, *pron.* of which, of whom, whose, whereof

czar, *m.* czar

Ch

ch/, cheque, check

chabacano, *adj.* coarse, awkward; *m.* (Mex.) apricot

chacarero, *m.* (Arg. Urug.) farmer on small scale

chacra, *f.* (Arg. Urug.) small size farm

chal, *m.* shawl

chalán, *m.* hawker, huckster; (Mex.) **chalán de río,** river ferry

chaleco, *m.* waistcoat, vest

chalina, *f.* scarf

chalupa, *f.* (Mex.) small canoe

chamaco, chamaca, *n.* (Mex.) small boy or girl

chamarra, *f.* mackinaw coat

chambón, chambona, *adj.* awkward, bungling; *n.* bungler

champaña, *m.* champagne

champú, *m.* shampoo

chamuscar, *va.* to singe, scorch

chancear, *vn., vr.* to joke, jest

chancla, *f.* old shoe

chanza, *f.* joke, jest, fun

chapa, *f.* thin metal plate flush on cheek; veneer

chaparro, *adj.* (Mex.) small or short (of a person)

chaparrón, *m.* violent shower of rain

chapulín, *m.* grasshopper

chaqueta, *f.* jacket, coat

charada, *f.* charade

charca, *f.* pool of water, pond

charco, *m.* pool of standing water

charla, *f.* idle chitchat, prattle, talk

charlatán, charlatana, *n.* idle talker; quack

charol, *m.* varnish; lacquer; enamel; patent leather

charro, *m.* churl; Mexican cowboy; *adj.* gaudy

chasco, *m.* joke, jest; disappointment; **llevarse chasco,** to be disappointed

chasis, *m.* chassis

chasquido, *m.* crack of a whip

chato, *adj.* flat, flattish; flat-nosed

chaveta, *f.* bolt, pin, pivot; **perder la chaveta,** to become rattled

chelín, *m.* shilling

cheque, *m.* (com.) check

chicle, *m.* chewing gum

chico, *adj.* little, small; *n.* little boy or girl

chícharo, *m.* pea

chicharrón, *m.* crackling, pork rind or fat cooked until crisp

chichón, *m.* lump on the head occasioned by a blow

chiflar, *vn.* to whistle; **chiflar-se,** (coll.) to become mentally unbalanced; to act silly

chile, *m.* (bot.) chili, red pepper

chileno, chilena, *n., adj.* Chilean

chillido, *m.* squeak, shriek

chimenea, *f.* chimney; smokestack; (naut.) funnel

chimpancé, *m.* chimpanzee

china, *f.* porcelain; pebble; (Cuba and P.R.) thin-skinned orange; **China,** China

chinche, *f.* bedbug; thumbtack

chinchilla, *f.* chinchilla

chinela, *f.* house slipper

chino, china, *n., adj.* Chinese; *m.* Chinese language

chiquillo, chiquilla, *n.* child, youngster

chiquito, chiquita, *adj.* little, small; *n.* little boy or girl

chiripa, *f.* fluke (in billiards); (coll.) fortunate chance; **de chiripa,** by mere chance

chisme, *m.* misreport; gossip

chismear, *va., vn.* to tattle, gossip

chismoso, *adj.* tattling, talebearing

chispa, *f.* spark; very small diamond; small particle; **¡chispas!** *interj.* blazes! **echar chispas,** to rave

chiste, *m.* joke, jest

chistoso, *adj.* funny, comical

chivo, chiva, *n.* kid, goat

chocante, *adj.* repugnant

chocolate, *m.* chocolate

chochear, *vn.* to dote

chochera, *f.* second childhood

chofer or **chófer,** *m.* chauffeur, driver

choque, *m.* shock; collision, crash, clash

chorizo, *m.* pork sausage

chorrear, *vn.* to drip from a spout, gush, drip; trickle

chorro, *m.* gush; **a chorros,** abundantly

chotear, *va.* to rib, kid, poke fun at

choza, *f.* hut, cabin

chuleta, *f.* chop; **chuleta de puerco,** pork chop

chulo, chula, *n.* jester, clown; *adj.* (Sp. Am.) pretty, darling

chusco, *adj.* pleasant, droll

chuzo, *m.* spear or pike; **llover a chuzos,** to rain heavily

D

D., Dn. or **D.ⁿ, Don,** Don, title equivalent to Mr., but used before given name

Da. or **D.ª, Doña,** Donna, title equivalent to Mrs. or Miss but used before given name

dádiva, *f.* gift, present; handout

dado, *m.* die (*pl.* dice); (*p.p.* of **dar**) **dado que** or **dado caso que,** in case that, provided that, since

daga, dagger

dalia, (bot.) dahlia

dama, lady, mistress; king (in checkers (theat. leading lady; **damas,** *pl.* checkers

danés, danesa, *n., adj.* Danish

Danubio, *m.* Danube

danza, *f.* dance

danzar, *vn.* to dance

dañar, *va.* to damage; to injure; to spoil

dañino, *adj.* harmful

daño, *m.* damage, injury

dar, *va., vn.* to give; to supply, **dar a conocer,** to make known; **dar prestado,** to lend; **darse por vencido,** to give up; **darse cuenta de,** to realize: **darse prisa,** to hurry

data, *f.* date; item in an account

datar, *va.* to date

dátil, *m.* (bot.) date

dato, *m.* datum; **datos,** *pl.* data

D. de J.C., después de Jesucristo, A.D. After Christ

DDT, DDT (insecticide)

de, *prep.* of; from; for

debajo, *adv.* under, underneath, below

debate, *m.* debate, contest

debe, *m.* (com.) debit; **debe y haber,** debit and credit

deber, *m.* obligation, duty; debt; *va.* to owe; to be obliged

debido, debida, *adj.* due; proper

débil, *adj.* feeble, weak

débito, *m.* debt; duty

debutar, *vn.* to make one's debut

década, *f.* decade

decadencia, *f.* decay, decline

decaer, *vn.* to decay, decline

decaído, *adj.* crestfallen

decano, *m.* senior, dean

decencia, *f.* decency

decente, *adj.* decent, honest

decididamente, *adv.* decidedly

decigramo, *m.* decigram

decimal, *adj.* decimal

décimo, *adj.* tenth

va. to say, tell, speak; **querer decir,** to mean; *m.* familiar saying

decisión, *f.* decision, determination

decisivo, *adj.* decisive

declamar, *vn.* to harangue, recite

declaración, *f.* declaration, statement, explation; (law) deposition; railroad bill of lading

declarar, *va.* to declare, state; (law) to depose upon oath; **declararse,** to declare one's opinion; (coll.) to declare one's love

declinación, *f.* decline; (gram.)

declension

declinar, *vn.* to decline; *va.* (gram.) to decline

declive, *m.* declivity, slope

decomisar, *va.* to confiscate

decoración, *f.* decoration, ornament; stage scenery

decorado, *m.* decoration, stage scenery

decorar, *va.* to decorate; to adorn; to illustrate

decoroso, *adj.* decorous, decent

decretar, *va.* to decree, decide; to determine

decreto, *m.* decree

dedal, *m.* thimble

dedicación, *f.* dedication; consecration

dedicado, *adj.* dedicated; destined

dedicar, *va.* to dedicate, devote, consecrate; **dedicarse,** to apply oneself to

dedicatoria, *f.* dedication

dedillo, *m.* little finger; **saber una cora al dedillo,** to know a thing perfectly

dedo, *m.* finger; toc; **dedo meñique,** little finger; **dedo pulgar,** thumb; **dedo del corazon,** middle finger; **dedo anular,** ring finger

deducción, *f.* deduction

deducir, *va.* to deduce, to subtract, deduct

defectivo, *adj.* defective

defectuoso, *adj.* defective

defender, *va.* to defend, uphold

defensa, *f.* defense, justification; apology; shelter, protection

defensiva, *f.* defensive

defensor, defensora, *n.* defender, supporter; lawyer

deferencia, *f.* deference

deficiencia, *f.* deficiency

deficiente, *adj.* deficient

déficit, *m.* deficit

definición, *f.* definition

definido, *adj.* definite

definir, *va.* to define, describe

definitivo, definitiva, *adj.* definitive, final; **en definiti-**

va, in short, definitely

deformado, *adj.* deformed

deformar, *va., vr.* to deform, disfigure

deforme, *adj.* deformed, ugly

deformidad, *f.* deformity

defraudar, *va.* to defraud

defunción, *f.* death

degenerar, *vn.* to degenerate

degollar, *va.* to behead

degradación, *f.* degradation

degradar, *va., vr.* to degrade

deidad, *f.* deity, divinity

dejado, *adj.* slovenly, indolent

dejar, *va.* to leave, let; to omit; to permit, allow; to forsake; to bequeath; **dejarse,** to abandon oneself (to)

del, of the (contraction of **de el**)

delantal, *m.* apron

delante, *adv.* ahead; **delante de,** *prep.* in front of

delantero, *adj.* foremost, first; **delantera,** *f.* forepart; lead, advantage; **tomar la delantera,** to take the lead

delatar, *va.* to accuse, denounce

delegación, *f.* delegation

delegado, delegada, *n.* delegate, deputy

delegar, *va.* to delegate, substitute

deleitar, *va.* to delight

deleite, *m.* pleasure, delight

deletrear, *va., vn.* to spell

delgado, *adj.* thin

deliberación, *f.* deliberation

deliberar, *vn.* to deliberate

delicadeza, *f.* delicacy, subtlety

delicado, *adj.* delicate, tender; fastidious; dainty

delicia, *f.* delight, pleasure

delicioso, *adj.* delicious, delightful

delincuencia, *f.* delinquency

delincuente, *m., f.* delinquent

delinquir, *vn.* to transgress the law

delirante, *adj.* delirious

delirar, *vn.* to be delirious

delirio, *m.* delirium; nonsense

delito, *m.* crime

delta, *f.* delta

demanda, *f.* demand, claim; lawsuit; request; **oferta y demanda,** supply and demand

demandado, demandada, *n.* defendant

demandar, *va.* to demand, petition, claim; to sue

demás, *adj.* other; **los** or **las demás,** the rest, the others; *adv.* besides; **y demás,** and so on; **por demás,** in vain, to no purpose

demasía, *f.* excess in the price; abundance, plenty

demasiado, *adj.* excessive, overmuch; *adv.* too much, excessively

demente, *adj.* mad, insane

democracia, *f.* democracy

demoler, *va.* to demolish

demonio, *m.* devil, demon; **¡demonio!** *interj.* the deuce!

demora, *f.* delay

demorar, *vn.* to delay, tarry

demostración, *f.* demonstration

demostrar, *va.* to prove, demonstrate, show

demostrativo, *adj.* demonstrative

denigrar, *va.* to blacken; to calumniate

denominación, *f.* denomination

denominador, *m.* (math.) denominator

denominar, *va.* to call, give a name to

denso, *adj.* dense, thick

dentadura, *f.* set of teeth

dental, *adj.* dental

dentición, *f.* dentition, teething

dentífrico, *m.* dentifrice; *adj.* for tooth cleaning

dentista, *m.* dentist

dentistería, *f.* dentistry

denuncia, *f.* denunciation

denunciar, *va.* to denounce

departamento, *m.* department; section, bureau; apartment; (rail.) compartment

dependencia, *f.* dependency; relation, affinity

depender, *vn.* to depend, be dependent on; **depender de,**

to count on

dependiente, *m.* dependent; subordinate; clerk

deplorable, *adj.* deplorable

deplorar, *va.* to deplore, regret

deponer, *va.* to depose, declare; to displace; *vn.* to evacuate the bowels

deportar, *va.* to deport, banish

deporte, *m.* sport, amusement

deportive, *adj.* sport, athletic

deposición, *f.* deposition; assertion, affirmation; evacuation of the bowels

depositar, *va.* to deposit

depósito, *m.* deposit; warehouse

depravar, *va.* to deprave, corrupt

depresión, *f.* depression

deprimir, *va.* to depress

derecha, *f.* right hand, right side; right wing (in politics)

derecho, *adj.* right, straight; *m.* right; law; just claim; tax duty; fee; **dar derecho** to entitle

derivado,*m.* by-product; (gram.) derivative; *adj.* derived

derivar, *va.,* *vn.* to derive; (naut.) to deflect from the course

derogar, *va.* to derogate, abolish

derramar, *va.* to drain off water; to spread; to spill; to shed; **derramarse,** to spill; to become scattered

derrame, *m.* leakage

derredor, *m.* circumference, circuit; **al derredor** or **en derredor,** about, around

derretir, *va.,* *vr.* to melt

derribar, *va.* to demolish; to overthrow

derrocar, *va.* to overthrow; to demolish

derrochar, *va.* to squander

derrota, *f.* defeat, rout (of an army, etc.)

derrotar, *va.* to cause (a ship) to fall off her course; to defeat

derrotero, *m.* ship's course; (fig.) course, way

derrumbar, *va.* to demolish; **derrumbarse,** to crumble

derrumbe, *m.* landslide

desabotonar, *va.* to unbutton

desabrido, *adj.* tasteless, insipid

desabrigar, *va.* to uncover, to

deprive of clothes or shelter

desabrochar, *va.* to unclasp, unbutton, unfasten

desacierto, *m.* error, blunder

desacomodar, *va.* to incommode, inconvenience; **desacomodarse,** to lose one's place

desacreditar, *va.* to discredit

desacuerdo, *m.* disagreement

desafiar, *va.* to challenge; to defy

desafinar, *vn., vr.* get out of tune

desafortunado, *adj.* unfortunate

desagradable, *adj.* disagreeable, unpleasant

desagradar, *va.* to displease, offend

desagradecido, *adj.* ungrateful; *n.* ingrate

desagrado, *m.* displeasure

desagüe, *m.* drain outlet

desahogado, *adj.* in comfortable circumstances

desahogar, *va.* to relieve; **desahogarse,** to unbosom

desahogo, *m.* ease, relief; unbosoming

desahuciar, *va.* to declare (a patient) incurable

desaire, *m.* disdain; slight

desalentar, *va.* to discourage; **desalentarse,** to lose hope, be discouraged

desaliento, *m.* dismay, discouragement, dejection

desaliñado, *adj.* slipshod

desalojar, *va.* to dislodge, evict; to displace

desamarrar, *va.* to untie

desamparar, *va.* to forsake

desanimado, *adj.* downhearted

desanimar, *va., vr.* to discourage

desapacible, *adj.* disagreeable, unpleasant

desaparecer, *vn.* to disappear

desaparición, *f.* disappearance

desapercibido, *adj.* unprepared, unguarded

desaplicado, *adj.* indolent, careless

desaprovechar, *va.* to misspend

desarmador, *m.* screwdriver

desarmar, va. to disarm; to disassemble; (fig.) to pacify

desarme, m. disarmament

desarreglado, adj. immoderate in eating, drinking, etc.; disarranged; slovenly

desarreglar, va. to disarrange

desarrollar, va., vr. to develop, unfold

desarrollo, m. development; evolution; developing of a photo

desarropar, va. to take off covers or blankets

desaseo, m. uncleanliness

desastrado, adj. wretched, miserable; ragged

desastre, m. disaster

desastroso, adj. disastrous

desatar, va. to untie, separate; desatarse, to lose all reserve

desatender, va. to pay no attention; to disregard, neglect

desatento, adj. inattentive, rude, uncivil

desatinado, adj. extravagant; tactless

desatino, m. extravagance, folly; nonsense, blunder

desavenencia, f. discord, disagreement

desayunarse, vr. to breakfast

desayuno, m. breakfast

desbandarse, vr. to disband

desbaratar, va. to destroy; to dissipate; desbaratarse, to break to pieces

desbocado, adj. wild (applied to a horse); foul-mouthed, indecent

desbordar, vn., vr. to overflow; to give vent to one's temper or feelings

desbordamiento, m. overflowing

descabellado, adj. disorderly; wild, unrestrained

descalabro, m. calamity, considerable loss

descalificar, va. to disqualify

descalzo, adj. barefooted

descansado, adj. rested, refreshed; quiet

descansar, vn. to rest; to repose, sleep

descanso, m. rest, repose

descarado, adj. bold, impudent

descaro, m. impudence

descarriar, va. to lead astray; descarriarse, to go astray; to deviate from justice or reason

descarrilar, vn., vr. (rail.) to jump the track; va. to derail

descartar, va. to discard; to dismiss

descendencia, f. descent, offspring

descender, vn. to descend; to be derived from

descendiente, adj., m. descending; descendant

descifrar, va. to decipher; to decode

descolgar, va. to unhang, take down

descolorido, adj. pale, colorless, faded

descollar, vn. to stand out; to excel, to surpass

descomponer, va. to spoil; to set at odds, disconcert; (chem.) to decompose; vn. to be indisposed; to change for the worse (of the weather); descomponerse, to get out of order; to become spoiled

descompuesto, adj. slovenly; out of order; spoiled (applied to food)

desconcertado, adj. baffled

desconcertar, va., vr. to disturb; to confound; to embarrass, disconcert

desconectar, va., vr. to disconnect

desconfiado, adj. suspicious, mistrustful

desconfianza, f. distrust, lack of confidence

desconfiar, vn. to mistrust, suspect

desconforme, adj. discordant; unlike; unsatisfied

desconocer, va. to disown, to disavow; to be ignorant of a thing; not to know a person; not to acknowledge (a favor)

desconocido, adj. unknown, unrecognizable; n. stranger

desconsiderado, *adj.* inconsiderate, imprudent

desconsolado, *adj.* disconsolate, dejected

desconsolador, *adj.* lamentable; disconsolate; disconcerting

desconsuelo, *m.* affliction; dejection, grief

descontar, *va.* to discount; to deduct

descontento, *m.* discontent, disgust; *adj.* unhappy, discontented

descontinuar, *va.* to discontinue

descorazonado, *adj.* depressed (in spirit)

descortés, *adj.* impolite

descortesía, *f.* discourtesy

descotado, *adj.* décolleté, low cut

descote, *m.* exposure of neck and shoulders

descrédito, *m.* discredit

describir, *va.* to describe

descripelón, *f.* description

descriptivo, *adj.* descriptive

descrito, *adj.* described

descuartizar, *va.* to quarter to divide the body into four parts); to carve

descubierto, *adj.* uncovered; bareheaded

descubrimiento, *m.* discovery, disclosure

descubrir, *va.* to discover, disclose; to uncover; to reveal; **descubrirse,** to take off one's hat

descuento, *m.* discount; decrease, rebate

descuidado, *adj.* careless, negligent

descuidar, *va., vn.* to neglect; **descuidarse,** to become negligent

descuido, *m.* indolence, negligence, forgetfulness

desde, *prep.* since, after, from; **desde luego,** of course

desdecirse, *vr.* to retract

desdén, *m.* disdain, scorn, contempt

desdeñar, *va.* to disdain

desdicha, *f.* misfortune

desdichado, *adj.* unfortunate, miserable

deseable, *adj.* desirable

desear, *va.* to desire, wish

desecar, *va.* to dry; to desiccate

desechar, *va.* to reject, refuse; to exclude

desembarcar, *va., vn.* to disembark

desembarque, *m.* landing

desembocar, *vn.* to flow into (as a river)

desembolso, *m.* disbursement, expenditure

desembuchar, *va.* to disgorge; (coll.) to unbosom

desempacar, *va.* to unpack

desempeñar, *va.* to perform (a duty); to discharge (any office)

desempeño, *m.* performance of an obligation

desempleo, *m.* unemployment

desencanto, *m.* disillusion

desenfrenado, *adj.* licentious, wanton

desenfrenar, *va.* to unbridle; **desenfrenarse,** to give full play to one's desires; to fly into a rage

desenfreno, *m.* licentiousness; unruliness

desengañar, *va., vr.* to disillusion, disappoint; to set right

desengaño, *m.* disillusion, disappointment

desenlace, *m.* denouement, outcome, conclusion

desenlazar, *va.* to unravel (a plot)

desenredar, *va.* to disentangle; **desenredarse,** to extricate oneself

desenterrar, *va.* to disinter, to dig up

desenvoltura, *f.* poise

desenvolver, *va.* to unwrap; to unroll; to develop; **desenvolverse,** to get along with assurance

desenvuelto, *adj.* poised

deseo, *m.* desire, wish

deseoso, *adj.* desirous

desequilibrio, *m.* unsteadiness, lack of balance

deserción, *f.* desertion

desertar, *va.* to desert; (law) to abandon a cause

desertor, *m.* deserter, fugitive

desesperación, *f.* despair, desperation; anger, fury

desesperadamente, *adv.* desperately

desesperado, *adj.* desperate, hopeless

desesperar, *vn., vr.* to despair; vex; *va.* to make desperate

desfalco, *m.* ebezzlement

desfallecer, *vn.* to pine, fall away, weaken

desfallecido, *adj.* faint, languid

desfallecimiento, *m.* languor, fainting, swoon

desfavorable, *adj.* unfavorable

desfigurar, *va.* to disfigure, deform; **desfigurarse,** to become disfigured or distorted

desfigurado, *adj.* deformed

desfile, *m.* parade

desganado, *adj.* having no appetite

desgano, *m.* lack of appetite; reluctance

desgarbado, *adj.* ungraceful, uncouth, gawky

desgarrado, *adj.* ripped, torn

desgarrador, *adj.* piercing; heartrending

desgarrar, *va.* to rend, tear

desgaste, *m.* wearing out, wastage

desgonzar, *va.* to separate; to unhinge; to disjoint

desgracia, *f.* misfortune, grief; disgrace; unpleasantness; **por desgracia,** unfortunately

desgraciado, *adj.* unfortunate, unhappy

desgreñar, *va.* to dishevel the hair

deshabitado, *adj.* deserted, desolate

deshecho, *adj.* undone, destroyed, wasted; melted; in pieces

deshelar, *va., vr.* to thaw

deshilachar, *va.* to ravel

deshilar, *va.* to ravel

deshojar, *va.* to strip off the leaves

deshonor, *m.* dishonor; insult

deshonra, *f.* dishonor; seduction of a woman

deshonroso, *adj.* dishonorable, indecent

deshuesar, *va.* to bone; to stone (fruit)

desidia, *f.* idleness, indolence

desidioso, *adj.* indolent, lazy, idle

desierto, *adj.* deserted, solitary; *m.* desert, wilderness

designación, *f.* designation

designar, *va.* to appoint; to name; to designate

designio, *m.* design, purpose

desigual, *adj.* unequal, unlike; uneven

desigualdad, *f.* inequality, dissimilitude; unevenness

desilusión, *f.* disillusion

desilusionar, *va., vr.* to disillusion

desinfectante, *m.* disinfectant

desinflamar, *va.* to cure an inflammation

desintegración, *f.* disintegration; fission

desintegrar, *vt., vi.* to disintegrate

desinterés, *m.* disinterestedness, unselfishness

desinteresado, *adj.* disinterested, unselfish

desistir, *vn.* to desist, cease, stop

deslave, *m.* washout

desleal, *adj.* disloyal; perfidious

deslealtad, *f.* disloyalty

desleír, *va.* to dilute, dissolve

deslenguado, *adj.* foulmouthed

desligar, *va.* to loosen, unbind, to extricate

desliz, *m.* slip, sliding; (fig.) slip, false step

deslizar, *vn., vr.* to slip, slide; to speak carelessly

deslucido, *adj.* unadorned; gawky; useless

deslumbrador, *adj.* dazzling

deslumbrar, *va.* to dazzle

desmantelado, *adj.* dismantled, stripped

desmañado, *adj.* clumsy, awkward

desmayar, *vn.* to be dispirited or fainthearted; **desmayarse,** to faint

desmayo, *m.* swoon; dismay, discouragement

desmedido, *adj.* out of proportion; excessive

desmejorar, *va.* to debase, make worse

desmembrar, *va.* to dismember; to curtail; to separate

desmemoriado, *adj.* forgetful

desmentir, *va.* to contradict

desmenuzar, *va.* to crumble, chip, to fritter; to examine minutely

desmerecer, *va., vn.* to become undeserving of; to compare unfavorably

desmesurado, *adj.* excessive; huge; immeasurable

desmoralizar, *va., vr.* to demoralize

desmoronar, *va.* to destroy little by little; **desmoronarse,** to decay, crumble

desnatar, *va.* to skim milk

desnivel, *m.* unevenness of the ground

desnudar, *va.* to denude, strip of clothes; to discover, reveal; **desnudarse,** to undress

desnudo, *adj.* naked, bare

desnutrición, *f.* malnutrition

desnutrido, *adj.* undernourished

desobedecer, *va.* to disobey

desobediencia, *f.* disobedience

desobediente, *adj.* disobedient

desocupar, *va.* to quit, empty; **desocuparse,** to quit an occupation

desodorante, *m.* deodorant

desolación, *f.* destruction; affliction

desolado, *adj.* desolate; lonely

desorden, *m.* disorder, confusion

desordenado, *adj.* disorderly, unruly

desordenar, *va., vr.* to disorder, disarrange

desorganización, *f.* disorganization

desorganizar, *va.* to disorganize

desorientado, *adj.* confused, having lost one's bearings

despacio, *adv.* slowly, leisurely

despacito, *adv.* gently, leisurely

despachar, *va.* to dispatch; to expedite; to dismiss

despacho, *m.* dispatch, expedition; cabinet; office

desparejar, *va.* to make unequal or uneven

desparpajo, *m.* pertness of speech or action

desparramar, *va.* to disseminate; to scatter, overspread; to squander

despavorido, *adj.* frightened, terrified

despecho, *m.* indignation, displeasure; despite, spite; **a despecho de,** in spite of

despedazar, *va.* to tear into pieces, cut asunder; to mangle

despedida, *f.* farewell, dismissal, leavetaking; close (of letter)

despedir, *va.* to discharge, dismiss from office; **despedirse,** to take leave

despegar, *va.* to unglue, detach; (avi.) to take off

despego, *m.* lack of love, coolness

despeinar, *va.* to entangle the hair

despejado, *adj.* sprightly, vivacious; clear, cloudless

despejar, *va.* to clear away obstructions; **despejarse,** to cheer up; to become clear weather

despejo, *m.* sprightliness; grace

despellejar, *va.* to skin

despensa, *f.* pantry, larder; provisions

despepitar, *va.* to remove the seeds from; despepitarse, to give vent to one's tongue

desperdiciar, *va.* to squander; not to avail oneself of

desperdicio, *m.* prodigality, profusion; remains; refuse

despertador, *m.* alarm clock

despierto, *adj.* awake; vigilant; brisk, sprightly

despilfarrar, *va.* to squander

despilfarro, *m.* slovenliness; waste

desplante, *m.* arrogant attitude

desplazado, *adj.* displaced

desplegar, *va.* to unfold, display; to explain, elucidate; to unfurl

desplomar, *va.* to make a wall bulge out; desplomarse, to bulge out; to collapse

desplome, *m.* downfall, collapse, tumbling down

despoblado, *m.* desert, uninhabited place; *adj.* depopulated

despoblar, *va., vr.* to depopulate; to desolate

despojar, *va.* to despoil; to deprive of, to strip; despojarse, to undress

despojos, *m. pl.* remains; debris, waste

desposado, *adj.* newly married; handcuffed

déspota, *m., f.* despot, tyrant

despótico, *adj.* despotic

despreciable, *adj.* contemptible, despicable, worthless

despreciar, *va.* to despise; to reject

desprecio, *m.* scorn, contempt

desprender, *va.* to unfasten, loosen, to separate; desprenderse, to give way, fall down; to extricate oneself; to be inferred

desprendimiento, *m.* alienation; unselfishness

despreocupado, *adj.* unconcerned, unconventional

desprestigio, *m.* loss of prestige

desprevenido, *adj.* unprepared

desproporción, *f.* disproportion

despropósito, *m.* absurdity, nonsense

desprovisto, *adj.* unprovided; devoid

después, *adv.* after, afterward, later; then; después de J.C. A.D., after Christ

desquitar, *va.* to retrieve a loss; desquitarse, to recoup; to retaliate, take revenge

desquite, *m.* revenge, retaliation

destacamento, *m.* (mil.) detachment

destacar, *va.* to build up, highlight; (mil.) to detach (a body of troops); destacarse, to stand out, be conspicuous

destapar, *va., vr.* to uncover

destartalado, *adj.* shabby; jumbled

destello, *m.* trickle; sparkle, gleam

destemplado, *adj.* inharmonious, out of tune; intemperate

destemplar, *va.* to distemper, alter, disconcert; to untune; destemplarse, to be ruffled; to be out of tune

desteñir, *va., vr.* to discolor, fade

desterrado, desterrada, *n.* exile; *adj.* exiled, banished

desterrar, *va.* to banish, exile

destierro, *m.* exile, banishment

destinar, *va.* to destine for, intend for

destinatario, destinataria, *n.* addressee, assignee

destino, *m.* destiny; fate, doom; destination; con destino a, bound for

destitución, *f.* destitution, abandonment

destituir, *va.* to deprive; to dismiss from office

destornillador, *m.* screwdriver

destornillar, *va.* to unscrew

destronar, *va.* to dethrone, to

depose
destrozado, *adj.* tattered, torn
destrozar, *va.* to destroy
destrucción, *f.* destruction, ruin
destructivo, *adj.* destructive
destruir, *va.* to destroy, ruin
desunir, *va.* to separate, to disunite
desuso, *m.* disuse; obsoleteness
desválido, *adj.* helpless, destitute
desvanecer, *va.* to cause to vanish; to remove; *vn., vr.* to faint ; to become insipid; to vanish
desvarío, *m.* delirium, raving; giddiness; extravagance
desvelar, *va.* to keep awake; **desvelarse,** to be watchful, spend a sleepless night
desvelo, *m.* lack of sleep; watchfulness; care
desventaja, *f.* disadvantage
desventura, *f.* misfortune, calamity
deoventurado, *adj.* unfortunate
desvergonzado, *adj.* impudent, shameless
desvergüenza, *f.* shame; impudence
desvestir, *vt.* to undress
desviar, *va., vr.* to deviate; to dissuade
detallar, *va.* to detail, relate minutely; to itemize
detalle, *m.* detail; retail
detallista, *m.* retailer
detención, *f.* detention, delay
detener, *va.* to stop, detain; to arrest; to withhold; **detener,** to tarry; to stop
detenido, *adj.* under arrest
deteriorar, *va., vr.* to deteriorate
deterioro, *m.* deterioration
determinación, *f.* determination; boldness
determinado, *adj.* determinate; specific; resolute
determinar, *va., vr.* to determine; to resolve

detestable, *adj.* detestable
detester, *va.* to detest, hate
detonador, *m.* detonator, fuse, blasting cap
detrás, *adv.* behind; behind one's back
detrimento, *m.* detriment, damage, loss
deuda, *f.* debt
deudor, deudora, *n.* debtor
devastar, *va.* to desolate, lay waste
devengar, *va.* to earn or draw (as salary, interest, etc.)
devoción, *f.* devotion, piety; strong affection
devolución, *f.* (law) devolution; restitution, return
devolutivo, *adj.* returnable
devolver, *va.* to return; to restore; to refund, repay; (coll.) to vomit
devoto, *adj.* devout, pious; devoted
D. F., Distrito Federal, Federal District
dia, *m.* day, daylight; **al dia,** up to date
diabetes, *f.* diabetes
diabético, *adj.* diabetic
diablo, *m.* devil, Satan
diablura, devilishness
diabólico, *adj.* diabolical, devilish
diadema, diadem
diagnóstico, *m.* diagnosis
diagonal, *adj.* diagonal
diagrama, *m.* diagram
dialecto, *m.* dialect
diamante, *m.* diamond
diámetro, *m.* diameter
diana, *f.* (mil.) reveille
diantre, *m.* deuce, devil
diapasón, *m.* (mus.) diapason, octave; tuning fork
diario, *m.* journal, diary; daily newspaper; daily expense; *adj.* daily
diarrea , diarrhea
dibujante, *m.* draftsman; one who draws
dibujar, *va.* to draw, design
dibujo, *m.* drawing, sketch, draft
dicción, *f.* diction

diccionario, m. dictionary

diciembre, m. December

dictado, m. dictate; dictation

dictador, m. dictator

dictadura, f. dictatorship

dictáfono, m. dictaphone

dictamen, m. opinion, notion; suggestion

dictar, va. to dictate

dicha, f. happiness, good fortune; **por dicha,** by chance, luckily

dicho, m. saying, sentence, proverb; declaration; adj. said; **dejar dicho,** to leave word

dichoso, adj. happy, prosperous, lucky

diecinueve or **diez y nueve,** m., adj. nineteen

dieciocho or **diez y ocho,** m., adj. eighteen

dieciseis or **diez y seis,** m., adj. sixteen

diecisiete or **diez y siete,** m., adj. seventeen

Diego, m. James

diente, m. tooth, fang, tusk, jag; **dientes postizos,** false teeth; **hablar** or **decir entre dientes,** to mumble, mutter

diestra, f. right hand

diestro, adj. clever, handy

dieta, f. diet, regimen

dietética, f. dietetics

diez, adj., m. ten

difamar, va. to defame, libel

diferencia, f. difference; **diferencias,** pl. controversies, disputes

diferencial, adj. differential, different; m. (auto.) differential

diferenciar, va., vr. to differ, differentiate

diferente, adj. different, unlike

diferir, va. to defer, put off; to differ

difícil, adj. difficult

dificultad, f. difficulty

dificultar, va. to raise difficulties; to render difficult

difteria, f. diphtheria

difundir, va. to diffuse, out-spread; to divulge

difunto, adj. dead, deceased; late; **difunta,** n. deceased person

difusión, diffusion, extension

difusora, (rad.) broadcasting station

digerible, adj. digestible

digerir, va. to digest; to think over, to examine carefully

digestión, f. digestion

digestivo, adj. digestive

digital, f. (bot.) digitalis, foxglove; adj. pertaining to the fingers; **impresiones** or **huellas digitales,** fingerprints

dignarse, vr. to condescend, deign

dignidad, f. dignity, rank

digno, adj. meritorious, worthy, deserving; **digno de confianza,** trustworthy, reliable

dije, m. charm, amulet; jewel

dilación, f. delay

dilatado, adj. large, extended; long delayed

dilatar, va. to dilate, expand; to spread out; to defer, to protract; **dilatarse,** to dilate; to delay

dilecto, adj. loved, beloved

diligencia, f. diligence; industriousness; errand; stagecoach

digente, adj. diligent, industrious

dilucidar, va. to elucidate

diluvio, m. deluge

dimanar, vn. to spring from; to originate; to flow

dimensión, f. dimension

dimes, m. pl. **andar en dimes y diretes,** (coll.) to contend, to argue back and forth

diminutivo, m., adj. diminutive

diminuto, adj. tiny, minute

dimitir, va. to resign; to abdicate

Dinamarca, f. Denmark

dinámica, f. dynamics

dinámico, adj. dynamic

dinamita, f. dynamite

dinamo, f. dynamo

dinastía, f. dynasty

dineral, *m.* large sum of money

dinero, *m.* coin, money, currency

dintel, *m.* doorframe

Dios, *m.* God; **Dios mediante**, God willing; **Dios quiera**, **Dios lo permita**, God grant

dios, **diosa**, *m., f.* god, goddess

diploma, *m.* diploma

diplomacia, *f.* diplomacy

diplomarse, *vr.* to be graduated

diplomático, *adj.* diplomatic; *m.* diplomat

diputado, *m.* delegate, representative

diputar, *va.* to depute

dique, *m.* dike, dam

dirección, *f.* direction; guidance, administration; management; manager's office; address, addressing

directivo, *adj.* managing; **directiva**, *f.* governing body

directo, *adj.* direct, straight, nonstop; apparent, evident

director, *m.* director; conductor; editor (of a publication); manager

directora, *f.* directress; principal (of a school)

directorio, *m.* directory; board of directors

dirigente, *adj.* directing, ruling

dirigible, *m.* airship, dirigible

dirigir, *va.* to direct; to conduct; to govern; **dirigir la palabra**, to address (someone); **dirigirse**, to turn, to go; to address; **dirigirse a**, to speak to, to turn to

discernir, *va.* to discern, to distinguish

disciplina, *f.* discipline

disciplinar, *va.* to discipline

discípulo, **discípula**, *n.* disciple, scholar, pupil

díscolo, *adj.* ungovernable; peevish

discordancia, *f.* disagreement, discord

discordante, *adj.* dissonant, discordant

discoteca, *f.* discotheque; record shop or library

discreción, *f.* discretion

disculpa, *f.* apology, excuse

disculpar, *va., vr.* to excuse, acquit, absolve

discurrir, *vn.* to discourse upon a subject; to discuss; *va.* to invent, to contrive

discurso, *m.* speech

discusión, *f.* discussion

discutir, *va., vn.* to discuss, argue

disección, *f.* dissection, anatomy

diseminar, *va.* to scatter as seed; to disseminate, propagate

disensión, *f.* dissension, strife

disentería, *f.* dysentery

diseñar, *va.* to draw, design

diseño, *m.* design, draft

disertar, *vn.* to discourse, debate

disfraz, *m.* mask, disguise; masquerade

disfrazar, *va., vr.* to disguise, conceal; to mask

disfrutar, *va.* to enjoy

disgustar, *va.* to displease; to offend; **disgustarse**, to be displeased, to be worried

disgusto, *m.* sorrow, grief; aversion

disimular, *va.* to dissemble; to pretend; to tolerate

disimulo, *m.* dissimulation; pretence

disipación, *f.* dissipation

disipar, *va., vr.* to dissipate

dislocación, *f.* dislocation

disminuir, *va.* to diminish

disoluto, *adj.* dissolute

disolver, *va.* to loosen, untie; to dissolve; to melt, liquefy; **disolverse**, to dissolve, to break up

disonante, *adj.* dissonant, inharmonious; (fig.) discordant

disparar, *va., vn.* to shoot

disparate, *m.* nonsense, absurdity; blunder

disparejo, *adj.* unequal, uneven

disparidad, *f.* disparity

disparo, *m.* shot; discharge, explosion

dispenser, *va.* to dispense; to excuse, absolve; to grant

dispensario, *m.* dispensary of drugs; clinic

dispersar, *va., vr.* to scatter

displicente, *adj.* disagreeable, peevish

disponer, *va., vn.* to arrange; to dispose, prepare; to dispose of; to resolve

disposición, *f.* disposition, arrangement; resolution; disposal, command

dispuesto, *adj.* disposed, fit, ready; **bien dispuesto,** favorably inclined; **mal dispuesto,** unfavorably disposed

disputar, *va., vn.* to dispute, question; to argue

distancia, *f.* distance

distante, *adj.* distant, far off

distinción, *f.* distinction; difference; prerogative

distinguido, *adj.* distinguished, prominent, conspicuous

distinguir, *va.* to distinguish; to show regard for; **distinguirse,** to distinguish oneself; to excel

distintivo, *m.* insignia

distinto, *adj.* distinct, different; clear

distracción, *f.* distraction; amusement, pastime

distraer, *va.* to distract; to amuse, entertain; **distraerse,** to be absent-minded; to enjoy oneself

distraído, *adj.* absentminded; inattentive

distribuidor, *m.* distributor

distribuir, *va.* to distribute, divide; to sort

distrito, *m.* district

disturbio, *m.* disturbance, interruption

disuadir, *va.* to dissuade

diurno, *adj.* diurnal, by day

diva, *f.* prima donna

divagación, *f.* wandering, digression

diván, *m.* sofa

divergencia, *f.* divergence

diversidad, *f.* diversity; variety of things

diversión, *f.* diversion, pastime, sport

diverso, *adj.* diverse, different; several, sundry

divertido, *adj.* amused; amusing

diverter, *va.* to divert (the attention); to amuse, entertain; **diverterse,** to have an enjoyable time

dividendo, *m.* (math., com.) dividend

dividir, *va., vr.* to divide, separate; to split, break up

divinidad, *f.* god; divinity; woman of exquisite beauty; **la Divinidad,** the Deity

divino, *adj.* divine, heavenly

divisa, *f.* motto, badge

divisar, *vn.* to perceive indistinctly

división, *f.* division; partition; separation; (gram.) hyphen

divociar, *va., vr.* to divorce, separate

divorcio, *m.* divorce

dls., dólares, $ or dol., dollars

dm., decímetro, dm. decimeter

do, *m.* (mus.) do

doblar, *va., vn.* to double, fold; to bend; to toll; **doblarla esquina,** to turn the corner; **doblarse,** to bend, submit

doblez, *m.* crease, fold; *m., f.* duplicity in dealing

doce, *adj., m.* twelve

docena, *f.* dozen

docente, *adj.* teaching; **personal docente,** teaching staff

dócil, *adj.* docile, obedient

docto, *adj.* learned

doctor, *m.* doctor; physician

doctrina, *f.* doctrine

documento, *m.* document

dogma, *m.* dogma

dogmático, *adj.* dogmatic

dólar, *m.* dollar

dolencia *f.* disease, affliction

doler, *vn., vr.* to feel pain; to ache; to be sorry; to repent

doliente, *adj.* suffering; sorrowful; *m.,* mourner

dolor, *m.* pain, aching, ache; grief; regret

doloroso, *adj.* sorrowful; painful

domar, *va.* to tame, subdue, master

domesticar, *va.* to domesticate, tame

doméstico, *adj.* domestic; *n.* domestic, menial

domicilio, *m.* domicile, home, abode

dominación, *f.* domination

dominante, *adj.* dominant, domineering

dominar, *va.* to dominate; to control; to master (a language or a subject); **dominarse,** to control oneself

domingo, *m.* Sunday

dominio, *m.* dominion, domination, power, authority; domain

dominó, *m.* domino (a masquerade garment); game of dominoes

don, *m.* Don, the Spanish title for a gentleman (used only before given name)

don, *m.* gift, quality; **el don de la palabra,** the gift of speech; **don de gentes,** savoir-faire, courteous, pleasant manners

donación, *f.* donation, gift

donaire, *m.* grace, elegance

donativo, *m.* free contribution

doncella, *f.* virgin, maiden; lady's maid

donde, *adv.* where

dondequiera, *adv.* anywhere; wherever

doña, *f.* lady, mistress; title, equivalent to Mrs. or Miss, used only before given name

doquier or **doquiera,** *adv.* anywhere

dorado, *adj.* gilded; *m.* gilding

dorar, *va.* to gild; to palliate

dormido, *adj.* asleep

dormilón, dormilona, *n.* (coll.) sleepyhead; *adj.* fond of sleeping

dormir, *vn.* to sleep; **dormir-**

se, to fall asleep

dormitar, *vn.* to doze, to be half asleep

dormitorio, *m.* dormitory, bedroom

dorsal, *adj.* dorsal; **espina dorsal,** spinal column

dorso, *m.* back

dos, *adj., m.* two; **de dos en dos,** by two's, two abreast

doscientos, doscientas, *m.,* *adj.* two hundred

dotar, *va.* to endow, to give a dowry to

dragón, *m.* dragon; dragoon

drama, *m.* drama

dramático, *adj.* dramatic

dramatizar, *va.* to dramatize

drástico, *adj.* drastic

drenaje, *m.* drainage

droga, *f.* drug; (coll.) nuisance

droguería, *f.* drugstore

ducha, *f.* shower bath; douche

duda, *f.* doubt, suspense, hesitation; **poner en duda,** to question; **no cabe duda,** there is no doubt

dudable, *adj.* dubious

dudar, *va., vn.* to doubt, waver

duelo, *m.* duel; grief; mourning

duende, *m.* elf, goblin

dueño, dueña, *n.* owner, master, proprietor; **dueño de sí mismo,** self-controlled

dueto, *m.* duet

dulce, *adj.* sweet; mild, soft, meek; *m.* candy, sweetmeat

dulcería, *f.* confectionery store

dulcificar, *va.* to sweeten

dulzura, *f.* sweetness; gentleness

duodeno, *m.* duodenum

duplicado, *m.* duplicate

duplicar, *va.* to double, duplicate

duque, *m.* duke

durable, *adj.* durable, lasting

duración, *f.* duration, term

duradero, *adj.* lasting, durable

durante, *pres. p.* of **durar,** during

durar, *vn.* to last, endure; to wear well (as clothes)

durazno, *m.* peach; peach tree

dureza, *f.* hardness
durmiente; *adj.* sleeping; *m.* (Sp. Am.) (rail.) cross tie
duro, *adj.* hard, solid; unjust; rigorous, cruel; stubborn; stale (of bread); *m.* peso, dollar
d/v., días vista, (com.) days' sight

E

e, *conj.* and (used only before words beginning with *i* or *hi,* when not followed by *e*)
ebanista, *m.* cabinetmaker
ébano, *m.* ebony
ebrio, *adj.* inebriated, drunk
eclesiástico, *m.* clergyman, ecclesiastic; *adj.* ecclesiastical
eclipsar, *va.* (ast.) to eclipse; to outshine; **eclipsarse,** to disappear
eclipse, *m.* eclipse
eco, *m.* echo
ecología, *f.* ecology
ecológico *adj.* ecological
economía, *f.* economy
económico, *adj.* economic; economical
economista, *m.* economist
economizar, *va.* to economize
ecuación, *f.* equation
ecuador, *m.* equator
ecuatorial, *adj.* equatorial
ecuestre, *adj.* equestrian
echar, *va.* to cast, throw, dart; to cast away; **echar a perder,** to spoil; **echar de menos,** to miss; **echarse,** to lie, stretch at full length
edad, *f.* age, era, time; **mayor de edad,** of age
Edén, *m.* Eden, paradise
edición, *f.* edition
edificar, *va.* to build
edificio, *m.* building, structure
editor, editora, *n.,* *adj.* publisher; publishing
educación, *f.* education; bringing up
educado, *adj.* educated
educando, educanda, *n.* pupil, scholar

educar, *va.* to educate, instruct
educative, *adj.* educational
EE. UU., E.U., E.U.A. or **E.U. de A., Estados Unidos, Estados Unidos de América,** U.S., United States, U.S.A., United States of America
efectivamente, *adv.* in effect, truly
efectivo, *adj.* effective, true, certain; *m.* cash; **hacer efectivo,** to cash
efecto, *m.* effect, consequence, purpose; **efectos,** *pl.* merchandise, wares, goods, belongings
efectuar, *va.* to effect, accomplish
efervescencia, *f.* effervescence
eficacia, efficacy
eficaz, *adj.* efficacious, effective
eficiente, *adj.* efficient, effective
efigie, *f.* effigy, image
efímero, *adj.* ephemeral, passing
egipcio, egipcia, *n.,* *adj.* Egyptian
Egipto, *m.* Egypt
egoísmo, *m.* selfishness, egoism
egoísta, *adj.* egoistic, selfish; *m., f.* self-seeker
egreso, *m.* debit, expense
eje, *m.* axle tree, axle, axis, shaft
ejecución, *f.* execution; performance
ejecutante, *m.* performer
ejecutar, *va.* to execute, perform, carry out; to put to death
ejecutivo, *adj.,* *m.* executive
ejemplar, *m.* copy; sample; *adj.* exemplary; excellent
ejemplo, *m.* example; comparison; pattern, copy; **por ejemplo,** for instance
ejercicio, *m.* exercise, practice; (mil.) drill
ejercitar, *va.* to exercise, to put into practice

ejército, *m.* army
ejido, *m.* common land
el, *art. m.* the
él, *pron.* he
elaborar, *va.* to elaborate; to manufacture
elasticidad, *f.* elasticity; resilience
elección, *f.* election; choice
electivo, *adj.* elective
electo, *adj.* elect
elector, *m.* elector
electorado, *m.* electorate
electoral, *adj.* electoral
electricidad, *f.* electricity
electricista, *m.* electrician
eléctrico, *adj.* electric, electrical
electrizar, *va.* to electrify
electrónica, *f.* electronics
electrotipo, in electrotype
elefante, *m.* elephant
elegancia, *f.* elegance
elegible, *adj.* eligible
elegir, *va.* to choose, elect
elemental, *adj.* elemental, elementary
elemento, *m.* element; ingredient; **clementos**, *pl.* elements; rudiments, first principles
elenco, *m.* catalogue, list, index
elevación, *f.* elevation; highness; exaltation, pride; height; (avi.) altitude
elevado, *adj.* elevated, lofty, high
elevador, *m.* elevator, hoist
elevar, *va.* to raise; to elevate; to heave; **elevarse**, to be enraptured; to be puffed up, to rise
eliminación, *f.* elimination
eliminar, *va.* to eliminate
elixir *or* elixir, *m.* elixir
elocución, *f.* elocution
elocuencia, *f.* eloquence
elocuente, *adj.* eloquent
elogiar, *va.* to praise, eulogize
elogio, *m.* eulogy, praise, compliment
elucidar, *va.* to elucidate, explain
eludir, *va.* to elude

ella, *pron.* she
ello, *neut. pron.* it, that
ellos, ellas, *pron. pl.* they (*masc.* and *fem.*)
emanar, *vn.* to emanate
emancipar, *va.* to emancipate
embajada, *f.* embassy
embajador, *m.* ambassador
embarazada, *adj.* pregnant
embarazo, *m.* embarrassment; obstacle; pregnancy
embarazoso, *adj.* difficult, intricate
embarcación, *f.* embarkation; any vessel or ship
embarcar, *va.* to embark, ship; **embarcarse**, to go on shipboard, embark; (fig.) to engage in any affair
embargar, *va.* to lay an embargo; to impede, restrain
embargo, *m.* embargo on shipping; **sin embargo**, however, nevertheless
embarque, *m.* shipment
embaucar, *va.* to deceive, to trick
embeberse, *vr.* to become absorbed
embelesar, *va., vr.* to amaze, astonish; to charm
embeleso, *m.* rapture, bliss, amazement
embellecer, *va.* to embellish, beautify, adorn
emblanquecer, *va., vr.* to whiten
emblema, *m.* emblem, symbol
embobar, *va.* to amuse, to distract; **embobarse**, to stand gaping
émbolo, *m.* (mech.) wrist pin; piston
emborrachar, *va., vr.* to intoxicate
emboscada, *f.* ambush
embotellar, *va.* to bottle
embragar, *va.* to put in gear
embrague, *m.* clutch, coupling
embriagar, *va., vr.* to intoxicate; to enrapture
embriaguez, *f.* intoxication, drunkenness; rapture
embrollar, *va.* to entangle, embroil

embrollo, *m.* tangle, trickery; embroiling

embromado, *adj.* vexed, annoyed

embrujar, *va.* to bewitch

embrutecer, *va.* to make stupid; **embrutecerse,** to become stupid

embudo, *m.* funnel

embuste, *m.* lie; fraud

embustero, embustera, *n.* impostor, cheat, liar

emergencia, *f.* emergency; emergence

emersión, *f.* emersion

emigración, *f.* emigration

emigrante, *m., f.* emigrant

emigrar, *vn.* to emigrate

eminencia, *f.* eminence

eminente, *adj.* eminent

emisario, *m.* emissary

emisora, *f.* broadcasting station

emocionar, *va., vr.* to touch, move, arouse emotion

empacho, *m.* indigestion; overloading; **sin empacho,** without ceremony; unconcernedly

empalagoso, *adj.* cloying

empalme, *m.* (rail.) junction; (rad.) hookup

empanada, *f.* meat tart

empanizado, *adj.* breaded

empañar, *va.* to dim, blemish; **empañarse,** to become tarnished

empapar, *va.* to soak, drench; **empaparse,** to be soaked; to go deeply into a matter

empapelar, *va.* to paper (a room, etc.)

empaque, *m.* packing

empaquetar, *va.* to make into a package

emparedado, *m.* sandwich

emparejar, *va.* to level; to match, fit; to equalize

empatar, *va.* to equal; to be a tie (in voting, in a game, etc.)

empate, *m.* equality of votes, tie

empeine, *m.* groin; instep; hoof

empellón, *m.* push, heavy

blow; **a empellones,** rudely, by dint of blows

empeñar, *va.* to pawn; **empeñarse,** to pledge himself; to persevere

empeño, *m.* obligation; perseverance; pawn

empeorar, *va.* to make worse; *vn.* to grow worse

emperador, *m.* emperor

emperatriz, *f.* empress

empero, *conj.* yet, however

empezar, *va.* to begin

empinar, *va.* to raise, lift; to exalt; **empinarse,** to stand on tiptoe

empleado, empleada, *n.* employee, clerk

emplear, *va.* to hire; to occupy; to use

empleo, *m.* employment, occupation

empobrecer, *va.* to reduce to poverty; *vn.* to become poor

empolvado, *adj.* powdered; dusty

empolvar, *va.* to powder; **empolvarse,** to become dusty

empollar, *va.* to brood, hatch

emprendedor, *adj.* enterprising

emprender, *va.* to undertake

empresa, *f.* enterprise, undertaking; business concern

empresario, *m.* impresario, contractor

empréstito, *m.* loan

empuje, *m.* impulsion, impulse, pushing

empujón, *m.* impulse, push; **a empujones,** pushingly, rudely

empuñar, *va.* to clinch, grip

emular, *va.* to emulate, rival

emulsión, *f.* emulsion

en, *prep.* in; for; on, upon

enagua, *f.,* **enaguas,** *pl.* underskirt, skirt

enaltecer, *va., vr.* to praise, exalt

enamorado, *adj.* in love, enamored, lovesick

enamorar, *va.* to inspire love; to woo; **enamorarse,** to fall in love

enano, *adj.* dwarfish; *n.* dwarf, midget

encabezamiento, *m.* headline; heading

encabezar, *va.* to head a list

encadenar, *va.* to chain, link together; to connect, unite

encajar, *va.* to enchase; to fit in; to push or force in; **encajarse,** to thrust oneself into some narrow place; (coll.) to intrude

encaje, *m.* chasing, inlaid work; lace; socket, groove

encallar, *vn.* (naut.) to run aground

encaminar, *va.* to guide, show the way; **encaminarse,** to take a road, to be on the way

encanecer, *vn.* to grow gray-haired

encantador, *adj.* charming, delightful, enchanting

encantar, *va.* to enchant, charm, delight; to cast a spell

encanto, *m.* enchantment, spell, charm; delightfulness

encapricharse, *vr.* to become stubborn

encaramarse, *vr.* to climb

encarar, *vn.* to face, come face to face

encarcelar, *va.* to imprison

encarecer, *va., vn.* to raise the price; to recommend strongly

encargar, *va.* to charge, commission; **encargarse,** to take upon oneself

encargo, *m.* charge, commission; order, request; responsibility; errand

encariñar, *va.* to inspire affection; **encariñarse con,** to become fond of

encarrilar, *va.,vr.* to place on the right track; to set right

encauzar, *va.* to channel, lead, direct

encendedor, *m.* lighter; cigarette lighter

encender, *va.* to kindle, light, to set on fire; to inflame, incite; **encenderse,** to fly into a rage

encendido, *adj.* inflamed, high-colored; *m.* ignition

encerado, *m.* oilcloth; blackboard

encerrar, *va.* to shut up, confine; to contain; **encerrarse,** to withdraw, go behind closed doors

encía, gum (of the teeth)

enciclopedia, *f.* encyclopedia

enciclopédico, *adj.* encyclopedic

encierro, *m.* confinement, enclosure; cloister; prison

encima, *adv.* above, over; at (the top);over and above, besides

encina, *f.* evergreen oak, live oak

encinta, *adj.* pregnant, expectant (mother)

enclenque, *adj.* feeble, sickly

encoger, *va.* to contract, shorten; to shrink; **encogerse,** to shrink

encogido, *adj.* shrunk; timid

encolerizar, *va., vr.* to provoke, to irritate

encomendar, *va.* to recommend; to instruct; **encomendarse,** to commit oneself to another's protection

encomiar, *va.* to praise

encomiástico, *adj.* complimentary, extolling

encomienda, *f.* commission, charge; message; **encomienda postal,** parcel post

encomio *m.* praise, commendation

encono, *m.* rancor, ill will

encontrar, *va., vn.* to meet, find, encounter; **encontrarse,** to clash; to be of contrary opinions; **encontrarse con,** to meet, come upon

encopetado, *adj.* presumptuous, boastful

encrespar, *va.* to curl, frizzle; **encresparse,** to become rough (as the sea)

encrucijada, *f.* crossroad; street intersection

encuadernador, *m.* book binder

encuadernar, *va.* to bind

books
encuentro, *m.* shock, jostle; encounter, meeting; **salir al encuentro,** to go to encounter; to go to meet a person
encumbrado, *adj.* high, elevated
encumbrar, *va.* to raise, elevate; to mount, ascend
encurtido, *m.* pickle
enchapar, *va.* to veneer, plate
enchilada, *f.* (Mex.) kind of pancake stuffed with various foods and chili
enchufe, *m.* socket joint
endemoniado, *adj.* possessed with the devil; devilish
enderezar, *va.* to rectify; to straighten; **enderezarse,** to stand upright
endiablado, *adj.* devilish, diabolical
endiosar, *va.* to deify; **endiosarse,** to be puffed up with pride
endorso, *m.* endorsement
endosar, *va.* to indorse a bill of exchange
endoso, *m.* endorsement.
endrogarse, *vr.* (Sp. Am.) to get into debt
endulzar, *va.* to sweeten; to soften
endurecer, *va.* to harden; **endurecerse,** to become cruel; to grow hard
endurecido, *adj.* inured, hardened
enemigo, *adj.* hostile, opposed; **enemiga,** *n.* enemy
enemistar, *va.* to make an enemy; *vn.* to become an enemy
energía, *f.* energy, power, vigor; **energía atómica,** atomic energy; **energía nuclear** or **nuclearia,** nuclear or atomic energy
enérgico, *adj.* energetic; expressive
enero, *m.* January
enfadar, *va., vr.* to vex, molest, trouble; to become angry
énfasis, *m.* emphasis,
enfático, *adj.* emphatic

enfermar, *vn.* to fall ill; *va.* to make sick
enfermería, *f.* infirmary
enfermero, **enfermera,** *n.* nurse; hospital attendant
enfermizo, *adj.* infirm, sickly
enfermo, *adj.* sick, diseased, indisposed; *n.* sick person, patient
enflaquecer, *va.* to make thin; **enflaquecerse,** to lose weight
enfocar, *va.* to focus
enfoque, *m.* focus
enfrenar, *va.* to bridle; to put on the brake; to curb, restrain
enfrentar, *va.* to encounter, face
enfrente, *adv.* opposite, in front
enfriamiento, *m.* refrigeration; cold, chin
enfriar, *va.* to cool, refrigerate; **enfriarse,** to cool down
enfurecer, *va.* to irritate, enrage; **enfurecerse,** to grow furious
engalanar, *va.* to adorn
enganchar, *va.* to hook; to hitch, connect; to ensnare
engañar, *va.* to deceive, cheat; **engañarse,** to be deceived; to make a mistake
engañoso, *adj.* deceitful, misleading
engatusar, *va.* to wheedle, coax
engendrar, *va.* to beget, engender
engordar, *a.* to fatten; to grow fat
engorroso, *adj.* troublesome, cumbrous
engranaje, *m.* gear, gearing
engrandecer, *va.* to augment; to exaggerate; to exalt
engrasar, *va.* to grease, oil
engreimiento, *m.* presumption, vanity; overindulgence
engreír, *va.* to make proud; to spoil, overindulge; **engreírse,** to become vain; to become spoiled or overindulged
enhebrar, *va.* to thread a needle

enhorabuena, *f.* congratulation; felicitation; *adv.* well and good

enhoramala, *adv.* in an evil hour

enigmático, *adj.* enigmatical

enjabonar, *va.* to soap, lather

enjambre, *m.* swarm of bees; crowd

enjaular, *va.* to shut up in a cage; to imprison

enjuagar, *va.* to rinse.

enjuague, *m.* rinsing; rinse

enjuiciar, *va.* to bring a lawsuit to trial; to pass judgment

enlace, *m.* link; kindred, affinity, wedding

enladrillar, *va.* to pave with bricks

enlazar, *va., vr.* to join, unite, connect; to be joined in wedlock

enlodar, *va.* to bemire

enloquecer, *va.* to madden; *vn.* to become insane; **enloquecerse,** to become insane; to become infatuated

enloquecido, *adj.* deranged

enmarañar, *va.* to entangle, involve in difficulties; to puzzle

enmendar, *va.* to correct reform

enmienda, *f.* correction, amendment

enmohecerse, *vr.* to grow moldy or musty; to rust

enmudecer, *vn.* to grow dumb; to become silent

enojado, *adj.* angry, cross

enojar, *va.* to irritate, make angry; to offend; **enojarse,** to become angry

enojo, *m.* peevishness; anger, displeasure

enorgullecer, *va., vr.* to fill with pride; to become proud

enorme, *adj.* enormous, vast, huge

enormidad, *f.* enormity

enredadera, *f.* climbing plant; vine

enredar, *va.* to entangle, ensnare; to puzzle; **enredarse,** to fall in love (unlawful love); to become entangled or involved

enredo, *m.* entanglement; plot of a play

enrejado, *m.* grating; railing (as a fence); trellis-work

enriquecer, *va.* to enrich; *vn.* to grow rich

enrojecer, *va., vr.* to blush

enrollar, *va.* to wind, roll, coil

enronquecer, *va.* to make hoarse; *vn.* to grow hoarse

ensalada, *f.* salad

ensalzar, *va.* to exalt, praise

ensanchar, *va.* to widen, enlarge

ensanche, *m.* widening; gore (in garments); increase

ensangrentar, *va., vr.* to stain with blood

ensayar, *va.* to rehearse; to try

ensenada, *f.* small bay

enseñanza, *f.* teaching, instruction

enseñar, *va.* to teach, instruct; to show

enseres, *m. pl.* chattels; implements, fixtures; household goods

enseriarse, *vr.* (Sp. Am.) to become earnest or serious

ensuciar, *va., vr.* to stain, soil

ensueño, *m.* dream, reverie, illusion

entablar, *va.* to cover with boards; to start (a conversation, debate, etc.)

entapizar, *va.* to cover with tapestry, upholster

entenado, entenada, *n.* stepson, stepdaughter

entender, *va., vn.* to understand, comprehend

entendimiento, *vr.* understanding, knowledge

enterar, *va.* to inform thoroughly; to instruct; to let know. **enterarse (de),** to find out, inform oneself; to be told

entereza, *f.* entireness, integrity; fortitude; uprightness

enternecer, *va.* to soften; to move to compassion; **enternecerse,** to be moved to pity, to be touched

entero, *adj.* whole, entire; perfect, complete; sound

enterrar, *va.* to bury

entidad, *f.* entity, real being; (fig.) consideration, importance

entierro, *m.* burial; interment funeral

entonación, *f.* modulation; intonation, tone, voice

entonar, *va.* to tune, intonate, chant

entonces, *adv.* then, at that time

entorpecer, *va.* to benumb; to stupefy; to hinder

entrada, *f.* entrance, entry, admission; **entradas y gastos,** receipts and expenses

entrañable, *adj.* intimate, affectionate

entrañas, *f. pl.* viscera, intestines; (fig.) heart

entrar, *va., vn.* to enter; to commence

entreacto, *m.* (theat.) intermission

entrecejo, *m.* the space between the eyebrows; frowning, supercilious look

entrega, delivery; surrender; **entrega inmediata,** special delivery

entregar, *va.* to deliver; to restore

entremés, *m.* appetizer

entremeter, *va.* to put one thing between others; **entremeterse,** to intrude

entremetido, entremetida, *n.* meddler, intruder; kibitzer; *adj.* meddling

entrenar, *va.* to train, coach

entrepaño, *m.* panel

entresacar, *va.* to sift, separate; to thin out (hair)

entresuelo, *m.* mezzanine; basement

entretanto, *adv.* meanwhile

entretela, *f.* interlining

entretener, *va.* to amuse; to entertain, divert; **entretenerse,** to amuse oneself

entretenido, *adj.* pleasant,

amusing

entretenimiento, *m.* amusement, entertainment

entretiempo, *m.* season between summer and winter (spring or autumn)

entrevista, *f.* interview

entronque, *m.* crossroads, junction

entumecer, *va.* to benumb; *vn.* to become numb; to swell

entusiasmar, *va.* to arouse enthusiasm, enrapture; **entusiasmarse,** to become enthusiastic

entusiasmo, *m.* enthusiasm

entusiasta, *m., f.* enthusiast; *adj.* enthusiastic

envanecer, *va.* to make vain; to swell with pride; **envanecerse,** to become proud or vain

envasar, *va.* to barrel; to bottle; to can

envase, *m.* packing, bottling; container

envejecer, *va.* to make old; *vn.* to grow old

envenenamiento, *m.* poisoning

envenenar, *va.* to poison

enviado, *m.* envoy, messenger

enviar, *va.* to send, transmit

enviciar, *va.* to corrupt; **enviciarse,** to become strongly addicted (to something)

envidia, *f.* envy; emulation

envidiable, *adj.* enviable

envidiar, *vn.* to envy; to grudge

envidioso, *adj.* envious, jealous

envío, *m.* sending, shipment, remittance

enviudar, *vn.* to become a widower or widow

envoltorio, *m.* bundle of goods

envoltura, *f.* wrapper

envolver, *va.* to involve; to wrap up

enyesar, *va.* to plaster; to put in a cast

epidemia, *f.* epidemic disease

epidermis, *f.* epidermis, cuti-

cle
epigrama, m. epigram
epilepsia, f. epilepsy
epílogo, m. epilogue
episodio, m. episode
epístola, f. epistle, letter
epitafio, m. epitaph
época, f. epoch; age, era
epopeya, f. epic; epic poem
equidad, equity, honesty
equilátero, adj. equilateral
equilibrado, adj. balanced
equilibrar, va. to balance; to counterbalance
equilibrio, m. equilibrium, balance
equinoccio, m. equinox
equipaje, m. baggage, luggage; equipment
equipar, va. to fit out, equip
equipo, m. equipment; (sports) team
equitación, f. horsemanship
equitativo, adj. fair, equitable
equivalente, adj. equivalent
equivocación, f. error, misunderstanding
equivocar, va., vr. to mistake, misconceive, misunderstand
era, f. era, age
erigir, va. to erect, build
ermitaño, m. hermit; hermit crab
erosión, f. erosion
erradicación, f. extirpation
errante, adj. errant, erring, roving
errar, va. vn. to err, commit errors
errata, f. error in printing
erróneo, adj. erroneous
error, m. error, mistake
erudito, adj. learned, lettered, erudite; m. sage, scholar
erupción, f. eruption, rash
eructar, **erutar**, to belch
esbelto, adj. svelte
esbozo, m. outline, sketch
escabroso, adj. rough, uneven; scabrous
escafandra, f. diving suit; **escafandra autónoma**, Scuba
escala, f. ladder; scale
escalafón, m. seniority scale; grade scale

escalar, va. to climb, scale
escalera, f. stairway; **escalera mecánica**, escalator; **escalera de mano**, stepladder
escalofrío, m. (med.) chill
escalón, m. step of a stair; degree of dignity; (mil.) echelon
escama, f. fish scale
escampar, vn. to stop raining
escandalizar, va., vr. to scandalize, shock
escándalo, m. scandal
escandaloso, adj. scandalous
escapada, f. escape, flight
escapar, vn., vr. to escape, flee
escaparate, m. show window, showcase; cupboard, cabinet
escape, m. escape, flight; exhaust; **a todo escape**, at full speed
escapulario, m. scapulary
escarbadientes, m. toothpick
escarbar, va. to scratch the earth (as chickens do)
escarcha, f. white frost
escardar, va. to weed
escarlata, f. scarlet color; scarlet cloth
escarlatina, f. scarlet fever
escarmentar, vn. to profit by experience; to take warning; va. to punish severely
escarmiento, m. warning, chastisement
escasear, vn. to grow less, decrease
escasez, f. scantiness, want
escatimar, va. to curtail, lessen; to skimp
escena, f. stage; scene; incident, episode
escenario, m. scenario, stage
escéptico, adj. skeptic, skeptical
esclarecer, va. to lighten, clear up; to illustrate
esclarecido, adj. illustrious, noble
esclavizar, va., vr. to enslave
esclavo, **esclava**, n. slave, captive
esclusa, f. lock; sluice, floodgate
escoba, f. broom
escocés, **escoesa**, n., adj.

Scotsman, Scotswoman; Scotch, Scottish

escoger, *va.* to choose, select

escogido, *adj.* choice, selected

escolar, *m.* scholar, student; *adj.* scholastic

escolástico, *adj.* scholastic

escolta, *f.* (mil.) escort convoy

escollo, *m.* sunken rock, reef; difficulty

escombro, *m.* rubbish, debris; mackerel

esconder, *va., vr.* to hide conceal

escondidas or **escondidillas,** *adv.* in a secret manner

escondido, *adj.* hidden

escopeta, *f.* gun, shotgun

escorbuto, *m.* scurvy

escorial, *m.* dump pile

escorpión, *m.* scorpion

escotado, *adj.* low-necked

escote, *m.* low-cut in a garment

escribano, *m.* notary; clerk

escribiente, *m., f.* amanuensis, clerk

escribir, *va.* to write; **escribir a máquina,** to typewrite

escrito,*m.* writing, manuscript; communication; (law) writ, brief; *p.p.* of **escribir,** written; **por escrito,** in writing

escritor, escritora, *n.* writer, author

escritorio, *m.* writing desk

escritura, *f.* writing; deed; **Escritura,** Scripture

escrúpulo, *m.* doubt, scruple

escrupuloso, *adj.* scrupulous; exact

escrutinio, *m.* scrutiny, inquiry

escuadra, *f.* square; squadron

escuchar, *va.* to listen

escudo, *m.* shield, buckler; coat of arms; scutcheon of a lock; escudo (Sp. coin)

escudriñar, *va.* to search, pry into

escuela, *f.* school; **escuela de párvulos,** kindergarten

escueto, *adj.* devoid of trimmings; unencumbered

esculpir, *va.* to sculpture, carve

escultor, *m.* sculptor, carver

escultura, *f.* sculpture; work of a sculptor

escupidera, *f.* spittoon

escupir, *va.* to spit

escurrir, *va.* to drain to the dregs; *vn.* to drop; to slip, slide; **escurrirse,** to slip away

ESE: estesudeste, ESE or E.S.E., east southeast

ese, esa, *adj.* and **ése, ésa,** *pron.* that; **esos, esas,** *pl.* those

esencia, *f.* essence

esencial, *adj.* essential; principal

esfera, *f.* sphere; globe; dial

esférico, *adj.* spherical

esforzar, *va.* to strengthen; **esforzarse,** to exert oneself, to make an effort

esfuerzo, *m.* effort

esfumarse, *vr.* to disappear, fade away

esgrima, *f.* fencing

eslabón, *m.* link of a chain

esmalte, *m.* enamel; fingernail polish

esmerado, *adj.* painstaking, carefully done

esmerarse, *vr.* to do one's best, to take pains

esmero, *m.* elaborate effort; neatness

eso, *dem. pron. neuter,* that (idea or statement); **por eso,** for that reason, therefore

esófago, *m.* gullet; throat, esophagus

espacial, *adj.* relating to space

espacio, *m.* space, capacity; distance

espacioso, *adj.* spacious

espada, *f.* sword; spade (in cards)

espalda, *f.* back; shoulders; **a espaldas,** behind one's back

espaldar, *m.* back of a seat

espantajo, *m.* scarecrow; bugaboo

espantar, *va.* to frighten, daunt; to chase or drive away

espanto, *m.* fright; menace, threat; wonder, surprise; apparition, spook

España, *f.* Spain

español, española, *n.,* *adj.* Spaniard; Spanish; *m.* Spanish language

esparcimiento, *m.* recreation, relaxation

esparcir, *va.* to scatter; to divulge

espárrago, *m.* asparagus.

espasmo, *m.* spasm

especial, *adj.* special, particular

especialidad, *f.* specialty

especialista, *m., f.* specialist

especializarse, *vr.* to specialize

especie, *f.* species; matter; motive; class, sort, kind

especificación, *f.* specification

especificar, *va.* to specify

específico, *adj.* specific; *m.* patented medicine

espécimen, *m.* specimen, sample

espectáculo, *m.* spectacle, sight; show

espectador, espectadora, *n.* spectator, onlooker

espectro, *m.* specter, phantom, apparition; spectrum

especulación, *f.* speculation

especular, *va.* to speculate

espejismo, *m.* mirage

espejo, *m.* looking glass, mirror

espera, *f.* stay, waiting; (law) adjournment, delay; **sala de espera,** waiting room

esperanto, *m.* Esperanto

esperanza, *f.* hope, expectation

esperar, *va.* to hope; to expect, to wait for

espesar, *va., vr.* to thicken, condense

espeso, *adj.* thick, dense

espía, *m., f.* spy

espiar, *va.* to spy, lurk

espiga, *f.* ear (of grain)

espina *f.* thorn; thistle; backbone; fishbone; **estar en espinas,** to be on needles and pins

espinaca, *f.* (bot.) spinach

espinazo, *m.* spine, backbone

espinoso, *adj.* thorny

espiral, *adj.* spiral

espirar, *va.* to exhale; *vn.* to breathe

espiritismo, *m.* spiritualism; spiritism

espíritu, *m.* spirit, soul; genius; ardor; courage; (chem.) spirits; **el Espíritu Santo,** the Holy Ghost

espiritual, *adj.* spiritual

esplendidez, *f.* splendor, magnificence

espléndido, *adj.* splendid

esplendor, *m.* radiance

esplín, *m.* melancholy

esponjar, *va.* to sponge; **esponjarse,** to get fluffy; to be puffed up with pride

esponjoso, *adj.* spongy

esponsales, *m. pl.* espousals, betrothal

espontáneo, *adj.* spontaneous

esposa, *f.* wife; **esposas,** *pl.* handcuffs

esposo, *m.* husband; **esposos,** *pl.* married couple

espuela, *f.* spur; stimulus; (bot.) larkspur

espumoso, *adj.* frothy, foamy

esputo, *m.* spit, sputum, saliva

esquela, *f.* note, slip of paper

esqueleto, *m.* skeleton

esquema, *m.* diagram, plan

esquiar, *vn.* to ski

esquilar, *va.* to shear

esquina, *f.* corner, angle; **doblar la esquina,** to turn the corner

esquivar, *va.* to shun, avoid, evade

esquivo, *adj.* shy, reserved

estabilizar, *va.* to stabilize

estable, *adj.* stable

establecer, *va.* to establish, found; to decree

establecimiento, *m.* establishment; founding; household

establo, *m.* stable

estación, *f.* station; position,

situation; season (of the year)

estacionamiento, *m.* parking

estacionar, *va.* to park

estacionario, *adj.* stationary

estadía, *f.* stay, sojourn

estadio, *m.* stadium

estadista, *m.* statesman

estadística, *f.* statistics

estadístico, *adj.* statistical

estado, *m.* state, condition; **estado de cuenta**, statement of an account; **ministro de Estado**, Secretary of State

Estados Unidos de América, *m. pl.* United States of America

estadounidense, *adj.* of the United States of America; *m.*, *f.* person from the U. S. A

estafa, *f.* trick; swindle

estafar, *va.* to deceive, defraud; to swindle

estallar, *vn.* to burst, explode

estallido, *m.* crash; outburst

estambre, *m.* fine wool; stamen of flowers

estampa, *f.* print, stamp

estampar, *va.* to print; to stamp; to imprint

estampido, *m.* report of a gun, etc.; crack, crash; **estampida**, *f.* stampede

estampilla, *f.* signet, rubber stamp; (Sp. Am.) postage stamp

estancia, *f.* stay, sojourn; mansion; (Sp. Am.) cattle ranch; living room

estandarte, *m.* banner, standard

estanque, *m.* pond, pool

estanquillo, *m.* cigar store

estante, *m.* shelf; bookcase

estar, *vn.* to be; to be in a place; **estar de prisa**, to be in a hurry; **estar bien**, to be well; **estar malo**, to be ill

estaroide, *m.* steroid

estatua, *f.* statue

estatura, *f.* stature

estatuto, *m.* statute, law, bylaw

este, *m.* east

este, esta, *adj.* and **éste, ésta**, *pron.* this; **estos, estas**, *pl.* these

estela de vapor, *f.* contrail

estenografía, *f.* stenography, shorthand

estenógrafo, estenógrafa, *n.* stenographer, shorthand writer

estenotipia, *f.* stenotyping

estera, *f.* mat,

estereofónico, estereofónica, *adj.* stereophonic

estereoscopio, *m.* stereoscope

estéril, *adj.* sterile; barren

esterilizar, *va.* to sterilize

esterlina, *adj.* sterling; **libra esterlina**, pound sterling

estero, *m.* estuary, firth; (Arg.) swamp

estética, *f.* aesthetics

estetoscopio, *m.* stethoscope

estiércol, *m.* dung; excrement, manure

estigma, *m.* birthmark; stigma, affront

estilo, *m.* stylus; style; use, custom

estima, *f.* esteem

estimable, *adj.* worthy of esteem

estimar, *va.* to estimate, value; to esteem; to judge

estimular, *va.* to encourage, stimulate

estímulo, *m.* stimulus, encouragement, inducement

estío, *m.* summer

estipular, *va.* to stipulate

estirado, *adj.* forced; taut

estirar, *va.* to dilate, stretch out

estirpe, *f.* race, origin, stock

esto, *pron.* neuter this; **en esto**, at this juncture; **por esto**, for this reason

estoico, *adj.* stoic, indifferent

estómago, *m.* stomach

estorbar, *va.* to hinder, obstruct; to molest

estorbo, *m.* hindrance, impediment

estornudar, *vn.* to sneeze

estornudo, *m.* sneeze

estrangulación, *f.* strangulation; **cuello de estrangulación**, bottleneck

estrategia, *f.* strategy
estratégico, *adj.* strategic
estrechar, *va.* to tighten: to contract, clasp
estrechez, *f.* tightness; narrowness; poverty
estrecho, *m.* strait; *adj.* narrow, close; tight; intimate
estrella, *f.* star
estrellado, *adj.* starry; dashed to pieces; **huevos estrellados,** fried eggs
estrellar, *va.* to dash to pieces; to crash, to hit against; to fry (eggs)
estremecer, *va.* to shake, make tremble; **estremecerse,** to shake; to thrill
estremecimiento, *m.* trembling, shaking, shiver, thrill
estrenar, *va.* to inaugurate; to use for the first time
estreno, *m.* début, first performance, premiere
estreñimiento, *m.* obstruction; constipation
estrépito, *m.* noise, clamor
estribar, *vn.* depend upon (a reason)
estricto, *adj.* strict; severe
estridente, *adj.* strident
estroboscopio, *m.* stroboscope
estrofa, *f.* (poet.) stanza
estropajo, *m.* dishrag; worthless thing
estropear, *va.* to spoil by rough usage
estructura, *f.* structure
estruendo, *m.* clamor, noise
estrujar, *va.* to press, squeeze
estuche, *m.* kit
estudiante, *m.* scholar, student
estudiar, *va.* to study
estudio, *m.* study; studio
estupefacto, *adj.* stupefied
estupendo, *adj.* stupendous
estupidez, *f.* stupidity
etapa, *f.* stage, station, step
etcétera, *f.* et cetera, and so on
éter, *m.* ether
etéreo, *adj.* ethereal
eternidad, *f.* eternity
eterno, *adj.* eternal

ético, *adj.* ethical, moral
etimología, *f.* etymology
etiqueta, *f.* etiquette, formality; label; **de etiqueta,** in formal dress
E.U.A., Estados Unidos de América, U.S.A., United States of America
eucalipto, *m.* eucalyptus
eufonía, euphony
Europa, Europe
europeo, europea, *n.,* *adj.* European
evacuar, *va.* to evacuate, empty
evangelio, *m.* gospel
evaporar, *va.,* *vn.* to evaporate
evasivo, *adj.* evasive, elusive
eventual, *adj.* eventual, fortuitous
evitable, *adj.* avoidable .
evocar, *va.* to call out; to invoke
evolución, *f.* evolution; evolvement
exactitud, *f.* exactness
exacto, *adj.* exact; punctual
exageración, *f.* exaggeration
exagerar, *va.* to exaggerate
exaltado, *adj.* hot-headed
exaltar, *va.* to exalt, elevate; to praise; **exaltarse,** to become excited and angry
examen, *m.* examination
exasperar, *va.* to exasperate
excavadora, *f.* excavating machine, steam shovel
excavar, *va.* to excavate
excedente, *adj.* excessive, exceeding; *m.* surplus, excess
exceder, *va.* to exceed
Excelencia, *f.* Excellency (title)
excelencia, *f.* excellence
excelente, *adj.* excellent
excelso, *adj.* elevated, lofty
excentricidad, *f.* eccentricity
excéntrico, *adj.* eccentric
excepción, *f.* exception
excepcional, *adj.* exceptional
excepto, *adv.* excepting
exceptuar, *va.* to except, exempt
excesivo, *adj.* excessive
exceso, *m.* excess

excitar, va. to excite, arouse; to urge

exclamación, f. exclamation

exclamar, va. to exclaim, cry out

excluir, va. to exclude

exclusión, f. exclusion; preclusion

exclusivo, adj. exclusive, select

excomulgar, va. to excommunicate

excomunión, f. excommunication

excremento, m. exerement

excursión, excursion, outing

excusa, f. excuse, apology

excusado, adj. excused; exempted; m. toilet, water closet

excusar, va. to excuse, pardon; to exempt; **excusarse,** to decline a request

exento, adj. exempt, free

exhausto, adj. exhausted

exhibición, f. exhibition, exposition

exhibir, va. to exhibit, display

exigencia, f. exigency, demand

exigente, adj. demanding

exigir, va. to demand, require

eximir, va. to exempt, excuse

existencia, f. existence; **en-existencia,** in stock

existir, vn. to exist, be

éxito, m. outcome; **buen éxito,** success

exorbitante, adj. exorbitant

exótico, adj. exotic, foreign

expansión, f. expansion, extension

expansivo, adj. effusive

expedición, f. expedition; shipment

expediente, m. expedient; pretext; proceedings

expedir, va. to expedite, dispatch, forward; to issue

expeler, va. to expel, eject

experiencia, f. experience

experimentado, adj. experienced, expert

experimentar, va. to experience; to experiment

experimento, m. experiment, trial

experto, adj. expert, experienced; **experta,** n. expert, old hand

expirar, vn. to expire

explayar, va. to extend, dilate; **explayarse,** to dwell upon, enlarge upon

explicable, adj. explainable

explicación, f. explanation

explicar, va. to explain, expound; **explicarse,** to explain oneself

explícito, adj. explicit

exploración, f. exploration

explorador, exploradora, n. explorer; scout; adj. exploring

explorer, va. to explore; to inquire

explosión, f. explosion

exponente, m., f. exponent; m. (math.) exponent

exponer, va. to expose; to explain

exportación, f. exportation, export

exportador, adj. exporting; m. exporter

exportar, va. to export

expresión, f. expression

expresivo, adj. expressive

exprimir, va. to wring

exprofeso, adv. on purpose

expropiar, va. to expropriate

expuesto, adj. exposed; **lo expuesto,** what has been stated

expulsar, va. to expel

exquisito, adj. exquisite

éxtasis, m. ecstasy, enthusiasm

extender, va. to extend, spread; **extenderse,** to spread out

extensión, f. extension; extent

extenso, adj. extensive, vast

extenuar, va. to extenuate

exterior, adj. exterior, external; m. exterior; abroad

exterminar, va. to exterminate

extinguir, va. to extinguish

extirpar, va. to extirpate

extra, *inseparable prep.* out of, beyond, extra (as a prefix); *adj.* unusually good

extracción, *f.* extraction

extractar, *vn.* to extract, abridge

extracto, *m.* extract

extraer, *va.* to extract

extranjero, *adj.* foreign; **extranjera,** *n.* foreigner, alien; **ir al extranjero,** to go abroad

extrañar, *va.* to miss; **extrañarse,** to be surprised, wonder at

extraordinario, *adj.* extraordinary, uncommon, odd

extrasensorio, extrasensoria, *adj.* extrasensory

extravagancia, *f.* folly, freak

extravagante, *adj.* freakish; eccentric

extraviar, *va.* to mislead; **extraviarse,** to lose one's way

extremidad, *f.* extremity

F

f., franco, (com.) free

f/, fardo, bl. bale; bdl. bundle

f.a.b., franco a bordo, (com.) f.o.b., free on board

fábrica, *f.* factory

fabricación, *f.* manufacture; **fabricación en serie** or **en gran escala,** mass production

fabricante, *m.* manufacturer

fabricar, *va.* to build, construct

facción, *f.* faction; **facciones,** *pl.* features, physiognomy

fácil, *adj.* facile, easy

facilidad, *f.* facility; ability; **facilidades,** *pl.* opportunities; conveniences

factible, *adj.* feasible

factor, *m.* factor, element; (math.) factor

factura, *f.* invoice, bill

facturar, *va.* to invoice; to check (baggage)

facultad, *f.* faculty, authority; ability

facultar, *va.* to authorize

facha, *f.* appearance, aspect

fachada, *f.* facade, face, front

fachendear, *vn.* to brag, boast

faena, *f.* work; fatigue

faisán, *m.* pheasant

faja, *f.* band, belt, sash; girdle

fajar, *va.* to swathe; to girdle

fajina, *f.* toil, chore; bugle call to mess; **hacer fajina,** (coll.) to clean house thoroughly

falsete, *m.* falsetto voice

falso, *adj.* false, untrue

falta, *f.* fault; mistake; want, lack; flaw; **hacer falta,** to be necessary; to be lacking; **sin falta,** without fail; **no faltaba más,** (coll.) that's the last straw

faltar, *vn.* to lack

falto, *adj.* devoid

fallar, *va.* to give sentence, judge; *vn.* to fail, miss

fallecer, *vn.* to die

fallo, *m.* judgment, sentence

familia, *f.* family; species

familiar, *adj.* familiar; colloquial; informal; *m.* member of one's family

familiaridad, *f.* familiarity

familiarizar, *va., vr.* to familiarize

fango, *m.* mire, mud

fantasma, *m.* phantom, ghost

fantástico, *adj.* fantastic; (coll.) superb

farmacéutico, *adj.* pharmaceutical; *m.* pharmacist

farmacia, *f.* pharmacy

faro, *m.* (naut.) lighthouse

farol, *m.* lantern, light

farsa, *f.* farce; sham

farsante, *m.* charlatan; *adj.* boastful; deceitful

fascinador, *adj.* fascinating

fascinar, *va.* to fascinate; to charm

fase, *f.* phase, aspect

fastidiar, *va.* to bore, to annoy

fastidio, *m.* boredom, ennui

fatiga, *f.* fatigue, weariness

fatigar, *va., vr.* to tire, harass

fausto, *adj.* happy, fortunate

favor, *m.* favor

favorable, *adj.* favorable, advantageous, propitious

favorecer, *va.* to favor, protect

favoritismo, _m._ favoritism
favorito, _adj._ favorite, beloved
faz, _f._ face, front
F.C. or f.c., ferrocarril, R.R.
or r.r., railway
fe, _f._ faith, belief; testimony;
dar fe, to certify
Febo or feb.°, febrero, Feb.
February
febrero, _m._ February
fecundar, _va._ to fertilize
fecundo, _adj._ fruitful, fertile
fecha, date (of letter, etc.)
fechar, _va._ to date (a letter,
document, etc.)
federación, _f._ federation
federal, _adj._ federal
felicidad, _f._ felicity, happiness
felicitar, _va._ to congratulate
feliz, _adj._ happy, fortunate
felpa, _f._ plush
femenino, _adj._ feminine, female
feminista, _m., f._ feminist
fenómeno, _m._ phenomenon
feo, _adj._ ugly; deformed
feraz, _adj._ fertile, fruitful (of
vegetation)
feria, _f._ fair, market
feriado, _adj._ suspended (applied to work); **dia feriado,**
holiday
fermentar, _vn._ to ferment
férreo, _adj._ iron, ferrous; **via
férrea,** railroad
ferretería, _f._ hardware store
ferrocarril, _m._ railroad
ferroviario, _adj._ railroad
fértil, _adj._ fertile, fruitful
fertilizar, _va._ to fertilize
ferviente, _adj._ fervent, ardent
fervor, _m._ fervor, ardor
festejar, _va._ to fete; to celebrate
festejo, _m._ feast, entertainment
festín, _m._ feast, banquet
festivo, _adj._ festive; gay, merry; **dia festivo,** holiday
fétido, _adj._ fetid, stinking
feto, _m._ fetus
fiado, _adj._ on trust, on credit
fiador, fiadora, _n._ bondsman,
surety (person); _m._ fastener;
catch of a lock

fiambre, _m._ cold lunch
fianza, _f._ security, bail
fiar, _va._ to bail; to sell on
credit; to commit to another;
_vn._ to confide, to trust
fiasco, _m._ failure
ficción, _f._ fiction
ficticio, _adj._ fictitious
ficha, _f._ counter (at games),
chip
fidedigno, _adj._ true; **fuente fi-
dedigna,** reliable source
fideos, _m. pl._ vermicelli, spaghetti, noodles
fiebre, _f._ fever; **fiebre aftosa,**
hoof-and-mouth disease
fiel, _adj._ faithful, loyal; **fieles,**
_m. pl._ the faithful
fieltro, _m._ felt; felt hat
fiera, _f._ wild beast; fiendish
person; (coll.) very able or
shrewd person
fiero, _adj._ fierce, ferocious
fiesta, _f._ fiesta; feast; festivity,
party; **dia de fiesta,** holiday
fig., figura, fig. figure
figura, _f._ figure, shape
figurado, _adj._ figurative
figurar, _va._ to shape, fashion;
_vn._ to figure, be conspicuous;
figurarse, to fancy, imagine
figurín, _m._ fashion plate
fijar, _va._ to fix, fasten; to determine; to post; **se prohibe
fijar carteles,** post no bills;
fijarse, to take notice(of)
fijo, _adj._ fixed, firm
fila, _f._ row, line (of soldiers,
etc.)
filantrópico, _adj._ philanthropic
filántropo, _m._ philanthropist
filarmónico, _adj._ philharmon-
ic
filatelia, _f._ philately
filete, _m._ loin, tenderloin
filial, _adj._ filial
filigrana, _f._ filigree
filipino, filipina, _n., adj._ Phil-
ippine
filo, _m._ edge (of a knife, etc.)
filosofía, _f._ philosophy
filosófico, _adj._ philosophical
filósofo, _m._ philosopher
filtrar, _va._ to filter, strain

filtro, *m.* filter

fin, *m.* end, conclusion; **al fin, por fin,** at last

finado, finada, *n., adj.* dead, deceased

final, *adj.* final; *m.* end, finale

finalidad, *f.* finality

finalizar, *va.* to finish, conclude

financiero, *adj.* financial

finca, *f.* land or house property; ranch

fineza, *f.* fineness, perfection; expression of courtesy; delicacy

fingido, *adj.* feigned, sham

fingir, *va., vr.* to feign

fino, *adj.* fine, perfect, pure; delicate; acute, sagacious

firma, *f.* signature; company, firm

firmar, *va.* to sign, subscribe

firme, *adj.* firm, secure; constant, resolute

firmeza, *f.* firmness

fiscal, *m.* attorney general, public prosecutor; *adj.* fiscal

fisco, *m.* exchequer

física, *f.* physics

físico, *adj.* physical; *m.* physicist; physique; (coll.) face, physiognomy

fisiología, *f.* physiology

flaco, *adj.* thin, meager

flamante, *adj.* flaming, bright; quite new

flautín, *m.* piccolo, fife

fleco, *m.* flounce, fringe; bangs (style of haircut)

flecha, *f.* arrow

flema, *f.* phlegm

flete, *m.* (naut.) freight; **flete aéreo,** air freight

flexible, *adj.* flexible

flojo, *adj.* loose; lazy

flor, *f.* flower; **echar flores,** to compliment, flatter

florecer, *vn.* to blossom, bloom

floreciente, *adj.* in bloom

florero, *m.* flower vase

florido, *adj.* florid, flowery

florista, *m., f.* florist

flota, *f.* fleet

flotador, *m.* float; **flotador de**

hidroavión, pontoon

flotar, *vn.* to float

flote, *m.* floating; **a flote,** buoyant, afloat

fluctuar, *vn.* to fluctuate

fluir, *vn.* to flow, run (as a liquid)

fluorización, *f.* fluoridation

fluorizar, *va.* to fluoridate

focal, *adj.* focal

foco, *m.* focus; center; bulb (electric light)

fogoso, *adj.* fiery, ardent, fervent; impetuous

follaje, *m.* foliage

folleto, *m.* pampblet

fomentar, *va.* to promote, encourage

fomento, *m.* promotion, fostering; improvement, development

fonda, *f.* hotel, inn

fondo, *m.* depth; bottom; rear; fund(s), capital, stock; essential nature; (art) background; **a fondo,** completely, fully

fonética, *f.* phonetics

fonógrafo, *m.* phonograph, gramophone

forastero, *adj.* strange, exotic; *n.* stranger, foreigner

forma, form, shape; way

formal, *adj.* formal; serious

formalidad, *f.* formality; punctuality; good behavior

formalizar, *va.* to make official; **formalizarse,** to settle down, become earnest

formar, *va.* to form, shape

formidable, *adj.* formidable; terrific

formón, *m.* chisel; punch

fórmula, *f.* formula

formular, *va.* to formulate, draw up

formulario, *m.* form (for filling in information)

foro, *m.* court of justice; bar; background of the stage; forum

forrar, *va.* to line (clothes, etc.); to cover (books, etc.)

fortalecer, *va.* to fortify, strengthen

fortaleza, *f.* fortitude,

strength, vigor; (mil. fortress
fortificar, *va.* to fortify
fortuna, *f.* fortune; **por fortuna**, fortunately
forzar, *va.* to force; to ravish
forzoso, *adj.* necessary
fosa, *f.* grave
fosforescente, *adj.* phosphorescent
fósforo, *m.* phosphorus; match
foso, *m.* pit; moat, ditch, fosse; **foso séptico**, septic tank
fotogénico, *adj.* photogenic
fotograbado, *m.* photoengraving, photogravure
fotografía *f.* photograph, picture
fotografiar, *va.* to photograph
fotógrafo, *m.* photographer
frac, *m.* evening coat, dress coat
fracasar, *vn.* to fail
fracaso, *m.* failure
fractura, fracture
fragancia, *f.* fragrance, perfume
fragante, *adj.* fragrant; flagrant
fragmento, *m.* fragment
frambuesa, *f.* raspberry
francés, **francesa**, *adj.* French; *m.* French language; Frenchman; *f.* Frenchwoman
Francia, *f.* France
franco, *adj.* frank, liberal, open, sincere; **franco a bordo**, free on board; **franco de porte**, postpaid; *m.* franc
franja, *f.* fringe; braid, border; stripe
franqueo, *m.* postage
franqueza, *f.* frankness
franquicia, *f.* franchise, grant; **franquicia postal**, free postage
frase, *f.* phrase, sentence
fraternal, *adj.* fraternal, brotherly
fraternidad, *f.* fraternity, brotherhood
fraudulento, *adj.* fraudulent
frazada, *f.* blanket
frecuencia, *f.* frequency; **con frecuencia**, frequently

frecuente, *adj.* frequent
freir, *va.* to fry
fréjol or **frijol**, bean
frenesí, *m.* frenzy
frente, *f.* face; forehead; **frente a frente**, face to face; *m.* (mil.) front line; **en frente**, in front, across the way
fresa,, *f.* strawberry
fresco *adj.* fresh, cool; new; bold; *m.* refreshing air; **tomar el fresco**, to enjoy the cool air
frescura, *f.* freshness, coolness; smart repartee
fresno, *m.* ash tree
frialdad, *f.* coldness; indifference
frijoles, *m. pl.* beans
frío, **fría**, *adj.* cold; indifferent; *m.* cold; **hacer frío** or **tener frío**, to be cold
frito, *adj.* fried
frívolo, *adj.* frivolous
frondoso, *adj.* leafy
frontera, *f.* frontier, border
frontón, *m.* wall of a handball court; pelota court
frotar, *va.* to rub
fructífero, *adj.* fruitful
frugal, *adj.* frugal, sparing
frugalidad, *f.* frugality
fruncir, *va.* to pleat; to gather, shirr; to pucker; to reduce to a smaller size; **fruncir las cejas**, to knit the eyebrows; **fruncir el ceño**, to frown
fruta, *f.* fruit
frutal, *adj.* fruit-bearing
frutera, *f.* fruit woman; fruit dish
frutería, *f.* fruit store
frutilla, *f.* small fruit; strawberry (in South America)
fruto, *m.* fruit; benefit
fuego, *m.* fire; skin eruption; ardor
fuelle, *m.* bellows, blower
fuente, *f.* fountain; source; issue; spring (of water); platter, dish
fuera, *adv.* outside; **fuera de sí**, frantic, beside oneself; **fuera de alcance**, beyond reach

fuerte, *m.* fortification; fort; *adj.* strong; loud; *adv.* strongly; loudly

fuerza, *f.* force, strength, vigor; violence, coercion; **a fuerza de,** by dint of; **fuerza mayor,** act of God

fuete, *m.* (Sp. Am.) horsewhip

fuga, *f.* flight, escape; leak; (mus.) fugue

fugarse, *vr.* to escape, flee

fugaz, *adj.* fugitive; volatile

fulano, fulana, or **Fulano de Tal,** *n.* John Doe, so-and-so

fulgor, *m.* glow, brilliancy

fulminante, *m.* percussion cap; *adj.* explosive

fumar, *va., vn.* to smoke (cigars ,etc.)

fumigación, *f.* fumigation

funcionamiento, *m.* functioning

funcionar, *vn.* to function; to work, run (as machines)

funcionario, *m.* official, functionary

funda, *f.* case, sheath; slip cover; **funda de almohada,** pillowcase

fundación, *f.* foundation

fundador, fundadora, *n.* founder

fundamental, *adj.* fundamental

fundamento, *m.* foundation, base, groundwork; reason; good behavior

fundar, *va.* to found; to establish

fundir, *va.* to melt metals

fúnebre, *adj.* mournful, sad; funeral

funesto, *adj.* funereal dismal; disastrous

furgón, *m.* baggage, freight,or express car

furor, *m.* fury

fusil, *m.* musket, rifle

fusilar, *va.* to shoot, execute

fusión, *f.* fusion, union

futbol, *m.* football, soccer

futuro, *adj., m.* future

G

g/, gramo, gr. gram

g/, giro, draft

gabardina, *f.* gabardine; raincoat

gabinete, *m.,* cabinet, study

gafas, *f. pl.* spectacles, goggles

galán, *m.* gallant, courtier; lover; actor

galante, *adj.* gallant, courtly; generous, liberal

galantear, *va.* to court, woo

galanteo, *m.* gallantry, courtship

galantería, *f.* gallantry; compliment

galera, *f.* galley

galería, *f.* gallery

galgo, *m.* greyhound

galón, *m.* braid; gallon

galope, *m.* gallop

galvanómetro, *m.* galvanometer

galleta, *f.* cracker; cookie

gallina, *f.* hen; coward

gallinero, *m.* hen coop

gallo, *m.* cock, rooster; **misa de gallo,** midnight mass

gama globulina, *f.* gamma globulin

gana, *f.* appetite; desire, mind; **tener gana,** to be willing; **de buena gana,** voluntarily; **de mala gana,** unwillingly

ganadería, *f.* cattle breeding

ganado, *m.* cattle

ganancia, *f.* gain, profit

ganar, *va.* to gain, win; to beat (in a game); to earn

ganga, *f.* bargain

ganso, gansa, *n.* gander; goose

garage or **garaje,** *m.* garage

garantía, *f.* guarantee, pledge

garantizar, *va.* to guarantee, warrant

garbanzo, *m.* chick-pea

garbo, *m.* gracefulness

garboso, *adj.* graceful

gardenia, *f.* gardenia

garganta, *f.* throat, gullet; gorge

gárgara, *f.* gargle

garrapata, *f.* tick (insect)

garrote, *m.* cudgel, club

gas, *m.* gas
gasolina, *f.* gasoline
gasolinera, *f.* gas station; motor launch
gasómetro, *m.* gas storage tank, gas holder
gastador, *adj.* extravagant
gastar, *va.* to spend; to wear out; to use up
gasto, *m.* expense, cost
gata, *f.* tabby; **a gatas**, on all fours
gatear, *vn.* to creep, crawl
gato, *m.* cat; tomcat; jack
gaucho, *m.* Argentine cowboy
gavilán, *m.* (orn.) hawk
gaviota, *f.* (orn.) gull, sea gull
gazapo, *m.* young rabbit; blunder
gelatina, *f.* gelatine, jelly
gemido, *m.* groan, moan
gemir, *vn.* to groan, moan
gen, *m.* gene
generación, *f.* generation
generador, *m.* generator
general, *m.* general; *adj.* general, usual; **por lo general**, as a rule
generosidad, *f.* generosity
generoso, *adj.* generous
Génesis, *f.* Genesis
genial, *adj.* outstanding
genio, *m.* genius; temper
genital, *adj.* genital
genocidio, *m.* genocide
gente, *f.* people
gentil, *adj.* courteous
gentileza, *f.* gentility; courteous gesture
gentío, *m.* crowd, multitude
gentuza, *f.* rabble, mob
genuino, *adj.* genuine
geografía, *f.* geography.
geográfico, *adj.* geographical
geología, *f.* geology
geólogo, *m.* geologist
geometría, *f.* geometry
gerencia, *f.* management
gerente, *m.* manager
germinar, *vn.* to germinate
gerundio, *m.* (gram.) gerund, present participle
gestión, *f.* action, step
gestionar, *va.* to take steps to obtain something

gesto, *m.* face, aspect; gesture
gigante, *m.* giant; *adj.* gigantic
gigantesco, *adj.* gigantic
gymnasia *f.* gymnastics
gimnasio, *m.* gymnasium
ginebra, *f.* gin
ginecólogo, *m.* gynecologist
girafa, *f.* giraffe
girar, *vn.* to rotate, revolve; (com.) to draw on
girasol, *m.* sunflower
giro, *m.* turn, bend; (com.) draft; **giro a la vista**, sight draft; **giro postal**, money order
gitano, gitana, *n.* gypsy
glacial, *adj.* icy
gladiolo, *m.* (bot.) gladiolus
glicerina, glycerine
glóbulo, *m.* globule
gloria, *f.* glory
glorificar, *va.* to glorify
glorioso, *adj.* glorious
glosario, *m.* glossary
glotón, glotona, *n., adj.* glutton; gluttonous
glucosa, *f.* glucose
gobernación, *f.* government; governor's office or mansion
gobernador, *m.* governor
gobernar, *va.* to govern; to regulate; to direct
gobierno, *m.* government
golfo, *m.* gulf
golondrina, *f.* (orn.) swallow
golosina, *f.* dainty, titbit
goloso, *adj.* gluttonous
golpe, *m.* blow, stroke, hit; knock; **de golpe**, all at once
golpear, *va., vn.* to beat, knock; to bruise; to tap
goma, *f.* gum; rubber; eraser
gordo, *adj.* fat; thick
gordura, *f.* grease; fatness
gorgojo, *m.* grub, weevil
gorila, *m.* (zool.) gorilla
gorra, *f.* cap, bonnet; **de gorra**, (coll.) at others' expense, sponging
gorro, *m.* cap or hood
gota, *f.* drop; gout
gotear, *vn.* to drip
gotera, *f.* leak, leakage
gozar, *va.* to enjoy
gozoso, *adj.* joyful

gr., gramo, gr., gram
grabación, *f.* recording; enraving
grabado, *m.* engraving, illustration; **grabado al agua fuerte**, etching
gracia, *f.* grace; pardon; **gracias**, *pl.* thanks
gracioso, *adj.* graceful; funny, pleasing; *m.* clown, buffoon
grada, *f.* step of a staircase; **gradas**, *pl.* seats of a stadium
grado, *m.* step; degree; grade. ,
graduación, *f.* graduation
gradual, *adj.* gradual
graduar, *va., vr.* to graduate; to grade
gráfico, *adj.* graphic; vivid
Gral. General, Gen. General
gramática, *f.* grammar
gramatical, *adj.* grammatical
gramo, *m.* gram
gran, *adj.* contraction of **grande**, great, large, big
granada, *f.* grenade, shell, pomegranate
Gran Bretaña, *f.* Great Britain
grande, *adj.* great; large, big
grandioso, *adj.* grand, magnificent
granero, *m.* granary
granito, *m.* granite
granizo, *m.* hail
granja, *f.* grange, farm
grano, *m.* grain, kernel; pimple; **ir al grano**, to get to the point
grasa, *f.* suet, fat, grease; shoe polish
gratificación, *f.* gratification; gratuity
gratificar, *va.* to gratify, reward
gratitud, *f.* gratitude
grato, *adj.* pleasant, pleasing; **su grata**, your favor (letter)
gratuito, *adj.* free
gravamen, *m.* charge, tax
gravar, *va.* to burden; to tax
grave, *adj.* grave, serious
Grecia, *f.* Greece
gremio, *m.* guild, trade union
griego, *adj.* Greek
grieta, *f.* opening, crack
grillo, *m.* cricket

gringo, gringa, *n.* (Sp. Am.) (coll.) foreigner (especially an Anglo-Saxon)
gripe, *f.* grippe, influenza
gris, *adj.* gray
gritar. *vn.* to scream
grito, *m.* cry, scream
grosería, *f.* insult; coarseness
grosero, *adj.* coarse, rude
grúa, *f.* crane, derrick
gruesa, *f.* gross
grueso, *adj.* thick, coarse
gruñido, *m.* grunt, growl
grupo, *m.* group
gruta, *f.* grotto
gsa., gruesa, gro., gross
gte., gerente, mgr., manager
guacamayo, *m.*, **guacamaya**, *f.* macaw
guante, *m.* glove
guapo, *adj.* courageous; bold; elegant, handsome
guarda, *m., f.* guard, keeper
guardabrisa, *m.* windshield
guardafango, *m.* fender; dashboard
guardar, *va.* to keep; to guard
guardarropa, *m., f.* keeper of a wardrobe; *m.* coatroom
guardia, *f.* guard; watch; *m.* guardsman
guasa, *f.* (coll.) fun, jest
guasón, guasona, *adj.* (coll.) fond of teasing
guatemalteco, guatemalteca, *n., adj.* Guatemalan
guayaba, *f.* guava (fruit); **guayabo**, *m.* guava (tree)
güero, güera, *n., adj.* (Mex.) blond, light-haired. *See* **huero**
guerra, war; **dar guerra**, to be a nuisance (usually a child)
guerrero, *m.* warrior; **guerrera**, *adj.* martial, warlike
guía, *m., f.* guide; guidebook
guiar, *va.* to guide, lead; to drive
Guillermo, William
guillotina, *f.* guillotine
guindar, *va.* to hang
guiñar, *va.* to wink
guión, *m.* hyphen; (rad.) script
guisado, *m.* stew
guisante, *m.* (bot.) pea

guisar, *va.* to cook, stew
guiso, *m.* any edible concoction
guitarra, *f.* guitar
gusano, *m.* maggot, worm
gustar, *va.*, *vn.* to like, be fond of
gusto, *m.* taste; pleasure, delight; choice
gustoso, *adj.* tasty; willing

H

h., **habitantes**, pop., population
haba, *f.* (bot.) navy bean
Habana, *f.* Havana
habanero, **habanera**, *n.*, *adj.* native of Havana; of Havana
habano, *m.* Havana cigar
haber, *va.* to have (as an auxiliary verb); to exist; *m.* (com.) credit; **haberes**, *m. pl.* property
habichuela, *f.* kidney bean; **habichuela verde**, string bean
hábil, *adj.* able, skillful
habilidad, *f.* ability, dexterity, aptitude
habilitar, *va.* to qualify, enable; to equip
habitación, *f.* dwelling
habitante, *m.*, *f.* inhabitant
habitar, *va.* to inhabit, reside
hábito, *m.* custom
habituarse, *vr.* to accustom oneself
habla, *f.* speech; language; **sin habla**, speechless
hablador, *adj.* talkative
hablar, *va.*, *vn.* to speak, talk
hacendado, *m.* landholder, farmer
hacendoso, *adj.* industrious, diligent
hacer, *va.*, *vn.* to make, do; to manufacture; **hacer alarde**, to boast; **hacer calor**, to be warm; **hacer frío**, to be cold
hacia, *prep.* toward; about
hacienda, *f.* landed property; farmstead
hada, *f.* fairy
halagar, *va.* to please; to flatter

halago, *m.* caress; flattery
halagüeño, *adj.* pleasing; flattering
halcón, *m.* falcon, hawk
haltera, *f.* barbell
hallar, *va.* to find; to discover; to come upon; **hallarse**, to be; **no hallarse**, to be out of sorts
hallazgo, *m.* finding, discovery
hambre, *f.* hunger; famine; **tener hambre**, to be hungry
hambriento, *adj.* hungry; starved
haragán, **haragana**, *n.* idler; *adj.* lazy
harapo, *m.* rag, tatter
harén, *m.* harem
harina, *f.* flour
harinoso, *adj.* mealy, starchy
harmonía, *f.* harmony
hartar, *va.*, *vr.* to cloy, satiate
harto, *adj.* satiated; sufficient; *adv.* enough
hasta, *prep.* till, until; *conj.* also, even
hazaña, *f.* exploit, feat
hazmerreir, *m.* laughingstock
he, *adv.* behold, look here (generally followed by **aquí** or **allí**); **he aquí**, here it is
hebilla, *f.* buckle
hebra, *f.* thread, filament
hebreo, **hebrea**, *n.* Hebrew; *m.* Hebrew language; *adj.* Hebraic, Judaical
hecatombe, *f.* massacre, slaughter
hectárea, *f.* hectare
hecho, *adj.* made, done; accustomed; *m.* fact; act, deed
hechura, *f.* making; workmanship
hediondo, *adj.* ill-smelling
helada, *f.* frost; nip
heladería, *f.* ice-cream parlor
helado, *adj.* frozen; icy; *m.* ice cream
helar, *va.*, *vn.* to congeal; to freeze, ice; to astonish, amaze; **helarse**, to be frozen; to congeal
hélice, *f.* propeller
helicóptero, helicopter

hembra, *f.* female; eye of hook; nut of a screw
hemisferio, *m.* hemisphere
hemorragia, *f.* (med.) hemorrhage
hemorroides, *f. pl.* piles, hemorrhoids
heno, *m.* hay
heredar, *va.* to inherit
hereditario, *adj.* hereditary
heredero, heredera, *n.* heir, heiress
hereje, *m., f.* heretic
herencia, *f.* inheritance, heritage; heirship
herida, *f.* wound, hurt
herir, *va.* to wound, to hurt; to offend
hermanastra, *f.* stepsister
hermanastro, *m.* stepbrother
hermano, hermana, *n.* brother, sister; **primo hermano,** or **prima hermana,** first cousin
hermético, *adj.* airtight
hermoso, *adj.* beautiful, handsome
hermosura, *f.* beauty
héroe, *m.* hero
heroico, *adj.* heroic
heroína, *f.* heroine
heroísmo, *m.* heroism
herradura, *f.* horseshoe
herramienta, *f.* tool, implement
herrería, *f.* ironworks
herrero, *m.* blacksmith
hervir, *vn.* to boil
hervor, *m.* boiling; fervor
hidroavión, *m.* seaplane
hidrógeno, *m.* hydrogen
hidropesía, *f.* dropsy
hidroplano, *m.* hydroplane (boat)
hiedra, *f.* ivy
hiel, *f.* gall, bile
hielo, *m.* frost, ice
hiena, *f.* hyena
hierba or **yerba,** *f.* herb; grass; weed
hierbabuena, *f.* (bot.) mint
hierro, *m.* iron; **hierros,** *pl.* fetters
hígado, *m.* liver
higiene, *f.* hygiene

hija, *f.* daughter; child
hijastra, *f.* stepdaughter
hijastro, *m.* stepson
hijo, *m.* son; child
hilar, *va.* to spin
hilera, *f.* row; ridgepole; (mech.) wire drawer
hilo, *m.* thread; linen; wire
hilvanar, *va.* to baste
himno, *m.* hymn; anthem
hincapié, *m.* stress; **hacer hincapié,** to emphasize
hincarse, *vr.* to kneel
hinchado, *adj.* swollen
hinchar, *va., vr.* to swell
hindú, *m., f.* Hindu
hipnotismo, *m.* hypnotism
hipnotizar, *va.* to hypnotize
hipo, *m.* hiccough
hipócrita, *adj., n.* hypocritical; hypocrite
hipopótamo, *m.* hippopotamus
hipoteca, *f.* mortgage
hirviente, *adj.* boiling
hispano, *adj.* Hispanic, Spanish
Hispanoamérica, *f.* Spanish America
hispanoamericano, hispanoamericana, *adj., n.* Spanish-American
histérico, *adj.* hysterical
historia, *f.* history; story
historiador, historiadora, *n.* historian
histórico, *adj.* historical
hocico, *m.* snout, muzzle
hogar, *m.* home; hearth
hoguera, *f.* bonfire; blaze
hoja, *f.* leaf; blade (of knife, sword, etc.); sheet (of paper or metal), **hoja de trébol,** cloverleaf
hohalata, *f.* tin plate
hojear, *va.* to turn the leaves of a book
Holanda, *f.* Holland
holandés, holandésa, *n., adj.* Dutch
holgado, *adj.* loose; in easy circumstances
holgazán, holgazana, *n.* idler
hollín, *m.* soot
hombre, *m.* man, human be-

ing

hombro, m. shoulder

homenaje, m. homage, tribute

homicida, m., f. murderer; adj. homicidal

homicidio, m. murder

hondo, adj. profound, deep

hondureño, hondureña, n.; adj. Honduran

honesto, adj. honest; modest

hongo, m. mushroom; fungus

honor, m. honor

honorable, adj. honorable

honorario, adj. honorary; m. honorarium, fee

honra, f. honor; chastity (in women); **honras,** pl. funeral honors

honrado, adj. honest, honorable

honrar, va. to honor; **honrarse,** to deem it an honor

hora, f. hour; time

horario, m. hour hand; time table; hours; schedule

horma, f. mold; **horma de zapatos,** shoe last

hormiga, f. ant

hormigón, m. concrete

hormigonera, f. concrete mixer

horno, m. oven; furnace; **alto horno,** blast furnace

horquilla, f. hairpin

horrible, adj. horrible

horror, m. horror, fright

horrorizar, va., vr. to horrify

hortaliza, f. vegetables

hospedaje, m. lodging

hospedar, va., vr. to lodge, board

hospicio, m. orphanage; old peoples home

hospital, m. hospital

hospitalidad, f. hospitality

hospitalización, f. hospitalization

hospitalizar, va. to hospitalize

hostia, f. host; wafer

hotel, m. hotel

hoy, adv. today

hoyo, m. hole, pit

hoz, f. sickle

huelga, f. strike of workmen

huella, f. track, trace

huérfano, huérfana, n., adj. orphan

huero, adj. empty, addle; **huevo huero,** rotten egg

huerta, orchard, vegetable garden

huerto, m. fruit garden

hueso, m. bone; stone, core

huésped, huéspeda, n. guest; boarder

huevo, m. egg

huida, f. flight, escape

huir, vn. to flee, escape

hule, m. rubber; oilcloth

humanidad, f. humanity, mankind; **humanidades,** pl. humanities, human learning

humanitario, humanitaria, n., adj. humanitarian

humano, adj. human; humane, kind

humedad, f. humidity, moisture, wetness

humedecer, va. to moisten, wet, soak

humedo, adj. humid, wet

humildad, f. humility, humbleness

humilde, adj. humble, meek

humillar, va., vr. to humble; to humiliate

humo, m. smoke; fume

humor, m. humor, disposition

hundir, vn., vr. to submerge; to sink

húngaro, húngara, adj., n. Hungarian

Hungría, f. Hungary

huracán, m. hurricane, storm

hurtar, va. to steal, rob

I

ibérico, adj. Iberian

id., idem, id., same, ditto

ida, f. departure; **idas y venidas,** comings and goings

idea, f. idea; scheme

ideal, m., adj. ideal

idealismo, m. idealism

idealista, n., adj. idealist; idealistic

idealizar, va., vn. to idealize

idear, va. to conceive; to think, to contrive, to plan

idem, item, the same, ditto

idéntico, *adj.* identical

identificar, *va., vr.* to identify

idioma, *m.* language

idiosincrasia, *f.* idiosyncrasy

idiota, *m., f.* idiot; *adj.* idiotic

idolatrar, *va.* to idolize

idolo, *m.* idol

iglesia, *f.* church

ignorancia, *f.* ignorance

ignorante, *adj.* ignorant

ignorar, *va.* to be ignorant of

igual, *adj.* equal, similar

igualar, *va.* to equalize, equal; **igualarse,** to place oneself on a level (with)

igualdad, *f.* equality

igualmente, *adv.* equally

ilegal, *adj.* illegal, unlawful

ilegítimo, *adj.* illegitimate

ileso, *adj.* unhurt

iluminación, *f.* illumination, lighting

iluminar, *va.* to illumine, illuminate

ilustración, *f.* illustration

ilustrar, *va.* to illustrate; to enlighten

ilustre, *adj.* illustrious

imagen, *f.* image

imaginación, *f.* imagination

imaginar, *va., vn.* to imagine

imaginario, *adj.* imaginary, fancied

imán, *m.* magnet

imbécil, *m., f.* imbecile, idiot; *adj.* feeble minded

imitación, *f.* imitation

imitar, *va.* to imitate

impaciencia, *f.* impatience

impaciente, *adj.* impatient

impar, *adj.* unequal, odd

imparcial, *adj.* impartial

impartir, *va.* to impart

impávido, *adj.* calm in the face of danger

impecable, *adj.* impeccable

impedir, *va.* to impede, prevent

imperar, *vn.* to rule, command; to reign; to prevail

imperativo, *adj.* imperative, pressing; *m.* (gram.) imperative (case)

imperdible, *m.* safety pin

imperdonable, *adj.* unpardonable

imperfecto, *adj.* imperfect

imperial, *adj.* imperial

imperialismo, *m.* imperialism

imperio, *m.* empire

imperioso, *adj.* imperious, pressing; arrogant

impermeable, *adj.* waterproof; *m.* raincoat

impersonal, *adj.* impersonal

impertinente, *adj.* impertinent; importunate

impertinentes, *m. pl.* lorgnette

impetu, *m.* impetus; impetuosity

impetuoso, *adj.* impetuous

implicar, *va., vn.* to impliclite, involve

implícito, *adj.* implicit

implorar, *va.* to implore

imponderabilidad, *f.* weightlessness

imponer, *va.* to impose; **imponerse,** to assert oneself

importador, importadora, *n.* importer

importancia, *f.* importance, import

importante, *adj.* important

importar, *vn.* to matter; to mind; to import

importe, *m.* amount, cost

imposibilidad, *f.* impossibility

imposible, *adj.* impossible

imposición, *f.* imposition

impostor, impostora, *n.* impostor

impotente, *adj.* impotent; helpless

impracticable, *adj.* impracticable

imprenta, *f.* printing; printing office

imprescindible, *adj.* indispensible, essential

impresión, *f.* impression; edition; presswork

impresionar, *va.* to impress

impresos, *m. pl.* printed matter

impresor, impresora, *n.* printer

imprevisto, *adj.* unforeseen

imprimir *va.* to print

impropio, *adj.* improper, unfit

improvisar, *va.* to improvise

improviso, *adj.* unforeseen; **de improviso,** unexpectedly

impuesto, *m.* tax, impost, duty; **impuesto sobre rentas,** income tax

impulsar, *va.* to further, impel; (mech.) to drive

impulso, *m.* impulse, impulsion, spur

impureza, *f.* impurity

inaccesible, *adj.* inaccessible

inaceptable, *adj.* unacceptable

inagotable, *adj.* inexhaustible

inalámbrico, *adj.* wireless

inaudito, *adj.* unheard of, unusual

inauguración, *f.* inauguration

inaugurar, *va.* to inaugurate

inca, *m.* Inca; Peruvian gold coin

incansable, *adj.* untiring

incapaz., *adj.* incapable, unable

incendiar, *va., vr.* to set on fire

incendio, *m.* fire, conflagration

incentivo, *m.* incentive

incertidumbre, *f.* uncertainty

incidente, *m.* incident

incienso, *m.* incense

incierto, *adj.* uncertain

incitar, *va.* to incite, stir

inclinar, *va., vn.* to incline, slope; **inclinarse por,** to be favorably disposed to

incluir, *va.* to include, comprise; to inclose

inclusive, *adv.* inclusive, including

incluso, inclosed

incógnito, *adj.* unknown

incoherente, *adj.* incoherent

incomodar, *va.* to inconvenience, disturb

incomodidad, *f.* inconvenience, annoyance

incómodo, *adj.* uncomfortable, inconvenient

incomparable, *adj.* incomparable

incompatible, *adj.* incompatible

incompetente, *adj.* incompetent

incompleto, *adj.* incomplete

incomprensible, *adj.* incomprehensible

inconcebible, *adj.* inconceivable

inconsciente, *adj.* unconscious

inconstante, *adj.* inconstant, fickle

inconveniencia, *f.* inconvenience

inconveniente, *adj.* inconvenient; inadvisable; *m.* obstacle; objection

incorporar, *va.* to incorporate; to join; **incorporarse,** to become incorporated; to sit up (in bed)

incorrecto, *adj.* incorrect

incorregible, *adj.* incorrigible

incrédulo, *adj.* incredulous

increíble, *adj.* incredible

incremento, *m.* increment, increase

incubar, *va.* to hatch

inculcar, *va.* to inculcate

incurable, *adj.* incurable

incurrir, *vn.* to incur

indagar, *va.* to investigate

indecente, *adj.* indecent

indeciso, *adj.* undecided

indefinido, *adj.* indefinite

indemnizar, *va.* to indemnify

independencia, *f.* independence

independiente, *adj.* independent

indescriptible, *adj.* indescribable

indicación, *f.* indication

indicar, *va.* to indicate

indicativo, *adj.* indicative; *m., adj.* (gram.) indicative

índice, *m.* mark, sign; hand of a watch or clock; index; forefinger

índico, *adj.* pertaining to the East Indies; **Océano Índico** or **Mar de las Indias,** Indian Ocean

indiferencia, *f.* indifference

indiferente, *adj.* indifferent

indígena, *adj., n.* indigenous, native

indigente, *adj.* indigent,

indigestión, *f.* indigestion

indigesto, *adj.* indigestible

indignación, *f.* indignation, anger

indio, india, *n., adj.* Indian

indirecta, *f.* hint, cue

indirecto, *adj.* indirect

indispensable, *adj.* indispensable

individual, *adj.* individual

individuo, *m.* individual

índole, *f.* disposition, temper; kind; nature

inducir, *va.* to induce

indudable, *adj.* undeniable; evident, certain

indulgencia, *f.* indulgence, forgiveness

industria, *f.* industry

industrial, *adj.* industrial

industrialización, *f.* industrialization

industrializer, *va.* to industrialize

industrioso, *adj.* industrious

inédito, *adj.* not published, unedited

inepto, *adj.* inept, unfit

inercia, *f.* inertia; inactivity

inesperado, *adj.* unexpected

inevitable, *adj.* inevitable

infame, *adj.* infamous, bad; *m., f.* wretch, scoundrel

infancia, *f.* infancy

infante, *m.* infant; any son of the king of Spain, except the heir apparent

infantil, *adj.* infantile

infección, *f.* infection

infectar, *va.* to infect

infeliz, *adj.* unhappy, unfortunate

inferior, *adj.* inferior; lower

inferioridad, *f.* inferiority

inferir, *va.* to infer; to inflict

infiel, *adj.* unfaithful

infierno, *m.* hell

ínfimo, *adj.* lowest

infinidad, *f.* infinity

infinitivo, *m.* (gram.) infinitive

infinito, *adj.* infinite, im-

mense; *adv.* infinitely, immensely; *m.* infinity

inflación, *f.* inflation

inflamable, *adj.* inflammable

intramar, *va.* to inflame; **intramarse,** to catch fire

inflar, *va., vr.* to inflate

influencia, *f.* influence

influenza, *f.* influenza

influir, *va.* to influence

influyente, *adj.* influential

información, *f.* information

informal, *adj.* not punctual; unreliable

informar, *va.* to inform, report

informe, *m.* information; report, account

infortunio, *m.* misfortune

infracción, *f.* violation

infructuoso, *adj.* fruitless

infundado, *adj.* groundless

infundir, *va.* to infuse; to instill

ingeniar, *va.* to conceive; to contrive

ingeniero, *m.* engineer

ingenio, *m.* wit, ingenuity; **ingenio de azúcar,** sugar mill

ingenioso, *adj.* ingenious, witty; resourceful

ingenuidad, *f.* candor, naiveté

ingenuo, *adj.* candid, naive

Inglaterra, *f.* England

inglés, inglesa, *n., adj.* Englishman, Englishwoman; English; *m.* English language

ingratitud, *f.* ingratitude

ingrato, *adj.* ungrateful

ingrediente, *m.* ingredient

ingreso, *m.* (com.) receipts, revenue; entrance

inhumano, *adj.* inhuman

inicial, *f., adj.* initial

iniciar, *va.* to initiate, begin; **iniciarse,** to be initiated

inciativa, *f.* initiative

injusticia, *f.* injustice

inmaculado, *adj.* immaculate

inmediato, *adj.* immediate, next

inmejorable, *adj.* unsurpassable

inmenso, *adj.* immense, infinite

inmersión, immersion, dip

inmigración, *f.* immigration
inmigrar, *vn.* to immigrate
inmoral, *adj.* immoral
inmoralidad, *f.* immorality
inmortal, *adj.* immortal
inmortalidad, *f.* immortality
inmóvil, *adj.* immovable, stable; death-like
inmueble, *adj.* (law) immovable (property); **bienes inmuebles,** real estate
inmundo, *adj.* filthy, dirty
inmune, *adj.* immune
innato, *adj.* inborn, natural
innovación, *f.* innovation
inocencia, *f.* innocence
inocente, *adj.* innocent
inodoro, *m.* water closet
inofensivo, *adj.* harmless
inolvidable, *adj.* unforgettable
inquietud, *f.* restlessness
inquilino, inquilina, *n.* tenant, renter
inquisición, *f.* inquisition
insaciable, *adj.* insatiable
inscribir, *va., vr.* register
inscripción, *f.* inscription
insecto, *m.* insect
inseguro, *adj.* uncertain
inseparable, *adj.* inseparable
inserción, *f.* insertion
insertar, *va.* to insert
inservible, *adj.* useless
insignia, *f.* badge, insignia
insignificante, *adj.* insignificant
insinuación, *f.* insinuation, hint
insinuar, *va.* to insinuate, hint; **insinuarse,** to ingratiate oneself
insistencia, *f.* persistence
insistir, *vn.* to insist
insolente, *adj.* insolent
insomnio, *m.* insomnia
inspección, *f.* inspection
inspector, *m.* inspector
inspiración, *f.* inspiration
inspirar, *va.* to inspire
instalación, *f.* installation
instalar, *va.* to install; **instalarse,** to settle
instantáneo, *adj.* instantaneous; **instantánea,** *f.* snapshot

instigar, *va.* to instigate
instintivo, *adj.* instinctive
instinto, *m.* instinct
institución, *f.* institution
instituto, *m.* institute
institutriz, *f.* governess
instrucción, *f.* instruction; education
instructor, *m.* instructor
instruido, *adj.* well-educated
instruir, *va.* to instruct
instrumento, *m.* instrument; machine
insubordinado, *adj.* insubordinate
insuficiente, *adj.* insufficient
insufrible, *adj.* insufferable
insuperable, *adj.* insurmountable
insurrecto, insurrecta, *n.,* *adj.* insurgent, rebel
intachable, *adj.* blameless; irreproachable
integridad, *f.* integrity, whole
íntegro, *adj.* entire
intelectual, *adj., n.* intellectual
inteligencia, *f.* intelligence; understanding
inteligente, *adj.* intelligent
intemperie, *f.* rough or bad weather; **a la intemperie,** outdoors
intempestivo, *adj.* inopportune
intención, intention
intensidad, intensity
intensificar, *va.* to intensify
intenso, *adj.* intense, ardent
intentar, *va.* to try; to intend
intento, *m.* intent, purpose
intercambio, *m.* interchange
interceder, *vn.* to intercede
interés, *m.* interest
interesante, *adj.* interesting
interesar, *vn., vr.* to be concerned or interested in; *va.* to interest
interino, *adj.* provisional, acting (of an employ or office)
interior, *adj.* interior, internal; **ropa interior,** underwear; *m.* interior
interjección, *f.* (gram.) interjection

intermediar, *va.* to interpose
intermedio, *adj.* intermediate; *m.* intermission; interlude, recess; **por intermedio de,** through, by means of
internacional, *adj.* international
internar, *va.* to intern; to place in a boarding school or asylum; *vn.* to pierce
interno, *adj.* interior, internal, inside; *n.* boarding-school student
interplanetario, interplanetaria, *adj.* interplanetary
interpretación, *f.* interpretation
interpretar, *va.* to interpret, explain; to translate
intérprete, *m.* interpreter
interrogación, *f.* interrogation
interrogar, *va.* to interrogate
interrumpir, *va.* to interrupt
interrupción, *f.* interruption
interruptor, *m.* (elec.) switch
intervalo, *m.* interval
intervención, *f.* intervention
intervenir, *vn.* to intervene, mediate
intestino, *m.* intestine
intimidad, *f.* intimacy
intolerable, *adj.* intolerable
intolerancia, *f.* intolerance
intranquilo, *adj.* restless
intransitive, *adj.* (gram.) intransitive
intriga, *f.* intrigue, plot
intrigante, *adj.* intriguing, scheming
intrínseco, *adj.* intrinsic
introducción, *f.* introduction
introducir, *va.* to introduce; **introducirse,** to gain access (to)
intruso, *adj.* intrusive, obtrusive; *n.* intruder
intuición, *f.* intuition
inundación, *f.* inundation, flood
inundar, *va.* to inundate
inútil, *adj.* useless
invadir, *va.* to invade
inválido, *adj.* invalid, null; *n.* invalid
invariable, *adj.* invariable

invasión, *f.* invasion
invencible, *adj.* invincible
invención, *f.* invention
inventar, *va.* to invent
inventario, *m.* inventory
invento, *m.* invention
invernadero, *m.* (mil). greenhouse
inverosímil, *adj.* unlikely, improbable
inversión, *f.* inversion; investment
invertir, *va.* to invert; (com.) to invest
investigación, *f.* investigation, research
investigar, *va.* to investigate
invierno, *m.* winter
invisible, *adj.* invisible
invitación, *f.* invitation
invitado, invitada, *n.* guest
invitar, *va.* to invite
invocar, *va.* to invoke
involuntario, *adj.* involuntary
inyección, *f.* injection
inyectar, *va.* to inject
ir, *vn.* to go; to walk; to progress; **irse,** to go away, depart
ira, *f.* anger, wrath
iris, *m.* rainbow; iris (of the eye)
Irlanda, *f.* Ireland
irlandés, irlandésa, *n.,* *adj.* Irishman, Irishwoman; Irish
ironía, *f.* irony
irónico, *adj.* ironical
irregular, *adj.* irregular
irremediable, *adj.* irremediable, helpless
irreparable; *adj.* irreparable
irresistible, *adj.* irresistible
irresponsable, *adj.* irresponsible
irrevocable, *adj.* irrevocable
irritación, *f.* irritation; wrath
irritar, *va.* to irritate
isla, *f.* isle,, island
israelita, *n.* *adj.* Israelite, Jew, Jewish
istmo, *m.* isthmus
Italia, *f.* Italy
italiano, italiana, *n.,* *adj.* Italian; *m.* Italian language
itinerario, *adj.,* *m.* itinerary

izar, *va.* (naut.) to hoist
izquierdo, *adj.* left; left-handed; **izquierda,** *f.* left wing in politics; left, left hand

J

jabalí, *m.* wild boar
jabón, *m.* soap
jacinto, *m.* hyacinth
jactarse, *vr.* to boast
jadeante, *adj.* panting
jal lai, *m.* Basque ball
jaiba, *f.* (Sp. Am.) crab
jalea, *f.* jelly
jamás, *adv.* never
jamón, *m.* ham
Japón, *m.* Japan
japonés, japonesa, *adj., n.* Japanese; *m.* japanese language
jaqueca, *f.* headache
jarabe, *m.* sirup; **jarabe tapatío,** Mexican regional dance
jardín, *m.* garden
jardinero, jardinera, *n.* gardener
jarra, *f.* jug, jar, pitcher
jarro, *m.* pitcher, jug
J.C., Jesucristo, J.C., Jesus Christ
jefatura, *f.* leadership; **jefatura de policía,** police headquarters
jeringa, *f.* syringe
Jesucristo, *m.* Jesus Christ
jesuita, *m., adj.* Jesuit
Jesús, *m.* Jesus; *interj.* goodness!
jinete, *m.* horseman, rider
jira, *f.* strip of cloth; tour; **jira campestre,** picnic
jirafa, *f.* giraffe
jocoso, *adj.* comical
jornada, *f.* one-day march; journey
joroba, *f.* hump
jorobado, *adj.* hunchbacked
jota, *f.* the letter **j;** Spanish dance; **no saber ni jota,** not to know a thing
joven, *adj.* young; *m., f.* young man, young woman
jovial, *adj.* jovial, gay

joya, *f.* jewel
joyería, *f.* jewelry store
joyero, *m.* jeweler
juanete, *m.* bunion
jubilar, *va., vr.* to pension off; to retire
júbilo, *m.* joy
judía, *f.* kidney bean; string bean; Jewess
judicial, *adj.* judicial, juridical
judío, *adj.* Jewish; *m.* Jew
jueves, *m.* Thursday
juez, *m.* judge
jugada, *f.* move (in a game); mean trick
jugar, *va., vn.* to play; to gamble
jugo, *m.* sap, juice
jugoso, *adj.* juicy
juguete, *m.* toy, plaything
juguetón, *adj.* playful
juicio, *m.* judgment, reason; trial
juicioso, *adj.* wise, prudent
julio, *m.* July
junio, *m.* June
junta, *f.* session, meeting; board; **junta directiva,** board of directors
juntar, *va.* to unite; to collect, gather; **juntarse,** to assemble
junto, *adv.* near, close; **junto, junta,** *adj.* united; **juntos,** *pl.* together, side by side
jurado, *m.* jury; juror, juryman
juramento, *m.* oath
jurar, *va., vn.* to swear, make oath; to curse
jurisdicción, *f.* jurisdiction
justicia, *f.* justice; fairness; **la justicia,** the police
justificación, *f.* justification
justificar, *va.* to justify
justo, *adj.* just; fair, upright; tight
juvenil, *adj.* juvenile, youthful
juventud, *f.* youthfulness, youth
juzgado, *m.* tribunal; court
juzgar, *va., vn.* to judge

K

kaki, *m., adj.* khaki

karate, m. karate
Kc., Kilociclo, kc., kilocycle
Kg. or **kg., kilogramo,** k. or
kg., kilogram
kilo, m. kilo, kilogram
kilociclo, m. kilocycle
kilogramo, m. kilogram
kilométrico, kilométrica, adj.
kilometric; (coll.) too long
kilómetro, m. kilometer
kilotón, m. kiloton
kilovatio, m. kilowatt
kiosco, m. kiosk, booth
Km. or **km., kilómetro,** km.,
kilometer,
kodak, m. kodak
kv. or **k.w., kilovatio,** kw.,
kilowatt

L

l., ley, law; **libro,** bk., book;
litro, l., liter
L/, 1.ª, 1.: letra, bill, draft,
letter
£, libra esterlina, £, pound
sterling
la, art. (fem. sing.) the pron.
(acc. fem. sing.) her, it, as **la
vio,** he saw her, **la compré,** I
bought it (casa)
laberinto, m. labyrinth, maze
labia, f. (coll.) gift of gab
labio, m. lip; edge of anything
labor, f. labor, task; needlework
laborar, va., vn. to work; to till
laboratorio, m. laboratory
laborioso, adj. industrious
labrador, labradora, n. farmer;
peasant
labrar, va. to work; to labor, to
cultivate the ground
laca, f. lac; lacquer
lacio, adj. straight (applied to
hair)
lacónico, adj. laconic
lactancia, f. time of suckling
lácteo, adj. lacteous, milky
ladino, adj. cunning, crafty
lado, m. side; party
ladrar, vn. to bark
ladrillo, m. brick
ladrón, m. thief, robber
lagartija, f. (zool.) eft, newt

lagarto, m. lizard; alligator;
(coll.) sly person
lago, m. lake
lágrima, f. tear
laguna, f. lagoon, pond; blank
space (as in a text), hiatus;
gap
lamentar, va. to lament, regret; vn., vr. to lament, complain, cry
lamer, va. to lick, to lap
lámina, f. plate, sheet of
metal; copper plate; print,
picture
lana, f. wool
lanar, adj. woolly; **ganado lanar,** sheep
lance, m. cast, throw; critical
moment; quarrel
lancha, f. barge, launch
langosta f. locust; lobster
lánguido, adj. languid
lanudo. adj. woolly, fleecy
lanza, f. lance, spear
lanzacohetes, m. rocket
launcher
lanzar, va. to throw, fling; to
launch
lapicero, m. pencil case
lápida, f. tombstone
larga, f. delay; **a la larga,** in
the long run
largar, va. to slacken; to let
go; **largarse,** (coll.) to get out,
leave
largo, adj. long; **larga ejecución (discos),** long-playing
(records); m. length
laringe, f. larynx
lástima, f. pity
lastimar, va. to hurt; to
wound; **lastimarse,** to be
hurt
lata, f. tin can; (coll.) nuisance
annoyance
latente, adj. dormant
lateral, adj. lateral
latido, m. pant, palpitation;
barking
latigazo, m. crack of a whip
látigo, m. whip
latín, m. Latin language
latino, latina, adj., n. Latin
Latinoamérica, f. Latin America

latinoamericano, latinoamericana, *adj.* Latin American
latir, *vn.* to palpitate; to howl (as dogs)
lntitud, *f.* latitude
latón, *m.* brass; brassie
latoso, *adj.* boring; **latosa,** *n.* bore
laurel, *m.* (bot.) laurel; laurel crown
lavado, *m.* washing, wash
lavamanos, *m.* wash bowl
lavandería, *f.* laundry
lavar, *va.* to wash
lavativa, *f.* enema
lavatorio, *m.* lavatory
laxante, *m., adj.* (med.) laxative
lazarillo, *m.* blind man's guide
lazo, *m.* lasso, lariat; tie; bond
lb., libra, lb., pound
Ldo., L.^{do}, or **l.**^{do}, **Licenciado,** (Sp. Am.) lawyer
le, *pron.* dative case of **él** or **ella**
leal, *adj.* loyal, faithful
lealtad, *f.* loyalty
lección, *f.* lesson
lector, lectora, *n.* reader
leche, *f.* milk
lechería, *f.* dairy
lechero, *m.* milkman, dairyman; *adj.* pertaining to milk
lecho, *m.* bed; litter
lechuga, *f.* lettuce
lechuza, *f.* owl
leer, *va.* to read
legación, *f.* legation, embassy
legal, *adj.* legal, lawful
legalizar, *va.* to legalize
legar, *va.* to depute; to bequeath
legendario. *adj.* legendary
legible, *adj.* legible
legión, *f.* legion
legislación, *f.* legislation
legislativo, *adj.* legislative
legislatura, *f.* legislature
legítimo, *adj.* legitimate
legumbre, *f.* legume; vegetable
leído, *adj.* well-read
lejano, *adj.* distant
lejos, *adv.* far off
lengua, *f.* tongue; language
lenguaje, *m.* language

lente, *m.* or *f.* lens; monocle; **lentes,** *m. pl.* eye glasses; **lentes de contacto,** contact lenses
lenteja, *f.* (bot.) lentil
lentitud, *f.* slowness
lento, *adj.* slow, lazy
leña, *f.* kindling wood
león, *m.* lion
leona, *f.* lioness
leopardo, *m.* leopard
lerdo, *adj.* slow, heavy
lesbiano, *adj.* lesbian
lesion, *f.* wound; injury
letargo, *m.* drowsiness
letra, *f.* letter; handwriting; (com.) draft; words in a song; **al pie de la letra,** literally; **letras,** *pl.* learning, letters
letrado, *adj.* learned, lettered; *m.* lawyer, jurist
letrero, *m.* inscription, label; poster
levadura, *f.* yeast
levantar, *va.* to raise; to impute falsely; **levantarse,** to rise, to get up
leve, *adj.* light; trifling
ley, *f.* law
liberal, *adj.* liberal, generous
libertad, *f.* liberty, freedom
libertinaje, *m.* licentiousness
libra, *f.* pound (weight); **libra esterlina,** pound sterling
librar, *va.* to free, rid
libre, *adj.* free; exempt; *m.* (Mex.) taxicab
librería, *f.* bookstore
librero, *m.* bookseller; bookcase
libreta, *f.* memorandum book
libro, *m.* book
Lic. or **Licdo., licenciado,** (Sp. Am.) lawyer
licencia, *f.* permission, license
licenciado, *m.* licentiate, title given a lawyer
liceo, *m.* lyceum, high school
lícito, *adj.* lawful, licit
licor, *m.* liquor
líder, *m., f.* leader; (labor) instigator, agitator; chief
liebre, *f.* hare
ligar, *va., vr.* to tie, bind; to alloy; to confederate

ligereza, *f.* lightness; levity; swiftness
ligero, *adj.* light, swift
lija, *f.* sandpaper
lima, *f.* file; sweet lime (fruit)
limar, *va.* to file; to polish
limeño, limeña, *n.* native of Lima; *adj.* from Litna
limitación, *f.* limitation
limitar, *va.* to limit
límite, *m.* limit, boundary
limón, *m.* lemon
limonada, *f.* lemonade
limosna, *f.* alms, charity
limosnero, limosnera, *n.* beggar
limpiabotas, *m.* boot-black
limpiar, *va.* to clean
limpieza, *f.* cleanliness
limpio, *adj.* clean
linaza, *f.* linseed
lindo, *adj.* pretty
lino, *m.* flax; linen
linóleo, *m.* linoleum
linotipo, *m.* linotype
linterna, *f.* lantern; **linterna de proyección,** slide projector
lío, *m.* bundle; mess; **armar un lío,** to cause trouble
liquidación, *f.* liquidation, settlement; clearance sale
liquidar, *va.* to liquidate; to settle, clear accounts
líquido, *adj.* liquid, net; *m.* liquid
lira, *f.* lyre
lírico, *adj.* lyrical, lyric
lirio, *m.* iris (flower); lily
Lisboa, *f.* Lisbon
lisiado, *adj.* crippled
liso, *adj.* flat, smooth
lisonja, *f.* flattery
lista, *f.* list; stripe; **pasar lista,** to call the roll
listo, *adj.* ready; alert
literal, *adj.* literal
literario, *adj.* literary
literato, literata, *n.* literary person, writer; *adj.* learned
literatura, *f.* literature
litografía, *f.* lithography
litro, *m.* liter
liviano, *adj.* light; unchaste
lo, *pron.* (acc. case third pers.

sing.) him, it; *art.* the (used before an adjective)
lobo, *m.* wolf
local, *adj.* local; *m.* place
localidad, *f.* locality; **localidades,** *pl.* accommodations, tickets, seats
localizar, *va.* to localize
loción, *f.* lotion, wash
loco, loca, *adj., n.* mad, crack-brained
locomotora, *f.* locomotive
locura, *f.* madness, folly; absurdity
locutor, locutora, *n.* (radio) announcer
lodo, *m.* mud, mire
logico, *adj.* logical
lograr, *va.* to gain, obtain
loma, *f.* hillock
lombriz, *f.* earthworm
lomo, *m.* loin
lona, *f.* canvas; saileloth
Londres, *m.* London
longitud, *f.* length; longitude
loro, *m.* parrot
losa, *f.* flagstone; slab
lote, *m.* lot; share
lotería, *f.* lottery; lotto
loza, *f.* chinaware
Ltda., Sociedad Limitada, (Sp. Am.) Inc., Incorporated
lubricante, *adj., m.* lubricant
lubricar, lubrificar, *va.* to lubricate
luciérnaga, *f.* firefly
lucir, *vn., vr.* to shine, be brilliant; show off
lucrativo, *adj.* lucrative
lucha, *f.* struggle; wrestling
luchar, *vn.* to struggle; to wrestle
luego, *adv.* presently; soon afterwards; **desde luego,** of course; **hasta luego,** good-by
lugar, *m.* place; space; cause, motive
lujo, *m.* luxury; **de lujo,** de luxe
lujoso, *adj.* luxurious
lumbre, *f.* fire; light
lumbrera, *f.* luminary
luna, *f.* moon; glass plate for mirrors; **luna de miel,** honeymoon

lunar, *m.* mole; blemish
lunes, *m.* Monday
luneta, *f.* orchestra seat
lustre, *m.* luster; splendor
lustroso, *adj.* bright
luto, *m.* mourning
luz, *f.* light; **dar a luz,** to give
  birth

LL

llaga, *f.* wound, sore
llama, *f.* flame; (zool.) llama
llamada, *f.* call
llamar, *va.* to call; to invoke;
  ¿como se llama Ud.? What
  is your name?
llamativo, *adj.* showy
llano, *m.* field, plain
llanta, *f.* tire
llanto, *m.* flood of tears
llanura, *f.* plain, field
llave, *f.* key; **llave inglesa,**
  monkey wrench
llavero, *m.* key ring
llegada, *f.* arrival
llegar, *vn.* to arrive; **llegar a**
  ser, to become
llenar, *va.* to fill
lleno, *adj.* full, replete
llevar, *va.* to carry, bear, take
  away; to wear (clothes)
llover, *v. imp.* to rain
lloviznar, *v. imp.* to drizzle
lluvia, *f.* rain
lluvioso, *adj.* rainy

M

m., masculino, *m.* masculine;
  metro, *m.* meter; **milla,** *m.*
  mile
maceta, *f.* flowerpot
macizo, *adj.* massive, solid
machacar, *va.* to pound,
  crush
macho, *m.* male animal; hook
  (of hook and eye); *adj.* masculine, male; vigorous
madrastra, *f.* stepmother
madre, *f.* mother
madreperla, *f.* mother of pearl
madreselva, *f.* honey-suckle
madrileño, madrileña, *n., adj.*
  inhabitant of Madrid; from

Madrid
madrina, *f.* godmother
madrugada, *f.* dawn
madrugar, *vn.* to get up early;
  to anticipate, beforehand
madurar, *va., vn.* to ripen; to
  mature
madurez, *f.* maturity
maduro, *adj.* ripe; mature
maestra, *f.* woman teacher
maestría, *f.* mastership skill
maestro, *m.* master; expert;
  teacher; **maestro, maestra,**
  adj. masterly; **obra maestro,**
  masterpiece
magia, *f.* magic
mágico, *adj.* magical
magnánimo, *adj.* magnanimous
magnetismo, *m.* magnetism
magnetófono, *m.* tape recorder
magnífico, *adj.* magnificent
magnitud, *f.* magnitude
maguey, *m.* (bot.) maguey,
  century plant
mahometano, mahometana,
  n., adj. Mohammedan
maíz, *m.* corn, maize
majar, *va.* to pound; to mash
majestad, *f.* majesty
mal, *m.* evil, hurt, injury; ill-
  ness; *adj.* (used only before
  masculine nouns) bad
malaria, *f.* malaria
malcriado, *adj.* ill-bred
maldad, *f.* wickedness
maldecir, *va.* to curse
maldición, *f.* curse
maldito, *adj.* wicked; damned,
  cursed
malestar, *m.* indisposition
maleta, *f.* suitcase, satchel
malgastar, *va.* to misspend
malicioso, *adj.* malicious
maligno, *adj.* malignant
malnutrido, *adj.* undernourished
malsano, *adj.* unhealthful
maltratar, *va.* to mistreat
mamá, *f.* mamma
mamar, *va., vn.* to suck
manada, *f.* flock, drove
manantial, *m.* source, spring
manar, *vn.* to spring from

manco, *adj.* one-handed
mandamiento, *m.* commandment
mandar, *va.* to command; to send; *va., vn.* to govern
mandíbula, *f.* jawbone
mando, *m.* authority, power
mandolina, *f.* mandolin
manecilla, *f.* hand of a clock
manejar, *va.* to manage, handle; to drive (a car, etc.); manejarse, to behave
manera, *f.* manner, mode
manga, *f.* sleeve
mango, *m.* handle, heft; mango (a fruit)
manguera, *f.* hose, hose pipe
maní, *m.* (Sp. Am.) peanut
manía, *f.* frenzy, madness
manicero, *m.* peanut vendor
manicomio, *m.* insane asylum
manifestar, *va.* to manifest, show
maniobra, *f.* maneuver
maniquí, *m.* mannikin
manjar, *m.* food; choic morsel
mano, *f.* hand; coat, layer
manómetro, *m.* pressure guage
manosear, *va.* to handle; to muss
mansión, *f.* mansion
manta, *f.* blanket
manteca, *f.* lard
mantel, *m.* tablecloth
mantener, *va., vr.* to maintain, support
mantequilla, *f.* butter
mantilla, *f.* mantilla, headshawl
manual, *adj.* manual, handy; manual
manubrio, *m.* handle bar
manufacturar, *va.* to manufacture
manuscrito, *m.* manuscript; manuscrito, manuscrita, *adj.* written by hand
manutención, *f.* maintenance
manzana, *f.* apple; block of houses
manzano, *m.* apple tree
maña, *f.* dexterity; skill, trick; evil habit
mañana, *f.* morning, pasado

mañana, day after tomorrow
maoísmo, *m.* Maoism
mapa, *m.* map
maquillaje, *m.* make-up
máquina, *f.* machine, engine; máquina de escribir, typewriter
maquinalmente, *adv.* mechanically
maquinaria, *f.* machinery
maquinista, *m.* machinist
mar, *m.* or *f.* sea
maravilla, wonder; a las mil maravillas, uncommonly well; exquisitely
maravillarse, *vr.* to wonder, be astonished
maravilloso, *adj.* marvelous
marcar, *va.* to mark
marco, *m.* frame
marcha, *f.* march; ponerse en marcha, to proceed, to start off
marchar, *vn.* to march; marcharse, to go away, leave
marchitar, *va., vn.* to wither
marchito, *adj.* faded, withered
marea, *f.* tide
marear, *va.* to molest, annoy. marearse, to become seasick
mareo, *m.* seasickness
marfil, *m.* ivory
margarita, *f.* daisy
margen, *m.* or *f.* margin; border
mariano, mariana, *adj.* marian, pertaining to the Virgin Mary
marido, *m.* husband
marimba, *f.* marimba
marina, *f.* navy; shipping
marinero, *m.* sailor
marino, *adj.* marine; *m.* seaman, sailor
mariposa, *f.* butterfly; braza mariposa, butterfly stroke
mariscal, *m.* marshal
marisco, *m.* shellfish
mármol, *m.* marble
marqués, *m.* marquis
marquesa, *f.* marchioness
marrano, *m.* pig, hog
marta, *f.* marten, marten fur
martes, *m.* Tuesday
martillo. *m.* hammer

marzo, *m.* March
mas, *conj.* but, yet
más, *adv.* more
masa, *f.* dough, paste; mass:
masaje, *m.* massage
mitscara, *m.* or *f.* masquer-
ader; *f.* mask
mascota, *f.* mascot
masculino, *adj.* masculine,
male
masonería, *f.* freemasonry
masticar, *va.* to chew
mata, *f.* plant, shrub
matadero, *m.* slaughterhouse
matanza, *f.* slaughtering; cattle to be slaughtered; massacre
matar, *va., vr.* to kill
matemática, or **matemáticas,**
f. mathematics
matemático, *adj.* mathematical; *m.* mathematician
materia, matter, material; subject; matter (pus)
material, *adj.* material; *m.* ingredient; cloth; material
maternal, *adj.* maternal
maternidad, *f.* motherhood
materno, *adj.* maternal, moth-
erly
matinié, *f.* matinée
matiz, *m.* shade of color;
shading
matorral, *m.* shrub, thicket
matrícula, *f.* register; license
number; roster; entrance fee
in a school
matricular, *va., vr.* to
matriculate, register
matrimonio, *m.* marriage,
matrimony
matriz, *f.* uterus, womb; mold,
die; *adj.* main, parent; **casa
matriz,** head or main office
matrona, *f.* matron
máxima, *f.* maxim, rule
máxime, *adv.* principally
máximo, *adj.* maximum
mayo, *m.* May
mayonesa, *f., adj.* mayonnaise
mayor, *adj.* greater, larger;
elder; **estado mayor,** military
staff; *m.* superior; major; **al
por mayor,** wholesale
mayordomo, *m.* steward, ma-

jordomo
mayoría, *f.* majority
mayúscula, *f.* capital letter
m/cta., mi cuenta, (com.) my
account
**m/cte., m/co., moneda co-
rriente,** cur., currency
me, *pron.* me (dative case)
mear, *vn.* to urinate
mecánicamente, *adv.* mechanically; automatically
mecánica, *f.* mechanics
mecánico, *adj.* mechanical; *m.*
mechanic
mecanismo, *m.* mechanism
mecanografía, *f.* typewriting
mecanógrafo, mecanógrafa,
n. typist
mecedora, *f.* rocking chair
mecer, *va.* to rock
medalla, *f.* medal
mediados, a mediados de,
adv. about the middle of
mediano, *adj.* moderate; medium
medianoche, *f.* midnight
mediante, *adv.* by means of,
through; **Dios mediante,**
God willing
mediar, *vn.* to mediate
medicina, *f.* medicine
médico, *m.* physician; **médica,** *adj.* medical
medida, *f.* measure
medidor, *m.* meter; gauge
medio, *adj.* half, halfway;
medium, average; **a medias,**
by halves; *m.* way, method;
medium; middle; **medios,** *m.*
pl. means
mediodía, *m.* noon, midday
medir, *va.* to measure; **medir-
se,** to be moderate
meditación, *f.* meditation
meditar, *va., vn.* to meditate
Mediterráneo, *m.* Mediterra-
nean
megatón, *m.* megaton
mejicano, mejicana, or **mexicano, mexicana,** *n., adj.*
Mexican
mejilla, *f.* cheek
mejor, *adj., adv.* better, best;
a lo mejor, when least ex-
pected

mejora, *f.* improvement
mejorar, *va.* to improve; *vn.*, *vr.* to improve (as to health)
mejoría, *f.* improvement
melancólico, *adj.* melancholy, sad
melocotón, *m.* peach
melodía, *f.* melody
melodioso, *adj.* melodious
melodrama, *m.* melodrama
melón, *m.* melon
mella, *f.* gap; **hacer mella**, to affect
mellizo, melliza, *n., adj.* twin
membrete, *m.* letterhead
membrillo, *m.* quince
memorable, *adj.* rnemorable
memorándum, *m.* memorandum
memoria, *f.* memory; memoir; report (of a conference, etc.)
memorial, *m.* memorial, brief
mencionar, *va.* to mention
mendigo, *m.* beggar
menear, *va.* to stir; **menearse**, (coll.) to wriggle, waddle
menester, *m.* necessity; **ser menester**, to be necessary
menor, *m., f.* minor (one under age); *adj.* less, smaller, minor
menos, *adv.* less; with exception of; **a lo menos**, or **por lo menos**, at least, however; **venir a menos-**, to grow poor; **a menos que**, unless; **echar de menos** to miss
mensaje, *m.* message, errand
mensajero, mensajera, *n.* messenger
menstruación, *f.* menstruation
mensual, *adj.* monthly
mensualidad, *f.* month's allowance; monthly installment
menta, *f.* (bot.) mint
mental, *adj.* mental
mentalidad, *f.* mentality
mentar, *va.* to mention
mente, *f.* mind
mentira, *f.* lie, falsehood; **parecer mentira**, to seem impossible
mentiroso, *adj.* lying, deceit-

ful; **mentiroso, mentirosa**, *n.* liar
menú, *m.* bill of fare
menudeo, *m.* retail
menudo, *adj.* small; minute; **a menudo**, repeatedly, often; *m.* small change (money); tripe, entrails
meñique, *m.* little finger
mercado, *m.* market
mercancía, *f.* merchandise
merced, *f.* favor, mercy; will, pleasure
mercenario, *adj.* mercenary
mercurio, *m.* mercury, quicksilver
merendar, *vn.* to lunch
merengue, *m.* meringue
meridiano, *m.* meridian; **pasado meridiano**, afternoon
meridional, *adj.* southern
merienda, *f.* luncheon, light repast
mérito, *m.* merit, desert
merma, *f.* decrease; waste, leakage; shortage
mes, *m.* month
mesa, *f.* table
mesada, *f.* monthly allowance
meseta, *f.* landing (of a staircase); tableland, plateau
Mesías, *m.* Messiah
mestizo, mestiza, *adj., n.* of mixed blood
meta, *f.* goal
metáfora, *f.* metaphor
metal, *m.* metal; voice timbre
metálico, *adj.* metallic, metal
metate, *m.* (Mex.) grinding stone
meter, *va.* to place, put; to introduce, to insert; **meterse**, to meddle, interfere
meticuloso, *adj.* conscientious
metiche, *m., f.* (coll.) prier, meddler
método, *m.* method
métrico, *adj.* metrical
metro, *m.* meter; verse; (Spain, coll.) subway
metrópoli, *f.* metropolis
Mex. or **Mej., Méjico**, Mex., Mexico
m/f., mi favor, my favor

mg., miligramo, mg., milli-gram

m/g, mi giro, (com.) my draft

mi, *pron.* my; *m.* (mus.) mi

mi, *pron.* me (objective case of the pronoun yo)

microbio, *m.* microbe

micrófono, *m.* microphone

microscopio, *m.* microscope; **microscopio electrónico,** electron microscope

miedo, *m.* fear, dread; **tener miedo,** to be afraid

miel, *f.* honey; **luna de miel,** honeymoon

miembro, *m.* member; limb

mientras, *adv.* in the mean-time; while; **mientras tanto,** meanwhile

miércoles, *m.* Wednesday

mierda, *f.* excrement, ordure

miga, *f.* crumb

migaja, *f.* scrap, crumb

mil, *m.* one thousand

milagro, *m.* miracle, wonder

milagroso, *adj.* miraculous

milésimo, *adj.* thousandth

milicia, *f.* militia

miligramo, *m.* milligram

milímetro, *m.* millimeter

militar, *adj.* military

milreis *m.* milreis (Portuguese and Brazilian coin)

milla, *f.* mile

millar, *m.* thousand

millón, *m.* million

millonario, millonaria, *n.* mil-lionaire

mimar, *va.* to flatter, spoil; to fondle, caress

mimbre, *m.* wicker

mimeógrafo, *m.* mimeograph

mina, *f.* mine

mineral, *adj.* mineral

minero, *m.* miner

miniatura, *f.* miniature

mínimo, *adj.* least, smallest

ministerio, *m.* ministry (of-fice), cabinet

ministro, *m.* minister; **Mini-stro de Estado,** Secretary of State

minoría, minoridad, minority

minucioso, *adj.* meticulous

minúscula, *adj.* small (applied to letters)

minutero, *m.* minute hand

minuto, *m.* minute

mío, mía, *pron.* mine

miope, *n., adj.* nearsighted; near-sighted person

miopía, *f.* nearsightedness

mirada, *f.* glance; gaze

mirar, *va.* to behold, look; to observe; **mirarse,** to look at oneself; to look at one an-other

mirlo, *m.* blackbird

misa, *f.* mass

misceláneo, *adj.* miscellane-ous

miserable, *adj.* miserable, wretched; avaricious

miseria, misery; trifle

misericordia, *f.* mercy

misión, *f.* mission

misionero, *m.* missionary

misterio, *m.* mystery

misterioso, *adj.* mysterious

mitad, *f.* half; middle

mitigar, *va.* to mitigate

mitología, *f.* mythology

mixto, *adj.* mixed, mingled

m/l or **m/L, mi letra,** my let-ter, my draft

ml., mililitro, ml., milliliter

mm, milímetro, mm., milli-meter

m/n, moneda nacional, na-tional currency

moco, *m.* mucus

mocoso, *adj.* sniveling, mu-cous; **mocoso, mocosa,** *n.* brat

mochila, *f.* knapsack

moda, *f.* fashion, mode

modales, *m. pl.* manners, breeding

moderación, *f.* moderation

moderado, *adj.* moderate

modernista, *adj.* modernistic

modernizar, *va.* to modernize

moderno, *adj.* modern

modestia, *f.* modesty; humil-ity

modesto, *adj.* modest; unas-suming

módico, *adj.* moderate, rea-sonable (as price)

modo, *m.* mode, manner;

mood; **de ningún modo,** by no means

mofa, *f.* mockery

mohoso, *adj.* musty; rusty

mojado, *adj.* wet

molar, *va., vr.* to wet, moisten

molde, *m.* mold; pattern (for a dress, etc.); matrix, cast

moldura, *f.* molding

mole, *m.* (Mex.) spicy sauce for fowl and meat

moler, *va.* to grind

molestar, *va.* to vex, tease; to trouble

molestia, *f.* trouble; inconvenience

molino, *m.* mill; **molino de viento,** windmill

momento, *m.* moment, while

mona, *f.* female monkey

monada, *f.* (coll.) pretty child or thing

monarca, *m.* monarch

monarquía, *f.* monarchy

mondongo, *m.* tripe

moneda, *f.* money, currency

monja, *f.* nun

monje, *m.* monk

monograma, *m.* monogram

monológo, *m.* monologue

monopolio, *m.* monopoly

monosílabo, *m.* monosyllable

monstruo, *m.* monster

montaña, *f.* mountain

montar, *vn.* to mount (on horseback); to amount to; *va.* to set (as diamonds)

monto, *m.* amount, sum

montón, *m.*heap, pile; **a montones,** abundantly, by heaps

monumento, *m.* monument

mora, *f.* blackberry, mulberry

morada, *f.* abode, residence

morado, *adj.* violet, purple

moral, *f.* morals, ethics; *adj.* moral

moralidad, *f.* morality, morals

moratorio, *f.* moratorium

mórbido, *adj.* morbid

mordaz, *adj.* sarcastic

morder, *va.* to bite

moreno, *adj.* brown, swarthy; brunet

moribundo, *adj.* dying

morir, *vn., vr.* to die, expire

moroso, *adj.* slow, tardy

mortal,*adj.*mortal; deadly

mosaic, *m.* tile

mosca, *f.* fly

mosquitero, *m.* mosquito net

mosquito, *m.* mosquito

mostaza, *f.* mustard

mostrador, *m.* counter

mostrar, *va.* to show, exhibit; **mostrarse,** to appear, show oneself

mota, *f.* powder puff

motín, *m.* mutiny, riot

motocicleta, *f.* motorcycle

motor, *m.* motor, engine

motriz, *adj.* motor, moving

mover, *va.* to move; to stir up

móvil, *m.* motive, incentive

movilizar, *va.* to mobilize

moza, *f.* girl, lass; maidservant

mozo, *m.* youth, lad; waiter

muchacha, *f.* girl, lass

mucliacho, *m.* boy, lad

muchedumbre, *f.* crowd

mucho, *adj., adv.* much, abundant

mudar, *va.* to change; to molt; **mudarse,** to change residence

mudo, *adj.* dumb; silent, mute

mueble, *m.* piece of ftirniture; **muebles,** *pl.* furniture

mueca, grimace

muela, molar tooth

muerte, *f.* death

muerto, *m.* corpse; *adj.* dead

mugre, *f.* dirt

mujer, *f.* woman; wife

mula, *f.* she-mule

mulato, mulata, *n., adj.* mulatto

muleta, *f.* crutch

multa, *f.* fine, penalty

multar, *va.* to fine

multiplicar, *va.* to multiply

mundial, *adj.* world-wide

mundo, *m.* world

municipal, *adj.* municipal

muñeca, *f.* wrist; doll

muralla, *f.* rampart, wall

murciélago, *m.* (zool.) bat

murmullo, *m.* murmur, mutter

murmurar, *vn.* to murmur; to gossip

muro, *m.* wall
muscular, *adj.* muscular
músculo, *m.* muscle
museo, *m.* museum
musgo, *m.* moss:
música, *f.* music
musical, *adj.* musical
músico, *m.* musician
mutación, *f.* mutation
mutuo, *adj.* mutual, reciprocal
muy, *adv.* very; greatly
Mzo. or **mzo., marzo,** Mar., March

N

N., norte, N., No. or no., north
n/, nuestro, our
nabo, *m.* turnip
Nac., nacional, nat., national
nácar, *m.* mother of pearl
nacer, *vn.* to be born
nacido, *adj.* born; *m.* tumor, abscess
nacimiento, *m.* birth; Nativity
nación, *f.* nation
nacional, *adj.* national
nacionalidad, *f.* nationality
nada, *f.* nothing; **de nada,** don't mention it
nadar, *vn.* to swim
nadie, *pron.* nobody, no one
nafta, *f.* naphtha; (Arg. Urug.) gasoline
naipe, *m.* playing card
nalga, *f.* buttock, rump
Nápoles, *m.* Naples
naranja, *f.* orange
naranjada, *f.* orangeade
naranjado, *adj.* orange-colored
naranjo, *m.* orange tree
narciso, *m.* daffodil
narcótico, *adj., m.* narcotic
nariz, *f.* nose
narrar, *va.* to narrate, tell
nasal, *adj.* nasal
nata, *f.* film formed on surface of milk when boiled; **la tor y nata,** the cream, the elite
natal, *adj.* natal, native
natalidad, *f.* birth rate
natalicio, *m.* birthday
natilla, *f. pl.* custard

natividad, *f.* nativity
nativo, *adj.* native
natural, *adj.* natural, native; unaffected
naturaleza, *f.* nature
naturalmente, *adv.* naturally
náusea, *f.* nausea
navaja, *f.* razor
naval, *adj.* naval
navegable, *adj.* navjgable
navegación, *f.* navigation, shipping
navegar, *vn.* to navigate
navidad, *f.* nativity; **Navidad,** Christmas
N.B., Nota Bene, (Latin) N.B., take notice
n/c., or **n/cta. nuestra cuenta,** (com.) our account
NE, nordeste, NE or N.E., northeast
neblina, *f.* fog; drizzle
nebuloso, *adj.* foggy, hazy
necedad, *f.* nonsense
necesario, *adj.* necessary
necesitar, *va., vn.* to need
necio, *adj.* ignorant, silly
néctar, *m.* nectar
negar, *va., vr.* to deny, refuse
negativo, *adj.* negative
negligencia, *f.* negligence
negociante, *m., f.* dealer, merchant
negocio, *m.* business; affair; negotiation; **hombre de negocios,** businessman
negro, *adj.* black; *n.* Negro
nene, nena, *n.* baby
neoyorquino, neoyorquina, *n., adj.* New Yorker
nervio, *m.* nerve
neto, *adj.* net
neumático, *m.* tire
neumonía, *f.* pneumonia
neutral, *adj.* neutral
neutralidad, *f.* neutrality
neutrino, *m.* neutrino
neutro, *adj.* neutral, neuter
nevada, *f.* snowfall
nevar, *vn. imp.* to snow
nevera, *f.* icebox
n/f., nuestro favor, our favor
n/g., nuestro giro, (com.) our draft
niacina, *f.* niacin

nido, m. nest
niebla, f. fog, mist
nieta, f. granddaughter
nieto, m. grandson
nieve, f. snow
ninfa, f. nymph
ningún, adj. (contraction of **ninguno**), no, not any (used only before masculine nouns); **de ningún modo**, in no way, by no means
ninguno, adj. none, neither; **en ninguna parte**, no place, nowhere
niña, f. little girl; **niña del ojo**, pupil of the eye; **niña de los ojos**, (coll.) apple of one's eye
niñez, f. childbood
niño, adj. childish; m. child, infant
niquel, m. nickel
nitido, adj. neat; clear
nitrato, m. (chem.) nitrate
nitrógeno, m. nitrogen
nivel, m. level, plane
nivelar, va. to level
n/l. or **n/L., nuestra letra**, (com.) our letter, our draft
NNE, nornordeste, NNE or N.N.E., north-northeast
NNO, nornoroeste, NNW or N.N.W., north-north-west
NO, noroeste, NW or N.W., northwest
No. or **N.º, número**, no., number
n/o., nuestra orden, (com.) our order
no, adv. no; not
noble, adj. noble; illustrious
nobleza, f. nobleness, nobility
noción, f. notion, idea
nocivo, adj. injurious
nocturno, adj. nightly; m. (mus.) nocturne
noche, f. night; **esta noche**, tonight; this evening; **Noche Buena**, Christmas Eve
nombramiento, m. nomination; appointment
nombrar, va. to name; to nominate; to appoint
nombre, m. name; reputation
nominativo, m. (gram.) nominative

non, adj. odd, uneven
nono, adj. ninth
non plus ultra, unexcelled, unsurpassed
nordeste, m. northeast
norma, f. standard, model, rule
nornoroeste, m. northnorthwest
noroeste, m. northwest
norte, m. north; guide
Norteamérica, f. North America
norteamericano, norteamericana, n., adj. North America, a native of U. S. A
Noruega, f. Norway
noruego, noruega, n., adj. Norwegian
nos, pron. dative of we
nosotros, nosotras, pron. we, ourselves
nostalgia, f. homesickess, nostalgia
nota, f. note, notice, remark; bill; **nota bene**, N. B. take notice
notable, adj. remarkable
notar, va. to note, observe, mark
notario, m. notary
noticia, f. notice; knowledge, information, news; **en espera de sus noticias**, (com.) awaiting your reply
noticiario, m. latest news, news report
notificar, va. to notify
notorio, adj. notorious:
Novbre., nov.ᶜ, noviembre, Nov., November
novecientos, novecientas, adj., m. nine hundred
novela, f. novel
novelista, m., f. novelist
novena, f. Novena
noveno, adj. ninth
noventa, m., adj. ninety
novia, f. bride; fiancée
noviembre, m. November
novillo, m. young bull
novio, m. bridegroom; fiancé, sweetheart (male); **viaje de novios**, honeymoon trip
n/r, nuestra remesa, (com.)

our remittance or our shipment

N.S., **Nuestro Señor**, Our
Lord

N.S.J.C., **Nuestro Señor Jesucristo**, Our Lord Jesus
Christ

nuclear, *adj.* nuclear

núcleo, *m.* nucleus, core

nudo, *m.* knot, gnarl

nuera, *f.* daughter-in-law

nuestro, nuestra, *adj., pron.*
our, ours

nueva, *f.* news

nueve, *m., adj.* nine

nuez, *f.* walnut; **nuez moscada**, nutmeg

nulidad, *f.* nonentity

nulo, *adj.* null, void

núm., número, no., number

numerar, *va.* to number, nu-
merate

número, *m.* number; cipher

numeroso, *adj.* numerous

nunca, *adv.* never

nupcial, *adj.* nuptial

nupcias, *f., pl.* nuptials, wedding

nutrición, *f.* nutrition, feeding

nutrir, *va.* to nourish

nutritivo, *adj.* nourishing

nylon, *m.* nylon

Ñ

ñame, *m.* (bot.) yam

ñato, ñata, (Sp. Am.) *n., adj.*
pug-nosed

O

o, (**ó** when between numbers)
conj. or

O., oeste, W., West

obedecer, *va.* to obey

obediencia, *f.* obedience

obediente, *adj.* obedient

obertura, *f.* (mus.) overture

obispo, *m.* bishop

objeción, *f.* objection

objetar, *va.* to object, oppose

objetivo, *adj.* objective; *m.*
objective, purpose

objeto, *m.* object, thing; purpose

oblicuo, *adj.* oblique

obligación, *f.* obligation

obligado, *adj.* obliged to; obli-
gated

oblongo, *adj.* oblong

obra, *f.* work, deed

obrar, *va.* to work; to operate,
act; *vn.* to act; to ease nature

obrero obrera, *n.* day laborer

obsceno, *adj.* obscene

obsequiar, *va.* to regale; to
fete; to make a present of

obsequio, *m.* gift

observación, *f.* observation;
remark

observador, observadora, *n.*
observer; *adj.* observing

observar, *va.* to observe,
watch

obstáculo, *m.* obstacle; **obstáculo sónico**, sonic barrier

obstante, participle of **obstar;
no obstante**, notwitbstand-
ing, nevertheless

obstar, *va.* to hinder

obstetricia, *f.* obstetrics

obstruir, *va., vr.* to obstruct

ocasión, *f.* occasion, chance;
de ocasión, used, secondhand

ocasionar, *va.* to cause, occasion

occidental, *adj.* western

occidente, *m.* occident, west

océano, *m.* ocean

ocio, *m.* leisure; idleness

ocioso, *adj.* idle

octava, *f.* octave

octavo, *adj.* eighth

Octbre, oct.ᵉ, octubre, Oct.,
October

octubre, *m.* October

oculto, *adj.* hidden, concealed

ocupación, *f.* occupation

ocupado, *adj.* busy; occupied

ocupar, *va., vr.* to occupy, be
occupied

ocurrencia, *f.* occurrence,
event, incident; witty remark

ochenta, *adj., m.* eighty

ocho, *m., adj.* eight

odiar, *va.* to hate; **odiarse**, to
hate one another

oeste, *m.* west; west wind

ofender, *va.* to offend; **ofen-**

derse, to take offense

ofensa, *f.* offensive, injury

oferta, *f.* offer; offering; **oferta y demanda,** supply and demand

oficial, *adj.* official; *m.* officer; official

oficiar, *va.* to officiate

oficina, *f.* office, bureau

oficio, *m.* employ, occupation; business; **oficios,** *pl.* divine service

ofrecer, *va.* to offer; **ofrecerse,** to offer one's services; to present itself

ofrecimiento, *m.* offering, promise

oído, *m.* hearing; ear

oir, *va.* to hear; to listen

ojal, *m.* buttonhole

¡ojalá! *interj.* God grant!

ojeada, *f.* glance, look

ojear, *va.* to eye, view; to glance

ojera, *f.* dark circle under the eye

ojo, *m.* eye; sight; eye of a needle

ola, *f.* wave, billow

oler, *va.* to smell, to scent; *vn.* to smell, to smack of

olivo, *m.* olive tree

olor, *m.* odor, scent

oloroso, *adj.* fragrant, odorous

olvidadizo, *adj.* forgetful

olvidar, *va., vr.* to forget

olla, *f.* kettle

ombligo, *m.* navel

omisión, *f.* omission

omitir, *va.* to omit

ómnibus, *m.* omnibus, bus

omnipotente, *adj.* omnipotent

once, *m., adj.* eleven

onceno, *adj.* eleventh

onda, *f.* wave

ondear, *va., vn.* to undu.late, wave

ondulado, *adj.* wavy

O.N.U., Organización de las Naciones Unidas, U.N., United Nations

onz., onza, oz., ounce

onza, *f.* ounce (weight)

opaco, *adj.* opaque, dark

ópalo, *m.* opal

opción, *f.* option, choice

ópera, *f.* opera

operación, *f.* operation; **operación cesarea,** Caesarean operation

operar, *va., vn.* to operate; **operarse,** (med.) to have an operation

opereta, *f.* operetta

opinar, *va., vn.* to give an opinion

opinión, *f.* opinion

opio, *m.* opium

oporto, *m.* port wine

oportunidad, *f.* opportunity

oportuno, *adj.* opportune

oposición, *f.* opposition

optar, *va.* to choose, elect

óptico, *adj.* optic, optical

optimismo, *m.* optimism

optimista, *m., f.* optimist; *adj.* optimistic

opuesto, *adj.* opposite, contrary

opulencia, *f.* wealth, riches

ora, *conj.* whether, either

oración, *f.* oration, speech; prayer; (gram.) sentence

orador, oradora, *n.* orator, speaker

oral, *adj.* oral

orar, *vn.* to pray

oratoria, *f.* oratory

orbe, *m.* earth, globe

orden, *m.* order, arrangement; *f.* order, command; **a sus órdenes,** at your service

ordenar, *va.* to arrange; to order, command

ordeñar, *va.* to milk

ordinario, *adj.* ordinary, usual, common; coarse

oreja, *f.* ear

orejón, *m.* preserved peach

organdí, *m.* organdy

orgánico, *adj.* organic

organismo, *m.* organism

organización, *f.* organization

organizar, *va.* to organize

órgano, *m.* organ

orgullo, *m.* pride, haughtiness

orgulloso, *adj.* proud, haughty

orientación, *f.* orientation; position

oriental, *adj.* oriental, eastern

orientar, *va.* to orient; **orientarse,** to find one's bearings
oriente, *m.* orient, east
original, *adj.* original, primitive; novel, new; *m.* original, first copy
originalidad, *f.* originality
orina, *f.* urine
orines, *m.*, *pl.* urine
orinar, *vn.* to urinate
ornamento, *m.* ornament
ornar, *va.* to trim, adorn
oro, *m.* gold; money
orquesta, *f.* orchestra
orquídea, *f.* orchid
ortografía, *f.* orthography, spelling
ortopédico, *adj.* orthopedic
oruga, *f.* (bot.) rocket; caterpillar
os, *pron.* dative of you, to you
osa, *f.* she-bear; **Osa Mayor,** (ast.) Great Bear, the Dipper
oscurecer, *va.*, *vn.*, *vr.* to darken; to become dark
oscurecimiento, *m.* blackout; darkening
oscuridad, *f.* darkness; obscurity
oscuro, *adj.* obscure, dark; **a oscuras,** in the dark
oso, *m.* bear
ostentar, *va.* to show, display; *vn.* to boast
ostra, *f.* oyster
otoño, *m.* autumn, fall
otro, otra, adj. another, other; **otra vez,** another time, once again
ovación, *f.* ovation
ovalado, *adj.* oval-shaped
ovario, *m.* ovary
oveja, *f.* sheep
oxidar, *va.*, *vr.* to rust
óxido, *m.* (chem.) oxide
oxígeno, *m.* oxygen; **oxígeno líquido,** liquid oxygen
oyente, *m.*, *f.* listener; **oyentes,** audience

P

pabellón, *m.* pavilion; flag
paciencia, *f.* patience
paciente, *adj.*, *m.*, *f.* patient

pacífico, *adj.* pacific, peaceful
pacto, *m.* contract, pact
padecer, *va.* to suffer
padrastro, *m.* stepfather; hangnail
padre, *m.* father; **padres,** *pl.* parents; ancestors
padrenuestro, *m.* the Our Father, the Lord's Prayer
padrino, *m.* godfather; sponsor, protector
paella, *f.* rice, seafood and chicken dish
pagadero, *adj.* payable
pagano, *m.* heathen, pagan
pagaré, *m.* promissory note; I. O. U
página, *f.* page of a book
pago, *m.* pay, payment; (Arg., Urug.) rural home place
paila, *f.* kettle
país, *m.* country, region
paisaje, *m.* landscape
paisano, paisana, *n.* countryman (or woman)
pájaro, *m.* bird
paje, *m.* page
palabra, *f.* word; **de palabra,** by word of mouth; **tener la palabra,** to have the floor
palacio, *m.* palace
paladar, *m.* palate; taste
palco, *m.* box in a theater
pálido, *adj.* pallid, pale
palillo, *m.* toothpick
paliza, *f.* whipping
palma, *f.* palm of the hand
palmera, *f.* palm tree
palmotear, *vn.* to clap hands, applaud
palo, *m.* stick; cudgel; post; blow with a stick
paloma, *f.* dove, pigeon
palomilla, *f.* (Mex.) boys' gang; one's social crowd
palomita, *f.* squab; **palomitas de maíz,** popcorn
palomo, *m.* cock pigeon
palpar, *va.* to feel, touch; to grope
palpitante, *adj.* palpitating; **cuestión palpitante,** important, live issue
palpitar, *vn.* to palpitate, beat, throb

paludismo, *m.* malaria

pampa, *f.* great plain, prairie

pámpano, *m.* pompano (a fish)

pan, *m.* bread

panadería, *f.* bakery

panadero, panadera, *n.* baker

páncreas, *m.* pancreas

pandereta, *f.* tambourine

pandilla, *f.* gang

pando, *adj.* bulging, conyex

pánico, *m.* panic, fright

panorama, *m.* panorama

pantalones, *m. pl.* trousers

pantalla, *f.* screen, fire screen; lamp shade

panteón, *m.* cemetery

pantera, *f.* panther

pantorrilla, *f.* calf (of the leg)

pantufla, *f.* slipper, shoe

panza, *f.* belly, paunch

pañal, *m.* diaper

paño, *m.* cloth

pañoleta, *f.* bandanna

pañuelo, *m.* handkerchief

papa, *m.* Pope; *f.* potato; soft food for babies; (coll.) fib, exaggeration

papá, *m.* papa, father

papada, *f.* double chin

papagayo, *m.* parrot

papaya, *f.* papaya

papel, *m.* paper; role, part

papelería, *f.* stationery; stationery store

papeleta, *f.* ballot

paquete, *m.* package, bundle

par, *adj.* par, equal; sin par, matchless; *m.* pair; par

para, *prep.* for, to, in order to

parabién, *m.* congratulation, felicitation

parabrisa, *m.* windshield

paracaídas, *m.* parachute

parada, *f.* halt; stop, pause; (mil.) parade

paradero, *m.* whereabouts

parado, *adj.* stopped (as a clock); (Sp. Am.) standing up

paradoja, *f.* paradox

paraguas, *m.* umbrella

paraíso, *m.* paradise

paralelo, *adj.*, *m.* parallel

parálisis, *f.* paralysis

paralizar, *va.* to paralyze; stop, impede; paralizarse, to become paralyzed

pararrayo, *m.* lightning rod

parásito, *m.* parasite

parasol, *m.* parasol

parche, *m.* patch; plaster

pardo, *adj.* brown

parecer, *m.* opinion, advice; al parecer, apparently; *vn.* to appear, seem; parecerse, to resemble

parecido, *m.* resemblance

pared, *f.* wall

pareja, *f.* pair; couple

parentela, *f.* relatives

parentesco, *m.* kingship

pares o nones, *m. pl.* even or odd

pariente, parienta, *n.* kinsman, kinswoman

parir, *va.*, *vn.* to give birth

parisiense, *m.*, *f.*, *adj.* Parisian

parodia, *f.* parody

parpadear, *vn.* to blink

párpado, *m.* eyelid

parque, *m.* park

parra, *f.* grapevine

párrafo, *m.* paragraph

parranda, *f.* spree, revel

parrandear, *vn.* to go on a spree

parrilla, *f.* gridiron, broiler

párroco, *m.* parson

parroquia, *f.* parish

parte, *f.* part; side

partera, *f.* midwife

partición, *f.* partition, division

participación, *f.* participation, share

participar, *va.*, *vn.* to participate, partake; to communicate

participio, *m.* participle

particular, *adj.* particular, special; *m.* civilian; topic

partida, *f.* departure; item, entry; game

partidario, partidaria, *n.* advocate

partido, *m.* party; match; sacarle partido a, to take advantage of

partir, *va.* to part, divide; *vn.* to depart; a partir de, beginning with

parto, *m.* childbirth

párvulo, m. child; **escuela de párvulos,** kindergarten

pasa, f. raisin; **ciruela pasa,** prune

pasadero, adj. supportable, passable

pasaje, m. passage; fare

pasajero, adj. transient, transitory; m. traveler, passenger

pasaporte, m. passport

pasar, va. to pass; to suffer; vn. to spend (time); v. imp. to happen; **pasar por alto,** to overlook; **¿qué pasa?** what is the matter?

pasatiempo, m. pastime

Pascua, f. Christmas; Easter

pase, m. permit

pasear, va., vn. to stroll; to ride; **pasearse,** to go out for amusement

paseo, m. walk, stroll, ride

pasión, f. passion

pasivo, adj. passive, inactive; m. liabilities of a business house

pasmar, va. to benumb; to chill; **pasmarse,** to be astonished

paso, m. pace, step; passage

pasta, f. paste; dough; binding for books

pastar, vn. to pasture

pastel, m. pie, cake; cray

pastelero, pastelera, n. pastry cook

pasterizar, va. to pasteurize

pastilla, f. tablet, lozenge

pasto, m. pasture

pastor, m. shepherd; pastor, minister

pata, f. foot and leg of an animal; female duck; **patas arriba,** topsy-turvy

patada, f. kick

patán, m. yokel, churl

patata, f. potato

patear, va., vn. to kick, stamp the feet

patente, adj. patent, manifest, evident; f. patent

paternal, adj. paternal

paterno, adj. paternal

patético, adj. pathetic

patín, m. ice skate; **patín de ruedas,** roller skate

patinar, vn. to skate; to skid; to spin

patineta, f. scooter

patio, m. yard, courtyard

pato, pata, n. duck

patria, f. native country

patriarca, m. patriarch

patriota, m., f. patriot

patriotismo, m. patriotism

patrocinar, va. to favor, sponsor

patrón, m. patron; employer; pattern

patrulla, f. patrol, squad

pausa, f. pause

pausar, vn. to pause

pauta, f. ruler; standard, model; (mus.) ruled staff

pavimentar, va. to pave

pavo, m. turkey; **pavo real,** peacock

pavor, m. fear, terror

payaso, m. clown

paz, f. peace

p/cta., por cuenta, (com.) on account, for account

P.D., posdata, P. S., postscript

pdo. or **p.do, pasado,** pt., past

peatón, m. pedestrian

peca, f. freckle, spot

pecado, m. sin

pecador, pecadora, n. sinner

pecar, vn. to sin

peculiar, adj. peculiar

pecuniario, adj. financial

pecho, m. breast; chest; teat; bosom

pechuga, f. breast of a fowl

pedagogía, f. pedagogy

pedal, m. pedal

pedante, adj. pedantic

pedazo, m. piece, bit

pedestal, m. pedestal

pedido, m. request, order

pedigüeño, adj. beggary

pedir, va. to ask, to beg; to demand;

pedir prestado, to borrow

pedrada, f. throw of a stone, blow

pegajoso, adj. sticky; contagious

pegar, va. to cement, stick, paste; to join, unite; to

spank; *vn.* to take root; **pegarse,** to adhere

peinado, *m.* hairdressing, coiffure

peinadora, *f.* hairdresser

peinar, *va., vr.* to comb (the hair)

peine, *m.* comb

pelado, pelada, *n.* (Mex.) person of the lower classes; ignorant peasant; *adj.* coarse, vulgar

pelea, *f.* fight, quarrel

pelear, *vn., vr.* to fight

película, *f.* film

peligro, *m.* danger, peril

peligroso, *adj.* dangerous

pelo, *m.* hair; pile; **tomar el pelo,** to tease

pelota, *f.* pelota, ball; **en pelota,** entirely naked

pelotera, *f.* quarrel, brawl, free-for-all

pelotón, *m.* large ball; crowd; (mil.) platoon

peluquería, *f.* barbershop

peluquero, *m.* barber, hairdresser

pellejo, *m.* skin, hide; pelt

pellizcar, *va.* to pinch

pena, *f.* embarrassment; trouble, affliction; **a duras penas,** with difficulty

penal, *adj.* penal

penalidad, *f.* suffering, trouble; penalty

pendiente, *adj.* pending; **pendiente de pago,** unpaid; *m.* pendant; earring, eardrop; *f.* slope, incline

péndulo, *m.* pendulum

pene, *m.* (anat.) penis

península, *f.* peninsula

penitencia, *f.* penitence, penance

penoso, *adj.* distressing, embarrassing

pensar, *vn.* to think; to intend

pensión, *f.* pension; annuity; price of board and tuition; boarding house

pentagrama, *m.* musical staff

peña, *f.* rock, large stone

peón, *m.* laborer; pawn (in chess)

peor, *adj., adv.* worse

pepino, *m.* cucumber

pepita, *f.* kernel; seed of some fruits; distemper in fowl

pequeño, *adj.* little, small; young

percal, *m.* percale

percance, *m.* misfortune

percepción, *f.* perception

percibir, *va.* to perceive, comprehend

percha, *f.* perch; clothes hanger

perder, *va.* to lose; **echar a perder,** to ruin; to spoil; **perderse,** to go astray

pérdida, *f.* loss, damage

perdiz, *f.* partridge

perdón, *m.* pardon, forgiveness

perdonar, *va.* to pardon, forgive

perecer, *vn.* to perish, die

pereza, *f.* laziness

perezoso, *adj.* lazy, idle

perfección, *f.* perfection

perfecto, *adj.* perfect

perfil, *m.* profile

perforadora, *f.* air drill

perforar, *va.* to perforate

perfumar, *va.* to perfume

perfume, *m.* perfume

pericia, *f.* skill, ability

perifonear, *va.* to broadcast (radio)

perilla, *f.* doorknob; goatee; **de perilla,** to the purpose, in time

periódico, *adj.* periodical; *m.* newspaper

periodismo, *m.* journalism

periodista, *m., f.* journalist

periodo, *m.* period, term

periscopio, *m.* periscope

perito, perita, *n., adj.* expert; skillful, experienced

perjudicar, *va.* to injure, hurt

perjudicial, *adj.* harmful, injurious

perjuicio, *m.* damage

perla, *f.* pearl; **de perlas,** just perfect

permanecer, *vn.* to remain, stay

permanente, *adj.* permanent

permiso, *m.* permission

permitir, *va.* to permit, allow; **permitirse**, to take the liberty; **Dios lo permita**, may God will it

perno, *m.* spike, bolt; (mech.) joint pin

pero, *conj.* but, yet, except; *m.* defect, fault; **poner peros**, to find fault

peróxido, *m.* peroxide

perpendicular, *adj.* perpendicular

perpetuo, *adj.* perpetual

perplejo, *adj.* perplexed

perra, *f.* female dog; bitch

perseguir, *va.* to pursue, persecute

perseverancia, *f.* perseverance, constancy

perseverante, *adj.* persevering

perseverar, *vn.* to persevere

persiana, *f.* venetian blind

persignarse, *vr.* to make the sign of the cross

persistente, *adj.* persistent, tenacious

persistir, *vn.* to persist

persona, *f.* person

personaje, *m.* personage; character (in a play)

personal, *adj.* personal; *m.* personnel, staff

personalidad, *f.* personality

perspectiva, *f.* perspective; prospect; sight, outlook

perspicaz, *adj.* perspicacious, keen

persuadir, *va.* to persuade

pertenecer, *vn.* to belong to

perturbar, *va.* to perturb, disturb

peruano, peruana, *adj., n.* Peruvian

perversidad, *f.* perversity

perverso, *adj.* perverse

pervertir, *va.* to pervert, corrupt

pesadez, *f.* heaviness, fatigue

pesadilla, *f.* nightmare

pesado, *adj.* heavy, weighty

pésame, *m.* message of condolence

pesar, *m.* sorrow, grief; regret, repentance; **a pesar de**, in spite of; *vn.* to weigh; to be heavy; *va.* to weigh

pesca, *f.* fishing, fishery

pescado, *m.* fish (when caught; in the water it is **pez**)

pescador, pescadora, *n.* fisher, fisherman (or woman)

pescar, *va.* to fish

pescuezo, *m.* neck

pesebre, *m.* manger

peseta, *f.* monetary unit of Spain

pesimista, *m., f.* pessimist; *adj.* pessimistic

pésimo, *adj.* very bad

peso, *m.* monetary unit of Sp. Am. countries with sign same as the U. S. dollar; weight, heaviness; balance; load

pestaña, *f.* eyelash

pestañear, *vn.* to wink, move the eyelids

peste, *f.* plague; stench

petaca, *f.* (Sp. Am.) suitcase

petate, *m.* straw sleeping mat

petición, *f.* petition, request, plea

petróleo, *m.* petroleum, oil, mineral oil

petunia, *f.* (bot.) petunia

pez, *m.* fish (in the water); *f.* pitch, tar

piadoso, *adj.* pious, merciful

pianista, *m., f.* pianist

piano, *m.* piano; **piano de cola**, grand piano

picadillo, *m.* mincemeat, hash

picadura, *f.* prick; puncture; bite (of an insect or snake)

picaflor, *m.* hummingbird; fickle person

picante, *adj.* sharp, pricking; hot, highly seasoned; piquant

picaporte, *m.* picklock; catch, bolt; doorlatch

picar, *va.* to prick; to sting; to mince; to itcb; **picarse**, to be piqued; to be motheaten; to begin to rot (as fruit)

picardía, *f.* roguery; mischievousness

pícaro, *adj.* roguish; mischievous, malicious; *m.* rogue

picazón, *f.* itching

pico, *m.* beak, bill; peak; pickax; point; odd; a bit over; **cien dólares y pico**, one hundred and odd dollars; **la una y pico**, few minutes past one (o'clock)

picoso, *adj.* (Mex. coll.) hot, highly seasoned:

pichón, *m.* young pigeon; young bird

pie, *m.* foot; base, foundation; **al pie de la letra**, literally; **ponerse de pie**, to stand up

piedad, *f.* mercy, pity

piedra, *f.* stone; gem

pierna, *f.* leg

pieza, *f.* piece; piece of furniture; room

pijamas, *m. pl.* pajamas

pila, *f.* font; pile, battery; heap; holy water basin; **nombre de pila**, Christian name

pilar, *m.* pillar

piloto, *m.* pilot; first mate

pillo, *adj.* roguish; *m.* rogue

pimienta, *f.* pepper

pimpollo, *m.* sprout, bud

pincel, *m.* artist's brush

pinchazo, *m.* puncture; prick

pinta, *f.* spot, blemish; pint

pintar, *va.* to paint, picture; to describe; **pintarse**, to paint one's face

pintor, **pintora**, *n.* painter, artist

pintoresco, *adj.* picturesque

pintura, *f.* painting; picture

pinzas, *f. pl.* forceps, tweezers

piña, *f.* pineapple; fir cone

piñata, *f.* potful of goodies broken by blindfolded children at games

piojo, *m.* louse

pipa, *f.* wine cask; tobacco pipe

pirámide, *f.* pyramid

pirata, *m.* pirate

piropo, *m.* compliment, flattery

pisada, *f.* footstep; footprint; footfall

pisapapeles, *m.* paperweight

pisar, *va.* to step, tread, trample

piscina, *f.* swimming pool

piso, *m.* floor, story

pisotear, *va.* to trample

pista, *f.* trace, footprint; racetrack

pito, *m.* whistle; **no me importa un pito**, I don't care a straw

pizarrón, *m.* blackboard

pl., **plural**, *pl.* plural

placa, *f.* plaque; sheet of metal

placer, *m.* pleasure, delight

plan, *m.* plan; design, plot

plancha, *f.* plate; flatiron; slab

planchar, *va.* to iron

planeador, *m.* (avi.) glider

planear, *vn.* to glide

planeta, *m.* planet

piano, *adj.* plane, level; *m.* plane; floorplan; **de piano**, frankly, plainly

planta, *f.* sole of the foot; plant

plantar, *va.* to plant; (coll.) to jilt; **plantarse**, to stand firm

plasma, *m.* plasma

plástico, *adj.* plastic

plata, *f.* silver; money

plataforma, *f.* platform

plátano, *m.* banana; plantain; plane tree

plateado, *adj.* silvery; silver-plated

platero: *m.* silversmith

plática *f.* chat, conversation

platicar, *vn.* to converse, chat

platillo, *m.* saucer; side dish; cymbal

Platino, *m.* platinum

plato, *m.* dish; plate; **lista de platos**, menu; **plato toca discos**, turntable,

playa, *f.* shore, beach

plaza, *f.* square, place; fortified place

plazo, *m.* term, date of payment; **a plazos**, on credit, on time

plegar, *va.* to fold; to pleat

plegaria, *f.* prayer

pleito, *m.* dispute; lawsuit

plenamente, *adv.* fully, completely

pliego, *m.* sheet of paper

plomero, *m.* plumber

plomo, *m.* lead (metal)

pluma, *f.* feather, plume; pen

plumaje, *m.* plumage

P.M. or **p.m., pasado meridiano,** P.M., afternoon

p/o or **P.O., por orden,** (com.) by order

población, *f.* population; town

poblado, *m.* town, village

poblar, *va.* to populate, people

pobre, *adj.* poor, indigent; deficient

pobreza, *f.* poverty

poco, *adj.* little, scanty; *m.* a small part; **pocos,** *pl.* few; **poco,** *adv.* little; **hace poco,** a short time ago

podar, *va.* to prune

poder, *m.* power, authority; command; **en poder de,** in the hands of; **por poder,** by proxy; *vn.* to be able; *v. imp.* to be possible

poderoso, *adj.* powerful

podrir, *vn.* **pudrir**

poema, *m.* poem

poesía, *f.* poetry

poeta, *m.* poet

poético, *adj.* poetic

poetisa, *f.* poetess

polaco, polaca, *n.* Pole; *adj.* Polish; *m.* Polish language

polar, *adj.* polar

Polea, *f.* pulley

policía, *f.* police; *m.* policeman

polígamo, polígama, *n., adj.* polygamist

política, *f.* politics; policy

político, *adj.* political; polite; *m.* politician

póliza, *f.* insurance policy

polo, *m.* pole; polo; **polo acuático,** water polo

Polonia, *f.* Poland

polonio, *m.* polonium

polvera, *f.* compact; vanity case

polvo, *m.* powder; dust

pólvora, *f.* gunpowder

polla, *f.* pullet; pool; (coll.) young girl

pollera, *f.* hen-coop; (Sp. Am.) wide skirt; national costume of Panama

pollo, *m.* young chicken; (coll.) young man

pomo, *m.* small bottle

pompón, *m.* pompon

pómulo, *m.* cheekbone

ponche, *m.* punch (drink)

ponchera, *f.* punchbowl

ponderar, *va.* to ponder, consider, weigh; to exaggerate

poner, *va.* to put, to place; to lay eggs; **poner al corriente,** to acquaint (with), to inform; **ponerse,** to become: to set (as the sun, etc.)

poniente, *m.* west; west wind; *adj.* setting (as sun, etc.)

popa, *f.* (naut.) poop, stern

popular, *adj.* popular

popularidad, *f.* popularity

populoso, *adj.* populous

poquito, *adj.* very little; *m.* a little; **poquito a poquito,** little by little

por, *prep.* for, by, about; through; on account of

porcelana, *f.* porcelain, china

porcentaje, *m.* percentage

porción, *f.* part, portion

pordiosero, pordiosera, *n.* beggar

porfiado, *adj.* obstinate

porfiar, *vn.* to dispute obstinately

pormenor, *m.* detail

poro, *m.* pore

porqué, *m.* cause, reason

¿por qué? *interr.* why?

portada, *f.* title page, frontispiece

portador, portadora, *n.* carrier, bearer

portal, *m.* porch; portico, piazza

portamonedas, *m.* purse, pocketbook

portar, *va.* to carry; to bear (arms, etc.); **portarse,** to behave, comport oneself

portátil, *adj.* portable

porte, *m.* portage, freight, postage; bearing, carriage

portero, portera, *n.* porter, janitor or janitress, concierge

portuario, portuaria, *adj.* relating to a seaport

porvenir, *m.* future

posada, *f.* boardinghouse; inn,

hotel; (Mex.) pre-Christmas party

posar, *vn.* to lodge; to sit down, repose

posdata, *f.* postscript

poseer, *va.* to possess, own

posesión, *f.* possession

posesivo, *adj.* possessive

posibilidad, *f.* possibility

posible, *adj.* possible

posición, *f.* position, place; posture; situation

positivo, *adj.* positive

posponer, *va.* to postpone

postal, *adj.* postal; **paquete postal,** parcel post

poste, *m.* post, pillar

postema, *f.* abscess, tumor

postergar, *va.* to defer, delay

posteridad, *f.* posterity

posterior, *adj.* back, rear

posteriormente, *adv.* later, subsequently

postizo, *adj.* artificial, false

postrarse, *vr.* to prostrate oneself; to kneel down

postre, *adj.* last in order; **a la postre,** at last; *m.* dessert

potasa, *f.* potash

pote, *m.* pot, jar; flowerpot

potencia, power; strength

potente, *adj.* potent, powerful, mighty

pozo, *m.* well; (min.) shaft, pit

P.P., porte pagado, p.p. postpaid

p. p., por poder, (law) by power of attorney or by proxy

ppdo., p.pdo or **p.ºp.ᵈᵒ, próximo pasado,** in the past month

practicante, *m., f.* (med.) intern

practicar, *va.* to practice; to exercise

práctico, *adj.* practical; skillful

precaución, *f.* precaution

precaver, *va.* to prevent, guard against

precedente, *adj.* precedent, foregoing

preceder, *va.* to precede

preciar, *va.* to value, appraise; **preciarse de,** to take pride

in, boast

precio, *m.* price, value

precioso, *adj.* precious; beautiful

precipitación, *f.* inconsiderate haste

precipitar, *va.* to precipitate; **precipitarse,** to run headlong to one's destruction

precisar, *va.* to compel, oblige; to necessitate; to state

precisión, *f.* preciseness; **con toda precisión,** on time, very promptly

preciso, *adj.* necessary, requisite; precise

precoz, *adj.* precocious

precursor, precursora, *n.* forerunner; *adj.* preceding

predicado, *m.* predicate

predicador, *m.* preacher

predicción, *f.* prediction

predilecto, *adj.* favorite

predispuesto, *adj.* biased, predisposed

predominar, *va., vn.* to predominate, prevail

prefacio, *m.* preface

preferencia, *f.* preference; **de preferencia,** preferably

preferente, *adj.* preferred, preferable

preferible, *adj.* preferable

preferir, *va.* to prefer

pregunta, *f.* question, inquiry

preguntar, *va.* to question, inquire

preguntón, preguntona, *n.* inquisitive person; *adj.* inquisitive

prehistórico, *adj.* prehistoric

prejuicio, *m.* prejudice

preliminar, *adj., m.* preliminary

preludio, *m.* prelude

prematuro, *adj.* premature

premeditar, *va.* to premeditate

premiar, *va.* to reward, remunerate

premio, *m.* reward, prize, recompense; (com.) premium; interest

prenda, *f.* pledge, forfeit; pawn; piece of jewelry

prender, *va.* to seize, catch; to imprison; *vn.* to catch or take fire; to take root

prensa, *f.* press, newspapers

preocupar, *va.* to preoccupy; **preocuparse,** to care about, worry

prep., preposición, *prep.,* preposition

preparación, *f.* preparation

preparar, *va., vr.* to prepare

preparativo, *m.* preparation

preposición, *f.* (gram.) preposition

prerrogativa, *f.* prerogative, privilege

presa, *f.* capture, seizure; prey; dike, dam

prescribir, *va.* to prescribe

presencia, *f.* presence

presenciar, *va.* to witness, see

presentación, *f.* presentation, introduction

presentar, *va.* to present, introduce; **presentarse,** to appear; to introduce oneself

presente, *adj.* present; *m.* present, gift; instant; **el 20 del presente,** the 20th instant; **hacer presente,** to call attention; **la presente,** the present writing; **tener presente,** to bear in mind

presentimiento, *m.* presentiment, misgiving

presentir, *va.* to have a presentiment

preservación, *f.* preservation

preservar, *va.* to preserve

presidencia, *f.* presidency; chairmanship

presidente, *m.* president; chairman

presidiario, *m.* convict

presidio, *m.* prison

presidir, *va.* to preside

presión, *f.* pressure, pressing; **presión arterial,** blood pressure

préstamo, *m.* loan

presto, *adj.* quick, prompt, ready; *adv.* soon, quickly

presumido, *adj.* presumptuous, arrogant

presupuesto, *m.* estimate; budget

pretender, *va.* to pretend, claim; to try, attempt

pretendiente, *m.* pretender; suitor; candidate, office seeker

pretérito, *adj.* preterit, past

pretexto, *m.* pretext, pretense

prevención, *f.* prevention

prevenir, *va.* to prepare; to foresee; to prevent; to warn; **prevenirse,** to be prepared

preventivo, *adj.* preventive

prever, *va.* to foresee

previo, *adj.* previous

provisión, *f.* foresight

previsor, *adj.* foreseeing, farseeing

prieto, *adj.* brackish, very dark; **prieta,** *n.* very dark person

prima, *f.* (mus.) treble; (com.) premium; female cousin

primario, *adj.* first; **escuela primaria,** elementary school

primavera, *f.* spring (the season)

primeramente, *adv.* in the first place, mainly

primero, *adj.* first, prior, former; **primeros auxilios,** first aid

primitivo, *adj.* primitive, original

primo, prima, *n.* cousin

primogénito, primogénita, *adj., n.* first-born

primoroso, *adj.* exquisite

princesa, *f.* princess

principal, *adj.* principal, main

príncipe, *m.* prince

principiar, *va.* to begin

principio, *m.* beginning; principle

prioridad, *f.* priority

prisa, *f.* hurry; haste; **a toda prisa,** at full speed; **darse prisa,** to hurry; **tener prisa,** to be in a hurry

prisión, *f.* prison; duress

prisionero, prisionera, *n.* prisoner

privado, *adj.* private

privar, *va., vr.* to deprive; to prohibit

privilegiado, *adj.* privileged

pro, *m.* or *f.* profit, benefit, advantage; **en pro de**, in behalf of; **el pro y el contra**, the pro and con

proa, *f.* (naut.) prow, bow

probabilidad, *f.* probability

probable, *adj.* probable, likely

probar, *va.* to try; to prove; to taste; *vn.* to suit, agree; **probarse**, to try on (clothes)

problema, *m.* problem

problemático, *adj.* problematical

procedencia, *f.* origin, source

procedente, *adj.* coming from, proceeding from

proceder, *m.* procedure; *vn.* to proceed, go on; to issue

procesar, *va.* to prosecute; to indict

procesión, *f.* procession

proceso, *m.* process, lawsuit

proclamar, *va.* to proclaim

procurador, *m.* procurer; solicitor; attorney; **procurador público**, attorney at law; **Procurador General**, Attorney General

prodigar, *va.* to waste, lavish

pródigo *adj.* prodigal

producción, *f.* production

producir, *va.* to produce, yield

productiveo, *adj.* productive, fertile; profitable

producto, *m.* product; amount

prof., profesor, prof., professor; **profeta**, prophet

profecía, *f.* prophecy

profesión, *f.* profession

profesor, profesora, *n.* professor, teacher

profesorado, *m.* body of teachers, faculty

profeta, *m.* prophet

profundidad, *f.* profoundness; depth; **carga de profundidad**, (mil.) ash can (depth charge)

progenitor, *m.* ancestor, forefather

programa, *m.* program

progresar, *vn.* to progress, to improve

progreso, *m.* progress, advancement

prohibición, *f.* prohibition

prohibir, *va.* to prohibit, forbid

prójimo, *m.* fellow creature; neighbor

prole, *f.* issue, offspring

prólogo, *m.* prologue

promedio, *m.* average

promesa, *f.* promise; pious offering

prometer, *va.* to promise, assure; *vn.* to be promising

prometido, prometida, *n., adj.* betrothed

prominente, *adj.* prominent

promoción, *f.* promotion

premover, *va.* to promote, further

pronombre, *m.* pronoun,

pronosticar, *va.* to predict, foretell

prontitud, *f.* promptness

pronto, *adj.* prompt, ready; soon; *adv.* promptly; quickly

pronunciar, *va.* to pronounce; **pronunciarse**, to rebel

propaganda, *f.* propaganda; advertising

propagandista, *m., f., adj.* propagandist

propagar, *va., vn.* to propagate, spread, disseminate

propicio, *adj.* propitious favorable

propiedad, *f.* property; propriety

propietario, *adj.* proprietary; *m.* proprietor; **propietaria**, *f.* proprietress

propina, *f.* tip, gratuity

propio, *adj.* proper; own; characteristic

proponer, *va.* to propose, suggest; **proponerse**, to intend, plan, be determined

proporción, *f.* proportion

proporcionar, *va.* to proportion; to adjust, adapt; to provide, supply

proposición, *f.* proposition

propósito, *m.* purpose; **a propósito**, adequate, fitting; **de propósito**, on purpose; **a propósito de**, apropos of

propuesta, *f.* proposal, offer, proposition; nomination

prorrata, *f.* quota; a prorrata, in proportion

prórroga, *f.* extension, renewal

prosa, *f.* prose

prosaico, *adj.* prosaic

proseguir, *va.* to pursue, prosecute; to continue

prosperar, *vn.* to prosper, thrive

prosperidad, *f.* prosperity

próspero, *adj.* prosperous

prostituta, *f.* prostitute

protección, *f.* protection

protector, protectora, *n.* protector

proteger, *va.* to protect

protegido, protegida, *n.* protegé

proteina, *f.* protein

protesta, *f.* protest

protestante, *n., adj.* Protestant

protestar, *va.* to protest

protocolo, *m.* protocol

prototipo, *m.* prototype

protuberancia, *f.* bulge

provecho, *m.* profit, benefit

provechoso, *adj.* beneficial

proveer, *va.* to provide; to provision

proverbio, *m.* proverb

providencia, *f.* providence

provincia, *f.* province

provocar, *va.* to provoke

prox., próximo, next, nearest

próximamente, *adv.* very soon; shortly

próximo, *adj.* next, nearest, following

proyectar, *va.* to project, plan

proyectil, *m.* projectile

proyecto, *m.* project, plan

proyector, *m.* projector; spotlight

prudente, *adj.* prudent, cautious

P. S., posdata, P.S., postscript

psiquiatría, *f.* psychiatry

pte., presente, pres. present

pto., puerto, pt., port; punto, pt., point

publicación, *f.* publication

publicar, *va.* to publish, reveal

publicidad, *f.* publicity

público, *adj.* public; *m.* attendance, audience

pudiente, *adj.* rich, opulent

pudín, *m.* pudding

pudor, *m.* modesty, decorum

pudrir, *vn.* to rot

pueblo, *m.* town, village; populace

puente, *m.* bridge; puente aéreo, airlift

puerca, *f.* sow

pueril, *adj.* childish

puerta, *f.* door, gateway

pues, *conj.* as, since, because, for; *adv.* then, therefore

puesta, *f.* (ast.) set, setting; puesta del sol, sunset

puesto, *m.* place; post; employment; booth; puesto, puesta, *adj.* put, set, placed; puesto que, since

pujar, *va.* to outbid; to push ahead, push through

pulcro, *adj.* neat, tidy

pulga, *f.* flea

pulgada, *f.* inch

pulmón, *m.* lung; pulmón de acero, iron lung

pulmonía, *f.* pneumonia

púlpito, *m.* pulpit

pulsera, *f.* bracelet

pulverizador, *m.* atomizer

pulverizar, *va.* to pulverize, to spray

punta, *f.* point, tip; punta de combate, warhead

puntada, *f.* stitch

puntapié, *m.* kick

puntería, *f.* aiming (of firearms); marksmanship

puntiagudo, *adj.* sharp-pointed

puntilla, *f.* small point; de puntillas, on tiptoe

punto, *m.* period; point, end; dot; estar a punto de, to be about to; son las dos en punto, it is exactly two o'clock

puntual, *adj.* punctual

punzada, *f.* prick, sting; sharp pain

puñado, *m.* handful

puñal, *m.* poniard, dagger

puño, *m.* fist; cuff
pupila, *f.* eyeball, pupil
pupilo, *m.* pupil; scholar; boarder; orphan ward (boy)
pupitre, *m.* writing desk
purga, *f.* physic; purge
purgar, *va.* to purge, purify; to administer a physic; to atone
purgatorio, *m.* purgatory
pus, *m.* pus, matter
puta, *f.* whore
pza.: pieza, pc. piece

g

q.e.p.d., que en paz descanse, may (he, she) rest in peace
ql. or q.¹, quintal, cwt., hundred-weight
qq., quintales, cwts., hundred-weights
que, *relative pron.* that, which, who, whom; qué, *interrogative and exclamatory pron.*, what; how; no hay de que, don't mention it; *conj.* that; than; whether; because
quebrada, *f.* brook
quebrado, *m.* (math.) fraction; *adj.* broken; bankrupt
quebrar, *va., vr.* to break; *vn.* to fail
quedar, *vn.* to stay, remain; to be left
quedo, *adj.* quiet, still; *adv.* softly, gently
quehacer, *m.* occupation, work; task, chore
queja, *f.* complaint
quejarse, *vr.* to complain of; to moan
quejido, *m.* groan, moan
quemar, *va., vr.* to burn; to kindle; *vn.* to be too hot
querella, *f.* complaint; quarrel
querer, *va.* to wish, desire; to like, love; querer decir, to mean, signify; sin querer, unwillingly; Dios quiera, God grant
querido, *adj.* dear, beloved; *n.* darling, lover
quetzal, *m.* (orn.) quetzal; monetary unit of Guatemala

quiebra, *f.* bankruptcy
quien, *pron.* who, which; ¿quién? who?
quienquiera, *pron.* whoever
quieto, *adj.* quiet, still
quietud, *f.* quietness, peace
quím., química, chem., chemistry
química, *f.* chemistry
químico, *m.* chemist; *adj.* chemical
quince, *adj., m.* fifteen
quincena, *f.* fortnight; semimonthly pay
quincenal, *adi.* semimonthly
quinientos, quinientas, *adj., m.* five hundred
quinina, quinine
quinta, country house; (mus.) fifth
quintal, *m.* hundredweight
quinto, *m., adj.* fifth
quintuplo, *adj.* quintuple, fivefold
quirófano, *m.* operating room
quirúrgico, *adj.* surgical
quitar, *va.* to remove, take away
quizá, *adv.* perhaps

R

R., Reverendo, Rev., Reverend; Respuesta, reply; Reprobado, not passing (in an examination)
rabia, *f.* rage, fury
rabioso, *adj.* rabid; furious
rabo, *m.* tail
racimo, *m.* bunch, cluster (of grapes, etc.)
raciocinio, *m.* reasoning
racional, *adj.* rational; reasonable
radar, *m.* radar
radiación, *f.* radiation
radiador, *m.* radiator
radical, *adj.* radical; *m.* (math.) radical; extremist
radicar, *vn.* to take root; radicarse, to take root; to settle, establish oneself
radio, *m.* or *f.* radio, receiver; radio broadcasting station; (math., anat.) radius; (chem.)

radium

radiodifusión, *f.* radio broadcasting

radiodifusora, *f.* broadcasting station

radioescucha, *m., f.* radio listener

radiorreceptor, *m.* radio receiving set

radiotelescopio, *m.* radio telescope

radioyente, *m., f.* radio listener

raja, *f.* splinter, chip of wood; slice (of fruit); fissure, crack

rajar, *va.* to split, chop

ralo, *adj.* thin, sparse

rama, *f.* branch (of a tree, of a family)

ramal, *m.* ramification

ramillete, *m.* bouquet

ramo, *m.* branch (of a tree); branch (of trade, art, etc.); bouquet

rampa, *f.* slope, ramp

rana, *f.* frog

rancio, *adj.* rank, rancid

ranchero, *m.* small farmer

rango, *m.* rank

ranura, *f.* groove

rapidez, *f.* rapidity, speed

rapiña, *f.* rapine, robbery; **ave de rapiña,** bird of prey

rapsodia, *f.* rhapsody

raqueta, *f.* racket; **de raqueta nieve.** snowshoe

raquítico, *adj.* rickety

rascacielos, *m.* skyscraper

rascar, *va.* to scratch, scrape

rasgado, *adj.* torn, open; **boca rasgada,** wide mouth; **ojos rasgados,** large eyes

rasgar, *va.* to tear, rend

rasgo, *m.* dash, stroke; kind gesture; feature, trait

rasguño, *m.* scratch

raso, *m.* satin, sateen; **raso, rasa,** *adj.* plain; flat

raspar, *va.* to scrape, rasp

rastrillo, *m.* hammer of a gun; rake

rastro, *m.* track; sledge; slaughterhouse; sign, token; trail

rata, *f.* (zool.) rat

ratero, *adj.* mean, vile; *m.* pickpocket

ratificar, *va.* to ratify

rato, *m.* while; moment

ratón, *m.* mouse

raya, *f.* stroke; stripe; streak; line; dash (in punctuation)

rayado, *adj.* striped

rayar, *va.* to draw lines, rule; to stripe; **rayar en,** to border on

rayo, *m.* ray, beam of light; flash of lightning; radius; **rayo equis,** X ray

rayón, *m.* rayon

raza, *f.* race, lineage

razón, *f.* reason; cause, motive; ratio, rate; **razón social,** firm name; **dar razón,** to inform, give account; **tener razón,** to be right

rezonable, *adj.* reasonable

razonamiento, *m.* reasoning

reacción, *f.* reaction; **propulsión por reacción,** jet propulsion

reaccionar, *vn.* to react

real, *adj.* real, actual; royal; **pavo real,** peacock

realce, *m.* luster, enhancement; **dar realce,** to highlight, give importance to

realidad, *f.* reality, fact

realismo, *m.* realism

realización, *f.* realization, fulfillment; bargain sale

realizar, *va.* to realize, fulfill

realmente, *adv.* really

realzar, *va.* to raise, elevate; to emboss; to heighten

reanudar, *va.* to renew, resume

rebaja, *f.* deduction; reduction, rebate

rebajar, *va.* to lessen, curtail; to lower (as price); **rebajarse,** to humble oneself

rebanada, *f.* slice

rebaño, *m.* flock of sheep, herd of cattle, drove

rebelarse, *vr.* to rebel

rebelde, *m.* rebel; *adj.* rebellious

rebotar, *va.* to repel; *vn.* to rebound

rebozo, *m.* woman's shawl

rebuznar, *vn.* to bray

recado, *m.* message

recaída, *f.* relapse

recalcar, *va.* to emphasize

recámara, *f.* boudoir, bedroom; chamber of a gun

recapacitar, *va.* to think over, meditate

recatado, *adj.* prudent, modest

recelo, *m.* suspicion, mistrust

recepción, *f.* reception

receptor, *m.* radio receiver

receso, *m.* withdrawal, retirement; recess

receta, *f.* recipe; prescription

recetar, *va.* to prescribe

recibir, *va.* to receive; to let in; to go to meet; **recibirse,** to graduate in a profession

recibo, *m.* receipt, voucher

recién, *adv.* recently, lately; **recién casado, recién casada,** newlywed

recio, *adj.* stout, strong; *adv.* loudly

recipiente, *m.* recipient, container

reciprocidad, *f.* reciprocity

recíproco, *adj.* reciprocal

recitar, *va.* to recite

reclamar, *va.* to claim, demand

recluir, *va., vr.* to seclude

reclutar, *va.* to recruit

recobrar, *va.* to recover

recoger, *va.* to take back; to gather, pick up; to shelter; **recogerse,** to take shelter or refuge; to retire, to rest

recomendación, *f.* recommendation

recomendar, *va.* to recommend

recompensa, *f.* recompense

reconciliación, *f.* reconciliation

reconciliar, *va., vr.* to reconcile

reconocer, *va.* to examine closely; to acknowledge favors received; to admit; to recognize; (mil.) to reconnoiter

reconocimiento, *m.* recogni-

tion; gratitude; reconnaissance; **reconocimiento médico,** medical examination

reconstituyente, *m.* (med.) tonic

reconstruir, *va.* to reconstruct

recopilar, *va.* to compile; to abridge

recordar, *va., vr.* to remind; to remember; *vn.* to call to mind

recorrer, *va.* to run over, peruse; to travel over

recorrido, *m.* run, line; expedition

recortar, *va.* to cut away, trim

recorte, *m.* cutting; **recorte de periódico,** newspaper clipping

recostar, *va.* to lean against; **recostarse,** to recline, rest

recrear, *va., vr.* to amuse, delight, recreate

recreo, *m.* recreation, pleasure; recess

rectamente, *adv.* justly, rightly

rectángulo, *m.* rectangle

rectificar, *va.* to rectify

recto, *adj.* straight, direct, right; just

recuerdo, *m.* remembrance, memory; souvenir; **recuerdos,** *pl.* regards

recuperar, *va.* to recover; **recuperarse,** to recover from sickness

recurso, *m.* recourse; resource; **recursos,** *pl.* means

rechazar, *va.* to repel, reject

red, *f.* net; web; network

redacción, *f.* editing; editor's office; editorial staff

redactar, *va.* to edit (a publication); to draw up, draft

redactor, *m.* editor

redimir, *va.* to redeem

redondo, *adj.* around; **a la redonda,** all around

reducción, *f.* reduction

reducir, *va.* to reduce

redundante, *adj.* redundant

reelección, *f.* re-election

reelegir, *va.* to re-elect

ref., referencia, ref., reference

refacción, *f.* repair; **piezas de**

refacción, spare parts
referencia, *f.* reference
referer, *va.* to refer, relate; **re-fererse,** to refer to, relate to
refinamiento, *m.* refinement
refinar, *va.* to refine
reflector, *m.* reflector, search light
reflejar, *va., vr.* to reflect
reflejo, *m.* reflex; reflection, light, glare
reflexionar, *vn.* to reflect, meditate
reforma, *f.* reform
reformar, *va., vr.* to reform, correct
reforzar, *va., vr.* to strengthen, fortify
refrán, *m.* proverb, saying
refrenar, *va.* to refrain, restrain
refrescante, *adj.* refreshing
refrescar, *va.* to refresh; *vn.* to cool; to take the air
refresco, *m.* refreshment; cold drink
refrigerador, *m.* refrigerator
refrigerar, *va.* to refrigerate
refuerzo, *m.* reinforcement
refugiado, refugiada, *n.* refugee
refugiar, *va.* to shelter; **refugiarse,** to take refuge
refuñfuñar, *vn.* to grumble
regadera, *f.* watering pot, sprinkler; (Sp. Am.) **baño de regadera,** shower bath
regalar, *va.* to make a present of
regalo, *m.* present, gift
regañar, *va.* to scold
regar, *va.* to water, irrigate; to spread
regateo, *m.* bargaining, act of haggling
regenerar, *va., vr.* to regenerate
regidor, *m.* governor, prefect
régimen, *m.* regime
regimiento, *m.* regiment
regio, *adj.* royal, kindly
región, *f.* region
regir, *va.* to rule, govern, direct; *vn.* to be in force
registrar, *va.* to register; in-

spect; to search; to record
registro, *m.* register, registration; record; inspection
regla, *f.* rule, statute, ruler
reglamento, *m.* by-law; regulations
regresar, *vn.* to return, go back
regreso, *m.* return, regression
regular, *va.* to regulate, adjust; *adj.* regular; ordinary
regularidad, *f.* regularity
rehabilitar, *va., vr.* to rehabilitate
rehusar, *va.* to refuse, decline
reina, *f.* queen
reinado, *m.* reign
reinar, *va.* to reign
reino, *m.* kingdom, reign
reintegrar, *va., vr.* to reintegrate, to restore
reir, *vn.* to laugh; **reirse de,** to laugh at
reiterar, *va.* to reiterate, repeat
reja, *f.* lattice; grating; railing
rejuvenecer, *vn.* to be rejuvenated
relación, *f.* relation; report; account; **relaciones,** connections
relacionar, *va.* to relate; to connect; to make acquainted
relámpago, *m.* flash of lightning
relatar, *va.* to relate
relatividad, *f.* relativity
relativo, *adj.* relative, pertaining
relato, *m.* account, narrative
relegar, *va.* to relegate, banish
relevar, *va.* to relieve, substitute
relevo, *m.* (mil.) relief
relieve, *m.* relief (sculpture); **bajo relieve,** bas-relief; **dar relieve,** to emphasize, highlight
religión, *f.* religion
religioso, *adj.* religious
reloj, *m.* clock, watch; **de reloj pulsera,** wrist watch
relojero, *m.* watchmaker
relucir, *vn.* to shine, glitter
rellenar, *va.* to refill; to stuff

remachar, va. to rivet

remangar, va. to tuck up (sleeves, dress, etc.)

remar, vn. to row

remetado, adj. utterly ruined; **loco remetado,** stark mad

rematar, va. to sell at auction; to finish

remate, m. end, conclusion; auction sale; **de remate,** absolutely, hopelessly

remediar, va. to remedy; to prevent

remedio, m. remedy, reparation; sin **remedio,** inevitable

remendar, va. to patch, mend

remesa, f. sending of goods; remittance of money

remiendo, m. patch, repair

reminiscencia, f. reminiscence

remitente, m., f. remitter, shipper, sender

remitir, va. to send, transmit

remojar, va. to soak

remolacha, f. beet

remolino, m. whirlwind; whirlpool

rémora, f. hindrance, cause of delay

remordimiento, m. remorse

remoto, adj. remote, distant

remunerar, va. to remunerate

Renacimiento, m. Renaissance

rencor, m. rancor, grudge

rendija, f. crevice, crack

rendir, va. to produce, yield; **rendirse,** to be fatigued; to surrender

renegar, va. to deny, disown; vn. to curse

renglón, m. written or printed line; (com.) part of one's income; items

reno, m. reindeer

renombre, m. renown

renovar, va. to renew, renovate, reform

renta, f. rent, income

renuncia, f. resignation

reñir, va., vn. to wrangle; to quarrel

reo, m. offender, criminal

Rep., República, Rep. Republic

reparar, va. to repair; to consider, serve

repartir, va. to distribute

reparto, m. distribution; (theat.) cast of characters

repasar, va., vn. to revise, review

repaso, m. revision, review

repente, de repente, adv. suddenly

repentino, adj. sudden

repercusión, f. reverberation, repercussion

repetictón, f. repetition

repetir, va. to repeat

repicar, va. to chime

repleto, adj. replete

réplica, f. reply, answer

replicar, vn. to reply, answer; to argue

repollo, m. cabbage head

reponer, va. to replace; to restore; **reponerse,** to recover lost health

reposo, m. rest, repose

representación, f. representation; performance

representante, m., f. representative

representar, va. to represent; to play on the stage

represión, f. repression

reprimir, va. to repress

reprochar, va. to reproach

reproducir, va. to reproduce

reptil, m. reptile

república, f. republic

repuesto, m. replacement; **piezas de repuesto,** spare parts

repugnante, adj. repugnant

reputación, f. reputation

requerir, va. to request, demand; to summon; to require

requisito m. requisite, requirement

res, f. head of cattle; beast; **carne de res,** beef

resaca, f. undertow

resaltar, vn. to rebound; to stand out; to be evident

resbalar, vn., vr. to slip, slide

rescate, m. ransom

resentimiento, m. resentment

resentirse, vr. to resent

reseña, *f.* brief description
reserva, *f.* reserve; reservation; **con** or **bajo la mayor reserva,** in strictest confidence
reservado, *adj.* reserved, cautious
reserver, *va.* to reserve
resfriado, *m.* cold (disease)
resfriarse, *vr.* to catch cold
resideneia, *f.* residence
residente, *m., f.* resident
residuo, *m.* residue
resignarse, *vr.* to be resigned
resistencia, *f.* resistance
resistir, *vn., va.* to resist, bear; to oppose
resolución, *f.* resolution
resolver, *va., vr.* to resolve, decide
resollar, *vn.* to breathe
resorte, *m.* spring (elastic body)
respaldar, *va.* to indorse; *m.* back (of seats)
respaldo, *m.* indorsement; back of a seat
respecto, *m.* relation, respect; **a** or **con respecto a,** in regard to
respetable, *adj.* respect
respetar, *va.* to respect
respetuoso, *adj.* respectful
respirar, *vn.* to breathe
resplandor, *m.* splendor, brilliance; light
responder, *va.* to answer
resbonsabilidad, *f.* responsibility
responsable, *adj.* responsible
respuesta, *f.* answer, reply
restante, *m.* rest, remainder
restar, *va.* to subtract; *vn.* to be left, remain
restaurante, *m.* restaurant
restaurar, *va.* to restore
restregar, *va.* to scrub, rub
restricción, *f.* restriction
restringir, *va.* to restrain
resucitar, *va., vn.* to revive
resuello, *m.* breath, breathing
resultado, *m.* result
resultar, *vn.* to result
resumen, *m.* summary
resumir, *va.* to resume
retar, *va.* to challenge

retardar, *va.* to retard, delay
retazo, *m.* remnant
retener, *va.* to retain
retina, *f.* retina
retirar, *va.* to withdraw, retire; **retirarse,** to retire, reretreat
reto, *m.* challenge
retocar, *va.* to retouch (a painting or a photograph)
retoño, *m.* sprout, shoot
retoque, *m.* finishing stroke; retouching
retórica, *f.* rhetoric
retornar, *va. vn.* to return, give back
retorno, *m.* return
retrasar, *va.* to defer, put off; **retrasarse,** to be late; to be backward
retraso, *m.* lateness; delay
retratar, *va.* to draw a portrait of; to photograph
retrato, *m.* portrait, photograph; effigy
retrete, *m.* water closet
retribución, *f.* retribution
reuma, *f.* rheumatism
reunión, *n. f.* meeting
reunir, *va., vr.* to reunite
reventar, *vn.* to burst
reverencia, *f.* reverence, respect; bow, curtsy
reverendo, *adj.* reverend
reverso, *m.* reverse
revés, *m.* reverse, wrong side; misfortune; **al revés,** backwards; inside out
revisar, *va.* to revise, review
revista, *f.* revision, review; magazine
revivir, *vn.* to revive
revolcarse, *vr.* to wallow
revolución, *f.* revolution
revolucionario, *adj., m.* revolutionary
revolver, *va.* to stir
revólver, *m.* revolver
rey, *m.* king
rezagado, *adj.* left behind; **cartas rezagadas,** unclaimed letters
rezar, *va.* to pray
riboflavina, *f.* riboflavin
rico, *adj.* rich, wealthy; delicious

ridiculizar, *va.* to ridicule
ridículo, *adj.* ridiculous
riego, *m.* irrigation, watering
riel, *m.* rail
rienda, *f.* rein of a bridle; **a rienda suelta,** without restraint
riesgo, *m.* risk, jeopardy
rifa, *f.* raffle, lottery
riguroso, *adj.* strict
rimar, *va., vn.* to rhyme
rinoceronte, *m.* rhinoceros,
riñón, *m.* kidney
río, *m.* river, stream
R. I. P., Requiescat In Pace, may (he, she) rest in peace
riqueza, *f.* riches, wealth
risa, *f.* laugh, laughter
risueño, *adj.* smiling, pleasant
ritmo *m.* rhythm; tempo
rito, *m.* rite, ceremony
rival, *m.*rival, competitor
rizo, *m.* curl, frizzle
róbalo or **robalo,** *m.* (zool.) bass
roble, *m.* oak tree
robo, *m.* robbery, theft
roca, *f.* rock, cliff
rociar, *va.* to sprinkle
rocío, *m.* dew
rodar, *vn.* to roll
rodear, *vn.* to encompass
rodilla, *f.* knee
rodillo, *m.* roller, cylinder
rogar, *va.* to entreat, beg; to pray
rojo, *adj.* red; ruddy; **Rojo,** *m.* Red (communist)
rol, *m.* list; roll; catalogue
rollo, *m.* roll; spiral
Roma, *f.* Rome
romance, *adj.* romance; *m.* Romance language; ballad; novel of chivalry
romano, romana, *adj., n.* Roman
romanticismo, *m.* romanticism
romántico, *adj.* romantic; *m.* romanticist
rompecabezas, *m.* riddle, puzzle
ron, *m.* rum
roncar, *vn.* to snore
ronquera, *f.* hoarseness

ropa, *f.* clothing
ropero, *m.* clothes closet
rosa, *f.* rose
rosado, *adj.* flushed; rosy, pink
rosario, *m.* rosary
rosbif, *m.* roast beef
rosca, *f.* screw and nut; rusk, twisted roll
roto, *adj.* broken; ragged; torn
rótula, *f.* kneecap
rotular, *va.* to self-address
rótulo, *m.* inscription, label; sign
rotura, *f.* fracture; breakage
r.p.m., revoluciones por minuto, r.p.m., revolutions per minute
rubí, *m.* ruby; **rubíes,** *pl.* jewels of a watch
rubia, *f.* blonde girl
rubio, *adj.* blond, fair
ruborizarse, *vr.* to blush, flush
rueda, *f.* wheel, circle
ruego, *m.* prayer; plea
ruido, *m.* noise –
ruina, *f.* ruin,,downfall
ruiseñor, *m.* nightingale
rumba, *f.* rumba
rumbo, *m.* course, direction; pomp, ostentation
rumboso, *adj.* magnificent, pompous; liberal
rumor, *m.* rumor, report
ruptura, *f.* rupture, break
rural, *adj.* rural
Rusia, *f.* Russia
ruso, rusa, *n., adj.* Russian
rustico, *adj.* rustic, rural; unbound or in a paper cover (of books)
ruta, *f.* route, road
rutina, *f.* routine, habit

S

S., San or **Santo,** St. Saint; **segundo,** second; **sur,** So. or so., south
s., sustantivo, *n.* noun
S.ª, Señora, Mrs. Mistress.
S. A., Sociedad Anónima, Inc. Incorporated; **Su Alteza,** His or Her Highness

sábado, *m.* Saturday
sábana, *f.* bed sheet
sábelotodo, *m.* know-it-all
saber, *va.* to know; to be able to; *vn.* to be very sagacious; **saber a,** to taste of; *m.* learning, knowledge; **a saber,** to wit
sabiduría, *f.* knowledge, wisdom
sabiendas, a sabiendas, *adv.* knowingly, with awareness
sabio, *adj.* sage, wise; *m.* sage, scholar
sabor, *m.* taste, flavor
saborear, *va.* to enjoy, relish
sabroso, *adj.* delicious
sacar, *va.* to draw out; to pull out
sacarina, *f.* saccharine
sacerdote, *m.* priest, clergyman
saciar, *va.* to satiate, quench
saco, *m.* sack, bag; man's coat; jacket
sacramento, *m.* sacrament
sacrificar, *va., vr.* to sacrifice
sacrificio, *m.* sacrifice
sacudir, *va.* to shake, jerk
sagrado, *adj.* sacred
sal, *f.* salt; wit, grace
sala, *f.* hall, parlor
salado, *adj.* salted, salty
salar, *va.* to salt
salario, *m.* salary
salchicha, *f.* sausage
saldar, *va.* to settle, pay
saldo, *m.* balance; **saldo acreedor,** credit balance; **saldo deudor,** debit balance
salero, *m.* saltcellar; (coll.) gracefulness
saleroso, *adj.* graceful
salir *vn.* to go out, leave; to appear; to be issued or published
saliva, *f.* saliva
salón, *m.* parlor, hall, salon; **salón de belleza,** beauty parlor
salsa, *f.* sauce, dressing
saltar, *vn.* to leap, jump
salto, *m.* jump; leap, dive; **salto con pértiga,** pole vault; **salto de altura,** high jump;

salto de longitud, broad jump
salud, *f.* health
saludable, *adj.* healthful
saludar, *va.* to greet
saludo, *m.* salute; greeting.
Salvador, *m.* Saviour
salvadoreño, salvadoreña, *n., adj.* Salvadorian
salvar, *va.* to save, rescue
salvavidas, *m.* life preserver
salvo, *adj.* saved, safe; **sano y salvo,** safe and sound; *adv.* excepting
san, *adj.* saint (before masculine proper names)
sanar, *va., vn.* to heal, recover (health)
sanatoria, *m.* sanitarium, sanatorium
sanción, *f.* sanction
sancionar, *va.* to sanction
sandalia, *f.* sandal
sandía, *f.* watermelon
sangrar, *va., vn.* to bleed
sangre, *f.* blood
sangriento, *adj.* bloody
sanitario, *adj.* sanitary
sano, *adj.* sane; healthy.
Santiago, James
santiguar, *va., vr.* to make the sign of the cross
santo, santa, *adj., m.* saint, holy; sacred
sapo, *m.* toad
S. A. R., Su Alteza Real, His or Her Royal Highness
sarampión, *m.* measles
serape, *m.* serape, shawl
sarcasmo, *m.* sarcasm
sarcástico, *adj.* sarcastic
sardina, *f.* sardine
sargento, *m.* sergeant
sartén, *f.* frying pan
sastre, *m.* tailor
Satanás, *m.* Satan
sátira. *f.* satire
satisfacción, *f.* satisfaction; amends, apology
satisfacer, *va.* to atone; **satisfacerse,** to satisfy oneself
satisfactorio, *adj.* satisfactory
satisfecho, *adj.* satisfied
sauce, *m.* (bot.) willow
saxofón, *m.* saxophone

sazonar, *va.* to season; to mature

Sbre., septiembre, Sept., September.

S. C., su casa, your house, (expresssion of kind hospitality)

s. c. or s/c., su cargo or su cuenta, (com.) your account; **su casa,** your house (expression of kind hospitality)

s/cta. or s/c., su cuenta, (com.) your account

SE, sudeste, SE or S.E., southeast

sé, second person imperative singular of **ser,** to be; first person indicative singular of **saber,** to know

se, the reflexive pronoun, possessive to the person or thing that governs the verb. It frequently introduces the passive form of a verb, as **Se dice,** It is said

sebo, *m.* suet; tallow

secante, *m.* blotter

sección, *f.* section

seco, *adj.* dry; arid

secretaria, *f.* secretariat; secretary's office

secretario, secretaria, *n.* occ retary

secreto, *adj.* secret; hidden; *m.* secret

secuestrar, *va.* to abduct

secundario, *adj.* secondary; **escuela secundaria,** high school

sed, *f.* thirst; **tener sed,** to be thirsty

seda, *f.* silk

sede, *f.* see, seat of episcopal power

sediento, *adj.* thirsty

sedimento, *m.* sediment

seducir, *va.* to seduce; to attract, charm

seductor, *adj.* attractive, fascinating; *m.* seducer

segregar, *va.* to segregate

seguida, *f.* following; succession; **en seguida,** immediately

seguir, *va.* to follow, pursue

según, *prep.* according to; **según aviso,** as per advice

segundo, *adj.* second; *m.* second (of time)

seguridad, *f.* security; certainty, safety, assurance

seguro, *adj.* secure, safe, sure; firm, constant; *m.* insurance

seis, *adj.* six, sixth (of the month); *m.* six

seiscientos, *adj.* six hundred

selección, *f.* selection

selecto, *adj.* select, choice

selva, *f.* forest

sellar, *va.* to seal, stamp

sello, *m.* seal; stamp; **sello de correo,** postage stamp

semana, *f.* week

semanal, *adj.* weekly

semanario, *adj.* weekly; *m.* weekly publication

sembrar, *va.* to sow, plant

semejante, *adj.* similar, like; *m.* fellow creature

semejanza, *f.* resemblance

semestral, *adj.* semiyearly

semestre, *m.* semester

semi, prefix denoting half

semianual, *adj.* semiannual

semifinal, *adj.* semifinal

senado, *m.* senate

senador, *m.* senator

sencillez, *f.* simplicity; naturalness, candor

sencillo, *adj.* simple; plain

senda, *f.* path, footpath

sendos, *adj. pl.* having one apiece

seno, *m.* breast, bosom; lap; sinus; asylum, refuge

sensación, *f.* sensation, feeling

sensato, *adj.* sensible, wise

sensible, *adj.* sensitive; regrettable; soft-hearted

sentado, *adj.* seated; **dar por sentado,** to take for granted

sentar, *va.* to sit; to seat; **sentarse,** to sit down

sentencia, *f.* sentence, opinion; verdict

sentenciar, *va.* to sentence, pass judgment

sentido, *m.* sense; reason; meaning

sentimental, *adj.* sentimental
sentimiento, *m.* sentiment; grief; feeling; sensation
sentir, *va.* to feel; to regret; to mourn; to think; to foresee; **sentirse,** to be hurt or offended
seña, *f.* sign, mark; password; **señas,** *pl.* address
señal, *f.* sign, signal
señalar, *va.* to mark; to point out
señor, *m.* lord; sir; master; **muy señor mio** or **nuestro,** dear sir; **el Señor,** the Lord
señora, *f.* lady; mistress\
señoría, *f.* lordship
señorita, *f.* young lady, miss
separación, *f.* separation
separado, *adj.* separate, apart; **por separado,** under separate cover
separar, *va.* to separate; **separarse,** to separate, to withdraw
sepelio, *m.* burial
septentrional, *adj.* northern
septiembre, *m.* September
séptimo, *adj.* seventh
sepulcro, *m.* sepulcher, grave, tomb
sequía, *f.* dryness; drought
ser, *vn.* to be; to exist; *m.* being, life
serenata, *f.* serenade
serenidad, *f.* serenity, quiet
sereno, *m.* night dampness; night watchman; *adj.* serene, calm; quiet
serie, *f.* series
seriedad, *f.* seriousness
serigrafía, *f.* silkscreen
serio, *adj.* serious, grave
serrucho, *m.* handsaw
servicial, *adj.* diligent
servicio, *m.* service
servidor, *m.* servant, waiter; **su servidor,** at your service; yours truly
servidora, *f.* maidservant; **su servidora,** at your service; yours truly
servil, *adj.* servile, cringing
servilleta, *f.* napkin
servir, *va.* to serve

sesenta, *m., adj.* sixty
sesgo, *m.* bias
sesión, *f.* session, meeting
seso, *m.* brain
setenta, *m., adj.* seventy
severo, *adj.* rigorous
sexagésimo, *adj.* sixtieth
sexismo, *m.* sexism
sexo, *m.* sex
sexto, *adj.* sixth
s/f., su favor, your favor
s/g: su giro, (com.) your draft
si, *conj.* if, whether; *m.* (mus.) si, seventh note of the scale
sí, *adv.* yes; indeed; *pron.* himself; herself; itself; themselves; **volver en sí,** to come to, to recover one's senses
sicoanalizar, *va.* to psychoanalyze
sicología, *f.* psychology
sideral, *adj.* sidereal, astral, space; **viajes siderales,** space travel
siderúrgico, siderúrgica, *adj.* pertaining to iron and steel
siempre, *adv.* always, ever
sien, *f.* temple (of the head)
sierra, *f.* saw; range of mountains
siete, *m., adj.* seven
sífilis, *f.* syphilis
siglo, *m.* century
significado, *m.* meaning
signo, *m.* sign, mark
siguiente, *adj.* following, successive
sílaba, *f.* syllable
silbido, *m.* hiss; whistling
sima, *f.* abyss, gulf
símbolo, *m.* symbol; device
símil, *m.* (rhet.) simile
similar, *adj.* similar
simpatía, *f.* sympathy; charm; **tener simpatía por,** to like someone, to find (someone) pleasant and congenial
simpático *adj.* sympathetic; likable, charming
simpatizar, *vn.* to sympathize; to be congenial
simple, *adj.* simple, silly; insipid
simplificar, *va.* to simplify
simultáneo, *adj.* simultaneous

sin, *prep.* without; **sin embargo,** notwithstanding, nevertheless
sinceridad, *f.* sincerity
sincero, *adj.* sincere, honest
sindicato, *m.* syndicate
sinfonía, *f.* symphony
singular, *adj.* singular; unique
siniestro, *adj.* left (side); sinister; unhappy
sinnúmero, *m.* no end; numberless quantity
sino, *conj.* (after a negative), but; except; besides; only; *m.* destiny, fate,
sinónimo, *m.* synonym; *adj.* synonymous
sintético, *adj.* synthetic
síntoma, *m.* symptom
sinvergüenza, *m.* cad, bounder
siquiatra, *m.* psychiatrist
siquiera, *conj.* at least; though, although; **ni siquiera,** not even
sirena, *f.* foghorn, siren; mermaid
sirviente, sirvienta, *n.* servant
sistema, *m.* system, plan
sistemático, *adj.* systematic
situación, *f.* situation, state, condition
ski, *m.* ski
s/l or **s/L, su letra** (com.) your letter or draft
S. M., Su Majestad, His or Her Majesty
smoking, *m.* Tuxedo coat.
SO, sudoeste, SW or S.W. Southwest
s/o, su orden, (com.) your order
so, *prep.* under; below; **so pena de multa** or **muerte,** under penalty of fine or death
sobaco, *m.* armpit
sobar, *va.* to massage
soberanía, *f.* sovereignty
soberano, soberana, *adj., n.* sovereign
soberbio, *adj.* proud, haughty
soborno, *m.* bribe
sobra, *f.* surplus, excess; remainder; **de sobra,** over and above
sobrante, *m.* residue, surplus
sobrar, *vn.* to have more than is necessary; to be more than enough; to remain
sobre, *prep.* above, over; on, about; *m.* envelope
sobrecama, *f.* bedspread
sobrehumano, *adj.* superhuman
sobrellevar, *va.* to suffer, tolerate
sobremanera, *adv.* exceedingly
sobremesa, *f.* table cover; dessert; **de sobremesa,** immediately after dinner
sobrenombre, *m.* nickname
sobreponerse, *vr.* to master; to show oneself superior to
sobresaliente, *adj.* outstanding, excellent
sobretodo, *m.* overcoat
sobreviviente, *m., f.* survivor
sobrevivir, *vn.* to survive
sobrina, *f.* niece
sobrino, *m.* nephew
sobrio, *adj.* sober, frugal.
Soc., Sociedad, Soc., Society; Co., Company
sociable, *adj.* sociable
social, *adj.* social; **razón social,** firm name
socialista, *m., f.* socialist; *adj.* socialistic
sociedad, *f.* society, company, partnership; **sociedad anónima,** corporation
socio, socia, *n.* associate, partner, member
sociológico, *adj.* sociological
socorrer, *va.* to succor, help, rescue
socorro, *m.* help, aid
sofá, *m.* sofa, couch; **sofá cama,** studio couch
sofocar, *va.* to suffocate; to harass
soga, *f.* rope
sol, *m.* sun; a silver coin of Peru; (mus.) sol
solapa, *f.* lapel
solar, *m.* plot of ground; lot; *adj.* solar; **luz solar,** sun-

shine
solaz, *m.* solace, consolation
soldado, *m.* soldier
soleded, *f.* solitude; lonely place; desert
solicitar, *va.* to solicit; to apply for
solícito, *adj.* solicitous
solicitud, *f.* solicitude, application, petition; **a solicitud,** on request
sólido, *adj.* solid
solitario, a *i.* solitary, lonely
solo, *m.* (mus.) solo; **sola,** *adj.* alone, single
sólo, *adv.* only
soltar, *va.* to untie, loosen, to set at liberty; **soltarse,** to get loose
soltero, *adj.* unmarried; *m.* bachelor; **soltera,** bachelor girl
sollozo, *m.* sob
sombra, *f.* shade, shadow
sombrerera, *f.* hatbox
sombrerería, *f.* hat shop
sombrero, *m.* hat
sombrilla, *f.* parasol
someter, *va.* to submit; to subject
son, *m.* sound, report; Cuban musical rhythm
sonar, *vn.* to sound; to ring; **sonarse,** to blow one's nose
soneto, *m.* sonnet
sonido, *m.* sound
sonoro, *adj.* sonorous
sonreir, *vn., vr.* to smile
sonrisa, *f.* smile
sonrojarse, *vr.* to blush
soñar, *va., vn.* to dream
sopa, *f.* soup
soplar, *va.* to blow; to prompt; **soplarse,** to swell up
sopor, *m.* drowsiness
soporte, *m.* support; brassière
soportar, *va.* to suffer, bear
sorber, *va.* to sip
sordera, *f.* deafness
sordo, *adj.* deaf
sordomudo, sordomuda, *n., adj.* deaf and dumb; mute
sorprendente, *adj.* surprising
sorprender, *va.* to surprise
sorpresa, *f.* surprise

sorteo, *m.* raffle
sortija, *f.* ring; hoop
soso, *adj.* insipid, tasteless
sospecha, *f.* suspicion
sospechar, *va., vn.* to suspect
sospechoso, *adj.* suspicious
sostén, *m.* support
sostenido, *m.* (mus.) sharp (#)
sostenimiento, *m.* sustenance; support
sótano, *m.* cellar, basement
soviet, *m.* soviet
soya, *f.* soybean
s/p, su pagaré, (com.) your promissory note
Sr. or S.^{r}, Señor, Mr., Mister
s/r, su remesa, (com.) your remittance or shipment
Sra. or S.^{ra}, Señora, Mrs., Mistress
Sres. or S.^{res}, Señores, Messrs., Messieurs
Sría., Secretaría, secretary's office
srio, or S.^{rio}, secretario, sec., secretary
Srta, or S.^{rta}, Señorita, Miss
S. S or s. s., seguro servidor, devoted servant
S. S., Su Santidad, His Holiness
SS.^{mo} P., Santísimo Padre, Most Holy Father
S.S.S. or s.s.s., su seguro servidor, your devoted servant, yours truly
SS. SS. SS. or ss. ss. ss., sus seguros servidores, your devoted servants, yours truly
Sto., Santo, St., Saint (masculine)
su, *pron.* his, her, its, one's; **sus,** their
suave, *adj.* smooth, soft
suavizar, *va., vr.* to soften
subasta, *f.* auction
subconsciente, *adj.* subconscious
súbdito, súbdita, *n., adj.* subject (of a king, etc.)
subgerente, *m.* assistant manager
subir, *vn.* to mount, climb; to increase
súbitamente, *adv.* suddenly

subjuntivo, *m.* (gram.) subjunctive
sublime, *adj.* sublime, exalted
submarino, *m.* submarine
subnormal, *adj.* subnormal
subordinar, *va.* to subordinate
subrayar, *va.* to underline
subsecuente, *adj.* subsequent
subsidio, *m.* subsidy, aid
subsiguiente, *adj.* subsequent
subsistir, *vn.* to subsist, last
subteniente, *m.* second lieutenant
subterfugio, *m.* subterfuge
subterráneo, *adj.* underground; *m.* subway; cave
suburbano, *adj.* suburban
suburbio, *m.* suburb
subvención, *f.* subsidy
subyugar, *va.* to subdue
suceder, *vn.* to succeed, inherit; to happen
sucesión, *f.* succession; issue,
offspring; hereditary succession
sucesivo, *adj.* successive; **en
lo sucesivo,** from now on
suceso, *m.* outcome, event
sucesor, sucesora, *n.* successor
sucio, *adj.* dirty filthy
sucre, *m.* sucre, monetary
unit of Ecuador
Suc.^res, **Sucesores,** succes-
sors
suculento, *adj.* succulent
sucumbir, *vn.* to succumb,
perish
sucursal, *adj.* subsidiary; *f.*
branch, annex
sud, *m.* south; south wind
(used instead of **sur,** when
joined to another word)
**sudamericano, sudamerica-
na,** *adj., n.* South American
sudar, *va., vn.* to sweat, perspire
sudeste, *m.* southeast
sudoeste, *m.* southwest
sudor, *m.* sweat, perspiration
Suecia, *f.* Sweden
sueco, sueca, *n., adj.* Swedish
suegra, *f.* mother-in-law
suegro, *m.* father-in-law
suela, *f.* sole of the shoe

sueldo, *m.* salary, pay
suelo, *m.* floor; ground
suelto, *adj.* loose; *m.* change
(money); newspaper item
sueño, *m.* sleep; vision,
dream; **tener sueño,** to be
sleepy
suero, *m.* whey; serum (of
blood)
suerte, *f.* chance, lot, fate; **tener suerte,** to be lucky
suficiente, *adj.* sufficient
sufijo, *m.* suffix
sufragio, *m.* vote, suffrage
sufrido, *adj.* long suffering
sufrimiento, *m.* sufferance,
patience
sufrir, *va.* to suffer, bear with
patience; to undergo
suicidarse, *vr.* to commit suicide
suicidio, *m.* suicide
Suiza, *f.* Switzerland
suizo, suiza, *n., adj.* Swiss
sujetar, *va.* to subdue; to subject; to hold; to fasten
sujeto, *adj.* subject, liable, exposed; *m.* subject, topic
sultán, *m.* sultan
suma, *f.* sum; substance
sumar, *va.* to add, sum up
sumario, *m.* summary
suministrar, *va.* to supply,
furnish
suntuoso, *adj.* sumptuous
superar, *va.* to surpass, excel
supercarretera, *f.* superhighway
superhombre, *m.* superman
superintendente, *m.* superintendent
superior, *adj.* superior; upper
(in geography); **parte superior,** topside; *m.* superior
superioridad, *f.* superiority
superlativo, *adj., m.* superlative
supermercado, *m.* supermarket
superstición, *f.* superstition
super.^te, **superintendente,**
supt., superintendent
suplente, *adj.* alternate
súplica, *f.* petition, request
suplicar, *va.* to entreat; to

pray, plead

suplir, *va.* to supply; to supplant

supl.ᵗᵉ, **suplente,** sub., substitute

suponer, *va.* to suppose, surmise

suposición, *f.* supposition, conjecture, basis

supremo, *adj.* supreme:

supresión, *f.* suppression

suprimir, *va.* to suppress; to abolish

supuesto, *m.* supposition; *adj.* supposed, false, assumed; **por supuesto,** of course

sur, *m.* south; south wind

suroeste, *m.* southwest

surtir, *va.* to supply, provide

susceptible, *adj.* susceptible

suscitar, *va.* to excite, stir up

suscribir, *va., vr.* to subscribe; to sign

suscripción, *f.* subscription

suscriptor, suscriptora, *n.* subscriber

susodicho, *adj.* above-mentioned, aforesaid

suspender, *va.* to suspend, stop, cease; to raise up

suspenso, *adj.* suspended, unfinished

suspicaz, *adj.* suspicious, distrustful

suspirar, *vn.* to sigh

suspiro, *m.* sigh

sustancia, *f.* substance

sustancioso, *adj.* substantial, nutritious

sustantivo, *adj., m.* noun

sustento, *m.* sustenance, support

sustitución, *f.* substitution

sustituir, *va.* to substitute

sustituto, sustituta, *adj., n.* substitute

susto, *m.* fright, terror

sustracción, *f.* subtraction

sustraer, *va.* to subtract; **sustraerse,** to retire, withdraw

sutil, *adj.* subtle

sutileza, *f.* subtlety, cunning; finesse; delicacy

suyo, suya, *adj.* his, hers, theirs, one's; his, her, its

own, one's own or their own; **los suyos,** *m. pl.* their own, close friends, relations

T

tabaco, *m.* tobacco

tabla, *f.* board; table; **las tablas,** the stage

tablero, *m.* chessboard; checkerboard; blackboard

tableta, *f.* tablet

tablilla, *f.* tablet, slab; bulletin board

taburete, *m.* stool

tacaño, *adj.* miserly, stingy

taco, *m.* stopper, stopple; wad; billiard cue; (Mex.) sandwich made with a **tortilla**

tacón, *m.* shoe heel

tacto, *m.* touch; tact

tacha, *f.* fault, defect

tachar, *va.* to find fault with; to blot, efface

tafetán, *m.* taffeta

tajada, *f.* slice

tajar, *va.* to cut, chop

tal, *adj.* such; **con tal que,** provided that; **¿qué tal?** how goes it? **tal vez,** perhaps

taladro, *m.* drill

talco, *m.* talc, talcum

talego, *m.* sack

talento, *m.* talent

talón, *m.* heel; (com.) receipt, check; check stub

talonario, *m.* check stubs; **libro talonario,** checkbook; receipt book

talla, *f.* stature, size

tallado, *adj.* cut, carved, engraved

tallar, *va.* to carve in wood

tallarín, *m.* noodle (for soup)

talle, *m.* shape, figure, size; waist

taller, *m.* workshop

tallo, *m.* shoot, sprout, stem

tamal, *m.* tamale

tamaño, *m.* size, shape

tambalear, *vn., vr.* to stagger, waver

también, *adv.* also, too, likewise; as well

tambor, *m.* drum; drummer;

iron cylinder

tamborito, *m.* national folk dance of Panama

tampoco, *adv.* neither, not either (used to enforce a foregoing negative)

tan, *adv.* so, so much, as well. as much; **tan pronto como,** as soon as

tanda, *f.* turn; rotation; shift

Tánger, Tangier

tangible, *adj.* tangible

tango, *m.* tango

tanque, *m.* tank; reservoir, pool

tanto, *m.* certain sum or quantity; *adj.* so much, as much; very great; *adv.* so, in such a manner; a long time; **mientras tanto,** meanwhile; **por lo tanto,** therefore; **tantos,** *pl.* score, points

tapa, *f.* lid, cover

tapacubos, *m.* hub cap

tapar, *va.* to cover; to close; to conceal, hide

tapete, *m.* rug; runner

tapizar, *va.* to upholster

tapón, *m.* cork, plug

taquigrafía, *f.* shorthand, stenography

taquígrafo, taquígrafa, *n.* stenographer

taquilla, *f.* box office

tararear, *va.* to hum (a tune)

tardanza, *f.* tardiness, delay

tardar, *vn.,* *vr.* to delay, put off; **a más tardar,** at the latest

tarde, *f.* afternoon, early evening **buenas tardes,** good afternoon; *adv.* late

tardío, *adj.* slow, tardy

tarea, *f.* task

tarifa, *f.* tariff, charge, rate, fare; price list

tarima, *f.* platform

tarjeta, *f.* card; **tarjeta, postal,** post card

tarro, *m.* jar; mug

tartamudear, *vn.* to stutter, stammer

tasar, *va.* to appraise, value

taxi, *m.* taxicab

taza, *f.* cup; cupful; bowl

te, *pron.* objective and dative cases of **tú** (thou)

té, *m.* tea

teatral, *adj.* theatrical

testro, *m.* theater

tecla, *f.* key of an instrument; key of a typewriter

teclado, *m.* keyboard

técnico, *adj.* technical; **técnica,** *f.* technique; *m.* technician

tecnológico, *adj.* technological

techo, *m.* roof, ceiling; (coll.) dwelling house; **bajo techo,** indoors

tedio, *m.* disgust; boredom

teja, *f.* roof tile

tejer, *va.* to weave, knit

tejido, *m.* texture, web; textile, fabric; (anat.) tissue

telaraña, *f.* cobweb

telef., teléfono, tel., telephone

telefonear, *va.,* *vn.* to telephone

telefonista, *m.,* *f.* telephone operator

teléfono, *m.* telephone

teleg., telegrama, tel., telegram; **telégrafo,** tel. telegraph

telegrafiar, *va.,* *vn.* to telegraph

telégrafo, *m.* telegraph

telegrama, *m.* telegram

telerreceptor, *m.* television set

telescopio, *m.* telescope

televisión, *f.* television

telón, *m.* curtain, backdrop in a theater

tema, *m.* theme; subject

temblor, *m.* trembling, tremor; earthquake

temer, *va.,* *vn.* to fear; to doubt

temeroso, *adj.* timid

temible, *adj.* dreadful, inspiring awe or fear

temor, *m.* dread, fear

témpano, *m.* tympanum; block; iceberg

temperatura, *f.* temperature

tempestad, *f.* tempest; storm

templo, *m.* temple, church

temporada, *f.* period, season

temporal, *adj.* temporary; *m.* tempest, storm

temprano, *adj.* early, anticipated; *adv.* early, prematurely

tenacidad, *f.* tenacity

tenaz, *adj.* tenacious; stubborn

tender, *va.* to spread, expand, extend; to have a tendency

tendón, *m.* tendon, sinew

tenedor, tenedora, *n.* holder; payee (of bill of exchange); **tenedor de libros,** bookkeeper, accountant; *m.* fork

tener, *va.* to take, hold; to possess; to have; **tener cuidado,** to be careful

tenería, *f.* tanyard, tannery

teniente, *m.* lieutenant

tenis, *m.* tennis

tenor, *m.* kind; condition, nature; meaning; (mus.) tenor

tensión, *f.* tension, strain

tentación, *f.* temptation

tentar, *va.* to touch; to grope; to tempt

tentativa, *f.* attempt, trial

ten.te, **teniente,** Lt. or Lieut., Lieutenant

tentempié, *m.* snack, bite

teñir, *va.* to tinge, dye

teoría, *f.* theory

tequila, *m.* tequila (a Mexican liquor)

tercero, *adj.* third; *m.* third person; mediator

tercio, *m., adj.* third

terciopelo, *m.* velvet

terco, *adj.* stubborn

terminante, *adj.* decisive; absolute, strict

terminar, *va.* to finish

término, *m.* term; end; boundary; limit; **término medio,** average

termómetro, *m.* thermometer

termos, *m.* thermos bottle

ternero, ternera, *n.* calf; veal; heifer

terneza, *f.* tenderness

ternura, *f.* tenderness

terquedad, *f.* obstinacy

terraza, *f.* terrace, veranda

terremoto, *m.* earthquake

terreno, *m.* land, ground

terrestre, *adj.* earthly

terrible, *adj.* terrible, dreadful

territorial, *adj.* territorial

territorio, *m.* territory

terror, *m.* terror, dread

terruño, *m.* native land

terso, *adj.* smooth, terse

tertulia, *f.* informal gathering; conversation

tesorería, *f.* treasury

tesorero, tesorera, *n.* treasurer

tesoro, *m.* treasure

testamento, *m.* will, testament

testar, *va., vn.* to make one's will; to bequeath

testarudo, *adj.* obstinate

testículo, *m.* testicle

testigo, *m.* witness

testimonio, *m.* testimony

teta, *f.* dug, teat

tétano, *m.* tetanus, lockjaw

tetera, *f.* teapot, teakettle

textil, *adj., m.* textile

texto, *m.* text

tez. *f.* complexion of the face; hue

ti, *pron.* objective or dative case of **tu**

tía, *f.* aunt

tibio, *adj.* lukewarm

tiburón, *m.* shark

tictac, *m.* ticktock

tiempo, *m.* time, term; season, weather; tempo

tienda, *f.* shop; tent

tierno, *adj.* tender; young; delicate, soft

tierra, *f.* earth; soil; land, ground; native country

tieso, *adj.* stiff, hard, firm; taut

tifoideo, *adj.* typhoid; **tifoidea,** *f.* typhoid fever

tigre, *m.* tiger

tijeras, *f. pl.* scissors

tilde, *f.* tilde, diacritical sign of the letter **ñ**

timbrazo, *n.* sharp bell ring

timbre, *m.* postage stamp; call bell; timbre

timidez, *f.* timidity

tímpano, m. kettledrum; eardrum

tina, f. tub; **tina de baño,** bathtub

tinaja, f. large earthen jar for water

tiniebla, f. darkness, obscurity

tino, m. good aim; tact; good judgment

tinta, f. tint, hue; ink

tinte, m. tint, dye

tintero, m. inkwell

tintorería, f. dry cleaning shop

tío, m. uncle

típico, adj. typical

tipo, m. type, model, pattern; rate, standard; **tipo de cambio,** rate of exchange

tipográfico, adj. typographical

tira, f. strip

tirabtizón, m. corkscrew

tirada, f. cast, throw; stroke (golf); edition, issue; presswork

tirador, m. doorknob; door knocker

tiranía, f. tyranny

tirano, adj. tyrannical; **tirana,** n. tyrant

tirante, adj. taut; **tirantes,** m. pl. suspenders

tirar, va. to throw, toss, cast; to pull, draw; to shoot; vn. to tend, incline

tiritar, vn. to shiver

tiro, m. cast, throw; shot

tiroides, adj., f. (anat.) thyroid (gland)

tirón, m. pull, haul, tug; **de un tirón,** all at once, at one stroke

tiroteo, m. random shooting, skirmish

tísico, adj. tubercular

tisis, f. consumption, tuberculosis

titubeo, m. hesitation, wavering

tiza, f. chalk

tobillera, f. anklet; bobbysoxer

tobillo, m. ankle

tocador, m. dressing table, boudoir

tocar, va. to touch; (mus.) to play; to ring a bell; vn. to belong; to behoove, fall to one's share

tocayo, tocaya, n. namesake

tocino, m. bacon, salt pork

todavía, adv. yet, still

todopoderoso, adj. almighty

tolerante, adj. tolerant

tolerar, vn. to tolerate

tomar, va. to take, seize; to drink

tomate, m. tomato

tomo, m. tome; volume

tonada, f. tune, melody, air

tonelada, f. ton

tónico, m. tonic

tontería, f. nonsense

tonto, adj. stupid, foolish; **tonto, tonta,** n. fool, dunce

tope, m. butt, rub; scuffle; **topes,** pl. (rail.) buffers; adj. high; **precio tope,** ceiling price

tópico, m. topic, subject

toque, m. touch; bell ringing; (mil.) call

torbellino, m. whirlwind

torcer, va. to twist; distort; **torcerse,** to go crooked or astray

torcido, adj. twisted

toreo, m. bullfighting

torero, m. bullfighter

tormenta, f. storm, tempest

tormento, m. torment

torneo, m. tournament

tornillo, m. bolt; screw

torno, m. lathe; wheel; wheel and axle; dentist's drill

toro, m. bull

toronja, f. grapefruit

torpe, adj. dull, heavy; stupid, awkward

torpeza, f. heaviness, stupidity

torrente, m. torrent

torso, m. trunk, torso

torta, f. tart, cake

tortilla, f. omelet; (Mex.) kind of pancake

tortuga, f. tortoise; turtle

tos, f. cough

toser, vn. to cough

tostada, f. slice of toast; (Mex.)

open-faced meat tart
tostador, *m.* toaster
tostar, *va.* to toast
total, *m.* whole, totality; *adj.* total, entire
totalmente, *adv.* totally
tr., transitive, tr., transitive
traba, *f.* obstacle
trabajar, *va., vn.* to work, labor
trabajo, *m.* work, labor, toil; workmanship; difficulty, trouble
trabajoso, *adj.* laborious
traducción, *f.* translation
traducir, *va.* to translate
traductor, traductora, *n.* translator
traer, *va.* to bring, carry, wear
tráfico, *m.* traffic, trade
tragaluz, *m.* skylight
tragar, *va.* to swallow, glut
trago, *m.* draft of liquor; drink
tragón, *adj.* gluttonous
traición, *f.* treason
traicionar, *va.* to betray
traidor, traidora, *n.* traitor; *adj.* treacherous
traje, *m.* dress, suit, costume; **traje espacial,** space suit
trajinar, *va.* to convey; to bustle about one's work
trama, *f.* plot, conspiracy; weft or woof (of cloth)
tramar, *va.* to weave; to plot
trámite, *m.* requirement; step, passage; (law) procedure
tramo, *m.* flight of stairs; span of a bridge; stretch, section
trampa, *f.* trap, snare; trap door; fraud; **hacer trampa,** to cheat
tramposo, *adj.* deceitful, swindling
trancar, *va.* to barricade
trance, *m.* danger; hypnotic condition; last stage of life; **a todo trance,** at all costs
tranquilidad, *f.* tranquility
tranquilizar, *va., vr.* to soothe, quiet
tranquilo, *adj.* calm, quiet
transacción, *f.* transaction; adjustment
transición, *f.* transition

transigir, *va.* to compromise; *vn.* to give in
tránsito, *m.* passage; road, way; traffic
tranvía, *m.* streetcar
trapo, *m.* rag, tatter
tras, *prep.* after, behind
trasatlántico, *adj., m.* transatlantic
trasbordar, *va.* to transfer, change cars
trascendencia, *f.* transcendency; importance
trascendental, *adj.* transcendental
trascribir, *va.* to transcribe, copy
trascurso, *m.* course (of time)
trasero, *adj.* hind, hinder; **asiento trasero,** back seat; *m.* buttock
trasferir, *va.* to transfer
trasformación, *f.* transformation
trasformar, *va.* to transform
trasfusión, *f.* transfusion
trasladar, *va.* to transport, transfer
trasmisión, *f.* transmission
trasmitir, *va.* to transmit, send
trasnochar, *vn.* to watch, sit up all night
trasparente, *adj.* transparent
traspasar, *va.* to pass over; to trespass; to transfer
trasplantar, *va.* to transplant
trasportar, *va.* to transport, convey; (mus.) to transpose
trasporte, *m.* transportation; transport
trastornado, *adj.* unbalanced, crazy
trastorno, *m.* confusion, upset, overthrow
tratable, *adj.* compliant, pliant; pleasant
tratado, *m.* treaty
tratar, *va.* to treat on a subject; to trade; to treat
trato, *m.* treatment; manner; deal; dealing
travesía, *f.* crossing, voyage; distance
trazar, *va.* to plan out; to pro-

ject; to trace

trébol, *m.* (bot.) clover; **hoja de trébol**, cloverleaf

trece, *m.*, *adj.* thirteen; thirteenth

trecientos, *adj.*, *m.* three hundred

tregua, *f.* truce, recess; **sin tregua**, unceasingly

treinta, *m.*, *adj.* thirty

tremendo, *adj.* tremendous

tren, *m.* train, retinue; (rail.) train

trepar, *vn.* to climb, crawl

tres, *adj.*, *m.* three

trescientos, *adj.*, *m.* three hundred

triangular, *adj.* triangular

triángulo, *m.* triangle

tribu, *f.* tribe

tribuna, *f.* tribune, rostrum

tribunal, *m.* tribunal, court of justice

tributar, *va.* to pay tribute

tributo, *m.* tribute; tax

tricolor, *adj.* tricolored

trigésimo, *adj.* thirtieth

trigueño, *adj.* swarthy, brunet

trimestre, *m.* quarter, space of three months

trinar, *vn.* to trill, quaver

trinchante, *m.* carver; carving knife

trinchera, *f.* trench

trineo, *m.* sleigh, sled

trío, *m.* (mus.) trio

tripa, *f.* gut, entrails, tripe, intestine

triple, *adj.* triple, treble

triplicar, *va.* to treble, triple

tripulación, *f.* crew of a ship

triste, *adj.* sad, mournful

tristeza, *f.* sadness

triunfal, *adj.* triumphal

triunfante, *adj.* triumphant

triunfar, *vn.* to triumph

triunfo, *m.* triumph; trump (in cards)

trivial, *adj.* trivial

triza, *f.* mite; bit, shred

trompa, *f.* trumpet; trunk (of elephants)

trompeta, *f.* trumpet, horn; *m.* trumpeter

trompo, *m.* spinning top

tronco, *m.* tree trunk; log of wood; origin

trono, *m.* throne

tropa, *f.* troop

tropezar, *vn.* to stumble

tropical, *adj.* tropical

trópico, *m.* tropics

tropiezo, *m.* stumble, trip

tropo, *m.* figu speech

trote, *m.* trot; **a trote**, in haste

trovador, **trovadora**, *n.* minstrel

trozo, *m.* piece, fragment

trucha, *f.* trout; crane

trueno, *m.* thunderclap

tu, *adj.* possessive sing. of pronoun **tú**

tú, *pron.* thou, you (*sing.* familiar form)

tuberculosis, *f.* tuberculosis

tubería, *f.* pipe line; tubing; piping

tubo, *m.* tube, pipe, duct

tuerca, *f.* nut (of a screw)

tuerto, *adj.* one-eyed; squint-eyed

tul, *m.* tulle (cloth)

tulipán, *m.* tulip

tullido, *adj.* crippled, maimed

tumba, *f.* tomb, grave

tumbar, *va.*, *vn.* to tumble

tumor, *m.* tumor

túnel, *m.* tunnel

túnica, *f.* tunic

turbante, *m.* turban

turborreactor, *m.* turbojet

turbulento, *adj.* turbid, muddy; stormy, turbulent

turco, **turca**, *n.*, *adj.* Turkish, Turk

turismo, *m.* touring, tourism

turista, *m.*, *f.* tourist

turnar, *vn.* to alternate

turno, *m.* turn; shift

turquesa, *f.* turquoise

turquí, *adj.* turquoise blue

Turquía, *f.* Turkey

turrón, *m.* nougat, candy

tutora, *f.* tutoress

tuyo, **tuya**, *adj.* thine; **los tuyos**, *pl.* thy family, thy people, etc

U

u, *conj.* or (used instead of **o**, when the following word begins with **o** or **ho**)

ubicar, *vn., vr.* to be located

ubre, *f.* dug, teat, udder

Ud., usted, *pron.* you (sing.)

Uds., ustedes, *pron.* you

úlcera, *f.* ulcer

últimamente, *adv.* lately

útimo, *adj.* last, latest; late, latter; remote, final

últ.°, último, ult. last

ultrajar, *va.* to outrage; to abuse

ultramar, *adj., m.* overseas

umbral, *m.* threshold, doorstep; beginning

un, una, *adj.* a, an; one

unánime, *adj.* unanimous

unanimidad, *f.* unanimity

undécimo, *adj.* eleventh

ungüento, *m.* ointment

único, *adj.* unique, only

unidad, *f.* unity; unit

uniforme, *adj., m.* uniform

uniformidad, *f.* uniformity

union, *f.* union

unir, *va.* to join, unite; **unirse,** to associate, get together

universal, *adj.* universal

universidad, *f.* university

universo, *m.* universe

uno, *m.* one; *adj.* one; sole, only

uña, *f.* nail; hoof; claw

urbanidad, *f.* good manners

urbe, *f.* metropolis

urgencia, *f.* urgency, need

urgente, *adj.* urgent

urinario, *adj.* urinary

urraca, *f.* magpie

uruguayo, uruguaya, *n., adj.* Uruguayan

usado, *adj.* used; worn

usar, *va.* to use, make use of; **usarse,** to be in use, be customary

uso, *m.* use, service; custom; mode

usted, *pron.* you (sing.); **ustedes,** you (plural); **usted mismo,** you yourself

útero, *m.* uterus, womb

útil, *adj.* useful, profitable; **útiles,** *m. pl.* utensils, tools

utilidad, *f.* utility; usefulness; profit

utilizar, *va.* to make use of

uva, *f.* grape

V

v., véase, vid., see, refer to; **verbo,** verb

v/, valor, val., value; amt., amount

V. A., Vuestra Alteza, Your Highness, **Versión Autorizada,** A. V., Authorized Version

vaca, *f.* cow

vacaciones, *f. pl.* holidays, vacations

vacante, *adj.* vacant; *f.* vacancy

vaciar, *va.* to empty, clear; to mold; *vn.* to fall, decrease (of waters)

vacilar, *vn.* to hesitate

vacío, *adj.* void, empty; unoccupied; *m.* vacuum; concavity

vacuna, *f.* vaccine

vacunar, *va.* to vaccinate

vacuno, *adj.* bovine

vagón, *m.* car, freight car, coach; **vagón cama,** sleeping car

vahido, *m.* dizziness

vainilla, *f.* vanilla

vaivén, *m.* fluctuation, motion

vajilla, *f.* table service, set of dishes

vale, *m.* promissory note, I.O.U

valenciano, valenciana, *adj., n.* Valencian, from Valencia

valentía, *f.* valor, courage

valer, *vn.* to be valuable, be deserving; to be valid; **valer la pena,** to be worthwhile; **valerse,** to employ; to have recourse to

vilidez, *f.* validity

válido, *adj.* valid; obligatory

valiente, *adj.* brave, courageous

vafija, *f.* valise; mail bag

valioso, *adj.* valuable

valor, *m.* value, price; courage, valor

valorar, *va.* to value

vals, *m.* waltz

valuación, *f.* valuation, appraisal

valle, *m.* valley

¡vamos! *interj.* well let's go! stop!

vanagloriarse, *vr.* to boast

vanidad, *f.* vanity

vanidoso, *adj.* vain, conceited

vano, *adj.* vain; useless; **en vano**, in vain

vapor, *m.* vapor, steam; steamer, steamship

vaquero, *m.* cowherd; herdsman, cowboy; *adj.* pertaining to cowboys

vara, *f.* rod; pole, staff; yard (measure); **vara alta**, sway, high hand

variación, *adj.* variation

variado, varied

variar, *va.* to vary, change; *vn.* to vary

varieded, *f.* variety; diversity

variedades, *f. pl.* variety show

varios, *adj. pl.* some, several

varón, *m.* man, male human being; man of respectability

varonil, *adj.* male, masculine; manful

vaselina, *f.* vaseline, petroleum jelly

vasija, *f.* pot

vaso, *m.* vessel; jar

vástago, *m.* bud, shoot; descendant

vasto, *adj.* vast, huge

¡vaya! *interj.* well, now!

Vd., **usted**, you (sing.)

vda., **viuda**, widow

Vds. or VV., **ustedes**, you (*pl.*)

V.E., **Vuestra Excelencia**, Your Excellency

véase, see, refer to

vecindad, *f.* neighborhood

vecindario, *m.* neighborhood

vecino, *adj.* neighboring; near; *m.* neighbor; inhabitant

vegetación, *f.* vegetation

vegetal, *adj.*, *m.* vegetable

vegetar, *vn.* to vegetate

vegetariano, **vegetariana**, *adj.*, *n.* vegetarian

vehículo, *m.* vehicle

veinte, *adj.*, *m.* twenty

veintena, *f.* score, twenty

vejez, *f.* old age

vejiga, *f.* bladder; blister

vela, *f.* watch; watchfulness; candle

velada, *f.* evening entertainment, soiree

velar, *vn.* to watch

velo, *m.* veil; pretext

velocidad, *f.* speed

veloz, *adj.* swift

vello, *m.* down; gossamer; short downy hair

velludo, *adj.* hairy

vena, *f.* vein, blood vessel

venado, *m.* deer; venison

vencer, *va.* to conquer, vanquish; *vn.* to fall due

vencido, *adj.* conquered; due; **darse por vencido**, to give up, yield

venda, *f.* bandage

vendaje, *m.* bandage

vendar, *va.* to bandage

vendedor, **vendedora**, *n.* seller

vender, *va.* to sell

veneciano, **veneciana**, *adj.*, *n.* Venetian

veneno, *m.* poison, venom

venenoso, *adj.* poisonous

veneración, *f.* veneration

venerar, *va.* to venerate

venério, *adj.* venereal

vengar, *va.* to revenge, avenge; **vengarse de**, to take revenge on

vengativo, *adj.* revengeful

venia, *f.* pardon; leave, permission; bow

venida, *f.* arrival; return

venidero, *adj.* future, coming, next; **próximo venidero**, the coming month

venir, *vn.* to come, arrive; to follow, succeed; to spring from

venta, *f.* sale; roadside inn

ventaja, *f.* advantage; handicap

ventajoso, *adj.* advantageous

ventana, *f.* window

ventarrón, *m.* violent wind
ventilación, *f.* ventilation
ventilador, *m.* ventilator; fan
ventilar, *va., vr.* to ventilate;
to fan; to air; to discuss
ventura, *f.* luck, fortune; **por
ventura,** by chance
venturoso, *adj.* lucky, fortunate; happy
ver, *va.* to see, look; to observe; **a ver,** let's see; **hacer
ver,** to pretend; *m.* sense of
sight, seeing; view; **a mi ver,**
in my opinion
veracidad, *f.* veracity
veraneo, *m.* summering; **lugar
de veraneo,** *m.* summer resort
verano, *m.* summer
veras, *f. pl.* truth, sincerity; **de
veras,** in truth, really
veraz, *adj.* truthful
verbal, *adj.* verbal, oral
verbigracia, *adv.* for example,
namely
verbo, *m.* (gram.) verb
verdad, *f.* truth, veracity
verdaderamente, *adv.* truly
verdadero, *adj.* true, real
verde, *m., adj.* green
verdor, *m.* verdure; green
verdulero, verdulera, *n.* vegetable seller
verdura, *f.* verdure; vegetables, garden stuff
vereda, *f.* path, trail
vergel, *m.* flower garden
vergonzoso, *adj.* bashful, shy;
shameful
vergüenza, *f.* shame; bashful-
ness; confusion
verídico, *adj.* truthful
verificar, *va.* to verify, check;
verificarse, to take place
verja, *f.* grate, lattice
verosímil, *adj.* plausible
verruga, *f.* wart, pimple
versión, *f.* version, interpretation
verso, *m.* verse, stanza
vértebra, *f.* vertebra
vertebrado, vertebrada, *m.,
adj.* vertebrate
verter, *va., vr.* to pour; *vn.* to
flow

vespertino, *adj.* evening
vestíbulo, *m.* vestibule, lobby
vestigio, *m.* vestige, trace
vestir, *va.* to clothe, dress
veterano, *adj.* experienced,
long practiced; *m.* veteran,
old soldier
vez, *f.* turn, time; **una vez,**
once; **a veces, algunas ve-
ces,** sometimes; **en vez de,**
instead of; **otra vez,** again;
tal vez, perhaps
vg., v.g., or **v.gr., verbigracia,**
e.g., for example
vía, *f.* way, road, route; (rail.)
railway, railway line; **vía
áerea,** air mail
viaducto, *m.* viaduct; overpass
viajar, *vn.* to travel
viaje, *m.* journey, voyage; **viaje sencillo,** one-way trip;
viaje redondo or **de ida y
vuelta,** round trip
viajero, viajera, *n.* traveler
víbora, *f.* viper
vicecónsul, *m.* vice-consul
vicepresidente, *m.* vice-president vice-chairman
viceversa: *adj.* vice versa
vicio, *m.* vice, folly
víctima, *f.* victim; **víctimas,**
pl. casualties
victoria, *f.* victory
victorioso, *adj.* victorious
vid, *f.* (bot.) vine
vida, *f.* life
vidriera, *f.* glass case; shop-
window
vidrio, *m.* glass
viejo, *adj.* old; ancient
vienés, vienesa, *adj., n.* Viennese
viento, *in.* wind; air
vientre, *m.* belly
viernes, *m.* Friday; **Viernes
Santo,** Good Friday
viga, *f.* beam (of timber)
vigente, *adj.* in force
vigésimo, *adj., m.* twentieth
vigilar, *va., vn.* to watch over
vigor, *m.* vigor, strength
vigoroso, *adj.* vigorous
villa, *f.* town
villano, *adj.* rustic, boorish;
m. villain

vinagre, *m.* vinegar
vincular, *va.* to link
vínculo, *m.* link, bond
vindicar, *va.* to vindicate; to avenge
vino, *m.* wine
viña, *f.* vineyard; grapevine
violación, *f.* violation
violar, *va.* to violate; to ravish
violencia, *f.* violence
violentar, *va.* to enforce by violent means
violento, *adj.* violent
violeta, *f., adj.* violet
violín, *m.* violin, fiddle
violinista, *m., f.* violinist
violón, *m.* bass viol
violonchelo, *m.* violoncello
virar, *va.* (naut.) to tack; *vn.* to turn around
virgen, *adj., f.* virgin
viril, virile, manly
virología, *f.* virology
virtud, *f.* virtue
virtuoso, *adj.* virtuous
viruela, *f.* smallpox; **viruelas locas**, chicken pox
visa, *f.* visa
visita, *f.* visit; visitor
visitante, *m., f.* visitor
visitar, *va.* to visit
víspera, *f.* evening before; day before; **víspera de Año Nuevo**, New Year's Eve
vistazo, *m.* glance
visto, *adj.* obvious; **visto que**, considering that; **por lo visto**, apparently; **visto bueno**, O.K., all right, correct
vistoso, *adj.* beautiful, showy
vital, *adj.* vital, essential
vitalicio, *adj.* during life
vitalidad, *f.* vitality
vitamina, *f.* vitamin
vitrina, *f.* showcase
viuda, *f.* widow
viudo, *m.* widower
¡viva! *interj.* hurrah! hail!
vivacidad, *f.* vivacity
víveres, *m. pl.* provisions
viveza, *f.* liveliness, perspicacity
vividor, vividora, *n.* sponger
vivienda, *f.* dwelling house
viviente, *adj.* alive, living

vivir, *vn.* to live
vivo, *adj.* living; lively; ingenious, bright
V. M., Vuestra Majestad, Your Majesty
V.º B.º, visto bueno, O.K., all correct
vocablo, *m.* word, term
vocabulario, *m.* vocabulary
vocación, *f.* vocation, calling
vocal, *f.* vowel; *m.* member of a board of directors; *adj.* vocal, oral
vol., volumen, vol., volume; **voluntad**, will; (com.) good will
volante, *m.* steering wheel; flier, note, memorandum; ruffle
volcán, *m.* volcano
volcar, *va., vr.* to upset
voltear, *va.* to whirl, over set; *vn.* to tumble
volumen, *m.* volume; size
voluminoso, *adj.* voluminous
voluntario, *adj.* voluntary; *n.* volunteer
voluntarioso, *adj.* willful
volver, *va., vn.* to return; to turn; **volver en sí**, to recover one's senses
vómito, *m.* vomiting
voraz, *adj.* voracious, greedy
vos, *pron.* you ye
vosotros, vosotroas, *pron, pl.* you
votación, *f.* voting
votante, *m., f.* voter
votar, *va., vn.* to vote
voto, *m.* vow; vote; wish; supplication to God; **hacer votos**, tc wish well
voz, *f.* voice; word, term
V.P., Vicepresidente, Vice Pres., Vice-President
vuelo, *m.* flight
vuelta, *f.* turn; circuit; detour; return; **dar la vuelta**, to turn around; to go out for a short walk or ride
vuelto, *p. p.* of **volver**; *m.* (sp. Am.) change (money back from a payment)
vuestro, vuestra, *pron.* your, yours

vulgar, *adj.* vulgar, common, ordinary

vulgaridad, *f.* vulgarity

vulgarismo, *m.* slang

vulgo, *m.* populace, mob

VV or V.V., ustedes, you (*pl.*)

W

wáter, *m.* lavatory

whiskey, *m.* whiskey

X

xenón, *m.* xenon

xilófono, *m.* (mus.) xylophone

xilografía, *f.* wood engraving

Y

y, *conj.* and

ya, *adv.* already; presently; immediately; **ya no,** no longer

yanqui, *adj., n.* Yankee

yarda, *f.* yard (measure)

yate, *m.* yacht

yedra, *f.* ivy

yelmo, *m.* helmet

yema, *f.* yolk

yerba or **hierba,** *f.* herb; grass; **yerba buena,** mint; **yerba mate,** Paraguay tea; **yerbas** *pl.* greens, vegetables

yerno, *m.* son-in-law

yeso, *m.* gypsum; plaster, plaster cast

yo, *pron.* I; **yo mismo,** I myself

yodo, *m.* iodine

yuca, *f.* (bot.) yucca

yugo, *m.* yoke

yunque, *m.* anvil

yunta, *f.* couple, yoke

yute, *m.* jute (fiber)

Z

zacate, *m.* (Mex.) hay, grass

zafiro, *m.* sapphire

zafra, *f.* sugar crop

zalamero, zalamera, *n., adj.* wheedler, flatterer

zambullirse, *vr.* to plunge into water, dive

zanahoria, *f.* carrot

zancada, *f.* long stride

zanco, *m.* stilt

zancudo, *adj.* long-shanked; wading (bird); *m.* (Sp. Am.) mosquito

zángano, *m.* drone; idler, sponger

zanja, *f.* ditch, trench

zapallo, *m.* (Sp. Am.) squash

zapatear, *va., vn.,* to strike with the shoe; to beat time with the sole of the shoe

zapatería, *f.* shoe store

zapatero, *m.* shoemaker; shoe seller

zapatilla, *f.* pump (shoe), slipper

zapato, *m.* shoe

zar, *m.* czar

zaraza, *f.* chintz; gingham

zarzamora, *f.* brambleberry; blackberry bush

zarzuela, *f.* variety of operetta, musical comedy

zeta, *f.* name of letter *z*

zigzag, *m.* zigzag

zona, *f.* zone, district

zoología, *f.* zoology

zoológico, *adj.* zoological

zoquete, *m.* block; (coll.) blockhead, numbskull

zorra, *f.* fox; (coll.) prostitute, strumpet

zorrillo, *m.* skunk

zorro, *m.* male fox; cunning fellow

zozobra, *f.* anxiety

zueco, *m.* wooden shoe

zumbar, *vn.* to resound, hum; to buzz; to ring (the ears)

zumbido, *m.* humming, buzzing sound

zumo, *m.* sap, juice

zurdo, *adj.* left; lefthanded

zurrapa, *f.* lees, dregs; trash

zurrar, *va.* to chastise with a whip; **zurrarse,** (coll.) to have an involuntary evacuation of the bowels

zutano, zutana, *n.* such a one; **zutano y fulano,** such and such a one, so and so

A

a, *art.* un, uno, una

A. B., Bachelor of Arts, Br. Bachiller

aback, *adv.* detrás, atrás; **to be taken aback,** quedar desconcertado

abandon, *vt.* abandonar

abate, *vt., vi.* minorar, disminuir

abbreviate, *vt.* abreviar

abbreviation, *n.* abreviación, abreviatura, *f.*

abdicate, *vt.* abdicar

abdomen, *n.* abdomen, vientre, *m.*

abduct, *vt.* secuestrar

abhor, *vt.* aborrecer

abide, *vi.* habitar, morar; **to abide by,** cumplir con; atenerse a

ability, *n.* habilidad, aptitud, *f.*

abnormal, *adj.* anormal

aboard, *adj.* abordo

abode, *n.* habitación,

abolish, *vt.* abolir

abominable, *adj.* abominable

abortion, *n.* aborto, *m.*

about, *prep.* cerca de; sobre; acerca; *adv.* aquí y allá; **to be about to,** estar a punto de

above, *prep.* encima, sobre; *adj.* arriba; **above all,** sobre todo, principalmente

aboveboard, *adj.* y *adv.* sincero, al descubierto

abreast, *adj.* de frente

abrupt, *adi.* repentino; rudo

abscess, *n.* absceso, *m.*

absence, *n.* ausencia, *f.*; **leave of absence,** licencia, *f.*

absent, *adj.* ausente

absent-minded, *adj.* distraído

abstain, *vi.* abstenerse

abstract, *vt.* abstraer; compendiar; *adj.* abstracto; *n.* extracto, *m.*

absurd, *adj.* absurdo

abundance, *n.* abundancia, *f.*

abundant, *adj.* abundante

abuse, *vt.* abusar; ultrajar; violar; *n.* abuso, engaño, *m.*

A.C., a.c., alternating current, C.A., corriente alterna

academic, *adj.* académico

academy, *n.* academia, *f.*

accede, *vi.* acceder

accelerator, *n.* acelerador, *m.*

accent, *n.* acento, *m.*; tono, *m.*; *vt.* acentuar

accentuate, *vt.* acentuar

accept, *vt.* aceptar; admitir

acceptance, *n.* aceptación, *f.*

access, *n.* acceso, *m.*; entrada, *f.*

accessory, *adj.* accesorio; *n.* cómplice, *m.* y *f.*

accident, *n.* accidente, *m.*; casualidad, *f.*

accidental, *adj.* accidental, casual

acclaim, *vt.* aclamar, aplaudir

accommodate, *vt.* acomodar, ajustar

accommodating, *adj.* servicial

accompaniment, *n.* (mus.) acompañamiento, *m.*

accompany, *vt.* acompañar

accomplice, *n.* cómplice, *m.* y *f.*

accomplish, *vt.* efectuar, realizar

accord, *n.* acuerdo, convenio, *m.*

accordance, *n.* conformidad, *f.*, acuerdo, *m.*

according, *adj.* conforme; **according to,** según; **accordingly,** *adv.* de conformidad, por consiguiente

account, *n.* cuenta, *f.*; cálculo, *m.*; narración, *f.*; **on account of,** a causa de

accountant, *n.* contador, tenedor de libros, *m.*

accounting, *n.* contabilidad, *f.*

accredited, *adj.* autorizado

accumulate, *vt.* y *vi.* acumular

accurate, *adj.* exacto; atinado

accusation, *n.* acusación, *f.*; cargo, *m.*

accusative, *n.* acusativo, *m.*

accuse, *vt.* acusar; culpar

accustom, *vt.* acostumbrar

ace, *n.* as (de naipe), *m.*; as, aviador sobresaliente, *m.*; *adj.* extraordinario

ache, *n.* dolor, *m.*; *vi.* doler

achieve, *vt.* ejecutar; lograr

achievement, *n.* ejecución, *f.*; hazaña, *f.*

acid, *n.* ácido, *m.*; *adj.* ácido, agrio

acknowledge, *vt.* reconocer; confesar; **acknowledge receipt,** acusar recibo

acoustics, *n.* acústica, *f.*

acquaint, *vt.* enterar, familiarizar; **to be acquainted,** conocer

acquaintance, *n.* conocimiento, *m.*; conocido, *m.*

acquire, *vt.* adquirir

acre, *n.* acre, *m.* (medida)

across, *adv.* al otro lado; *prep.* a través de

acrylic, *adj.* acrílico

act, *vt.* representar; obrar; *vi.* hacer; *n.* acto, hecho, *m.*

ACTH, *n.* (med.) ACTH

acting, *adj.* interino, suplente

action, *n.* acción, operación, *f.*; batalla, *f.*; proceso, *m.*; actividad, *f.*

active, *adj.* activo; eficaz

activity, *n.* actividad, *f.*

actual, *adj.* real; efectivo

acute, *adj.* agudo; ingenioso

A.D.: (in the year of our Lord), D. de J. C. (después de J. C.)

ad, *n.* anuncio, aviso, *m.*

adamant, *adj.* inflexible

adapt, *vt.* adaptar

add, *vt.* sumar; agregar

adding, *n.* suma, *f.*; **adding machine,** calculadora, *f.*

addition, *n.* adición, *f.*

address, *vt.* hablar, dirigir la palabra; *n.* discurso, *m.*; direceión, *f.*

addressee, *n.* destinatario, *m.*

adhere, *vi.* adherir

adhesion, *n.* adherencia, *f.*

adhesive, *adj.* pegajoso, tenaz; **adhesive plaster, adhesive tape,** esparadrapo, *m.*

adjacent, *adj.* adyacente, contiguo

adjective, *n.* adjetivo, *m.*

adjourn, *vt.* y *vi.* clausurar (una reunión, etc.)

adjust, *vt.* ajustar, acomodar

adjustment, *n.* ajuste, arreglo, *m.*

Adm., Admiral, Almte., almirante

administer, *vt.* administrar

administration, *n.* administración

admirable, *adj.* admirable

admiral, *n.* almirante, *m.*

admiration, *n.* admiración, *f.*

admire, *vt.* admirar; contemplar

admirer, *n.* admirador, *m.*; pretendiente, *m.*

admission, *n.* admisión, entrada, *f.*

admit, *vt.* admitir, dar entrada; reconocer

adolescence, *n.* adolescencia, *f.*

adopt,, *vt.* adoptar

adoption, *n.* adopción, *f.*

adrift, *adj.* y *adv.* flotante, al garete

adult, *adj.* y *n.* adulto, adulta

advance, *vt.* avanzar; pagar adelantado; *vi.* progresar; *n.* adelanto, *m.*

advantage, *n.* ventaja, *f.*; provecho, *m.*; **to take advantage of,** aprovecharse de

advantageous, *adj.* ventajoso, útil

adventure, *n.* aventura, *f.*

adventurer, *n.* aventurero, *m.*

adverb. *n.* adverbio, *m.*

adversity, *n.* adversidid, *f.*

advertise, *vt.* avisar, anunciar

advertisement, *n.* aviso, anuncio, *m.*

advice, *n.* consejo, *m.*; parecer, *m.*

advisable, *adj.* prudente, conveniente

advise, *vt.* aconsejar; avisar

adviser, *n.* consejero, *m.*

advisory, *adj.* consultivo

aerial, *adj.* aéreo; *n.* antena, *f.*

aeronautics, *n.* aeronautica, *f.*

aerosol bomb, *n.* bomba de aerosol, *f.*

aerospace, *n.* atmósfera y espacio exterior

affair, *n.* asunto, *m.*

affect, *vt.* conmover; afectar

affected, adj. afectado, fingido
affection, n. amor, afecto, m.
affectionate, adj. afectuoso
affiliation, n. afiliación, f.
affirmative, adj. afirmativo
affix, vt. anexar, fijar
afflict, vt. afligir
afford, vt. dar; proveer; tener los medios
afraid, adj. miedoso; **to be afraid,** tener miedo
Afro, adj. afro
after, prep. después de, detrás; adv. después
afternoon, n. tarde, f.
afterward, afterwards, adv. después
again, adv. otra vez
against, prep. contra
age, n. edad, f.; **of age,** mayor de edad; vi. envejecer
agent, n. agente, m.
aggravate, vt. agravar
aggression, n. agresión, f.
ago, adv. pasado, tiempo ha; **long ago,** hace mucho
agony, n. agonía, f.
agrarian, adj. agrario
agree, vi. convenir; conocntir
agreeable, adj. agradable
agreement, n. acuerdo, m.; conformidad, f.
agricultural, adj. agrario, agrícola
agriculture, n. agricultura, f.
aid, vt. ayudar, socorrer; n. ayuda, f.; auxilio, m.
ailment, n. dolencia, f.
aim, vt. apuntar; aspirar a; n. designio, intento, m.; puntería, f.
air, n. aire, m.; tonada, f.; **air brush,** aerógrafo, m.; **air drill,** perforadora, f.; **air freight,** flete aéreo, m. **air-conditioned,** adj. con aire acondicionado
airlift, n. puente aéyeo, m.
airplane, n. aeroplano, m.
airport, n. aeropuerto, m.
airtight, adj. herméticamente cerrado
aisle, n. pasillo, m.; pasadizo, m.
alarm, n. alarma, f.; **alarm**

clock, reloj despertador, m.; vt. alarmar
album, n. álbum, m.
alcoholic, adj. alcohólico
alderman, n. concejal, m.
ale, n. varieded de cerveza
alert, adj. alerto, vivo
algebra, n. álgebra, f.
alibi, n. (law) coartada, f.
alien, n. extranjero, extranjera
alike, adj. semejante, igual
alive, adj. vivo, viviente
all, adj. todo; adv. enteramente; **all right,** bueno, satisfactorio; n. todo, m.
allege, vt. alegar, declarar
allegiance, n. lealtad, f.
allegory, n. alegoria f.
allergen, n. alergeno, m.
allergic, adj. alérgico
alley, n. callejón, m.
allied, adj. aliado
alligator, n. lagarto, caimán, m.; **alligator pear,** aguacate, m.
allot, vt. asignar, repartir
allotment, n. asignación, f.; parte, porción, f.
allow, vt. conceder; permitir
allowance, n. ración, f.; mesada, f.
allude, vt. aludir
alluring, adj. seductor
ally, n. aliado, asociado, m.; vt. vincular
almanac, n. almanaque, m.
almighty, adj. omnipotente, todopoderoso
almond, n. almendra, f.
almost, adv. casi, cerca de
alms, n. limosna, f.
alone, adj. solo; adv. a solas
along, adv. a lo largo; junto con
aloof, adj. reservado, apartado
aloud, adv. recio; en voz alta
alphabet, n. alfabeto, m.
Alps, Alpes, m. pl.
already, adv. ya
also, adv. también
alter, vt. alterar, modificar
alteration, n. alteración, f.
alternate, vt. alternar, variar; n. suplente, m. y f.
altimeter, n. altimetro, m.

altitude, *n.* altitud, *f.*
alto, *n.* contralto, *f.*
aluminum, *n.* aluminio, *m.*
always, *adv.* siempre
A.M., **Master of Arts**, Maestro o Licenciado en Artes
A.M., **a.m.**, **before noon**, A.M. antemeridiano
am (1ª persona del singular de indicativo del verbo **to be**), soy; estoy
amateur, *n.* aficionado, aficionada
amaze, *vt.* asombrar
amazing, *adj.* asombroso
ambassador, *n.* embajador, *m.*
ambition, *n.* ambición, *f.*
ambitious, *adj.* ambicioso
ambulance, *n.* ambulancia, *f.*
amen, *interj.* amén
amend, *vt., vi.* enmendar
amendment, *n.* enmienda, reforma, *f.*
American, *n.* y *adj.* americano, americana
amiable, *adj.* amable
amid, **amidst**, *prep.* entre, en medio de
amino acid, *n.* aminoácido, *m.*
ammonia, *n.* amoniaco, *m.*
ammunition, *n.* munición, *f.*
among, **amongst**, *prep.* entre, en medio de
amount, *n.* suma, *f.;* monto, *m.; vi.* importar
ample, *adj.* amplio, vasto
amplify, *vt.* ampliar, extender
amputate, *vt.* amputar
amt., **amount**, v/ valor
amuse, *vt.* divertir
amusement, *n.* diversión, *f.*, pasatiempo, *m.*
amusing, *adj.* divertido
an, *art.* un, uno, una
analysis, *n.* análisis, *m.* y *f.*
analyze, *vt.* analizar
anatomy, *n.* anatomia, *f.*
ancestors, *n. pl.* antepasados, *m. pl.*
ancestry, *n.* linaje, *m.*
anchor, *n.* ancla, áncora, *f.; vi.* echar anclas
ancient, *adj.* antiguo
and, *conj.* y; e (antes de palabras que empiezan con *i* o *hi*,

con excepción de *hie*)
Andalusian, *n.* y *adj.* andaluz, andalza
anecdote, *n.* anécdota, *f.*
anesthetic, *adj.* y *n.* anestésico, *m.*
angel, *n.* ángel, *m.*
anger, *n.* ira, cólera, *f.; vt.* enojar, encolerizar
Anglo-Saxon, *n.* y *adj.* anglosajón, anglosajona
angry, *adj.* enojado
anguish, *n.* ansia, angustia, *f.*
animal, *n.* y *adj.* animal, *m.*
animation, *n.* animación, *f.*
ankle, *n.* tobillo, *m.*
anniversary, *n.* aniversario, *m.*
announce, *vt.* anunciar, publicar; notificar, avisar
announcement, *n.* aviso, anuncio, *m.*, notificación, *f.*
announcer, *n.* anunciador, anunciadora; locutor, locutora
annoy, *vt.* molestar; fastidiar
annoyance, *n.* molestia, *f.;* fastidio, *m.;* (coll.) lata,
annual, *adj.* anual
annuity, *n.* pension, anualidad *f.*
annul, *vt.* anular, aniquilar
annulment, *n.* anulación, *f.*
anonymous, *adj.* anónimo
another, *adj.* otro, diferente
answer, *vi.* responder, contestar; *vt.* refutar; contestar; *n.* respuesta, contestación, *f.*
ant, *n.* hormiga, f
antenna, *n.* antena, *f.*
antibiotic, *n.* y *adj.* antibiótico, *m.*
anticipate, *vt.* anticipar, prevenir
antihistamine, *n.* antihistamina, *f.*
antiknock, *n.* antidetonante, *m.*
antimatter, *n.* antimateria, *f.*
antique, *adj.* antiguo; *n.* antigüedad, *f.*
antiseptic, *adj.* antiséptico
antitank gun, *n.* cañón anticarro o antitanque, *m.*
anvil, *n.* yunque, *m.*

anxiety, *n.* ansiedad, *f.*
anxious, *adj.* ansioso
any, *adj.* cualquier, algún
anyhow, *adv.* de cualquier modo; de todos modos
anyone, *pron.* alguno, cualquiera
anything, *pron.* algo
anyway, *adv.* como quiera; de todos modos
apart, *adv.* aparte; separadamente
apartment, *n.* departamento, apartamento, apartamiento
ape, *n.* mono, *m.*; *vt.* imitar
apiece, *adv.* por cabeza, por persona
apologize, *vi.* disculparse
apology, *n.* disculpa, *f.*
apostle, *n.* apóstol, *m.*
apparatus, *n.* aparato, *m.*
apparel, *n.* vestido, *m.*; ropa, *f.*
apparent, *adj.* evidente, aparente
appeal, *vi.* apelar; recurrir; atraer; *n.* súplica, *f.*; (law) apelación, *f.*; simpatía, atracción, *f.*
appear, *vi.* aparecer; ser evidente; salir
appearance, *n.* apariencia, *f.*; aspecto, *m.*
appease, *vt.* apaciguar, aplacar
appendicitis, *n.* apendicitis, *f.*
appendix, *n.* apéndice, *m.*
appetite, *n.* apetito, *m.*
appetizer, *n.* aperitivo, *m.*; entremés, *m.*
applaud, *vt.* aplaudir; aclamar
applause, *n.* aplauso, *m.*
apple, *n.* manzana, *f.*
appliance, *n.* utensilio, aparato, *m.*, herramienta, *f.*
application, *n.* solicitud, *f.*; aplicación, *f.*
apply, *vt.* aplicar; **to apply for**, solicitar; *vi.* dirigirse a, recurrir a
appoint, *vt.* nombrar, designar
appointment, *n.* nombramiento, *m.*; cita, *f.*, compromiso, *m.*
appraise, *vt.* tasar; valuar
appreciate, *vt.* apreciar

apprentice, *n.* aprendiz, *m.*
approach, *vt.* y *vi.* abordar; aproximarse; *n.* acercamiento, *m.*
appropriate, *vt.* apropiar, asignar (una partida); *adj.* apropiado
appropriation, *n.* apropiación, partido, *f.*
approval, *n.* aprobación, *f.*
approve, *vt.* aprobar
approximate, *adj.* aproximado
apricot, *n.* albaricoque, *m.*; (Mex.) chabacano, *m.*
April, *n.* abril, *m.*
apron, *n.* delantal, *m.*
apt, *adj.* apto, idóneo
aptitude, *n.* aptitud, *f.*
aquarium, *n.* acuario, *m.*
aqueduct, *n.* acueducto, *m.*
Arab, Arabian, *n.* y *adj.* árabe, *m.* y *f.*, arábigo, arábiga
arbitrary, *adj.* arbitrario
arbitration, *n.* arbitraje, *m.*
arbor, *n.* enramada, *f.*
arc, *n.* arco, *m.*
arch, *n.* arco (de círculo, de puente, etc.), *m.*
archbishop, *n.* arzobispo, *m.*
archipelago, *n.* archipiélago *m.*
architect, *n.* arquitecto, *m.*
architecture, *n.* arquitectura *f.*
arctic, *adj.* ártico
ardent, *adj.* ardiente, apasionado
ardor, *n.* ardor, *m.*; pasión, *f.*
are, plural y 2ª persona del singular de indicativo del verbo **to be**
area, *n.* área, *f.*; espacio, *m.*; superfide, *f.*
arena, *n.* pista, *f.*
argue, *vi.* disputar, argüir
argument, *n.* argumento, *m.*, controversia, *f.*
arid, *adj.* árido, seco
arise, *vi.* levantarse
aristocracy, *n.* aristocracia, *f.*
aristocrat, *n.* aristócrata, *m.* y *f.*
arithmetic, *n.* aritmética, *f.*
ark, *n.* arca, *f.*
arm, *n.* brazo, *m.*; arma, *f.*

armament, n. armamento, m.
armistice, n. armisticio, m.
armor, n. armadura, f.
armored, adj. blindado, acorazado
army, n. ejército, m.
around, prep. en, cerca; adv. al rededor
arrange, vt. arreglar
arrangement, n. arreglo. m.
arrest, n. arresto, m.; detención, f.; vt. arrestar, prender-
arrival, n. arribo, m.; llegada, f.
arrive, vi. arribar; llegar
arrow, n. flecha, f.; dardo, m.
arsenic, n. arsénico, m.
art, n. arte, m. y f.; ciencia, f.; **the fine arts,** las bellas artes
artery, n. arteria, f.
arthritis, n. artritis, f.
article, n. artículo, m.
artillery, n. artillería, f.
artisan, n. artesano, m.
artist, n. artista, m. y f.; pintor, pintora
artistic, adj. artístico
as, conj. y adv. como; mientras; pues; visto que, pues que; **as much,** tanto; **as far as,** hasta; **as to,** en cuanto a
ascend, vi. ascender, subir
ascent, n. subida, f.
ash, n. (bot.) fresno, m.; **ashes,** pl. ceniza, f.; **ash tray,** cenicero, m.
ashamed, adj. avergonzado; **to be ashamed,** tener vergüenza
ashore, adv. en tierra, a tierra
Asiatic, n. y adj. asiático, asiática
aside, adv. al lado, aparte
ask, vt. y vi. pedir; interrogar
asleep, adj. dormido; **to fall asleep,** dormirse
asparagus, n. espárrago, m.
aspect, n. aspecto, m.
aspire, vi. aspirar, desear
aspirin, n. aspirina, f.
ass, n. borrico, asno, m.
assail, vt. asaltar, atacar ·
assassin, n. asesino. m.
assassinate, vt. asesinar
assault, n. asalto, m.; vt. aco-

meter, asaltar
assemble, vt. congregar, convocar; esamblar, armar; vi. juntarse
assembly, n. asamblea, junta, f.; congreso, m.; montaje, m.; **assembly line,** línea de montaje
assert, vt. sostener, mantener; afirmar
assertion, n. aserción.
assessment, n. impuesto, m.; catastro, m.
assessor, n. asesor, m.
asset, n. algo de valor; ventaja, f.; **assets,** pl. (com.) haber, activo, capital, m.
assign, vt. asignar, destinar
assignment, n. asignación, f.; tarea escolar, f.
assimilate, vt. asimilar
assist, vt. asistir, ayudar
assistance, n. asistencia, f.; socorro, m.
assistant, n. asistente, ayudante, m.
associate, vt. asociar; acompañar; adj. asociado; n. socio, compañero, m.
association, n. asociación, agrupación, f.; club, m.
assume, vt. asumir
assumption, n. suposición, f.; **Assumption,** n. Asuncion, f.
assurance, n. seguridad, convicción, f.
assure, vt. asegurar, afirmar
asthma, n. asma, f.
astonishing, adj. asombroso
astounding, adj. asombroso
astray, adj. y adv. extraviado, descaminado; **to lead astray,** desviar, seducir
astringent, adi. astringente
astronomy, n. astronomía, f.
astute, adj. astuto; aleve
asylum, n. asilo, refugio, m.; **insane asylum,** manicomio, m.
at, prep. a, en; **at once,** al instante; **at last,** al fin, por último
ate, pretérito del verbo **eat**
athlete, n. atleta, m. y f.
athletics, n. pl. deportes. m.

pl.
Atlantic, *n.* y *adj.* Atlántico
atmosphere, *n.* atmósfera, *f.,* ambiente, *m.*
atom, *n.* átomo, *m.;* **atom bomb,** bomba atómica
atomic, *adj.* atómico
atomizer, *n.* pulverizador, *m.*
atone, *vt.* expiar, pagar
attach, *vt.* prender; juntar, adherir; embargar
attachment, *n.* anexo, *m.*
attack, *vt.* atacar; *n.* ataque, *m.*
attain, *vt.* obtener, alcanzar
attempt, *vt.* probar, experimentar; procurar; *n.* tentative, *f.;* prueba, *f.*
attend, *vt.* asistir; *vi.* prestar atención
attendance, *n.* asistencia, *f.*
attention, *n.* atención,
attest, *vt.* atestiguar; dar fe
attire, *n.* atavío, *m.; vt.* adornar, ataviar
attitude, *n.* actitud, *f.*
attorney, *n.* abogado, *m.*
attract, *vt.* atraer
attraction, *n.* atracción, *f.,* atractivo, *m.*
attractive, *adj.* atractivo, seductor
attribute, *vt.* atribuir, imputar; *n.* atributo, *m.*
auburn, *adj.* y *n.* castaño rojizo
auction, *n.* subasta, *f.,* remate, *m.*
audacious, *adj.* audaz, temerario
audience, *n.* audiencia, *f.;* auditorio, *m.;* concurrencia, *f.*
audition, *n.* audición, *f.; vt.* conceder audición; *vi.* presentar audición
auditor, *n.* contador, *m.*
audio-visual, *adj.* audio-visual
August, *n.* agosto (mes), *m.*
aunt, *n.* tía.
auspices *n. pl.* auspicio, *m.;* protección
austere, *adj.* austero
austerity, *n.* austeridad, crueldad, severidad, *f.*

authentic, *adj.* auténtico
author, *n.* autor, escritor, *m.*
authority, *n.* autoridad, *f.*
authorization, *n.* autorización, *f.*
authorize, *vt.* autorizar
autobiography, *n.* autobiografía, *f.*
auto, *n.* auto, *m.*
autograph, *n.* y *adj.* autógrafo, *m.*
automate, *vt.* automatizar
automatic, *adj.* automático
automobile, *n.* automóvil, *m.*
autumn, *n.* otoño, *m.*
auxiliary, *adj.* auxiliar, asistente
avail, *vt.* aprovechar; *vi.* servir, ser ventajoso; *n.* provecho, *m.*
ave., avenue, av. avenida
avenue, *n.* avenida, *f.*
average, *n.* término medio, promedio, *m.; adj.* medio, mediano, común y corriente
aviation, *n.* aviación, *f.*
aviator, *n.* aviador, *m.*
avocado, *n.* aguacate, *m.*
avocation, *n.* diversión, afición, *f.*
avoid, *vt.* evitar, escapar
await, *vt.* aguardar; **awaiting your reply,** en espera de sus noticias
awake, *vt.* y *vi.* despertar; *adj.* despierto
award, *vt.* otorgar, adjudicar; *n.* premio, *m.,* adjudicación, *f.*
aware, *adj.* enterado; consciente
away, *adv.* ausente, fuera
awe, *n.* miedo, pavor, *m.;* temor reverencial, *m.*
awhile, *adv.* por un rato
awkward, *adj.* tosco, torpe
awning, *n.* toldo, *m.*
ax, axe, *n.* segur, *f.;* hacha, *f.*
axis, *n.* eje, *m.;* alianza, *f.*
axle, *n.* eje de una rueda
aye, ay, *adv.* sí

B

B.A., Bachelor of Arts, Br.

Bachiller
babe, *n.* nene, bebé, *m.*
baby, *n.* nene, infante, *m.*
baby-sit, *vi.* servir de niñera
bachelor, *n.* soltero, *m.*; bachiller, *m.*
back, *n.* dorso, *m.*; espalda, *f.*; lomo, *m.*; *adj.* posterior;*vt.* sostener, apoyar; *adv.* atrás, detrás
backbone, *n.* espinazo, *m.*, espina dorsal *f.*
background, *n.* fondo, *m.*; ambiente, *m.*; antecedentes, *m. pl.*; educación, *f.*
backlash, *n.* reacción, *f.*
backup, *n.* (mil.) apoyo, *m.*; (com.) acumulación, congestión, *f.*; *adj.* suplente
backward, *adj.* retrógrado; **backwards,** *adv.* hacia atrás
bacon, *n.* tocino, *m.*
bacteria, *n. pl.* bacterias, *f. pl.*
badge, *n.*divisa, *f.*
baffle, *vt.* eludir; confundir
bag, *n.* saco, *m.*; bolsa, *f.*
baggage, *n.* equipaje, *m.*
bail, *n.* fianza, *f.*; fiador, *m.*; **to go bail for,** salir fiador
bait, *vt.* cebar; atraer; *n.* carnada, *f.*
bake, *vt.* cocer en horno
baker, *n.* panadero, *m.*
bakery, *n.* panadería, *f.*
balance, *n.* equilibria *m.*; resto, *m.*; balance, *m.*; saldo, *m.*; *vt.* equilibrar; saldar; considerar
balcony, *n.* balcón, *m.*; galería, *f.*
bald, *adj.* calvo
bale, *n.* bala, *f.*; paca, *f.*; *vt.* embalar
balk, *vi.* rebelarse (un caballo, etc.)
ball, *n.* bola, *f.*; pelota, *f.*; baile, *m.*
ballad, *n.* balada, *f.*; romance, *m.*
ballet, *n.* ballet, *m.*
ballot, *n.* balota, papeleta, *f.*
ballroom, *n.* salón de baile, *m.*
balm, *n.* bálsamo, *m.*
bamboo, *n.* bambú, *m.*
ban, *n.* edicto, *m.*; prohibición,

f.; *vt.* prohibir; excomulgar
banana, *n.* plátano, *m.*
band, *n.* venda, faja, *f.*; cuadrilla, *f.*; banda, *f.*; orquesta, *vt.* unir, juntar
bandage, *n.* venda, *f.*; vendaje, *m.*; *vt.* vendar
bandit, *n.* bandido, bandida
bane, *n.* veneno, *m.*; calamidad, *f.*
banish, *vt.* desterrar
banister, *n.* pasamano, *m.*
bank, *n.* orilla (de rio), ribera, *f.*; montón de tierra; banco, *m.*; **savings bank,** banco de ahorros; *vt.* poner dinero en un banco
banker, *n.* banquero, *m.*
banking, *n.* banca, *f.*; *adj.* bancario
bankrupt, *adj.* quebrado, en bancarrota
banner, *n.* bandera, estandarte, *m.*
banquet, *n.* banquete, *m.*
baptism, *n.* bautismo, bautizo, *m.*
baptize, *vt.* bautizar
bar, *n.* barra, *f.*; foro, *m.*; obstáculo, *m.*; cantina, *f.*; *vt.* impedir; excluir; **bars,** rejas, *f. pl.*
barbaric, *adj.* bárbaro, cruel, fiero
barbecue, *n.* barbacoa, *f.*
barbell, *n.* haltera, *f.*
barber, *n.* barbero, peluquero, *m.*
barbershop, *n.* peluquería, barbería, *f.*
bare, *adj.* desnudo, descubierto; simple; *vt.* desnudar, descubrir
barefoot, *adj.* descalzo
barely, *adv.* apenas
bargain, *n.* ganga, *f.*; *vi.* regatear
barge, *n.* chalupa, *f.*
baritone, *n.* barítono, *m.*
bark, *n.* corteza, *f.*; ladrido, *m.*; *vi.* ladrar
barley, *n.* cebada, *f.*
barn, *n.* granero, establo, *m.*
barnyard, *n.* corral, *m.*
barometer, *n.* barómetro, *m.*

barrack, n. cuartel, m.; barraca, f.

barrel, n. barril, m.; cañón de escopeta, m.

barren, adj. estéril; seco

barrier, n. barrera, f.

bartender, n. cantinero, m.

barter, vt. cambiar, trocar

base, n. fondo, m.; base, f.; contrabajo, m.; vt. apoyar; basar; adj. bajo, vil

baseball, n. baseball, beisbol, m.; pelota de baseball

basement, n. sótano, m.

bashful, adj. vergonzoso

basic, adj. fundamental

basis, n. base, f.

basket, n. cesta, canasta, f.

basketball, n. baloncesto, m.; juego de balón, m.

bass, n. (mus.) contrabajo, m.; bajo, m.; (zool.) lobina, f., róbalo or robalo, m.; adj. bajo; **bass viol,** violonchelo, m.

bassinet, n. cesta-cuna, f.

basso, n. (mus.) bajo, m.

bastard, n. y adj. bastardo, bastarda

baste, vt. pringar la carne; hilvanar

bat, n. (baseball) bate, m.; murciélago, m.

batch, n. hornada, f.; conjunto, m.

bath, n. baño, m.

bathe, vt. y vi. bañar, bañarse

bathrobe, n. bata de baño, f.

bathroom, n. cuarto de baño,

bathtub, n. bañera, f.; tina de baño, f.

baton, n. batuta, f.

battalion, n. batallón, m.

batter, n. pasta culinaria, f.; (baseball) bateador, m.

battery, n. acumulador, m.

battle, n. batalla, f.

bawl, vi. gritar, vocear; chillar

bay, n. bahía, f.

bazaar, n. bazar, m.

bbl., barrel, brl., barril

B. C., Before Christ, A. de J.C., antes de Jesuscristo

beach, n. playa, f.

beacon, n. faro, m.

bead, n. cuenta, chaquira, f.

beak, n. rayo de luz, m.; vi. brillar

bean, n. (bot.) haba, habichuela, f.; frijol, m.

bear, n. oso, m.; vt. soportar; parir; **to bear in mind,** tener presente

bearer, n. portador, portadora

bearing, n. comportamiento, m.; relación, f.

beast, n. bestia, f.

beastly, adj. bestial, brutal

beat, vt. golpear; batir; ganar (en un juigo); vi. pulsar, palpitar; n. pulsación, f.; (mus) compás, m.

beater, n. batidor, m.

beautiful, adj. hermoso, hello

beautify, vt. embellecer

beauty, n. hermosura, belleza, f.; beauty parlor, salón de belleza, m.

beck, n. seña, f.; **at one's beck and call,** a la mano, a la disposición

beckon, vi. llamar con señas

become, vt. sentar, quedar bien; vi. hacerse, convertirse; llegar a ser

becoming, adj. que sienta o cae bien; decoroso

bed, n. cama

bedclothes, n. pl. cobertores, m. pl.; mantas, colchas, f. pl.

bedding, n. ropa de cama, f.

bedridden, adj. postrado en cama

bedroom, n. dormitorio, m.

bedspread, n. sobrecama, f.

bee, n. abeja, f.

beech, n. (bot.) haya, f.

beef, n. carne de res, f.

beefsteak, n. biftec, bistec, m.

beehive, n. colmena, f.

been, p. p. del verbo **be**

beer, n. cerveza, f.

beet, n. remolacha, betarraga, f.; (Mex.) betabel, m.

beetle, n. escarabajo, m.

befall, vi. sobrevenir

before, adv. más adelante; prep. antes de, ante; conj. antes que

beforehand, adv. de antemano

beg, *vt.* mendigar, pedir

began, *pretérito* del verbo **begin**

beggar, *n.* mendigo, mendiga; limosnero, limosnera

begin, *vt.* y *vi.* comenzar, principiar

beginning, *n.* principio, comienzo, *m.*

begun, *p. p.* del verbo begin

behalf, *n.* favor, patrocinio, *m.*; **in behalf of,** en pro de

behave, *vi.* comportarse

behavior, *n.* comportamiento, *m.*

behind, *prep.* detrás; atrás; *adv.* atrás

behold, *vt.* ver, contemplar

beige, *n.* color arena, *m.*

being, *n.* ser, *m.*; existencia, *f.*

belated, *adj.* atrasado

belch, *vi.* eructar (or erutar

Belgium, Bélgica

believe, *vt.* y *vi.* creer; pensar

bell, *n.* campana, *f.*; timbre, m.

bellow, *vi.* bramar; rugir

bellows, *n.* fuelle, *m.*

belly, *n.* vientre, *m.*; panza, barriga, *f.*

belong, *vi.* pertenecer

belongings, *n. pl.* propiedad, *f.*; efectos, *m. pl.*

beloved, *adj.* querido, amado

below, *adv.* y *prep.* debajo, inferior; abajo

belt, *n.* cinturón, *m.*; correa, *f.*

bend, *vt.* doblar, plegar; *vi.* inclinarse

beneath, *adv.* y *prep.* debajo, abajo

benediction, *n.* bendición, *f.*

benefactor, *n.* bienhechor, bienhechora

beneficial, *adj.* beneficioso, útil

beneficiary, *n.* beneficiario, beneficiaria

benefit, *n.* beneficio, *m.*; utilidad, *f.*; provecho, *m.*; *vt.* y *vi.* beneficiar

benevolent, *adj.* benévolo

bequest, *n.* legado, *m.*

bereavement, *n.* luto, duelo, *m.*

beret, *n.* boina, *f.*

berry, *n.* baya, *f.*

berth, *n.* litera, *f.*; camarote, *m.*

beseech, *vt.* suplicar, rogar

beside, besides, *prep.* al lado de; fuera de; *adv.* además

best, *adj.* y *adv.* mejor; **best man,** padrino de boda

bestow, *vt.* otorgar

bet, *n.* apuesta, *f.*; apostar

betatron, *n.* betatrón

betray, *vt.* traicionar; divulgar (algún secreto)

betrothed, *adj.* comprometido, prometido; *n.* prometido, prometida

better, *adj.* y *adv.* mejor; *vt.* mejorar; **betters,** *n. pl.* superiores, *m. pl.*

beverage, *n.* bebida, *f.*

bewail, *vt.* y *vi.* lamentar, deplorar

beware, *vi.* tener cuidado

bewilder, *vt.*, *vi.* turbar; confundirse

beyond, *prep.* más allá; fuera de

bias, *n.* parcialidad, *f.*; sesgo, *m.*; **on the bias,** al sesgo; *vt.* inclinar, influir

biased, *adj.* predispuesto

bib, *n.* babero, *m.*

Bible, *n.* Biblia, *f.*

bicker, *vi.* reñir, disputar

bicycle, *n.* bicicleta, *f.*

bid, *vt.* convidar; mandar, ordenar; ofrecer; *n.* licitación, oferta *f.*

bide, *vi.* esperar, aguardar

biennial, *adj.* bienal

big, *adj.* grande

bile, *n.* bilis, *f.*; cólera, *f.*

bilingual, *adj.* bilingüe

bill, *n.* pico de ave, *m.*; cuenta, *f.*; factura, *f.*; **bill of fare,** menú, *m.*; *vt.* facturar; *vi.* arrullar

billfold, *n.* billetera, *f.*

billiards, *n.* billar, *m.*

billion, *n.* billón, *m.*, millón de millones (en España, Inglaterra, y Alemania); mil millones (en Francia y los Estados Unidos)

bimonthly, *adj.* bimestral

bind, *vt.* atar; unir; encuadernar; obligar; *vi.* ser obligatorio

binder, *n.* encuadernador, *m.*

binding, *n.* venda, fala, *f.*; encuademación, *f.*

binoculars, *n. pl.* gemelos, binóculos, *m. pl.*

bioastronautics, *n. pl.* bioastronáutica, *f.*

biochemical, *adj.* bioquímico

biodegradable, *adj.* biodegradable, hecho de compuestos que se descomponen por bacterias

biography, *n.* biografía, *f.*

biology, *n.* biología, *f.*

biopsy, *n.* biopsia, *f.*

biosphere, *n.* biosfera, *f.*

birch, *n.* (bot.) abedul, *m.*

bird, *n.* ave, *f.*; pájaro, *m.*

birth, *n.* nacimiento, *m.*; origen, *m.*; parto, *m.*; linaje, *m.*; **to give birth**, dar a luz, parir

birthday, *n.* cumpleaños, natalicio, *m.*; **to have a birthday**, cumplir años

birthmark, *n.* lunar, *m.*

birthplace, *n.* lugar de naci miento, *m.*

biscuit, *n.* galleta

bishop, *n.* obispo, *m.*; alfil (en el ajedrez), *m.*

bit, *n.* pedacito, *m.*; **two bits** (coll. E.U.A.), 25¢ (moneda de E.U.A.); *pretérito* del verbo **bite**

bite, *vt.* morder; *n.* mordida, *f.*; tentempié, *m.*

bitten, *p. p.* del verbo **bite**

bitter, *adj.* amargo

bitterness, *n.* amargor, *m.*; amargura, *f.*

biweekly, *adj.* quincenal; *adv.* quincenalmente

B/L, b.l., bill of lading, conto., conocimiento de embarque

blab, *vt., vi.* charlar, divulgar; chismear

black, *adj.* negro; oscuro; *n.* negro, *m.*

blackberry, *n.* zarzamora, mora, *f.*

blackboard, *n.* pizarra, *f.*; en-

cerado, pizarrón, tablero, *m.*

blacksmith, *n.* herrero, *m.*

bladder, *n.* vejiga, *f.*

blade, *n.* brizna, hoja, *f.*

blame, *vt.* culpar

blameless, *adj.* inocente, intachable

bland, *adj.* blando, suave

blank, *adj.* en blanco; **blank form**, blanco, esqueleto, *m.*; *n.* blanco, espacio en blanco, *m.*

blanket, *n.* frazada, manta, *f.*; *adj.* general

blasé, *adj.* abúlico

blast, *n.* explosión, *f.*; chorro, *m.*; **blast furnace**, alto horno, *m.*

blaze, *n.* fuerg *m.*; incendio, *m.*; hoguera, *f.*; *vi.* resplandecer

bleach, *vt., vi.* blanquear

bleat, *n.* balido, *m.*; *vi.* balar

bled, *pretérito* y *p. p.* del verbo **bleed**

bleed, *vt., vi.* sangrar

blemish, *vt.* manchar; infamar; *n.* tacha, *f.*; infamia, *f.*; lunar, *m.*

blend, *vt.* mezclar, combinar; *vi.* armonizar; *n.* mezcla, *f.*; ammonía, *f.*

bless, *vt.* bendecir, santiguar

blessing, *n.* bendición, *f.*

blind, *adj.* ciego; oculto; *vt.* cegar; deslumbrar; *n.* subterfugio, *m.*; **Venetian blinds**, persianas

blindfold, *vt.* vendar los ojos

bink, *vi.* guiñar, parpadear

bliss, *n.* felicidad, *f.*; embeleso, *m.*

blister, *n.* vejiga, ampolla, *f.*; *vi.* ampollarse

bloat, *vi.* abotagarse

bloc, *n.* bloque, *m.*

block, *n.* bloque, *m.*; obstáculo, *m.*; manzana (de una calle), *f.*; *vi.* bloquear

blond, blonde, *n.* y *adj.* rubio, bia; (Mex.) güero, güera

blood, *n.* sangre, *f.*

blood bank, *n.* banco de sangre, *m.*

bloody, *adj.* sangriento

bloom, n. flor, f.; florecimiento, m.; vi. florecér

blossom, n. flor, f.; capullo, botón, m.; vi. florecer

blot, vt. manchar (lo escrito); cancelar; n. mancha, f.

blotter, n. papel secante, m.

blouse n. blusa, f.

blow, n. golpe, m.; vi. soplar, sonar; vt. soplar; inflar

blowout, n. reventazón, f.; (auto.) ruptura de neumático o llanta

blue, adj. azul, celeste

bluebird, n. (orn.) azulejo, m.

blues, n. pl. (coll.) melancolía, f.; tipo de jazz melancólico

bluff. n. risco escarpado, morro, m.; fanfarronada, f.; vi. engañar, hacer alarde

bluing, blueing, n. añil, m.

blunder, n. desatino, disparate, m.; vt. y vi. desatinar, equivocarse

blur, n. mancha, f.; vt. manchar; infamar

blvd., boulevard, bulevar, m.

boar, n. verraco, m.; **wild boar,** jabalí, m.

board, n. tabla, f.; mesa, f.; (naut.) bordo, m.; **board of directors,** directorio, m., junta directiva, f.;vt.abordar; entablar; vi. residir en casa de huéspedes; recibir huéspedes

boardinghouse, n. casa de huéspedes, pensión, f.

boast, n. jactancia, ostentación, f.; vi. presumir; jactarse

boastful. adj. iactancioso

boat, n. barco, m., embarcación, f.; barca, f.

bob, vi. menearse

bobby pin, n. horquilla, f.

bode, vt. y vi. presagiar

bodily, adj. y adv. corpóreo; en peso

body, n. cuerpo, m.; individuo, m.; gremio, m.

bodyguard, n. (mil.) guardaespaldas, m.

boil, vi. hervir, bullir; vt. cocer; n. (med.) nacido, m.

boiler, n. caldera, f.

boisterous, adj. ruidoso

bold, adj. audaz

bolt, n. tornillo, m.; cerrojo, m.

bom n. bomba, f.

bond, n. vínculo, lazo, m.; (com.) bono, m.

bone, n. hueso, m.; vt. deshuesar

boneless, adj. sin huesos, deshuesado

bonfire, n. hoguera, fogata, f.

bonnet, n. gorra, f.; bonete, m.

bony, adj. huesudo

boob, booby, n. tonto, tonta

book, n. libro, m.; vt. asentar en un libro, inscribir

bookcase, n. librero, m.

bookkeeper, n. tenedor de libros, m.

booklet, n. folleto, m.

bookstore, n. librería, f.

boom, n. estampido, m.; auge industrial, m.

boon, n. favor, m.

boost, vt. levantar; vi. aprobar con entusiasmo; n. ayuda, f., empuje, m.

boot, n. bota, f.; **to boot,** además, por añadidura

bootblack, n. limpiabotas, m.

booth, n. puesto, m.; cabina, f.; reservado, m.

bootlegger, n. contrabandista (usualmente de licores), m.

booty, n. botín, m.; presa, f.; saqueo, m.

border, n. orilla, f.; borde, m.; frontera, f.; vi. confinar; bordear

borderline, n. límite, m., orilla, f.; adj. incierto

boric, adj. bórico; **boric acid,** ácido bórico

boring, adj. fastidioso, latoso

born, adj. nacido; destinado; **to be born,** nacer

borne, p. p. del verbo **bear**

borrow, vt. pedir prestado

bosom, n. seno, pecho, m.

botanical, adj. botátnico

botany, n. botánica, f.

both, pron. y adj. ambos, ambas

bother, vt. molestar; incomodar; n. estorbo, m.; molestia, f.

bottle, *n.* botella, *f.*; *vt.* embotellar

bottleneck, *n.* cuello de botella, *m.*; cuello de estrangulación, *m.*

bottom, *n.* fondo, *m.*

bottomless, *adj.* insondable; sin fondo

boudoir, *n.* tocador, *m.*, recámara, *f.*

bough, *n.* rama (de un árbol), *f.*

bought, *pretérito* y *p. p.* del verbo **buy**

bouillon, *n.* caldo, *m.*

boulevard, *n.* paseo, bulevar, *m.*

bounce, *vi.* arremeter, brincar

bouncing, *adj.* fuerte, robusto

bound, *n.* límite, *m.*; salto, *m.*; *vt.* confinar, limitar; *vi.* brincar; *pretérito* y *p. p.* del verbo **bind**; *adj.* destinado; **bound for**, con rumbo

boundary, *n.* límite, *m.*; frontera, *f.*

boundless, *adj.* ilimitado, infinito

bouquet, *n.* ramillete de flores, ramo, *m.*

bout, *n.* encuentro, combate, *m.*

bow, *vi.* encorvarse; hacer reverencia; *n.* reverencia, inclinación, *f.*

bow, *n.* arco, *m.*; lazo (de cinta, etc.), *m.*; (naut.) proa, *f.*

bowels, *n. pl.* intestinos, *m. pl.*; entrañas, *f. pl.*

bowl, *n.* taza, *f.*; **wash bowl**, lavamanos, *m.*; *vi.* jugar boliche o bolos

bowlegged, *adj.* patizambo

box, *n.* caja, *f.*; cofre, *m.*; **box office**, taquilla, *f.*; *vi.* boxear

boxer, *n.* boxeador, pugilista, *m.*

boxing, *n.* boxeo, pugilato, *m.*

boy, *n.* muchacho, *m.*; niño, *m.*; **boy scout**, muchacho explorador, *m.*

boycott, *n.* boicot, boicoteo, *m.*

boyhood, *n.* niñez (varones), *f.*

boyish, *adj.* pueril, propio de un niño varón

bra, *n.* brassière, *m.*, soporte (para senos), *m.*

bracelet, *n.* brazalete, *m.*, pulsera, *f.*

bracket, *n.* ménsula, *f.*; (fig.) categoría, *f.*; **brackets**, *pl.* (print.) corchetes, *m. pl.*

brag, *n.* jactancia, *f.*; *vi.* jactarse

brain, *n.* cerebro, *m.*

brake, *n.* freno, *m.*

branch, *n.* rama (de árbol), *f.*

brand, *n.* marca, *f.*; nota de infamia, *f.*; marca de fíbrica, *f.*; *vt.* herrar (ganado); infamar

brandy, aguardiente, *m.*; coñac, *m.*

brass, *n.* latión, bronce, *m.*

brave, *adj.* valiente

brawl, *n.* pelotera, *f.*

bray, *vi.* rebuznar; *n.* rebuzno (del asno), *m.*

breach, *n.* rotura, brecha, *f.*; violación, *f.*

bread, *n.* pan, *m.*

break, *vt.* y *vi.* quebrar; violar; *n.* rotura, *f.*; intrrrupción, *f.*

break-even point, *n.* punto en que un negocio empieza a cubrir los gastos que ocasiona

breakfast, *n.* almuerzo, desayuno, *m.*

breast, *n.* pecho, seno, *m.*; tetas, *f. pl.*

breath, *n.* aliento, *m.*, respiración, *f.*; soplo (de aire), *m.*

breathe, *vt.* y *vi.* respirar; resollar

breathing, *n.* respiración, *f.*

breathless, *adj.* falto de aliento

bred, *pretérito* y *p. p.* del verbo **breed**; **well bred**, bien educado, de buenos modales

breech, *n.* trasero, *m.*

breeches, *n. pl.* calzones, *m. pl.*

breed, *n.* casta, raza, *f.*; *vt.* procrear, engendrar; educar

breeder reactor, *n.* reactor reproductor, *m.*

breeding, *n.* crianza, *f.*; moda-

les, *m. pl.*
breeze, *n.* brisa, *f.*
brewery, *n.* cervecería, *f.*
bribe, *n.* cohecho, soborno, *m.*; *vt.* sobornar
brick, *n.* ladrillo, *m.*
bricklayer, *n.* albañil, *m.*
bridal, *adj.* nupcial
bride, *n.* novia, desposada, *f.*
bridegroom, *n.* novio, desposado, *m.*
bridesmaid, *n.* madrina de boda, *f.*
bridge, *n.* puente, *m.*
bridgework, *n.* puente dental, *m.*
bridle, *n.* brida, *f.*, freno, *m.*; *vt.* embridar; reprimir, refrenar
brief, *adj.* breve, sucinto; *n.* compendio *m.*; (law) escrito, *m.*; **brief case,** portapapeles, *m.*
brig, *n.* bergantín, *m.*
bright, *adj.* claro, brillante; vivo
brighten, *vt.* pulir, dar lustre; *vi.* aclarar
brightness, *n.* esplendor, *m.*, brillantez, *f.*
brilliance, brilliancy, *n.* brillantez, *f.*, brillo, esplendor, *m.*
brilliant, *adj.* brillante; luminoso; resplandeciente; *n.* brillante, *m.*
brim, *n.* borde, extremo *m.*; orilla, *f.*; ala (de sombrero), *f.*
bring, *vt.* llevar, traer; **to bring about,** efectuar; **to bring up,** educar
brink, *n.* orilla, *f.*; margen, *m.* y *f.*, borde, *m.*
broad, *adj.* ancho; **broad jump,** salto de longitud, *m.*
broadcast, *n.* radiodifusión, *f.*; *vt.* radiodifundir, perifonear
broaden, *vi.* ensancharse
broad-minded, *adj.* tolerante
broil, *vt.* asar (carne, etc.)
broiler, *n.* parrilla, *f.*
broke, *pretérito* del verbo **break**; *adj.* (coll.) en bancarrota; sin dinero
broken, *adj.* roto, quebrado

broker, *n.* corredor, agente, *m.*
bronchitis, *n.* bronquitis, *f.*
brooch, *n.* broche, *m.*
brood, *n.* cría, nidada, *f.*
brook, *n.* arroyo, *m.*, quebrada, *f.*
broom, *n.* escoba, *f.*
broth, *n.* caldo, *m.*
brother, *n.* hermano, *m.*
brotherhood, *n.* hermandad; fraternidad, *f.*
brother-in-law, *n.* cuñado, *m.*
brotherly, *adj.* fraternal
brought, *pretérito y p. p.* del verbo **bring**
brow, *n.* ceja , *f.*; frente, *f.*
brown, *adj.* castaño, pardo; *vt.* dorar, tostar
bruise, *vt.* magullar; *n.* magulladura, contusión, *f.*
brunet, brunette, *n., adj.* trigueño, trigueña, moreno, morena
brush, *n.* escobilla, *f.*; brocha, *f.*; cepillo, *m.*; *vt.* acepillar
brutal, *adj.* brutal, bruto
brute, *n.* bruto, *m.*; *adj.* feroz, bestial
B.S., Bachelor of Science, Br. en C., Bachiller en Ciencias
bu., bushel, medida de áridos (Ingl. 36.37 litros; E.U. 35.28 litros)
bubble, *n.* burbuja, *f.*; *vi.* bullir; **bubble over,** borbotar; hervir
buckle, *n.* hebilla, *f.*; *vt.* afianzar
bud, *n.* pimpollo, botón, *m.*; capullo, *m.*
buddy, *n.* hermano, compañero, muchachito, *m.*
budget, *n.* presupuesto, *m.*
buffalo, *n.* búfalo, *m.*
buffers, *n. pl.* (rail.) parachoques, *m. pl.*
buffet, *n.* aparador, *m.*; ambigú, *m.*
bug, *n.* insecto, *m.*
bugle, *n.* clarín, *m.*; corneta, *f.*
bugler, *n.* corneta, trompetero, *m.*
build, *vt.* edificar; construir
builder, *n.* arquitecto, constructor, *m.*

building, *n.* edificio, *m.*; construcción, *f.*

bulb, *n.* bulbo, *m.*; **electric light bulb**, foco o bombilla de luz eléctrica

bulge, *vi.* combarse

bulk, *n.* masa, *f.*; bulto, volumen, *m.*; **in bulk**, a granel

bull, *n.* toro, *m.*

bulldog, *n.* bulldog, *m.*

bulldoze, *vt.* intimidar

bullet, *n.* bala, *f.*

bulletin, *n.* boletín, *m.*; **bulletin board**, tablilla para noticias, *f.*

bulletproof, *adj.* a prueba de bala

bullfight, *n.* corrida de toros, *f.*

bullfighter, *n.* torero, toreador, *m.*

bully, *n.* valentón, *m.*; rufián, *m.*; *vi.* fanfarronear

bulwark, *n.* baluarte, *m.*; *vt.* fortificar

bum, *n.* hombre vago, *m.*

bumblebee, *n.* abejón, abejorro, zángano, *m.*

bump, *n.* hinchazón, *f.*; golpe, *m.*; *vt.* y *vi.* chocar contra

bumper, *n.* amortiguador de golpes, *m.*; (auto) defensa, *f.*

bunch, *n.* ramo, racimo, *m.*

bundle, *n.* haz (de leña, etc.), *m.*; bulto, *m.*; *vt.* atar, hacer un lío o un bulto; **bundle up**, envolver; abrigarse

bunion, *n.* juanete, *m.*

bunk, *n.* (coll.) cama, *f.*; patraña, *f.*

buoy, *n.* boya, *f.*

burden, *n.* carga, *f.*, cargo, *m.*; *vt.* cargar; gravar

bureau, *n.* armario, *m.*; tocador, *m.*, cómoda, *f.*, oficina, *f.*; departamento, *m.*

burglar, *n.* ladrón, *m.*

burial, *n.* entierro, *m.*

burlap, *n.* arpillera, *f.*

burlesque, *adj.* burlesco; *vt.* y *vi.* burlarse; parodiar

burn, *vt.* quemar, incendiar; *vi.* arder; *n.* quemadura, *f.*

burst, *vi.* reventar; abrirse; *n.* reventón, *m.*

bury, *vt.* enterrar, sepultar

bus, *n.* ómnibus, camión, *m.*

bushel, *n.* medida de áridos (Ingl. 36.37 litros; E.U. 35.28 litros)

business, *n.* negocio, *m.*, ocupación, *f.*

businessman, *n.* comerciante, *m.*

businesswoman, *n.* mujer de negocios

bust, *n.* busto, *m.*

bustle, *n.* confusión, *f.*; ruido, *m.*

busy, *adj.* ocupado; atareado

busybody, *n.* entremetido, entremetida

but, *prep.* excepto; *conj.* y *adv.* menos; pero; solamente

butcher, *n.* carnicero, *m.*; *vt.* matar atrozmente

butt, *n.* cabezada (golpe de la cabeza), *f.*; colilla (de cigarro), *f.*

butter, *n.* mantequilla, manteca, *f.*

butterfly, *n.* mariposa, *f.*

buttermilk, *n.* suero de mantequilla, *m.*; (Mex.) jocoqui, *m.*

butterscotch, *n.* especie de dulce de azúcar y mantequilla

buttock, *n.* nalga, *f.*; anca, *f.*

button, *n.* botón, *m.*; *vt.* abotonar

buttonhole, *n.* ojal, *m.*

buxom, *adj.* robusto y rollizo

buy, *vt.* comprar

buzz, *n.* susurro, soplo, *m.*; *vi.* zumbar, cuchichear

buzzer, *n.* zumbador, *m.*

by, *prep.* por; a, en; de, con; al lado de, cerca de; *adv.* cerca, al lado de

bygone, *adj.* pasado

bylaws, *n. pl.* estatutos, *m. pl.*, reglamento, *m.*

by-pass, *n.* desviación, *f.*; *vt.* evadir, eludir

by-product, *n.* derivado, *m.*

C

C., centigrade, C., centigrado;

current, corrte., cte., corriente
C.A., Central America, C.A.
Centro América
cab, n. coche de plaza, coche
de alquiler, m.
cabdriver, n. cochero, m.;
(auto.) taxista, m. y f.
cabana, n. cabaña, f.
cabaret, n. cabaret, m.
cabbage, n. repollo, m.; berza,
col, f.
cabin, n. cabaña, cabina, barraca, f.; camarote, m.
cabinet, n. gabinete, m.; ministerio, m.
cabinetmaker, n. ebanista, m.
cable, n. cable, cablegrama, m.
cablegram, n. cablegrama, m.
cackle, vi. cacarear, graznar;
n. cacareo, m.; charla, f.
cactus, n. (bot.) cacto, m.
cad, n. sinvergüenza, m.
cadence, n. cadencia, f.
cadet, n. cadete, m.
café, n. café, restaurante, m.
cafeteria, n. restaurante en
donde se sirve uno mismo
cake, n. bollo, m.; torta, f.; bizcocho, pastel, m.; vi. endurecerse; coagularse
calamity, n. calamidad, miseria f.
calcimine, n. lechada, f.
calcium, n. calcio, m.
calculate, vt. calcular, contar
calendar, n. calendario, m.
calf, n. ternero, ternera; cuero
de ternero; **calf of the leg,**
pantorrilla, f.
calfskin, n. piel de ternera, f.;
becerro, m.
caliber, n. calibre, m.
calisthentics, n. pl. calisténica, gimnasia
call, vt. llamar nombrar; convocar, citar; n. llamada, f.;
vocación, profesión, f.
calling, n. profesión, vocación,
f.
callous, adj. calloso, endurecido; insensible
calm, n. calma, tranquilidad,
f.; vt. calmar; aplacar; **to
calm down,** serenar, sere-

narse
camera, n. cámara, f.
camouflage, n. (mil.) camufla-
ge, m., simulación, f., engaño, m.
camp, n. campamento, campo,
m.; vi. acampar
campaign, n. campaña, f.
campfire, n. hoguera en el
campo
camphor, n. alcanfor, m.
campus, n. patio o terrenos de
una universidad, etc
can, vi. poder, saber; vt. envasar en latas; n. lata, f., bote
de lata; **can opener,** abrelatas, m.
Canada, Canadá, m.
Canadian, n. y adj. canadiense
canal, n. canal, m.
Canal Zone, Zona del Canal, f.
Canaries, Canary Islands, Las
Canarias, Islas Canarias, f.
pl.
canary, n. canario, m.
canasta, n. canasta, f. (juego
de naipes)
cancel, vt. cancelar, borrar;
anular
cancer, n. cáncer, m.
candid, adj. cándido, ingenuo
candidate, n. candidato, candidata, aspirante (a un puesto, cargo, etc.), m. y f.
candied, adj. garapiñado, en
almíbar
candle, n. vela, bujía, f.
candlestick, n. candelero, m.
candy, n. confite, bombón,
dulce, m.
cane, n. caña, f.; bastón, m.
cannibal, n. caníbal, m., an-
tropófago, antropófaga
cannon, n. cañón, m.
canoe, n. canoa, f.; bote, m.;
(Mex.) chalupa, f.; piragua, f.
canonize, vt. canonizar
cantaloupe, n. melón de verano, m.
canteen, n. (mil.) cantina, f.,
especie de tienda de provisio-
nes para soldados; cantim-
plora, f.
canvas, n. lona

canvass, vi. solicitar votos, etc

canyon, n. desfiladero, cañon, m.

cap, n. goffa, f., cachucha, f.; **cap and gown,** traje académico o toga y birrete

cap., capital letter, may., letra mayúscula

capable, adj. capaz

capacity, n. capacidad, f.; inteligencia, habilidad, f.; **seating capacity,** cabida, f., cupo, m.

cape, n. cabo, m.; capa, f.; capota, f.; capote, m.

Cape Horn, Cabo de Hornos, m.

Cape of Good Hope, Cabo de Buena Esperanza, m.

caper, n. travesura, f.; alcaparra, f.

capital, adj. capital, excelente; principal; **capital punishment,** pena de muerte; n. (arch.) capitel, m.; capital (la ciudad principal), f.; capital, fondo, m.; mayuscula, f.

capitalist, n. capitalista, m. y f.

captain, n. capitán, m.

capricious, adj. caprichoso

capsize, vt., vr. volcar, volcarse

capt., Captain, cap., capitán

captain, n. capitán, m.

captivate, vt. cautivar

captive, n. cautivo, va, esclavo, esclava

capture, n. captura, f.; toma, f.; vt. apresar; capturar

car, n. carreta, f.; carro, m.; coche, m.

caravan, n. caravana, f.

carbon, n. carbón, m.; **carbon paper,** papel carbón

carburetor, n. carburador, m.

carcass, n. animal muerto, m.; casco, m.; armazón, m.

card, n. naipe, m., carta, f.; tarjeta, f.

cardinal, adj. cardinal, principal; rojo, purpurado; n. cardenal, m.; (orn.) cardenal, m.

care, n. cuidado, m.; cargo, m.; vigilancia, f.; vt. cuidar, tener cuidado

career, n. carrera, profesión, f.

carefree, adj. sin cuidados

careful, adj. cuidadoso, solícito

careless, adj. descuidado

caress, n. caricia, f.; vt. acariciar, halagar

caretaker, n. velador, m.

carfare, n. pasaje (de tranvía), m.

carnation, n. (bot.) clavel, m.

carnival, n. carnaval, m.

carol, n. villancico, m.

carpenter, n. carpintero, m.

carpet, n. tapiz, m.; **carpet sweeper,** barredor de alfombra, m.

carport, n. cobertizo para auto

carriage, n. porte, talante, m.; coche, carruaje, m.; cureña de cañón, f.

carrier, n. portador, carretero, m.; **aircraft carrier,** porta aviones, m.; **carrier pigeon,** paloma mensajera, f.

carrot, n. zanahoria,

carry, vt. llevar, conducir; portar; cargar; **to carry on,** continuar; **to carry out,** llevar a cabo, realizar

cart, n. carro, m.; carreta, f.; carretón, m.; vt. y vi. acarrear

cartload, n. carretada,

cartoon, n. caricatura, f.

cartridge, n. cartucho, m.; **cartridge shell,** cápsula, f.

carve, vt. cincelar; trinchar, tajar; grabar; vi. esculpir

case, n. estado, m.; situación, f.; caso, m.; estuche, m., caja, f.; (gram.) caso, m.

cash, n. dinero contante o efectivo; vt. cobrar o hacer effectivo (un cheque, etc.)

cashier, n. cajero, cajera

cashmere, n. casimir (tela), m.

cask, n. barril, tonel, m.

casket, n. ataúd, m.

casserole, n. cacerola, f.

cast, vt. tirar, lanzar; echar; modelar; n. tiro, golpe, m.; (theat.) reparto, m.; adj. fundido, **cast iron,** hierro colado; **cast steel,** acero fundido

castanets, n. pl. castañuelas, f. pl.

Castile, Castilla, f.

Castilian, n. y adj. castellano, castellana

castle, n. castillo, m.

castor, adj. descartado

castor, n. castor, m.; sombrero castor; **castor oil,** aceite de ricino, m.

casual, adj. casual, fortuito

casualty, n. casualidad, f.; acaso, accidente, m.; caso, m.; **casualties,** n. pl. victimas de accidentes o de guerra, etc

cat, n. gato, m., gata, **to let the cat out of the bag,** revelar un secreto

cat., catalog, catálogo; **catechism,** catecismo

catalogue, n. catálogo, m.

Catatonia, Cataluña, f.

Catalonian, n. y adj. catalán, catalana

cataract, n. cascada, catarata, f.; (med.) catarata, f.

catarrh, n. catarro, m.

catastrophe, n. catástrofe, f.

catch, vt. coger, agarrar; atrapar; vi. pegarse, ser contagioso; **to catch cold,** resfriarse; n. botín, m., presa, f.; captura, f.; trampa, f.

catcher, n. (bascball) parador de la pelota, m.

catching, adj. contagioso

catchy, adj. atrayente, pegajoso

catechism, n. catecismo, m.

category, n. categoría, f.

caterpillar, n. oruga, f.

cathartic, adj. (med.) catártico; n. purgante, laxante, m.

cathedral, n. catedral, f.

catholic, n. y adj. católico, católica

catholicism, catolicismo, m.

catsup, n. salsa de tomate, f.

cattle, n. ganado, m.

caught, pretérito y p. p. del verbo **catch**

cauliflower, n. coliflor, f.

cause, n. causa, f.; razón, f.; motivo, m.; vt. motivar, cau-

sar

caution, n. prudencia, precaución, f.; aviso, m.; vt. advertir

cautious, adj. prudente, cauto

cavalier, n. caballero, m.

cavalry, n. caballería,

cave, n. caverna, f.

cc., c.c., cubic centimeter, centímetro cúbico

C.E., Civil Engineer, Ing. Civil, Ingeniero Civil

cede, vt. ceder, trasferir

ceiling, n. techo o cielo raso, m.; (avi.) cielo máximo; adj. máximo

celebrate, vt. celebrar

celebration, n. celebración, f.

celebrity, n. celebridad, fama, f.; persona célebre

celestial, adj. celestial

cell, n. celda, f.; célula, f.

cellar, n. sótano, m., bodega, f.

cello, n. violonchelo, m.

cement, n. cemento, m.; vt. cimentar

cemetery, n. cementerio, m.

cen., cent., central, cent. central

censor, n. censor, m.; crítico, m.

censorship, n. censura, f.

censure, n. censura, represión, f.; vt. censurar, criticar

census, n. censo, encabezamicnto, m.

cent, n. centavo, m.; céntimo, m.; per por ciento

cent., centigrade, C. centigrado; **century,** siglo

centennial, n. y adj. centenario, m.

center, n. centro, m.; vt. centrar; reconcentrar; vi. colocarse en el centro, reconcentrarse

centigrade, adj. centígrado

centigram, n. centigramo, m.

centimeter, n. centímetro, m.

centipede, n. ciempiés, m.

central, adj. central; céntrico

Central America, América Central, f.

centralize, vt. centralizar

century, n. centuria, f.; siglo, m.

ceramics, *n.* cerámica, *f.*
cereal, *n.* cereal, *m.*
cerebral, *adj.* cerebral
ceremony, *n.* ceremonia,
certain, *adj.* cierto, evidente
certainty, *n.* certeza, seguridad, *f.*; certidumbre, *f.*
certificate, *n.* certificado, *m.*; (com.) bono, *m.*; certificación, *f.*
certified, *adj.* certificado
certify, *vt.* certificar, afirmar; dar fe
chagrin, *n.* mortificación, *f.*; disgusto, *m.*
chain, *n.* cadena, *f.*; serie, sucesión, *f.*; *vt.* encadenar
chair, *n.* silla
chairman, *n.* presidente (de una reunión o junta) *m.*
chalk, *n.* greda, *f.*; tiza, *f.*; yeso, *m.*
challenge, *n.* desafío, *m.*; *vt.* desafiar; retar
chamber, *n.* cámara, *f.*; aposento, *m.*
champagne, *n.* vino de Champaña, champaña, *m.*
champion, *n.* campeón, campeona
championship, *n.* campeonato, *m.*
chance, *n.* ventura, suerte, oportunidad, casualidad, *f.*, acaso, *m.*; riesgo, *m.*; **by chance,** si acaso; *vi.* acaecer, acontecer; *adj.* fortuito, casual
change, *vt.* cambiar; variar; *vi.* variar, alterarse; *n.* cambio, *m.*
channel, *n.* canal, *m.*; conducto, *m.*
chaos, *n.* caos, *m.*
chapel, *n.* capilla, *f.*
chaperon, *n.* dueña, *f.*; acompañante de respeto
chaplain, *n.* capellán, *m.*
chapter, *n.* capítulo, *m.*
character, *n.* carácter, *m.*; letra, *f.*; calidad, *f.*; (theat.) papel, *m.*; personaje, *m.*
characteristic, *adj.* característico; típico; *n.* rasgo, *m.* peculiaridad, *f.*

charge, *vt.* encargar, comisionar; cobrar; cargar; acusar, imputar; *n.* cargo, cuidado, *m.*; acusación, *f.*; costo, *m.*; ataque, *m.*
charity, *n.* caridad, beneficencia, *f.*
charm, *n.* encanto, *m.*; atractivo, *m.*; *vt.* encantar; seducir
charming, *adj.* seductor; simpático, encantador
charter, *n.* carta constitucional, *f.*; *vt.* fletar (un barco, etc.); estatuir; **charter member,** miembro o socio fundador, *m.*
chase, *vt.* cazar; perseguir; *n.* caza, *f.*
chaste, *adj.* casto; puro
chastise, *vt.* castigar
chastity, *n.* castidad, *f.*
chat, *vi.* charlar, platicar; *n.* plática, charla, conversación, *f.*
chauffeur, *n.* chofer, *m.*
cheap, *adj.* barato
cheapen, *vt.* abaratar; denigrar
cheat, *vt.* engañar, hacer trampa; *n.* trampista, trápala, *m. y f.*
check, *vt.* reprimir, refrenar; verificar, comprobar; *n.* cheque, *m.*; restrición, *f.*; freno, *m.*
checkers, *n.* juego de damas, *m.*
checkroom, *n.* guardarropa, *m.*
cheek, *n.* cachete, carrillo, *m.*, mejilla, *f.*
cheer, *n.* alegría, *f.*; *vt.* animar, alentar; *vi.* regocijarse
cheerful, *adj.* alegre, jovial
chef, *n.* cocinero, *m.*
chemical, *adj.* químico; *n.* sustancia química,
chemist, *n.* químico, química
chemistry, *n.* química, *f.*
cherish, *vt.* estimar
cherry, *n.* cereza, *f.*; *adj.* bermejo, rojo cereza
chess, *n.* juego de ajedrez, *m.*
chest, *n.* pecho, *m.*; cofre, *m.*; **chest of drawers,** cómoda, *f.*

chestnut, *n.* castaña, *adj.* castaño

chewing gum, *n.* chicle, *m.*

chick, *n.* pollito, polluelo, *m.*

chicken, *n.* pollo, *m.*; (fig.) joven, *m.* y *f.*; **chicken pox,** viruelas locas, varicela, *f.*

chief, *adj.* principal, capital; *n.* jefe, *m.*

child, *n.* niño, niña

childbirth, *n.* parto, alumbramiento, *m.*

childhood, *n.* infancia, niñez, *f.*

childish, *adj.* frívolo, pueril

children, *n. pl.* niños, *m. pl.*; hijos, *m. pl.*

Chilean, *n.* y *adj.* chileno, chilena

chill, *adj.* frío; *n.* frío, *m.*; escalofrío, *m.*; *vt.* enfriar; helar

chimney, *n.* chimenea, *f.*

chin, *n.* barba, *f.*

china, chinaware, *n.* porcelana, loza, *f.*

chintz, *n.* zaraza,

chip, *vi.* astillarse; *n.* astilla, *f.*; raspadura, *f.*

chirp, *m.* chirriar, gorjear; *n.* gorjeo, chirrido, *m.*

chisel, *n.* cincel, *m.*; *vt.* cincelar, grabar; (coll.) estafar, engañar

chivalrous, chivalric, *adj.* caballeroso

chivalry, *n.* caballería, *f.*; hazaña, *f.*

chives, *n.* cebolleta, *f.*

chlorine, *n.* cloro, *m.*

chloroform, *n.* cloroformo, *m.*

chocolate, *n.* chocolate, *m.*

choice, *n.* selección, *f.*; preferencia, *f.*; *adj.* selecto, escogido

choir, *n.* coro, *m.*

choose, *vt.* escoger, elegir

chop, *vt.* tajar, cortar; picar; *n.* chuleta, *f.*

choral, *adj.* coral

chord, *n.* (mus.) acorde, *m.*; cuerda, *f.*

chore, *n.* quehacer, *m.*; **chores,** *n. pl.* quehaceres de la casa, *m. pl.*

chorus, *n.* coro, *m.*

chose, *pretérito* del verbo **choose**

Christ, *n.* Jesucristo, Cristo, *m.*

christening, *n.* bautismo, bautizo, *m.*

Christian, *n.* y *adj.* cristiano, cristiana; **Christian name,** nombre de pila, *m.*

Christianity, *m.* cristianismo, *m.*

Christmas, *n.* Navidad, Pascua, *f.*; **Christmas gift,** aguinaldo, *m.*; **Christmas Eve,** Nochebuena, *f.*

chromium, *n.* cromo, *m.*

chronic, *adj.* crónico

chronicle, *n.* crónica, *f.*, informe, *m.*

chubby, *adj.* gordo, rechoncho

chuckle, *vi.* reírse entre dientes

chum, *n.* camarada, *m.* y *f.* compañero, compañera

church, *n.* iglesia, *f.*; templo, *m.*

C.I.F., c.i.f., cost, insurance and freight, c.s.f., costo, seguro y flete

cigar, *n.* cigarro, puro, *m.*

cigarette, *n.* cigarrillo, cigarro, *m.*

cinema, *n.* cinematógrafo, *m.*

CIO, C.I.O., Congress of Industrial Organizations, C.I.O., Congreso de Organizaciones Industriales (de E.U.A.)

cipher, *n.* cifra, *f.*, número, *m.*; cero, *m.*

circle, *n.* círculo, *m.*; rueda, *f.*; *vt.* circundar; cercar

circuit, *n.* circuito, *m.*

circular, *adj.* circular, redondo; *n.* carta circular, *f.*

circulate, *vi.* circular

circulation, *n.* circulación, *f.*

circumference, *n.* circunferencia, *f.*

circumstance, *n.* circunstancia, condición, *f.*; incidente, *m.*

circus, *n.* circo, *m.*

cite, *vt.* citar (a juicio); citar, referirse a

citizen, *n.* ciudadano, ciudadana

citizenship, *n.* ciudadanía, *f.*; nacionalidad, *f.*

citric, *adj.* cítrico

city, *n.* ciudad, *f.*; **city hall**, ayuntamiento, palacio municipal, *m.*

civic, *adj.* cívico; civics, *n.* instrucción cívica, *f.*

civil, *adj.* civil, cortés

civilian, *n.* particular, *m.*

civilization, *n.* civilización, *f.*

civilize, *vt.* civilizar

clad, *adj.* vestido, cubierto

claim, *vt.* reclamar; *n.* pretensión, *f.*; derecho, *m.*; reclamo, *m.*

clam, *n.* almeja, *f.*

clamorous, *adj.* clamoroso, estrepitoso

clamp, *n.* grapa, laña, *f.*; sujetador, *m.*; *vt.* sujetar, afianzar

clan, *n.* familia, tribu, *f.*

clandestine, *adj.* clandestino

clap, *vi.* palmotear, aplaudir

clapping, *n.* aplauso, palmoteo, *m.*

clarify, *vt.* y *vi.* clarificar, aclarar

clarinet, *n.* clarinete, *m.*

clash, *vi.* encontrarse; chocar; *n.* estrépito, *m.*; disputa, *f.*; choque, *m.*

clasp, *n.* broche, *m.*; hebilla, *f.*; sujetador, *m.*; abrazo, *m.*; *vt.* abrochar; abrazar

class, *n.* clase, *f.*; género, *m.*; categoría, *f.*

classic, *adj.* clásico; *n.* autor clásico; obra clásica

classical, *adj.* clásico

classify, *vt.* clasificar, graduar

classmate, *n.* condiscípulo, la

classroom, *n.* sala de clase, *f.*

clean, *adj.* limpio; casto; *vt.* limpiar

cleaning, *n.* limpieza, *f.*

cleanliness, *n.* limpieza, *f.*; aseo *m.*

clear: *adj.* claro, lúcido; neto; *vt.* clarificar, aclarar; absolver; *vi.* aclararse

clef, *n.* (mtis.) clave, *f.*

clemency, *n.* clemencia, *f.*

clergy, *n.* clero, *m.*

clergyman, *n.* eclesiástico, *m.*

clerical, *adj.* clerical, eclesiástico; **clerica work**, trabajo de oficina

clerk, *n.* escribiente, *m.*; dependiente, *m.*

clever, *adj.* hábil; inteligente

cliff, *n.* precipicio, *m.*, barranca, *f.*

climate, *n.* clima, *m.*,

climax, *n.* culminación, *f.*

climb, *vt.* escalar, trepar; *vi.* subir

cling, *vi.* adherirse, pegarse

clinic, *adj.* clínico; *n.* clínica, *f.*; consultorio, *m.*

clip, *vt.* cortar a raíz; *n.* tijeretada, *f.*; grapa, *f.*, gancho, *m.*

clipper, *n.* (avi.) clíper, *m.*; trasquilador, *m.*; **clippers**, *n. pl.* tijeras podadoras, *f. pl.*

clipping, *n.* recorte, *m.*

cloak, *n.* capa, *f.*; capote, *m.*

cloakroom, *n.* guardarropa, *m.*

clock, *n.* reloj, *m.*; **alarm clock**, despertador, *m.*

clog, *n.* obstáculo, *m.*; *vt.* obstruir; *vi.* coagularse

close, *vt.* cerrar, tapar; *vi.* cerrarse; *adj.* avaro; *adv.* cerca

closet, *n.* ropero, *m.*

close-up, *n.* fotografía de cerca, *f.*

clot, *n.* coagulación, *f.*; *vi.* cuajarse, coagularse

cloth, *n.* paño, *m.*; mantel, *m.*; lienzo, *m.*; material, *m.*

clothe, *vt.* vestir, cubrir.

clothes, *n. pl.* vestidura, *f.*; ropaje, *m.*; **clothes closet**, ropero, *m.*

clothespin, *n.* gancho para tender la ropa, *m.*

clothing, *n.* ropa, *f.*

clove, *n.* (bot.) clavo, *m.*

clover, *n.* trébol, *m.*

cloverleaf, *n.* hoja de trébol, *f.*; **cloverleaf (highway crossing)**, *n.* hoja de triébol, *f.*

clown, *n.* payaso, payasa

club, *n.* club, *m.*, agrupación, *f.*; garrote, *m.*

clue, *n.* seña, *f.*; indicio, *m.*

clutch, *n.* (auto.) embrague,

m.; *vt.* embragar; agarrar

clutter, *vt.* poner en desorden; *vi.* atroparse

Co., co., company, Cía., Comp., Compania; **county,** condado

coach, *n.* coche, *m.*; carroza, *f.*; vagón, *m.*; entrenador (en un deporte), *m.*; *vt.* entrenar, preparar

coarse, *adj.* basto; ordinario; rústico

coast, *n.* costa, *f.*

coat, *n.* saco, *m.*, casaca, *f.*; abrigo, *m.*

cobbler, *n.* remendón, *m.*

cobweb, *n.* telaraña,

cock, *n.* gallo, *m.*

cockroach, *n.* cucaracha, *f.*

cocktail, *n.* cocktail, coctel, *m.*

cocoa, *n.* cacao, *m.*; chocolate

coconut, *n.* coco, *m.*

cocoon, *n.* capullo, *m.*

cod, *n.* bacalao, *m.*

C.O.D., c.o.d., cash on delivery, collect on delivery, C.A.E., cóbrese al entregar

code, *n.* código, *m.*; clave, *f.*

codfish, *n.* bacalao, *m.*

cod-liver oil, *n.* aceite de hígado de bacalao, *m.*

coeducational, *adj.* coeducativo

coffee, *n.* café, *m.*

coffeepot, *n.* cafetera, *f.*

cog, *n.* diente (de rueda), *m.*

cogwheel, *n.* rueda dentada, *f.*

coherence, *n.* coherencia, *f.*

cohesion, *n.* coherencia, cohesión, *f.*

coiffure, *n.* peinado, tocado, *m.*

coil, *vt.* recoger; enrollar; *n.* (elec.) carrete, *m.*; bobina, *f.*

coin, *n.* cuña, *f.*; moneda acuñada; dinero, *m.*; *vt.* inventar

coincide, *vi.* coincidir

coincidence, *n.* coincidencia, *f.*; casualidad, *f.*

Col., Colonel, Cnel. Coronel

colander, *n.* coladera, colador, *m.*

cold, *adj.* frío; **to be cold,** hacer frío; tener frío; *n.* frío, *m.*; frialdad, *f.*; (med.) res-

friado, *m.*

coleslaw, *n.* ensalada de col cruda y picada

collaborate, *vt.* colaborar

collapse, *vi.* desplomarse; desmayarse; *n.* colapso, *m.*; derrumbe, desplome, *m.*

collapsible, *adj.* plegadizo

collar, *n.* collar, *m.*; cuello, *m.*

collarbone, *n.* clavícula,

collect, *vt.* recoger; cobrar

collection, *n.* colección, *f.*; colecta, *f.*; cobro, *m.*

collective, *adj.* colectivo

collectivization, *n.* colectivización, *f.*

collectivize, *vt.* colectivizar

collector, *n.* colector, *m.*; agente de cobros, *m.*

college, *n.* colegio, *m.*; escuela superior, universidad, *f.*

collie, *n.* perro de pastor, *m.*

collision, *n.* colisión, choque, *m.*

colon, *n.* colon, *m.*; dos puntos (signo de puntuación)

colonel, *n.* coronel, *m.*

colonial, *adj.* colonial

colony, *n.* colonia, *f.*

color, *n.* color, *m.*

colored, *adj.* colorado, pintado, teñido; de raza negra; con prejuicio

colorful, *adj.* pintoresco

coloring, *n.* colorido, *m.*; colorante, *m.*

colorless, *adj.* descolorido

colossal, *adj.* colosal

Columbus, Colón

column, *n.* columna, *f.*

columnist, *n.* diarista, *m.* y *f.*, periodista encargado de una sección especial

Com., Commander, jefe

coma, *n.* (med.) coma, *f.*; letargo, *m.*

comb, *n.* peine, *m.*; *vt.* peinar; cardar (la lana)

combat, *n.* combate, *m.*; batalla, *f.*; *vt.* y *vi.* combatir; resistir

combine, *vt.* combinar; *vi.* unirse

combustible, *adj.* y *n.* combustible, *m.*

combustion, *n.* combustión, *f.*

Comdr., Commander, jefe

come, *vi.* venir, acontecer; originar

comedian, *n.* comediante, *m.* y *f.*, cómico, cómca

comedy, *n.* comedia, *f.*

comfort, *n.* consuelo, *m.*; comodidad, *f.*; *vt.* confortar; consolar

comfortable, *adj.* cómodo

comforter, *n.* colcha, *f.*

comforting, *adj.* consolador

comical, *adj.* chistoso, gracioso, bufo

coming, *n.* venida, llegada, *f.*; *adj.* venidero, entrante

comma , *n.* (gram.) coma, *f.*

command, *vt.* ordenar; mandar; *n.* orden, *f.*

commander, *n.* jefe, *m.*, comandante, *m.*

commandment, *n.* mandamiento, *m.*

commemorate, *vt.* conmemorar; celebrar

comment, *n.* comentario, *m.*; *vt.* comentar

commentator, *n.* comentador, comentadora; (rad.) locutor, *m.*

commerce, *n.* comercio, *m.*

commercial, *adj.* comercial; *n.* (rad.) anuncio comercial, *m.*

commission, *n.* comisión, *f.*; *vt.* comisionar; encargar

commissioner, *n.* comisionado, delegado, *m.*

commit, *vt.* cometer; encargar; **to commit to memory,** aprender de memoria

committee, *n.* comité, *m.*, comisión, junta, *f.*

commodity, *n.* mercancías, *f. pl.*

common, *adj.* común, público, general; ordinario

Common Market, *n.* Mereado Común, *m.*

commonwealth, *n.* república, *f.*; estado, *m.*; nación, *f.*

communicate, *vt.* comunicar, participar; *vi.* comunicarse

communication, *n.* comunicación, *f.*; **communications**

satellite, satélite de radiodifusión;

communion, *n.* comunion, *f.*; **to take communion,** comulgar

communism, *n.* comunismo, *m.*

communist, *n.* comunista, *m.* y *f.*

community, *n.* comunidad, *f.*; colectividad, *f.*; *adj.* comunal

commute, *vt.* conmutar; *vi.* viajar diariamente de un lugar a otro

compact, *adj.* compacto; sólido; *n.* polvera, *f.*; (auto.) coche o carro compacto

companion, *n.* companero, companera; acompañante, *m.* y *f.*

companionship, *n.* camaradería, *f.*, compañerismo *m.*

company, *n.* compañía, *f.*; sociedad, *f.*

compare, *vt.* comparar; confrontar

compartment, *n.* compartimiento, compartimento, *m.*

compass, *n.* compás, *m.* piedad, *f.*

compel, *vt.* obligar

compensate, *vt.* y *vi.* compensar

compensation, *n.* compensación

competent, *adj.* competente, capaz

competition, *n.* competencia, *f.*

competitor, *n.* competidor, competidora; rival, *m.* y *f.*

compile, *vt.* compilar

complain, *vi.* quejarse, lamentarse

complaint, *n.* queja, *f.*

complement, *n.* complemento, *m.*

complete, *adj.* completo; *vt.* completar, acabar

complex, *adj.* complejo, compuesto; *n.* complejo *m.*

compliance, *n.* condescendencia, *f.*; consentimiento, *m.*; **in compliance with,** de acuerdo con, aocediendo (a sus deseos, etc.)

complicate, *vt.* complicar

compliment, *n.* lisonja, *f.*; piropo, requiebro, *m.*

comply, *vi.* cumplir; condescender

compose, *vt.* componer; sosegar; **to compose oneself**, serenarse

composed, *adj.* sosegado, moderado; **to be composed of**, componerse de

composer, *n.* autor, autora; compositor, compositora

composite, *n.* compuesto, *m.*; mezcla, *f.*

composure, *n.* calma, tranquilidad, *f.*

compound, *vt.* combinar; *adj.* compuesto; *n.* compuesto, *m.*

comprehend, *vt.* comprender; contener

comprehension, *n.* comprensión, *f.*

compress, *vt.* comprimir, estrechar; *n.* (med.) fomento, *m.*

comprise, *vt.* comprender, incluir

compromise, *n.* compromiso, convenio, *m.*; *vt.* transigir

compulsory, *adj.* obligatorio, compulsivo

compute, *vt.* computar, calcular

computer, (electronic) *n.* calculador electrónico, *m.*

comrade, *n.* camarada, *m.* y *f.*; compañero, compañera

con., **against**, contra; **conclusion**, conclusión

concede, *vt.* conceder, admitir

conceit, *n.* presunción, *f.*

conceive, *vt.* concebir

concentrate, *vt.* y *vi.* concentrar

concentration, *n.* concentración, *f.*

concept, *n.* concepto, *m.*

conception, *n.* concepción, *f.*; concepto, *m.*

concern, *vt.* concernir, importar; pertenecer; *n.* negocio, *m.*; interés, *m.*

concerned, *adj.* interesado; mortificado

concerning, *prep.* tocante a, respecto a

concession, *n.* concesión, cesión, *f.*

conciliation, *n.* conciliación, *f.*

concise, *adj.* conciso, sucinto

conclude, *vt.* concluir

concord, *n.* concordia, armonía, *f.*

concrete, *adj.* concreto; *n.* hormigón, cemento, *m.*; **concrete mixer**, hormigonera, *f.*

concussion, *n.* concusión, *f.*

condemn, *vt.* condenar

condense, *vt.* condensar; comprimir

condescend, *vi.* condescender; consentir

condescending, *adj.* complaciente, afable

condition, *n.* condición, *f.*; requisto, *m.*; estado, *m.*

condolence, *n.* pésame, *m.*, condolencia, *f.*

condominium, *n.* condominio, *m.*, propiedad horizontal

conduct, *n.* conducta, *f.*; conducción (de tropas), *f.*; **safe conduct**, salvoconducto, *m.*

conduct, *vt.* conducir, guiar

conductor, *n.* conductor, *m.*; guía, director, *m.*

confection, *n.* confitura, *f.*; confección, *f.*; confite, *m.*

confederate, *vi.* confederarse; *adj.* confederado; *n.* confederado, *m.*

confederation, *n.* federación, confederación, *f.*

confer, *vi.* conferenciar; consultarse; *vt.* otorgar

conference, *n.* conferencia, *f.*; sesión, junta, *f.*

confess, *vt.* y *vi.* confesar, confesarse

confession, *n.* confesión,

confide, *vt.* y *vi.* confiar; fiarse

confidence, *n.* confianza, seguridad, *f.*

confident, *adj.* cierto; seguro; confiado

confidential, *adj.* confidencial

confine, *vt.* limitar; aprisionar; *vi.* confinar

confinement, *n.* prisión, *f.*; encierro, *m.*; parto, *m.*

confirm, *vt.* confirmar; ratificar

confirmation, *n.* confirmación, *f.*; ratificación, *f.*

confiscate, *vt.* confiscar, decomisar

conflict, *n.* conflicto, *m.*; *vt.* estar en conflicto

conform, *vt.* y *vi.* conformar

conformity, *n.* conformidad, *f.*

confound, *vt.* confundir; **confound it!** *interj.* ¡caracoles!

confront, *vt.* confrontar, comparar

comfrontation, *n.* enfrentamiento, *m.*; careo, *m.*

confuse, *vt.* confundir; desordenar

confused, *adj.* confuso, desorientado

confusion, *n.* confusión, *f.*

congeal, *vt.* y *vi.* congelar

congenial, *adj.* congenial, compatible; **to be congenial**, simpatizar

congratulate, *vt.* felicitar

congregate, *vt.* congregar, reunir

congregation, *n.* congregación, reunión, *f.*

congress, *n.* congreso, *m.*

conjecture, *n.* conjetura, suposición, *f.*; *vt.* conjeturar; pronosticar

conjugate, *vt.* conjugar

conjunction, *n.* conjunción, *f.*

connect, *vt.* juntar, enlazar; relacionar

connection, *n.* conexión, *f.*; **connections**, *n. pl.* relaciones, *f. pl.*

connoisseur, *n.* perito, perita, conocedor, conocedora

conquer, *vt.* conquistar; vencer

conqueror *n.* vencedor, conquistador, *m.*

conquest, *n.* conquista, *f.*

conscience, *n.* conciencia, *f.*; escrúpulo, *m.*

conscientious, *adj.* concienzudo

conscious, *adj.* consciente;

consciously, *adv.* a sabiendas

consciousness, *n.* conocimiento, sentido, *m.*

conscription, *n.* reclutamiento obligatorio, *m.*

consecrate, *vt.* consagrar; dedicar

consecutive, *adj.* consecutivo

consent, *n.* consentimiento, *m.*; aprobación, *f.*; *vi.* consentir; aprobar

consequence, *n.* consecuencia, *f.*; importancia, *f.*

consequent, *adj.* consecutivo; consiguiente

conservation, *n.* conservación, *f.*

conservative, *adj.* conservador

conservatory, *n.* conservatorio, *m.*; invernadero, *m.*

conserve, *vt.* conservar, cuidar; hacer conservas

consider, *vt.* considerar, examinar; *vi.* pensar, deliberar; reflexionar

considerable, *adj.* considerable; importante; bastante

considerate, *adj.* considetado, prudente

considcration, *n.* considcración, *f.*; deliberación, *f.*

considering, *prep.* en vista de

consign, *vt.* consignar

consignee, *n.* consignatario, consignataria

consist, *vi.* consistir

consistent, *adj.* consistente; congruente

consolation, *n.* consuelo, *m.*

console, *vt.* consolar

consolidate, *vt.* y *vi.* consolidar, consolidarse

consort, *n.* consorte, *m.* y *f.*; esposo, esposa

conspicuous, *adj.* conspicuo, llamativo

conspiracy, *n.* conspiración, *f.*; trama, *f.*; complot, *m.*

conspire, *vt.* y *vi.* conspirar, maquinar

constant, *adj.* constante; fiel

consternation, *n.* consternación, *f.*

constipation, *n.* estreñimiento, *m.*

constitute, *vt.* constituir

constitution, *n.* constitución, *f.*

constitutional, *adj.* constitucional, legal

constrain, *vt.* constreñir; restringir

construct, *vt.* construir

construction, *n.* construcción, *f.*

construe, *vt.* interpretar

consul, *n.* cónsul, *m.*

consulate, *n.* consulado, *m.*

consult, *vt.* y *vi.* consultar

consultation, *n.* consulta, deliberación, *f.*

consume, *vt.* y *vi.* consumir

consumer, *n.* consumidor, consumidora

consumption, *n.* consumo, *m.*; consunción, tisis, *f.*

contact, *n.* contacto, *m.*; **contact lenses,** lentes de contacto; *vt.* y *vi.* tocar; poner en contacto

contagious, *adj.* contagioso

contain, *vt.* contener, comprender; caber; reprimir

container, *n.* envase, *m.*; recipiente, *m.*

contaminate, *vt.* contaminar

contemplate, *vt.* contemplar; *vi.* meditar, pensar

contempt, *n.* desprecio, desdén, *m.*

contend, *vi.* contender, disputar, afirmar

content, *adj.* contento, satisfecho; *vt.* contentar; *n.* contento, *m.*; satisfacción, *f.*

content, *n.* contento, *m.*; contenido, *m.*; **contents,** *pl.* contenido, *m.*

contention, *n.* contención, *f.*

contentment, *n.* contentamiento, placer, *m.*

contest, *vt.* disputar, litigar; *n.* concurso, *m.*; competencia, *f.*

contestant, *n.* contendiente, litigante, *m.* y *f.*; concursante, *m.* y *f.*

continent, *n.* continente, *m.*

continental, *adj.* continental

contingent, *n.* contingente, *m.*; cuota, *f.*

continuation, *n.* continuación, *f.*; serie, *f.*

continue, *vt.* continuar; *vi.* durar, perseverar, persistir

continuity, *n.* continuidad, *f.*

continuous, *adj.* continuo

contour, *n.* contorno, *m.*

contract, *vt.* contraer; abreviar; contratar; *vi.* contraerse; *n.* contrato, pacto, *m.*

contraction, *n.* contracción, *f.*; abreviatura, *f.*

contradict, *vt.* contradecir

contradiction, *n.* contradicción, oposición, *f.*

contrail, *n.* estela de vapor, *f.*

contralto, *n.* contralto (voz), *m.*; contralto (persona), *m.* y *f.*

contrary, *adj.* contrario, opuesto; **on the contrary,** al contrario

contrast, *n.* contraste, *m.*; oposición, *f.*; *vt.* contrastar, oponer

contribute, *vt.* contribuir, ayudar

contributor, *n.* contribudador, contribudadora, contribuyente, *m.* y *f.*

contrite, *adj.* contrito, arrepentido

contrive, *vt.* inventar, maquinar

control, *n.* inspección, *f.*; control, *m.*; gobierno, *m.*; *vt.* restringir; gobernar; **to control oneself,** contenerse

convalescence, *n.* convalecencia, *f.*

convalescent, *adj.* convaleciente

convene, *vt.* convocar; *vi.* juntarse

convenience, *n.* conveniencia, comodidad, *f.*

convenient, *adj.* conveniente, cómodo

convent, *n.* convento, monasterio, *m.*

convention, *n.* convención, *f.*

conventional, *adj.* convencional; tradicional

conversation, *n.* conversación, plática, *f.*

converse, *vi.* conversar, platicar

convert, *vt.* convertir, reducir; *vi.* convertirse; *n.* converso, convertido , *m.*

convey, *vt.* trasportar; trasmitir; conducir

convict, *n.* reo, convicto, presidiario, *m.*

conviction, *n.* convicción,

convince, *vt.* convencer

convincing, *adj.* convincente

convulsion, *n.* convulsión, *f.*

cook, *n.* cocinero, cocinera; *vt., vi.* cocinar, guisar, cocer

cookbook, *n.* libro de cocina, *m.*

cooking, *n.* cocina, *f.*; arte de cocinar, *m.*

cool, *adj.* fresco; indiferente; *vt.* enfriar, refrescar

coop, *n.* gallinero, *m.*; *vt.* enjaular, encarcelar

cooperate, *vi.* cooperar

cooperation, *n.* cooperación *f.*

co-ordinate, *vt.* coordinar

co-ordination, *n.* coordinación, *f.*

cop, *n.* (coll.) policía, gendarme, *m.*

copper, *n.* cobre, *m.*; cobre (color), *m.*

copy, *n.* copia, *f.*; original, *m.*; ejemplar de algún libro; *vt.* copiar; imitar

copyright, *n.* propiedad de una obra literaria; derechos de autor, *m. pl.*; patente, *f.*

coquette, *n.* coqueta, *f.*

coral, *n.* coral, *m.*; *adj.* de coral

cord, *n.* cuerda, *f.*; cordel, *m.*; cordón, pasamano, *m.*

cordial, *adj.* cordial, amistoso; *n.* cordial (licor), *m.*

core, *n.* cuesco, *m.*; interior, corazón, *m.*; núcleo, *m.*

cork, *n.* corcho, *m.*

corkscrew, *n.* tirabuzón, *m.*

corn, *n.* maíz, *m.*; callo, *m.*

corncob, *n.* mazorca, *f.*

corned beef, *n.* cecina, *f.*, carne de vaca en salmuera

corner, *n.* ángulo, *m.*; rincón, *m.*; esquina, *f.*

cornstalk, *n.* tallo de maíz

cornstarch, *n.* almidón de maíz, *m.*

Corp., corp., corporal, cabo; **corporation,** S.A. sociedad anónima

corporal, *n.* (mil.) cabo, *m.*; *adj.* corpóreo, corporal; material, físico

corporate, *adj.* colectivo

corporation, *n.* corporación, *f.*; gremio, *m.*; sociedad anónima, *f.*

corps, *n.* regimiento, *m.*; cuerpo, *m.*; **air corps,** cuerpo de aviación, *m.*

correct, *vt.* corregir, castigar; rectificar; *adj.* correcto, cierto

correction, *n.* corrección, *f.*

correspond, *vi.* corresponder; sostener correspondencia

correspondence, *n.* correspondencia, *f.*; reciprocidad, *f.*

correspondent, *n.* corresponsal, *m.*

corrugated, *adj.* corrugado

corrupt, *vt.* y *vi.* corromper; sobornar; *adj.* corrompido

corruption, *n.* corrupción, *f.*

cosmetic, *adj.* y *n.* cosmético, *m.*

cosmopolitan, cosmopolite, *n.* y *adj.* cosmopolita, *m.* y *f.*

cost, *n.* coste, costo, precio, *m.*; expensas, *f. pl.*; *vi.* costar

costly, *adj.* costoso, caro

costume, *n.* traje, *m.*; ropa, *f.*; disfraz, *m.*

cottage, *n.* cabaña, choza, *f.*; **cottage cheese,** requesón, *m.*

cotton, *n.* algodón, *m.*

couch, *n.* canapé, sofá, *m.*

cough, *n.* tos, *f.*; *vi.* toser

council, *n.* concilio, concejo, *m.*

counsel, *n.* consejo, aviso, *m.*; abogado, *m.*

counselor, counsellor, *n.* consejero, abogado, *m.*

count, *vt.* contar, numerar;

calcular; **to count on**, confiar, depender de; *n.* cuenta, *f.*; cálculo, *m.*; conde (título), *m.*

countdown, *n.* conteo, *m.*

counter, *n.* mostrador, *m.*

counteract, *vt.* contrarrestar

counterfeit, *adj.* falsificado

countless, *adj.* innumerable

country, *n.* país, *m.*; campo, *m.*; patria, *f.*; *adj.* campestre, rural

countryman, *n.* paisano, paisana, compatriota, *m.* y *f.*

county, *n.* condado, *m.*

couple, *n.* par, *m.*; *vt.* unir, parear, casar; *vi.* juntarse

coupon, *n.* cupón, talón, *m.*

courage, *n.* valor, *m.*

courageous, *adj.* valiente

course, *n.* curso, *m.*; carrera, *f.*; ruta, *f.*; rumbo, *m.*; plato, *m.*; **of course**, por supuesto

court, *n.* corte, *f.*; juzgado, tribunal, *m.*; palacio, *m.*; patio, *m.*; cortejo, *m.*; *vt.* cortejar

courteous, *adj.* cortés

courtesy, *n.* cortesía, *f.*

courtship, *n.* cortejo, *m.*; galantería, *f.*

cousin, *n.* primo, ma; **first cousin**, primo hermano, prima hermana

cover, *n.* cubierta, *f.*; *vt.* cubrir; tapar; ocultar

cow, *n.* vaca, *f.*

coward, *n.* cobarde, *m.* y *f.*

cowardice, *n.* cobardía,

cowardly, *adj.* cobarde

cowboy, *n.* vaquero, *m.*

cowhide, *n.* cuero, *m.*

co-worker, *n.* colaborador, colaboradora, compañero o compañera de trabajo

cozy, *adj.* cómodo y agradable

C.P.A., **Certified Public Accountant**, C.P.T., Contador Público Titulado

crab, *n.* cangrejo, *m.*; (Sp. Am.) jaiba, *f.*; **crab apple**, manzana silvestre, *f.*

crack, *n.* crujido, *m.*; hendedura, raja, *f.*; *vt.* hender, rajar; romper; *vi.* agrietarse

cracked, *adj.* quebrado, raja-

do; (coll.) demente

cracker, *n.* galleta, *f.*

cradle, *n.* cuna, *f.*

craft, *n.* arte, *m.*; artificio, *m.*; astucia, *f.*

crafty, *adj.* astuto

cramp, *n.* calambre, *m.*

crane, *n.* (orn.) grulla, *f.*; (mech.) grúa, *f.*

cranium, *n.* craneo, *m.*

crank, *n.* manivela, *f.*; manija, *f.*; (coll.) maniático, maniática

crash, *vi.* estallar, rechinar; estrellar; *n.* estallido, choque, *m.*

crazy, *adj.* loco

cream, *n.* crema, *f.*; nata, *f.*

creamy, *adj.* cremoso

crease, *n.* pliegue, *m.*; *vt.* plegar

create, *vt.* crear; causar

creation, *n.* creación, *f.*

creative, *adj.* creador

creator, *n.* criador, criadora; **the Creator**, el Criador

credit, *n.* crédito, *m.*; **credit card**, tarjeta de crédito, *f.*; *vt.* creer, fiar, acreditar

creditor, *n.* acreedor, acreedora

creep, *vi.* arrastrar; gatear

cremate, *vt.* incinerar cadáveres

cretonne, *n.* cretona, *f.*

crevice, *n.* raja, hendidura, *f.*

crew, *n.* (naut.) tripulación, *f.*

crime, *n.* crimen, delito, *m.*

criminal, *adj.* criminal, reo; *n.* reo convicto, criminal, *m.* y *f.*

crimson, *adj.* carmesi, bermejo

crinoline, *n.* crinolina, *f.*

cripple, *n.* lisiado, lisiada; *vt.* tullir

crisis, *n.* crisis, *f.*

crisp, *adj.* crespo; fresco, terso (aplicase, a la lechuga, el apio, etc.)

crisscross, *adj.* entrelazado

criterion, *n.* criterio, *m.*

critic, *n.* crítico, *m.*

critical, *adj.* critico; delicado

criticism, *n.* crítica, *f.*; censura, *f.*

criticize, vt. criticar, censurar

crochet, n. labor con aguja de gancho; vt. tejer con aguja de gancho

crocodile, n. cocodrilo, m.

crony, n. amigo (o conocido) antiguo

crook, n. gancho, m.; curva, f.; ladrón, ladrona

crooked, adj. torcido; perverso; tortuoso

crop, n. cosecha, f.; cabello cortado corto

cross, n. cruz, f.; adj. enojado; mal humorado; vt. atravesar, cruzar

crossing, n. (rail.) cruce, m.

crossword puzzle, n. crucigrama, rompecabezas, m.

crow, n. (orn.) cuervo, m.; canto del gallo; vi. cantar el gallo; alardear

crowd, n. multitud, f.; vt. amontonar

crowded, adj. concurrido, lleno de gente

crown, n. corona, f.; vt. coronar; recompensar

crown prince, n. príncipe heredero, m.

crucifix, n. crucifijo, m.

crucify, vt. crucificar; atormentar

crude, adj. crudo, tosco; **crude (ore, oil, etc.)** (mineral, petróleo, etc.) bruto

cruel, adj. cruel, inhumano

cruelty, n. crueldad, f.

cruise, n. travesía marítima; excursión, f.; vi. navegar; cruzar (el mar o el país)

crumb n. miga, f.

crumble, vt. desmigajar, desmenuzar; vi. desmoronarse

crumple, vt. arrugar, ajar

crunch, vi. crujir

crusade, n. cruzada, f.

crush, vt. apretar, oprimir; machacar

crust, n. costra, f.; corteza, f.

crutch, n. muleta, f.

cry, vt. y vi. gritar; exclamar; llorar; n. grito, m.; llanto, m.

crystal, n. cristal, m.

C.S.T., Central Standard Time, hora normal del centro (de E.U.A.)

cub, n. cachorro, m.

Cuban, n. y adj. cubano, cubana

cubbyhole, n. casilla, f.

cube, n. cubo, m.

cubic, cubical, adj. cúbico

cucumber, n. pepino, m.

cuddle, vt. y vi. abrazar; acariciarse

cue, n. rabo, m., coleta, f.; apunte de comedia, m.; taco (de billar), m.

cuff, n. puño de camisa o de vestido, m.; **cuff links,** gemelos, m. pl.; (Sp. Am.) mancuernillas, f. pl.

culinary, adj. culinario

culminate, vi. culminar

culprit, n. delincuente, criminal, m.

cult, n. culto, m.

cultivate, vt. cultivar

cultivation, n. cultivo, m.

cultural, adj. cultural

culture, n. cultura, civilización, f.

cumbersome, adj. engorroso

cunning, adj. astuto; intrigante; n. astucia, sutileza, f.

cup, n. taza, f.

cupboard, n. armario, aparador, m., alacena, f.

cupful, n. taza (medida), f.

cupola, n. cúpula, f.

curb, n. freno, m.; restricción, f.; orilla de la acera, f.; vt. refrenar

curdle, vt. y vi. cuajar, coagular

cure, n. remedio, m.; vt. curar, sanar

cure-all, n. panacea, f.

curiosity, n. curiosidad, f.; rareza, f.

curious, adj. curioso

curl, n. rizo, m.; vt. rizar (el cabello); vi. rizarse, encresparse

currency, circulación, f.; moneda corriente, f., dinero m.

current, adj. corriente, del día; n. corriente, f.

curse, vt. maldecir; n. maldición, f.

curtain, n. cortina, f., telón (en los teatros), m.

curve, vt. encorvar; n. curva, combadura, f.

cushion, n. cojín, m., almohada, f.

custody, n. custodia, f.; cuidado, m.

custom, n. costumbre, f.; uso, m.; **customs,** n. pl. aduana, f.

customary, adj. usual, acostumbrado

customer, n. cliente, m. y f.

customhouse, n. aduana, f.

cut, vt. cortar; herir; **to cut short,** interrumpir; n. cortadura, f.; herida, f.; (print.) grabado, m.

cute, adj. gracioso, chistoso

cutlery, n. cuchilleria, f.

cutlet, n. costilla, chuleta, f.

cutting, adj. cortante; sarcástico

cwt., hundredweight, ql., quintal

cycle, n. ciclo, m.

cyclone, n. ciclón, m.

cyclotron, n. ciclotrón, m.

cylinder, n. cilindro, m.

cypher, cipher, n. cifra, cero. m.

cyst, n. quiste, m.; lobanillo, m.

C. Z., Canal Zone, Z. del C. Zona del Canal

czar, n. zar, m.

D

d., date, fha., fecha; **daughter,** hija; **day,** día; **diameter,** diámetro; **died,** murió

D.A., District Attorney, fiscal

d/a, days after acceptance, d/v, dias vista

dad, daddy, n. papá, m.

daffodil, n. (bot.) narciso, m.

dagger, n. daga, f., puñal, m.

dahlia, n. (bot.) dalia, f.

daily, adj. diario, cotidiano; adv. diariamente

dainty, adj. delicado; meticuloso, refinado

dairy, n. lechería, f.

daisy, n, margarita, f.

dam, n. dique, m.; presa, f.; represa, f.; vt. represar; tapar

damage, n. daño, detrimento, m.; perjuicio, m.; **damages,** n. pl. daños y perjuicios, m. pl.; vt. dañar

damask, n. damasco, m.

dame, n. dama, señora, f.

damn, vt. condenar; maldecir; **damn!, damn it!** interj. ¡maldito sea!

damp, adj. húmedo

dampen, vt. humedecer; desanimar

dampness, n. humedad, f.

dance, n. danza, f.; baile, m.; vi. bailar

dancer, n. danzarín, danzarina, bailarín, bailarina

dandelion, n. diente de león, amargón, m.

dandy, n. petimetre, m.; adj. (coll.) excelente

danger, n. peligro, riesgo, m.

dangerous, adj. peligroso

Danish, n. y adj. danés, danesa, dinamarqués, dinamarquesa

D.A.R., Daughters of the American Revolution, Organización "Hijas de la Revolución Norteamericana."

dare, vi. atreverse, arriesgarse; vt. desafiar, provocar; n. reto, m.

daredevil, n. temerario, temeraria; calavera, m.

daring, n. osadía, f.; adj. temerario; emprendedor

dark, adj. oscuro, opaco; moreno, trigueño; n. oscuridad, f.; ignorancia, f.

darken, vt. y vi. oscurecer

darkness, n. oscuridad. f.; tinieblas, f. pl.

darling, n. predilecto, predilecta, favorito, favorita; adj. querido, amado

dash, n. arranque, m.; acometida, f.; (gram.) raya, f.; vt. arrojar, tirar; chocar, estrellar

data, n. pl. datos, m. pl.; **data**

processing, proceso de datos, proceso de información por computadoras

date, n. fecha, f.; cita, f.; (bot.) dátil, m.

dated, adj. fechado

daughter, n. hija, f.; **daughter-in-law,** nuera, f.

daunt, vt. intimidar

dauntless, adj. intrépido, affojado

davenport, n. sofá, m.

dawn, n. alba, f.; madrugada f.; vi. amanecer

day, n. día, m.; **day after tomorrow,** pasado mañana

daylight, n. día, m., luz del día, luz natural, f.

daze, vt. atolondrar

dazzle, vt. deslumbrar

D.C., District of Columbia, D.C., Distrito de Columbia, E.U.A.

d.c., direct current, C.D. corriente directa; C.C. corriente continua

DDT, DDT (insecticida), m.

dead, adj. muerto; marchito; **dead letter,** carta no reclamada

deaden, vt. amortecer

deadlock, n. paro, m.; desacuerdo, m.

deadly, adj. mortal

deaf, adj. sordo

deaf-mute, n. sordomudo, sordomuda

deafness, n. sordera, f.

deal, n. negocio, convenio, m.; (com.) trato, m.; mano (en el juego de naipes), f.; vt. tratar; dar (las cartas)

dealer, n. comerciante, m.

dealing, n. trato, m.; comercio, m.; **dealings,** n. pl. transacciones, f. pl.; relaciones, f. pl.

dean, n. deán, decano, m.

dear, adj. querido; costoso, caro

death, n. muerte,

debate, n. debate, m.; vt. y vi. deliberar; disputar

debit, n. debe, cargo, m.; vt. adeudar

debris, n. despojos, escom-

bros, m. pl.

debt, n. deuda, f.; débito, m.

debtor, n. deudor, deudora

debut, n. estreno, debut, m.

debutante, n. debutante, f.

Dec., December, dic., diciembre

decade, n. década, f.

decay, vi. decaer, declinar; degenerar; n. decadencia, f.; (dent.) caries, f.

deceased, n. y adj. muerto, muerta, difunto, difunta

deceit, n. engaño, fraude, m.

deceitful, adj. fraudulento, engañoso

December, n. diciembre, m.

decency, n. decencia, f.; modestia, f.

decent, adj. decente, razonable

decimal, adj. decimal

decipher, vt. descifrar

decision, n. decisión, determinación, resolución, f.

decisive, adj. decisivo

deck, n. (naut.) bordo, m., cubierta, f.; baraja de naipes, f.; vt. adornar

declare, vt. declarar, manifestar

decline, vt. (gram.) declinar; rehusar; vi. decaer; n. declinación, f.; decadencia, f.; declive, m.

decorate, vt. decorar, adornar; condecorar

decoy, vt. atraer (algún pájaro); embaucar, engañar

decrease, vt. y vi. disminuir, reducir

decree, n. decreto, edicto, m.; vt. decretar, ordenar

dedicate, vt. dedicar; consagrar

dedication, n. dedicación, f.; dedicatoria, f.

deduct, vt. deducir, sustraer

deduction, n. deducción, rebaja, f.; descuento, m.

deed, n. hecho, m.; hazaña, f.; (com.) escritura, f.

deem, vi. juzgar, estimar

deep, adj. profundo; subido (aplícase al color); intenso

deepen, *vt.* profundizar
deepfreeze, *n.* congeladora, *f.*
deer, *n. sing. y pl.* ciervo, ciervos, venado, venados, *m.*
deface, *vt.* desfigurar
defame, *vt.* difamar; calumniar
default, *n.* defecto, *m.*, falta, *f.*; *vt. y vi.* faltar, delinquir
defeat, *n.* derrota, *f.*; *vt.* derrotar; frustrar
defend, *vt.* defender; proteger
defendant, *n.* (law) demandado, demandada, acusado, acusada
defender, *n.* defensor, abogado, *m.*
defer, *vt.* diferir, posponer
deference, *n.* deferencia, *f.*; respeto, *m.*
defiance, *n.* desafío, *m.*
deficiency, *n.* deficiencia, *f.*
deficit, *n.* déficit, *m.*
define, *vt.* definir; determinar
definite, *adj.* definido; concreto
definition, *n.* definición, *f.*
deform, *vt.* deformar, desfigurar
deformity, *n.* deformidad, *f.*
defraud, *vt.* defraudar; frustrar
defray, *vt.* costear; sufragar
defrost, *vt.* descongelar, deshelar
defy *vt.* desafiar, retar
degrade, *vt.* degradar; deshonrar
degree, *n.* grado, *m.*; rango, *m.*; **by degrees**, gradualmente
deject, *vt.* abatir, desanimar
del., delegate, delegado; **delete**, suprímase
delay, *vt.* retardar; *vi.* demorar; *n.* demora, *f.*
delegate, *vt.* delegar, diputar; *n.* delegado, delegada, diputado, diputada
delegation, *n.* delegación, *f.*
delete, *vt.* suprimir
deliberate, *vt.* deliberar, considerar; *adj.* premeditado
deliberation, *n.* delibera ción, *f.*

delicacy, *n.* delicadeza, *f.*; manjar, *m.*
delicate, *adj.* delicado
delicious, *adj.* delicioso
delight, *n.* delicia, *f.*; deleite, *m.*; *vt. y vi.* deleitar
delightful, *adj.* delicioso; deleitable
delinquency, *n.* delincuencia,
delinquent, *n. y adj.* delincuente, *m. y f.*
deliver, *vt.* entregar; libertar; relatar; partear
delivery, *n.* entrega, *f.*; liberación, *f.*; parto, *m.*
deluxe, *adj.* de lujo
demand, *n.* demanda, *f.*; *vt.* pedir, exigir
demented, *adj.* demente, loco
demitasse, *n.* tacita (de café), *f.*
democracy, *n.* democracia, *f.*
democrat, *n.* demócrata, *m. y f.*
demolish, *vt.* demoler, arrasar
demon, *n.* demonio, diablo, *m.*
demonstrate, *vt.* demostrar
demonstration, *n.* demostración, *f.*
demonstrative, *adj.* demostrativo, expresivo
demotion, *n.* (mil.) degradación, *f.*; descenso de rango
den, *n.* caverna, *f.*; cuarto de lectura o de estudio, *m.*
denim, *n.* mezclilla, tela gruesa de algodón, *f.*
Denmark, Dinamarca
denomination, *n.* denominación, *f.*
denominational, *adj.* sectario
denominator, *n.* (math.) denominador, *m.*
denote, *vt.* denotar, indicar
denounce, *vt.* denunciar
dense, *adj.* denso, espeso; estúpido
dent, *n.* abolladura, *f.*; mella, *f.*; *vt.* abollar
dental, *adj.* dental
dentifrice, *adj. y n.* dentífrico, *m.*
dentist, *n.* dentista, *m.*
denture, *n.* dentadura postiza, *f.*

deodorant, *adj.*, *m.* desodorante

depart, *vi.* partir; irse, salir; morir

department, *n.* departamento, *m.*

departure, *n.* partida, salida, *f.*; desviación, *f.*

depend, *vi.* depender

dependable, *adj.* digno de confianza

dependent, *n.* dependiente, *m.*

depict, *vt.* pintar, retratar; describir

deplete, *vt.* agotar, vaciar

deplorable, *adj.* deplorable

deplore, *vt.* deplorar, lamentar

deport, *vt.* deportar

deportment, *n.* conducta, *f.*

deposit, *vt.* depositar; *n.* depósito, *m.*

depot, *n.* (rail.) estación, *f.*

depressed, *adj.* deprimido

depression, *n.* depresión, *f.*

deprive, *vt.* privar, despojar

dept., **department**, dep., depto., departamento

depth, *n.* profundidad, *f.*; abismo, *m.*

deputy, *n.* diputado, delegado, *m.*

derail, *vt.* descarrilar

derivation, *n.* derivación, *f.*

derive, *vt.* y *vi.* derivar; proceder

descend, *vi.* descender

descendant, *n.* descendiente, *m.* y *f.*

describe, *vt.* describir

description, *n.* descripción, *f.*

desert, *n.* desierto, *m.*; merecimiento, *m.*; *vt.* abandonar; *vi.* (mil.) desertar

desertion, *n.* deserción, *f.*

design, *vt.* designar, proyectar; diseñar; *n.* diseño, plan, *m.*

designate, *vt.* designar, señalar

designer, *n.* dibujante, proyectista, *m.* y *f.*

desire, *n.* deseo, *m.*; *vt.* desear

desk, *n.* escritorio, pupitre, *m.*

desolation, *n.* desolación, destrucción, *f.*

despair, *n.* desesperación, *f.*; *vi.* desesperar

desperate, *adj.* desesperado; furioso

desperation, *n.* desesperación, *f.*

despise, *vt.* despreciar; desdeñar

despite, *n.* despecho, *m.*; *prep.* a despecho de

despondent, *adj.* abatido, desalentado

despot, *n.* déspota, *m.* y *f.*

dessert, *n.* postre, *m.*

destination, *n.* destino, *m.*

destine, *vt.* destinar, dedicar

destiny, *n.* destino, hado, *m.*; suerte, *f.*

destitute, *adj.* carente; necesitado

destroy, *vt.* destruir

destruction, *n.* destrucción, ruina, *f.*

detach, *vt.* separar, desprender

detail, *n.* detalle, *m.*; particularidad, *f.*; (mil.) destacamento, *m.*; **in detail**, al por menor; detalladamente; *vt.* detallar

detect, *vt.* descubrir; discernir

detective, *n.* detective, *m.*

détente, *n.* relajación en la tensión, distensión, *f.*

deter, *vt.* disuadir

deteriorate, *vt.* deteriorar

determination, *n.* determinación, *f.*

determine, *vt.* determinar, decidir; **to be determined**, proponerse

detest, *vt.* detestar, aborrecer

detract, *vt.* disminuir; *vi.* denigrar

detriment, *n.* detrimento, perjuicio *m.*

develop, *vt.* desarrollar; revelar (una fotografía)

development, *n.* desarrollo, *m.*

deviate, *vi.* desviarse

device, *n.* invento, *m.*; aparato, mecanismo, *m.*

devil, *n.* diablo, demonio, *m.*

devise, *vt.* inventar; idear

devoid, *adj.* vacío; carente
devote, *vt.* dedicar; consagrar
devotion, *n.* devoción, *f.*; dedicación, *f.*
devout, *adj.* devoto, piadoso
dew, *n.* rocío, *m.*
diabetes, *n.* diabetes, *f.*
diabolic, diabolical, *adj.* diabólico
diagnose, *vt.* diagnosticar
diagnosis, *n.* diagnosis, *f.*
diagonal, *n.* y *adj.* diagonal, *f.*
diagram, *n.* diagrama, *m.*
dial, *n.* esfera de reloj, *f.*; cuadrante, *m.*; **dial telephone,** teléfono automático, *m.*
dialect, *n.* dialecto, *m.*
diameter, *n.* diámetro, *m.*
diamond, *n.* diamante, *m.*; brillante, *m.*; oros (de baraja), *m. pl.*
diaper, *n.* pañal, *m.*
diarrhea, *n.* diarrea, *f.*
diary, *n.* diario, *m.*
dictate, *vt.* dietar
dictation, *n.* dictado, *m.*
dictator, *n.* dictador, *m.*
dictatorship, *n.* dictadura, *f.*
diction, *n.* dicción, *f.*
dictionary, *n.* diccionario, *m.*
did, *pretérito* del verbo **do**
die, *vi.* morir, expirar; marchitarse; *n.* dado, *m.*; molde, *m.*, matriz, *f.*
diet, *n.* dieta, *f.*; régimen, *m.*; *vi.* estar a dieta
differ, *vi.* diferenciarse; contradecir
difference, *n.* diferencia, *f.*
different, *adj.* diferente
difficult, *adj.* difícil
difficulty, *n.* dificultad, *f.*
digest, *vt.* digerir, clasificar; *vi.* digerir; *n.* extracto, compendio, *m.*
digestion, *n.* digestión, *f.*
dignified, *adj.* serio, grave
dignity, *n.* dignidad, *f.*
dike, *n.* dique, canal, *m.*
dilate, *vt.* y *vi.* dilatar, extender
diligent, *adj.* diligente, aplicado
dim, *adj.* turbio de vista; oscuro; *vt.* oscurecer

dime, *n.* moneda de plata de diez centavos en E. U. A.
dimension, *n.* dimensión, *f.*
diminish, *vt.* y *vi.* disminuir
diminutive, *adj.* y *n.* diminutivo, *m.*
dine, *vi.* comer, cenar
diner, *n.* coche comedor, *m.*
dining, *adj.* comedor; **dining car,** coche comedor; **dining room,** comedor, *m.*
dinner, *n.* comida, cena, *f.*
dip, *vt.* remojar, sumergir; *vi.* sumergirse; inclinarse; *n.* inmersión, *f.*
diphtheria, *n.* difteria, *f.*
diploma, *n.* diploma, *m.*
diplomacy, *n.* diplomacia, *f.*
diplomat, *n.* diplomático, *m.*
diplomatic, *adj.* diplomático
direct, *adj.* directo, derecho, recto; *vt.* dirigir
direction, *n.* dirección, manejo, *m.*; rumbo, *m.*
director, *n.* director, *m.*
directory, *n.* directorio, *m.*; *f.* guía,
dirt, *n.* suciedad, mugre, *f.*
dirty, *adj.* sucio; vil, bajo; *vt.* ensuciar
disadvantage, *n.* desventaja, *f.*
disagree, *vi.* discordar, estar en desacuerdo; hacer daño (el alimento)
disagreeable, *adj.* desagradable
disagreement, *n.* desacuerdo, *m.*
disappear, *vi.* desaparecer
disappearance, *n.* desaparición, *f.*
disappoint, *vt.* decepcionar
disappointment, *n.* decepción, *f.*
disapproval, *n.* desaprobación, censura, *f.*
disapprove, *vt.* desaprobar
disarmament, *n.* desarme, *m.*
disaster, *n.* desastre, *m.*
disastrous, *adj.* desastroso
disbursement, *n.* desembolso, *m.*
discard, *vt.* descartar; *n.* descarte (en el juego de naipes), *m.*

discharge, *vt.* descargar, pagar (una deuda, etc.); despedir; *n.* descarga, *f.*; descargo, *m.*

disciple, *n.* discípulo, *m.*

discipline, *n.* disciplina, *f.*; *vt.* disciplinar

disclose, *vt.* descubrir, revelar

discomfort, *n.* incomodidad, *f.*

disconnect, *vt.* desunir, separar

discontent, *n.* descontento, *m.*; *adj.* malcontento

discontinue, *vt.* descontinuar

discotheque, *n.* discoteca, *f.*

discount, *n.* descuento, *m.*; rebaja, *f.*; *vt.* descontar

discourage, *vt.* desalentar, desanimar

discouragement, *n.* desaliento, *m.*

discover, *vt.* descubrir

discovery, *n.* descubrimiento, *m.*

discretion, *n.* discreción, *f.*

discriminate, *vt.* distinguir

discrimination, *n.* discriminación, *f.*

discuss, *vt.* discutir

discussion, *n.* discusión, *f.*

disease, *n.* mal, *m.*; enfermedad, *f.*

diseased, *adj.* enfermo

disfigure, *vt.* desfigurar, afear

disgrace, *n.* deshonra, *f.*; desgracia, *f.*; *vt.* des honrar

disgraceful, *adj.* deshonroso, vergonzoso

disguise, *vt.* disfrazar; simular; *n.* disfraz, *m.*; máscara, *f.*

disgust, *n.* disgusto, *m.*; aversión, *f.*; *vt.* disgustar, repugnar

dish, *n.* fuente, *f.*, plato, *m.*

dishearten, *vt.* desalentar, descorazonar

disillusion, *n.* desengaño, *m.*, desilusión, *f.*; *vt.* desengañar

disinfect, *vt.* desinfectar

disinfectant, *n.* desinfectante, *m.*

disloyal, *adj.* desleal; infiel

disloyalty, *n.* deslealtad, *f.*

disobedient, *adj.* desobediente

disobey, *vt.* desobedecer

disorder, *n.* desorden, *m.*

disorderly, *adj.* desarreglado, confuso

dispatch, *n.* despacho, *m.*; embarque, *m.*; *vt.* despachar; embarcar; remitir

dispel, *vt.* disipar, dispersar

dispensary, *n.* dispensario, *m.*

dispensation, *n.* dispensa, *f.*

dispense, *vt.* dispensar; distribuir

displaced, *adj.* desplazado, dislocado

display, *vt.* desplegar; exponer; ostentar; *n.* exhibición, *f.*; ostentación, *f.*

displease, *vt.* disgustar; ofender; desagradar

dispose, *vt.* disponer; dar; *vi.* vender; trasferir

disposition, *n.* disposición, *f.*; índole, *f.*; carácter, *m.*

dispute, *n.* disputa, controversia, *f.*; *vt.* y *vi.* disputar

disqualify, *vi.* inhabilitar

disregard, *vt.* desatender, desdeñar; *n.* desatención, *f.*

disreputable, *adj.* despreciable

disrupt, *vt.* y *vi.* desbaratar, hacer pedazos; desorganizar

dissatisfaction, *n.* descontento, disgusto, *m.*

disseminate, *vt.* diseminar, propagar

dissension, *n.* disensión, discordia, *f.*

dissipation, *n.* disipación, *f.*; libertinaje, *m.*

dissolve, *vt.* y *vi.* disolver

dissuade, *vt.* disuadir

distance, *n.* distancia, *f.*

distant, *adj.* distante, lejano; esquivo

distasteful, *adj.* desagradable

distinct, *adj.* distinto, diferente; claro, sin confusión

distinction, *n.* distinción, diferencia, *f.*

distinguish, *vt.* distinguir; discernir; **distinguished**, *adj.* distinguido, eminente

distress, *n.* aflicción, *f.*; *vt.* angustiar, acongojar

distribute, *vt.* distribuir, repartir

distributor, *n.* distribuidor, distribuidora

district, *n.* distrito, *m.*

distrust, *vt.* desconfiar; *n.* desconfianza, *f.*

disturb, *vt.* perturbar, estorbar

ditch, *n.* zanja, *f.*

dive, *vi.* sumergirse, zambullirse; bucear; *n.* zambullidura, *f.*; (Mex.) clavado, *m.*

diver, *n.* buzo, *m.*

diversion, *n.* diversión, *f.*; pasatiempo, *m.*

diversity, *n.* diversidad, *f.*

divert, *vt.* desviar; divertir

divide, *vt.* dividir; repartir; desunir; *vi.* dividirse

dividend, *n.* dividendo, *m.*

divine, *adj.* divino; sublime

diving, *n.* buceo, *m.*; **diving suit**, escafandra, *f.*

divinity, *n.* divinidad, *f.*

division, *n.* división, *f.*

divorce, *n.* divorcio, *m.*; *vt.* y *vi.* divorciar, divorciarse

DNA, deoxyribonucleic acid, ácido ribonucleico

do, *vt.* hacer, ejecutar; *vi.* obrar

docile, *adj.* dócil, apacible

doctor, *n.* doctor, médico, *m.*

doctrine, *n.* doctrina, *f.*

document, *n.* documento, *m.*

dodge, *vt.* evadir, esquivar

does, tercera persona del singular del verbo **do**

dog, *n.* perro, *m.*

doghouse, *n.* perrera, *f.*, casa de perro; (coll.) **to be in the doghouse**, estar castigado, estar en desgracia

dolly, *n.* pañito de adorno, *m.*

doings, *n. pl.* hechos, *m. pl.*

doll, *n.* muñeca, *f.*

dollar, *n.* dólar, peso (moneda de E.U.A.), *m.*

dome, *n.* cúpula, *f.*

domestic, *adj.* doméstico

domesticate, *vt.* domesticar

dominate, *vt.* y *vi.* dominar

domination, *n.* dominación. *f.*

domineering, *adj.* tiránico

Dominican Republic, República Dominicana, *f.*

domino, *n.* dominó, *m.*

donate, *vt.* donar, contribuir

donation, *n.* contribución, donación, *f.*

done, *adj.* hecho; cocido, asado; *p. p.* del verbo **do**

donkey, *n.* burro, asno, *m.*

doom, *n.* condena, *f.*; suerte, *f.*; *vt.* sentenciar, condenar

door, *n.* puerta, *f.*

doorbell, *n.* timbre de llamada, *m.*

doorknob, *n.* tirador, *m.* perilla, *f.*

doorman, *n.* portero, *m.*

doorstep, *n.* umbral, *m.*

doorway, *n.* puerta de entrada, *f.*

dope, *n.* narcótico, *m.*, droga heroica; (coll.) información, *f.*

dormitory, *n.* dormitorio, *m.*

dot, *n.* punto, *m.*

doubt, *n.* duda, sospecha, *f.*; *vt.* y *vi.* dudar

doubtful, *adj.* dudoso

doubtless, *adj.* indudable

dough, *n.* masa, pasta, *f.*

doughnut, *n.* rosquilla, *f.*, especie de buñuelo

dove, *n.* paloma, *f.*

dowdy, *adj.* desaliñado

down, *n.* plumón, *m.*; bozo, vello, *m.*; **ups and downs**, vaivenes, *m. pl.*; *adv.* abajo

downcast, *adj.* cabizbajo

downfall, *n.* ruina, decadencia, *f.*

downpour, *n.* aguacero, *m.*

downstairs, *adv.* abajo; *n.* piso inferior, *m.*

downtown, *n.* centro, *m.*, parte céntrica de una ciudad

doze, *vi.* dormitar

dozen, *n.* docena, *f.*

D.P., displaced person, persona desplazada

Dr., Doctor, Dr., Doctor

draft, *n.* dibujo, *m.*; (com.) giro, *m.*; corriente de aire; (mil.) conscripción, *f.*; **rough draft**, borrador, *m.*; *vt.* dibujar; redactar

draftsman, *n.* dibujante, *m.*

drag, *vt.* arrastrar; *vi.* arrastrarse; *n.* rémora, *f.*; (coll.) influencia, *f.*

dragon, *n.* dragón, *m.*

dragonfly, *n.* libélula, *f.*

drain, *vt.* desaguar; colar; *n.* desaguadero, *m.*

drainage, *n.* desagüe, *m.*; saneamiento, *m.*

drake, *n.* ánade macho, *m.*

drama, *n.* drama, *m.*

dramatic, dramatical, *adj.* dramático

dramatics, *n.* arte dramático; deciamación, *f.*

drank, *pretérito* del verbo **drink**

drape, *n.* cortina, *f.*; *vt.* vestir, colgar decorativamente

drapery, *n.* cortinaje, *m.*

draw, *vt.* tirar, traer; atraer; dibujar; girar, librar una letra de cambio

drawback, *n.* desventaja, *f.*

drawer, *n.* gaveta, *f.*; **drawers,** *n. pl.* calzones, *m. pl.*; calzoncillos, *m. pl.*

drawing, *n.* dibujo, *m.*; rifa, *f.*; **drawing room,** sala de recibo, *f.*

dread, *n.* miedo, terror, *m.*; *vt.* y *vi.* temer

dreadful, *adj.* terrible, espantoso

dream, *n.* suero, *m.*; fantasía, *f.*; *vi.* soñar; imaginarse

dreary, *adj.* espantoso, triste

dregs, *n. pl.* heces, *f. pl.*; escoria, *f.*

drench, *vt.* empapar, molar

dress, *n.* vestido, *m.*; traje, *m.*; *vt.* vestir, ataviar; curar (las heridas); *vi.* vestirse

dresser, *n.* tocador, *m.*

dressing, *n.* curación, *f.*; salsa, *f.*

dressy, *adj.* (coll.) vistoso; te, de vestir

drift, *n.* significado, *m.*; (naut.) deriva, *f.*

drill, *n.* taladro, *m.*, barrena, *f.*; (mil.) instrucción de reclutas; *vt.* taladrar; (mil.) disciplinar reclutas

drink, *vt.* y *vi.* beber; embriagarse; *n.* bebida, *f.*

drip, *vt.* y *vi.* gotear, destilar; *n.* gotera, *f.*

drive, *n.* paseo, *m.*; pulso, *m.*; *vt.* y *vi.* impeler; guiar, manejar, conducir; (mech.) impulsar; andar en coche

drive-in, *n.* restaurante o cine para automovilistas

driven, *p. p.* del verbo **drive**

driver, *n.* cochero, *m.*; carretero, *m.*; conductor, *m.*; chofer, *m.*

driving, *adj.* motriz; conductor; impulsor; **driving school,** autoescuela, *f.*, escuela de manejo

drizzle, *vi.* lloviznar; *n.* llovizna, *f.*

drone, *n.* zangano de colmena, *m.*; haragán, *m.*

droop, *vi.* inclinarse, colgar; desanimarse

drop, *n.* gota, *f.*; **letter drop,** buzón, *m.*; *vt.* soltar; cesar; dejar caer

dropsy, *n.* hidropesía,

drove, *n.* manada, *f.*; rebaño, *m.*; *pretérito* del verbo **drive**

drown, *vt.* y *vi.* sumergir; anegar

drudgery, *n.* trabajo arduo y monótono

drug, *n.* droga, *f.*, medicamento, *m.*; *vt.* narcotizar

druggist, *n.* farmacéutico, boticario, *m.*

drugstore, *n.* botica, *f.*

drum, *n.* tambor, *m.*; tímpano (del oído), *m.*

drumstick, *n.* palillo de tambor; pata (de ave cocida), *f.*

drunk, *adj.* borracho, ebrio, embriagado; *p. p.* del verbo **drink**

drunkard, *n.* borrachón, *m.*

dry, *adj.* árido, seco; aburrido; **dry cleaning,** lavado en seco; *vt.* y *vi.* secar; enjugar

D.S.T., Daylight Saving Time, hora oficial (aprovechamiento de luz del día)

duck, *n.* ánade, *m.* y *f.*, pato, pata; *vt.* zambullir; *vi.* zambullirse; agacharse

due, *adj.* debido, adecuado; **to**

become due, (com.) vencerse (una deuda, un plazo, etc.);
dues, n. pl. cuota, f.
dumb, adj. mudo; (coll.) estúpido
dump, n. vaciadero, depósito, m.; **dumps,** n. pl. abatimiento, m., murria, f.
dumpling, n. empanada, f.
dunce, n. tonto, tonta
dungeon, n. calabozo, m.
dupe, n. bobo, boba; víctima, f.; vt. engañar, embaucar
duplicate, n. duplicado, m.; copia, f.; vt. duplicar
durable, adj. durable, duradero
duration, n. duración, f.
during, prep. durante
dusk, n. crepúsculo, m.
dusky, adj. oscuro
dust, n. polvo, m.
duster, n. plumero, m.; bata corta de mujer
dusty, adj. polvoriento; empolvado
Dutch, adj. holandés, holandesa
duty, n. deber, m.; obligación, f.; **custom duties,** derechos de aduana
dwarf, n. enano, enana
dwell, vi. habitar, morar
dwelling, n. habitación, residencia, f.
dye, vt. teñir, colorar; n. tinte, colorante, m.
dying, adj. agonizante, moribundo
dynamic, adj. dinámico, enérgico
dynamite, n. dinamita, f.
dynasty, n. dinastía, f.
dysentery, n. disentería, f.

E

E., east, E., este, oriente
ea., each, c/u., cada uno
each, adj. cada; pron. cada uno, cada una, cada cual
eager, adj. deseoso, ansioso
eagle, n. águila, f.
ear, n. oreja, f.; oído, m.; (bot.) espiga f.

earache, n. dolor de oído, m.
eardrum, n. tímpano, m.
early, adj. y adv. temprano
earmuff, n. orejera, f.
earn, vt. ganar, obtener
earnest, adj. fervoroso; serio
earnings, n. pl. ingresos, m. pl., ganancias, f. pl.
earphone, n. audífono, auricular, m.
earth, n. tierra, f.
earthly, adj. terrestre, mundano
earthquake, n. terremoto, m.
ease, n. facilidad, f.; **at ease,** sosegado; vt. aliviar
easel, n. caballete, m.
easily, adv. fácilmente
east, n. oriente, este, m.
Easter, n. Pascua de Resurrección, f.
easterly, eastern, adj. oriental, del este
easy, adj. fácil
eat, vt. comer
ebony, n. ébano, m.
eccentric, adj. excéntrico
ecclesiastic, adj. y n. eclesiástico, m.
echo, n. eco, m.; vi. resonar, repercutir (la voz)
eclipse, n. eclipse, m.; vt. eclipsar
ecological, adj. ecológico
ecology, n. ecología, f.
economic, economical, adj. económico
economics, n. economía, f.
economize, vt. y vi. economizar
economy, n. economía, f.; frugalidad, f.
edit, vt. redactar; dirigir (una publicación); revisar o corregir (un artículo, etc.)
edition, n. edición, f.; publicación, f.; impresión, f.; tirada, f.
editor, n. director, redactor (de una publicación), m.
editorial, n. editorial, m.
educate, vt. educar; enseñar
educated, adj. educado, instruido
education, n. educación, f.;

crianza, *f.*

educational, *adj.* educativo

eel, *n.* anguila, *f.*

efface, *vt.* borrar, destruir

effect, *n.* efecto, *m.*; realidad, *f.*; **effects**, *n. pl.* efectos, bienes, *m. pl.*; *vt.* efectuar, ejecutar

effective, *adj.* eficaz; efectivo; real

effervescent, *adj.* efervescente.

efficiency, *n.* eficiencia, *f.*

efficient, *adj.* eficaz; eficiente

effort *n.* esfuerzo, empeño, *m.*

effusive, *adj.* efusivo, expansivo

e.g., for example, p.ej., por ejemplo, vg. verbigracia

egg, *n.* huevo, *m.*

eggplant, *n.* (bot.) berenjena, *f.*

eggshell, *n.* cáscara o cascarón de huevo

egg-yolk, *n.* yema de huevo, *f.*

ego, *n.* ego, yo, *m.*

egoism, egotism, *n.* egoísmo, *m.*

Egypt, Egipto

Egyptian, *n.* y *adj.* egipcio, egipcia

eight, *adj.* y *n.* ocho, *m.*

eighteen, *adj.* y *n.* dieciocho, *m.*

eighteenth, *adj.* y *n.* décimoctavo, *m.*

eighth, *adj.* y *n.* octavo, *m.*

eighty, *adj.* y *n.* ochenta, *m.*

either, *pron.* y *adj.* cualquiera, uno de dos; *conj.* o, sea, ya, ora

elaborate, *vt.* elaborar; *adj.* elaborado, trabajado, primoroso

elapse, *vi.* pasar, trascurrir (el tiempo)

elated, *adj.* exaltado, animoso

elder, *adj.* que tiene más edad, mayor; *n.* anciano, antepasado, *m.*; eclesiástico, *m.*; (bot.) saúco, *m.*

elderly, *adj.* de edad madura

eldest, *adj.* el mayor, el más anciano

elect, *vt.* elegir

election, *n.* elección, *f.*; **elections**, elecciones, *f. pl.*

electoral, *adj.* electoral

electric, electrical, *adj.* eléctrico

electrician, *n.* electricista, *m.*

electricity, *n.* electricidad, *f.*

electrocute, *vt.* electrocutar

electronics, *n.* electrónica, *f.*

elegance, *n.* elegancia, *f.*

elegant, *adj.* elegante

element, *n.* elemento, *m.*; principio, *m.*

elemental, *adj.* elemental

elementary, *adj.* simple

elephant, *n.* elefante, *m.*

elevate, *vt.* elevar, alzar

elevation, *n.* elevación, *f.*; altura, *f.*

elevator, *n.* ascensor, elevador, *m.*

eleven, *n.* y *adj.* once, *m.*

eleventh, *n.* y *adj.* onceno, undécimo, *m.*

eligible, *adj.* elegible; deseable

eliminate, *vt.* eliminar, descartar

elope, *vi.* fugarse con un amante

elopement, *n.* fuga, huida (con un amante), *f.*

eloquence, *n.* elocuencia,

eloquent, *adj.* elocuente

else, *adj.* otro; *adv.* en lugar distinto; en forma distinta; **nothing else**, nada más; *conj.* de otro modo; si no

elsewhere, *adv.* en otra parte

elude, *vt.* eludir, evadir

elusive, *adj.* evasivo

emanate, *vi.* emanar

emancipation, *n.* emancipación, *f.*

embankment, *n.* dique, *m.*, presa, *f.*; terraplén, *m.*

embargo, *n.* embargo, *m.*; *vt.* embargar

embark, *vt.* y *vi.* embarcar; embarcarse

embarrass, *vt.* avergonzar, desconcertar

embarrassing, *adj.* penoso

embarrassment, *n.* vergüenza, pena, *f.*

embassy, *n.* embajada, *f.*

embezzle, *vt.* desfalcar
emblem, *n.* emblema, *m.*
embrace, *vt.* abrazar; contener; *n.* abrazo, *m.*
embroider, *vt.* bordar
emerge, *vi.* salir, surgir
emergency, *n.* emergencia, *f.*
emigrate, *vi.* emigrar
eminence, *n.* eminencia, excelencia, *f.*
eminent, *adj.* eminente
emotion, *n.* emoción, *f.*
emperor, *n.* emperador, *m.*
emphasis, *n.* énfasis, *m.*
emphasize, *vt.* recalcar
emphatic, *adj.* enfático
empire, *n.* imperio, *m.*
employ, *vt.* emplear, ocupar; *n.* empleo, *m.*
employee, *n.* empleado, empleada
employer, *n.* amo, patrón, *m.*
employment, *n.* empleo, *m.*; ocupación, *f.*
empress, *n.* emperatriz, *f.*
empty, *adj.* vacío; vano; *vt.* vaciar, verter
enable, *vt.* habilitar; facilitar
enamel, *n.* esmalte, charol, *m.*
enchanting, *adj.* encantador
encircle, *vt.* circundar
enclose, *vt.* cercar, circundar; incluir
enclosure, *n.* cercado, *m.*; anexo (en una carta), *m.*
encounter, *n.* encuentro, *m.*; duelo, *m.*; pelea, *f.*; *vi.* encontrarse
encourage, *vt.* animar, alentar
encouragement, *n.* estímulo, aliento, *m.*
encouraging, *adj.* alentador
encyclopedia, *n.* enciclopedia, *f.*
end, *n.* fin, *m.*; término, *m.*; propósito, intento, *m.*; *vt.* matar, concluir; terminar; *vi.* acabarse
endeavor, *vi.* esforzarse; intentar; *n.* esfuerzo, *m.*
ending, *n.* conclusión, *f.*; muerte, *f.*
endless, *adj.* infinito, perpetuo, sin fin
endorse, *vt.* endosar (una letra

de cambio)
endorsement, *n.* endorso o endoso, *m.*
endurance, *n.* duración, *f.*; paciencia, resistencia, *f.*
endure, *vt.* sufrir, aguantar, soportar; *vi.* durar
ENE, E.N.E., east-north-east, ENE, estenordeste
energetic, *adj.* enérgico, vigoroso
enforce, *vt.* poner en vigor
enforcement, *n.* compulsión, *f.*; cumplimiento (de una ley), *m.*
engage, *vt.* empeñar, obligar; ocupar; *vt.* comprometerse
engaged, *adj.* comprometido
engagement, *n.* noviazgo, compromiso, *m.*; cita, *f.*
engine, *n.* máquina, *f.*; locomotora, *f.*
engineer, *n.* ingeniero, *m.*; maquinista, *m.*
engineering, *n.* ingeniería, *f.*
England, Inglaterra, *f.*
English, *n. y adj.* inglés, *m.*; **English Channel**, Canal de la Mancha
Englishman, *n.* inglés, *m.*
Englishwoman, *n.* inglesa, *f.*
enjoy, *vt.* gozar; disfrutar de
enjoyable, *adj.* agradable
enjoyment, *n.* goce, disfrute, *m.*; placer, *m.*
enlarge, *vt.* ampliar; *vi.* extenderse, dilatarse
enlargement, *n.* aumento, *m.*; ampliación, *f.*
enlist, *vt.* alistar, reclutar; *vi.* inscribirse como recluta, engancharse
enliven, *vt.* animar; avivar
enormous, *adj.* enorme
enough, *adj.* bastante, suficiente; *adv.* suficientemente
enroll, *vt.* registrar, inscribir
ensemble, *n.* conjunto, *m.*
entangle, *vt.* enmarañar, embrollar
enter, *vt.* entrar, admitir; *vi.* entrar
enterprise, *n.* empresa, *f.*
enterprising, *adj.* emprendedor

entertain, *vt.* entretener; agasajar; divertir

entertaining, *adj.* divertido, chistoso

entertainment, *n.* festejo, *m.*; diversión, *f.*, entretenimiento, *m.*

enthusiasm, *n.* entusiasmo, *m.*

enthusiastic, *adj.* entusiasmado, entusiasta

entire, *adj.* entero

entrance, *n.* entrada, *f.*; admisión, *f.* ingreso, *m.*

entreat, *vt.* rogar, suplicar,

entrust, *vt.* confiar

entry, *n.* entrada, *f.*; (com.) partida, *f.*

envious, *adj.* envioso

environment, *n.* ambiente, *m.*

environmental, *adj.* ambiental

envy, *n.* envidia, *f.*; *vt.* envidiar

epic, *adj.* épico; *n.* epopeya, *f.*

epidemic, *adj.* epidémico; *n.* epidemia, *f.*

epileptic, *adj.* y *n.* epiléptico, *m.*

episode, *n.* episodio, *m.*

epoch, *n.* época, era, *f.*

equal, *adj.* igual; semejante; *n.* igual, *m.*; *vt.* igualar

equality, *n.* igualdad, *f.*

equator, *n.* ecuador, *m.*

equilibrium, *n.* equilibrio, *m.*

equipment, *n.* equipo, *m.*

equitable, *adj.* equitativo

equivalent, *n.* y *adj.* equivalente, *m.*

era, *n.* edad, época, era, *f.*

erase, *vt.* borrár

eraser, *n.* goma de borrar, *f.*, borrador, *m.*

erect, *vt.* erigir; establecer; *adj.* derecho, erguido

erosion, *n.* erosión, *f.*

err, *vi.* errar; desviarse

errand, *n.* recado, mensaje, *m.*

erroneous, *adj.* erróneo; falso

error, *n.* error, yerro, *m.*

eruption, *n.* erupción, *f.*

escalate, *vi.* crecer

escalator, *n.* escalera mecánica, *f.*

escapade, *n.* travesura, *f.*

escape, *vt.* evitar; escapar; *vi.* evadirse, salvarse; *n.* escapada, huida, fuga, *f.*

escort, *n.* escolta, *f.*; acompañant *m.*; *vt.* escoltar, acompañar

especial, *adj.* especial, excepcional; **especially,** *adv.* particularmente; sobre todo

essay, *n.* ensayo literario, *m.*

essence, *n.* esencia, *f.*

essential, *adj.* esencial

E.S.T., Eastern Standard Time, hora normal de la region oriental de E.U.A

establish, *vt.* establecer

establishment, *n.* establecimiento, *m.*

estate, *n.* patrimonio, *m.*; bienes, *m. pl.*; predio, *m.*

esteem, *vt.* estimar; *n.* consideración, *f.*

esthetic, *adj.* estético; **esthetics,** *n.* estética, *f.*

estimate, *vt.* estimar, apreciar, tasar; *n.* cálculo, *m.*; presupuesto, *m.*

estrogen, *n.* estrogeno, *m.*

etching, *n.* aguafuerte, *f.*

eternal, *adj.* eterno

eternity, *n.* eternidad, *f.*

ether, *n.* éter, *m.*

etiquette, *n.* etiqueta, *f.*

Europe, Europa *f.*

European, *n.* y *adj.* europeo, europea

evacuate, *vt.* evacuar

evacuation, *n.* evacuación, *f.*

evaluate, *vt.* avaluar, evaluar

evaporate, *vi.* evaporarse; **evaporated milk,** leche evaporada

even, *adj.* llano, igual; *adv.* aun, aun cuando; *vt.* igualar, allanar

evening, *adj.* vespertino; *n.* tarde, noche, *f.*

event, *n.* evento, acontecimiento, *m.*

eventful, *adj.* memorable

eventual, *adj.* eventual, fortuito; **eventually,** *adv.* finalmente, con el tiempo

ever, *adj.* siempre; **ever since,**

desde que

everlasting, *adj.* eterno

every, *adj.* todo, cada; **every day,** todos los días

everybody, *pron.* cada uno, cada una; todo el mundo

everyday, *adj.* ordinario, rutinario

everything, *n.* todo, *m.*

everywhere, *adv.* en todas partes

evil, *adj.* malo; *n.* maldad, *f.*; daño, *m.*; mal, *m.*

evoke, *vt.* evocar

evolution, *n.* evolución, desarrollo, *m.*

exact, *adj.* exacto, puntual; *vt.* exigir

exacting, *adj.* exigente

exaggerate, *vt.* exagerar

exaggeration, *n.* exageración, *f.*

examination, *n.* examen, *m.*

examine, *vt.* examinar

exasperation, *n.* exasperación, irritación, *f.*

excavate, *vt.* excavar

excavation, *n.* excavación, *f.*; cavidad, *f.*

exceed, *vt.* exceder

exceedingly, *adv.* altamente

excel, *vt.* sobresalir, superar

excellent, *adj.* excelente; sobresaliente

except, *vt.* exceptuar, excluir

exception, *n.* excepción, exclusión, *f.*

exceptional, *adj.* excepcional

excerpt, *vt.* extraer; extractar; *n.* extracto, *m.*

excess, *n.* exceso, *m.*

exchange, *vt.* cambiar; *n.* cambio, *m.*; bolsa, lonja, *f.*

excite, *vt.* excitar; estimular

excitement, *n.* excitación, *f.*, comoción, *f.*

exclaim, *vi.* exclamar

exclamation, *n.* exclamación, *f.*; **exclamation mark, exclamation point,** punto de admiraión

exclude, *vt.* excluir

exclusion, *n.* exclusión, exclusiva, *f.*; excepción, *f.*

exclusive, *adj.* exclusivo

excrement, *n.* excremento, *m.*

excursion, *n.* excursión, expedición, *f.*

excuse, *vt.* excusar; perdonar; *n.* excusa, *f.*

execute, *vt.* ejecutar; llevar a cabo, cumplir

execution, *n,* ejecución, *f.*

executioner, *n.* verdugo, *m.*

executive, *adj.* y *n.* ejecutivo, *m.*

exemplify, *vt.* ejemplificar

exempt, *adj.* exento; *vt.* eximir, exentar

exemption, *n.* exención, franquicia, *f.*

exercise, *n.* ejercicio, *m.*; ensayo, *m.*; práctica, *f.*; *vi.* hacer ejercicio; *vt.* ejercer

exhaust, *n.* (auto., avi.) escape, *m.*; *vt.* agotar, consumir

exhausting, *adj.* agotador

exhibit, *vt.* exhibir; mostrar; *n.* exhibición, *f.*

exhibition, *n.* exhibición, presentación, *f.*; espectáculo, *m.*

exile, *n.* destierro, *m.*; desterrado, *m.*; *vt.* desterrar, deportar

exist, *vi.* existir

existence, *n.* existencia, *f.*

existing, *adj.* actual, presente

exit, *n.* salida, *f.*

exorbitant, *adj.* exorbitante, excesivo

exotic, *adj.* exótico, extranjero

expand, *vt.* extender, dilatar

expansion, *n.* expansión, *f.*

expect, *vt.* esperar

expectant, *adj.* que espera; encinta, embarazada

expedite, *vt.* acelerar; expedir

expel, *vt.* expeler, expulsar

expenditure, *n.* gasto, desembolso, *m.*

expense, *n.* gasto, *m.*

expensive, *adj.* caro, costoso

experience, *n.* experiencia, *f.*; práctica, *f.*; *vt.* experimentar; saber

experienced, *adj.* experimentado; versado, perito

experiment, *n.* experimento, *m.*; prueba, *f.*; *vt.* experimentar

expert, *adj.* experto, diestro; perito; *n.* maestro, maestra; conocedor, conocedora; perito, perita

expiration, *n.* expiración, *f.*; muerte, *f.*; vencimiento (de una letra o pagaré, etc.), *m.*

expire, *vi.* expirar, morir

explain, *vt.* explicar

explanation, *n.* explicación, aclaración, *f.*

explode, *vt.* y *vi.* volar, estallar, hacer explosión

explore, *vt.* explorar

explorer, *n.* explorador, *m.*

explosion, *n.* explosión, *f.*

export, *vt.* exportar

export, exportation, *n.* exportación, *f.*

expose, *vt.* exponer; mostrar; descubrir

exposition, *n.* exposición, exhibición, *f.*

express, *vt.* expresar, exteriorizar; *adj.* expreso, claro, a propósito; *n.* expreso, correo expreso, *m.*

expression, *n.* expresión, *f.*

expressive, *adj.* expresivo

expressway, *n.* autopista, *f.*

expropriate, *vt.* expropiar, confiscar

exquisite, *adj.* exquisito

extemporaneous, *adj.* extemporáneo, improviso

extend, *vt.* extender; **to extend (time),** prorrogar (un plazo)

extension, *n.* extensión, *f.*; prórroga, *f.*

extensive, *adj.* extenso; amplio

extent, *n.* extensión, *f.*; grado, *m.*

exterior, *n.* y *adj.* exterior, *m.*

exterminate, *vt.* exterminar

external, *adj.* externo, exterior

extinguish, *vt.* extinguir; suprimir

extra, *adj.* extraordinario, adicional; *n.* suplemento extraordinario de un periódico

extract, *vt.* extraer; extractar; *n.* extracto, *m.*; compendio, *m.*

extraction, *n.* extracción, *f.*

extraordinary, *adj.* extraordinario

extrasensory, *adj.* extrasensorio, extrasensoria

extravagance, *n.* extravagancia, *f.*; derroche, *m.*

extravagant, *adj.* extravagante, singular, excesivo; derrochador

extreme, *adj.* extremo; último; *n.* extremo, *m.*

extremity, *n.* extremidad, *f.*

exuberance, *n.* exuberancia, *f.*

exult, *vi.* regocijarse

eye, *n.* ojo, *m.*, vista, *f.*

eyeball, *n.* niña del ojo, *f.*

eyebrow, *n.* ceja, *f.*

eyeglass, *n.* anteojo, *m.*

eyelash, *n.* pestaña, *f.*

eyelid, *n.* párpado, *m.*

eyesight, *n.* vista, *f.*

eyestrain, *n.* cansancio o tensión de los ojos

F

F., Fellow, miembro de una sociedad científica o académica; **Fahrenheit,** Fahrenheit; **Friday,** vier., viernes

f., following, sig.^{te}, siguiente; **feminine,** *f.*, femenino; **folio,** fol., folio

fabricate, *vt.* fabricar, edificar; inventar (una leyen da, una mentira, etc.)

face, *n.* cara, faz, *f.*; fachada, *f.*; frente, *f.*; **to lose face,** sufrir pérdida de prestigio; **face value,** valor nominal o aparente; *vt.* encararse; hacer frente

facilitate, *vt.* facilitar

fact, *n.* hecho, *m.*; realidad, *f.*; **in fact,** en efecto, verdaderamente

factor, *n.* factor, *m.*; agente, *m.*

factory, *n.* fábrica, *f.*, taller, *m.*

faculty, *n.* facultad, *f.*; profesorado, *m.*

fade, *vi.* marchitarse; desteñirse

fail, *vt.* abandonar; decepcionar; reprobar (a un estudiante); *vi.* fallar, fracasar; *n.* falta, *f.*

failure, *n.* fracaso, *m.*; quiebra, bancarrota,

faint, *vi.* desmayarse

fair, *adj.* hermoso, bello; blanco; rubio; justo; *n.* feria, exposición, *f.*

fairly, *adv.* claramente; bastante; **fairly well,** bastante bien

fairness, *n.* hermosura, *f.*; equidad, *f.*

fairy, *n.* hada, *f.*, duende, *m.*; **fairy tale,** cuento de hadas, *m.*

faith, *n.* fe, *f.*

faithful, *adj.* fiel, leal

faithless, *adj.* infiel

fake, *adj.* (coll.) falso, fraudulento; *vt.* (coll.) engañar; imitar

faker, *n.* farsante, *m.* y *f.*

fall, *vi.* caer, caerse; *n.* caída, *f.*; otoño, *m.*

false, *adj.* falso, pérfido; postizo

falsehood, *n.* falseded, *f.*; mentira, *f.*

familiar, *adj.* familiar, casero, conocido

familiarity, *n.* familiaridad, *f.*

family, *n.* familia, *f.*; linaje, *m.*; clase, especie, *f.*

famine, *n.* hambre, *f.*; carestía, *f.*

fan, *n.* abanico, *m.*; ventilador, *m.*; aficionado, aficionada; *vt.* abanicar

fancy, *n.* fantasía, imaginación, *f.*; capricho, *m.*; *adj.* de fantasía; *vt.* y *vi.* imaginar; gustar de; suponer

far, *adv.* lejos; *adj.* lejano, distante, remoto

faraway, *adj.* lejano

fare, *n.* alimento, *m.*, comida, *f.*; pasaje, *m.*, tarifa, *f.*

farewell, *n.* despedida, *f.*

farfetched, *adj.* forzado, traído de los cabellos

farm, *n.* hacienda, granja, *f.*

farmer, *n.* labrador, labradora; hacendado, hacendada; agricultor, agricultora

farming, *n.* agricultura, cultivo, *m.*

far-off, *adj.* remoto, distante

far-reaching, *adj.* de gran alcance, trascendental

farsighted, *adj.* présbita, présbite; (fig.) precavido

farther, *adj.* y *adv.* mas lejos; más adelante

farthest, *adj.* más distante, más remoto; *adv.* a la mayor distancia

fascinate, *vt.* fascinar, encantar

fascinating, *adj.* fascinador, seductor

fashion, *n.* moda, *f.*; uso, *m.*, costumbre, *f.*; *vt.* formar, amoldar

fashionable, *adj.* en boga, de moda; elegante

fast, *vi.* ayunar; *n.* ayuno, *m.*; *adj.* firme, estable; veloz; *adv.* de prisa

fasten, *vt.* afirmar, fijar

fat, *adj.* gordo; **to get fat,** engordar; *n.* gordo, *m.*, gordura, *f.*; grasa, manteca, *f.*; sebo, *m.*

fate, *n.* hado, destino, *m.*

fateful, *adj.* funesto

father, *n.* padre, *m.*

father-in-law, *n.* suegro, *m.*

fatherland, *n.* patria *f.*

fatherless, *adj.* huérfano de padre

fatherly, *adj.* paternal

fatigue, *n.* fatiga, *f.*, cansancio, *m.*

fatten, *vt.* cebar, engordar

faucet, *n.* grifo *m.*; **water faucet,** toma, llave, *f.*, caño de agua, *m.*

favor, *n.* favor, beneficio, *m.*; **your favor,** su grata (carta); *vt.* favorecer, proteger, apoyar

favorable, *adj.* favorable, propicio; provechoso

favorite, *n.* y *adj.* favorito, favorita

FBI, Federal Bureau of Investigation, Departamento Federal de Investigación

fear, *vt.* y *vi.* temer, tener miedo; *n.* miedo, terror, pavor, *m.*

fearful, *adj.* temeroso; tímido
fearless, *adj.* intrépido
feasible, *adj.* factible, práctico
feast, *n.* banquete, festín, *m.*; fiesta, *f.*; *vt.* festejar; *vi.* comer opíparamente
feat, *n.* hecho, *m.*; acción, hazaña, *f.*
feather, *n.* pluma (de ave) *f.*
featherweight, *n.* peso pluma, *m.*
feature, *n.* facción del rostro; rasgo, *m.*; atracción principal; **double feature,** función de dos películas, *f.*; **features,** *n. pl.* facciones, *f. pl.*, fisonomía, *f.*
February, febrero, *m.*
federal, *adj.* federal
federation, *n.* confedera.ción, federación, *f.*
fee, *n.* paga, gratificación, *f.*; honorarios, derechos, *m. pl.*
feeble, *adj.* flaco, débil
feeble-minded, *adj.* retardado mentalmente
feed, *vt.* pacer; nutrir; alimentar; *n.* alimento, *m.*; pasto, *m.*
feeding, *n.* nutrición, alimento, *m.*
feel, *vt.* sentir; palpar
feeling, *n.* tacto, *m.*; sensibilidad, *f.*; sentimiento, *m.*
feet, *n. pl.* de **foot,** pies, *m. pl.*
feign, *vt.* y *vi.* inventar, fingir; simular
felicitation, *n.* felicitación, *f.*
fellow, *n.* compañero, camarada, *m.*; sujeto, *m.*; becario, *m.*
fellowship, *n.* beca (en una universidad), *f.*; camaradería, *f.*
female, *n.* hembra, *f.*; *adj.* femenino
feminine, *adj.* femenino
fence, *n.* cerca, valla, *f.*; *vt.* cercar; *vi.* esgrimir
fencing, *n.* esgrima, *f.*
fender, *n.* guardafango, *m.*
fertile, *adj.* fértil, fecundo
fertilizer, *n.* abono, *m.*
fervent, *adj.* ferviente; fervoroso
fervor, *n.* fervor, ardor, *m.*
festival, *n.* fiesta, *f.*

festive, *adj.* festivo, alegre
festivity, *n.* festividad, *f.*
fever, *n.* fiebre, *f.*
fiancé, *n.* novio, *m.*
fiancée, *n.* novia, *f.*
fickle, *adj.* voluble, inconstante
fiction, *n.* ficción, *f.*; invención, *f.*
fictitious, *adj.* ficticio; fingido
fiddle, *n.* violín, *m.*
fiddler, *n.* violinista, *m.* y *f.*
field, *n.* campo, *m.*; *adj.* campal
fierce, *adj.* fiero, feroz
fiery, *adj.* fogoso
fifteen, *n.* y *adj.* quince, *m.*
fifteenth, *n.* y *adj.* décimoquinto, *m.*
fifth, *n.* y *adj.* quinto, *m.*; quinto de galón (medida de vinos y licores)
fiftieth, *n.* y *adj.* quincuagésimo, *m.*
fifty, *n.* y *adj.* cincuenta, *m.*
fifty-fifty, *adj.* y *adv.* mitad y mitad
fight, *vi.* pelear; reñir; luchar; *n.* pelea, *f.*
fighter, *n.* luchador, luchadora; **fighter plane,** caza, *m.*
figure, *n.* figura, *f.*; cifra, *f.*; *vt.* figurar
file, *n.* archivo, *m.*; (mil.) fila, hilera, *f.*; lima, *f.*; *vt.* archivar; limar
filial, *adj.* filial
fill, *vt.* y *vi.* llenar, henchir; hartar; **to fill out,** llenar (un cuestionario, etc.)
filling, *n.* relleno, *m.*; orificación (de un diente), *f.*; **filling station,** estación de gasolina, *f.*
filly, *n.* potranca, *f.*
film, *n.* película, *f.*; membrana, *f.*
filter, *n.* filtro, *m.*; **filter-tip,** *adj.* de boquilla-filtro; *vt.* filtrar
filthy, *adj.* sucio, puerco
final, *adj.* final, útimo; definitivo; **finally,** *adv.* finalmente, por útimo; **finals,** último examen, juego, etc.

finality, *n.* finalidad, *f.*
finance, *n.* finaizas, *f. pl.*
financial, *adj.* financiero
find, *vt.* hallar, descubrir; *n.* hallazgo, descubrimiento, *m.*
fine, *adj.* fino; bueno; **the fine arts,** las bellas artes; *n.* multa, *f.*; *vt.* multar
finesse, *n.* sutileza, *f.*
finger, *n.* dedo, *m.*
fingernail, *n.* uña, *f.*
fingerprints, *n. pl.* impresiones digitales, *f. pl.*
finish, *vt.* acabar, terminar; *n.* conclusión, *f.*, final, *m.*
fire, *n.* fuego, *m.*; candela, *f.*; incendio, *m.*; *vi.* (mil.) tirar, hacer fuego
firearms, *n. pl.* armas de fuego, *f. pl.*
firefly, *n.* luciérnaga, *f.*, cocuyo, cucuyo, *m.*
fireman, *n.* bombero, *m.*; (rail.) fogonero, *m.*
fireplace, *n.* hogar, *m.*, chimenea, *f.*
fireplug, *n.* boca de incendios, toma de agua, *f.*
fireproof, *adj.* a prueba de fuego, refractario
fireside, *n.*sitio cerca a la chimenea u hogar; vida de hogar
fireworks, *n. pl.* fuegos artificiales, *m. pl.*
firm, *adj.* firme, estable; *n.* (com.) empresa, razón social, *f.*
firmament, *n.* firmamento, *m.*
first, *adj.* primero; primario; delantero; **first aid,** primeros auxilios; *adv.* primeramente
first-class, *adj.* de primera clase
firsthand, *adj.* directo, de primera mano
fiscal, *adj.* fiscal, del fisco
fish, *n.* pez, *m.*; pescado, *m.*; *vt.* y *vi.* pescar
fisherman, *n.* pescador, *m.*
fishing, *n.* pesca, *f.*
fist, *n.* puño, *m.*
fit, *adj.* apto, idóneo, capaz; *n.* convulsión, *f.*; ataque, *m.*; *vt.* ajustar, acomodar, adaptar;

sentar, quedar bien
five, *n.* y *adj.* cinco, *m.*
fix, *vt.* fijar, establecer; componer
fixtures, *n. pl.* enseres, *m. pl.*; instalación (eléctrica), *f.*
flag, *n.* bandera, *f.*; pabellon, *m.*
flagpole, *n.* asta de bandera, *f.*
flamingo, *n.* (orn.) flamenco, *m.*
flap, *n.* bragueta, *f.*; solapa, *f.*; aleta, *f.*; *vt.* y *vi.* aletear; sacudir
flash, *n.* relámpago, *m.*; llamarada, *f.*; destello, *m.*; *vi.* relampaguear; brillar
flashback, *n.* interrupción de la continuidad de un relato
flashlight, *n.* linterna, linterna eléctrica de bolsillo, *f.*
flat, *adj.* plano; insipido; **flat tire,** llanta desinflada, neumático desinflado; *n.* (mus.) bemol, *m.*; apartamiento, apartamento, *m.*
flatten, *vt.* allanar; aplastar
flatter, *vt.* adular
flavor, *n.* sabor, gusto, *m.*
flavoring, *n.* condimento, *m.*
flaw, *n.* falta, tacha,
flawless, *adj.* sin tacha
flax, *n.* lino, *m.*
flaxseed, *n.* semill de lino, *f.*
flea, *n.* pulga, *f.*
flee, *vi.* escapar; huir
fleecy, *adj.* lanudo
fleeting, *adj.* pasajero, fugitivo
flesh, *n.* carne, *f.*
flew, *pretérito* del verbo **fly**
flexible, *adj.* flexible
flicker, *vi.* aletear, fluctuar; *n.* aleteo, *m.*; **flicker of an eyelash,** pestañeo, *m.*
flier, *n.* aviador, aviadora; tren muy rápido
flight, *n.* buida, fuga, *f.*; vuelo, *m.*
fling, *vt.* lanzar, echar; *vi.* lanzarse con violencia; *n.* tiro, *m.*; tentativa, *f.*
flirt, *vi.* coquetear; *n.* coqueta, *f.*
flirtation, *n.* coqueteria, *f.*
float, *vi.* flotar; *n.* carro alegó-

rico, *m.*; flotador, *m.*

flock, *n.* manada, *f.*; rebaño, *m.*; gentío, *m.*; *vi.* congregarse

flood, *n.* diluvio, *m.*; inundación, *f.*; *vt.* inundar

floor, *n.* suelo, piso, *m.*

flounder, *n.* (pez) rodaballo, *m.*

flour, *n.* harina, *f.*

flourish, *vi.* prosperar; *n.* floreo de palabras; rasgo (de una pluma), *m.*; lozanía, *f.*

flow, *vi.* fluir, manar; *n.* flujo, *m.*, corriente, *f.*

flower, *n.* flor, *f.*

flowery, *adj.* florido

flu, *n.* (coll.) influenza, gripe, *f.*, trancazo, *m.*

fluent, *adj.* fluido; fluente, fácil; **fluently,** *adv.* con fluidez

fluorescent, *adj.* fluorescente; **fluorescent lighting,** aluminado fluorescente, *m.*

fluoridate, *vt.* fluorizar

fluoridation, *n.* fluoruración, *f.*

flush, *vt.* limpiar con un chorro de agua (por ej., un inodoro); *vi.* sonrojarse, ruborizarse; *n.* rubor, *m.*

fluster, *vt.* confundir, atropellar; *vi.* confundirse

flutter, *vt.* turbar, desordenar; *vi.* revolotear; flamear

fly, *vt.* y *vi.* volar; huir; *n.* mosca, *f.*; volante, *m.*

flying, *n.* vuelo, *m.*; aviación, *f.*; *adj.* volante, volador; de pasada

F.M. or **f.m., frequency modulation,** (rad.) modulación de frecuencia

f.o.b. or **F.O.B., free on board,** L.A.B., libre a bordo o f.a.b. franco a bordo

focus, *n.* foco, *m.*, punto céntrico; enfoque, *m.*; *vt.* enfocar

foe, *n.* adversario, adversaria, enemigo, enemiga

fog, *n.* niebla, *f.*

foil, *vt.* vencer; frustrar

fold, *n.* redil, *m.*; plegadura, *f.*, doblez, *m.*; *vt.* plegar, doblar

folder, *n.* folleto, *m.*; papelera, *f.*

foliage, *n.* follaje, *m.*

folk, *n.* gente, *f.*; **folk music,** música tradicional, *f.*; **folk song,** romance, *m.*, copla, *f.*

folklore, *n.* folklore, *m.*, tradiciones populares, *f. pl.*

follow, *vt.* seguir; *vi.* seguirse, resultar, provenir

following, *n.* séquito, cortejo, *m.*; profesión, *f.*; *adj.* próximo, siguiente

follow-up, *adj.* que sigue

fond, *adj.* afectuoso; aficionado; **to be fond of,** aficionarse, tener simpatía por

fondle, *vt.* mimar, acariciar

fondness, *n.* debilidad, *f.*; afición, *f.*

food, *n.* alimento, *m.*; comida, *f.*

fool, *n.* loco, loca, tonto, tonta, bobo, boba; *vt.* engañar; *vi.* tontear

foolish, *adj.* bobo, tonto, majadero

foolproof, *adj.* muy evidente, fácil hasta para un tonto

foot, *n.* pie, *m.*

football, *n.* futbol americano, *m.*; pelota de futbol, *f.*

footlights, *n. pl.* luces del proscenio; (fig.) el teatro, las tablas

footmark, *n.* huella, *f.*

footnote, *n.* anotación, glosa, *f.*; nota, *f.*

footprint, *n.* huella, pisada, *f.*

footstep, *n.* paso, *m.*; pisada, *f.*

footwear, *n.* calzado, *m.*

for, *prep.* para; por; *conj.* porque, pues; **what for?** ¿para qué?

forbear, *vt.* y *vi.* cesar, detenerse; abstenerse

forbearance, *n.* paciencia, *f.*

forbid, *vt.* prohibir; **God forbid!** Dios no quiera!

forbidden, *adj.* prohibido

force, *n.* fuerza, *f.*; poder, vigor, *m.*; valor, *m.*; **forces,** tropas, *f. pl.*; *vt.* forzar, violentar; obligar

forceful, *adj.* fuerte, poderoso; dominante

forceps, *n. pl.* pinzas, *f. pl.*

forearm, *n.* antebrazo, *m.*

forebear, *n.* antepasado, *m.*

foreboding, *n.* corazonada, *f.*

forecast, *vt.* y *vi.* proyectar, prever; *n.* previsión, *f.*; profecia *f.*; **weather forecast,** pronóstico del tiempo, *m.*

foreclosure, *n.* juicio hipotecario, *m.*

forefather, *n.* abuelo, antepasado, *m.*

forefinger, *n.* índice, *m.*

foregoing, *adj.* anterior, precedente

foreground, *n.* delantera, *f.*; primer plano, *m.*

foreign, *adj.* extranjero

foreigner, *n.* extranjero, extranjera, forastero, forastera

foreman, *n.* capataz, *m.*

forenoon, *n.* la mañana, las horas antes del mediodía

forerunner, *n.* precursor, precursora; predecesor, predecesora

foresee, *vt.* prever

foresight, *n.* previsión, *f.*

forest, *n.* bosque, *m.*; selva, *f.*

foreword, *n.* prefacio, prólogo, preámbulo, *m.*

forfeit, *n.* multa, *f.*; prenda, *f.*; *vt.* decomisar; perder

forget, *vt.* olvidar; descuidar

forgetful, *adj.* olvidadizo

forget-me-not, *n.* (bot.) nomeolvides, *f.*

forgive, *vt.* perdonar

forgiveness, *n.* perdón, *m.*

forgot, *pretérito* del verbo **forget**

forlorn, *adj.* abandonado, perdido

form, *n.* forma, *f.*; esqueleto, modelo, *m.*; modo, *m.*; **form letter,** carta circular, *f.*; *vt.* formar; concebir; *vi.* formarse

formal, *adj.* formal, metódico ceremonioso

formality, *n.* formalidad, *f.*

formation, *n.* formación, *f.*

former, *adj.* precedente; previo; **formerly,** *adv.* antiguamente, en tiempos pasados

formidable, *adj.* formidable, terrible

forsaken, *adj.* desamparado

fort, *n.* fortaleza, *f.*, fuerte, *m.*

forth, *adv.* en adelante; afuera; **and so forth,** y así sucesivamente, et cétera

forthcoming, *adj.* próximo

fortieth, *n.* y *adj.* cuadragésimo, *m.*

fortify, *vt.* fortificar

fortnight, *n.* quincena, *f.*, quince días; dos semanas

fortress, *n.* (mfl.) fortaleza, *f.*

fortunate, *adj.* afortunado, dichoso; **fortunately,** *adv.* felizmente, por fortuna

fortune, *n.* fortune, *f.*; suerte, *f.*

forty, *n.* y *adj.* cuarenta, *m.*

forum, *n.* foro, tribunal, *m.*

forward, *adj.* delantero; precoz; atrevido; *adv.* adelante, más allá; *vt.* expedir, trasmitir

forwards, *adv.* adelante

foul, *adj.* sucio, detestable; **foul ball,** pelota *foul* (que cae fuera del primer o tercer ángulo del rombal de baseball); **foul play,** conducta falsa y pérfida; jugada sucia, *f.*

found, *vt.* fundar, establecer; basar

foundation, *n.* fundación, *f.*; fundamento, *m.*, pie, *m.*; fondo, *m.*

founder, *n.* fundador, fundadora

fountain, *n.* fuente, *f.*; manantial, *m.*; **fountain pen,** plumafuente, estilográfica, *f.*

four, *n.* y *adj.* cuatro, *m.*

fourteen, *n.* y *adj.* catorce, *m.*

fourteenth, *n.* y *adj.* décimocuarto, *m.*

fourth, *n.* y *adj.* cuarto, *m.*

fox, *n.* zorra, *f.*, zorro, *m.*

foxy, *adj.* astuto

fracture, *n.* fractura, *f.*; *vt.* fracturar, romper

fragment, *n.* fragmento, trozo, *m.*

fragrance, *n.* fragancia, *f.*

fragrant, *adj.* fragante, oloroso

frame, *n.* marco, *m.*; bastidor,

m.; armazón, f.
France, Francia
franchise, n. franquicia, inmunidad, f.
frank, adj. franco, sincero;
frankly, adv. francamente
frankfurter, n. salchicha, f.
fraternal, adj. fraternal
fraternity, n. fraternidad, f.
freak, n. monstruosidad, f.
freakish, adj. estrambótico
freckle, n. peca, f.
free, adj. libre; liberal; gratuito, gratis; vt. libertar; librar;
eximir
freedom, n. libertad, f.
freethinker, n. librepensador,
librepensadora
freeze, vi. helar, helarse; vt.
helar, congelar
freezer, n. congelador, m.;
deep freezer, congeladora, f.,
congelador, m.
freezing, n. congelación, f.
freight, n. carga, f.; flete, m.;
porte, m.
French, adj. francés, francesa
Frenchman, n. francés, m.
frenzy, n. frenesí, m.; locura,
f.
frequency, n. frecuencia, f.
frequent, adj. frecuente; frequently, adv. con frecuencia
fresh, adj. fresco; nuevo; atrevido
freshen, vt. refrescar
freshman, n. estudiante de
primer año; novicio, novicia
fretful, adj. enojadizo
Friday, n. viernes, m.; Good
Friday, Viernes Santo
fried, adj. frito
friend, n. amigo, amiga
friendless, adj. sin amigos
friendly, adj. amigable, amistoso
friendship, n. amistad, f.
fright, n. susto, terror, m.
frighten, vt. espantar
frightful, adj. espantoso
frivolous, adj. frívolo, vano
frolic, n. alegría, f.; travesura,
f.; vi. retozar, juguetear
from, prep. de; desde; from
now on, en lo sucesivo

front, n. frente, m.
frontier, n. frontera, f.
frontispiece, n. frontispicio,
m.; portada, f.
frost, n. helada, f.
frosting, n. confitura o betún
(para pasteles)
froth, n. espuma (de algún líquido), f.
frown, vi. fruncir el entrecejo;
n. ceño, m.; mala cara, f.
froze, pretérito del verbo
freeze
frozen, adj. helado; congelado
fruit, n. fruto, fruta; producto,
m.
fruitcake, n. torta o pastel de
frutas
fruitful, adj. fructífero, fértil
fruitless, adj. estéril; inútil
frustration, n. contratiempo,
chasco, m.
fry, vt. freir
frying pan, n. sartén, f.
fudge, n. varieded de dulce de
chocolate
fulfil, vt. cumplir, realizar
full, adj. lleno, repleto
full grown, adj. desarrollado,
crecido, maduro
fumigate, vt. fumigar
fun, n. chanza, burla, f.; diversión, f.; to make fun of, burlarse de; to have fun, diver-
tirse
fund, n. fondo, (dinero), m.
fundamental, adj. fundamental, básico
funnel, n. embudo, m.
funny, adj. cómico
furlough, n. (mil.) licencia, f.;
permiso, m.
furnace, n. horno, m.; caldera,
f.
furnish, vt. proveer; equipar
furnished, adj. amueblado
furniture, n. mobiliario, m.,
muebles, m. pl.
furor, n. rabia, f.; entusiasmo,
m.
further, adj. ulterior, más
distante; adv. más lejos, más
allá; aun; vt. adelantar, promover
furthermore, adv. además

furthest, *adj.* y *adv.* más lejos, más remoto

fuss, *n.* (coll.) alboroto, *m.*; *vi.* preocuparse por pequeñeces

fussy, *adj.* melindroso; exigente

future, *adj.* futuro, venidero; *n.* lo futuro, porvenir, *m.*

G

gain, *n.* ganancia, *f.*; interés, beneficio, *m.*; *vt.* ganar; conseguir

gall, *n.* hiel, *f.*; rencor, odio, *m.*; **gall bladder,** vesícula biliar, *f.*

gallant, *adj.* galante; *n.* galán, *m.*

gallantry, *n.* galantería, *f.*

gallery, *n.* galería,

galley, *n.* (naut.) galera, *f.*; **galley roof,** (print.) galerada, *f.*, primera prueba

gallon, *n.* galón, *m.*

gallop, *n.* galope, *m.*; *vi.* galopar

gallstone, *n.* cálculo biliario, *m.*

galvanometer, *n.* galvanómetro, *m.*

gamble, *vi.* jugar por dinero; aventurar

gambling, *n.* juego por dinero, *m.*

game, *n.* juego, *m.*

gamma globulin, *n.* gama globulina, *f.*

gang, *n.* cuadrilla, banda, pandilla, *f.*

gangster, *n.* rufián, *m.*

gap, *n.* boquete, *m.*; brecha, *f.*; laguna, *f.*

gape, *vi.* bostezar, boquear

garage, *n.* garaje, garage, *m.* cochera, *f.*

garb, *n.* vestidura, *f.*

garbage, *n.* basura, *f.*

garden, *n.* huerto, *m.*; jardín, *m.*

gardener, *n.* jardinero, jardinera

gardenia, *n.* gardenia, *f.*

gargle, *vt.* y *vi.* hacer gárgaras; *n.* gárgara, *f.*

garlic, *n.* (bot.) ajo, *m.*

garment, *n.* vestidura, *f.*

garrison, *n.* (mil.) guarnición, *f.*; fortaleza, *f.*

gas, *n.* gas, *m.*; **gas station,** gasolinera, *f.*

gasoline, *n.* gasolina, *f.*

gas-storage tank, *n.* gasómetro, *m.*

gate, *n.* puerta, *f.*

gateway, *n.* entrada, *f.*

gather, *vt.* recoger, amontonar, reunir; inferir; *vi.* juntarse

gathering, *n.* reunión, *f.*

gaze, *vi.* contemplar

gear, *n.* engtanaje, *m.*; **to put in gear,** embragar

geese, *n. pl.* de **goose,** gansos, *m. pl.*

gelatine, *n.* gelatina, *f.*

gem, *n.* joya, *f.*

Gen., General, Gral., General

gender, *n.* género, *m.*

gene, *n.* gen, *m.*

general, *adj.* general, común, usual; *n.* general, *m.*; **in general,** por lo común

generation, *n.* generación, *f.*

generator, *n.* generador, *m.*

generosity, *n.* generosidad, *f.*

generous, *adj.* generoso

genetics, *n.* genética, *f.*

genius, *n.* genio, *m.*

genocide, *n.* genocidio, *m.*

genteel, *adj.* gentil, elegante

Gentile, *n.* gentil, *m.* y *f.*

gentle, *adj.* suave, dócil

gentleman, *n.* caballero, *m.*

gentleness, *n.* gentileza, *f.*

genuine, *adj.* genuino, puro

geographic, geographical, *adj.* geográfico

geography, *n.* geografía, *f.*

geology, *n.* geología, *f.*

geometric, geometrical, *adj.* geométrico

geometry, *n.* geometría, *f.*; **solid geometry,** geometría del espacio

German, *n.* y *adj.* alemán, alemana

Germany, Alemania, *f.*

gesture, *n.* gesto, movimiento, *m.*

get, *vt.* obtener, conseguir; *vi.* llegar; ponerse

ghastly, *adj.* pálido, cadavérico

ghost, *n.* espectro, *m.*; fantasma, *m.*

giant, *n.* gigante, *m.*

gift, *n.* don, *m.*; presente, obsequio, *m.*

gifted, *adj.* hábil, talentoso

gigantic, *adv.* gigantesco

gin, *n.* ginebra, *f.*

ginger, *n.* jengibre, *m.*

gingerly, *adv.* cautelosamente; *adj.* cauteloso

gingham, *n.* zaraza, *f.*

giraffe, *n.* jirafa, *f.*

girdle, *n.* faja, cinturón, *m.*

girl, *n.* muchacha, niña, *f.*

girlhood, *n.* niñez, *f.*, juventud femenina

give, *vt.* y *vi.* dar, conceder; **to give birth,** dar a luz; **to give up,** rendirse, darse por vencido

given, *p. p.* del verbo **give**

gladiolus, *n.* gladiolo, *m.*

gladness, *n.* alegría, *f.*, regocijo, placer, *m.*

glamor, glamour, *n.* encanto, hechizo, *m.*, elegancia, *f.*

glamorous, *adj.* fascinador, encantador

glance, *n.* vistazo, *m.*; ojeada, *f.*; **at first glance,** a primera vista; *vt.* verligeramente

glare, *n.* deslumbramiento, *m.*; reflejo, *m.*; mirada penetrante; *vi.* relumbrar, brillar; echar miradas de indignación

glaring, *adj.* deslumbrante; penetrante

glass, *n.* vidrio, *m.*; vaso para beber; espejo, *m.*; **glasses,** *n. pl.* anteojos, *m. pl.*; *adj.* de vidrio

glassful, *n.* vaso, *m.*, vaso lleno

glassware, *n.* cristalería, *f.*

glee, *n.* alegría, *f.*; gozo, *m.*; **glee club,** coro, *m.*

glide, *vi.* deslizarse; planear

glider, *n.* (avi.) planeador, *m.*

glint, *n.* lustre, brillo, *m.*

glisten, *vi.* centellear

glitter, *vi.* destellar; *n.* destello

globe, *n.* globo, *m.*; esfera, *f.*; orbe, *m.*

gloom, *n.* oscuridad, melancolía, tristeza, *f.*

gloomy, *adj.* sombrio oscuro; triste, melancólico

glorify, *vt.* glorificar, celebrar

glorious, *adj.* glorioso

glory, *n.* gloria, fama, *f.*

glossy, *adj.* lustroso, brillante

glove, *n.* guante, *m.*

glow, *vi.* arder; relucir

glowworm, *n.* luciérnaga, *f.*

glue, *n.* cola, *f.*, sustancia glutinosa; *vt.* encolar, pegar

glutton, *n.* glotón, glotona

gm., gram, g., gramo

G-Man, *n.* (E. U. A.) miembro de la policía secreta

go, *vi.* ir, irse, andar, caminar; partir; huir; to awa marcharse, salir; **to go away,** marcharse, salir; **to go back,** regresar; *n.* (coll.) energía, *f.*; **on the go,** en plena actividad

goal, *n.* meta, *f.*; fin, *m.*

goat, *n.* cabra, chiva, *f.*

gobbler, *n.* pavo, *m.*; glotón, glotona

goblet, *n.* copa, *f.*; cáliz, *m.*

goblin, *n.* duende, *m.*

God, *n.*; Dios, *m.*; **God willing,** Dios mediante

god, *n.* dios *m.*

godchild, *n.* ahijado, ahijada

godess, *n.* diosa, *f.*

godfather, *n.* padrino, *m.*

godmother, *n.* madrina, *f.*

godsend, *n.* bendición, cosa llovida del cielo

Godspeed, *n.* bienandanza, *f.*

goes, 3ª persona del singular del verbo **go**

gold, *n.* oro, *m.*

golden, *ddj.* de oro; excelente

goldenrod, (bot.) vara de San José, vara de oro, *f.*

goldfish, *n.* carpa dorada, *f.*

goldsmith, *n.* orfebre, *m.*

good, *adj.* bueno; bondadoso; apto; perito

good-bye, *n.* adiós, *m.*

good-looking, *adj.* bien pare-

cido, guapo
goodness, *n.* bondad, *f.*
goose, *n.* ganso, *m.*
gorge, *n.* barranco, *m.*
gorgeous, *adj.* primoroso
gorilla, *n.* (zool.) gorila,
gospel, *n.* evangelio, *m.*
gout, *n.* (med.) gota, *f.*
govern, *vt.* y *vi.* gobernar
governess, *n.* institutriz, *f.*
government, *n.* gobierno, *m.*
governor, *n.* gobernador, *m.*;
gobernante, *m.*
grace, *n.* gracia, *f.*; favor, *m.*;
to say grace, bendecir la mesa; *vt.* agraciar
graceful, *adj.* agraciado
gracious, *adj.* gentil, afable
grade, *n.* grado, *m.*; pendiente,
f.; nivel, *m.*; calidad, *f.*; **grade
school,** escuela premaria, *f.*
gradual, *adj.* gradual
graduate, *vt.* y *vi.* graduar,
graduarse, recibirse; *n.* gra-
duado, graduada
graduation, *n.* graduación, *f.*
grain, *n.* grano, *m.*; semilla, *f.*
gram, *n.* gramo (peso), *m.*
grammar, *n.* gramática, *f.*;
grammar school, escuela
primaria o elemental, *f.*
grammatical, *adj.* gramatical
grand, *adj.* grande, ilustre; espléndido; **grand piano,** piano
de cola, *m.*
grandchild, *n.* nieto, nieta
granddaughter, *n.* nieta, *f.*
grandeur, *n.* pompa, *f.*
grandfather, *n.* abuelo, *m.*
grandmother, *n.* abuela, *f.*
grandparent, *n.* abuelo, abuela
grandson, *n.* nieto, *m.*
granite, *n.* granito, *m.*
grant, *vt.* conceder; conferir;
granting that, supuesto que;
to take for granted, dar por
sentado; *n.* subvención, *f.*
grape, *n.* uva, *f.*
grapefruit, *n.* toronja, *f.*
graph, *n.* diagrama, *m.*; gráfico, *m.*
graphic, *adj.* gráfico; pintoresco
grasp, *vt.* empuñar, agarrar;

comprender; *n.* puño, puñado, *m.*; dominio, *m.*
grasping, *adj.* codicioso
grass, *n.* hierba, *f.*; yerba, *f.*,
césped, *m.*
grasshopper, *n.* saltamontes,
m.
grate, *n.* reja, verja, rejilla, *f.*;
vt. rallar; irritar
grateful, *adj.* agradecido
gratify, *vt.* gratificar
gratis, *adj.* gratuito, gratis;
adv. gratis, de balde
gratitude, *n.* gratitud, *f.*
grave, *n.* sepultura, *f.*; tumba,
fosa, *f.*; *adj.* grave, serio
graveyard, *n.* cementerio, *m.*
gravity, *n.* graveded, *f.*; seriedad, *f.*
gravy, *n.* jugo de la carne, *m.*,
salsa, *f.*
graze, *vt.* pastorear; tocar ligeramente; *vi.* rozar; pacer
grease, *n.* grasa, *f.*; *vt.* engrasar, lubricar
greasy, *adj.* grasiento
great, *adj.* gran, grande; ilustre; **greatly,** *adv.* grandemen-
te, muy, mucho
Great Britain, Gran Bretaña,
f.
great-grandchild, *n.* biznieto,
biznieta
great-grandparent, *n.* bisabuelo, bisabuela
Grecian, *n.* y *adj.* griego, griega
Greece, Grecia, *f.*
greed, greediness, *n.* voraci-
dad, *f.*; codicia, *f.*
greedy, *adj.* voraz, goloso; codicioso
Greek, *n.* *adj.* griego, griega
green, *adj.* verde, fresco; no
maduro; *n.* verde, *m.*, verdor,
m.; **greens,** *n. pl.* verduras,
hortalizas, *f. pl.*
Greenland, Groenlandia, *f.*
greet, *vt.* saludar
greeting, *n.* saludo, *m.*
grew, *pretérito* del verbo **grow**
greyhound, *n.* galgo, lebrel, *m.*
grief, *n.* dolor, *m.*, aflicción, *f.*
grieve, *vt.* agraviar, afligir; *vi.*
afligirse, llorar

grill, *vt.* asar en parrillas; *n.* parrilla, *f.*

grim, *adj.* feo; austero

grimace, *n.* mueca, *f.*

grime, *n.* suciedad,

grimy, *adj.* sucio

grin, *n.* risa franca, *f.*; *vi.* reirse francamente

grind, *vt.* moler; afilar

grinder, *n.* molinillo, *m.*; amolador, *m.*

grip, *vt.* agarrar, empuñar; *n.* maleta, *f.*

grippe, *n.* gripe, *f.*; influenza, *f.*

gripping, *adj.* emocionante

gristle, *n.* cartílago, *m.*

gritty, *adj.* arenoso

groan, *vi.* gemir; *n.* gemido, quejido, *m.*

grocer, *n.* abacero, *m.*; (Sp. Am.) abarrotero, *m.*

grocery, *n.* abacería, *f.*; **grocery store**, tienda de comestibles, *f.*; (Sp. Am.) tienda de abarrotes, *f.*

groom, *n.* criado, *m.*; mozo de caballos; novio, *m.*

gross, *n.* gruesa, *f.*; todo, *m.*

ground, *n.* tierra, *f.*; país, *m.*; terreno, suelo, *m.*

groundless, *adj.* infundado

group, *n.* grupo, *m.*

grow, *vt.* cultivar; *vi.* crecer

grown, *p. p.* del verbo **grow**

grown-up, *adj.* mayor de edad, maduro; *n.* persona mayor de edad

growth, *n.* crecimiento, *m.*; nacencia, *f.*, tumor, *m.*

grudge, *n.* rencor, odio, *m.*; envidia

grudgingly, *adv.* con repugnancia, de mala gana

gruff, *adj.* ceñudo, brusco

grumble, *vi.* gruñir; murmurar

grumpy, *adj.* regañón, quejoso

guarantee, *vt.* garantizar

guaranty, *n.* garante, *m.*; garantía, *f.*

guard, *n.* guarda, guardia, *f.*, centinela, *m.* y *f.*; vigilante, *m.*; *vt.* defender; custodiar; *vi.* guardarse; prevenirse; velar

guardian, *n.* tutor, *m.*; guardián, *m.*

guess, *vt.* y *vi.* conjeturar; adivinar; *n.* conjetura, *f.*

guest, *n.* huésped, huéspeda, invitado, invitada, convidado, convidada

guide, *vt.* guiar, dirigir; *n.* guía, *m.* y *f.*

guilt, *n.* delito, *m.*; culpa, *f.*

guilty, *adj.* culpable

guitar, *n.* guitarra, *f.*

gulf, *n.* golfo, *m.*; abismo , *m.*

Gulf Stream, *n.* corriente del Golfo de México, *f.*

gum, *n.* gorna, *f.*; encía, *f.*; **chewing gum**, chicle, *m.*, goma de mascar, *f.*

gumbo, *n.* (bot.) quimbombó, *m.*

gumption, *n.* (coll.) iniciativa, inventiva, *f.*

gun, *n.* arma de fuego; fusil, *m.*; escopeta, *f.*; pistola, *f.*, revólver, *m.*

gunpowder, *n.* pólvora, *f.*

gust, *n.* soplo de aire, *m.*; ráfaga, *f.*

gusto, *n.* gusto, placer, *m.*

gut, *n.* intestino, *m.*, cuerda de tripa, *f.*; **guts**, *n. pl.* (coll.) valor, *m.*, valentía, *f.*

gutter, *n.* zanja, *f.*; caño, *m.*

guy, *n.* tipo, sujeto, *m.*

gymnasium, *n.* gimnasio, *m.*

gypsy, *n.* y *adj.* gitano, gitana

H

habit, *n.* hábito, vestido, *m.*; costumbre, *f.*

habitation, *n.* habitación, *f.*; domicilio, *m.*

habitual, *adj.* habitual

had, *pretérito* y *p. p.* del verbo **have**

haddock, *n.* (pez) merluza, *f.*

Hades, *n. pl.* los infiernos, *m. pl.*

hag, *n.* bruja, hechicera, *f.*

haggard, *adj.* ojeroso, trasnochado

hail, *n.* granizo, *m.*; saludo, *m.*; *vt.* saludar; *vi.* granizar; **hail!** *interj.* ¡viva!

hair, *n.* cabello pelo, *m.*

hairbrush, *n.* cepillo para el cabello, *m.*

hair-do, *n.* (coll.) peinado, *m.*

hairdresser, *n.* peluquero, *m.*; peinador, peinadora

hairpin, *n.* horquilla, *f.*

hairy, *adj.* peludo

hale, *adj.* sano, vigoroso

half, *n.* mitad, *f.*; *adj.* medio

half-breed, *n.* y *adj.* mestizo, mestiza

halfhearted, *adj.* indiferente, sin entusiasmo

half-hour, *n.* media hora, *f.*

halfway, *adv.* a medio camino, a medias

hall, *n.* vestíbulo, *m.*, sala, *f.*; salón, colegio, *m.*; sala, *f.*; cámara, *f.*

hallow, *vt.* consagrar, santificar

Halloween, *n.* víspera de Todos los Santos, *f.*

hallway, *n.* vestíbulo, atrio, *m.*

halo, *n.* halo, nimbo, *m.*, corona, *f.*

halves, *n. pl.* de **half,** mitades, *f. pl.*, **by halves,** a medias

ham, *n.* jamón, *m.*

hamburger, *n.* carne picada de res; emparedado de carne molida

hammer, *n.* martillo, *m.*; *vt.* martillar

hamper, *n.* cesto grande (para ropa, etc.); *vt.* estorbar, impedir

hand, *n.* mano, *f.*; obrero, *m.*; mano o manecilla (de un reloj), *f.*; **at hand,** a la mano, *vt.* alargar; entregar

handbag, *n.* bolsa, *f.*; maletilla, *f.*

handcuff, *n.* manilla, *f.*; esposas, *f. pl.*

handful, *n.* puñado, *m.*

handicap, *n.* obstáculo, *m.*; ventaja, *f.* (en juegos)

handiwork, *n.* obra manual, *f.*

handkerchief, *n.* pañuelo, *m.*

handle, *n.* mango, *m.*, asa, manigueta, *f.*; *vt.* manejar; tratar

handmade, *adj.* hecho a mano

handshake, *n.* apretón de manos, *m.*

handsome, *adj.* hermoso, bello

handwork, *n.* trabajo a mano, *m.*

handwriting, *n.* escritura, *f.*; caligrafía, *f.*; letra, *f.*

handy, *adj.* manual; diestro, hábil

hang, *vt.* colgar, suspender; ahorcar; *vi.* colgar; ser ahorcado; pegarse

hangnail, *n.* uñero, padrastro, *m.*

haphazard, *adj.* casual, descuidado

happen, *vi.* acontecer, suceder

happening, *n.* suceso, acontecimiento, *m.*

happily, *adv.* felizmente

happiness, *n.* felicidad, dicha, *f.*

happy, *adj.* feliz

hard, *adj.* duro, firme; difícil; severo, rígido

hard-boiled, *adj.* cocido hasta endurecerse; **hard-boiled eggs,** huevos duros, *m. pl.*

harden, *vt.* y *vi.* endurecer, endurecerse

hardly, *adv.* apenas

hardship, *n.* injusticia, *f.*; trabajo, *m.*

hardtop, *n.* toldo rígido; *adj.* con toldo rígido

hardware, *n.* ferretería, *f.*

hardy, *adj.* fuerte, robusto

hare, *n.* liebre, *f.*

harem, *n.* harén, *m.*

harm, *n.* mal, daño, *m.*; perjuicio, *m.*; *vt.* dañar, injuriar

harmful, *adj.* perjudicial

harmless, *adj.* inofensivo

hormonize, *vt.* y *vi.* armonizar

harmony, *n.* armonía, *f.*

harp, *n.* arpa, *f.*

harsh , *adj.* áspero, austero

harvest, *n.* cosecha, *f.*

has, 3ª persona del singular del verbo **have**

hash, *n.* jigote, picadillo, *m.*

hassock, *n.* cojín para los pies, *m.*

haste, *n.* prisa, *f.*

hasten, *vt.* y *vi.* acelerar, apresurar

hastily, *adv.* precipitadamente

hasty, *adj.* apresurado

hat, *n.* sombrero, *m.*

hatch, *vt.* criar pollos; empollar

hate, *n.* odio, *m.*; *vt.* odiar, detestar

hateful, *adj.* odioso, detestable

haul, *vt.* tirar, halar; acarrear

haunt, *vt.* frecuentar, rondar; perseguir; *n.* guarida, *f.*

haunted, *adj.* encantado, frecuentado por espantos

Havana, Habana

haven, *n.* puerto, *m.*; abrigo, asilo, *m.*

Hawaiian Islands, Islas Hawaianas, *f. pl.*

hawk, *n.* (orn.) halcón, gavilán, *m.*

hay, *n.* heno, *m.*; **hay fever,** romadizo, *m.*, fiebre del heno, *f.*

hazard, *n.* acaso, accidente, *m.*; riesgo, *m.*; *vt.* arriesgar; aventurar

haze, *n.* niebla, bruma, *f.*

hazel, *n.* avellano, *m.*; *adj.* castaño

hazelnut, *n.* avellano, *f.*

hazy, *adj.* anieblado, oscuro

H-Bomb, *n.* bomba H, *m.*

he, *pron.* él

head, *n.* cabeza, *f.*; jefe, *m.*; *vt.* gobernar, dirigir

headache, *n.* dolor de cabeza, *m.*; jaqueca, *f.*

headfirst, *adv.* de cabeza

headgear, *n.* tocado, *m.*

heading, *n.* título, membrete, *m.*

headline, *n.* encabezamiento, título (de un periódico, etc.), *m.*

headquarters, *n.* (mil.) cuartel general, *m.*; jefatura, administración, *f.*

headstrong, *adj.* testarudo, cabezudo

heal, *vt.* y *vi.* curar, sanar; cicatrizar

health, *n.* salud, sanidad, *f.*

healthy, *adj.* sano; saludable

heap, *n.* montón, *m.*; *vt.* amontonar, acumular

hear, *vt.* y *vi.* oir; escuchar

hearing, *n.* oído, *m.*, oreja, *f.*; audiencia, *f.*

hearsay, *n.* rumor, *m.*

hearse, *n.* carroza fúnebre, *f.*

heart, *n.* corazón, *m.*; alma, *f.*; interior, centro, *m.*; animo, valor, *m.*; **by heart,** de memoria; **heart attack,** ataque al corazón; **heart transplant,** trasplante de corazón, trasplante cardíaco

heartbroken, *adj.* transido de dolor

heartburn, *n.* acedía, *f.*

heartfelt, *adj.* expresivo, sentido, sincero

hearth, *n.* hogar, fogón, *m.*, chimenea, *f.*

heartless, *adj.* inhumano, cruel

heart-to-heart, *adj.* sincero, abierto; confidencial

hearty, *adj.* cordial

heat, *n.* calor, *m.*; ardor, *m.*; *vt.* calentar

heater, *n.* calorífero, *m.*; **hot-air heater,** calorífero de aire caliente

heathen, *n.* gentil, *m.* y *f.*, pagano, pagana

heating, *n.* calefacción, *f.*

heave, *vt.* alzar; elevar; (naut.) virar para proa; *vi.* palpitar

heaven, *n.* cielo, *m.*

heavenly, *adj.* celeste, divino

heaviness, *n.* pesadez, *f.*

heavy, *adj.* pesado

heavyweight, *n.* boxeador de peso mayor, *m.*

hectic, *adj.* inquieto, agitado

heed, *vt.* atender, observar; *n.* cuidado, *m.*; atención. precaución, *f.*

heel, *n.* talón, carcañal, calcañar, *m.*; tacón, *m.*; (coll.) canalla, *m.*

height, *n.* altura, elevación, *f.*

heighten, *vt.* realzar

heir, *n.* heredero, *m.*

heiress, *n.* heredera, *f.*

heirloom, *n.* reliquia de familia, *f.*

helicopter, *n.* helicóptero, *m.*

hell, *n.* infierno, *m.*

hello, *interj.* ¡qué hay! ¡qué hubo! (expresión de saludo)

helmet, *n.* yelmo, casco, *m.*

help, *vt.* y *vi.* ayudar, socorrer; aliviar, remediar; evitar; *n.* ayuda, *f.*; socorro, remedio, *m.*

helpful, *adj.* util, provechoso

helpless, *adj.* irremediable

hem, *n.* bastilla, *f.*; *vt.* bastillar

hemisphere, *n.* hemisferio, *m.*

hemoglobin, *n.* (med.) hemoglobina, *f.*

hemorrhage, *n.* hemorragia, *f.*

hemorrhoids, *n.* *pl.* hemorroides, almorranas, *f.* *pl.*

hemp, *n.* ciñamo, *m.*

hemstitch, *n.* (costura) vainica, *f.*; *vt.* (costura) hacer una vainica

hen, *n.* gallina, *f.*

henceforth, *adv.* de aquí en adelante; en lo sucesivo

hencoop, *n.* gallinero, *m.*

her, *pron.* su, ella, de ella, a ella

herald, *n.* heraldo, *m.*

herb, *n.* yerba, hierba, *f.*

herd, *n.* hato, rebaño, *m.*; manada, *f.*

here, *adv.* aquí, acá

hereabouts, *adv.* aqui al rededor

hereafter, *adv.* en lo futuro; *n.* estado venidero, el futuro, *m.*

hereditary, *adj.* hereditario

heredity, *n.* derecho de su cesión, *m.*; herencia, *f.*

heretofore, *adv.* antes, en tiempos pasados; hasta ahora

heritage, *n.* herencia, *f.*

hermetic, *adj.* hermético

hermit, *n.* ermitaño, *m.*

hero, *n.* héroe, *m.*

heroic, *adj.* heroico; **heroics,** *n.* *pl.* expresión o acto extravagantes

heroine, *n.* heroína, *f.*

heroism, *n.* heroísmo, *m.*

heron, *n.* garza, *f.*

herring, *n.* arenque, *m.*

hers, *pron.* suyo, de ella

herself, *pron.* sí, ella misma

hesitate, *vi.* vacilar, titubear

hesitation, *n.* duda, *f.*, titubeo, *m.*

hiccough, *n.* hipo, *m.*; *vi.* tener hipo

hid, *pretérito* del verbo **hide**

hidden, *adj.* escondido; secreto

hide, *vt.* esconder; *vi.* esconderse; *n.* cuero, *m.*; piel, *f.*

hide-and-seek, *n.* escondite, *m.*

hideous, *adj.* horripilante

high, *adj.* alto, elevado; **high jump,** salto de altura, *m.*

highball, *n.* highball, *m.*, bebida compuesta de aguardiente con soda

high-grade, *adj.* de alta calidad, excelente

highland, *n.* tierra montañosa

Highness, *n.* Alteza, *f.*

highness, *n.* altura, *f.*

high-strung, *adj.* nervioso, excitable

highway, *n.* carretera, *f.*

hike, *n.* paseo a pie, *m.*

hilarious, *adj.* alegre y bullicioso

him, *pron.* le, a él

himself, *pron.* sí, él mismo

hinder, *vt.* impedir, estorbar

hindrance, *n.* impedimento, obstáculo, *m.*; rémora, *f.*

hint, *n.* seña, *f.*; sugestión, insinuación, *f.*; *vt.* insinuar; sugerir; hacer señas

hip, *n.* cadera, *f.*

hippopotamus, *n.* hipopótamo, *m.*

hippie, hippy, *n.* hippie, *m.* y *f.*

hire, *vt.* alquilar; arrendar; *n.* alquiler, *m.*; salario, *m.*

his, *pron.* su, suyo, de él

historian, *n.* historiador, *m.*

historic, historical, *adj.* histórico

history, *n.* historia, *f.*

hit, *vt.* golpear; atinar; *n.* golpe, *m.*; (coll.) éxito, *m.*

hive, *n.* colmena, *f.*

hives, n. (med.) urticaria, f., ronchas, f. pl.

hoard, n. montón, m.; tesoro escondido, m.; vt. atesorar, acumular

hoax, n. burla, f.; petardo, m.; vt. engañar, burlar

hobby, n. afición, f.

hockey, n. hockey, m. juego de patinadores sobre el hielo

hog, n. cerdo, puerco, m.

hoist, vt. alzar; (naut.) izar; n. grúa, f.; cabria, f.; montacargas, m.

hold, vt. tener, asir; detener; sostener; contener; sujetar; pl. mantenerse

holdup, n. asalto, robo, m.

hole, n. agujero, m.; hoyo, m.; hueco, m.

holiday, n. día de fiesta, día festivo, m.; **holidays,** n. pl. vacaciones, f. pl.

Holland, Holanda

holly, n. (bot.) acebo, m.

holster, n. funda de pistola

holy, adj. santo

homage, n. homenaje, culto, m.

home, n. casa, morada, f., hogar, m.; adj. doméstico

homeland, n. patria, f.

homeless, adj. sin hogar

homely, adj. feo

homemade, adj. hecho en casa; casero

homemaker, n. ama de casa, f.

homesick, adj. nostálgico

homesickness, n. nostalgia, f.

homework, n. tarea, f.

homicide, n. homicidio, m.; homicida, m. y f.

honest, adj. honesto, probo; honrado; justo

honesty, n. honestidad, justicia, probidad, f.; honradez, f.

honey, n. miel, f.; dulzura, f.

honeybee, n. abeja obrera

honeycomb, n. panal, m.

honeysuckle, n. (bot.) madreselva, f.

honor, n. honra, f., honor, lauro, m.; vt. honrar; **to honor (a draft),** (com.) aceptar

(un giro o letra de cambio)

honorable, adj. honorable; ilustre; respatable

honorary, adj. honorario

hood, n. caperuza, f.; gorro, m.; (auto.) cubierta del motor

hoodlum, n. (coll.) pillo, tunante, m.

hook, n. gancho, m.; anzuelo, m.; vt. enganchar

hop, n. salto m.; **hops,** (bot.) lúpulo, m.; vi. saltar, brincar

hope, n. esperanza, f.; vi. esperar

hopeless, adj. desesperado; sin remedio

hormone, n. hormón, m., hormona, f.

horn, n. cuerno, m.; corneta, f.; trompeta, f.; bocina, f.; klaxon, m.

hornet, n. abejón, m.

horoscope, n. horóscopo m.

horrible, adj. horrible

horrid, adj. horroroso

horrify, va. horrorizar

horror, n. horror, terror, m.

hors d'oeuvre, n. pl. entremés, m.

horse, n. caballo, m.

horseback, n. espinazo del caballo; **on horseback,** a caballo

horseman, n. jinete, m.

horsepower, n. caballo de fuerza o potencia, m.

horseshoe, n. herradura de caballo, f.

horticulture, n. horticultura, jardinería, f.

hose, n. medias, f. pl.; manguera, f.; tubo flexible, m.

hosiery, n. medias, f. pl.; calcetines, m. pl.

hospitable, adj. hospitalario

hospital, n. hospital, m.

hospitality, n. hospitalidad, f.

hospitalization, n. hospitalización, f.

hospitalize, vt. hospitalizar

host, n. anfitrión, m.; huésped, m.; hostia, f.

hostel, n. posada, hostería, f., hotel, m.

hostess, n. anfitriona, f.

hot, *adj.* caliente, cálido; ardiente; picante; (coll.) excitante agitado, violento; **hot line**, línea de emergencia

hotel, *n.* posada, fonda, *f.*, hotel, *m.*

hot-tempered, *adj.* colérico

hound, *n.* sabueso, *m.*

hour, *n.* hora, *f.*

hourly, *adv.* a cada hora; frecuentemente; *adj.* por hora, frecuente

house, *n.* casa, *f.*; linaje, *m.*; cámara (del parlamento), *f.*; **House of Representatives**, Cámara de Representantes; **to keep house**, ser ama de casa; *vt.* y *vi.* albergar, residir

housecoat, *n.* bata de casa

household, *n.* familia, *f.*; casa, *f.*; establecimiento, *m.*; **household management**, manejo doméstico, *m.*

housekeeper, *n.* ama de casa, jefe de familia, *f.*; ama de llaves, *f.*

housewife, *n.* ama de casa, *f.*

housework, *n.* quehaceres domésticos, *m. pl.*

housing, *n.* alojamiento, *m.*

how, *adv.* cómo, cuán; cuánto

however, *adv.* como quiera, como quiera que sea; sin embargo, no obstante

hub, *n.* cubo, *m.*; centro, *m.*; **hub cap**, tapacubos, *m.*

hubbub, *n.* alboroto, tumulto, *m.*

hue, *n.* color, *m.*; tez del rostro, *f.*; matiz, *m.*

hug, *vt.* abrazar, acariciar; *n.* abrazo, *m.*

huge, *adj.* vasto, enorme

hull, *n.* cáscara, *f.*; (naut.) casco (de un buque), *m.*; *vt.* descortezar, pelar

hullabaloo, *n.* tumulto, alboroto, *m.*

hum, *vi.* zumbar, susurrar, murmurar; *vt.* tararear (una canción, etc.); *n.* zumbido, *m.*

human, *n.* y *adj.* humano, humana

humane, *adj.* humano

humanitarian, *n.* filántropo,

filántropa; *adj.* humanitario

humanity, *n.* humanidad *f.*

humankind, *n.* el género o linaje humano *m.*

humble, *adj.* humilde, modesto; *vt.* humillar; **to humble oneself**, humillarse

humid, *adj.* humedo

humidity, *n.* humedad, *f.*

humiliate, *vt.* humillar

humiliation, *n.* humillación, mortificación, *f.*

humility, *n.* humildad, *f.*

humor, *n.* humor, *m.*; *vt.* complacer, dar gusto

humorist, *n.* humorista, *m.* y *f.*

humorous, *adj.* chistoso, jocoso

hump, *n.* giba, joroba, *f.*

hunch, *n.* giba, *f.*; (coll.) idea, *f.*

hunchback, *n.* joroba, *f.*; jorobado, jorobada

hundred, *adj.* cien, ciento; *n.* centenar, *m.*

hundredth, *n.* y *adj.* centésimo, *m.*

hundredweight, *n.* quintal, *m.*

hung, *pretérito* y *p.p.* del verbo **hang**

Hungary, Hungría

hunger, *n.* hambre, *f.*

hungry, *adj.* hambriento; **to be hungry**, tener hambre

hunk, *n.* pedazo grande, *m.*

hunt, *vt.* cazar; perseguir; buscar; *n.* caza, *f.*

hunter, *n.* cazador, *m.*; perro de monte, perro de caza, *m.*

hunting, *n.* montería, caza, *f.*

hurdle, *n.* valla, *f.*; obstáculo; **hurdles**, *pl.* carrera de vallas, *f.*

hurrah! *interj.* ¡viva!

hurricane, *n.* huracán, *m.*

hurry, *vt.* acelerar, apresurar, precipitar; *vi.* atropellarse, apresurarse; *n.* precipitación, *f.*; urgencia, *f.*

hurt, *vt.* dañar, hacer daño, herir; ofender; *n.* mal, daño, perjuicio, *m.*; herida, *f.*; *adj.* sentido; lastimado; perjudicado

husband, *n.* marido, esposo, *m.*

husky, *adj.* fuerte; robusto

hustle, *vt.* y *vi.* bullir; apurar (un trabajo); apurarse, andar de prisa

hut, *n.* cabaña, choza, *f.*

hydraulic, *adj.* hidráulico

hydrofoil, *n.* aereodeslizador, hidrofoil, *m.*

hydrogen, *n.* (chem.) hidrógeno, *m.;* **hydrogen bomb,** bomba de hidrógeno

hydroplane, *n.* (naut.) hidroplano, *m.;* (avi.) hidroavión, *m.*

hygiene, *n.* higiene, *f.*

hygienic, *adj.* higiénico

hymn, *n.* himno, *m.*

hyphen, *n.* guión, *m.*

hypnotic, *adj.* hipnótico

hypnotize, *vt.* hipnotizar

hypocrite, *n.* hipócrita, *m.* y *f.*

hypocritical, *adj.* hipócrita, disimulado

hypodermic, *adj.* hipodérmico

hysteria, *n.* histeria, *f.,* histerismo, *m.*

hysteric, hysterical, *adj.* histérico

hysterics, *n. pl.* paroxismo histérico, *m.*

I

I, *pron.* yo

ICBM, I.C.B.M., **intercontinental ballistic missile,** cohete balístico intercontinental

ice, *n.* hielo, *m.;* **ice skate,** patín de hielo, *m.;* **ice water,** agua helada

iceberg, *n.* témpano de hielo, *m.*

icebox, *n.* refrigerador, *m.,* nevera, *f.*

ice cream, *n.* helado, mantecado, *m.,* nieve, *f.*

iceman, *n.* repartidor de hielo, *m.*

icicle, *n.* carámbano, *m.*

icing, *n.,* betún o confitura (para pasteles)

icy, *adj.* helado; frio; (fig.) indiferente

idea, *n.* idea, *f.;* concepto, *m.*

ideal, *adj.* ideal

idealism, *n.* idealismo, *m.*

idealistic, *adj.* idealista

identical, *adj.* idéntico

identification, *n.* identificación, *f.*

identify, *vt.* identificar

idiomatic, idiomatical, *adj.* idiomático

idiot, *n.* idiota, *m.* y *f.*

idiotic, *adj.* tonto, bobo

idle, *adj.* ocioso, perezoso

idleness, *n.* ociosidad, pereza, *f.*

idol, *n.* idolo, *m.;* imagen, *f.*

idolize, *vt.* idolatrar

idyl, *n.* idilio, *m.*

i.e., that is, i.e., es decir, esto es

if, *conj.* si; aunque, supuesto que

ignorance, *n.* ignorancia, *f.*

ignorant, *adj.* ignorante, inculto

ignore, *vt.* pasar por alto, desconocer

ill, *adj.* malo, enfermo; *adv.* mal, malament

ill-bred, *adj.* malcriado, descortés

illegal, *adj.* ilegal

illegible, *adj.* ilegible

illegitimate, *adj.* ilegítimo

ill-gotten, *adj.* mal habido

ill-humored, *adj.* malhumorado

illiterate, *adj.* analfabeto

ill-mannered, *adj.* malcriado, descortés

illuminate, *vt.* iluminar

illumination, *n.* iluminación, *f.;* alumbrado, *m.*

illumine. *vt.* iluminar

illustrate, *vt.* ilustrar; explicar

illustrated, *adj.* ilustrado, de grabados

illustration, *n.* ilustración, *f.;* ejemplo, *m.;* grabado, *m.*

illustrious, *adj.* ilustre, célebre

image, *n.* imagen, estatua, *f.*

imaginary, *adj.* imaginario

imagination, *n.* imaginación, *f.*

imagine, *vt.* imaginar; idear, inventar

imbecile, *n.* y *adj.* imbécil, *m.* y *f.*

imitate, *vt.* imitar, copiar

imitation, *n.* imitación, copia, *f.*

imitator, *n.* imitador, imitadora

immaculate, *adj.* inmaculado, puro

immature, *adj.* inmaturo

immediate, *adj.* inmediato; **immediately,** *adv.* en seguida

immense, *adj.* inmenso

immensity, *n.* inmensidad, *f.*

immerse, *vt.* sumergir

immersion, *n.* inmersión,

immigrant, *n.* inmigrante, *m.* y *f.*

immigrate, *vi.* inmigrar

immigration, *n.* inmigración, *f.*

imminent, *adj.* inminente

immobile, *adj.* inmóvil

immoral, *adj.* immoral, depravado

immorality, *n.* inmoralidad *f.*

immortal, *adj.* immortal

immune, *adj.* inmune, exento

immunity, *n.* inmunidad, franquicia, *f.*

immunize, *vt.* inmunizar

impair, *vt.* deteriorar; disminuir

impart, *vt.* comunicar

impartial, *adj.* imparcial

impartiality, *n.* imparcialidad, *f.*

impassable, *adj.* intransitable

impassive, *adj.* impasible

impatience, *n.* impaciencia, *f.*

impatient, *adj.* impaciente

impediment, *n.* impedimento, obstáculo, *m.*

impel, *vt.* impeler, impulsar

imperative, *adj.* imperativo, imprescindible

imperfect, *adj.* imperfecto, defectuoso; *n.* (gram.) pretérito imperfecto

imperfection, *n.* imperfección, *f.*, defecto, *m.*

impersonate, *vt.* personificar; representar

impersonation, *n.* personificación, *f.*; (theat.) representación, *f.*

impertinence, *n.* impertinencia, *f.*; descaro, *m.*

impertinent, *adj.* impertinente

impetuous, *adj.* impetuoso

implement, *n.* herramienta, *f.*; utensilio, *m.*; *vt.* ejecutar, completar

implicate, *vt.* implicar, envolver

implicit, *adj.* implícito

implied, *adj.* implícito

implore, *vt.* implorar, suplicar

imply, *vt.* implicar

impolite, *adj.* descortés

import, *vt.* importar; significar; *n.* importancia, *f.*; importe, *m.*; sentido, *m.*; **import duties,** derechos de importación, *m. pl.*

importance, *n.* importancia, *f.*

important, *adj.* importante

importing, *adj.* importador; *n.* importación, *f.*

impose, *vt.* imponer

imposing, *adj.* imponente

imposition, *n.* imposición, carga, *f.*

impossibility, *n.* imposibilidad, *f.*

impossible, *adj.* imposible

impostor, *n.* impostor, impostora

impotent, *adj.* impotente; incapaz

impress, *vt.* imprimir, estampar

impression, *n.* impresión, *f.*

impressive, *adj.* imponente

imprint, *vt.* imprimir; estampar; *n.* impresión, *f.*; huella, *f.*

imprisonment, *n.* prisión, *f.*, encierro, *m.*

improbable, *adj.* inverosímil

impromptu, *adj.* extemporáneo

improper, *adj.* impropio, indecente

improve, *vt.* y *vi.* mejorar, perfeccionar; *vi.* progresar

improvement, *n.* mejoramiento, perfeccionamiento, *m.*

improvise, *vt.* improvisar

impulse, *n.* impulso, *m.*; impetu, *m.*

in., inch, pulgada; *pl.* das **inches**, plgs., pulgadas

inability, *n.* incapacidad, *f.*

inaccurate, *adj.* inexacto

inactive, *adj.* inanimado

inaugurate, *vt.* inaugurar

inauguration, *n.* inauguración, *f.*

Inc., Incorporated, (Sp. Am.) S.A., Sociedad Anónima, Ltda., Sociedad Limitada

incapable, *adj.* incapaz

incense, *n.* incienso, *m.*; *vt.* exasperar, provocar

incentive, *n.* incentivo, estímulo, *m.*

inch, *n.* pulgada, *f.*

incident, *n.* incidente *m.*

incidental, *adj.* accidental, casual

incite, *vt.* incitar, estimular

inclination, *n.* inclinación, propensión, *f.*; declive, *m.*

incline, *vt.* inclinar; *vi.* inclinarse; *n.* pendiente, *f.*

include, *vt.* incluir

inclusion, *n.* inclusión, *f.*

inclusive, *adj.* inclusivo

incognito, *adj.* y *adv.* de incógnito

incoherent, *adj.* incoherente

income, *n.* renta, *f.*, entradas, *f. pl.*; **income tax**, impuesto sobre rentas

incomparable, *adj.* incomparable

incompatible, *adj.* incompatible

incompetent, *adj.* incompetente

incomplete, *adj.* incompleto

inconceivable, *adj.* inconcebible

inconvenience, *n.* incomodidad, *vt.* incomodar

inconvenient, *adj.* inconveniente

incorporate, *vt.* y *vi.* incorporar

incorporation, *n.* incorpora-

ción, *f.*

incorrect, *adj.* incorrecto

incorrigible, *adj.* incorregible

increase, *vt.* aumentar; *vi.* crecer, aumentarse; *n.* aumento, *m.*

incredible, *adj.* increíble

incubator, *n.* incubadora, *f.*

incur, *vt.* incurrir; ocurrir

incurable, *adj.* incurable

indebted, *adj.* endeudado, obligado,

indebtedness, *n.* deuda, obligación, *f.*

indecent, *adj.* indecente

indecision, *n.* indecisión, *f.*

indeed, *adv.* verdaderamente, de veras; sí

indefinite, *adj.* indefinido

indelible, *adj.* indeleble

indentation, *n.* margen, *m.*

independence, *n.* independencia ,

independent, *adj.* independiente

indescribable, *adj.* indesriptible

indestructible, *adj.* indestructible

index, *n.* índice, elenco, *m.*

India, *n.* India, *f.*

Indian, *n.* y *adj.* indiano, indiana; indio, india

indicate, *vt.* indicar

indication, *n.* indicación, *f.*; indicio, *m.*; señal, *f.*

indicative, *n.* (gram.) indicativo, *m.*; *adj.* indicativo

indict, *vt.* procesar

indictment, *n.* denuncia, *f.*

indifference, *n.* indiferencia, apatía, *f.*

indigenous, *adj.* indígena

indigent, *adj.* indigente, pobre

indigestion, *n.* indigestión, *f.*

indignation, *n.* indignación, *f.*

indignity, *n.* indignidad, *f.*

indirect, *adj.* indirecto

indiscreet, *adj.* indiscreto

indiscretion, *n.* indiscreción, imprudencia, *f.*

indispensable, *adj.* indispensable

indisposed, *adj.* indispuesto, achacoso

indistinct, *adj.* confuse; borroso

individual, *adj.* individual; *n.* individuo, *m.*

induce, *vt.* inducir, persuadir

inducement, *n.* motivo, móvil, aliciente, *m.*

indulgence, *n.* indulgencia, *f.*, mimo, *m.*

indulgent, *adj.* indulgente

industrial, *adj.* industrial

industrialization, *n.* industrialización, *f.*

industrialize, *vt.* industrializar

industrious, *adj.* hacendoso; trabajador

industry, *n.* industria, *f.*

inefficiency, *n.* ineficacia, *f.*

inefficient, *adj.* ineficaz

inept, *adj.* inepto

inescapable, *adj.* ineludible

inevitable, *adj.* inevitable

inexcusable, *adj.* inexcusable

inexhaustible, *adj.* inagotable

inexpensive, *adj.* barato

inexperienced, *adj.* inexperto, sin experiencia

infallible, *adj.* infalible

infamy, *n.* infamia, *f.*

infancy, *n.* infancia, *f.*

infant, *n.* infante, m; niño, niña

infantile, *adj.* pueril, infantil; **infantile paralysis,** parálisis infantil, *f.*

infantry, *n.* infantería,

infect, *vt.* infectar

infection, *n.* infección,

infer, *vt.* inferer, deducir

inferior, *adj.* inferior

inferiority, *n.* inferioridad, *f.*; **inferiority complex,** complejo de inferioridad, *m.*

infinite, *adj.* infinito; **infinitely,** *adv.* infinitamente

infinitive, *n.* infinitivo, *m.*

infinity, *n.* infinidad, eternidad,. *f.*

infirmary, *n.* enfermería,

inflame, *vt.* y *vi.* inflamar

inflammable, *adj.* inflamable

inflation, *n.* inflación, *f.*

inflection, *n.* inflexión, modulación de la voz, *f.*

inflict, *vt.* castigar; infligir (penas corporales, etc.)

influence, *n.* influencia, *f.*; *vt.* influir

influential, *adj.* influyente

influenza, *n.* (med.) influenza, gripe, *f.*, trancazo, *m.*

inform, *vt.* informar

informal, *adj.* íntimo, sin formulismos

information, *n.* información, instrucción, *f.*; informe, *m.*; aviso, *m.*

ingenious, *adj.* ingenioso

ingenuity, *n.* ingeniosidad, inventiva, *f.*

ingratitude, *n.* ingratitud, *f.*

ingredient, *n.* ingrediente, *m.*

ingrown, *adj.* crecido hacia dentro; **ingrown nail,** uñero, *m.*

inhabit, *vt.* habitar

inhabitant, *n.* habitante, residente, *m.* y *f.*

inherent, *adj.* inherente

inherit, *vt.* heredar

inheritance, *n.* herencia, *f.*; patrimonio, *m.*

inhibition, *n.* inhibición, *f.*

inhuman, *adj.* inhumano

initial, *n.* y *adj.* inicial, *f.*

initiation, *n.* iniciación, *f.*

initiative, *n.* iniciativa, *f.*

inject, *vt.* inyectar

injection, *n.* inyección, *f.*

injure, *vt.* injuriar, ofender; hacer daño

injurious, *adj.* perjudicial, nocivo

injury, *n.* perjuicio, *m.*; daño, *m.*

injustice, *n.* injusticia, *f.*

ink, *n.* tinta, *f.*

inkling, *n.* insinuación, noción vaga, *f.*

inkstand, *n.* tintero, *m.*

inmate, *n.* inquilino, inquilina; preso, presa

inn, *n.* posada, *f.*

inner, *adj.* interior

innocence, *n.* inocencia, *f.*

innocent, *adj.* inocente

innovation, *n.* innovación, *f.*

inoculate, *vt.* inocular; inyectar

inoffensive, *adj.* inofensivo

input, *n.* (elec.) entrada, *f.*; (fig.) gasto, *f.*

inquest, *n.* indagación, *f.*

inquire, *vt.* preguntar (alguna cosa); *vi.* inquirir, examinar

inquiry, *n.* pregunta, *f.*; investigación,*f.*

inquisition, *n.* inquisición *f.*

inquisitive, *adj.* curioso, preguntón

insane, *adj.* loco, demente

insanity, *n.* locura, *f.*

inscription, *n.* inscripción, letra, leyenda, *f.*; letrero, *m.*; dedicatoria, *f.*

insect, *n.* insecto, bicho, *m.*

insecurity, *n.* inseguridad, *f.*

inseparable, *adj.* inseparable

insert, *vt.* insertar, meter

insertion, *n.* inserción, *f.*

inside, *n.* y *adj.* interior, *m.*; **insides,** (coll.) entrañas, *f. pl.*; **on the inside,** por dentro; *adv.* adentro, dentro; **inside out,** al revés

insignia, *n. pl.* insignias, *f. pl.*; estandartes, *m. pl.*

insignificant, *adj.* insignificante; trivial

insincere, *adj.* insincero

insincerity, *n.* insinceridad, *f.*

insinuate, *vt.* insinuar; *vi.* congraciarse

insinuation, *n.* insinuación, *f.*

insist, *vi.* insistir, persistir

insistence, *n.* insistencia, *f.*

insistent, *adj.* insistente, persistente

insolent, *adj.* insolente

insomnia, *n.* insomnio, *m.*

inspect, *vt.* inspeccionar

inspection, *n.* inspección, *f.*

inspector, *n.* inspector, *m.*

inspiration, *n.* inspiración, *f.*

inspire, *vt.* inspirar

installation, *n.* instalación *f.*

installment, instalment, *n.*; plazo, *m.*; **monthly installment,** mensualidad, *f.*

instant, *adj.* instante, urgente; presents; **the 20th instant,** el 20 del presente; **instantly,** *adv.* un instante; *n.* instante, momento, *m.*

instead, *adv.* en lugar de, en vez de

instigate, *vt.*, instigar

instinct, *n.* instinto, *m.*

instinctive, *adj.* instintivo

institute, *vt.* instituir, establecer; *n.* instituto, *m.*

institution, *n.* institución, *f.*

instruct, *vt.* instruir, enseñar

instruction, *n.* instrucción, enseñanza, *f.*

instructor, *n.* instructor, *m.*

instrument, *n.* instrumento, *m.*

insufferable, *adj.* insufrible, insoportable

insufficient, *adj.* insuficiente

insulating, *adj.* (elec.) aislante

insurance, *n.* seguro, *m.*; **life insurance,** seguro de vida, *m.*

integration, *n.* integración, *f.*

integrity, *n.* integridad, *f.*

intellect, *n.* intelecto, *m.*

intellectual, *n.* intelectual, *m.* y *f.*; *adj.* intelectual, mental

intelligence, *n.* inteligencia, *f.*

intelligent, *adj.* inteligente

intend, *vt.* intentar; *vi.* proponerse

intense, *adj.* intenso; vehemente

intensify, *vt.* intensificar

intensive, *adj.* completo, concentrado

intent, *adj.* atento, cuidadoso; *n.* intento, designio, *m.*

intention, *n.* intención, *f.*; designio, *m.*; (fig.) mira, *f.*

intentional, *adj.* intencional

intercede, *vi.* interceder, mediar

interest, *vt.* interesar; empeñar; *n.* interés, provecho, *m.*

interesting, *adj.* interesante, atractivo

interfere, *vi.* intervenir

interference, *n.* mediación, ingerencia, *f.*

interjection, *n.* (gram.) interjección, *f.*

interlining, *n.* entretela, *f.*

interlude, *n.* intermedio, *m.*

intermediary, *adj.* y *n.* intermediario, intermediaria

interment, *n.* entierro, *m.*; sepultura, *f.*

interminable, *adj.* interminable

intermission, *n.* intermedio, *m.*

intern, *vt.* internar; encerrar; *n.* (med.) practicante, *m.*; médico interno (en un hospital), *m.*

international, *adj.* internacional

interpret, *vt.* interpretar

interpretation, *n.* interpretación, *f.*; versión, *f.*

interpreter, *n.* intérprete, *m.* y *f.*

interrogate, *vt.* interrogar, examinar

interrogation, *n.* interrogación, pregunta, *f.*

interrupt, *vt.* interrumpir

interruption, *n.* interrupción, *f.*

intersection, *n.* intersección, *f.*; bocacalle, *f.*

interval, *n.* intervalo, *m.*

intervene, *vi.* intervenir

intervention, *n.* intervención, *f.*

interview, *n.* entrevista, *f.*; *vt.* entrevistar

intestinal, *adj.* intestinal

intestine, *adj.* intestino; **intestines,** *n. pl.* intestinos, *m. pl.*

intimacy, *n.* intimidad, confianza, *f.*; familiaridad, *f.*

intimate, *adj.* íntimo, familiar; *vt.* insinuar, dar a entender

intolerable, *adj.* intolerable

intolerance, *n.* intolerancia, *f.*

intolerant, *adj.* intolerante

intoxicant, *n.* bebida alcohólica, *f.*

intoxicated, *adj.* ebrio, borracho

intoxicating, *adj.* embriagante

intoxication, *n.* embriaguez, *f.*; intoxicación, *f.*

intransitive, *adj.* (gram.) intransitivo

intrepid, *adj.* arrojado, intrépido

intricate, *adj.* complicado; complejo

intrigue, *n.* intriga, *f.*

introduce, *vt.* introducir, meter; **to introduce (a person),** presentar (a una persona)

introduction, *n.* introducción, *f.*; presentación, *f.*; prólogo, preámbulo, *m.*

intrude, *vi.* entremeterse, introducirse

intuition, *n.* intuición,

inundate, *vt.* inundar

inundation, *n.* inundación, *f.*

invade, *vt.* invadir

invalid, *adj.* inválido; nulo; *n.* inválido, inválida

invaluable, *adj.* inapreciable

invariable, *adj.* invariable

invasion, *n.* invasion, *f.*

inveigle, *vt.* persuadir

invent, *vt.* inventar

invention, *n.* invención, *f.*; invento, *m.*

inventor, *n.* inventor, *m.*

inventory, *n.* inventario, *m.*

invert, *vt.* invertir

invest, *vt.* investir; invertir

investigate, *vt.* investigar

investigation, *n.* investigación,

investment *n.* inversión, *f.*

invisible, *adj.* invisible

invitation, *n.* invitación, *f.*

invite, *vt.* convidar, invitar

invoice, *n.* factura, *f.*; *vt.* facturar

invoke, *vt.* invocar

involuntary, *adj.* involuntario

involve, *vt.* envolver, implicar

iodine, *n.* yodo, *m.*

I.O.U., IOU, I owe you, pagaré, vale

Ireland, Irlanda, *f.*

iris, *n.* arco iris, *m.*; (anat.) iris, *m.*; (bot.) flor de lis, *f.*

Irish, *n.* y *adj.* irlandés, irlandesa

iron, *n.* hierro, *m.*; *vt.* planchar

ironical, *adj.* irónico

ironing, *n.* planchado, *m.*

irony, *n.* ironía, *f.*

irradiate, *vt.* y *vi.* irradiar, brillar

irregular, *adj.* irregular

irrelevant, *adj.* no aplicable
irreproachable, *adj.* irreprochable
irresistible, *adj.* irresistible
irresponsible, *adj.* irresponsable
irrigation, *n.* riego, *m.*; irrigación, *f.*
irritate, *vt.* irritar, exasperar
is, 3ª persona del singular del verbo **be**
island, *n.* isla, *f.*
isolate, *vt.* aislar, apartar
isolation, *n.* aislamiento, *m.*
isthmus, *n.* istmo, *m.*
it, *pron.* él, ella, ello, lo, la le
italic, *n.* bastardilla, *f.*
Italy, Italia, *f.*
itch, *n.* picazón, *f.*; *vi.* picar
item, *n.* artículo, suelto, *m.*; (com.) renglón, *m.*
itinerary, *n.* itinerario, *m.*
its, *pron.* su, suyo
itself, *pron.* el mismo, la misma, lo mismo; si; **by itself,** de por sí
ivory, *n.* marfil, *m.*
ivy, *n.* hiedra, *f.*

J

jack, *n.* (mech.) gato, *m.*; sota, *f.*; **jack pot,** premio grande, *m.*
jackass, *n.* burro, asno, *m.*
jacket, *n.* chaqueta, *f.*, saco, *m.*; envoltura, *f.*
jail, *n.* cárcel , *f.*
jam, *n.* compotá, conserva, *f.*; apretadura, *f.*; aprieto, *m.*; *vt.* apiñar, apretar
janitor, *n.* portero, conserje, *m.*
January, *n.* enero, *m.*
Japan, japón, *m.*
Japanese, *n.* y *adj.* japonés, japonesa, nipón, nipóna
jar, *vi.* chocar; discordar; *n.* jarro, *m.*
jct., junction emp. empalme, *m.*; confluencia, *f.*
jealous, celoso
jealousy, *n.* celos, *m. pl.*
jeans, *n. pl.* pantalones ajustados de dril, generalmente azules

jelly, *n.* jalea, gelatina, *f.*
jest, *n.* chanza, burla, *f.*; *vi.* chancear
Jesuit, *n.* jesuita, *m.*
Jesus Christ, Jesucristo
jet, *n.* (min.) azabache, *m.*; (mech.) mechero, *m.*; boquilla, *f.*; **jet plane,** avión de retropropulsión, *m.*; **jet propulsion,** propulsión por reacción, *f.*
Jew, *n.* judío, judía
jewel, *n.* joya, alhaja, *f.*; rubi (de un reloj), *m.*
jeweler, *n.* joyero, *m.*
jewelry, *n.* joyería, *f.*
Jewish, *adj.* judío
jiffy, *n.* (coll.) tris, momentito, *m.*
jilt, *vt.* dar calabazas, plantar
jingle, *vi.* retiñir, resonar; *n.* retintín, *m.*
job, *n.* empleo, *m.*; (Mex. coll.) chamba, *f.*
jockey, *n.* jinete, *m.*
join, *vt.* y *vi.* juntar, unir
joint, *n.* coyuntura, articulación, *f.*; *adj.* unido; participante; **jointly,** *adv.* conjuntamente, en común,
joke, *n.* chanza, chiste, *m.*; *vi.* chancear, bromear
jolly, *adj.* alegre, jovial
jolt, *vt.* y *vi.* sacudir; *n.* sacudida, *f.*
journal, *n.* diario, periódico, *m.*
journalism, *n.* periodismo, *m.*
journalist, *n.* periodista, *m.* y *f.*
journey, *n.* jornada, *f.*; viaje, *m.*; *vi.* viajar
jowl, *n.* quijada, *f.*
joy, *n.* alegría, *f.*; júbilo, *m.*
joyful, joyous, *adj.* alegre
judge, *n.* juez *m.*; *vi.* juzgar; inferir
judgment, judgement, *n.* juicio, *m.*; opinión, *f.*
judicial, *adj.* judicial
jug, *n.* jarro, *m.*
juice, *n.* zumo, jugo, *m.*
juicy, *adj.* jugoso
jukebox, *n.* sinfonola, *f.*

July, *n.* (mes) julio, *m.*

jumble, *n.* mezcla, confusión, *f.*

jump, *vi.* saltar, brincar; *n.* salto, *m.*

junction, *n.* empalme, *m.*; bifurcación, *f.*

June, *n.* (més) junio, *m.*

jungle, *n.* matorral, *m.*

junior, *adj.* más joven; *n.* estudiante de tercer año

junk, *n.* chatarra, *f.*, hierro viejo, *m.*; baratijas, *f. pl.*

jury, *n.* jurado, *m.*

just, *adj.* justo; *adv.* sólo

justice, *n.* justicia, *f.*, derecho, *m.*; juez, *m.*

justify, *vt.* justificar

juvenile, *adj.* juvenil

K

karate, *n.* karate, *m.*

kc., **kilocycle**, kc., kilociclo

keen, *adj.* agudo; penetrante, sutil, vivo

keep, *vt.* mantener, retener; guardar; **to keep accounts**, llevar cuentas; *n.* manutención, *f.*

keepsake, *n.* recuerdo, *m.*

kettle, *n.* caldera, olla, *f.*

key, *n.* llave, *f.*; (mus.) clave, *f.*; tecla, *f.*

keyboard, *n.* teclado, *m.*

keyhole, *n.* agujero de la llave, *m.*

kg., **kilogram**, kg., kilogramo

kick, *vt.* patear, acocear; *vi.* patear; (coll.) reclamar, objetar; *n.* puntapié, *m.*, patada, *f.*; (coll.) efecto estimulador, *m.*

kid, *n.* cabrito, *m.*; (coll.) muchacho, muchacha

kidnap, *vt.* secuestrar

kidney, *n.* riñón, *m.*, **kidney bean**, variedad de frijol

kill, *vt.* matar, asesinar

kilocycle, *n.* kilociclo, *m.*

kilogram, *n.* kilogramo, *m.*

kilometer, *n.* kilómetro, *m.*

kiloton, *n.* kilotón. *m.*

kilowatt, *n.* kilovatio, *m.*

kin, *n.* parentesco, *m.*; afini-

dad, *f.*

kind, *adj.* benévolo, bondadoso; *n.* género, *m.*; clase, *f.*

kindergarten, *n.* escuela de párvulos, *f.*, jardín de la infancia, *m.*

kindness, *n.* benevolencia, *f.*

king, *n.* rey, *m.*

kingdom, *n.* reino, *m.*

kinky, *adj.* grifo; ensortijado

kinsfolk, *n.* parientes, *m. pl.*

kiss, *n.* beso, *m.*; *vt.* besar

kitchen, *n.* cocina, *f.*

kite, *n.* cometa, birlocha, *f.*

kitten, *n.* gatito, gatita

km., **kilometer**, km., kilómetro

knack, *n.* maña, destreza, *f.*

knee, *n.* rodilla, *f.*

kneecap, *n.* rótula,

kneel, *vi.* arrodillarse

knew, *pretérito* del verbo **know**

knife, *n.* cuchillo, *m.*

knight, *n.* caballero, *m.*

knit, *vt. y vi.* enlazar; tejer

knitting, *n.* tejido con agujas, *m.*

knives, *n. pl.* de **knife**, cuchillos, *m. pl.*

knock, *vt. y vi.* tocar; pegar; *n.* golpe, *m.*; llamada, *f.*

knockout, *n.* golpe decisivo, (en el boxeo), *m.*

knot, *n.* nudo, *m.*; lazo, *m.*; *vt.* anudar

know, *vt. y vi.* conocer, saber

know-how, *n.* conocimiento práctico, *m.*

knowledge, *n.* conocimiento, saber, *m.*

knuckle, *n.* coyuntura, *f.*

L

£, pound, £, libra esterlina, *f.*

label, *n.* marbete, *m.*, etiqueta, *f.*; rótulo, *m.*; *vt.* rotular

labor, *n.* trabajo, *m.*; labor, *f.*; **to be in labor**, estar de parto; *vt. y vi.* trabajar; afanarse

laboratory, *n.* laboratorio, *m.*

laborer, *n.* trabajador, obrero, *m.*

lace, *n.* lazo, cordón, *m.*; enca-

je, *m.*; *vt.* amarrar (los cordo-
nes de los zapatos, etc.)

lack, *vt.* y *vi.* carecer; faltar
algo; *n.* falta, carencia, *f.*

lacquer, *n.* laca, *f.*

lad, *n.* mozo, muchacho, *m.*

ladder, *n.* escalera portátil, *f.*

ladle, *n.* cucharón, cazo, *m.*

lady, *n.* señora, senorita, dama, *f.*

lagoon, *n.* laguna, *f.*

laid, *pretérito* y *p.p.* del verbo
lay

lain, *p.p.* del verbo **lie**

lake, *n.* lago, *m.*

lamb, *n.* cordero, *m.*

lament, *vt.* y *vi.* lamentar; *n.*
lamento, *m.*

land, *n.* país, *m.*; región, *f.*; territorio, *m.*; tierra, *f.*; *vt.* y *vi.*
desembarcar; saltar en tierra

landlady, *n.* affendadora, *f.*

landlord, *n.* propietario, casero, *m.*

landmark, *n.* señal, marca, *f.*;
hecho o acontecimiento importante, *m.*

landslide, *n.* derrumbe, *m.*;
(pol.) mayoría de votos abru-
madora, *f.*

language, *n.* lengua, *f.*; lenguaje, idioma, *m.*

lantern, *n.* linterna, *f.*; farol,
m.

lapel, *n.* solapa, *f.*

lapse, *n.* lapso, *m.*; *vi.* caducar
(un plazo, etc.)

large, *adj.* grande, amplio

lark, *n.* (orn.) alondra, *f.*

larynx, *n.* laringe, *f.*

laser, *n.* rayo laser

last, *n.* doncella, moza, *f.*

last, *adj.* último; **at last,** al fin,
por último; *vi.* durar; subsis-
tir; *n.* horma de zapato, *f.*

late, *adj.* tardo, lento; difunto;
adv. tarde; **lately,** *adv.* re-
cientemente

later, *adj.* posterior; *adv.* más
tarde

lateral, *adj.* lateral

latest, *adj.* último; más reciente; **at the latest,** a mis
tardar

Latin, *n.* latín (lenguaje), *m.*;

n. y *adj.* latino, latina

Latin American, *n.* latinoamericano, latinoamericana

latitude, *n.* latitud, *f.*

latter, *adj.* posterior, último

laugh, *vi.* reir; *n.* risa, risota-
da, *f.*

laughter, *n.* risa, *f.*

laundress, *n.* lavandera, *f.*

laundry, *n.* lavandería, *f.*

lavatory, *n.* lavabo, lavatorio,
m.

lavish, *adj.* pródigo; gastador;
vt. disipar, prodigar

law, *n.* ley, *f.*; derecho, *m.*

lawful, *adj.* legal; legitimo

lawn, *n.* prado, césped, *m.*

lawsuit, *n.* pleito, *m.*, demanda, *f.*

lawyer, *n.* abogado, *m.*

laxative, *n.* y *adj.* purgante,
laxante, *m.*

lay, *vt.* poner, colocar; poner
(un huevo)

lay, *adj.* laico, secular, seglar;
pretérito del verbo **lie**

layer, *n.* capa, *f.*, estrato, *m.*

lazy, *adj.* perezoso

lb., pound, lb. libra

lead, *vt.* conducir, guiar; *vi.*
mandar, tener el mando; sobresalir, ser el primero; *n.* de
lantera, *f.*

lead, *n.* plomo, *m.*; **lead pencil,** lápiz, *m.*

leader, *n.* líder, guía, *m.*

leadership, *n.* capacidad dirigente, *f.*

leading, *adj.* principal

leaf, *n.* hoja (de una planta), *f.*;
hoja (de un libro), *f.*

leafy, *adj.* frondoso

league, *n.* liga, alianza, *f.*; le-
gua, *f.*

leak, *n.* fuga, *f.*, goteo, *m.*; *vi.*
gotear, salirse o escaparse (el
agua, gas, etc.)

lean, *vt.* y *vi.* inclinar, apoyarse

leap, *vi.* saltar, brincar; *n.* salto, *m.*; **leap year,** año bisiesto, *m.*

learn, *vt.* y *vi.* aprender, conocer; saber

learning, *n.* erudición, *f.*; saber, *m.*

lease, *n.* contrato, arrendamiento, *m.*; *vt.* arrendar

least, *adj.* mínimo; *adv.* en el grado mínimo

leave, *n.* licencia, *f.*, permiso, *m.*; despedida, *f.*; *vt.* y *vi.* dejar, abandonar; salir

leaves, *n. pl.* de **leaf,** hojas, *f. pl.*

left, *adj.* izguierdo; *n.* izquierda, *f.*

leg, *n.* pierna, *f.*

legacy, *n.* legado, *m.*

legal, *adj.* legal, legitimo

legation, *n.* legación, embajada, *f.*

legislation, *n.* legislación *f.*

legislature, *n.* legislatura, *f.*

legitimate, *adj.* legitimo

leisure, *n.* ocio, *m.*; comodidad, *f.*; **at leisure,** cómodamente, con sosiego; **leisure hours,** horas o ratos libres

lemon, *n.* limón, *m.*

lemonade, *n.* limonada, *f.*

length, *n.* longitud, *f.*; duración, *f.*; distancia, *f.*

lengthen, *vt.* y *vi.* alargar

lengthy, *adj.* largo

Lent, *n.* cuaresma, *f.*

leopard, *n.* leopardo, *m.*

leprosy, *n.* lepra, *f.*

lesbian, *adj.* lesbiano

lesion, *n.* lcsión, *f.*

less, *adj.* inferior, menos; *adv.* menos

lessen, *vt.* y *vi.* disminuir

lesson, *n.* lección, *f.*

let, *vt.* dejar, permitir; arrendar

letter, *n.* letra, *f.*; carta, *f.*

letterhead, *n.* membrete, *m.*

lettering, *n.* inscripción, leyenda, *f.*

lettuce, *n.* lechuga, *f.*

level, *adj.* llano, plano; *vt.* allanar; nivelar

liability, *n.* responsabilidad, *f.*; **liabilities,** (com.) pasivo, *m.*, créditos pasivos

liable, *adj.* sujeto, expuesto a; responsable; capaz

liar, *n.* mentiroso, mentirosa

liberal, *adj.* liberal; generoso

liberate, *vt.* libertar

liberty, *n.* libertad, *f.*

librarian, *n.* bibliotecario, bibliotecaria

library, *n.* biblioteca,. *f.*

license, licence, *n.* licencia, *f.*; permiso, *m.*

lick, *vt.* lamer, chupar; (coll.) golpear; derrotar (en una pelea, etc.)

lid, *n.* tapa, *f.*, tapadera, *f.*

lie, *n.* mentira, *f.*; *vi.* mentir, acostarse; descansar

lieutenant, *n.* teniente, *m.*

life, *n.* vida, *f.*; ser, *m.*

lifeboat, *n.* bote de salvamento, *m.*

lifeguard, *n.* vigilante, *m.*

lifeless, *adj.* muerto, inanimado

lift, *vt.* alzar, elevar

lift-off, *n.* despegue, lanzamiento, *m.*

light, *n.* luz, *f.*; claridad, *f.*; *adj.* ligero, liviano; claro; blondo; *vt.* encender; alumbrar

lighten, *vt.* iluminar; aligerar; aclarar

lighthouse, *n.* faro, *m.*

lighting, *n.* iluminación, *f.*

lightning, *n.* relámpago, *m.*

likable, *adj.* simpático. agradable

like, *adj.* semejante; igual; *adv.* como; *vt.* y *vi.* querer; gustar, agradar alguna cosa

likely , *adj.* probable

likeness, *n.* semejanza,. *f.*

lily, *n.* lirio, *m.*

limb, *n.* miembro (del cuerpo), *m.*; pierna, *f.*; rama (de un árbol), *f.*

lime, *n.* cal, *f.*; limón mexicano, *m.*

limelight, *n.* centro de atención pública

limit, *n.* límite, término, *m.*; *vt.* restringir

limited, *adj.* limitado

limp, *vi.* cojear; *n.* cojera, *f.*; *adj.* flojo, blando

linen, *n.* lienzo, lino, *m.*; tela de hilo; ropa blanca

linger, *vi.* demorarse

lingerie, n. ropa íntima, f.

link, n. eslabón, m.; vínculo, m.; vt. y vi. unir, vincular

linkup, n. acoplamiento, enlace, m., unión, f.

lion, n. león, m.

lip, n. labio borde, m.

lipstick, n. lápiz para los labios, lápiz labial, m.

liquid, adj.y n. líquido, m.

liquor, n. licor, m.

Lisbon, Lisboa

lisp, vi. cecear

list, n. lista, f., elenco, m.; catálogo, m.; vt. poner en lista; registrar

listen, vi. escuchar

liter, n. litro, m.

literal, adj. literal

literary, adj. literario

literature, n. literatura, f.

little, adj. pequeño; poco; chico; n. poco, m.

live, vi. vivir

live, adj. vivo

lively, adj. vivo, alegre

liver, n. hígado, m.

lives, n. pl. de **life,** vidas, f. pl.

livestock, n. ganado, m.; ganadería, f.

living, n. subsistencia, f.

lid, n. lagarto, m., lagartija, f.

llama, n. (zool.) llama, f.

L.L.D., Doctor of Laws, Doctor en Derecho

load, vt. cargar; n. carga, f.

loaf, n. pan, m.; vi. holgazanear

loan, n. préstamo, m.; vt. prestar

loathe, vt. aborrecer, detestar

loaves, n. pl. de **loaf,** panes, m. pl.

lobby, n. vestíbulo, m.

lobster, n. langosta, f.

local, adj. local

locality, n. localidad; f.

locate, vt. ubicar, colocar

location, n. ubicación, f.

lock, n. cerradura, cerraja, f.; compuerta, f.; vt. y vi. cerrar con llave

locker, n. armario, m.; gaveta, f.

locket, n. medallón, guardape-

lo, m.

lockjaw, n. tétano, m.

locksmith, n. cerrajero, m.

locomotive, n. locomotora, f.

lodge, n. casita en el bosque, f.; logia, f.; vt. alojar; fijar en la memoria; vi. residir

lodging, n. hospedaje, m.

lofty, adj. alto, sublime

logic, n. lógica, f.

logical, adj. lógico

loin, n. ijada, f., ijar, m.; **loins,** n. pl. lomos, m. pl.

loiter, vi. holgazanear

London, Londres

lone, adj. solitario

loneliness, n. soledad, f.

lonely, adj. **lonesome**

lonesome, adj. solitario, triste

long, adj. largo, prolongado; adv. durante mucho tiempo

longing, n. anhelo, m.

long-playing (records), adj. (discos) de larga ejecución

look, vt. y vi. mirar; parecer; buscar; n. aspecto, m.; mirada, f.

loom, n. telar, m.

loose, adj. suelto, desatado

loosen, vt. aflojar, desatar

loot, n. pillaje, botín, m.

lord, n. señor m.; amo, dueño, m.; lord (título de nobleza inglés), m.

lose, vt. y vi. perder, perderse

loss, n. pérdida, f.; **to be at a loss,** estar perplejo

lot, n. suerte, f.; lote, m.

lotion, n. loción f.

lottery, n. lotería. rifa, f.

loud, adj. ruidoso; fuerte, recio, alto; chillón

loudspeaker, n. altoparlante, altavoz, m.

lounge, n. sofá, canapé, m.; salón social, m.

louse, n. (pl. **lice**), piojo, m.

lovable, adj. digno de ser querido

love, n. amor, cariño, m.; vt. amar; querer

lovely, adj. bello

lover, n. amante, galán, m.

low, adj. bajo, pequeño; abatido; vil ; adv. a precio bajo; en

posición baja
lower, adj. más bajo; vt. bajar; disminuir
lowly, adj. humilde
lox, (liquid oxygen) n. oxígeno líquido, m.
loyal, adj. leal, fiel
loyalty, n. lealtad, f.
L.P., long-playing, L.E., larga ejecución (discos)
lubricant, n. y adj. lubricante, m.
luck, n. suerte, f.
luckily, adv. afortunadamente
lucky, adj. afortunado
lukewarm, adj. tibio
lullaby, n. canción de cuna
lumber, n. madera de construcción, f.
lump, n. protuberancia, f.; **lump of sugar,** terrón de azúcar, m.; vi. aterronarse; agrumarse
lunatic, adj. y n. loco, loca
lunch, n. merienda, f., almuerzo, m.; vi. almorzar, merendar
luncheon, n. almuerzo, m.
lung, n. pulmón, m.
lure, n. señuelo, cebo, m.; vt. atraer, seducir
lurk, vi. espiar
luscious, adj. delicioso, atractivo
luster, lustre, n. lustre, m., brillantez, f.
luxuriant, adj. exuberante
luxurious, adj. lujoso
luxury, n. lujo, m.
lyric, lyrical, adj. lírico

M

macaroni, n. macarrones, m. pl.
machine, n. máquina, f.; **machine gun,** ametralladora, f.
machinery, n. maquinaria, f.
machinist, n. maquinista, mecánico, m.
mackerel, n. (pez) escombro, m., caballa, f.
mad, adj. loco, furioso
madam, madame, n. madama, señora, f.

made, adj. hecho, fabricado
made-to-order, adj. hecho a la medida o a la orden
made-up, adj. ficticio; pintado
madness, n. locura, f.
magazine, n. revista, f.
magic, n. magia, f.; adj. mágico
magician, n. mago, nigromante, m.
magistrate, n. magistrado, m.
magnanimous, adj. magnánimo
magnesia, n. magnesia, f.
magnet, n. imán, m.
magnetism, n. magnetismo, m.
magnificent, adj. magnífico
magnify, vt. magnificar
magnitude, n. magnitud. f.
magnolia, n. magnolia, f.
magpie, n. urraca, f.
mahogany, n. caoba, f.
maid, maiden, n. doncella, joven, f.; moza, criada, f.
maiden, adj. virgen, virginal; **maiden name,** nombre de soltera; n. doncella, joven, f.
mail, n. correo, m.; correspondencia, f.
mailbox, n. buzón, m.
mailman, n. cartero, m.
main, adj. principal; esencial; **main office,** casa matriz; **mainly,** adv. principalmente
maintain, vt. y vi. mantener, sostener; conservar
maintenance, n. mantenimiento m.
maize, n. maíz, m.
majestic, majestical, adj. majestuoso
majesty, n. majestad, f.
major, adj. mayor; n. (mil.) mayor, m.
majority, n. mayoría, f.; pluralidad, f.
make, vt. hacer, fabricar; obligar, forzar; n. hechura, f.
make-up, n. maquillaje, m.
malaria, n. paludismo, m.
male, adj. masculino; n. macho, m.
malice, n. malicia, f.
malicious, adj. malicioso

malignant, *adj.* maligno
malt, *n.* malta, *f.*
maltreat, *vt.* maltratar
mamma, mama, *n.* mamá, *f.*
mammal, *n.* mamífero, *m.*
man, *n.* hombre, *m.*; marido, *m.*
manage, *vt.* y *vi.* manejar, administrar
management, *n.* manejo. *m.*, administración, dirección, *f.*; gerencia, *f.*
manager, *n.* administrador, director, *m.*; gerente, *m.*
mandolin, *n.* mandolina, *f.*
maneuver, *n.* maniobra, *f.*; *vt.* y *vi.* manjobrar
manger, *n.* pesebre, *m.*
mangle, *n.* planchadora mecánica, *f.*; *vt.* mutilar
manhood, *n.* virilidad, *f.*; edad viril, hombría, *f.*
manicure, *n.* manicuro, manicura; arte de arreglar las uñas; *vt.* arreglar las uñas
manifest, *adj.* manifiesto, patente
manikin, *n.* maniquí, *m.*
mankind, *n.* género humano, *m.*, humanidad, *f.*
manly, *adj.* varonil
manner, *n.* manera, *f.*, modo, *m.*; forma, *f.*; método, *m.*; **manners,** *n. pl.*, modales, *m. pl.*
mansion, *n.* mansión, residencia, *f.*
manual, *n.* manual, *m.*; *adj.* manual; **manual training,** instrucción en artes y oficios
manufacture, *n.* manufactura, fabricación, *f.*; *vt.* fabricar, manufacturar
manuscript, *n.* manuscrito, escrito, *m.*; original, *m.*
many, *adj.* muchos. muchas
Maoism, *n.* maoismo, *m.*
map, *n.* mapa, *m.*
maple, *n.* arce, *m.*
marble, *n.* mármol, *m.*; canica, bola, *f.*
March, *n.* marzo, *m.*
march, *n.* marcha, *f.*; *vi.* marchar, caminar
margin, *n.* margen, *m.* y *f.*;
borde, *m.*
marimba, *n.* marimba, *f.*
marina, *n.* estación de gasolina para los botes
marine, *n.* marina, *f.*; soldado de marina, *m.*; *adj.* marino
mariner, *n.* marinero, *m.*
marionette, *n.* títere, *m.*
maritime, *adj.* marítimo
mark, *n.* marca, *f.*; señal, nota, *f.*; seña, *f.*; calificación, *vt.* marcar; advertir
market, *n.* mercado, *m.*
marquis, *n.* marqués, *m.*
marriage, *n.* matrimonio, casamiento, *m.*
marry, *vt.* y *vi.* casar, casarse
marshal, *n.* mariscal, *m.*
martial, *adj.* marcial, guerrero
marvel, *n.* maravilla, *f.*, prodigio, *m.*; *vi.* maravillarse
marvelous, *adj.* maravilloso
mascot, *n.* mascota, *f.*
masculine, *adj.* masculino; varonil
mash, *vt.* majar
mask, *n.* máscara, *f.*; *vt.* enmascarar; disimular
mason, *n.* albañil, *m.*; masón, *m.*
masquerade, *n.* mascarada, *f.*
mass, *n.* misa, *f.*; masa, *f.*, bulto, *m.*; **masses,** *n. pl.* las masas, *f. pl*
massage, *n.* masaje, *m.*, soba, *f.*; *vt.* sobar
massive, *adj.* macizo, sólido
master, *n.* amo, dueño, *m.*; maestro, *m.*; señor, *m.*; señorito, *m.*; patrón, *m.*; *vt.* dominar, dominar
mat, *n.* estera, esterilla, *f.*
match, *n.* fósforo, *m.*; cerilla, *f.*, cerillo, *m.*; partido, *m.*; contrincante, *m.*, casamiento, *m.*; *vt.* igualar; aparear
mate, *n.* consorte, *m.* o *f.*; compañero, compañera; piloto, *m.*; *vt.* desposar; igualar
material, *adj.* material, físico; *n.* material, *m.*, tela, *f.*
maternal, *adj.* maternal, materno
maternity, *n.* maternidad, *f.*
mathematical, *adj.* matemáti-

co

mathematics, *n. pl.* matemáticas, *f. pl.*
matinee, *n.* matiné, *f.*
matriculate, *vt.* matricular
matrimony, *n.* matrimonio, *m.*
matter, *n.* materia, sustancia, *f.*; asunto, objeto, *m.*; **what is the matter?** ¿de qué se trata?; *vi.* importar, ser importante
maximum, *adj.* máximo
May, *n.* mayo, *m.*
may, *vi.* poder; ser posible
maybe, *adv.* quizás, tal vez
mayonnaise, *n.* mayonesa, *f.*
mayor, *n.* corregidor, alcalde, *m.*
maze, *n.* laberinto, *m.*
M.C., Master of Ceremonies, Maestro de Ceremonias
M.D., Doctor of Medicine, Doctor en Medicina
me, *pron.* mí; me
meadow, *n.* prado, *m.*
meal, *n.* comida, *f.*; harina, *f.*
mean, *adj.* bajo, vil, despreciable; **means**, *n. pl.* medios, recursos, *m. pl.*; **by all means**, sin falta; **by no means**, de ningún modo; *vt.* y *vi.* significar; querer decir
meaning, *n.* significado, *m.*
meantime, *adv.* mientras tanto
meanwhile, *adv.* entretanto, mientras tanto
measles, *n. pl.* sarampión, *m.*; rubeola, *f.*
measure, *n.* medida, *f.*; (mus.) compás, *m.*; *vt.* medir
measurement, *n.* medición, *f.*; medida, *f.*
meat, *n.* carne, *f.*
mechanic, *n.* mecánico, *m.*
mechanical, *adj.* mecánico; rutinario
mechanics, *n. pl.* mecánica, *f.*
mechanism, *n.* mecanismo, *m.*
medal, *n.* medalla, *f.*
mediate, *vi.* mediar
medical, *adj.* médico
medicare, *n.* asistencia médica estatal para personas ma-

yores de 65 años
medicine, *n.* medicina, *f.*
mediocre, *adj.* mediocre
meditation, *n.* meditación, *f.*
medium, *n.* medio, *m.*; *adj.* mediano
meet, *vt.* y *vi.* encontrar, convocar, reunir
meeting, *n.* sesión, reunión, *f.*
melancholy, *n.* melancolía, *f.*
melodious, *adj.* melodioso
melodrama, *n.* melodrama, *m.*
melody, *n.* melodía, *f.*
melon, *n.* melón, *m.*
member, *n.* miembro, socio, *m.*
membership, *n.* personal de socios, *m.*
memo., memorandum, memorándum, *m.*
memorable, *adj.* memorable
memorandum, *n.* memorándum, volante, *m.*
memorial, *n.* memoria, *f.*; memorial, *m.*; *adj.* conmemorativo
Memorial Day, *n.* Día de los soldados muertos en la guerra (30 de mayo)
memorize, *vt.* memorizar, aprender de memoria
memory, *n.* memoria, *f.*; recuerdo, *m.*; retentiva, *f.*
men, *n. pl.* de **man**, hombres, *m. pl*
menstruation, *n.* menstruación, *f.*
mentality, *n.* mentalidad, *f.*
mention, *n.* mención, *f.*; *vt.* mencionar; **don't mention it**, no hay de qué
menu, *n.* menú, *m.*
merchandise, *n.* mercancía, *f.*
merchant, *n.* comerciante, *m.*
merciful, *adj.* misericordioso
merciless, *adj.* inhumano
mercury, *n.* mercurio, *m.*
mercy, *n.* misericordia, *f.*
merge, *vt.* unir, combinar; *vi.* absorberse, fundirse, converger
meridian, *n.* meridiano, *m.*
meringue, *n.* merengue, *m.*
merit, *n.* mérito, *m.*; merecimiento, *m.*; *vt.* merecer

merry, adj. alegre, jovial
merry-go-round, n. caballitos, m. pl., tiovivo, m.
mess, n. (mil.) comida, f.; confusión, f.; aprieto, lío, m.; suciedad, f.
message, n. mensaje, m.
messenger, n. mensajero, mensajera
metal, n. metal,. m.; **metal shears,** cizalla, f.
meter, n. medidor, contador, m.; metro, m.
method, n. método, m.
methodical. adj. metódico
meticulous, adj. metictiloso
metric, adj. métrico
metropolis, n. metrópoli, capital, f.
Mexico, Méjico
mezzanine, n. (theat.) entresuelo, m., mezanina, f.
mfg., manufacturing, manuf., manufactura
mfr., manufacturer, fab. fabricante
mg., milligram, mg. miligramo
mioe, n. pl. dc **mouse,** ratones, m. pl.
microbe, n. microbio, m.
microphone, n. micrófono, m.
microscope, n. microscopio, m.
midday, n. mediodía, m.
middle, n. medio, centro, m., mitad, f.
middle-aged, adj. entrado en años, de edad madura
middle class, n. clase media, f.
midnight, n. media noche, f.
midwife, n. partera, f.
might, n. poder, m., fuerza, f.; pretérito del verbo **may**
mighty, adj. fuerte, potente
migraine, n. jaqueca, f.
migrate, vi. emigrar
mild, adj. apacible, suave
mile, n. milla , f.
mileage, n. kilometraje, m.
military, adj. militar
milk, n. leche, f.; vt. ordeñar
milkman, n. lechero, m.
milky, adj. lácteo; lechoso; lechero

Milky Way, n. Vía Láctea, f.
mill, n. molino, m.
milligram, n. miligramo, m.
millimeter, n. milímetro, m.
millinery, n. confección de sombreros para señora
million, n. millón, m.
millionaire, n. y adj. millonario, millonaria
mind, n. mente, f.; intención, f.; opinión, f.; ánimo, m.; vt. importar; obedecer; vi. tener cuidado; preocuparse;
mine, pron. mío, mía, míos, mías; n. mina, f.
miner, n. minero, m.
mineral, adj. y n. mineral, m.
miniature, n. miniatura, f.
minimum, n. mínimum, mínimo, m.; adj. mínimo:
mining, n. minería, f.
minister, n. ministro, pastor, m.
ministry, n. ministerio, m.
minnow, n. varieded de pez pequeño
minor, adj. menor, pequeño; (mus.) menor; n. menor (de edad), m. y f.
minority, n. minoridad, f.; minoría, f.
mint, n. (bot.) menta, f.; casa de moneda, f.; vt. acuñar
minuet, n. minué, m.
minus, prep. menos; adj. negativo; n. (math.) el signo menos
minute, adj. menudo, pequeño
minute, n. minuto, m.
miracle, n. milagro, m.; maravilla, f.
miraculous, adj. milagroso
mirror, n. espejo, m.
misbehave, vi. portarse mal
miscarriage, n. aborto, malparto, m.
miscellaneous, adj. misceláneo, mezclado
mischief, n. travesura, f.
mischievous, adj. travieso, pícaro
misdeed, n. delito, m.
miser, n. avaro, avara

miserable, *adj.* miserable, infeliz

miserly, *adj.* tacaño

misery, *n.* miseria, *f.*; infortunio, *m.*

misfortune, *n.* infortunio, *m.*; calamidad, *f.*

misgiving, *n.* recelo, *m.*; presentimiento, *m.*

mishap, *n.* desventura, *f.*; contratiempo, *m.*

misleading, *adj.* engañoso, desorientador

miss, *n.* señorita, *f.*; pérdida, falta, *f.*; *vt.* errar; echar de menos

missile, *n.* proyectil, *m.*

missing, *adj.* que falta; perdido

mission, *n.* misión, comisión, *f.*; cometido, m.

missionary, *n.* misionero, *m.*

missive, *n.* carta, misiva, *f.*

misspell, *vt.* deletrear mal, escribir con mala ortografía

mistake, *n.* equivocación, *f.*, error, *m.*; *vt.* equivocar; *vi.* equivocarse, engañarse

Mister, *n.* Señor (título), *m.*

mistress, *n.* ama, *f.*; señora, *f.*; concubina, *f.*

misunderstand, *vt.* entender mal una cosa

misunderstanding, *n.* mal entendimiento, *m.*

mm., millimeter, mm., milímetro

moan, *n.* lamento, gemido, *m.*; *vi.* afligirse,quejarse

mob, *n.* populacho, *m.*

mobile, *adj.* movedizo, móvil

mobilize, *vt.* movilizar

mock, *vt.* mofar, burlar; *n.* mofa, burla, *f.*; *adj.* ficticio, falso

mockingbird, *n.* (orn.) sinsonte, arrendajo, *m.*

mode, *n.* modo, *m.*; forma, *f.*; manera, *f.*

moderate, *adj.* moderado; módico

moderation, *n.* moderación, *f.*

modern, *adj.* moderno

modernistic, *adj.* modernista

modest, *adj.* modesto

modesty, *n.* modestia, decencia, *f.*, pudor, *m.*

modify, *vt.* modificar

moist, *adj.* húmedo, mojado

moisten, *vt.* humedecer

moisture, *n.* humedad, *f.*; jugosidad, *f.*

molar, *adj.* molar; **molar teeth,** muelas, *f. pl.*

molasses, *n.* melaza, *f.*

mold, *n.* moho, *m.*; molde, *m.*; matriz, *f.*; *vt.* enmohecer, moldar; formar; *vi.* enmohecerse

molding, *n.* molduras, *f. pl*

moldy, *adj.* mohoso

mole, *n.* topo, *m.*; lunar, *m.*

molt, *vi.* mudar, estar de muda las aves

moment, *n.* momento, rato, *m.*

momentary, *adj.* momentáneo

momentous, *adj.* importante

monarch, *n.* monarca, *m.*

monarchy, *n.* monarquía, *f.*

monastery, *n.* monasterio, *m.*

Monday, *n.* lunes, *m.*

monetary, *adj.* monetario

money, *n.* moneda, *f.*; dinero, *m.*; plata, *f.*; **paper money,** papel moneda

monk, *n.* monje, *m.*

monkey, *n.* mono, mona; simio, mia; **monkey wrench,** llave inglesa, *f.*

monogram, *n.* monograma, *m.*

monologue, *n.* monólogo, *m.*

monopolize, *vt.* monopolizar, acaparar

monopoly, *n.* monopolio, *m.*

monster, *n.* monstruo, *m.*

month, *n.* mes, *m.*

monthly, *adj.* mensual

monument, *n.* monumento, *m.*

mood, *n.* humor, talante, *m.*

moody, *adj.* caprichoso, veleidoso

moon, *n.* luna, *f.*

moonlight, *n.* luz de la luna *f.*

moose, *n.* (zool.) alce, *m.*

mop, *n.*(Sp. Am.) trapeador, *m.*; *vt.* (Sp. Am.) trapear

moral, *adj.* moral, ético; *n.* moraleja, *f.*; **morals,** *n. pl.* moralidad, conducta, *f.*

morale, n. moralidad, f.; animación, f.

morality, n. ética, moralidad, f.

moratorium, n. moratoria, f.

more, adj. más, adicional; adv. más, en mayor grado

moreover, adv. además

morning, n. mañana, f.; **good morning**, buenos días; adj. matutino

morphine, n. morfina, f.

mortal, adj. mortal; humano; n. mortal, m.

mortgage, n. hipoteca, f.; vt. hipotecar

mosquito, n. mosquito, m.

most, adj. más; adv. sumamente, en sumo grado; n. los más; mayor número; mayo valor; **mostly**, adv. por lo común; principalmente

motel, n. hotel para automovilistas, m.

mother, n. madre, f.

motherhood, n. maternidad, f.

mother-in-law, n. suegra, f.

motherless, adj. huérfana de madre

motif, n. motivo, tema, m.

motion, n. movimiento, m., moción, f.; **motion picture**, cinema, cinematógrafo, m.; vt. proponer

motionless, adj. inmóvil

motor, n. motor, m.

motorcade, n. procesión o desfile de automóviles

motorcar, n. automóvil, m.

motorcycle, n. motocicleta, f.

motorist, n. automovilista, motorista, m. y f.

motorman, n. motorista, m.

mountain, n. montaña, sierra, f., monte, m.

mountainous, adj. montañoso

mourn, vt. deplorar; vi. lamentar; llevar luto

mourning, n. luto, m.

mouse, n. ratón, m.

mouth, n. boca, f.

mouthful, n. bocado, m.

mouthpiece, n. boquilla, f.

move, vt. mover; proponer; emocionar;vt. moverse, me-

nearse; n. movimiento

movement, n. movimiento, m.; moción, f.

movie, n. **movies**, n. pl. (coll.) cine, cinema, cinematógrafo, m.

moving, adj. conmovedor; **moving picture**, cine, cinema, cinematógrafo, m.

mow, vt. guadañar, segar

mph, **m.p.h.**, **miles per hour**, m.p.h. millas por hora

much, adj. y adv. mucho

mucous, adj. mocoso, viscoso

mud, n. lodo, m.

muddle, vt. enturbiar; confundir

muffin, n. bizcochuelo, m.

muffler, n. (auto.) silenciador, m., sordina, f.; desconectador, m.

mule, n. mula, f.

multimillionaire, n. multimillonario, multimillonaria

multiplication, n. multiplicación, f.

multiply, vt. y vi. multiplicar

mumble, vt. y vi. gruñir; murmurar

municipal, adj. municipal

munition, n. municiones, f. pl.

murder, n. asesinato, homicidio, m.; vt. asesinar

murderer, n. asesino, asesinar

murmur, n. murmullo, m.; cuchicheo, m.; vi. murmurar

muscle, n. músculo, m.

muscular, adj. muscular

museum, n. museo, m.

mushroom, n. hongo, m.

music, n. música, f.

musical, adj. musical

musician, n. músico, m.

mustard, n. mostaza, f.

mute, adj. mudo, silencioso

mutilate, vt. mutilar

mutiny, n. motín, tumulto, m.

mutter, vt. y vi. murmurar, hablar entre dientes

mutton, n. carnero, m.

mutual, adj. mutuo, recíproco

my, pron. mi, mis

myself, pron.yo mismo

mysterious, adj. misterioso

mystery, n. misterio, m.

myth, *n.* fábula, *f.*, mito, *m.*
mythology, *n.* mitología,

N

nab, *vt.* atrapar, prender
nag, *n.* jaca, *f.*, jaco, *m.*; *vt.* y *vi.* regañar, sermonear
nail, *n.* uña, *f.*; garra, *f.*; clavo, *m.*; *vt.* clavar
naked, *adj.* desnudo
name, *n.* nombre, *m.*; fama, reputación, *f.*
nameless, *adj.* sin nombre
namely, *adv.* a saber
namesake, *n,* tocayo, tocaya
nap, *n.* siesta, *f.*; pelo (de una tela), *m.*
napkin, *n.* servilleta,
narcotic, *adj.* narcótico
narrate, *vt.* narrar, relatar
narrative, *n.* relato, *m.*
narrow, *adj.* angosto, estrecho
narrowminded, *adj.* intolerante
NASA, National Aeronautics and Space Administration, Administración Nacional de Aeronáutica y del Espacio
nasal, *adj.* nasal
nasty, *adj.* sucio, puerco; desagradable
natal, *adj.* nativo; natal
nation, *n.* nación, *f.*
national, *adj.* nacional
nationality, *n.* nacionalidad, *f.*
native, *adj.* nativo; *n.* natural, *m.* y *f.*
NATO, North Atlantic Treaty Organization, OTAN, Organización del Tratado del Atlántico Norte
natural, *adj.* natural; sencillo; *n.* (mus.) becuadro, *m.*
nature, *n.* naturaleza, *f.*; indole, *f.*; **good nature,** buen humor, *m.*
naught, *n.* nada, *f.*; cero, *m.*
naughty, *adj.* travieso, pícaro
nausea, *n.* náusea, basca, *f.*
naval, *adj.* náutico, naval
navel, *n.* ombligo, *m.*
navigable, *adj.* navegable
navigate, *vt.* y *vi.* navegar
navigation, *n.* navegación, *f.*

navy, *n.* marina, *f.*
NE, N.E., n.e., northeast, N.E., nordeste
near, *prep.* cerca de, junto a; *adv.* casi; cerca, cerca de; *adj.* cercano
nearby, *adj.* cercano, próximo; *adv.* cerca, a la mano
neat, *adj.* pulido; ordenado
necessary, *adj.* necesario
necessity, *n.* necesidad, *f.*
neck, *n.* cuello, *m.*
necklace, *n.* collar, *m.*
necktie, *n.* corbata, *f.*
nectar, *n.* néctar, *m.*
negative, *adj.* negativo; *n.* negativa, *f.*
neglect, *vt.* descuidar, desatender; *n.* negligencia, *f.*
negligee, *n.* bata de casa, *f.*
negligence, *n.* negligencia, *f.*
negotiation, *n.* negociación, *f.*
negro, *n.* negro, negra
neighbor, *n.* vecino, vecina
neighborhood, *n.* vecindad, *f.*; vecindario, *m.*; inmediación, cercanía, *f.*
neither, *conj.* ni; *adj.* ninguno; *pron.* ninguno, ni uno ni otro
nephew, *n.* sobrino, *m.*
nerve, *n.* nervio, *m.*; (coll.) descaro, *m.*
nest, *n.* nido, *m.*
net, *n.* red, *f.*; malla, *f.*; *adj.* neto, líquido
Netherlands, Países Bajos, *m. pl.*
network, *n.* red radiodifusora o televisora, *f.*
neuralgia, *n.* neuralgia, *f.*
neutral, *adj.* neutral
neutrality, *n.* neutralidad, *f.*
neutron bomb, *n.* bomba de neutrón
never, *adv.* nunca, jamas; **never mind,** no importa
nevertheless, *adv.* no obstante
new, *adj.* nuevo
newcomer, *n.* recién llegado, recién llegada
newlywed, *n.* recién casado, recién casada
news, *n. pl.* novedad, *f.*, nuevas, noticias, *f. pl.*

newsboy, *n.* vendedor de periódicos, *m.*

newspaper, *n.* gaceta, *f.*; periódico, *m.*; diario, *m.*

next, *adj.* próximo; entrante, venidero; *adv.* inmediatamente después

niacin, *n.* niacina, *f.*

nice, *adj.* fino; elegante

nickel, *n.* níquel, *m.*

nickel-plated, *adj.* niquelado

nickname, *n.* apodo, *m.*

niece, *n.* sobrina, *f.*

night, *n.* noche, *f.*; **good night,** buenas noches

nightgown, *n.* camisón, *m.*, camisa de dormir, *f.*

nightingale, *n.* ruiseñor, *m.*

nightmare, *n.* pesadilla, *f.*

nimble, *adj.* ligero, ágil

nine, *n.* y *adj.* nueve, *m.*

nineteen, *n.* y *adj.* diez y nueve, diecinueve, *m.*

nineteenth, *n.* y *adj.* décimonono, *m.*

ninety, *n.* y *adj.* noventa, *m.*

ninth, *n.* y *adj.* nono, noveno, *m.*

nitrogen, *n.* nitrógeno, *m.*

no, *adv.* no; *adj.* ningún, ninguno; **by no means, in no way,** de ningún modo

No., north, N., norte

nobility, *n.* nobleza, *f.*

noble, *n.* y *adj.* noble, *m.* y *f.*

nobody, *pron.* nadie, ninguno, ninguna; *n.* persona insignificante, *f.*

noise, *n.* ruido, *m.*

noiseless, *adj.* sin ruido

noisy, *adj.* ruidoso

nominate, *vt.* nombrar, proponer (a alguien para un pueso, cargo, etc.)

nominative, *n.* (gram.) nominativo, *m.*

none, *pron.* nadie, ninguno

nonsense, *n.* tontería, *f.*; disparate, absurdo, *m.*

nonsensical, *adj.* absurdo; tonto

nonstop, *adj.* directo, sin parar

noodle, *n.* tallarín, fideo, *m.*

noon, *n.* mediodía, *m.*

noonday, *n.* mediodía, *m.*

north, *n.* norte, *m.*; *adj.* septentrional

northeast, *n.* nordeste, *m.*

northerly, northern, *adj.* septentrional

North Pole, *n.* Polo Artico, Polo Norte, *m.*

northward, northwards, *adv.* hacia el norte

northwest, *n.* noroeste, *m.*

Norway, Noruega

nose, *n.* nariz, *f.*; olfato, *m.*

not, *adv.* no

notary, notario, *m.*

note, *n.* nota, *f.*; billete, *m.*; consecuencia, *f.*; comentario, *m.*; (mus.) nota, *f.*; *vt.* notar, observar

notebook, *n.* librito de apuntes, *m.*

noted, *adj.* afamado, célebre

noteworthy, *adj.* notable

nothing, *n.* nada, *f.*

notice, *n.* noticia, *f.*; aviso, *m.*; nota, *f.*; *vt.* observar

noticeable, *adj.* notable, reparable

notify, *vt.* notificar

notion, *n.* noción, *f.*; opinion, *f.*; idea, *f.*; **notions,** *n.* *pl.* mercería, *f.*

notorious, *adj.* notorio

notwithstanding, *conj.* no obstante, aunque

noun, *n.* sustantivo, *m.*

nourish, *vt.* nutrir, alimentar

nourishing, *adj.* nutritivo

novel, *n.* novela, *f.*; *adj.* novedoso, original

novelist, *n.* novelista, *m.* y *f.*

novice, *n.* novicio, novicia

nowadays, *adv.* hoy día

nowhere, *adv.* en ninguna parte

nucleus, *n.* núcleo, *m.*

nude, *adj.* desnudo

nuisance, *n.* estorbo, *m.*; (coll.) lata, *f.*

null, *adj.* nulo, inválido

numb, *adj.* entumecido; *vt.* entumecer

number, *n.* número, *m.*; cantidad, *f.*; cifra, *f.*; *vt.* numerar

numeral, *adj.* numeral; *n.* nú-

mero, *m.*, cifra, *f.*
numerator, *n.* (math.) nume-
rador, *m.*
numerical, *adj.* numérico
nun, *n.* monja, *f.*
nuptial, *adj.* nupcial; **nuptials,** *n. pl.* nupcias, *f. pl.*
nurse, *n.* enfermera, *f.*; miñe-
ra, *f.*; **wet nurse,** nodriza,
nutriz, *f.*; *vt.* criar, amamantar; cuidar (un enfermo)
nursery, *n.* cuarto de los niños, *m.*; criadero, *m.*
nursemaid, *n.* niñera, aya, *f.*;
(Sp. Am.) nana, *f.*
nut, *n.* nuez, *f.*; tuerca, *f.*
nutmeg, *n.* nuez moscada, *f.*
nutrition, *n.* nutrición, *f.*
nutritious, nutritive, *adj.* nutritivo, alimenticio
NW., N.W., n.w., north-west,
NO, noroeste
nylon, *n.* nylon, *m.*
nymph, *n.* ninfa, *f.*

O

oak, *n.* roble, *m.*, encina, *f.*
oasis, *n.* oasis, *m.*
oath, *n.* juramento, *m.*; blasfemia, *f.*
obedience, *n.* obediencia, *f.*
obedient, *adj.* obediente
obey, *vt.* obedecer
object, *n.* objeto, *m.*; punto,
m.; (gram,) complemento, *m.*;
vt. objetar
objection, *n.* objeción, *f.*
objective, *n.* meta, *f.*; objetivo,
m.
obligation, *n.* obligación, *f.*;
compromiso, *m.*
oblige, *vt.* obligar; complacer,
favorecer
obliging, *adj.* servicial; con-
descendiente
obscene, *adj.* obsceno
obscure, *adj.* oscuro
obscurity, *n.* oscuridad, *f.*
observation, *n.* observación, *f.*
observatory, *n.* observatorio,
m.
observe, *vt.* observer, mirar;
notar; guarder (una fiesta,
etc.)

obsession, *n.* obsesión, *f.*
obsolete, *adj.* anticuado
obstacle, *n.* obstáculo, *m.*
obstetrician, *n.* partera, *m.*
obstinate, *adj.* terco, porfiado
obstruction, *n.* obstrucción,
occasion, *n.* ocasión, *vt.* ocasionar causar
occasional, *adj.* ocasional, casual
occident, *n.* occidente, *m.*
occupation, *n.* ocupación, *f.*;
empleo, *m.*; quehacer, *m.*
occupy, *vt.* ocupar, emplear
ocean, *n.* océano, *m.*
o'clock, del reloj; por el reloj;
at two o'clock, a las dos
October, *n.* octubre, *m.*
odds, *n. pl.* differencia, disparidad, *f.*; **odds and ends,** tro-
zos o fragmentos sobrantes
odor, odour, *n.* olor, *m.*; fragancia, *f.*
off, *adj. y adv.* lejos, a distancia; **hands off,** no tocar
offend, *vt.* ofender, irritar
offense, *n.* ofensa, *f.*; crimen,
delito, *m.*
offensive, *adj.* ofensivo; *n.*
(mil.) ofensiva, *f.*
offer, *vt.* ofrecer; *vi.* ofrecerse;
n. oferta, propuesta, *f.*
office, *n.* oficina, *f.*; cargo, *m.*
officer, *n.* oficial, *m.*; funcionario, *m.*; **agente de policía,**
m.
official, *adj.* oficial; *n.* oficial,
funcionario, *m.*; **officially,**
adv. oficialmente
offset, *vt.* balancear, compensar
offspring, *n.* prole, *f.*; descendencia, *f.*
oft, often, oftentimes, *adv.*
muchas veces, frecuente-
mente, a menudo
ogre, *n.* ogro, *m.*
oil, *n.* aceite, *m.*; petróleo, *m.*;
vt. aceitar, engrasar
oilcloth, *n.* encerado, hule, *m.*
oily, *adj.* aceitoso
ointment, *n.* ungüento, *m.*
O. K., all correct, correcto,
V.º B.º, visto bueno
okay, *adj. y adv.* bueno, está

bien; *vt.* aprobar; dar el visto
bueno; *n.* aprobación, *f.*, visto bueno
okra, *n.* (bot.) quimbombó, *m.*
old, *adj.* viejo; antiguo
old-fashioned, *adj.* anticuado,
fuera de moda
olive, *n.* olivo, *m.*; oliva, aceituna, *f.*; **olive oil**, aceite de
oliva
omelet, omelette, *n.* tortilla
de huevos, *f.*
omen, *n.* agüero, *m.*
omission, *n.* omisión, *f.*; descuido, *m.*
omit, *vt.* omitir
omnibus, *n.* ómnibus, *m.*
on, *prep.* sobre, encima, en;
de; a; *adv.* adelante, sin cesar
once, *adv.* una vez; **at once,**
en seguida
one, *adj.* un, uno
oneself, *pron.* sí mismo
one-sided, *adj.* unilateral, parcial
one-way, *adj.* en una sola dirección
onion, *n.* cebolla, *f.*
only, *adj.* único, solo; mero;
adv.; solamente
opal, *n.* ópalo, *m.*
open, *adj.* abierto; sincero,
franco; cándido; *vt.* abrir;
descubrir; *vi.* abrirse
opening, *n.* abertura
open-minded, *adj.* liberal; imparcial
opera, ópera, *f.*
operate, *vi.* obrar; operar
operating room, *n.* quirófano,
m.
operation, *n.* operación, *f.*;
funcionamiento, *m.*
opponent, *n.* antagonista, *m.*
y *f.*; contendiente, *m.* y *f.*
opportune, *adj.* oportuno
opposite, *adj.* opuesto; contrario; frente; *n.* antagonista,
m. y *f.*, adversario, adversaria
opposition, *n.* oposición
optic, optical, *adj.* óptico
optimism, *n.* optimismo, *m.*
optimistic, *adj.* optimista
or, *conj.* o; ó (entre números);

u (antes de o y ho)
oral, *adj.* oral, vocal; **orally,**
adv. oralmente, de palabra
orange, *n.* naranja, *f.*
orangeade, *n.* naranjada, *f.*
oration, *n.* oración, *f.*, discurso, *m.*
orator, *n.* orador, oradora
orchestra, *n.* orquesta, *f.*
orchid, *n.* orquídea, *f.*
order, *n.* orden, *m.* y *f.*; man-
dato, *m.*; encargo, *m.*; (com.)
pedido, *m.*; **out of order,**
descompuesto; *vt.* ordenar,
arreglar; hacer un pedido
ordinary, *adj.* ordinario
organ, *n.* órgano, *m.*
organdy, *n.* organdí, *m.*
organ-grinder, *n.* organillero,
m.
organic, *adj.* orgánico
organism, *n.* organismo, *m.*
organist, *n.* organista, *m.* y *f.*
organization, *n.* organización,
organize, *vt.* organizar
orient, *n.* oriente, *m.*
oriental, *adj.* oriental
origin, *n.* origen, principio, *m.*
original, *adj.* original
originality, *n.* originalidad, *f.*
originate, *vt.* y *vi.* originar;
provenir
ornament, *n.* adorno, *m.*
orphan, *n.* y *adj.* huérfano,
huérfana
orphanage, *n.* orfanato, *m.*
ostrich, *n.* avestruz, *m.*
other, *pron.* y *adj.* otro
otherwise, *adv.* de otra manera, por otra parte
ounce, *n.* onza, *f.*
our, ours, *pron.* nuestro,
nuestra, nuestros, nuestras
ourselves, *pron. pl.* nosotros
mismos
out, *adv.* fuera, afuera; *adj.* de
fuera; **out!** *interj.* ¡fuera!
outcome, *n.* consecuencia, *f.*
resultado, *m.*
outdoor, *adj.* al aire libre, fuera de casa
outdoors, *adv.* al aire libre, a
la intemperie
outer, *adj.* exterior
outfit, *n.* vestido, *m.*, vesti-

menta, *f.*; *vt.* equipar, ataviar

outgoing, *adj.* saliente, de salida

outgrow, *vt.* quedar chico (vestido, calzado, etc.)

outing, *n.* excursión campestre, *f.*

outlaw, *n.* bandido, *m.*

outlet, *n.* salida, *f.*; desagüe, *m.*; sangrador, tomadero, *m.*

outline, *n.* contorno, *m.*; bosquejo, *m.*; silueta, *f.*; *vt.* esbozar

outlook, *n.* perspectiva, *f.*

out-of-date, *adj.* anticuado

outrage, *n.* ultraje, *m.*

outrageous, *adj.* atroz

outside, *n.* superficie, *f.*; exterior, *m.*; *adv.* afuera

outskirts, *n. pl.* suburbios, *m. pl.*; afueras, *f. pl.*

outstanding, *adj.* sobresaliente, notable

oval, *n.* óvalo, *m.*; *adj.* oval, ovalado

ovary, *n.* ovario, *m.*

oven, *n.* horno, *m.*

over, *prep.* sobre, encima; **all over,** por todos lados; **over and over,** repetidas veces

overboard, *adv.* (naut.) al agua, al mar

overcoat, *n.* abrigo, *m.*

overcome, *vt.* vencer; superar; salvar (obstáculos)

overeat, *vi.* hartarse, comer demasiado

overflow, *vi.* rebosar; desbordar; *n.* superabundancia, *f.*

overkill, *n.* capacidad destructiva superior a la necesaria

overlook, *vt.* pasar por alto, tolerar; descuidar

overnight, *adv.* durante o toda la noche; *adj.* de una noche

overpass, *n.* paso superior, *m.*

overpower, *vt.* predominar

oversea, overseas, *adv.* ultramar; *adj.* de ultramar

oversight, *n.* equivocación, *f.*; olvido, *m.*

overthrow, *vt.* derribar, derrocar; *n.* derrocamiento, *m.*

overtime, *n.* trabajo en exceso

de las horas regulares

overture, *n.* (mus.) obertura, *f.*

overweight, *n.* exceso de peso

overwhelming, *adj.* abrumador

overwork, *vt.* hacer trabajar demasiado; *vi.* trabajar demasiado

owe, *vt.* deber, tener deudas; estar obligado

owl, owlet, *n.* lechuza, *f.*

own, *adj.* propio; **my own,** mío, mía; *vt.* poseer; **to own up,** confesar

owner, *n.* dueño, dueña, propietario, propietaria

ox, *n.* buey, *m.*

oxygen, *n.* oxígeno, *m.*

oyster, *n.* ostra, *f.*, ostión, *m.*

oz., ounce, ounces, onz., onza, onzas

P

pace, *n.* paso, *m.*, marcha, *f.*; *vi.* pasear

pacemaker, *n.* (med.) aparato cardiocinético, *m.*, marcador de paso, marcapasos, *m.*

Pacific, *n.* Pacífico, *m.*

package, *n.* bulto, *m.*; paquete, *m.*

packing, *n.* envase, *m.*; empaque, *m.*; relleno, *m.*

pad, *n.* cojincillo, *m.*, almohadilla, *f.*, relleno, *m.*; **pad (of paper),** bloc (de papel), *m.*; *vt.* rellenar

paddle, *vi.* remar; *n.* canalete (especie de remo), *m.*; pala (para remar), *f.*

page, *n.* página, *f.*; paje, *m.*

pageant, *n.* espectáculo público, *m.*, procesión, *f.*

pail, *n.* cubo, *m.*

pain, *n.* dolor, *m.*

painful, *adj.* doloroso; penoso

painstaking, *adj.* laborioso

paint, *vt.* y *vi.* pintar; *n.* pintura, *f.*

painter, *n.* pintor, pintora

painting, *n.* pintura, *f.*

pair, *n.* par, *m.*; *vt.* parear; *vi.* aparearse

pajamas, *n. pl.* pijamas, *m. pl.*

pal, n. compañero, compañera, gran amigo, gran amiga

palace, n. palacio, m.

palate, n. paladar, m.

pale, adj. pálido

paleness, n. palidez, f.

palm, n. (bot.) palma, f.; palma (de la mano), f.

Palm Sunday, n. domingo de Ramos, m.

pamper, vt. mimar

pamphlet, n. folleto, libreto, m.

Panama, Panama

Panamanian, n. y adj. panameño, panameña

pancake, n. especie de tortilla de masa que se cuece en una plancha metálica

pant, vi. palpitar; jadear; n. jadeo, m.; **pants**, n. pl. pantalones, m. pl.

panther, n. pantera, f.

panties, n. pl. pantalones (de mujer), m. pl.

pantry, n. despensa, f.

pants, n. pl. pantalones, m. pl.

paper, n. papel, m.; periódico, m.; vt. empapelar

paprika, n. pimentón, m.

par, n. equivalencia, f.; igualdad, f.; **at par**, a la par

parade, n. desfile, m.

paradise, n. paraíso, m.

paragraph, n. párrafo, m.

parallel, n. línea paralela, f.; adj. paralelo; vt. parangonar; ser paralelo a

paralysis, n. parálisis, f.

paralytic, paralytical, adj. paralítico

paralyze, vt. paralizar

paramount, adj. supremo, superior

parasite, n. parásito, m.

parcel, n. paquete, m.; bulto, m.; **parcel post**, paquete postal, m.

pardon, n. perdón, m., gracia, f.; vt. perdonar

parent, n. padre, m.; madre, f.; **parents**, n. pl. padres, m. pl.

parental, adj. paternal; maternal

parish, n. parroquia, f.

park, n. parque, m.; vt. estacionar (vehículos)

parking, n. estacionamiento (de automóviles), m.

parlor, n. sala, f.

parochial, adj. parroquial

parole, n. libertad condicional que se da a un prisionero; vt. y vi. libertar bajo palabra

parrot, n. papagayo, loro, m.

parson, n. párroco, m.

part, n. parte, f.; papel (de un actor), m.; obligación, f.; **in part**, parcialmente; vt. partir, separar, desunir; vi. separarse

participate, vt. participar

participle, n. (gram.) participio, m.

particular, adj. particular, singular

parting, n. separación, partida, f.; raya (en el cabello), f.

partition, n. partición, separación, f.; tabique, m.

party, n. partido, m.; fiesta, tertulia, f.

pass, vt. pasar; traspasar; vi. pasar, ocurrir, trascurrir; n. paso, camino, m.; pase, m.

passage, n. pasaje, m.; travesía, f.; pasadizo, m.

passenger, n. pasajero, pasajera

passing, adj. pasajero, transitorio; n. paso, m.; **in passing**, al pasar

passion, n. pasión, f.

passive, adj. pasivo

passport, n. pasaporte, m.

password, n. contraseña, f.

past, adj. pasado; **past tense**, (gram.) pretérito, m.; n. pasado, m.; prep. más allá de

paste, n. pasta, f.; engrudo, m.; vt. pegar (con engrudo)

pasteurize, vt. pasterizar

pastime, n. pasatiempo, m.

pastry, n. pastelería, f.

pasture, n. pasto, m.; vt. y vi. pastar, pacer

patch, n. remiendo, parche, m.; vt. remendar

patent, n. patente, f., vt. patentar

paternal, *adj.* paternal
path, *n.* senda, *f.*, sendero, *m.*
patient, *adj.* paciente, sufrido; *n.* enfermo, enferma; paciente, doliente, *m.* y *f.*
patriot, *n.* patriota, *m.*
patriotic, *adj.* patriótico
patriotism, *n.* patriotismo, *m.*
patrol, *n.* patrulla, *f.*
patron, *n.* patrón, protector, *m.*; patron saint, santo patrón, *m.*
patronize, *vt.* patrocinar
pattern, modelo, *m.*; patrón, *m.*; muestra, *f.*
pauper, *n.* pobre, *m.* y *f.*, limosnero, limosnera
pause, *n.* pausa, *f.*; *vi.* pausar; deliberar
paw, *n.* garra, *f.*
pawn, *n.* prenda, *f.*; peón (de ajedrez), *m.*; *vt.* empeñar
pawnshop, *n.* casa de empeño, *f.*
pay, *vt.* pagar; saldar; *n.* paga, *f.*, pago, *m.*
payable, *adj.* pagadero
payload, *n.* carga útil, *f.*
payment, *n.* pago, *m.*; paga, *f.*; recompensa, *f.*
payola, *n.* cohecho, soborno *m.*
pea, *n.* guisante, *m.*; (Mex.) chícharo, *m.*
peace, *n.* paz, *f.*; Peace Corps, Cuerpo de Paz
peaceful, *adj.* pacífico, apacible
peach, *n.* melocotón, durazno, *m.*
peacock, *n.* pavo real, *m.*
peanut, *n.* cacahuate, cacahuete, maní, *m.*
peasant, *n.* campesino, campesina
pebble, *n.* guijarro, *m.*, piedrecilla, *f.*
peculiar, *adj.* peculiar, singular
pedal, *n.* pedal, *m.*
peddler, *n.* buhonero, *m.*
pedestal, *n.* pedestal, *m.*
pedestrian, *n.* peatón, peatona
pediatrician, *n.* (med.) pedia-

tra, *m.* y *f.*
pedigreed, *adj.* de casta escogida
peel, *vt.* descortezar, pelar; *n.* corteza, *f.*
peerless, *adj.* sin par
pen, *n.* pluma, *f.*; corral, *m.*
penalty, *n.* pena, *f.*; castigo, *m.*; multa, *f.*
pencil, *n.* pince, *m.*; lápiz, *m.*
pending, *adj.* pendiente
penetrate, *vt.* y *vi.* penetrar
penicillin, *n.* penicilina, *f.*
peninsula, *n.* península, *f.*
penitence, *n.* penitencia,
penitentiary, *n.* penitenciaría, *f.*
penknife, *n.* cortaplumas, *m.*
penmanship, *n.* caligrafía, *f.*
penniless, *adj.* indigente
penny, *n.* centavo, *m.*
pension, *n.* pensión, *f.*; *vt.* pensionar
people, *n.* gente, *f.*; pueblo, *m.*; nación, *f.*
pep, *n.* (coll.) energía, *f.*, entusiasmo, *m.*
pepper, *n.* pimienta, *f.*
peppermint, *n.* menta, *f.*
per, *prep.* por; per capita, por persona, por cabeza; per cent, por ciento (%)
perceive, *vt.* percibir, comprender
percentage, *n.* porcentaje, *m.*
perception, *n.* percepción, *f.*
percussion, *n.* percussión *f.*; percussion section, (mus.) batería, *f.*
perfect, *adj.* perfecto; *vt.* perfeccionar
perfection, *n.* perfección, *f.*
perforate, *vt.* perforar
perforation, *n.* perforación, *f.*
perform, *vt.* ejecutar; efectuar; realizer; *vi.* (theat.) representar
performance, *n.* ejecución, *f.*; cumplimiento, *m.*; actuación, *f.*; representación teatral, funcion, *f.*
perfume, *n.* perfume, *m.*
perhaps, *adv.* quizá, tal vez
peril, *n.* peligro, riesgo, *m.*
period, *n.* periodo, *m.*; época,

f.; punto, *m.*
periodic, *adj.* periódico
periodical, *n.* periódico, *m.*; *adj.* periodico
perish, *vi.* perecer
permanent, *adj.* permanente; **permanent wave,** ondulado permanente, *m.*
permission, *n.* permiso, *m.*, licencia, *f.*
permit, *vt.* permitir; *n.* permiso, *m.*
peroxide, *n.* peróxido, *m.*
perpendicular, *adj.* perpendicular
perpetual, *adj.* perpetuo
persecute, *vt.* perseguir
persecution, *n.* persecución, *f.*
perseverance, *n.* perseverancia, *f.*
persist, *vi.* persistir
persistent, *adj.* persistente
person, *n.* persona, *f.*
personal, *adj.* personal
personality, *n.* personalidad, *f.*
personnel, *n.* personal, *m.*
perspective, *n.* perspectiva, *f.*
perspiration, *n.* traspiración, *f.*, sudor, *m.*
perspire, *vi.* traspirar, sudar
persuade, *vt.* persuadir
pertain, *vi.* relacionar, tocar
perturb, *vt.* perturbar
perverse, *adj.* perverso
perversion *n.* perversión, *f.*
perversity, *n.* perversidad, *f.*
pervert, *vt.* perverter, corromper
pessimist, *n.* pesimista, *m.* y *f.*
pessimistic, *adj.* pesimista
pest, *n.* reste, pestilencia, *f.*
pet, *n.* favorito, favorita; *vt.* mimar
petition, *n.* petición, súplica, *f.*; *vt.* suplicar, pedir
pew, *n.* banco de iglesia, *m.*
phantom, *n.* espectro, fantasma, *m.*
pharmacist, *n.* boticario, farmacéutico, *m.*
pharmacy, *n.* farmacia, botica, *f.*
phase, *n.* fase, *f.*, aspecto, *m.*
philanthropic, philanthropi-

cal, *adj.* filantrópico
philately, *n.* filatelia, *f.*
Philippines, Filipinas
philosopher, *n.* filósofo *m.*
philosophy, *n.* filosofía *f.*
phone, *n.* (coll.) teléfono, *m.*; *vt.* (coll.) telefonear
phonetics, *n. pl.* fonética, *f.*
photo, *n.* (coll.) **photograph**
photogenic, *adj.* fotogénico
photograph, *n.* fotografía, *f.*; retrato, *m.*; *vt.* fotografiar, retratar
photographer, *n.* fotógrafo, *m.*
physic, *n.* purgante, *m.*, purga, *f.*; **physics,** *n. pl.* física, *f.*; *vt.* purgar, dar un purgante
physical, *adj.* físico
physician, *n.* médico, *m.*
physics, *n.* física, *f.*
physiology, *n.* fisiología, *f.*
physique, *n.* físico, *m.*
pianist, *n.* pianista, *m.* y *f.*
piano, *n.* piano, *m.*
pickle, *n.* encurtido, *m.*
pickpocket, *n.* ratero, ratera, ladrón, ladrona
picnic, *n.* merienda campestre, *f.*; día de campo, *m.*
picture, *n.* retrato, *m.*; fotografía, *f.*; cuadro, *m.*; **motion picture,** película, *f.*
picturesque, *adj.* pintoresco
pie, *n.* pastel, *m.*
piece, *n.* pedazo, *m.*; pieza, obra, *f.*
pier, *n.* muelle, *m.*
pig, *n.* cerdo, *m.*, puerco, puerca
pigeon, *n.* palomo, *m.*, paloma, *f.*
pile, *n.* pila, *f.*; montón, *m.*; **piles,** *n. pl.* hemorroides, almorranas, *f. pl.*; *vt.* amontonar, apilar
pill, *n.* píldora, *f.*
pillar, *n.* pilar, poste, *m.*, columna, *f.*
pillow, *n.* almohada, *f.*, cojín, *m.*
pillowcase, pillowslip, *n.* funda, *f.*
pilot, *n.* piloto, *m.*
pimento, *n.* pimiento, *m.*
pimple, *n.* grano, barro, *m.*

pin, *n.* alfiler, *m.*, prendedor, *m.*; **safety pin**, imperdible, alfiler de gancho; *vt.* asegurar con alfileres; fijar con clavija

pinafore, *n.* delantal de niña, *m.*

pinch, *vt.* pellizcar; *vi.* escatimar gastos; *n.* pellizco, *m.*; aprieto, *m.*

pineapple, *n.* piña, *f.*; ananá, ananás, *f.*

pink, *n.* (bot.) clavel, *m.*; *adj.* rosado, sonrosado

pint, *n.* pinta (medida de líquidos), *f.*

pious, *adj.* piadoso

pipe, *n.* tubo, conducto, caño, *m.*; pipa para fumar, *f.*

pirate, *n.* pirata, *m.*

pit, *n.* hoyo, *m.*

pitcher, *n.* cántaro, *m.*; (baseball) lanzador de pelota

pitiful, *adj.* lastimoso

pity, *n.* piedad, compasión, *f.*; *vt.* compadecer

pkg., **package**, bto., bulto, paquete

place, *n.* lugar, sitio, *m.*; local, *m.*; **to take place**, verificarse; *vt.* colocar; poner

plague, *n.* peste, plaga, *f.*; *vt.* atormentar

plain, *adj.* sencillo; simple; evidente; *n.* llano, *m.*

plan, *n.* plan, *m.*; *vt.* planear, proyectar

plane, *n.* (avi.) avión, *m.*; plano; *m.*; cepillo, *m.*

planet, *n.* planeta, *m.*

plant, *n.* planta, *f.*

plasma, *n.* plasma. *m.*

plastic, *adj.* plástico

plate, *n.* placa, *f.*; clisé, *m.*; plato, *m.*

platform, *n.* plataforma, tarima, *f.*

platter, *n.* fuente, *f.*, plato grande, *m.*

play, *n.* juego, *m.*; recreo, *m.*; comedia, *f.*; *vt.* y *vi.* jugar; (mus.) tocar

playback, *n.* reproducción en magnetófono

playboy, *n.* muchacho travieso, hombre de mundo, cala-

vera, *m.*

playful, *adj.* juguetón, travieso

playground, *n.* campo de deportes o de juegos, *m.*

playmate, *n.* compañero o compañera de juego

plaything, *n.* juguete, *m.*

plea, *n.* ruego, *m.*; súplica, *f.*; petición, *f.*

plead, *vt.* alegar; suplicar

please, *vt.* agradar, complacer

pleasing, *adj.* agradable, grato

pleasure, *n.* placer, *m.*

plot, *n.* pedazo pequeño de terreno; trama, *f.*; complot, *m.*; *vt.* y *vi.* conspirar, tramar

plug, n: tapón, *m.*; (elec.) clavija, *f.*; *vt.* tapar; (elec.) conectar

plumber, *n.* plomero, *m.*

plunge, *vt.* y *vi.* sumergir, precipitarse

plus, *prep.* más

p.m., **afternoon**, p.m., pasado meridiano, tarde

pneumonia, *n.* neumonia, pulmonía, *f.*

pocket, *n.* bolsillo, *m.*

pocketbook, *n.* portamonedas, *m.*, cartera, *f.*; (fig.) dinero, *m.*

pocketknife, *n.* cortaplumas, *m.*

poem, *n.* poema, *m.*

poet, *n.* poeta, *m.*

poetic, **poetical**, *adj.* poético

poetry, *n.* poesía, *f.*

point, *n.* punta, *f.*; punto, *m.*; **point of view**, punto de vista; *vt.* apuntar; **to point out**, señalar

poison, *n.* veneno, *m.*; *vt.* envenenar

poker, *n.* hurgón, *m.*; póker (juego de naipes), *m.*

Poland, Polonia

polar, *adj.* polar; **polar bear**, oso blanco, *m.*

Pole, *n.* polaco, polaca

pole, *n.* polo, *m.*; palo, *m.*; **pole vault**, salto con pértiga, *m.*

police, *n.* policía, *f.*

policeman, *n.* policía, *m.*

policewoman, *n.* mujer policía, *f.*

policy, *n.* póliza, *f.*; política, *f.*: sistema, *m.*

polite, *adj.* cortés

politeness, *n.* cortesía, *f.*

political, *adj.* político

politician, *n.* político, *m.*

politics, *n. pl.* política, *f.*

pond, *n.* charca, *f.*

ponder, *vt.* y *vi.* ponderar

pontoon, *n.* (avi.) flotador de hidroavión, *m.*

pony, *n.* caballito, *m.*

pool, *n.* charco. *m.*

poor, *adj.* pobre; deficiente

popcorn, *n.* palomitas de maíz, *f. pl.*

Pope, *n.* papa, *m.*

poplar, *n.* álamo temblón, *m.*

poppy, *n.* amapola, *f.*

popular, *adj.* popular

popularity, *n.* popularidad, *f.*

population, *n.* población, *f.*, número de habitantes, *m.*

populous, *adj.* populoso

porcelain, *n.* porcelana, *f.*

porch, *n.* pórtico, vestíbulo, *m.*

pork, *n.* carne de puerco, *f.*

port, *n.* puerto, *m.*; vino de Oporto, *m.*

portable, *adj.* portátil

porter, *n.* portero, *m.*; mozo, *m.*

portion, *n.* porción, ración, *f.*

portrait, *n.* retrato, *m.*

Portuguese, *n.* y *adj.* portugués, portuguesa

pose, *n.* postura, actitud

position, *n.* posición, situación, *f.*

positive, *adj.* positive, real

possess, *vt.* poseer

possession, *n.* posesión, *f.*

possessive, *adj.* posesivo

possibility, *n.* posibilidad, *f.*

possible, *adj.* posible

post, *n.* correo, *m.*; puesto, *m.*; empleo, *m.*; poste, *m.*; *vt.* fijar; **post no bills,** se prohibe fijar carteles

postage, *n.* franqueo, *m.*

postal, *adj.* postal; **postal card,** tarjeta postal, *f.*

poster, *n.* cartel, cartelón, *m.*

posterity, *n.* posteridad, *f.*

postman, *n.* cartero, *m.*

postmark, *n.* sello o marca de la oficina de correos

post office, *n.* correo, *m.*, oficina postal, *f.*

postpaid, *adj.* franco; con porte pagado

postpone, vt. posponer

postscript, *n.* posdata, *f.*

postwar, *n.* postguerra, *f.*

pot, *n.* olla, *f.*

potato, *n.* patata, papa, *f.*

potent, *adj.* potente

pouch, *n.* buche, *m.*; bolsa, *f.*

poultry, *n.* aves de corral, *f. pl.*

pound, *n.* libra, *f.*; **pound sterling,** libra esterlina, *f.*; *vt.* machacar

pour, *vt.* verter; *vi.* fluir con rapidez; llover a cántaros

poverty, *n.* pobreza, *f.*

POW, (prisoner of war), *n.* prisionero de guerra, *m.*

powder, *n.* polvo, *m.*; pólvora, *f.*; **powder puff,** borla o mota de empolvarse; *vt.* pulverizar; empolvar

power, *n.* poder, *m.*; potencia, *f.*

powerful, *adj.* poderoso

powerless, *adj.* impotente

pp., pages, págs., páginas; **past participle,** p. pdo., participio pasado

practice, *n.* práctica, *f.*; costumbre, *f.*; *vt.* y *vi.* practicar, ejercer; ensayar

praise, *n.* alabanza, *f.*; *vt.* alabar, ensalzar

pray, *vt.* y *vi.* rezar, rogar

prayer, *n.* oración, súplica, *f.*; **the Lord's Prayer,** el Padre Nuestro, *m.*

preach, *vt.* y *vi.* predicar

preacher, *n.* predicador, *m.*

preamble, *n.* preámbulo, *m.*

precaution, *n.* precaución, *f.*

precede, *vt.* preceder

precedent, *adj.* y *n.* precedente, *m.*

preceding, *adj.* precursor

precious, *adj.* precioso; valioso

precipitation, *n.* precipitación, *f.*

precise, *adj.* preciso, exacto

predecessor, n. predecesor, predecesora, antecesor, antecesora

predict, vt. predecir

predominate, vt. predominar

preface, n. prefacio, m.

prefer, vt. preferir

preferable, adj. preferible

preference, n. preferencia, f.

pregnant, adj. encinta

prejudice, n. prejuicio, m.

preliminary, adj. preliminar

premature, adj. prematuro

premier, n. primer ministro, m.

premiere, n. estreno, m.

premium, n. premio, m.; prima, f.

premonition, n. presentimiento, m.

preparation, n. preparación, f.; preparativo, m.

prepare, vt. preparar; vi. prepararse

preposition, n. preposición, f.

prescribe, vt. y vi. prescribir; recetar

prescription, n. receta medicinal, f.

presence, n. presencia, f.; **presence of mind,** serenidad de ánimo, f.

present, n. presente, regalo, m.; adj. presente; vt. presentar, regalar

presentable, adj. presentable, decente

preserve, vt. preserver, conservar; n. conserva, confitura, f.

preside, vi. presidir

presidency, n. presidencia, f.

president, n. presidente, m.

press, vt. planchar; oprimir; compeler; n. prensa, f.; imprenta, f.

pressing, urgente

pressure, n. presión, f.; **pressure gauge,** manómetro, m.

pretend, vt. simular, fingir

pretense, pretence, n. pretexto, m.; pretensión, f.

pretext, n. pretexto, m.

pretty, adj. bonito

prevent, vt. prevenir

prevention, n. prevención , f.

preventive, adj. y n. preventivo, m.

preview, n. exhibición preliminar, f.

previous, adj. previo

price, n. precio, valor, m.

priceless, adj. inapreciable

priest, n. sacerdote, cura, m.

primary, adj. primario

primitive, adj. primitivo

princess, n. princesa, f.

principal, adj. principal; n. principal, jefe, m.; rector, director (de un colegio), m.; capital (dinero empleado), m.

principle, n. principio, fundamento, m.

print, vt. estampar, imprimir; n. impresión, estampa, f.

printed, adj. impreso; **printed matter,** impresos, m. pl.

printer, n. impresor, m.

prison, n. prisión, cárcel, f.

prisoner, n. prisionero, prisionera

private, adj. privado; secreto; particular; **private enterprise,** empresa particular, f.; n. soldado raso, m.

prize, n. premio, m.

prizefighter, n. pugilista, boxeador, m.

pro, prep. para, pro; adj. en el lado afirmativo (de un debate, etc.); **the pros and cons,** el pro y el contra

probability, n. probabilidad, f.

probable, adj. probable

probation, n. prueba, f.; libertad condicional, f.

problem, n. problema, m.

proceed, vi. proceder; **proceeds,** n. pl. producto, rédito, m.

process, n. proceso, m.

procession, n. procesión, f.

produce, vt. producir; rendir

product, n. producto, m.

production, n. producción, f.

Prof., prof., professor, Prof., profesor

profit, n. ganancia, f.; provecho, m.; vt. y vi. aprovechar

profitable, adj. provechoso,

productivo

program, n. programa, m.; vt. programar

progress, vt. progreso, m.; adelanto, m.; vi. progresar

prohibit, vt. prohibir

prohibition, n. prohibición, f.

project, vt. proyectar, trazar; n. proyecto, m.

prominent, adj. prominente

promise, n. promesa, f.; vt. prometer

promising, adj. prometedor

promote, vt. promover

promotion, n. promoción, f.

prompt, adj. pronto, listo; **promptly,** adv. pronto; vt. apuntar (en el teatro)

pronoun, n. pronombre, m.

pronounce, vt. pronunciar

pronunciation, n. pronunciación, f.

proof, n. prueba, f.

proofread, vt. corregir pruebas

propaganda, n. propaganda, f.

propagandist, adj. y n. propagandista, propagador, m.

proper, adj. propio; debido

property, n. propiedad, f.

prophecy, n. profecía, f.

prophet, n. profeta, m.

proportion, n. proporción, f.

proposal, n. propuesta, proposición, f.; oferta, f.

propose, vt. proponer

proposition, n. proposición, propuesta, f.

proprietor, n. propietario, propietaria, dueño, dueña

prose, n. prosa, f.

prosecutor, n. acusador, m.

prospect, n. perspectiva, f.

prosper, vt. y vi. prosperar

prosperity, n. prosperidad, f.

prosperous, adj. próspero

prostitution, n. prostitución, f.

prostrate, adj. decaído, postrado

protect, vt. proteger, amparar

protection, n. protección,

protector, n. protector, protectora

protein, n. proteína, f.

protest, vt. y vi. protestar; n.

protesta, f.

Protestant, n. y adj. protestante, m. y f.

prove, vt. probar

proverb, n. proverbio, m.

provide, vt. proveer, surtir

provided, adj. provisto; **provided that,** con tal que

providence, n. providencia, f.; economía, f.

province, n. provincia, f.; jurisdicción, f.

provision, n. provisión, f.; **provisions,** n. pl. comestibles, m. pl.

provisional, adj. provisional

proxy, n. apoderado, apoderada; **by proxy,** por poder

P.S., postscript, P.D., posdata

psalm, n. salmo, m.

psychiatry, n. siquiatría, f.

psychoanalyze, vt. sicoanalizar

psychology, n. sicología, f.

P. T. A.: Parent-Teacher Association, Asociación de Padres y Maestros

public, adj. y n. público, m.

publication, n. publicación, f.

publicity, n. publicidad, f.

publish, vt. publicar

puff, n. bufido, soplo, m.; bocanada, f.; **powder puff,** mota o borla para polvos, f.; vt. y vi. hinchar; soplar

puffy, adj. hinchado

pull, vt. tirar, halar.; n. tirón, m.. influencia. f.

pulpit, n. púlpito, m.

pump, n. bomba, f.; zapatilla, f.; vt. sondear; sonsacar

pumpkin, n. calabaza, f.

pun, n. equívoco, chiste, m.; juego de palabras, m.

punch, n. puñetazo, m.; ponche, m.

punctual, adj. puntual

punctuation, n. puntuación, f.

puncture, n. pinchazo, m.

punish, vt. castigar

punishment, n. castigo, m.

pupil, n. (anat.) pupila, f.; pupilo, m.; discípulo, discípula; **pupil of the eye,** niña del ojo, *f.*

puppy, *n.* perrillo, cachorro, *m.*

purgatory, *n.* purgatorio, *m.*

purple, *adj.* morado

purpose, *n.* intención, *f.*; **on purpose,** de propósito

purse, *n.* bolsa, *f.*, portamonedas, *m.*

pursue, *vt.* y *vi.* perseguir; seguir

pursuit, *n.* persecución, *f.*

puss, pussy, *n.* micho, gato, *m.*

put, *vt.* poner, colocar

puzzle, *n.* rompecabezas, *m.*; *vt.* y *vi.* confundir

pyramid, *n.* pirámide,

Q

qt., quantity, cantidad; **quart,** cuarto de galón.

quail, *n.* codorniz, *f.*

quake, *vi.* temblar, tiritar; *n.* temblor, *m.*

Quaker, *n.* y *adj.* cuáquero, cuáquera

qualification, *n.* aptitud, *f.*; requisito, *m.*

quantity, *n.* cantidad, *f.*

quarantine, *n.* cuarentena, *f.*

quarrel, *n.* riña, pelea, *f.*; *vi.* reñir, disputar

quart, *n.* un cuarto de galón, *m.*

quarter, *n.* cuarto, *m.*; cuarta parte; cuartel, *m.*; moneda de E.U.A. de 25 centavos de dólar

quarterly, *adj.* trimestral

quartet, *n.* cuarteto, *m.*

queen, *n.* reina, *f.*; dama (en el juego de aiedrez), *f.*

queenly, *adj.* majestuoso, como una reina

question, *n.* cuestión, *f.*; asunto, *m.*; duda, *f.*; pregunta, *f.*; *vi.* preguntar; *vt.* desconfiar, poner en duda

questionable, *adj.* dudoso

questionnaire, *n.* cuestionario, *m.*

quick, *adj.* veloz; ligero, pronto; **quickly,** *adv.* rápidamen-

te

quiet, *adj.* quieto, tranquilo, callado; *n.* calma, serenidad, *f.*; *vt.* tranquilizar

quinine, *n.* quinina, *f.*

quiz, *vt.* examinar; *n.* examen *m.*

quorum, *n.* quórum, *m.*

quota, *n.* cuota, *f.*

quotation, *n.* cotización, cita, *f.*; **quotation marks,** comillas, *f. pl.*

quote, *vt.* citar; **to quote (a price),** cotizar (precio)

quotient, *n.* cuociente o cociente, *m.*

R

rabbit, *n.* conejo, *m.*

race, *n.* raza, *f.*; carrera, corrida, *f.*; *vi.* correr

rack, *n.* (mech.) cremallera, *f.*

racket, *n.* raqueta, *f.*

radar, *n.* radar, *m.*

radiance, *n.* esplendor, *m.*

radiator, *n.* calentador, *m.*; (auto.) radiador, *m.*

radio, *n.* radio. *m.* y *f.*

radio telescope, *n.* radiotelescopio *m.*

radius, *n.* (math., anat.) radio, *m.*

rage, *n.* rabia, *f.*; furor, *m.*, cólera, *f.*; *vt.* rabiar, encolerizarse

rail, *n.* balaustrada, *f.*; (rail.) carril, riel, *m.*; **by rail,** por ferrocarril

railing, *n.* baranda, *f.*, barandal *m.*; carril, *m.*

railroad, *n.* ferrocarril, *m.*

railway, *n.* ferrocarril, *m.*

rain, *n.* lluvia, *f.*; *vi.* llover

rainbow, *n.* arco iris, *m.*

raincoat, *n.* impermeable, *m.*

raindrop, *n.* gota de lluvia, *f.*

rainy, *adj.* lluvioso

raise, *vt.* levantar, alzar

raisin, *n.* pasa, *f.*

ran, *pretérito* del verbo **run**

ranch, *n.* hacienda, *f.*; rancho, *m.*

random, *n.* ventura, casualidad, *f.*; **at random,** al azar

rang, *pretérito* del verbo **ring**

range, *vt.* clasificar; *vi.* fluctuar; alcance, *m.*; cocina económica, estufa, *f.*

rank, *n.* fila, hilera, *f.*; clase, *f.*; grado, rango, *m.*

ransom, *vt.* rescatar; *n.* rescate, *m.*

rape, *n.* fuerza, *f.*; estupro, *m.*; *vt.* estuprar

rash, *adj.* precipitado, temerario; *n.* roncha, *f.*; erupción, *f.*; sarpullido, *m.*

raspberry, *n.* frambuesa, *f.*

rat, *n.* rata, *f.*

rate, *n.* tipo, *m.*, tasa, *f.*; precio, valor, *m.*; **at the rate of,** a razón de; *vt.* tasar, apreciar; calcular, calificar

rather, *adv.* más bien; bastante; mejor dicho

ratify, *vt.* ratificar

rattle, *vt.* y *vi.* hacer ruido; **to become rattled,** confundirse; *n.* sonajero, *m.*; matraca, *f.*

rattlesnake, *n.* culebra de cascabel, *f.*

raw, *adj.* crudo; en bruto; **raw materials,** primeras materias, *f. pl.*

ray, *n.* rayo (de luz), *m.*

rayon, *n.* rayón, *m.*

razor, *n.* navaja de afeitar, *f.*

rd., road, camino; **rod,** pértica

reach, *vt.* alcanzar; *vi.* extenderse, llegar

read, *vt.* leer; interpretar

reader, *n.* lector, lectora

readily, *adv.* prontamente; de buena gana

reading, *n.* lectura, *f.*

real, *adj.* real, verdado, efectivo; **real estate,** bienes raíces o inmuebles, *m. pl.*

realistic, *adj.* realista; natural

reality, *n.* realidad, *f.*

realize, *vt.* realizer; darse cuenta de

really, *adv.* realmente

reap, *vt.* segar

rear, *n.* retaguardia, *f.*; parte posterior, *f.*; *adj.* posterior; *vt.* criar, educar

reason, *n.* razón, *f.*; motivo,

m.; *vt.* razonar, raciocinar

reasonable, *adj.* razonable

reassure, *vt.* volver a asegurar

rebate, *n.* rebaja, *f.*

rebel, *n.* rebelde, *m.* y *f.*; *adj.* insurrecto; *vi.* rebelarse; insubordinarse

rebirth, *n.* renacimiento, *m.*

rebuild, *vt.* reconstruir

receipt, *n.* recibo, *m.*; receta, *f.*

receive, *vt.* recibir; admitir

receiver, *n.* receptor, *m.*; recipiente, *m.*; audífono, *m.*

reception, *n.* recepción, *f.*

receptionist, *n.* recepcionista, *m.* y *f.*, recibidor, m

recess, *n.* receso, recreo, *m.*

recipe, *n.* receta de cocina, *f.*

recipient, *n.* receptor, receptora

reciprocal, *adj.* recíproco

reciprocate, *vi.* corresponder

recital, *n.* recitación, *f.*; concierto, *m.*

recitation, *n.* recitación,

recite, *vt.* recitar; declamar

recognition, *n.* reconocimiento, *m.*; agradecimiento, *m.*

recognize, *vt.* reconocer

recommend, *vt.* recomendar

recommendation, *n.* recomendación, *f.*

recompense, *n.* recompensa, *f.*; *vt.* recompensar

reconciliation, *n.* reconciliación, *f.*

record, *vt.* registrar; grabar; *n.* registro, archivo, *m.*; disco, *m.*; *adj.* sin precedente; **off-the-record,** confidencial, extraoficial

recover, *vt.* recobrar; *vi.* restablecerse

recovery, *n.* restablecimiento, *m.*

recruit, *vt.* reclutar; *n.* (mil.) recluta, *m.*

rectangle, *n.* rectángulo, *m.*

rectangular, *adj.* rectangular

rectify, *vt.* rectificar

recuperate, *vi.* restablecerse; *vt.* recobrar, recuperar

red, *adj.* rojo; colorado; **Red, (communist),** *n.*, *adj.* rojo (communista)

redbreast, *n.* petirrojo, pechirrojo, *m.*

redden, *vi.* enrojecer

redeem, *vt.* redimir

redeemer, *n.* redentor, redentora, salvador, salvadora; the **Redeemer,** el Redentor

red-haired, *adj.* pelirrojo

reduce, *vt.* reducir

reduction, *n.* reducción, rebaja, *f.*

refer, *vt.* y *vi.* referir, dirigir

referee, *n.* árbitro, *m.*

reference, *n.* referencia, *f.*

refill, *vt.* rellenar; *n.* relleno, *m.*

refine, *vt.* y *vi.* refinar, purificar

refinement, *n.* refinamiento, *m.*

reflect, *vt.* y *vi.* rerejar; reflexionar

reflection, *n.* reflexión, meditación, *f.*; reflejo, *m.*

reflex, *adj.* reflejo

reform, *vt.* y *vi.* reformar; *n.* reforma, *f.*

reformatory, *n.* reformatorio *m.*

refrain, *vi.* abstenerse; *n.* estribillo, *m.*

refresh, *vt.* refrescar

refreshment, *n.* refresco, refrigerio, *m.*

refrigerate, *vt.* refrigerar

refrigeration, *n.* refrigeración, *f.*

refrigerator, *n.* refrigerador, *m.*

refuge, *n.* refugio, asilo, *m.*

refugee, *n.* refugiado, refugiada

refuse, *vt.* rehusar, repulsar; *n.* desecho, *m.*, sobra, *f.*

regard, *vt.* estimar; considerar; *n.* consideración, *f.*; respeto, *m.*; **regards,** *m. pl.* , recuerdos, *m. pl.*, memorias, *f. pl.*; **in regard to,** en cuanto a, respecto a, con respecto a; **in this regard,** a este respecto

regime, *n.* régimen. *m.*

regiment, *n.* regimiento, *m.*

region, *n.* región, *f.*

regional, *adj.* regional

register, *n.* registro, *m.*; **cash register,** caja registradora, *f.*; *vt.* registrar; certificar (una carta); *vi.* matricularse, registrarse

regret, *n.* arrepentimiento, *m.*; pesar, *m.*; *vt.* lamentar, deplorar

regrettable, *adj.* lamentable, deplorable

regular, *adj.* regular; ordinario

regularity, *n.* regularidad, *f.*

rehabilitation, *n.* rehabilitación, *f.*

rehearsal, *n.* (theat.) ensayo, *m.*

rehearse, *vt.* (theat.) ensayar

reign, *n.* reinado, reino, *m.*; *vi.* reinar, prevalecer, imperar

reimburse, *vt.* rembolsar

rein, *n.* rienda, *f.*

reindeer, *n. sing.* y *pl.*. reno(s), rangifero(s), *m.*

reinforced, *adj.* reforzado

relate, *vt.* referir

related, *adj.* emparentado

relation, *n.* relación, *f.*; parentesco, *m.*

relative, *adj.* relativo; *n.* pariente, *m.* y *f.*

relax, *vt.* aflojar; *vi.* descansar, reposar

relaxation, *n.* reposo, descanso, *m.*

relay, *n.* trasmisión, *f.*; **relay race,** carrera de relevos, *f.*

release, *vt.* soltar, libertar; dar al público

relentless, *adj.* inflexible

relevant, *adj.* pertinente; concerniente

reliable, *adj.* digno de confianza, responsable

relief, *n.* alivio, consuelo, *m.*

relieve, *vt.* aliviar; relevar

religion, *n.* religión, *f.* ; culto, *m.*

religious, *adj.* religioso

relish, *n.* sabor, *m.*; gusto, deleite, *m.*; condimento, *m.*

relocate, *vt.* establecer de nuevo

remain, *vi.* quedar, restar, permanecer

remark, *n.* observación, nota,

f., comentario, *m.*

remarkable, *adj.* notable, interesante

remedy, *n.* remedio, medicamento, *m.*; *vt.* remediar

remember, *vt.* recordar, tener presente; dar memorias; *vi.* acordarse

remit, *vt.* y *vi.* remitir

remittance, *n.* remesa, *f.*; remisión, *f.*

remorse, *n.* remordimiento, *m.*

remote, *adj.* remoto, lejano

remove, *vt.* remover, alejar; quitar

render, *vt.* rendir

rendezvous, *n.* cita (particularmente amorosa), *f.*

renew, *vt.* renovar

renewal, *n.* prórroga,

rent, *n.* renta, *f.*, alquiler, *m.*; *vt.* arrendar, alquilar

repair, *vt.* reparar; *n.* remiendo, *m.*, reparación, compostura, *f.*

repeal, *vt.* abrogar, revocar; *n.* revocación, *f.*

repeat, *vt.* repetir

repent, *vi.* arrepentirse

repentance, *n.* arrepentimiento, *m.*

repertoire, *n.* repertorio, *m.*

repetition, *n.* repetición, *f.*

reply, *vt.* replicar, contestar, responder; *n.* respuesta, contestación, *f.*

report, *vt.* informar; dar cuenta; *n.* rumor, *m.*; informe, *m.*

reporter, *n.* reportero, *m.*; periodista, *m.* y *f.*

represent, *vt.* representar

representation, *n.* representación, *f.*

representative, *adj.* representativo; *n.* representante, *m.* y *f.*; **House of Representatives,** Cámara de Representantes

reprint, *n.* reimpresión, *f.*

reproduce, *vt.* reproducir

reptile, *n.* reptil, *m.*

republic, *n.* república,

reputation, *n.* reputación, *f.*

request, *n.* solicitud, súplica, *f.*; *vt.* suplicar; pedir, solicitar

require, *vt.* requerir, demandar

requirement, *n.* requisito, *m.*

rescue, *n.* rescate, *m.*; *vt.* socorrer; salvar

research, *n.* investigación, *f.*

resemblance, *n.* semejanza, *f.*

resemble, *vi.* parecerse a

resent, *vt.* resentir

resentment, *n.* resentimiento, *m.*

reservation, *n.* reservación, *f.*

reserve, *vt.* reservar; *n.* reserva, *f.*

residence, *n.* residencia, *f.*

resident, *n.* y *adj.* residente, *m.* y *f.*

residential, *adj.* residencial

resign, *vt.* y *vi.* resignar, renunciar, ceder; conformarse

resignation, *n.* resignación, *f.*; renuncia, *f.*

resist, *vt.* y *vi.* resistir; oponerse

resistance, *n.* resistencia, *f.*

resolution, *n.* resolución, *f.*

resolve, *vt.* resolver; decretar; *vi.* resolverse

resort, *vi.* recurrir; *n.* recurso; **summer resort,** lugar de veraneo, *m.*

resource, *n.* recurso, *m.*

resourceful, *adj.* ingenioso, hábil

respect, *n.* respecto, *m.*; respeto, *m.*; *vt.* apreciar; respetar

respectable, *adj.* respetable; decente

respectful, *adj.* respetuoso;

respectfully, *adv.* respetuosamente

respond, *vt.* responder

response, *n.* respuesta, réplica, *f.*

responsibility, *n.* responsabilidad, *f.*

responsible, *adj.* responsable

rest, *n.* reposo, *m.*; resto, restante, *m.*; **rest room,** sala de descanso, *f.*; *vt.* poner a descansar; apoyar; *vi.* resposar, recostar

restaurant, *n.* restaurante, *m.* fonda, *f.*

restless, *adj.* inquieto

restore, *vt.* restaurar, restituir

restrain, vt, restringir

restrict, *vt.* restringir, limitar

result, *n.* resultado, *m.*; consecuencia, *f.*; *vi.* resultar

resurrect, *vt.* resucitar

retail, *n.* venta al por menor *f.*, menudeo, *m.*

retain, *vt.* retener, guardar

retire, *vt.* retirar; *vi.* retirarse, sustraerse

return, *vt.* devolver; *n.* retorno, *m.*; vuelta, *f.*

reunion, *n.* reunión, *f.*

Rev., Reverend, R., Reverendo

revelation, *n.* revelación, *f.*

reverend, *adj.* reverendo; venerable; *n.* sacerdote, *m.*

reverse, *n.* reverso (de una moneda), *m.*; revés, *m.*; *adj.* inverso; contrario

review, *n.* revista, *f.*; reseña, *f.*; repaso, *m.*; *vt.* (mil.) revistar; repasar

revise, *vt.* revisar

revoke, *vt.* revocar, anular

revolt, *vi.* rebelarse; *n.* rebelión, *f.*

revolting, *adj.* repugnante

revolution, *n.* revolución, *f.*

revolutionary, *n.* y *adj.* revolucionario, revolucionaria

revolve, *vi.* girar

revolver, *n.* revólver, *m.*, pistola, *f.*

reward, *n.* recompensa, *f.*; *vt.* recompensar

RFD, r.f.d., rural free delivery, distribución gratuita del correo en regiones rurales

rhinoceros, *n.* rinoceronte, *m.*

rhyme, *n.* rima, *f.*; *vi.* rimar

rhythm, *n.* ritmo, *m.*

rib, *n.* costilla, *f.*

riboflavin, *n.* riboflavina, *f.*

rice, *n.* arroz, *m.*

rich, *adj.* rico; opulento

riches, *n. pl.* riqueza, *f.*; bienes, *m. pl.*

rid, *vt.* librar, desembarazar

riddle, *n.* enigma, rompecabezas, *m.*

ride, *vi.* cabalgar; andar en coche; *n.* paseo a caballo o en coche

ridge, *n.* espinazo, lomo, *m.*; cordillera, *f.*

ridiculous, *adj.* ridículo

riding, *n.* paseo a caballo o en coche; *adj.* relativo a la equitación

rifle, *n.* fusil, *m.*

right, *adj.* derecho, recto; justo; *adv.* rectamente; **to be right,** tener razón; *n.* justicia, *f.*; derecho, *m.*; mano derecha, *f.*; (pol.) derecha, *f.*

ring, *n.* círculo, cerco, *m.*; anillo, *m.*; campaneo, *m.*; *vt.* sonar; **to ring the bell,** tocar la campanilla, tocar el timbre; *vi.* resonar

rinse, *vt.* enjuagar

riot, *n.* pelotera, *f.*; motín, *m.*

ripe, *adj.* maduro, sazonado

ripen, *vt.* y *vi.* madurar

rise, *vi.* levantarse; nacer, salir (los astros); rebelarse; ascender; *n.* levantamiento, *m.*; subida, *f.*; salida (del sol), *f.*

risen, *p. p.* del verbo **rise**

risk, *n.* riesgo, peligro, *m.*; *vt.* arriesgar

risky, *adj.* peligroso

rival, *n.* rival, *m.* y *f.*

river, *n.* río, *m.*

R.N., registered nurse, enfermera titulada, *f.*

RNA, ribonucleic acid, *n.* ácido ribonucleico

roach, *n.* cucaracha, *f.*

road, *n.* camino, *m.*

roar, *vi.* rugir; bramar; *n.* rugido, *m.*

roast, *vt.* asar

rob, *vt.* robar, hurtar

robber, *n.* ladrón, ladrona

robbery, *n.* robo, *m.*

robe, *n.* manto, *m.*; toga, *f.*

robin, *n.* (orn.) petirrojo, pechirrojo, pechicolorado, *m.*

rock, *n.* roca, *f.*; *vt.* mecer; arrullar; *vi.* balancearse

rock n' roll, rock-and-roll, *n.* música y baile popular, rock, *m.*

rocket, *n.* cohete, *m.*; **rocket launcher,** lanzacohetes, *m.*

rocky, *adj.* peñascoso, rocoso. roqueño

rode, *pretérito* del verbo **ride**

role, *n.* papel, *m.*, parte, *f.*

roll, *vt.* rodar; arrollar, enrollar; *vi.* rodar; girar; *n.* rollo, *m.*; lista, *f.*; panecillo, *m.*

Roman, *adj.* romano; manesco; *n.* y *adj.* romano, romana

romance, *n.* romance, cuento, *m.*; idilio, *m.*; aventura romántica, *f.*

romantic, *adj.* romántico; sentimental

roof, *n.* tejado, techo, *m.*; azotea, *f.*; paladar, *m.*

room, *n.* cuarto, *m.*, habitación, cámara, *f.*; lugar, espacio, *m.*

roommate, *n.* compañero o compañera de cuarto

roomy, *adj.* espacioso

rooster, *n.* gallo, *m.*

rope, *n.* cuerda, *f.*

rosary, *n.* rosario, *m.*

rose, *n.* (bot.) rosa, *f.*; color de rosa; *pretérito* del verbo **rise**

rotary engine, *n.* máquina rotativa, máquina alternativa

rotate, *vt.* y *vi.* girar, alternarse

rotten, *adj.* podrido, corrompido

rough, *adj.* áspero; brusco

round, *adj.* redondo

rout, *vt.* derrotar

route, *n.* ruta, vía, *f.*

routine, *n.* rutina, *f.*

row, *n.* riña, pelea, *f.*

row, *n.* hilera, fila, *f.*; *vt.* y *vi.* remar, bogar

rowboat, *n.* bote de remos *m.*

royal, *adj.* real; regio

royalty, *n.* realeza, *f.*; **royalties,** *n. pl.* regalías, *f. pl.*

R.R., railroad, f.c., ferrocarril; **Right Reverend,** Reverendísimo

R.S.V.P., please answer, sírvase enviar respuesta

rub, *vt.* frotar, restregar,

rubber, *n.* goma, *f.*, caucho, *m.*; **rubbers,** *n. pl.* chanclos, zapatos de goma, *m. pl.*; *adj.* de goma, de caucho

rubbish, *n.* basura, *f.*; desechos, *m. pl.*

ruby, *n.* rubí, *m.*

rude, *adj.* rudo, grosero

rug, *n.* alfombra, *f.*

ruin, *n.* ruina, *f.*; perdición, *f.*; *vt.* arruinar; echar a perder

rule, *n.* mando, *m.*; regla, *f.*; norma, *f.*; *vt.* y *vi.* gobernar; dirigir

ruler, *n.* gobernante, *m.*; regla, *f.*

Rumanian, *n.* y *adj.* rumano, rumana

rumba, *n.* rumba, *f.*

rumor, *n.* rumor, runrún, *m.*

run, *vi.* correr; fluir, manar

rural, *adj.* rural, rústico

rush, *n.* prisa, *f.*; *vi.* ir de prisa, apresurarse

Russia, Rusia

Russian, *n.* y *adj.* ruso, rusa

rusty, *adj.* mohoso, enmohecido

rut, *n.* rutina, *f.*; brama, *f.*

ruthless, *adj.* cruel

rye, *n.* centeno, *m.*

S

S.A., Salvation Army, Ejército de Salvación; **South America,** S.A., Sud América; **South Africa,** Sud Africa

sabotage, *n.* sabotaje, *m.*

saccharine, *n.* sacarina, *f.*

sack, *n.* saco, talego, *m.*

sacrament, *n.* sacramento, *m.*

sacred, *adj.* sagrado

sacrifice, *n.* sacrificio, *m.*; *vt.* y *vi.* sacrificar

sad, *adj.* triste

sadness, *n.* tristeza, *f.*

safe, *adj.* seguro; salvo; *n.* caja fuerte, *f.*

safeguard, *vt.* proteger

safety, *n.* seguridad, *f.*; **safety pin,** alfiler de gancho, imperdible, *m.*

sage, *n.* y *adj.* sabio, *m.*

sail, *n.* vela, *f.*; *vi.* navegar

sailboat, *n.* buque de vela, *m.*

sailor, *n.* marinero, *m.*

saint, *n.* santo, santa

sake, *n.* causa, razón, *f.*; amor,

_m._, consideración, _f._
salad, _n._ ensalada, _f._
salary, _n._ salario, sueldo, _m._
sale, _n._ venta, _f._; barata, _f._
salesman, _n._ vendedor, _m._
saliva, _n._ saliva, _f._
saloon, _n._ cantina, taberna, _f._
salt, _n._ sal, _f._
salty, _adj._ salado
salute, _vt._ saludar; _n._ saludo, _m._
salvation, _n._ salvación, _f._
salve, _n._ ungüento, _m._, pomada _f._
sanatorium, _n._ sanatorio, _m._
sanction, _n._ sanción, _vt._ sancionar
sandal, _n._ sandalia, _f._
sandwich, _n._ sandwich, emparedado, _m._
sane, _adj._ sano, sensato
sanetarium, _n._ sanatorio, _m._
sanitary, _adj._ sanitario
sanity, _n._ cordura, _f._
sap, _n._ savia, _f._
sapphire, _n._ zafiro, _m._
sarcasm, _n._ sarcasmo, _m._
sarcastic, _adj._ sarcástico
sardine, _n._ sardina, _f._
sat, _pretérito y p. p._ del verbo **sit**
Sat., Saturday, sáb. sábado
Satan, _n._ Satanás, _m._
satin, _n._ raso, _m._
satisfaction, _n._ satisfacción, _f._
satisfactory, _adj._ satisfactorio
satisfy, _vt._ satisfacer
Saturday, _n._ sábado, _m._
sauce, _n._ salsa, _f._
sausage, _n._ salchicha, _f._
save, _vt._ salvar; economizar
saving, _adj._ económico; **savings,** _n. pl._ ahorros, _m. pl._
Saviour, _n._ Redentor, _m._
saw, _n._ sierra, _f._; _vt._ serrar; _pretérito_ del verbo **see**
scaffold, _n._ andamio, _m._
scald, _vt._ escaldar
scale, _n._ balanza, _f._; báscula, _f._; escala, _f._; escama, _f._; _vt._ escalar
scalp, _n._ cuero cabelludo, _m._
scandal, _n._ escándalo, _m._
Scandinavia, Escandinavia
scant, scanty, _adj._ escaso, parco

scarce, _adj._ raro; **scarcely,** _adv._ apenas, escasamente
scare, _n._ susto, _m._; _vt._ espantar
scarf, _n._ bufanda, _f._
scarlet, _n._ y _adj._ escarlata, _f._; **scarlet fever,** escarlatina, _f._
scatter, _vt._ y _vi._ esparcir, derramarse
scene, _n._ escena, _f._
scenery, _n._ vista, _f._; (theat.) decoración, _f._
schedule, _n._ plan, programa, _m._
scheme, _n._ proyecto, plan, _m._
scholar, _n._ estudiante, _m._ y _f._; erudito, erudita
scholarly, _adj._ erudito
scholarship, _n._ beca, _f._
school, _n._ escuela, _f._; **high school,** escuela secundaria, _f._
schoolteacher, _n._ maestro o maestra de escuela
science, _n._ ciencia, _f._
scientific, _adj._ científico
scissors, _n. pl._ tijeras, _f. pl._
scoff, _vi._ mofarse
scold, _vt._ y _vi._ regañar
scooter, _n._ patineta, _f._
scope, _n._ alcance, _m._
scorched, _adj._ chamuscado
score, _n._ veintena, _f._; (mus.) partitura, _f._; tanteo, _m._; _vt._ tantear; calificar; _vi._ hacer tantos
scorn, _vt._ y _vi._ despreciar; _n._ desdén, menosprecio, _m._
Scotland, Escocia
scoundrel, _n._ infame, _m._ y _f._
scout, _n._ (mil.) centinela avanzada; **boy scout,** niño explorador; **girl scout,** niña exploradora; _vi._ (mil.) explorar
scrap, _n._ migaja, _f._
scrapbook, _n._ álbum de recortes, _m._
scrape, _vt._ y _vi._ raspar; arañar; _n._ dificultad, _f._, lío, _m._
scratch, _vt._ rascar, raspar; borrar
scream, _vi._ chillar; _n._ chillido, grito, _m._
screen, _n._ tamiz, _m._; biombo,

m.; pantalla, *f.*; *vt.* tamizar

screw, *n.* tornillo, *m.*; clavo de rosca, *m.*; **screw driver,** destornillador, *m.*; **to screw in,** atornillar

Scripture, *n.* Escritura Sagrada, *f.*

scuba, *n.* escafandra autónoma, *f.*

sculptor, *n.* escultor, *m.*

sculptress, *n.* escultora, *f.*

sculpture, *n.* escultura, *f.*

sea, *n.* mar, *m.* y *f.*; **sea plane,** hidroavión, *m.*

seal, *n.* sello, *m.*; (zool.) foca, *f.*; *vt.* sellar

seam, *n.* costura, *f.*

seamstress, *n.* costurera, *f.*

search, *vt.* examinar, registrar; escudriñar; busca, *f.*

seasick, *adj.* mareado

season, *n.* estación, *f.*; tiempo, *m.*; *vt.* sazonar

seasoning, *n.* condimento, *m.*

seat, *n.* silla, *f.*; localidad, *f.*

seat belt, *n.* cinturón de seguridad, cinturón de asiento

second, *adj.* segundo; *n.* segundo, *m.*; *vt.* apoyar

secondary, *adj.* secundario

secondhand, *adj.* de ocasión; de segunda mano

secrecy, *n.* secreto, *m.*

secret, *n.* secreto, *m.*; *adj.* privado

secretariat, *n.* secretaría, *f.*

secretary, *n.* secretario, secretaria

sect, *n.* secta, *f.*

section, *n.* sección, *f.*

secure, *adj.* seguro; salvo; *vt.* asegurar; conseguir

security, *n.* seguridad, *f.*; defensa, *f.*; fianza, *f.*

sedative, *n.* y *adj.* sedante, calmante, *m.*

seduce, *vt.* seducir

see, *vt.* y *vi.* ver, observar

seem, *vi.* parecer

seen, *p. p.* del verbo **see**

seep, *vi.* colarse, escurrirse

segregation, *n.* segregación, *f.*

seize, *vt.* agarrar, prender

seldom, *adv.* rara vez

select, *vt.* elegir, escoger; *adj.* selecto, escogido

selection, *n.* selección, *f.*

self, *adj.* propio, mismo

self-controlled, *adj.* dueño de sí mismo

self-defense, *n.* defensa propia, *f.*

self-denial, *n.* abnegación, *f.*

selfish, *adj.* egoísta

semester, *n.* semestre, *m.*

semicolon, *n.* punto y coma, *m.*

semifinal, *adj.* semifinal

semimonthly, *adj.* quincenal

seminary, *n.* seminario, *m.*

Sen., sen., Senate, senado; **Senator,** senador; **senior,** padre; socio más antiguo o más caracterizado

senate, *n.* senado, *m.*

senator, *n.* senador, *m.*

send, *vt.* enviar, mandar

senior, *adj.* mayor; *n.* estudiante de cuarto año, *m.*

seniority, *n.* antigüedad, *f.*

sense, *n.* sensatez, *f.*; **common sense,** sentido común, *m.*

sensible, *adj.* juicioso

sensitive, *adj.* sensible; sensitivo

sentence, *n.* sentencia, *f.*; (gram.) oración, *f.*; *vt.* sentenciar, condenar

sentiment, *n.* sentimiento, *m.*; opinión, *f.*

sentimental, *adj.* sentimental

separate, *vt.* y *vi.* separar; *adj.* separado

separation, *n.* separación, *f.*

September, *n.* septiembre, *m.*

serenade, *n.* serenata, *f.*; (Mex.) gallo, *m.*

serene, *adj.* sereno

serenity, *n.* serenidad, *f.*

series, *n.* serie, cadena, *f.*

serious, *adj.* serio, grave

sermon, *n.* sermon, *m.*

serpent, *n.* serpiente, *f.*

servant, *n.* criado, criada; sirviente, sirvienta

serve, *vt.* y *vi.* servir

service, *n.* servicio, *m.*; servidumbre, *f.*

session, *n.* sesión, *f.*

set, vt. poner, colocar, fijar; vi. ponerse (el sol o los astros); cuajarse; n. juego, m., colección, f.

settle, vt. arreglar; calmar; solventar (deudas); vi. establecerse, radicarse; sosegarse

settlement, n. establecimiento, m.; liquidación, f.

seven, n. y adj. siete, m.

seventeen, adj. y n. diez y siete, diecisiete, m.

seventeenth, adj. décimoséptimo

seventh, adj. séptimo

seventy, n. y adj. setenta, m.

several, adj. diversos, varios

severe, adj. severo

sew, vt. y vi. coser

sewage, n. inmundicias, f. pl.; **sewage system,** alcantarillado, m.

sewer, n. cloaca, alcantarilla, f.; caño, m.

sewing, n. costura, f.; **sewing machine,** máquina de coser, f.

sex, n. sexo, m.

sexual, adj. sexual

shabby, adj. destartalado

shack, n. choza, cabaña, f.

shade, n. sombra, f.; matiz, m.

shadow, n. sombra, f.

shady, adj. opaco; sospechoso

shake, vt. sacudir; agitar; vi. temblar; **to shake hands,** darse las manos; n. sacudida, f.

shape, vt. y vi. formar; n. forma, figura, f.

share, n. parte, cuota, f.; (com.) acción, f.; participación, f.; vt. y vi. compartir

shark, n. tiburón, m.

sharp, adj. agudo, astuto; afilado; n. (mus.) sostenido, m.; **two o'clock sharp,** las dos en punto

sharpener, n. afilador, amolador, m.; **pencil sharpener,** tajalápices, m.

shatter, vt. y vi. destrozar, estrellar

shawl, n. chal, mantón, m.

she, pron. ella

sheep, n. sing. y pl. oveja(s), f.; carnero, m.

sheepish, adj. tímido, cortado

sheet, n. pliego (de papel), m.; **bed sheet,** sábana, f.

shell, n. cáscara, f.; concha, f.; vt. descascarar, descortezar

shelter, n. asilo, refugio, m.

shepherd, n. pastor, m.

sheriff, n. alguacil, m., funcionario administrativo de un condado

sherry, n. jerez, m.

shield, n. escudo, m.; vt. defender; amparar:

shift, vt. y vt. cambiarse; ingeniarse; n. tanda, f.

shin, n. espinilla, f.

shine, vi. lucir, brillar; vt. dar lustre (a los zapatos , etc.); n. brillo, m.

shining, adj. reluciente

shiny, adj. brillante

ship, n. buque, barco, m.; vt. embarcar; expedir

shipment, n. embarque, m., remesa, f.

shirk, vt. esquivar, evitar

shirt, n. camisa, f.

shock, n. choque, m.; conmoción, f.; vt. chocar; sacudir; conmover; **shock absorber,** amortiguador, m.

shocking, adj. ofensivo

shoe, n. zapato, m.

shoemaker, n. zapatero, m.

shone, pretórito y p. p. del verbo **shine**

shop, n. tienda, f.; vt. hacer compras

shopping, n. compras, f. pl.

short, adj. corto; conciso

shorten, vt. acortar; abreviar

shortening, n. acortamiento, m.; manteca o grasa vegetal, f.

shorthand, n. taquigrafía, f.

shorts, n. pl. calzoncillos, m. pl.; pantalones cortos, m. pl.

shortsighted, adj. miope

shot, n. tiro, m.

shotgun, n. escopeta, f.

should, subj. y condicional de **shall;** úsase como auxiliar de otros verbos

shoulder, n. hombro, m.
shout, vi. aclamar; gritar
shovel, n. pala, f.
show, vt. mostrar, enseñar, probar; n. espectáculo, m. función, f.
shower, n. aguacero, m.; vi. llover; vt. derramar profusamente
shrank, pretérito del verbo **shrink**
shred, n. triza, f.; jirón, m.; vt. picar, rallar
shrimp, n. camarón, m.
shrink, vi. encogerse
shrunk, p. p. del verbo **shrink**
shudder, vi. estremecerse
shut, vt. cerrar, encerrar
shy, adj. tímido
sick adj. malo, enfermo
sickly, adj. enfermizo
sickness, n. enfermedad, f.
side, n. lado, m.; costado, m.; facción, f.; partido, m.; adj. lateral
sidewalk, n. banqueta, acera, f.
sideways, adv. de lado
sift, vt. cerner; cribar
sigh, vi. suspirar, gemir; n. suspiro, m.
sign, n. señal, f., indigo, m.; signo, m.; letrero, m.; vt. y vi. firmar
signal, n. señal, seña, f.
signature, n. firma, f.
significance, n. importancia, significación, f.
silence, n. silencio, m.
silent, adj. silencioso
silk, n. seda, f.
silkscreen, n. serigrafia, f.
silky, adj. sedoso
sill, n. alfeiza, f.
silly, adj. tonto, bobo
silver, n. plata, f.
silvery, adj. plateado
similar, adj. similar
simple, adj. simple
simplicity, n. simplicidad, f.
simplify, vt. simplificar
simply, adv. simplemente
simultaneous, adj. simultáneo
sin, n. pecado, m., culpa, f.; vi.

pecar, faltar
since, adv. desde entonces; conj. puesto que; prep. desde, después
sincere, adj. sincere, franco
sincerity, n. sinceridad, f.
sinew, n. tendón, m.
sinful, adj. pecaminoso
sing, vt. y vi. cantar
singe, vt. chamuscar
singer, n. cantante, m. y f.
singing, n. canto, m.
single, adj. solo; soltero, soltera
sink, vt. y vi. hundir; n. fregadero, m.
sinner, n. pecador, pecadora
sinus, n. seno (cavidad) m.
sip, vt. y vi. sorber; n. sorbo, m.
sir, n. señor, m.
siren, n. sirena, f.
sister, n. hermana, f.
sister-in-law, n. cuñada, f.
sit, vi. sentarse
situation, n. situación, f.
six, n. y adj. seis, m.
sixteen, n. y adj. diez y seis, dieciseis
sixteenth, adj. y n. décimosexto, m.
sixth, n. y adj. sexto, m.
sixty, n. y adj. sesenta, m.
size, n. tamaño, m., talla, f.
sizzle, vi. chamuscar
skate, n. patín, m.; **ice skate,** patin de hielo, m.; **roller skate,** patín de ruedas, m.; vi. patinar
skeleton, n. esqueleto, m.; **skeleton key,** llave maestra, f.
sketch, n. esbozo, m.; bosquejo, m.; vt. bosquejar, esbozar
skill, n. destreza, pericia, f.
skillet, n. cazuela, sartén, f.
skillful, skilful, adj. práctico, diestro
skin, n. cutis, m.; piel, f.
skinny, adj. flaco
skip, vi. saltar, brincar; vt. pasar, omitir; n. salto, brinco, m.
skunk, n. zorrillo, zorrino, m.
sky, n. cielo, m.

skylight, n. claraboya, f.
skyscraper, n. rascacielos, m.
slander, vt. calumniar, infamar; n. calumnia, f.
slang, n. vulgarismo, m.
slap, n. manotada, f.; **slap on the face,** bofetada, f.; vt. dar una bofetada
slave, n. esclavo, esclava
slavery, n. esclavitud, f.
slay, vt. matar
slayer, n. asesino, m.
sleep, vi. dormir; n. sueño, m.
sleepless, adj. desvelado
sleepy, adj. soñoliento
sleet, n. cellisca, aguanieve, f.
sleeve, n. manga, f.
sleeveless, adj. sin mangas
slender, adj. delgado
slice, n. rebanada, f.; vt. rebanar, tajar
slide, vt. correr; vi. deslizarse; n. diapositiva, f.; **slide projector,** linterna de proyección, f.
slight, adj. leve; n. desaire, m.; vt. desairar
slim, adj. delgado, sutil
sling, n. honda, f.
slip, n. resbalón, m.; enagua, f.; vi. resbalar
slipper, n. zapatilla, f.
sloppy, adj. desaliñado
slot, n. hendedura, f.
slow, adj. tardío, lento; adv. despacio
slums, n. pl. barrios bajos, m. pl.; viviendas escuálidas, f. pl.
slumber, vi. dormitar; n. sueño ligero
slush, n. lodo, cieno, m.
sly, adj. astuto; furtivo
small, adj. pequenño, chico
smallpox, n. viruelas, f. pl.
smart, adj. inteligente; elegante
smear, vt. manchar; calumniari,
smell, vt. y vi. oler; olfatear; n. olfato, m.; olor, m.; hediondez, f.
smile, vi. sonreir, sonreirse; n. sonrisa, f.
smoke, n. humo, m.; vt. y vi. ahumar; fumar (tabaco)
smooth, adj. liso, pulido
smother, vt. sofocar
smuggling, n. contrabando, m.
snake, n. culebra, f.
snap, vt. y vi. romper; chasquear
snappy, adj. vivaz, animado
snapshot, n. instantánea, fotografía, f.
snare, n. trampa, f.
snarl, vi. enredar
snatch, vt. arrebatar
sneeze, vi. estornudar; n. estornudo, m.
sniff, vt. olfatear
snoop, vi. espiar, acechar
snooze, vi. dormitar
snore, vi. roncar
snow, n. nieve, f.; vi. nevar
snowfall, n. nevada, f.
snowflake, n. copo de nieve, m.
snowmobile, n. vehículo automotor para marchar sobre la nieve
snowshoe, n. raqueta de nieve, f.
so, adv. así; tal
So., South, S., Sur
soak, vt. y vi. remojar
soap, n. jabón, m.
soar, vi. remontarse
sob, n. sollozo, m.; vi. sollozar
sober, adj. sobrio; serio
soccer, n. futbol, m.
sociable, adj. sociable
social, adj. social; sociable; **social worker,** asistente social
socialism, n. socialismo, m.
socialize, vt. socializar; **socialized medicine,** medicina estatal
society, n. sociedad, f.; compañía, f.
sociology, n. sociología, f.
sock, n. calcetín, m.
socket, n. enchufe, m.; cuenca (del ojo), f.
sod, n. césped, m.; tierra, f.
soda, n. sosa, soda, f.; **baking soda,** bicarbonato de sosa o de soda
sofa, n. sofá, m.

soft, *adj.* blando, suave
soft-boiled, *adj.* pasado por agua
soften, *vt.* ablandar
soggy, *adj.* empapado
soil, *vt.* ensuciar, emporcar; *n.* tierra, *f.*
solar, *adj.* solar; **solar battery,** batería solar; **solar energy,** energía solar
sold, *p. p.* vendido
soldier, *n.* soldado, *m.*
sole, *n.* planta, *f.*; suela, *f.*; *adj.* único, solo
solicit, *vt.* solicitar; pedir
solid, *adj.* sólido, compacto; entero; *n.* sólido, *m.*
solid-fuel space rocket, *n.* cohete especial de combustible sólido, *m.*
solitary, *adj.* solitario
solitude, *n.* soleded, *f.*
solo, *n.* y *adj.* solo, *m.*
solve, *vt.* resolver, solucionar
some, *adj.* algún; cierto; algo de
somebody, *pron.* alguno, alguna
somehow, *adv.* de algún modo
something, *n.* alguna cosa; algo, *m.*; **something else,** alguna otra cosa
sometimes, *adv.* a veces
somewhere, *adv.* en alguna parte
son, *n.* hijo, *m.*
sonic barrier, *n.* obstáculo sonic *m.*
sonic boom, *n.* trueno sónico, estrépito sónico, *m.*
son-in-law, *n.* yerno, *m.*
soothe, *vt.* calmar, sosegar
sophisticated, *adj.* refinado; complicado
soprano, *n.* soprano, tiple, *m.* y *f.*
sore, *n.* llaga, úlcera, *f.*; *adj.* doloroso penoso; (coll.) enojado, resentido
sorority, *n.* hermandad de mujeres, *f.*
sorry, *adj.* triste; afligido
soul, *n.* alma, *f.*; esencia, *f.*
sound, *adj.* sano; entero; *n.* sonido, *m.*; *vt.* sondar; *vi.* so-

nar, resonar
soup, *n.* sopa, *f.*
sour, *adj.* agrio, ácido; *vt.* y *vi.* agriar, agriarse
south, *n.* sur, sud, *m.*
southeast, *n.* sureste, sudeste, *m.*
southern, *adj.* meridional
southwest, *n.* sudoeste, *m.*
souvenir, *n.* recuerdo, *m.*
sovereign, *n.* y *adj.* soberano, soberana
soviet, *n.* soviet, *m.*
sow, *n.* puerca, marrana, *f.*
sow, *vt.* sembrar, sementar
soybean, *n.* soya, *f.*
space, *n.* espacio, *m.*; lugar, *m.*; **space capsule,** cabina espacial; **space travel,** viajes espaciales o siderales
spaceship, *n.* astronave, *f.*
spacious, *adj.* espacioso
spade, *n.* azadón, *m.*; espada (naipe),
Spain, España, *f.*
span, *n.* espacio, trecho, *m.*
Spaniard, *n.* y *adj.* español, española
Spanish, *adj.* español
spank, *vt.* pegar, dar nalgadas
spare, *vt.* y *vi.* ahorrar, evitar; *adj.* de reserva; **spare time,** tiempo desocupado; **spare tire,** neumático o llanta de repuesto
spark, *n.* chispa, *f.*
spat, *n.* riña, *f.*; *vi.* reñir
spats, *n. pl.* polainas, *f. pl.*
speak, *vt.* y *vi.* hablar
speaker, *n.* orador, oradora
spear, *n.* lanza, *f.*; pica, *f.*
spearmint, *n.* hierbabuena, *f.*
special, *adj.* especial
specialize, *vt.* y *vi.* especializar
specimen, *n.* muestra, *f.*
spectacle, *n.* espectáculo, *m.*; **spectacles,** *n. pl.* anteojos, espejuelos, *m. pl.*
spectacular, *adj.* espectacular
spectator, *n.* espectador, espectadora
speculate, *vi.* especular
speech, *n.* habla, *f.*; discurso, *m.*

speechless, *adj.* sin habla

speed, *n.* rapidez, *f.*; *vt.* apresurar; *vi.* darse prisa

speedy, *adj.* veloz

spell, *n.* hechizo, encanto, *m.*; *vt.* y *vi.* deletrear

spelling, *n.* ortografia, *f.*; deletreo, *m.*

spend, *vt.* gastar; consumir

spendthrift, *n.* botarate, *m.* y *f.*

sphere, *n.* esfera, *f.*

spider, *n.* araña, *f.*

spill, *vt.* derramar, verter

spin, *vt.* hilar; *vt.* y *vi.* girar; *n.* vuelta, *f.*; paseo, *m.*

spinach, *n.* espinaca, *f.*

spinal, *adj.* espinal; **spinal column**, columna vertebral, espina dorsal, *f.*

spine, *n.* espina, *f.*

spiral, *adj.* espiral

spirit, *n.* espíritu, *m.*; ánimo, valor, *m.*; fantasma, *m.*

spirited, *adj.* vivo, brioso

spiritual, *adj.* espiritual

spit, *vt.* y *vi.* escupir

spite, *n.* rencor, *m.*; **in spite of**, a pesar de

spiteful, *adj.* rencoroso

splash, *vt.* salpicar

splendid, *adj.* espléndido

splint, *n.* astilla, *f.*; **splints**, *n. pl.* tablillas para entablillar

splinter, *n.* astilla, *f.*

split, *vt.* y *vi.* hender, rajar; *n.* hendidura, raja, *f.*

spleen, *n.* bazo, *m.*; esplín, *m.*

spoil, *vt.* y *vi.* dañar; pudrir; mimar demasiado; **spoils**, *n. pl.* despojo, botín, *m.*

spoke, *n.* rayo de rueda, *m.*; *pretérito* del verbo **speak**

sponsor, *n.* fiador, *m.*; padrino, *m.*; garante, *m.* y *f.*; anunciante (de un programa de radio, etc.), *m.*

spontaneous, *adj.* espontáneo

spool, *n.* bobina, carrete, carretel, *m.*

spoon, *n.* cuchara, *f.*

spoonful, *n.* cucharada, *f.*

sport, *n.* recreo, pasatiempo, *m.*; deporte, *m.*

sportsman, *n.* deportista, *m.*

spot, *n.* mancha, *f.*; sitio, lugar, *m.*; *vt.* manchar

spotless, *adj.* sin mancha

spotlight, *n.* proyector, *m.*

spouse, *n.* esposo, esposa

sprain, *vt.* dislocar; *n.* torcedura, *f.*

sprang, *pretérito* del verbo **spring**

spray, *vt.* rociar, pulverizar

spread, *vt.* y *vi.* extender; *n.* sobrecama, colcha, *f.*

spring, *vi.* brotar; provenir; saltar, brincar; *n.* primavera, *f.*; elasticidad, *f.*; muelle, resorte, *m.*

sprinkle, *vt.* rociar; salpicar; *vi.* lloviznar

spur, *n.* espuela, *f.*; **on the spur of the moment**, en un impulso repentino; *vt.* estimular

sputnik, *n.* sputnik, *m.*, satélite artificial

spy, *n.* espía, *m.* y *f.*; *vt.* y *vi.* espiar

sq., **square**, cuadrado, *m.*; plaza, *f.*

squabble, *vi.* reñir; *n.* riña, *f.*

squander, *vt.* malgastar

square, *adj.* cuadrado; equitativo; *n.* cuadro, *m.*; plaza, *f.*; *vt.* cuadrar; ajustar

squaw, *n.* mujer india de E.U.A

squeal, *vi.* gritar; delatar

squeeze, *vt.* apretar, estrechar; *n.* abrazo, *m.*; apretón, *m.*

squirrel, *n.* ardilla, *f.*

S.S., **steamship**, v., vapor; **Sunday School**, escuela dominical

St., **Saint**, Sto., San, Santo; Sta., Santa; **Strait**, Estrecho; **Street**, Calle

stable, *n.* establo, *m.*; *adj.* estable

stadium, *n.* estadio, *m.*

staff, *n.* báculo, palo, *m.*; personal, *m.*

stag, *n.* ciervo, *m.*; **stag party**, tertulia para hombres, *f.*

stage, *n.* escenario, *m.*; teatro, *m.*, las tablas, *f. pl.*; *vt.* poner

en escena
stagecoach, n. diligencia, f.
stagger, vi. vacilar, titubear;
vt. escalonar, alternar
stainless, adj. limpio, inmaculado; inoxidable
stair, n. escalón, m.; **stairs,** n.
pl. escalera, f.
stairway, n. escalera, f.
stake, n. estaca, f.; vt. apostar;
arriesgar
stale, adj. viejo, rancio
stamina, n. resistencia, f.
stamp, vt. patear, dar golpes
(con los pies); estampar, imprimir, sellar; n. sello, m.; estampa, f.; timbre, m.; **postage stamp,** sello de correo,
m.
stand, vi. estar en pie o derecho; sostenerse; resistir; pararse; n. puesto, sitio, m.; tarima, f.
standard, n. norma, f.; **standard of living,** nivel o norma
de vida; adj. normal
starch, n. almidón, m.; vt. almidonar
stare, vt. clavar la vista; n. mirada fija, f.
start, vi. sobrecogerse, estremecerse; vt. comenzar; n. sobresalto, m.; principio, m.
starter, n. iniciador, iniciadora; (auto.) arranque, m.
starve, vi. perecer de hambre
state, n. estado, m.; condición,
f.; vt. declarar
statement, n. estado de cuenta, m.; declaración, f.
stateroom, n. camarote, m.;
compartimiento, m.
statesman, n. estadista, m.
station, n. estación, **station
wagon,** camioneta, f.
stationary, adj. estacionario,
fijo
stationery, n. papel de escribir, m.
statistics, n. pl. estadística, f.
statue, n. estatua, f.
staunch, adj. firme; fiel
stay, n. permanencia, f.; vi.
quedarse, permanecer
steady, adj. firme, fijo

steak, n. bistec, m.
steam, n. vapor, m.; **steamroller,** apisonadora, f.
steamship, n. vapor, m.
steep, adj. empinado
steeple, n. campanario, m.
steer, n. novillo, m.; vt. guiar,
dirigir
stenographer, n. taquígrafo,
taquígrafa, estenógrafo, estenógrafa; mecanógrafo, mecanógrafa
stenography, n. taquigrafía,
estenografía,
step, n. paso, escalón, m.; trámite, m.; gestión, f.; vi. dar
un paso; andar; vt. pisar
stepbrother, n. medio hermano, hermanastro, m.
stepdaughter, n. hijastra, f.
stepfather, n. padrastro, m.
stepladder, n. escalera de mano, f.
stepmother, n. madrastra, f.
stepson, n. hijastro, m.
stereophonic, adj. estereofónico, estereofónica
sterling, adj. genuino, verdadero; **sterling silver,** plata
esterlina,
stern, adj. austero, severo; n.
(naut.) popa, f.
stew, vt. guisar; n. guisado,
guiso, m.
streward, n. mayordomo, m.
stewardess, n. (avi.) azafata,
aeromoza, f.
stick, palo, bastón, m.; vi. pegarse
sticky, adj. pegajoso
stiff, adj. tieso; rígido
stifle, vt. sofocar
still, vt. aquietar, aplacar; destilar; adj. silencioso, tranquilo; adv. todavía; no obstante
stilt, n. zanco, m.
stimulate, vt. estimular
stimulation, n. estímulo, m.
sting, vt. picar o morder (un
insecto); n. aguijón m.
stingy, adj. tacaño, avaro
stipulate, vt. y vi. estipular
stir, vt. agitar; revolver; incitar
stirring, adj. emocionante
stitch, vt. coser; n. puntada,

f.; punto, *m.*

stock, *n.* linaje, *m.*; (com.) capital, principal, *m.*; (com.) acción, *f.*; ganado, *m.*; proveer, abastecer

stockholder, *n.* accionista, *m.* y *f.*

stole, *n.* estola, *f.*; *pretérito* del verbo **steal**

stomach, *n.* estómago, *m.*

stone, *n.* piedra, *f.*; hueso de fruta, *m.*; *vt.* apedrear; deshuesar

stood, *pretérito* y *p. p.* del verbo **stand**

stool, *n.* banquillo, *m.*; evacuación, *f.*

stop, *vt.* cesar, suspender, *vi.* pararse, hacer alto; *n.* parada, *f.*

store, *n.* almacén, *m.*; *vt.* proveer, abastecer

storeroom, *n.* deposito, *m.*

stork, *n.* cigüeña,

storm, *n.* tempestad, *f.*; *vi.* haber tormenta

stormy, *adj.* tempestuoso

story, *n.* cuento, *m.*; piso de una casa, *m.*

straight, *adj.* derecho, recto; *adv.* directaménte, en línea recta

straighten, *vt.* enderezar

strain, *vt.* colar, filtrar; *vi.* esforzarse; *n.* tensión, tirantez, *f.*

strainer, *n.* colador, *m.*

strange, *adj.* extraño; raro

stranger, *n.* extranjero, extranjera

strap, *n.* correa, *f.*

strategy, *n.* estrategia, *f.*

strawberry, *n.* fresa; (Sp. Am.) frutilla, *f.*

stray, *vi.* extraviarse

stream, *n.* arroyo, *m.*; corriente, *f.*

streamline, *vt.* simplificar

street, *n.* calle, *f.*

streetcar, *n.* tranvía, *m.*

strength, *n.* fuerza, *f.*

strengthen, *vt.* reforzar

strenuous, *adj.* estrenuo

stress, *n.* fuerza, *f.*; acento, *m.*; tensión *f.*; *vt.* acentuar, dar

énfasis

stretch, *vt.* y *vi.* tirar; extenderse

stretcher, *n.* estirador, *m.*; camilla, *f.*

strict, *adj.* estricto, riguroso

stride, *n.* tranco, *m.*; adelanto, avance, *m.*; *vt.* cruzar, pasar por encima; *vi.* andar a pasos largos

strike, *vt.* y *vi.* golpear; declararse en huelga

striking, *adj.* llamativo

string, *n.* cordón, *m.*; cuerda, *f.*; hilera, *f.*; **string bean,** habichuela verde, judia, *f.*, (Mex.) ejote, *m.*

strip, *n.* tira, faja, *f.*; *vt.* desnudar, despojar

stripe, *n.* raya, lista, *f.*

striped, *adj.* rayado

stroboscope, *n.* estroboscopio, *m.*

stroke, *n.* golpe, *m.*; caricia, *f.*; *vt.* acariciar

stroll, *vi.* vagar, pasearse, *m.*

strong, *adj.* fuerte

structure, *n.* edificio, *m.*

struggle, *n.* lucha, *f.*; *vi.* luchar

stubborn, *adj.* testarudo

student, *n.* estudiante, estudianta, alumno, alumna

studio couch, *n.* sofá cama

study, *n.* estudio, *m.*; gabinete, *m.*; *vt.* estudiar

stuff, *n.* materia, *f.*; *vt.* llenar; rellenar; *vi.* abracarse; tragar

stuffing, *n.* relleno, *m.*

stumble, *vt.* tropezar

stupendous, *adj.* estupendo

stupid, *adj.* estúpido

stupidity, *n.* estupidez, *f.*

sturdy, *adj.* fuerte, robusto

style, *n.* estilo, *m.*; moda, *f.*

stylish, *adj.* elegante, de moda

subconscious, *adj.* subconsciente

subject, *n.* tema, tópico, *m.*; asignatura, *f.*; *adj.* sujeto, sometido a; *vt.* sujetar, someter

submarine, *n.* y *adj.* submarino, *m.*

submerge, *vt.* sumergir

submission, *n.* sumisión, *f.*

submit, *vt.* someter, rendir
subordinate, *n.* y *adj.* subalterno, *m.*; *vt.* subordinar
subscribe, *vt.* y *vi.* suscribir
subscriber, *n.* suscriptor, suscriptora, abonado, abonada
subscription, *n.* suscripción, *f.*, abono, *m.*
subsequent, *adj.* subsiguiente, subsecuente
subsist, *vi.* subsistir; existir
substance, *n.* sustancia, *f.*
substantive, *n.* sustantivo, *m.*
substitute, *vt.* sustituir; *n.* suplente, *m.*
substitution, *n.* sustitución, *f.*
subtle, *adj.* sutil
subtract, *vt.* sustraer; restar
subtraction, *n.* sustracción, *f.*; resta, *f.*
suburb, *n.* suburbio, *m.*
suburban, *adj.* suburbano
subway, *n.* túnel, *m.*; ferrocarril subterráneo, *m.*
sucaryl, *n.* nombre comercial de un compuesto ezucarado parecido a la sacarina
succeed, *vt.* y *vi.* lograr, tener éxito; seguir
success, *n.* buen éxito, *m.*
successful, *adj.* próspero, dichoso; **to be successful,** tener buen éxito
succession, sucesión, *f.*; herencia, *f.*
successor, *n.* sucesor, sucesora
such, *adj.* y *pron.* tal, semejante
sudden, *adj.* repentino; **suddenly,** *adv.* de repente
sue, *vt.* y *vi.* demandar, poner pleito
suffer, *vt.* y *vi.* sufrir
suffice, *vt.* y *vi.* bastar
sufficient, *adj.* suficiente
suffocate, *vt.* y *vi.* sofocar
sufrage, *n.* sufragio, voto, *m.*
sugar, *n.* azúcar, *m.* y *f.*
suicide, *n.* suicidio, *m.*; suicida, *m.* y *f.*
suit, *n.* vestido, *m.*; traje, *m.*; pleito, *m.*; *vt.* y *vi.* adaptar; ajustarse; *vt.* sentar, caer bien

suitable, *adj.* adecuado
suitcase, *n.* maleta, *f.*
sulky, *adj.* malhumorado
sulphur, *n.* azufre, *m.*
sum, *n.* suma, *f.*
summary, *n.* sumario, *m.*
summer, *n.* verano, *m.*
summertime, *n.* verano, *m.*
summit, *n.* cumbre, *f.*
summon, *vt.* citar, convocar
sun, *n.* sol, *m.*
sunbeam, *n.* rayo de sol, *m.*
Sunday, *n.* domingo, *m.*
sunflower, *n.* girasol, *m.*
sung, *p. p.* del verbo **sing**
sunken, del verbo **sink**
sunlight, *n.* luz del sol, *f.*
sunny, *adj.* asoleado; alegre
sunrise, *n.* salida del sol, *f.*
sunset, *n.* ocaso, *m.*
sunshine, *n.* luz del sol, *f.*
sunstroke, *n.* insolación, *f.*
superb, *adj.* excelente
superhighway, *n.* supercarretera, *f.*
superhuman, *adj.* sobrehumano
superintendent, *n.* superintendente, mayordomo, *m.*
superior, *n.* y *adj.* superior, *m.*
superiority, *n.* superioridad, *f.*
superlative, *adj.* y *n.* superlativo, *m.*
superman, *n.* superhombre, *m.*
supermarket, *n.* supermercado, *m.*
supernatural, *adj.* sobrenatural
superpower, *n.* superpotencia, *f.*
superstitious, *adj.* supersticioso
supervise, *vt.* inspeccionar
supervision, *n.* dirección, inspección, *f.*
supervisor, *n.* superintendente, *m.* y *f.*; inspector, inspectora
supper, *n.* cena, *f.*
supply, *vt.* suplir, proporcionar; *n.* surtido, *m.*; provisión, *f.*; **supply and demand,** oferta y demanda
support, *vt.* sostener; sopor-

tar; basar; *n.* sustento, *m.*; apoyo, *m.*

suppose, *vt.* suponer

supposition, *n.* suposición, *f.*, supuesto, *m.*

suppress, *vt.* suprimir; reprimir

supremacy, *n.* supremacia, *f.*

supreme, *adj.* supremo

Supt., supt., superintendent, super.te, superintendente

sure, *adj.* seguro, cierto; **surely,** *adv.* sin duda

surgeon, *n.* cirujano, *m.*

surgery, *n.* cirugía, *f.*

surgical, *adj.* quirúrgico

surname, *n.* apellido, *m.*

surplus, *n.* sobrante, *m.*

surprise, *vt.* sorprender; *n.* sorpresa, *f.*

surprising, *adj.* sorprendente

surrender, *vt.* y *vi.* rendir; renunciar; *n.* rendición, *f.*

surround, *vt.* circundar, rodear

surroundings, *n. pl.* cercanías, *f. pl.*; ambiente, *m.*

survey, *vt.* inspeccionar, examinar; *n.* inspección, *f.*; apeo (de tierras), *m.*

surveying, *n.* agrimensura, *f.*

survive, *vi.* sobrevivir

survivor, *n.* sobreviviente, *m.* y *f.*

susceptible, *adj.* susceptible

suspect, *vt.* y *vi.* sospechar

suspend, *vt.* suspender, colgar

suspenders, *n. pl.* tirantes, *m. pl.*

suspense, *n.* incertidumbre, *f.*

suspicion, *n.* sospecha, *f.*

suspicious, *adj.* sospechoso

sustain, *vt.* sostener, sustentar

sustenance, *n.* sostenimiento, sustento, *m.*

SW, S.W., s.w., southwest, SO., Sudoeste

swallow, *n.* golondrina, *f.*; bocado, *m.*; *vt.* tragar

swam, *pretérito* del verbo **swim**

swan, *n.* cisne, *m.*

swap, *vt.* y *vi.* (coll.) cambalachear, cambiar

swarm, *n.* enjambre, *m.*; gentío, *m.*

swear, *vt.* y *vi.* jurar; juramentar

sweat, *n.* sudor, *m.*; *vi.* sudar; trasudar

sweater, *n.* suéter, *m.*

Sweden, Suecia

sweet, *adj.* dulce; grato

sweeten, *vt.* endulzar

sweetheart, *n.* novio, novia

sweetness, *n.* dulzura, *f.*

swell, *vi.* hincharse; *adj.* (coll.) espléndido

swelling, *n.* hinchazón, *f.*

swelter, *vi.* ahogarse de calor

swim, *vi.* nadar

swimming, *n.* natación, *f.*

swindle, *vt.* estafar; *n.* estafa, *f.*, petardo, *m.*

swing, *vi.* balancear, oscilar; mecerse; columpio, *m.*

switch, *n.* (elec.) interruptor, conmutador, *m.*; *vt.* desviar

switchboard, *n.* conmutador telefónico, *m.*

Switzerland, Suiza

swivel, *vt.* y *vi.* girar

swollen, *adj.* hinchado, inflado

sword, *n.* espada, *f.*

swordfish, *n.* pez espada, *m.*

swore, *pretérito* del verbo **swear**

sworn, *p. p.* del verbo **swear**

syllable, *n.* sílaba, *f.*

symbol, *n.* símbolo, *m.*

symbolic, *adj.* simbólico

sympathize, *vi.* simpatizar

sympathy, *n.* compasión, condolencia, *f.*; simpatía, *f.*

symphony, *n.* sinfonía, *f.*

symptom, *n.* síntoma, *m.*

syndicate, *n.* sindicato, *m.*

synonym, *n.* sinónimo, *m.*

synopsis, *n.* sinopsis, *f.*

synthesis, *n.* síntesis,

synthetic, *adj.* sintético

syrup, *n.* jarabe, *m.*

system, *n.* sistema, *m.*

T

table, *n.* mesa, *f.*

tablecloth, *n.* mantel, *m.*

tablespoon, *n.* cuchara, *f.*
tablespoonful, *n.* cucharada, *f.*
tablet, *n.* tableta, *f.*; pastilla, *f.*; (med.) oblea, *f.*
taboo, tabu, *n.* tabú, *m.*: *adj.* prohibido
tact, *n.* tacto, *m.*
tactful, *adj.* prudente
tactics, *n. pl.* táctica, *f.*
tactless, *adj.* sin tacto
taffeta, *n.* tafetán, *m.*
tail, *n.* cola, *f.*, rabo, *m.*
tailor, *n.* sastre, *m.*
take, *vt.* tomar, coger, asir
talcum, *n.* talco, *m.*
tale, *n.* cuento, *m.*
talent, *n.* talento, *m.*; ingenio, *m.*; capacidad, *f.*
talk, *vi.* hablar, conversar; *n.* plática, charla, *f.*
tall, *adj.* alto, elevado
tallow, *n.* sebo, *m.*
tambourine, *n.* pandereta, *f.*
tame, *adj.* domesticado; manso; *vt.* domesticar
tang, *n.* sabor, *m.*
tangerine, *n.* mandarina *f.*
tangle, *vt.* y *vi.* enredar, embrollar
tango, *n.* tango, *m.*
tank, *n.* (mil) tanque, *m.*
tantalizing, *adj.* atormentador
tap, *vt.* tocar o golpear ligeramente; *n.* palmada suave, *f.*; **tap dance**, baile zapateado (de E. U. A.)
tape, *n.* cinta, *f.*; *vt.* vendar; grabar; **tape recorder**, magnetófono, *m.*
tar, *n.* alquitrán, *m.*
tardiness, *n.* tardanza, *f.*
tardy, *adj.* tardío; lento
target, *n.* blanco, *m.*; meta, *f.*
tariff, *n.* tarifa, *f.*
taste, *n.* gusto, *m.*; sabor, *m.*; *vt.* y *vi.* probar; tener sabor
tasteful, *adj.* de buen gusto
tasteless, *adj.* insípido
tasty, *adj.* gustoso
tattered, *adj.* andrajoso
tattletale, *n.* chismoso, chismosa
tavern, *n.* taberna, *f.*
tax, *n.* impuesto, *m.*, contribu-

ción, *f.*; **income tax**, impuesto de rentas; *vt.* imponer tributos
taxi, *n.* taxímetro, *m.*
taxicab, *n.* taxímetro, automóvil de alquiler, *m.*; (Mex.) libre, *m.*
tea, *n.* té, *m.*
teach, *vt.* enseñar, instruir
teacher, *n.* maestro, maestra, profesor, profesora
teaching, *n.* enseñanza, *f.*
teacup, *n.* taza para té, *f.*
teakettle, *n.* tetera, *f.*
team, *n.* tiro de caballos, *m.*; (deportes) equipo, *m.*
teapot, *n.* tetera, *f.*
tear, *vt.* despedazar; *n.* rasgón, jirón, *m.*
tear, *n.* lágrima, *f.*
tearoom, *n.* salón de té, *m.*
teaspoon, *n.* cucharita, *f.*
teat, *n.* ubre, *f.*; teta, *f.*
technical, *adj.* técnico
technician, *n.* técnico, *m.*
technique, *n.* técnica, *f.*
tedious, *adj.* fastidioso
teen-ager, *n.* adolescente, *m.* y *f.*
teens, *n. pl.* números y años desde 13 hasta 20; periodo de trece a diecinueve años de edad
teeth, *n. pl.* de **tooth**, dientes, *m. pl.*
telecast, *vt.* y *vi.* televisar; *n.* teledifusión, *f.*
telegram, *n.* telegrama, *m.*
telegraph, *n.* telégrafo, *m.*; *vi.* telegrafiar
telepathy, *n.* telepatía, *f.*
telephone, *n.* teléfono, *m.*; **dial telephone**, teléfono automático, *m.*; *vt.* y *vi.* telefonear
teleprompter, *n.* apuntador electrónico, *m.*
telescope, *n.* telescopio, *m.*
television, *n.* televisión *f.*; **television set**, telerreceptor, aparto de televisión
temper, *n.* temperamento, *m.*; humor, genio, *m.*
temperament, *n.* temperamento, *m.*; carácter, genio, *m.*

temperate, *adj.* templado, moderado, sobrio
temperature, *n.* temperatura, *f.*
tempest, *n.* tempested, *f.*
temple, *n.* templo, *m.*; sien, *f.*
temporarily, *adj.* temporalmente
tempt, *vt.* tentar; provocar
temptation, *n.* tentación, *f.*
tempting, *adj.* tentador
ten, *n.* y *adj.* diez, *m.*
tenant, *n.* inquilino, inquilina
tendency, *n.* tendencia, *f.*
tender, *adj.* tierno, delicado
tenderloin, *n.* filete, solomillo, *m.*
tenderness, *n.* terneza, *f.*
tennis, *n.* tenis, *m.*
tenor, *n.* (mus.) tenor, *m.*
tense, *adj.* tieso; tenso; *n.* (gram.) tiempo, *m.*
tension, *n.* tensión, *f.*
tent, *n.* tienda de campaña, *f.*
tentative, *adj.* tentativo
tenth, *n.* y *adj.* décimo, *m.*
tepid, *adj.* tibio
term, *n.* plazo, *m.*; tiempo, periodo, *m.*; **terms of payment**, condiciones de pago, *f. pl.*
terminate, *vt.* y *vi.* terminar
terrace, *n.* terraza, *f.*
terrestrial, *adj.* terrestre
terrible, *adj.* terrible
terrify, *vt.* espantar, llenar de terror
territory, *n.* territorio, *m.*
terror, *n.* terror, *m.*
test, *n.* ensayo, *m.*, prueba, *f.*; examen, *m.*; *vt.* ensayar, probar; examinar
Testament, *n.* Testamento, *m.*
testament, *n.* testamento, *m.*
testify, *vt.* testificar, atestiguar
testimony, *n.* testimonio, *m.*
text, *n.* texto, *m.*; tema, *m.*
textbook, *n.* libro de texto, *m.*
texture, *n.* textura, *f.*
than, *conj.* que o de (en sentido comparativo)
thank, *vt.* dar gracias; **thanks**, *n. pl.* gracias, *f. pl.*
thankful, *adj.* agradecido
Thanksgiving,   **Thanksgiving**

Day, *n.* dia de dar gracias (en Estados Unidos)
that, *dem. pron.* ése, ésa, eso; aquél, aquélla, aquello; *rel. pron.* que, quien, el cual, la cual, lo cual; *conj.* que, por que, para que; *adj.* ese, esa, aquel, aquella
the, *art.* el, la, lo; los, las
theater, *n.* teatro, *m.*
theatrical, *adj.* teatral
thee, *pron.* (acusativo de **thou**) ti, a ti
theft, *n.* hurto, robo, *m.*
their, *adj.* su, suyo, soya; sus, suyos, suyas; **theirs**, *pron.* el suyo, la suya, los suyos, las suyas
them, *pron.* (*acusativo y dativo* de they) los, las, les; ellos, ellas
theme, *n.* tema, asunto, *m.*; (mus.) motivo, *m.*
themselves, *pron. pl.* ellos mismos, ellas mismas; sí mismos
then, *adv.* entonces, después; **now and then**, de cuando en cuando
theology, *n.* teologia, *f.*
there, *adv.* allí, allá
thereafter, *adv.* después; subsiguientemente
thereby, *adv.* por medio de eso
therefore, *adv.* por lo tanto
thermometer, *n.* termómetro, *m.*
these, *pron. pl.* éstos, éstas; *adj.* estos, estas
thick, *adj.* espeso, grueso
thicken, *vt.* y *vi.* espesar
thief, *n.* ladrón, ladrona
thin, *adj.* delgado, flaco
thing, *n.* cosa, *f.*
think, *vt.* y *vi.* pensar; creer
thinking, *n.* pensamiento, *m.*; opinión, *f.*
third, *n.* y *adj.* tercero, *m.*
thirst, *n.* sed, *f.*
thirsty, *adj.* sediento; **to be thirsty**, tener sed
thirteen, *n.* y *adj.* trece, *m.*
thirteenth, *n.* y *adj.* décimotercio, *m.*

thirtieth, *n.* y *adj.* treintavo, *m.; adj.* trigésimo

thirty, *n.* y *adj.* treinta. *m.*

this, *adj.* este, esta; esto; *pron.* éste, ésta

thorn, *n.* espina, *f.*

those, *adj. pl.* de **that,** aquellos, aquellas; esos, esas; *pron.* aquéllos, aquéllas; ésos, ésas

though, *conj.* aunque; *adv.* (coll.) sin embargo

thought, *n.* pensamiento, *m.;* concepto, *m.; pretérito* y *p. p.* del verbo **think**

thoughtful, *adj.* pensativo; considerado

thoughtless, *adj.* inconsiderado

thousand, *n.* mil, *m.;* millar, *m.*

thousandth, *n.* y *adj.* milésimo, *m.*

threader, *n.* (mech.) terraja, *f.*

threat, *n.* amenaza,

threaten, *vt.* amenazar

three, *n.* y *adj.* tres, *m.*

thresh, *vt.* trillar

threshold, *n.* umbral, *m.*

threw, *pretérito* del verbo **throw**

thrice, *adv.* tres veces

thrift, *n.* frugalidad, *f.*

thrifty, *adj.* ahorrativo, frugal

thrill, *vt.* emocionar; *vi.* estremecerse; *n.* emoción, *f.*

thrilling, *adj.* emocionante

thrive, *vi.* prosperar

throat, *n.* garganta, *f.*

throb, *vi.* palpitar, vibrar

throne. *n.* trono, *m.*

throng, *n.* gentío, *m.*

throttle, *n.* válvula reguladora, *f.;* acelerador, *m.*

through, *prep.* a través, por medio de; por

throw, *vt.* echar, arrojar; *n.* tiro, *m.*, tirada *f.*

thrown, *p. p.* del verbo **throw**

thumbtack, *n.* chinche, tachuela, *f.*

thunder, *n.* trueno, *m.;* estrépito, *m.; vt.* y *vi.* tronar

Thursday, *n.* jueves, *m.*

thwart, *vt.* frustrar

ticket, *n.* billete, *m.;* (Sp. Am.) boleto, *m.,* boleta, *f.*

tickle, *vt.* hacer cosquillas a alguno; *vi.* tener cosquillas

tide, *n.* marea, *f.*

tidings, *n. pl.* noticias, *f. pl.*

tidy, *adj.* pulcro

tie, *vt.* atar; enlazer; *n.* nudo, *m.;* corbata, *f.*

tiger, *n.* tigre, *m.*

tight, *adj.* tieso; apretado; (coll.) tacaño

tighten, *vt.* estirar; apretar

tigress, *n.* tigre hembra

tile, *n.* teja, *f.;* azulejo, *m.*

till, *prep.* y *conj.* hasta que, hasta; *vt.* cultivar, labrar

time, *n.* tiempo, *m.;* (mus.) compás, *m.;* edad, época, *f.;* hora, *f.;* vez, *f.*

timely, *adj.* oportuno

timetable, *n.* itinerario, *m.*

timid, *adj.* tímido

tin, *n.* estaño, *m.;* hojalata, *f.;*

tin can, lata, *f.*

tingle, *vi.* latir, punzar

tint, *n.* tinte, *m.; vt.* teñir, colorar

tiny, *adj.* pequeño, chico

tip, *n.* punta, extremidad, *f.;* gratificación, propina, *f.;* información oportuna; *vt.* dar propina; ladear; volcar

tiptoe, *n.* punta del pie, *f.;* **on tiptoe,** de puntillas

tire, *n.* llanta, goma, *f.;* neumático, *m.* ; *vt.* cansar, fatigar; *vi.* cansarse

tired, *adj.* cansado

tissue, *n.* (anat.) tejido, *m.;*

tissue paper, papel de seda, *m.*

title, *n.* título, *m.*

to, *prep.* a. para; por; de; hasta; en; con; que; *adv.* hacia determinado objeto; **he came to,** volvió en sí

toad, *n.* sapo, *m.*

toast, *vt.* tostar; brindar; *n.* tostada, *f.,* pan tostado, *m.;* brindis, *m.*

toaster, *n.* tostador, *m.*

toastmaster, *n.* maestro de ceremonias, *m.*

tobacco, *n.* tabaco , *m.*

today, n. y adv. hoy m.
toddle, vi. tambalearse
toe, n. dedo del pie, m.
toenail, n. uña del dedo del pie, f.
together, adv. juntamente
toil, vi. afanarse; n. fatiga, f.; afán, m.
toilet, n. tocado, m.; excusado; retrete, m.
token, n. símbolo, m.; recuerdo, m.
told, pretérito del verbo **tell**
tolerence, n. tolerancia, f.
tolerate, vt. tolerar
toll, n. peaje, portazgo, m.; tañido, m.; **toll call,** llamada telefónica de larga distancia; vi. sonar las campanas
tomato, n. tomate, m.
tomb, n. tumba, f.
tomorrow, n. y adv. mañana, f.
ton, n. tonelada, f.
tongue, n. lengua, f.
tonic, n. tónico, reconstituyente, m.; (mus.) tónica, f.
tonight, n. y adv. esta noche
tonsil, n. amígdala, f.
too, adv. demasiado; también
took, pretérito del verbo **take**
tool, n. herramienta, f.
toot, vt. y vi. sonar una bocina
tooth, n. diente, m.
toothache, n. dolor de muelas, m.
toothbrush, n. cepillo de dientes, m.
toothpaste, n. pasta dentífrica, f.
toothpick, n. escarbadientes, palillo de dientes, m.
top, n. cima, cumbre, f.; trompo, m.
topaz, n. topacio, m.
topcoat, n. sobretodo, abrigo, m.
topic, n. tópico, asunto, m.
topsy-turvy, adv. patas arriba, desordenadamente
torch, n. antorcha, f.
tore, pretérito del verbo **tear**
toreador, n. torero, m.
torment, n. tormento, m.; vt. atormentar

torn, adj. destrozado; descosido; p. p. del verbo **tear**
torpedo, n. torpedo, m.
tortoise-shell, adj. de carey
torture, n. tortura, f., martirio, m.; vt. atormentar, torturar
toss, vt. tirar, lanzar, arrojar; agitar, sacudir; vi. agitarse; menearse
tot, n. niñito, niñita
total, n. total, m.; adj. entero, completo
totter, vi. tambalear
touch, vt. tocar, palpar; emocionar, conmover; n. tacto, m.; toque, contacto, m.
touching, adj. conmovedor
tough, adj. tosco; correoso; fuerte, vigoroso
toughen, vi. endurecerse; vt. endurecer
touring, n. turismo, m.
tourist, n. turista, m. y f.; viajero, viajera; **tourist court,** posada para turistas, f.
tournament, n. torneo, concurso, m.
toward, towards, prep. hacia, con dirección a
town, n. pueblo, m., población, f.
trace, n. huella, pisada, f.; vestigio, m.; vt. delinear, trazar
track, n. vestigio, m.; huella, pista, f.; vía f.
trade, n. comercio, tráfico, m.; negocio, trato, m.; vt. comerciar, negociar
trade-mark, n. marca de fábrica, f.
traffic, n. tráfico, m.
trail, vt. y vi. rastrear; arrastrar; n. rastro, m.; pisada, f.; sendero, m.
trailer, n. carro de remolque, m.
train, vt. enseñar, adiestrar; entrenar; n. tren, m.; cola (de vestido), f.
training, n. educación, disciplina, f.; entrenamiento, m.
traitor, n. traidor, m.
transact, vt. negociar, transi-

gir

transaction, *n.* transacción, *f.*

transatlantic, *adj.* trasatlántico

transfer, *vt.* trasferir; *n.* traspaso, *m.*; trastado, *m.*

transform, *vt.* y *vi.* trasformar

transfusion, *n.* trasfusión, *f.*

transient, *adj.* pasajero, transitorio

transit, *n.* transito, *m.*

transition, *n.* transición, *f.*

transitive, *adj.* transitivo

translate, *vt.* traducir

translation, *n.* traducción, *f.*

translator, *n.* traductor, traductora

transmission, *n.* (mech.) caja de cambios, *f.*

transmit, *vt.* trasmitir

transom, *n.* travesaño, *m.*

transparent, *adj.* trasparente

transport, *vt.* trasportar

transportation, *n.* trasportación, *f.*, trasporte, *m.*

trap, *n.* trampa, *f.*; *vt.* atrapar

trapeze, *n.* trapecio, *m.*

trash, *adj.* despreciable

travel, *vt.* y *vi.* viajar

traveler, *n.* viajero, viajera

tray, *n.* bandeja, *f.*; (Mex.) charola, *f.*

treacherous, *adj.* traidor

treachery, *n.* traición, *f.*

tread, *vt.* y *vi.* pisar, hollar; *n.* pisada, *f.*

treason, *n.* traición, *f.*

treasure, *n.* tesoro, *m.*; *vt.* atesorar; apreciar

treasurer, *n.* tesorero, tesorera

treasury, *n.* tesorería, *f.*

treat, *vt.* y *vi.* tratar; regalar; *n.* convite, *m.*

treatment, *n.* trato, *m.*; tratamiento, *m.*

treaty, *n.* tratado, *m.*

tree, *n.* árbol, *m.*

tremble, *vi.* temblar

tremendous, *adj.* tremendo; inmenso

trench, *n.* trinchera, *f.*

trespass, *vt.* traspasar, violar

trial, *n.* prueba, *f.*; ensayo, *m.*; (law) juicio, *m.*

triangle, *n.* triángulo, *m.*

triangular, *adj.* triangular

tribe, *n.* tribu, *f.*

tribulation, *n.* tribulación, *f.*

tribunal, *n.* tribunal, *m.*

tribute, *n.* tributo, *m.*

tricycle, *n.* triciclo, velocípedo, *m.*

trill, *n.* trino, *m.*

trillion, *n.* trillón, *m.*, la tercera potencia de un millón, o 1,000,000,000,000,000,000 (en la América Ibera, España Inglaterra, y Alemania); un millón de millones, o 1,000,000,000,000 (en Francia y los Estados Unidos)

trim, *adj.* bien ataviado; *n.* adorno, *m.*; *vt.* adornar, ornar; recortar

trinket, *n.* joya, alhaja, *f.*

trio, *n.* terceto, trío, *m.*

trip, *vt.* saltar, brincar; hacer tropezar; *vi.* tropezar; *n.* viaje, *m.*

triple, *adj.* triple

triplicate, *vt.* triplicar; *adj.* triplicado

trite, *adj.* trivial, banal

triumph, *n.* triunfo, *m.*; *vi.* triunfar; vencer

triumphant, *adj.* triunfante

trivial, *adj.* trivial, vulgar

trolley, *n.* tranvía, *m.*

trombone, *n.* trombón, *m.*

troop, *n.* tropa, *f.*

tropics, *n. pl.* trópico, *m.*

tropical, *adj.* tropical

troubadour, *n.* trovador, *m.*

trouble, *vt.* incomodar, molestar; *vi.* incomodarse; *n.* pena, *f.*; molestia, *f.*; trabajo, *m.*

troubled, *adj.* afligido

troublesome, *adj.* molesto, fastidioso

trousers, *n. pl.* calzones, pantalones, *m. pl.*

trousseau, *n.* ajuar de novia, *m.*

trout, *n.* trucha, *f.*

truce, *n.* tregua, *f.*

truck, *n.* camión, *m.*

true, *adj.* verdadero, cierto

truly, *adv.* en verdad

trumpet, *n.* trompeta, trompa, *f.*

trunk, *n.* tronco, *m.*; baúl, cofre, *m.*; **trunk (of an elephant),** trompa, *f.*

trunks, *n. pl.* calzones, *m. pl.*

trust, *n.* confianza, *f.*; crédito, *m.*; *vt.* y *vi.* confiar

trustee, *n.* fideicomisario, depositario, *m.*

trustworthy, *adj.* digno de confianza

truth, *n.* verdad, *f.*

truthful, *adj.* verídico, veraz

truthfulness, *n.* veracidad, *f.*

try, *vt.* y *vi.* probar; experimentar; intentar

trying, *adj.* cruel, penoso

tub, *n.* tina, *f.*

tube, *n.* tubo, caño, *m.*

tuberculosis, *n.* tuberculosis, tisis, *f.*

tug, *vt.* tirar con fuerza; arrancar

tugboat, *n.* remolcador, *m.*

tuition, *n.* instrucción, enseñanza, *f.*

tumble, *vi.* caer, voltear; *n.* caída, *f.*

tumor, *n.* tumor, *m.*

tuna, *n.* (bot.) tuna, *f.*; **tuna fish,** atún, *m.*

tune, *n.* tono, *m.*; tonada, *f.*; *vt.* afinar (un instrumento musical)

tunic, *n.* túnica, *f.*

tunnel, *n.* túnel, *m.*

turban, *n.* turbante, *m.*

turbojet, *n.* turborreactor, *m.*

turf, *n.* césped, *m.*

turkey, *n.* pavo, *m.*

Turkey, *n.* Turquía, *f.*

Turkish, *adj.* turco

turmoil, *n.* confusión, *f.*

turn, *vt.* volver, trocar; *vi.* volver, girar, voltear; *n.* vuelta, *f.*; giro, *m.*; turno, *m.*

turnip, *n.* (bot.) nabo, *m.*

turquoise, *n.* turquesa, *f.*

turtle, *n.* tortuga, *f.*

turtledove, *n.* tórtola, f

tuxedo, *n.* smoking, *m.*

tweezers, *n. pl.* pinzas, *f. pl.*; tenacillas, *f. pl.*

twelfth, *n.* y *adj.* duodécimo, *m.*

twelve, *n.* y *adj.* doce, *m.*

twentieth, *n.* y *adj.* vigésimo, *m.*

twenty, *n.* y *adj.* veinte, *m.*

twice, *adv.* dos veces

twig, *n.* varita, varilla, *f.*

twilight, *n.* crepúsculo, *m.*

twine, *vt.* torcer, enroscar; *vi.* entrelazarse

twinge, *n.* punzada, *f.*; *vi.* arder; sufrir dolor (de una punzada, etc.)

twinkle, *vi.* parpadear; *n.* pestañeo, *m.*

twinkling, *n.* pestañeo, *m.*; momento, *m.*

twirl, *vt.* voltear; hacer girar

twist, *vt.* y *vi.* torcer

two, *n.* y *adj.* dos , *m.*

type, *n.* tipo, *m.*; clase, *f.*; *vt.* y *vi.* escribir en máquina

typewrite, *vt.* escribir a máquina

typewriter, *n.* máquina de escribir, *f.*

typhoid, *adj.* tifoideo; **typhoid fever,** fiebre tifoidea, *f.*

typical, *adj.* típico

typing, *n.* mecanografía, *f.*

typist, *n.* mecanógrafo, mecanógrafa

typographical, *adj.* tipográfico

tyranny, *n.* tiranía, *f.*

tyrant, *n.* tirano, *m.*

U

U., University, Universidad

udder, *n.* ubre, *f.*

ugliness, *n.* fealdad, *f.*

ugly, *adj.* feo

ulcer , *n.* úlcera, *f.*

ultimatum, *n.* ultimátum, *m.*

ultra, *adj.* extremo, excesivo

ultrasonic, *adj.* ultrasónico

umbrella, *n.* paraguas, *m.*

umpire, *n.* árbitro, *m.*; *vt.* arbitrar

UN, United Nations, N.U., Naciones Unidas

unable, *adj.* incapaz

unanimity, *n.* unanimidad, *f.*

unanimous, *adj.* unánime

unarmed, *adj.* desarmado

unassuming, *adj.* sin pretensiones

unattached, *adj.* separado; disponible

unattainable, *adj.* inasequible

unavoidable, *adj.* inevitable

unawares, *adv.* inadvertidamente

unbalanced, *adj.* trastornado

unbearable, *adj.* intolerable

unbiased, *adj.* imparcial

unbutton, *vt.* desabotonar

uncertain, *adj.* inseguro

uncertainty, *n.* incertidumbre, *f.*

uncle, *n.* tío, *m.*

uncomfortable, *adj.* incómodo

unconcerned, *adj.* indiferente

unconditional, *adj.* incondicional

unconscious, *adj.* inconsciente

undecided, *adj.* indeciso

under, *prep.* debajo de, bajo; *adv.* abajo

underage, *adj.* menor de edad

underclothing, *n.* ropa interior, *f.*

undergo, *vt.* sufrir; sostener

underground, *adj.* subterráneo

underhanded, *adj.* clandestino

underline, *vt.* subrayar

underneath, *adv.* debajo

underprivileged, *adj.* desvalido, necesitado

underscore, *vt.* subrayar

undershirt, *n.* camiseta, *f.*

undersigned, *n.* y *adj.* suscrito, suscrita

underskirt, *n.* enagua, *f.*; fondo, *m.*

understand, *vt.* entender, comprender

understanding, *n.* entendimiento, *m.*; *adj.* comprensivo

undertake, *vt.* y *vi.* emprender

undertaker, *n.* empresario o director de pompas fúnebres

undertaking, *n.* empresa, obra, *f.*

undertow, *n.* resaca, *f.*

underwear, *n.* ropa interior, *f.*

underweight, *adj.* de bajo peso

undesirable, *adj.* nocivo

undivided, *adj.* entero

undress, *vt.* desvestir; desnudar

unearth, *vt.* desenterrar; reveler, divulgar

unemployed, *adj.* desocupado

unending, *adj.* sin fin

unequal, *adj.* desigual

uneven, *adj.* desigual

unexpected, *adj.* inesperado

unfailing, *adj.* infalible

unfair, *adj.* injusto

unfamiliar, *adj.* desconocido

unfavorable, *adj.* desfavorable

unfit, *adj.* inepto, incapaz; indigno

unfold, *vt.* desplegar

unforeseen, *adj.* imprevisto

unforgettable, *adj.* inolvidable

unfortunate, *adj.* desafortunado, infeliz

unfounded, *adj.* infundado

unfurl, *vt.* desplegar

ungrounded, *adj.* infundado

unhappy, *adj.* infeliz

unharmed, *adj.* ileso, incólume

unhealthy, *adj.* malsano

unheard (of), *adj.* inaudito

unhurt, *adj.* ileso

uniform, *n.* y *adj.* uniforme, *m.*

uniformity, *n.* uniformidad, *f.*

union, *n.* unión, *f.*

unique, *adj.* único; singular

unison, *n.* concordancia, *f.*; **in unison,** al unisono

unit, *n.* unidad, *f.*

unite, *vt.* y *vi.* unir, juntarse

united, *adj.* unido, junto

United States of America, Estados Unidos de América

unity, *n.* unidad, *f.*; unión, *f.*

universal, *adj.* universal; **universal joint,** cardán, *m.*

universe, *n.* universo, *m.*

university, *n.* universidad, *f.*

unkind, *adj.* cruel

unknowingly, *adv.* sin saberlo

unknown, *adj.* desconocido

unlike, *adj.* desemejante

unlikely, *adj.* improbable

unlimited, *adj.* ilimitado

unlock, *vt.* abrir alguna cerradura

unlucky, *adj.* desafortunado
unmarried, *adj.* soltero, soltera
unnatural, *adj.* artificial
unnecessary, *adj.* innecesario
unofficial, *adj.* extraoficial
unpack, *vt.* desempacar
unpaid, *adj.* sin pagar, pendiente de pago
unpopular, *adj.* impopular
unprincipled, *adj.* sin escrúpulos
unravel, *vt.* desenredar; resolver
unreal, *adj.* fantástico, ilusorio
unreserved, *adj.* franco, abierto
unscrew, *vt.* destornillar
unscrupulous, *adj.* sin escrúpulos
unseemly, *adj.* indecoroso
unseen, *adj.* no visto
unselfish, *adj.* desinteresado
unsettled, *adj.* incierto, indeciso; **unsettled accounts**, cuentas por pagar
unsightly, *adj.* feo
unskilled, *adj.* inexperto
unsound, *adj.* inestable; falso
unsuitable, *adj.* inadecuado
untangle, *vt.* desenredar
untie, *vt.* soltar, desamrrar
until, *prep.* y *conj.* hasta, hasta que
untimely, *adj.* intempestivo
untold, *adj.* no relatado
unusual, *adj.* inusitado, poco común
unveil, *vt.* y *vi.* descubrir; revelar; estrenar
unwilling, *adj.* sin deseos; **unwillingly**, *adv.* de mala gana
unwind, *vt.* desenrollar
unwise, *adj.* imprudente
unworthy, *adj.* indigno, vil
unwritten, *adj.* verbal, no escrito
up, *adv.* arriba, en lo alto; *prep.* hasta; **to make up**, hacer las paces; inventar; compensar; maquillarse; **to bring up**, criar, educar; **to call up**, telefonear
upbringing, *n.* educación,

crianza, *f.*
upholster, *vt.* entapizar
upkeep, *n.* mantenimiento, *m.*
upon, *prep.* sobre encima
upper, *adj.* superior; más elevado
upright, *adj.* derecho, recto
uproar, *n.* tumulto, alboroto, *m.*
upset, *vt.* y *vi.* volcar, trastornar; *adj.* mortificado
upside-down, *adj.* al revés; de arriba abajo
upstairs, *adv.* arriba
up-to-date, *adj.* moderno, de ultima moda, reciente
upward, *adv.* hacia arriba
uranium, *n.* uranio, *m.*
urban, *adj.* urbano
urge, *vt.* y *vi.* incitar, instar
urgent, *adj.* urgente
urinate, *vi.* orinar, mear
urine, *n.* orina, *f.*, orines, *m. pl.*
U.S.A., **United States of America**, E.U.A. Estados Unidos de América
usable, *adj.* utilizable
usage, *n.* uso, *m.*
use, *n.* uso, *m.*, servicio, *m.*; *vt.* y *vi.* usar, emplear; acostumbrar
used, *adj.* gastado, usado
useful, *adj.* útil
usefulness, *n.* utilidad, *f.*
useless, *adj.* inútil
usher, *n.* acomodador, *m.*
usual, *adj.* común, ordinario; **usually**, *adv.* de costumbre
utensil, *n.* utensilio, *m.*
utility, *n.* utilidad, *f.*; **public utilities**, servicios públicos *m. pl.*

V

vacancy, *n.* vacante, *f.*
vacant, *adj.* vacío, vacante
vacation, *n.* vacación, *f.*
vaccinate, *vt.* vacunar
vaccination, *n.* vacuna, *f.*; vacunación, *f.*
vaccine, *n.* vacuna, *f.*
vacuum, *n.* vacío, *m.*; **vacuum cleaner**, aspiradora, *f.*, barre-

dor al vacio, *m.*

vain, *adj.* vano, inútil; vanidoso, presentuoso

valet, *n.* criado, camarero, *m.*

valid, *adj.* válido

valley, *n.* valle, *m.*

valuable, *adj.* valioso; **valuables,** *n. pl.* tesoros, *m. pl.*, joyas, *f. pl.*

value, *n.* valor, precio, importe, *m.*; *vt.* valuar, apreciar

vanilla, *n.* vainilla, *f.*

vanish, *vi.* desaparecer

vanity, *n.* vanidad, *f.*; **vanity case,** polvera, *f.*

variety, *n.* variedad, *f.*

various, *adj.* diferentes

varnish, *n.* barniz, *m.*; *vt.* barnizer; charolar

vary, *vt.* y *vi.* variar

vase, *n.* jarrón, florero, *m.*

vast, *adj.* vasto; inmenso

vault, *n.* bóveda, *f.*

veal, *n.* ternera, *f.*; **veal cutlet,** chuleta de ternera, *f.*

vegetable, *adj.* vegetal; *n.* vegetal, *m.*; **vegetables,** *n. pl.* verduras, hortalizas, *f. pl.*

vegetation, *n.* vegetación, *f.*

vehicle, *n.* vehículo, *m.*

veil, *n.* velo, *m.*; *vt.* encubrir, ocultar

vein, *n.* vena, *f.*

velocity, *n.* velocidad, *f.*

velvet, *n.* terciopelo, *m.*

velveteen, *n.* pana, *f.*

venerate, *vt.* venerar, honrar

veneration, *n.* veneración, *f.*

Venetian, *n.* y *adj.* veneciano, veneciana

Venezuelan, *n.* y *adj.* venezolano, venezolana

vengeance, *n.* venganza, *f.*

Venice, Venecia

venison, *n.* carne de venado, *f.*

ventilate, *vt.* ventilar

ventilation, *n.* ventilación, *f.*

veracity, *n.* veracidad, *f.*

veranda, *n.* terraza, *f.*

verb, *n.* (gram.) verbo, *m.*

verbal, *adj.* verbal, literal; **verbally,** *adv.* oralmente, de palabra

verbatim, *adv.* palabra por palabra

verdict, *n.* (law) veredicto, *m.*; sentencia, *f.*, dictamen, *m.*

verify, *vt.* verificar

versatile, *adj.* hábil para muchas cosas

verse, *n.* verso, *m.*

version, *n.* versión, traducción, *f.*

vessel, *n.* vasija, *f.*, vaso, *m.*; buque, *m.*

vest, *n.* chaleco, *m.*

vestibule, *n.* zaguán, *m.*

vestige, *n.* vestigio, *m.*

vest-pocket, *adj.* propio para el bolsillo del chaleco; pequeño; **vest-pocket edition,** edición en miniatura, *f.*

veteran, *n.* y *adj.* veterano, veterana

vex, *vt.* contrariar; **vexed,** *adj.* molesto, contrariado

via, *prep.* por la vía de; por; **via airmail,** por vía aérea

viaduct, *n.* viaducto, *m.*

vice, *n.* vicio, *m.*

vice-consul, *n.* vicecónsul, *m.*

vice-president, *n.* vice-presidente, *m.*

vicinity, *n.* vecindad, proximidad, *f.*

victim, *n.* víctima, *f.*

victorious, *adj.* victorioso

victory, *n.* victoria, *f.*

video, *n.* televisión, *f.*

Vienna, Viena, *f.*

Viennese, *n.* y *adj.* vienés, vienesa

view, *n.* vista, *f.*; paisaje, *m.*; *vt.* mirar, ver

viewpoint, *n.* punto de vista, *m.*

vigor, *n.* vigor, *m.*

vigorous, *adj.* vigoroso

villa, *n.* quinta, *f.*

village, *n.* aldea, *f.*

villain, *n.* malvado, *m.*

vim, *n.* energía, *f.*, vigor, *m.*

vindicate, *vt.* vindicar, defender

vine, *n.* vid, *f.*

vinegar, *n.* vinagre, *m.*

vineyard, *n.* viña, *f.*, viñedo, *m.*

viol, *n.* (mus.) violón, *m.*

viola, *n.* (mus.) viola, *f.*

violate, *vt.* violar
violation, *n.* violación, *f.*
violence, *n.* violencia, *f.*
violent, *adj.* violento
violet, *n.* (bot.) violeta, *f.*
violin, *n.* violín, *m.*
violinist, *n.* violinista, *m.* y *f.*
virgin, *n.* virgen, *f.*; *adj.* virginal; virgen
virology, *n.* virología, *f.*
virtue, *n.* virtud, *f.*
virtuous, *adj.* virtuoso
virus, *n.* (med.) virus, *m.*
visa, *n.* visa, *f.*
viscount, *n.* vizconde, *m.*
vision, *n.* visión, *f.*
visit, *vt.* y *vi.* visitar; *n.* visita, *f.*
visitor, *n.* visitante, *m.* y *f.*
visualize, *vt.* vislumbrar
vital, *adj.* vital; **vital statistics,** estadística demográfica, *f.*
vitality, *n.* vitalidad, *f.*
vitamin, *n.* vitamina, *f.*
vivacious, *adj.* vivaz
vivacity, *n.* vivacidad, *f.*
vivid, *adj.* vivo, vivaz; gráfico
viz., *adv.* a saber, esto es
vocabulary, *n.* vocabulario, *m.*
vocal, *adj.* vocal
vocalist, *n.* cantante, *m.* y *f.*
vocation, *n.* vocación, carrera, profesión, *f.*; oficio, *m.*
vocational, *adj.* práctico, profesional; **vocational school,** escuela de artes y oficios, escuela práctica, *f.*
vogue, *n.* moda, *f.*; boga, *f.*
voice, *n.* voz, *f.*
void, *n.* y *adj.* vacío, *m.*; *vt.* anular
volcano, *n.* volcán, *m.*
volleyball, *n.* balonvolea, *m.*
volume, *n.* volumen, *m.*
voluntarily, *adv.* voluntariamente
volunteer, *n.* voluntario, *m.*
vote, *n.* voto, sufragio, *m.*; *vt.* votar
voter, *n.* votante, *m.* y *f.*
voucher, *n.* comprobante, recibo, *m.*
vow, *n.* voto, *m.*; *vt.* y *vi.* dedicar, consagrar; hacer votos;

jurar
vowel, *n.* vocal, *f.*
voyage, *n.* viaje marítimo, *m.*
v.t., transitive verb, v.tr., verbo transitivo
vulgar, *adj.* vulgar, cursi
vulgarity, *n.* vulgaridad, *f.*

W

w., week, semana; **west,** O., oeste; **width,** ancho; **wife,** esposa
wafer, *n.* hostia, *f.*; oblea, *f.*; galletica, *f.*
wag, *vt.* mover ligeramente; **to wag the tail,** menear la cola; *n.* meneo, *m.*
wage, *vt.* apostar; emprender; **wages,** *n. pl.* sueldo, salario, *m.*
wager, *n.* apuesta, *f.*; *vt.* apostar
wagon, *n.* carreta, *f.*; vagón, *m.*
wail, *vi.* lamentarse
waist, *n.* cintura, *f.*
waistline, *n.* cintura, *f.*
wait, *vi.* esperar, aguardar
waiter, *n.* sirviente, mozo, *m.*
waitress, *n.* camarera, criada, mesera, *f.*
wake, *vi.* velar; despertarse; *vt.* despertar; *n.* vigilia, *f.*; velorio *m.*
walk, *vt.* y *vi.* pasear, andar, caminar; *n.* paseo, *m.*, caminata, *f.*
wallet, *n.* cartera, *f.*
walnut, *n.* nogal, *m.*; nuez, *f.*
wand, *n.* vara, varita, *f.*; batuta, *f.*
wander, *vi.* vagar, rodar; extraviarse
wanderer, *n.* peregrino, *m.*
want, *vt.* y *vi.* desear, querer, anhelar; faltar; *vi.* estar necesitado; *n.* falta, carencia, *f.*
war, *n.* guerra, *f.*
warden, *n.* custodio, guardián, *m.* alcalde, *m.*
wardrobe, *n.* guardarropa, *f.*, ropero, *m.*; vestuario, *m.*
warehouse, *n.* almacén, depósito, *m.*, bodega, *f.*
warhead, *n.* punta de comba-

te, *f.*

warm, *adj.* caliente; abrigador; cordial, caluroso; **to be warm,** hacer calor; tener calor; *vt.* calentar

warmth, *n.* calor, *m.*; ardor, fervor, *m.*

warn, *vt.* avisar; advertir

warrant, *vt.* autorizar; garantizar; *n.* decreto de prisión, *m.*; autorización, *f.*

warship, *n.* barco de guerra, *m.*

wart, *n.* verruga, *f.*

wartime, *n.* época de guerra, *f.*

was, 1ª y 3ª persona del singular del pretérito del verbo **be**

wash, *vt.* y *vi.* lavar; *n.* loción, ablución, *f.*; lavado, *m.*

washable, *adj.* lavable

washer, *n.* máquina lavadora, *f.*; (mech.) arandela, *f.*

washing, *n.* lavado, *m.*; ropa para lavar; **washing machine,** máquina de lavar, lavadora, *f.*

wasp, *n.* avispa, *f.*

waste, *vt.* desperdiciar; malgastar; *vi.* gastarse; *n.* desperdicio, *m.*; despilfarro, *m.*

wastebasket, *n.* cesta para papeles

wasteful, *adj.* despilfarrador

wastepaper, *n.* papel de desecho, *m.*

watch, *n.* vigilia, vela, *f.*; centinela, *f.*; reloj de bolsillo, *m.*; **wrist watch,** reloj de pulsera, *m.*;*vt.* observar; *vi.* velar, custodiar

water, *n.* agua, *f.*; **running water,** agua corriente, *f.*; **water closet,** retrete, *m.*; **water color,** acuarela, *f.*; **water meter,** contador de agua, *m.*; **water polo,** polo acuático, *m.*; **water skiing,** esquí náutico o acuático, *m.*; *vt.* irrigar, regar

watermelon, *n.* sandía, *f.*

waterproof, *adj.* a prueba de agua; impermeable

watery, *adj.* aguado

watt, *n.* vatio, *m.*

wattmeter, *n.* vatímetro, *m.*

wave, *n.* ola, onda, *f.*; *vt.* agitar, menear; *vi.* ondear; saludar

wavy, *adj.* ondeado, ondulado

wax, *n.* cera, **wax paper,** papel encerado, *m.*; *vt.* encerar

way, *n.* camino, *m.*, senda, ruta, *f.*; modo, *m.*, forma, *f.*; medio, *m.*; **by the way,** a propósito

we, *pron.* nosotros, nosotras

weak, *adj.* débil

weaken, *vt.* y *vi.* debilitar

wealth, *n.* riqueza, *f.*; bienes, *m. pl.*

wealthy, *adj.* rico, adinerado

weapon, *n.* arma, *f.*

wear, *vt.* gastar, consumir; llevar puesto, traer; *vi.* gastarse; *n.* uso, *m.*

weariness, *n.* cansancio, *m.*

weather, *n.* tiempo, *m.*, temperatura, *f.*

weave, *vt.* tejer; trenzar

web, *n.* red, *f.*

wed, *vt.* y *vi.* casar, casarse

wedding, *n.* boda, *f.*, casamiento, matrimonio, *m.*

wedge, *n.* cuña, *f.*; *vt.* acuñar; apretar

Wednesday, *n.* miércoles, *m.*

wee, *adj.* pequeñito

weed, *n.* mala hierba, *f.*

week, *n.* semana, *f.*

weekday, *n.* día de trabajo, *m.*

week-end, *adj.* de fin de semana

weekly, *adj.* semanal, semanario; *adv.* semanalmente

weigh, *vt.* y *vi.* pesar; considerar

weight, *n.* peso, *m.*; pesadez, *f.*

weightlessness, *n.* imponderabilidad, *f.*

weird, *adj.* extraño, sobrenatural, misterioso

welcome, *adj.* bienvenido; *n.* bienvenida, *f.*; *vt.* dar la bienvenida

weld, *vt.* soldar

welfare *n.* bienestar, *m.*

well, *n.* pozo, *m.*; *adj.* bueno, sano; *adv.* bien

well-being, *n.* felicidad, prosperidad, *f.*

well-bred, *adj.* bien educado, de buenos modales
well-done, *adj.* bien hecho; bien cocido
well-timed, *adj.* oportuno
well-to-do, *adj.* acomodado, rico
wench, *n.* mozuela, *f.*
went, *pretérto* del verbo **go**
were, 2ª persona del singular y plural del *pretérto* del verbo **be**
west, *n.* poniente, occidente, oeste, *m.*
westerly, **western**, *adj.* occidental
West Indies, Antillas, *f. pl.*
wet, *adj.* húmedo, mojado; *vt.* molar, humedecer
whale, *n.* ballena, *f.*
wharf, *n.* muelle, *m.*
what, *pron.* qué; lo que, aquello que; **what is the matter?** ¿qué pasa?
whatever, *pron.* y *adj.* cualquier cosa, lo que sea
wheat, *n.* trigo, *m.*
wheel, *n.* rueda, *f.*
wheelbarrow, *n.* carretilla, *f.*
when, *adv.* cuando; cuándo
whence, *adv.* de donde; de quien
whenever, *adv.* siempre que
where, *adv.* donde; dónde
whereabouts, *n.* paradero, *m.*; *adv.* por donde, hacia donde
whereas, *conj.* por cuanto, mientras que; considerando
whereby, *adv.* con lo cual
wherein, *adv.* en lo cual
whereof, *adv.* de lo cual
whereon, *adv.* sobre lo cual
whereupon, *adv.* entonces, en consecuencia de lo cual
wherever, *adv.* dondequiera que
whet, *vt.* afilar, amolar; exciter
whether, *conj.* que; si; ora
whey, *n.* suero, *m.*
which, *pron.* que, el cual, la cual, los cuales, las cuales; cuál
whichever, *pron.* y *adj.* cualquiera que
whiff, *n.* bocanada de humo,

fumada, *f.*
while, *n.* rato, *m.*; vez, *f.*; momento, *m.*; **to be worth while**, valer la pena; *conj.* mientras, durante
whim, *n.* antojo, capricho, *m.*
whimsical, *adj.* caprichoso, fantástico
whip, *n.* azote, látigo, *m.*; *vt.* azotar
whipped cream, *n.* crema batida, *f.*
whirl, *vt.* y *vi.* girar; hacer girar; moverse rápidamente; *n.* remolino, *m.*; vuelta, *f.*
whirlwind, *n.* torbellino, remolino, *m.*
whisker, *m.* patilla, *f.*
whiskey, **whisky**, *n.* whiskey, *m.*
whisper, *vi.* cuchichear; *n.* cuchicheo, secreto, *m.*
whistle, *vt.* y *vi.* silbar; chiflar; *n.* silbido, *m.*; pito, *m.*
white, *adj.* blanco, pálido; cano, canoso; puro; *n.* color blanco; clara (de huevo)
white-haired, *adj.* canoso
whiten, *vt.* y *vi.* blanquear; blanquearse
who, *pron.* quien, que; quién
whoever, *pron.* quienquiera
whole, *adj.* todo, total; entero; *n.* todo, total, *m.*; **the whole**, conjunto, *m.*
wholehearted, *adj.* sincero, cordial
wholesale, *n.* venta al por mayor, *f.*
wholesome, *adj.* sano, saludable
whole-wheat, *adj.* de trigo entero
wholly, *adv.* totalmente
whom, *pron.* acusativo de **who** (quien)
whooping cough, *n.* tosferina, *f.*
whore, *n.* puta, *f.*
whose, *pron.* (genitivo de **who** y **which**) cuyo, cuya, cuyos, cuyas, de quien de quienes
why, *adv.* ¿por qué?
wicked, *adj.* malvado, perverso

wide, *adj.* ancho, extenso;
widely, *adv.* ampliamente
wide-awake, *adj.* despierto,
alerta
widen, *vt.* ensanchar, ampliar
widespread, *adj.* diseminado
widow, *n.* viuda, *f.*
widower, *n.* viudo, *m.*
width, *n.* anchura, *f.*
wield, *vt.* manejar, empuñar
wife, *n.* esposa, mujer, *f.*
wild, *adj.* silvestre; salvaje
wilderness, *n.* desierto, *m.*,
selva, *f.*
wilful, *adj.* voluntarioso
will, *n.* voluntad, *f.*; capricho,
m.; testamento, *m.*; *vt.* legar,
dejar en testamento; verbo
auxiliar que indica futuro
willing, *adj.* deseoso, listo;
willingly, *adv.* de buena gana
willow, *n.* (bot.) sauce, *m.*
win, *vt.* y *vi.* ganar, obtener
wind, *n.* viento, *m.*; pedo, *m.*
wind, *vt.* enrollar; dar cuerda
(a un reloj, etc.); torcer; envolver; *vi.* serpentear
winded, *adj.* sin fuerzas
window, *n.* ventana, *f.*
windpipe, *n.* (anat.) tráquea, *f.*
windshield, *n.* parabrisas, *m.*
wine, *n.* vino, *m.*
wing, *n.* ala, *f.*; lado, costado,
m.; **wings,** *pl.* (theat.) bastidores, *m. pl.*
wink, *vt.* y *vi.* guiñar, pestañear
winner, *n.* vencedor, vencedo-
ra
winning, *adj.* atractivo; **win-
nings,** *n. pl.* ganancias, *f. pl.*
winsome, *adj.* simpático
winter, *n.* invierno, *m.*
winterize, *vt.* acondicionar
para uso invernal
wipe, *vt.* secar, limpiar; borrar;
to wipe out, obliterar; arruinar
wire, *n.* alambre, *m.*; *vt.* alam-
brar; *vi.* (coll.) telegrafiar, cablegrafiar
wireless, *n.* telegrafía inalám-
brica, *f.*
wisdom, *n.* sabiduría, *f.*; jui-

cio, *m.*
wisdom tooth, *n.* muela del
juicio, muela cordal, *f.*
wise, *adj.* sabio, juicioso, prudente
wish, *vt.* desear, querer; *n.* anhelo, deseo, *m.*
wishful, *adj.* deseoso; **wishful
thinking,** ilusiones, *f. pl.*
wisp, *n.* fragmento, *m.*; pizca,
f.
wit, *n.* ingenio, *m.*, agudeza,
sal, *f.*; **to wit,** a saber
witch, *n.* bruja, hechicera, *f.*
with, *prep.* con; por; de; a
withdraw, *vt.* quitar; retirar;
vi. retirarse, apartarse
wither, *vi.* marchitarse
withhold, *vt.* detener, retener
within, *prep.* dentro, adentro
without, *prep.* sin; fuera,
afuera; *adv.* exteriormente
withstand, *vt.* oponer, resistir
witness, *n.* testimonio, *m.*;
testigo, *m.*; *vt.* atestiguar,
testificar; *vi.* servir de testigo;
presenciar
witty, *adj.* ingenioso
wives, *n. pl.* de **wife,** esposas,
mujeres, *f. pl.*
wizard, *n.* hechicero, mago, *m.*
wobble, *vt.* bambolear
woe, *n.* dolor, *m.*, aflicción, *f.*
wolf, *n.* lobo, *m.*
wolves, *n. pl.* de **wolf,** lobos,
m. pl.
woman, *n.* mujer, *f.*
womanhood, *n.* la mujer en
general
womanly, *adj.* femenino
womb, *n.* útero, *m.*, matriz, *f.*
women, *n. pl.* de **woman,** mujeres, *f. pl.*
wonder, *n.* milagro, *m.*; prodigio, *m.*; maravilla, *f.*; *vi.* maravillarse (de)
wonderful, *adj.* maravilloso
won't, contracción de **will not**
woo, *vt.* cortejar
wood, *n.* madera, *f.*; leña, *f.*;
woods, *pl.* bosque, *m.*
woodchuck, *n.* (zool.) marmo-
ta, *f.*
woodcutter, *n.* leñador, *m.*
wooded, *adj.* arbolado

wooden, *adj.* de madera

woodland, *n.* bosque, *m.*, selva, *f.*

woodman, *n.* cazador, *m.*; guardabosque, *m.*

woodpecker, *n.* (orn.) picamaderos, *m.*

wool, *n.* lana, *f.*

woolen, *adj.* de lana

word, *n.* palabra, voz, *f.*; *vt.* expresar

wore, *pretérito* del verbo **wear**

work, *vi.* trabajar; funcionar; *vt.* trabajar; *n.* trabajo, *m.*

worker, *n.* trabajador, obrero, *m.*

workingman, *n.* obrero, *m.*

workroom, *n.* taller, *m.*

works, *n.* fábrica, *f.*, taller, *m.*

workshop, *n.* taller, *m.*

world, *n.* mundo, *m.*

worldly, *adj.* mundano

world-wide, *adj.* mundial

worm, *n.* gusano, *m.*

worn, *p. p.* del verbo **wear**

worn-out, *adj.* rendido, gastado

worry, *n.* cuidado, *m.*; preocupación, ansia, *f.*; *vt.* molestar, atormentar; *vi.* preocuparse

worse, *adj.* y *adv.* peor

worship, *n.* culto, *m.*; adoración, *f.*; *vt.* adorar, venerar

worst, *adj.* pésimo, malísimo; *n.* lo peor, lo más malo

worth, *n.* valor, precio, *m.*; mérito, *m.*, valía, *f.*; *adj.* meritorio, digno; **to be worth while,** merecer o valer la pensa

worthless, *adj.* inservible, sin valor

would, *pret.* y *subj.* de **will,** para expresar deseo, condición, acción

wound, *n.* herida, llaga, *f.*; *vt.* herir

wove, *pretérito* del verbo **weave**

woven, *p. p.* del verbo **weave**

wrangle, *vi.* reñir, discutir

wrap, *vt.* arrollar; envolver; *n.* abrigo, *m.*

wrapping, *n.* envoltura, *f.*

wrath, *n.* ira, cólera, *f.*

wreath, *n.* corona, guirnalda *f.*

wreck, *n.* naufragio, *m.*; destrucción, *f.*; colisión, *f.*, *vt.* arruinar; destruir

wren, *n.* (orn.) reyezuelo, *m.*

wrench, *vt.* arrancar; torcer; *n.* torcedura (del pie, etc.); destornillador, *m.*; **monkey wrench,** llave inglesa, *f.*

wrest, *vt.* arrancar, quitar a fuerza

wrestle, *vi.* luchar a brazo partido; *n.* lucha, *f.*

wrestling, *n.* lucha, *f.*

wretch, *n.* infeliz, *m.*; infame, *m.*

wretched, *adj.* infeliz, mísero

wriggle, *vi.* retorcerse; menearse

wring, *vt.* exprimir, torcer

wringer, *n.* torcedor, *m.*

wrinkle, *n.* arruga, *f.*; *vt.* arrugar

wrist, *n.* muñeca (de la mano), *f.*; **wrist watch,** reloj de pulsera, *m.*

write, *vt.* escribir

writer, *n.* escritor, escritora, autor, autora; novelista, *m.* y *f.*

writhe, *vt.* torcer; *vi.* contorcerse,

written, *p. p.* del verbo **write**

wrong, *n.* perjuicio, *m.*; injusticia, *f.*; error, *m.*; *adj.* incorrecto, erróneo; injusto; falso; *vt.* hacer un mal, injuriar; agraviar; **wrongly,** *adv.* mal, injustamente; al revés

wrote, *pretérito* del verbo **write**

wt., weight, P. peso

X

Xmas, Christmas, Navidad, Pascua de Navidad

X ray, *n.* rayo X o Roentgen; **X-ray picture,** radiografía, *f.*; *vt.* examinar con rayos X, radiografiar

Y

yacht, *n.* (naut.) yate, *m.*

yam, *n.* (bot.) batata, *f.*; (Sp. Am.) camote, *m.*

yank, *vt.* (coll.) sacudir, tirar de golpe; *n.* abreviatura de **yankee**

yankee, *n.* y *adj.* yanqui, *m.* y *f.*

yard, *n.* corral, *m.*; patio, *m.*; yarda (medida), *f.*

yardstick, *n.* yarda de medir, *f.*

yarn, *n.* estambre, *m.*; (coll.) cuento exagerado, *m.*

yawn, *vi.* bostezar; *n.* bostezo, *m.*

yd., yard, yd., yarda

year, *n.* año, *m.*

yearly, *adj.* anual; *adv.* anualmente

yearn, *vi.* anhelar

yearning, *n.* anhelo, *m.*

yeast, *n.* levadura, *f.*

yell, *vi.* aullar, gritar; *n.* grito, aullido, *m.*

yellow, *adj.*, *n.* amarllo, *m.*

yelp, *vi.* latir, ladrar; *n.* aullido, latido, *m.*

yes, *adv.* sí

yesterday, *adv.* aycr; **day before yesterday,** anteayer

yet, *adv.* todavía, aún; *conj.* sin embargo

yield, *vt.* y *vi.* producir, rendir

yoke, *n.* yugo, *m.*; yunta, *f.*

yolk, *n.* yema (de huevo) *f.*

you, *pron.* tú, usted; vosotros, vosotras, ustedes

young, *adj.* joven; **young man,** joven, *m.*; **young woman,** joven, señorita, *f.*

youngster, *n.* jovencito, jovencita, chiquillo, chiquilla, muchacho , muchacha

your, yours, *pron.* tu, su, vuestro, de ustedes, de vosotros

yourself, *pron.* usted mismo; **yourselves,** ustedes mismos

youth, *n.* juventud, adolescencia, *f.*; joven, *m.*

youthful, *adj.* juvenil

Z

zeal, *n.* celo, ardor, ahinco , *m.*

zebra, *n.* cebra, *f.*

zero, *n.* cero, *m.*

zest, *n.* gusto, fervor, *m.*

zigzag, *n.* zigzag, *m.*

zinc, *n.* (chem.) cinc, zinc, *m.*; **zinc chloride,** cloruro de cinc, *m.*

zipper, *n.* cremallera, *f.*; cierre automático, *m.*

zone, *n.* zona, *f.*

zoo, *n.* jardín zoológico, *m.*

zoological, *adj.* zoológico

zoology, *n.* zoología, *f.*

A Taste of Spain

Spain offers a variety of food and that echoes throughout the western world. In the Americas, the Spanish style is reflected in the traditional dishes of Central and South America, as well as those of the Caribbean. We thought you might enjoy a sampling, some familiar and some not so familiar, but all guaranteed to be delicious.

Chili con Queso

2 tablespoons olive oil
½ cup onion, finely chopped
1 tablespoon flour
2 cups canned tomatoes, finely chopped, with liquid
½ cup green chilies, finely chopped
1 teaspoon chili powder
3 cups Monterey Jack cheese, shredded

1. Heat olive oil in a heavy skillet and sauté the onion until tender. Stir in flour and continue cooking for 2 minutes.
2. Stir in tomatoes, chilies, and chili powder. Simmer, stirring often, for 15 minutes or until the mixture has thickened somewhat.
3. Reduce the heat and add the cheese, stirring until melted. Serve warmed with fresh vegetables, tortilla chips, or bread for dipping.

Refried Beans

4 tablespoons bacon fat
2 tablespoons onions, finely chopped
2 cups kidney or pinto beans, cooked & drained
Salt

1. Heat the fat in a heavy skillet and sauté the onion just until soft.
2. Add beans to the pan and cook while mashing with a fork until all of the fat is absorbed and the beans are fairly dry.
3. Salt to taste.

NOTES: Flavor the beans with a bit of tomato paste, hot chili powder, or salsa.

—Spread refried beans over tortillas, or thin with a bit of broth to serve as a dip.

Party Quesadillas

This simplified version of the traditional Mexican preparation, sort of a cross between a quesadilla and a tostada, is a great way to add variety to a buffet or snack table.

½ cup mayonnaise
¼ cup salsa
2½ cups cheese, shredded
8 10-inch flour tortillas
Olive oil

1. Combine mayonnaise, salsa, and cheese.
2. Spread cheese mixture over 4 tortillas and cover with remaining 4 tortillas.
3. Brush tops with olive oil and brown under the broiler for about 1 minute. Turn, brush with olive oil, and brown the other side.
4. Cut into wedges and serve.

NOTES: Use any cheese that melts well such as Jack, Muenster, or cheddar.

For variety, garnish each serving with a thin avocado slice or spread with guacamole.

—Spread a thin layer of refried beans over the second tortilla before putting the sandwich together.

Easy Salsa

1 cup canned tomatoes, diced or crushed
¼ cup onions, finely chopped
1 small hot red or green pepper, minced
½ teaspoon coriander
1 clove garlic, minced
Pinch of cloves
Salt & pepper

Combine all measured ingredients well. Season with salt and pepper to taste. Refrigerate 1 to 2 hours to blend flavors. Serve with chips for dipping or over cold meat, poultry, or fish.

Chicken with Salsa

Serves 4

1 or 2 large chicken breasts, about 2 pounds
2 bay leaves
Pinch of thyme
¼ cup parsley, chopped

1. Place chicken breasts in a skillet with about ½ inch of water containing 1 bay leaf and a pinch of thyme. Bring water to a boil; reduce heat and simmer covered for 20 to 30 minutes or until cooked through. Set aside to cool.
2. While chicken cooks, prepare *Easy Salsa*.
3. Remove skin from chicken and carefully cut the flesh into ¼-inch-thick slices. Overlap slices on a serving platter or on individual plates and spread salsa over. Sprinkle with parsley. Serve cold.

For variety, green olives may be added to the sauce.

Spanish Chicken

Serves 4

2 tablespoons olive oil
2½ to 3 pound chicken, cut into serving pieces
1½ cups onions, sliced
¾ cup green peppers, cut into strips
½ cup lean smoked ham, finely chopped
1 teaspoon garlic, minced
4 cups tomatoes, fresh or canned, peeled, seeded, & finely chopped
Salt & pepper
12 each black & green olives, sliced

1. Heat 1 tablespoon olive oil in a heavy skillet and brown chicken lightly on all sides, adding more oil if needed. Remove chicken from the pan and set aside.
2. Add onion, pepper, ham, and garlic to the pan and sauté until the vegetables are barely soft.
3. Add tomatoes to the pan and bring to a boil.
4. Return chicken to the pan, turning to coat with sauce. Cook for 30 minutes, or until chicken is cooked through.
5. Remove chicken from the pan and boil until the sauce has thickened. Season to taste with salt and pepper. Stir in the olives, and serve.

Chicken with Green Chilies

¼ cup canned green chili peppers
1 cup onion, chopped
1 teaspoon garlic, crushed
¾ cup chicken broth
1 tablespoon vinegar
1 teaspoon sugar
½ teaspoon coriander seeds, finely ground
¼ teaspoon cinnamon, finely ground
¼ teaspoon cloves, finely ground
1 cup tomatoes, crushed or diced, drained
2 tablespoons olive oil
1 chicken, about 3 pounds, cut into serving pieces
Salt & pepper

1. In a blender, purée the chili peppers, onion, and garlic with the chicken broth or force the ingredients through a food mill and a strainer.
2. In a large bowl, combine purée with the vinegar, sugar, coriander, cinnamon, cloves and tomatoes; set aside.
3. Have ready a baking dish large enough to hold the chicken in one layer. In a heavy skillet, heat the olive oil and sauté the chicken a few pieces at a time, turning to brown well on all sides. As chicken pieces are ready, dip them in the bowl to coat with sauce and place them in the baking dish.
4. Pour remaining sauce over the chicken and bake at 350° for about 1 hour, or until chicken is cooked through. About 45 minutes into the baking, baste chicken parts with the sauce or turn them over.
5. When chicken is done, remove to a serving platter. Skim off fat and boil liquid in a sauce pan to reduce it. Serve over the chicken.

Skimming fat from pan juices is easier if the liquid is poured into a heatproof container and placed in the freezer. After a few minutes, fat will rise to the top. If time permits, chill for about 30 minutes and the fat will solidify.

Paella

A classic Spanish dish.

Serves 8

¼ cup olive oil
1 frying chicken, cut up, or about 3 pounds of chicken parts
½ cup onion, sliced or chopped
2 cloves garlic, minced
½ pound tomatoes, peeled, fresh or canned
2 cups rice, uncooked
1 teaspoon saffron dissolved in 4 cups water
Salt & pepper
1 cup peas, fresh or frozen
1 sweet red pepper, cut into strips
¼ pound medium shrimp, shelled
8 each clams and mussels in the shell

---

1. In a large skillet or kettle, heat the olive oil and brown the chicken on all sides.

2. Add the onion and continue to cook while stirring until the onion is transparent.

3. Add garlic, tomatoes, rice, saffron, and water. Stir to combine. Add salt and pepper to taste. Cover and cook for 15 minutes over low heat.

4. Stir the pot from top to bottom to prevent rice from browning. Arrange peas and red pepper strips over the top of the rice and cook for 10 more minutes.
   Note: If canned peas are used, add them with the seafood.

5. Arrange shrimp, clams, and mussels on top of the rice. Cover and cook for 5 to 10 minutes, or until the shellfish open. Serve in the skillet or kettle and enjoy!
   Note: Check the rice to be sure that it does not overcook. If the rice is already tender, steam the seafood in a separate pot with a small amount of water. If rice is very firm, cook for about 5 minutes longer before adding seafood.

NOTE: The traditional paella pan is a large covered skillet with metal handles on two sides, somewhat like a heavy wok with a flat bottom, although an iron kettle also serves very well.

Cocido (Spanish Stew)

Another classic, not so well known as paella, but one that qualifies as our all–time favorite. Don't let the long list of ingredients daunt you. Works great in a crock pot as well, using canned chick peas—merely combine all the ingredients and cook on low for several hours.

Serves 4

1 pound dried chick peas
1 pound lean beef, cut into 1-inch cubes
1 cup onion, chopped
1 cup fresh tomato, diced
¼ cup green pepper, chopped
1 clove garlic, minced
¼ pound Canadian bacon, diced
½ pound pumpkin, cut into 1-inch cubes
½ cup carrots, sliced thick
2 Spanish or Italian sausages, sliced thick
1 pound potatoes, peeled & cubed
½ pound green beans, cut in 1-inch pieces
½ teaspoon cumin
Salt & pepper

1. Soak chick peas overnight or boil for 2 minutes, then cover and allow to rest for 1 hour.
2. Add the beef, onion, tomatoes, green pepper, garlic, and Canadian bacon to the pot with the beans. Pour in sufficient water to cover and simmer with the pot covered, until the chick peas are tender, about 1 hour. If necessary, add more water as the beans cook.
3. Stir in the pumpkin, carrots, sausage, potatoes, green beans, and cumin. Cook for an additional 30 minutes, or until vegetables are tender.
4. Correct the seasoning and serve.

Tex-Mex Chili

3 thin strips bacon
1½ pounds lean beef, chuck or round, diced; or 1½
   pounds lean ground beef
1 cup onion, minced
2 cups tomatoes, canned, crushed or diced, with juice
1 bay leaf
½ teaspoon each cinnamon & salt
1 tablespoon cumin
3 tablespoons chili powder, or to taste

1. Over low heat in a large skillet, fry bacon until crisp and set aside.
2. In fat remaining in the pan, sauté beef, shaking the pan to brown on all sides. Add onion and continue cooking until lightly colored.
3. Crumble the bacon and return to the pan with tomato, bay leaf, cinnamon, salt, cumin, and chili powder. Cover and simmer for 1 hour.
4. Correct seasoning and serve with tortillas or crackers, chopped onion, and shredded cheese.

NOTES: If ground meat is used, brown in a small amount of oil, then pour off the rendered fat before combining with bacon fat and sautéed onions.

—Serve chili over beans, spaghetti, or rice.

—Beans can be cooked with the chili—add 3 to 4 cups of cooked kidney, navy, or pinto beans for the final 30 minutes of cooking.

—For a spicier dish, add chopped jalapeños or pepper sauce.

—If chili is too thick, stir in a little water and cook for 5 to 10 minutes to blend flavors.

HEALTH NOTE: 2 tablespoons olive oil can be substituted for the bacon and bacon fat.

For variety, use a mixture of beef and pork.

—Minced green peppers can be sautéed with the onions.

—A clove of garlic, minced, can be added to the pan with the tomatoes and beans.

Arroz con Pollo (Chicken with Rice)

Serves 4

¼ cup olive oil
2½ to 3 pound chicken, cut into serving pieces
1 cup rice, uncooked
¼ cup onion, finely chopped
1 clove garlic, minced
2 cups canned tomatoes, diced, with liquid
½ teaspoon oregano
Dash of hot sauce
Salt & pepper
1 cup canned peas or frozen & cooked peas

1. Heat olive oil in a large, heavy skillet and brown chicken pieces on all sides. Remove chicken and set aside.
2. In the same pan, heat rice, onion, and garlic, stirring until onion is softened and the rice takes on a bit of color.
3. Return the chicken to the pan with tomatoes, oregano, hot sauce, and 1 cup water. Cover and simmer gently for 20 minutes or just until rice is soft, chicken is cooked through and most of the liquid has been absorbed.
4. Season with salt and pepper to taste and carefully mix in the peas. Continue cooking just to heat through.

Turkey Españole

Serves 4

½ pound loose sausage, preferable Spanish
1 cup rice, uncooked
1 cup tomatoes, crushed or diced
¼ teaspoon saffron
2 cups chicken broth
1½ cups cooked turkey, diced
½ cup green peppers, cut into thin strips
¼ cup onion, finely chopped
½ teaspoon ground cumin
1 clove garlic, minced
2 tablespoons pimientos, chopped

more...

1. Brown the sausage in a large heavy skillet.
2. Add rice and cook until the rice takes on a bit of color.
3. Add tomatoes and cook for 5 minutes.
4. Dissolve saffron in the then add to the pan with turkey, peppers, onion, cumin, and garlic. Cook, covered, over low heat for 40 minutes or until rice is tender. Stir in pimientos and continue cooking just to heat through.

Pork Mexicaine

Serves 4

1 cup flat beer
2 tablespoons soy sauce
2 tablespoons brown sugar
1 tablespoon dry mustard
2 cloves garlic, minced
Hot pepper sauce or chili peppers
Salt & pepper
1½ pounds lean pork, sliced or cubed
1 fresh lime

1. Combine the beer, soy sauce, sugar, mustard, garlic, and hot sauce or peppers to taste in a saucepan. Heat briefly and stir just to combine flavors. Season with salt and pepper to taste. Set aside to cool.
2. Cover meat with the marinade and refrigerate overnight, stirring occasionally.
3. Thread meat on skewers or place loose in a broiler pan. Broil about 4 inches from the heat, basting often with the marinade, for 15 minutes or until the meat is cooked through.
4. Sprinkle with lime juice and serve.

NOTE: If wooden skewer are used, soak them in water for at least an hour ahead of time.

Chili Bake

1 pound lean ground beef
2 thin strips bacon
½ cup onion, minced
¼ cup green pepper, minced
¾ cup tomatoes, canned, crushed, with juice
¼ teaspoon each cinnamon, allspice, & salt
2 teaspoons chili powder, or to taste
Tortilla chips, about 5 ounces
½ cup cheddar cheese, shredded

1. In a large skillet, brown beef using a little oil if necessary. Drain off oil and set beef aside.

2. Over low heat in the same skillet, fry bacon until crisp and set aside.

3. Sauté onion and pepper in bacon grease, just until soft. Crumble bacon and return to pan with meat, tomato, cinnamon, allspice, salt, and chili powder. Simmer for about 1 hour covered.

4. In an oven dish, place alternating layers of chips and chili, beginning with chips and ending with chili. Cover with cheese and bake at 350° for 20 to 30 minutes.

THE NEW INTERNATIONAL
WEBSTER'S
GUIDE TO
ENGLISH
SPELLING

TRIDENT
PRESS
INTERNATIONAL

Published by
Trident Press International
2002 Edition

Cover Design Copyright • Trident Press International
Copyright © Trident Press International

ISBN 1582794391

aard´vark
aard´wolf
a·back´
ab´a-cus
a·bac-te´ri·al
a·baft´
ab-a-lo´ne
a·ban´don
a·ban´don-a·ble
a·ban´doned
a·ban´don·er
a·ban´don-ment
a·base´
a·based´
a·bas´ed·ly
a·base´ment
a·bas´er
a·bash´
a·bash´ed·ly
a·bash´ment
a·bas´ing
a·bat´a·ble
a·bate´
a·bate´ment
a·bat´er
a·bat´ing
ab-ax´i·al
ab´ba·cy
ab-bé´
ab´bess
ab´bey
ab´bot
ab´bot·cy
ab-bre´vi-ate
ab-bre´vi-at·ed
ab-bre´vi-at-ing
ab-bre-vi-a´tion

ab-bre´vi-a-tor
ab-bre´vi-a-to·ry
ab´di-ca·ble
ab´di-cate
ab´di-cat-ing
ab-di-ca´tion
ab´di-ca-tive
ab´di-ca-tor
ab´do-men
ab-dom´i-nal
ab-dom´i-nal·ly
ab-du´cent
ab-duct´
ab-duc´tion
ab-duc´tor
a·beam´
a·be-ce-dar´i·an
a·bcd´
ab-er´rance
ab-er´ran·cy
ab-er´rant
ab-er´rant·ly
ab-er-ra´tion
ab·er·ra´tion·al
a·bet´
a·bet´ment
a·bet´tal
a·bet´ted
a·bet´ting
a·bet´tor
a·bey´ance
a·bey´ant
ab-hor´
ab-horred´
ab-hor´rence
ab-hor´rent
ab-hor´rent·ly

ab-hor´ring
a·bid´ance
a·bide´
a·bid´ing
a·bid´ing·ly
a·bid´ing-ness
a·bil´i-ties
a·bil´i·ty
a·bi-o-gen´e-sis
a·bi-o-ge-net´ic
a·bi-o-gen´ic
a·bi-og´e-nist
a·bi-ot´ic
ab-ject´, ab´ject
ab-jec´tion
ab-ject´ly
ab-ject´ness
ab-ju-ra´tion
ab-jur´a-to·ry
ab-jure´
ab-jur´er
ab-jur´ing
ab-late´
ab-la´tion
ab´la-tive
ab´laut
a·blaze´
a´ble
able–bodied
a´bler
a´blest
a·bloom´
ab´lu-ent
ab-lu´tion
ab-lu´tion-ar·y
a´bly
ab´ne-gate

1

ab-ne-ga´tion
ab´ne-ga-tive
ab´ne-ga-tor
ab-nor´mal
ab-nor-mal´i-ties
ab-nor-mal´i·ty
ab-nor´mal·ly
ab-nor´mal-ness
ab-nor´mi·ty
a·board´
a·bode´
a·boil´
a·bol´ish
a·bol´ish-a·ble
a·bol´ish·er
a·bol´ish-ment
ab-o-li´tion
ab-o-li´tion-ism
ab-o-li´tion-ist
a·bom´i-na·ble
a·bom´i-na·ble-ness
a·bom´i-na·bly
a·bom´i-nate
a·bom´i-nat·ed
a·bom-i-na´tion
ab-o-rig´i-nal
ab-o-rig-i-nal´i·ty
ab-o-rig´i-nal·ly
ab-o-rig´i·ne
a·bort´
a·bor´ti-cide
a·bor´ti-fa´cient
a·bor´tion
a·bor´tion-ist
a·bort´ive

a·bor´tive·ly
a·bor´tive-ness
a·bound´
a·bound´ing
a·bound´ing·ly
a·bout´
about–face
a·bove´
a·bove´board
a·bove´ground
a·bove´men-tioned
ab-ra-ca-dab´ra
a-brad´a·ble
a·brad´ant
a·brade´
a·brad´ed
a·brad´er
a·brad´ing
a·bran´chi·an
a·bran´chi-ate
a·bra-si-om´e-ter
a·bra´sion
a·bra´sive
a·bra´sive·ly
a·bra´sive-ness
ab-re-act´
ab-re-ac´tion
ab-re-ac´tive
a·breast´
a·bridge´
a·bridge´a·ble
a·bridg´er
a·bridg´ing
a·bridg´ment
a·bris´tle
a·broach´

a·broad´
ab´ro-ga·ble
ab´ro-gate
ab´ro-gat·ed
ab´ro-gat-ing
ab-ro-ga´tion
ab´ro-ga-tive
ab´ro-ga-tor
ab-rupt´
ab-rup´tion
ab-rupt´ly
ab-rupt´ness
ab´scess
ab´scessed
ab-scise´
ab-scis´sa
ab-scis´sion
ab-scond´
ab-scond´ed
ab-scond´ence
ab-scond´er
ab´sence
ab´sent *(adj.)*
ab-sent´ *(v.)*
ab-sen-ta´tion
ab-sen-tee´
ab-sen-tee´ism
ab´sent·ly
ab´sent-mind·ed
ab´sent-ness
ab´sinthe
ab-sin´thi-an
ab´so-lute
ab´so-lute´ly
ab-so-lute´ness
ab´so-lu´tion
ab´so-lut-ism

2

ab´so-lut-ist
ab-so-lu-tis´tic
ab´so-lu-tive
ab´so-lut-ize
ab-sol´u-to·ry
ab-solv´a·ble
ab-solve´
ab-solved´
ab-sol´vent
ab-solv´er
ab-solv´ing
ab-sorb´
ab-sorb´a·ble
ab-sorb-a-bil´i·ty
ab-sorb´ance
ab-sorbed´
ab-sorb´ed·ly
ab-sorb´ed-ness
ab-sorb´en·cy
ab-sorb´ent
ab-sorb´er
ab-sorb´ing
ab-sorb´ing·ly
ab-sorp´tance
ab-sorp´tion
ab-sorp´tive
ab-stain´
ab-stained´
ab-stain´er
ab-ste´mi-ous
ab-ste´mi-ous·ly
ab-sten´tion
ab-sten´tious
ab-ster´gent
ab-ster´sion
ab´sti-nence
ab´sti-nent

ab´sti-nent·ly
ab´stract *(n.,*
   adj.)
ab-stract´ *(v.)*
ab-stract´ed
ab-stract´ed·ly
ab-stract´er
ab-strac´tion
ab-strac´tion·al
ab-strac´tive
ab-strac´tive·ly
ab´stract·ly
ab´stract-ness
ab-stric´tion
ab-struse´
ab-struse´ly
ab-struse´ness
ab-surd´
ab-surd´ism
ab-surd´i·ty
ab-surd´ly
ab-surd´ness
a·bub´ble
a·bu´li·a
a·bu´lic
a·bun´dance
a·bun´dant
a·bun´dant·ly
a·bus´a·ble
a·buse´
a·bused´
a·bus´er
a·bus´ing
a·bu´sive
a·bu´sive·ly
a·bu´sive-ness
a·but´

a·but´ment
a·but´tal
a·but´ted
a·but´ter
a·but´ting
a·buzz´
a·bysm´
a·bys´mal
a·bys´mal·ly
a·byss´
a·byss´al
a·ca´cia
ac´a-deme
ac-a-de´mi·a
ac-a-dem´ic
ac-a-dem´i-cal
ac-a-dem´i-cal·ly
ac-a-de-mi´cian
ac-a-dem´ics
a·cad´e·my
a·cap-pel´la
a·cau´dal
a·cau´date
a·cau-les´cent
a·cau´line
a·caus´al
a·cau-sal´i·ty
ac-cede´
ac-ced´ence
ac-ce-le-ran´do
ac-cel´er-ant
ac-cel´er-ate
ac-cel-er-a´tion
ac-cel´er-a-tive
ac-cel´er-a-tor
ac-cel´er-a-to·ry
ac´cent *(n., v.)*

3

ac-cent´ *(v.)*
ac-cen´tu-ate
ac-cen-tu-a´tion
ac-cept´
ac-cept-a-bil´i·ty
ac-cept´a·ble
ac-cept´a·bly
ac-cept´ance
ac-cept´ant
ac-cep-ta´tion
ac-cept´ed
ac-cep´tor
ac´cess
ac-ces´sa·ry
ac-ces-si-bil´i·ty
ac-ces´si·ble
ac-ces´si·bly
ac-ces´sion
ac-ces-so´ri·al
ac-ces´so-ri·ly
ac-ces´so-rize
ac-ces´so·ry
ac´ci-dence
ac´ci-dent
ac-ci-den´tal
ac-ci-den´tal·ly
ac-cip´i-tral
ac-claim´
ac-claim´ing
ac-cla-ma´tion
ac-clam´a-to·ry
ac-cli´mat-a·ble
ac-cli´mate
ac-cli´mat·ed
ac-cli-ma´tion
ac-cli-ma-ti-
  za´tion

ac-cli´ma-tize
ac-cliv´i·ty
ac-cli´vous
ac-co-lade´
ac´co-lade
ac-com´mo-date
ac-com´mo-dat-
  ing
ac-c o m - m o -
  da´tion
ac-com´pa-nied
ac-com´pa-nies
ac-com´pa-ni-
  ment
ac-com´pa-nist
ac-com´pa·ny
ac-com´plice
ac-com´plish
ac-com´plished
ac-com´plish-
  ment
ac-compt´
ac-cord´
ac-cord´a·ble
ac-cord´ance
ac-cord´ant
ac-cord´ed
ac-cord´ing
ac-cord´ing·ly
ac-cor´di·on
ac-cor´di-on-ist
ac-cost´
ac-couche-ment´
ac-cou-cheur´
ac-count´
ac-count-a·bil´-
  i·ty

ac-count´a·ble
ac-count´a·bly
ac-count´an·cy
ac-count´ant
ac-count´ing
ac-cou´ter
ac-cou´ter-ment
ac-cred´it
ac-cres´cence
ac-crete´
ac-cre´tion
ac-cre´tive
ac-cru´al
ac-crue´
ac-crue´ment
ac-cru´ing
ac-cul-tur-a´tion
ac-cum´ben·cy
ac-cum´bent
ac-cu´mu-late
ac-cu´mu-lat-ing
ac-cu´mu-la´tion
ac-cu´mu-la-tive
ac-cu´mu-la-tor
ac´cu-ra·cy
ac´cu-rate
ac´cu-rate·ly
ac´cu-rate-ness
ac-curs´ed
ac-curs´ed·ly
ac-cus´al
ac-cu-sa´tion
ac-cu´sa-tive
ac-cu´sa-tive·ly
ac-cus´a-to·ry
ac-cuse´
ac-cused´

4

ac-cus´er
ac-cus´ing
ac-cus´ing·ly
ac-cus´tom
ac-cus´tomed
ace
ac´er-bate
a·cer´bic
a·cer´bi·ty
ac´er-ose
ache
ached
a·che´ni·al
a·chiev´a·ble
a·chieve´
a·chieved´
a·chieve´ment
a·chiev´ing
ach´i·ness
ach´ing·ly
ach-ro-mat´ic
a·chro´ma-tism
a·chro´ma-tize
a·chro´ma-tous
ach´y
ac´id
a·cid´ic
a-cid´i-fi-a·ble
a·cid-i-fi-ca´tion
a·cid´i-fied
a·cid´i·fy
a·cid´i·ty
ac-i-doph´i-lus
a·cid´u-late
a·cid-u-la´tion
a·cid´u-lous
acid–washed

ac-knowl´edge
ac-knowl´edge-
   a·ble
ac-knowl´edged
ac-knowl´edg-
   ing
ac-knowl´edg-
   ment
a·clin´ic
ac´me
ac´ne
ac´o-lyte
a´corn
a·cous´tic
a·cous´ti-cal
a·cous´ti-cal·ly
ac-ous-ti´cian
ac-quaint´
ac-quaint´ance
ac-quaint´ance-
   ship
ac-quaint´ed
ac-qui-esce´
ac-qui-es´cence
ac-qui-es´cent
ac-qui-es´cent·ly
ac-qui-esc´ing
ac-qui-esc´ing·ly
ac-quir-a-bil´i·ty
ac-quir´a·ble
ac-quire´
ac-quire´ment
ac-quir´er
ac-quir´ing
ac-qui-si´tion
ac-qui-si´tion·al
ac-quis´i-tive

ac-quis´i-tor
ac-quit´
ac-quit´tal
ac-quit´ted
ac-quit´ting
a´cre
a´cre-age
ac´rid
a·crid´i·ty
ac´rid·ly
ac´rid‒ness
ac-ri-mo´ni-ous
ac´ri-mo·ny
ac´ro-bat
ac-ro-bat´ic
ac´ro-nym
ac-ro-pho´bi·a
ac-ro-pho´bic
a·cross´
a·cryl´ic
act
act´able
act´ing
ac´tion
ac´tion-a·ble
ac´tion-less
ac´ti-vate
ac-ti-va´tion
ac´ti-va-tor
ac´tive
ac´tive·ly
ac´tive-ness
ac´tiv-ism
ac´tiv-ist
ac-tiv´i-ties
ac-tiv´i·ty
ac´tor

5

ac´tress
ac´tu·al
ac-tu-al´i·ty
ac-tu-al-i-za´tion
ac´tu-al-ize
ac´tu-al·ly
ac´tu-al-ness
ac-tu-ar´i·al
ac´tu-ar-ies
ac´tu-ar·y
ac´tu-ate
ac´tu-at-ing
ac-tu-a´tion
ac´tu-a-tor
ac´u-ate
a·cu´i·ty
a·cu´men
ac´u-pres-sure
ac´u-punc-ture
ac´u-punc-tur-
   ist
a·cute´
a·cute´ly
a·cute´ness
ad´age
ad´a-man·cy
ad´a-mant
ad-a-man´tine
ad´a-mant·ly
a·dapt´
a·dapt-a-bil´i·ty
a·dapt´a·ble
ad-ap-ta´tion
ad-ap-ta´tion·al
a·dapt´er
a·dapt´ive
a·dap´tive·ly

a·dap´tive-ness
ad-ap-tiv´i·ty
a·dap´tor
ad-ax´i·al
add´a·ble
add´ed
ad´dend
ad-den´da
ad-den´dum
ad´dict *(n.)*
ad-dict´ *(v.)*
ad-dict´ed
ad-dic´tion
ad-dic´tive
ad-di´tion
ad-di´tion·al
ad-di´tion-al·ly
ad´di-tive
ad´dle
ad´dled
add–on
ad-dress´
ad-dress´a·ble
ad-dress-ee´
ad-dress´er
ad-dress´ing
ad-dres´sor
ad-duce´
ad-du´cent
ad-duc´i·ble
ad-duc´ing
ad-duct´ *(v.)*
ad´duct *(n.)*
ad-duc´tion
ad-duc´tor
a·dept´ *(adj.)*
ad´ept *(n.)*

a·dept´ly
a·dept´ness
ad´e-qua·cy
ad´e-quate
ad´e-quate·ly
ad´e-quate-ness
ad-here´
ad-her´ence
ad-her´ent
ad-her´ent·ly
ad-her´ing
ad-he´sion
ad-he´sive
ad hoc
a·dieu´
ad in-fi-ni´tum
ad in´ter·im
a·dios´
ad-ja´cen·cy
ad-ja´cent
ad-ja´cent·ly
ad-jec-ti´val
ad´jec-tive
ad-join´
ad-joined´
ad-join´ing
ad-journ´
ad-journed´
ad-journ´ment
ad-judge´
ad-judg´ing
ad-ju´di-cate
ad-ju´di-cat-ing
ad-ju-di-ca´tion
ad-ju´di-ca-tive
ad-ju´di-ca-tor
ad-ju´di-ca-to·ry

ad´junct
ad-junc´tion
ad-junc´tive
ad-junct´ly
ad-ju-ra´tion
ad-jur´a-to·ry
ad-jure´
ad-ju´ror
ad-just´
ad-just-a-bil´i·ty
ad-just´a·ble
ad-just´er
ad-just´ment
ad-jus´tor
ad´ju-tant
ad´ju-vant
ad–lib *(v., adj.)*
ad lib´i-tum
ad-min´is-ter
ad-min´is-trate
ad-min-is-tra´-
　tion
ad-min´is-tra-
　tive
ad-min´is-tra-
　tive·ly
ad-min´is-tra-tor
ad´mi-ra·ble
ad´mi-ra·bly
ad´mi-ral
ad´mi-ral·ty
ad-mi-ra´tion
ad-mire´
ad-mired´
ad-mir´er
ad-mir´ing
ad-mir´ing·ly

ad-mis-si-bil´i·ty
ad-mis´si·ble
ad-mis´sion
ad-mis´sive
ad-mit´
ad-mit´tance
ad-mit´ted
ad-mit´ted·ly
ad-mit´ting
ad-mix´
ad-mix´ture
ad-mon´ish
a d - m o n ´ i s h -
　ing·ly
a d - m o n ´ i s h -
　ment
ad-mo-ni´tion
ad-mon´i-to·ry
a·do´
a·do´be
ad-o-les´cence
ad-o-les´cent
ad-o-les´cent·ly
a·dopt´
a·dopt´a·ble
a·dopt´er
a·dop´tion
a·dop´tive
a·dop´tive·ly
a·dor´a·ble
a·dor´a·bly
ad-o-ra´tion
a·dore´
a·dored´
a·dor´er
a·dor´ing
a·dor´ing·ly

a·dorn´
a·dorned´
a·dorn´ing
a·dorn´ment
a·down´
ad-ren´a-lin
a·drift´
a·droit´
a·droit´ly
a·droit´ness
ad-sorb´
ad-sorb´ent
ad-sorp´tion
ad-sorp´tive
ad´u-late
ad-u-la´tion
ad´u-la-to·ry
a·dult´
a·dul´ter-ant
a·dul´ter-ate
a·dul-ter-a´tion
a·dul´ter-a-tor
a·dul´ter·er
a·dul´ter-ess
a·dul´ter-ous
a·dul´ter·y
a·dult´hood
ad va-lo´rem
ad-vance´
ad-vanced´
ad-vance´ment
ad-vanc´ing
ad-van´tage
ad-van´taged
ad-van-ta´geous
ad´vent
ad-ven-ti´tious

ad-ven´ture
ad-ven´tur·er
a d - v e n ´ t u r e -
  some
ad-ven´tur-ous
ad´verb
ad-verb´i·al
ad´ver-sar-ies
ad´ver-sar·y
ad´verse
ad´verse·ly
ad-verse´ness
ad-ver´si·ty
ad-vert´
ad-vert´ence
ad-vert´en·cy
ad-vert´ent
ad-vert´ent·ly
ad´ver-tise
ad-ver-tise´ment
ad´ver-tis·er
ad´ver-tis-ing
ad-vice´
ad-vis-a-bil´i·ty
ad-vis´a·ble
ad-vis´a·ble-ness
ad-vis´a·bly
ad-vise´
ad-vised´
ad-vis´ed·ly
ad-vise´ment
ad-vis´er
ad-vis´ing
ad-vi´sor
ad-vis´o·ry
ad´vo-ca·cy
ad´vo-cate

ad-vo-ca´tion
ad´vo-ca-tor
ad-voc´a-to·ry
adz, adze
aer´ate
aer-a´tion
aer´a-tor
aer´i·al
aer´i-al-ist
ae´rie
aer-o-bat´ics
aer-o´bic
aer·o-dy-nam´ic
aer´o-naut
aer·o-nau´ti-cal
aer-o-pho´bi·a
aer´o-plane
aer´o-sol
aer´o-space
a´er·y
aes´thete
aes-thet´ic
aes-thet´i-cal
aes-thet´i-cal·ly
aes-thet´ics
ae´ther
a·far´
af-fa-bil´i·ty
af´fa-ble
af´fa-bly
af-fair´
af-fect´
af-fec-ta´tion
af-fect´ed
af-fect´ing
af-fect´ing·ly
af-fec´tion

af-fec´tion-ate
af-fec´tion-ate·ly
af´fer-ent
af-fi´ance
af-fi´anced
af-fil´i-ate
af-fil´i-at·ed
af-fil-i-a´tion
af-fin´i-ties
af-fin´i-tive
af-fin´i·ty
af-firm´
af-firm´a·ble
af-firm´a·bly
af-fir-ma´tion
af-firm´a-tive
af-firm´a-tive·ly
af-firm´ing·ly
affix´ *(v.)*
af´fix *(n.)*
af-flict´
af-flic´tion
af-flict´ive
af´flu-ence
af´flu-en-cy
af´flu-ent
af´flu-ent·ly
af-ford´
af-ford-a-bil´i·ty
af-ford´a·ble
af-ford´a·bly
af-fray´
af-fright´
af-front´
af-front´ive
a·fi-cio-na´do
a·field´

a·fire´
a·flame´
a·float´
a·flut´ter
a·foot´
a·fore´men-
  tioned
a·fore´said
a·fore´thought
a·fore´time
a·foul´
a·fraid´
a·fresh´
af´ter
af´ter-birth
af´ter-burn·er
af´ter-care
af´ter-deck
af´ter-ef-fect
af´ter-glow
after–hours
af´ter-im-age
af´ter-life
af´ter-math
af-ter-noon´
af´ter-shave
af´ter-shock
af´ter-taste
af´ter-thought
af´ter-ward
af´ter-wards
a·gain´
a·gainst´
a·gape´ *(ajar)*
a·ga´pe *(love)*
a-gaze´
age

aged, ag´ed
age´less
a´gen-cies
a´gen·cy
a·gen´da
a·gen´dum
a´gent
ag-glom´er-ate
ag-glom-er-a´-
  tion
ag-grade
ag-gran´dize
ag-gran´dize-
  ment
ag´gra-vate
ag´gra-vat·ed
ag´gra-vat-ing
ag´gra-va´tion
ag´gra-va-tor
ag´gre-gate
ag´gre-gate·ly
ag´gre-gat-ing
ag-gre-ga´tion
ag´gre-ga-tive
ag´gre-ga-to·ry
ag-gress´
ag-gres´sion
ag-gres´sive
ag-gres´sive·ly
ag-gres´sive-
  ness
ag-gres´sor
ag-griev´ance
ag-grieve´
ag-grieved´
a·ghast´
ag´ile

ag´ile·ly
ag´ile-ness
a·gil´i·ty
ag´ing
ag´i-tate
ag´i-tated
ag´i-tat-ed·ly
ag´i-tat-ing
ag-i-ta´tion
ag´i-ta-tive
ag´i-ta-tor
a·gleam´
a·glow´
ag-nos´tic
ag-nos´ti-cism
a·go´
a·gog´
ag´o-nist
ag-o-nis´tic
ag´o-nize
ag´o-niz-ing
ag´o·ny
ag-o-ra-pho´bi·a
a·grar´i·an
a·gree´
a·gree´a·ble
a·gree´a·bly
a·greed´
a·gree´ing
a·gree´ment
ag´ri-bus·i-ness
ag-ri-cul´tur·al
ag-ri-cul´ture
ag-ri-cul´tur-ist
a·gron´o-mist
a·gron´o·my
a·ground´

a´gue
a´gue-weed
a´gu-ish
a·head´
a·hoy´
aide–de–camp
ail´ment
aim´less
aim´less·ly
aim´less-ness
air´brush
air´craft
air´field
air´flow
air´foil
air force
air´freight
air´i·ly
air´i-ness
air´ing
air´less
air´lin·er
air´ lock
air´mail
air´man
air´plane
air pock´et
air´port
air pres´sure
air´show
air´sickness
air´speed
air´stream
air´strip
air´tight
air´ traf-fic
air´waves

air´way
air´wor·thy
air´y
aisle
a·jar´
a·kim´bo
a·kin´
al´a-bas-ter
à la carte
a·lac´ri·ty
à la king
à la mode
a·larm´
a·larm´ing
a·larm´ing·ly
a· larm´ist
a·las´
al´ba-tross
al-bi´no
al´bum
al-bu´men *(egg
white)*
al-bu´min *(pro-
tein)*
al´che-mist
al´che·my
al´co-hol
al-co-hol´ic
al-co-hol-ic´i·ty
al´co-hol-ism
al´cove
al-co-vi-nom´e-
ter
al den´te
al´der
al´der-man
al-der-man´ic

ale
ale´house
a·lert´
a·lert´ly
a·lert´ness
al-fres´co
al´ga, al´gae
al´ge-bra
al-ge-bra´ic
al-ge-bra´i-cal
al-ge-bra´i-cal·ly
al´go-rithm
a´li·as
al´i·bi
al´i-bi-ing
al´ien
al´ien-a·ble
al´ien-ate
al´ien-at-ing
al´ien-a´tion
al´ien-ist
a·light´
a·lign´
a·lign´ment
a·like´
al´i-ment
al-i-men´ta·ry
al-i-men-ta´tion
al´i-mo·ny
a·line´
a·line´ment
a·live´
al´ka·li
al´ka-line
al-ka-lin´i·ty
al´ka-loid
all–around

al-lay´
al-lay´ing
all–day
al-le-ga´tion
al-lege´
al-lege´a·ble
al-leged´
al-leg´ed·ly
al-le´giance
al-leg´ing
al-le-gor´ic
al-le-gor´i-cal
al-le-gor´i-cal·ly
al´le-go-ries
al´le-go-rize
al´le·go·ry
al´ler-gen
al´ler-gen´ic
al´ler´gic
al´ler-gist
al´ler·gy
al-le´vi-ate
al-le´vi-at-ing
al-le-vi-a´tion
al-le´vi-a-tive
al´ley
al´ley-way
al-li´ance
al-lied´
al-lies´
al´li-ga-tor
all–important
al-lit´er-ate
al-lit-er-a´tion
al-lit´er-a-tive
all–night
al´lo-cate

al´lo-cat-ing
al-lo-ca´tion
al-lot´
al-lot´ment
al-lot´ted
al-lot´ting
all–out
all–over
al-low´
al-low´a·ble
al-low´ance
al-lowed´
al´loy
all–powerful
all–purpose
all right
all–round
all-spice
all–star
al-lude´
al-lure
al-lured´
al-lure´ment
al-lur´ing
al-lu´sion
al-lu´sive
al-lu´sive·ly
al-lu´sive-ness
al´ly (n.)
al·ly´ (v.)
al-ly´ing
al´ma-nac
al-might´y
al´mond
al´mo-ner
al´most
a·loft´

a·lone´
a·long´
a·long-side´
a·loof´
a·loof´ness
a·loud´
al´pha
al´pha-bet
al-pha-bet´ic
al´pha-bet´i-cal
al´pha-bet-ize
al-read´y
al-right´
al´tar
al´tar-piece
al´ter
al-ter-a-bil´i·ty
al´ter-a-ble
al-ter-a´tion
al´ter-cate
al-ter-ca´tion
al´ter-nate
al´ter-nat·ed
al´ter-nate·ly
al´ter-nat-ing
al-ter-na´tion
al-ter´na-tive
al´ter-na-tor
al-though´
al´ti-tude
al´to
al´to-geth·er
al´tru-ism
al´tru-ist
al-tru-is´ti-cal·ly
al-u-min´i·um
a·lum´ni

11

a·lum´nus
al´ways
a·mal´ga-mate
a·mal-ga-ma´-
　tion
a·mal´ga-ma-tor
a·man-u-en´sis
am-a-ret´to
a·mass´
a·mass´a·ble
a·mass´ment
am´a-teur
am´a-teur-ish
am´a-teur-ism
am´a-to·ry
a·maze´
a·mazed´
a·maz´ed·ly
a·maze´ment
a·maz´ing
a·maz´ing·ly
am-bas´sa-dor
am-bas-sa-do´
　ri·al
am´bi-ance
am-bi-dex´trous
am´bi-ence
am´bi-ent
am-bi-gu´i·ty
am-big´u-ous
am-bi´tion
am-bi´tious
am-biv´a-lence
am-biv´a-lent
am´ble
am´bled
am´bling

am-bro´si·a
am´bu-lance
am´bu-la-to·ry
am´bush
am´bushed
am´bush·er
a·me´lio-rate
a·me-lio-ra´tion
a·me´lio-ra-tive
a·me´lio-ra-tor
a´men´
a·me-na-bil´i·ty
a·me´na·ble
a·mend´
a·mend´a·ble
a·mend´a-to·ry
a·mend´ed
a·mend´ment
a·mends´
a·men´i-ties
a·men´i·ty
a·mi-a-bil´i·ty
a´mi-a·ble
a´mi-a·bly
am-i-ca-bil´i·ty
am´i-ca·ble
am´i-ca·bly
a·mid´
a·midst´
a·miss´
am´i·ty
am-ne´sia
am-ne´si·ac
am´nes·ty
a·moe´ba
a·mong´
a·mongst´

a·mor´al
a·mo-ral´i·ty
a·mor´al·ly
am-o-ret´to
am´o-rous
a·mor´phous
am´or-tize
am´or-tiz-ing
a·mount´
am´per-age
am´pere
am´per-sand
am-phet´a-mine
am-phib´i·an
am-phib´i-ous
am-phib´i-ous·ly
am´phi-the-a-ter
am´ple
am´ple-ness
am-pli-fi-ca´tion
am´pli-fied
am´pli-fi·er
am´pli-fy
am´pli-fy-ing
am´pli-tude
am´ply
am´pu-tate
am´pu-tat-ing
am-pu-ta´tion
am´pu-tee´
a·muck´
am´u-let
a·muse´
a·muse´ment
a·mus´ing
a·nach´ro-nism
a·nach-ro-nis´tic

a·nae´mi·a *(Br.)*
an-al-ge´sic
an´a-log
a·nal´o-gies
a·nal´o-gize
a·nal´o-gous
a·nal´o-gous·ly
an´a-logue
a·nal´o·gy
an´a-lyse *(Br.)*
a·nal´y-ses
a·nal´y-sis
an´a-lyst
an-a-lyt´ic
an-a-lyt´i-cal
an-a-lyt´i-cal·ly
an´a-lyze
an´a-lyz-ing
an´ar-chism
an´ar-chist
an-ar-chis´tic
an´ar-chy
a·nath´e·ma
an-a-tom´i-cal
a·nat´o-mist
a·nat´o-mize
a·nat´o·my
an´ces-tor
an-ces´tral
an´ces-try
an´chor
an´chor-age
an´cho-ret
an´cho-vies, an-
  cho´vies
an´cho-vy
an-cho´vy

an´cient
an´cil-lar·y
and´i-ron
an´droid
an´ec-dot·al
an´ec-dote
a·ne´mi·a
a·ne´mic
an-es-the´sia
an-es-the-si-ol´-
  o-gist
an-es-thet´ic
a·nes´the-tist
a·nes´the-tize
an´eu-rysm
a·new´
an´gel
an´gel-fish
an-gel´ic
an´ger
an-gi´na
an-gi-os´to·my
an´gle
an´gler
an´gle-worm
an´gling
an´gri·ly
an´gri-ness
an´gry
an´guish
an´guished
an´gu-lar
an-gu-lar´i·ty
an´i-mal
an´i-mal-ism
an´i-mate
an´i-mat·ed

an´i-mat-ed·ly
an´i-mat-ing
an-i-ma´tion
an´i-ma-tor
an-i-mos´i·ty
an´i-mus
an´ise
an´i-seed
an-i-sette´
an´kle
an´klet
an´nal
an-neal´
an-nealed´
an-nex´ *(v.)*
an´nex *(n.)*
an-nex-a´tion
an-ni´hi-late
an-ni-hi-la´tion
an-ni´hi-la-tor
an-ni-ver´sa-ries
an-ni-ver´sa·ry
an´no-tate
an-no-ta´tion
an´no-ta-tor
an-nounce´
an-nounce´ment
an-nounc´er
an-nounc´ing
an-noy´
an-noy´ance
an-noyed´
an-noy´ing
an´nu·al
an´nu-al-ize
an´nu-al·ly
an-nu´i·ty

13

an-nul´
an-nulled´
an-nul´ling
an-nul´ment
an´num
an-nun´ci-ate
an-nun-ci-a´tion
an-nun´ci-a-tor
a·noint´
a·noint´ed
a·noint´er
a·noint´ment
a·nom´a-lous
a·nom´a-lous·ly
a·nom´a·ly
an-o-nym´i·ty
a·non´y-mous
a·non´y-mous·ly
an-o-rex´i·a
an-o-rex´ic
an-oth´er
an´swer
an´swer-a·ble
an´swered
an´swer-ing
an-tag´o-nism
an-tag´o-nist
an-tag-o-nis´tic
an-tag´o-nize
an´te
an´te-bel´lum
an-te-cede´
an-te-ced´ence
an-te-ced´ent
an´te-cham-ber
an´te-date
an-ten´na

an-te´ri·or
an´te-room
an´them
an-thol´o·gy
an´thro-poid
an-thro-po-log´i-
  cal
an-thro-pol´o-
  gist
an-thro-pol´o·gy
an-thro-po-
  morph´ic
an-thro-po-
  mor´phize
an´ti
an-ti-bi-ot´ic
an´ti-bod-ies
an´ti-bod·y
an´tic
an-tic´i-pate
an-tic´i-pat·ed
an-tic´i-pat-ing
an-tic-i-pa´tion
an-tic´i-pa-tive
an-tic´i-pa-to·ry
an-ti-cli´max
an´ti-dote
an´ti-freeze
an-ti-grav´i·ty
an-ti-his´ta-
  mine
an´ti-mat-ter
an-ti-pas´to
an-tip´a-thy
an´ti-quate
an´ti-quat·ed
an´ti-quat-ing

an-tique´
an-tiq´ui·ty
an-ti-sep´tic
an-ti-so´cial
an-tith´e-sis
an-ti-thet´ic
an-ti-thet´i-cal
an-ti-thet´i-cal·ly
an-ti-trust´
an´to-nym
an´vil
anx-i´e·ty
anx´ious
anx´ious·ly
an´y
an´y-bod·y
an´y-how
an-y-more´
an´y-one
an´y-place
an´y-thing
an´y-time
an´y-way
an´y-where
a·part´
a·part´heid
a·part´ment
ap-a-thet´ic
ap-a-thet´i-cal·ly
ap´a-thy
a ·pér-i-tif´
ap´er-ture
a´pex
aph´o-rism
aph-o-ris´tic
a´pi-ar·y
a·piece´

a·poc´a-lypse
a·poc-a-lyp´tic
a·poc´ry-phal
a-po-lit´i-cal
a·pol-o-get´ic
a·pol-o-get´i-cal·ly
ap-o-lo´gi·a
a·pol´o-gies
a·pol´o-gise *(Br.)*
a·pol´o-gist
a·pol´o-gize
a·pol´o-giz-ing
a·pol´o·gy
ap-os-tol´ic
ap-os-tol´i-cal
a·pos´tro-phe
a·poth´e-car·y
ap-pal´ *(Br.)*
ap-pall´
ap-pall´ing
ap-pall´ing·ly
ap-pa-rat´us
ap-par´el
ap-par´ent
ap-par´ent·ly
ap-pa-ri´tion
ap-peal´
ap-pealed´
ap-peal´er
ap-peal´ing
ap-peal´ing·ly
ap-pear´
ap-pear´ance
ap-peared´
ap-pear´ing
ap-pease´

ap-pease´ment
ap-peas´er
ap-peas´ing
ap-pel´lant
ap-pel´late
ap-pel-la´tion
ap-pend´
ap-pend´age
ap-pend´ed
ap´pe-tite
ap´pe-tiz·er
ap´pe-tiz-ing
ap-plaud´
ap-plaud´er
ap-plaud´ing
ap-plause´
ap´ple
ap´ple-jack
ap´ple-sauce
ap-pli´ance
ap-pli-ca-bil´i·ty
ap´pli-ca·ble
ap´pli-ca·bly
ap´pli-cant
ap´pli-ca´tion
ap´pli-ca-tor
ap´pli-ca-to·ry
ap-plied´
ap-pli´er
ap-pli-que´
ap-ply´
ap-ply´ing
ap-point´
ap-point´ed
ap-poin-tee´
ap-point´er
ap-point´ing

ap-point´ment
ap-por´tion
ap-por´tioned
ap-por´tion·er
ap-por´tion-ment
ap-pos´a·ble
ap-pose´
ap´po-site
ap-po-si´tion
ap-pos´i-tive
ap-prais´al
ap-praise´
ap-praised´
ap-prais´er
ap-prais´ing
ap-pre´cia·ble
ap-pre´ci-ate
ap-pre´ci-at·ed
ap-pre´ci-at-ing
ap-pre-ci-a´tion
ap-pre´cia-tive
ap-pre´cia-tive·ly
ap-pre-hend´
ap-pre-hend´ed
ap-pre-hend´ing
ap-pre-hen´si·ble
ap-pre-hen´sion
ap-pre-hen´sive
ap-pre-hen´sive·ly
ap-pren´tice
ap-pren´ticed
ap-pren´tice-ship
ap-prise´

15

ap-prised´
ap-pris´ing
ap-prize´
ap-proach´
ap-proach-a-
bil´i·ty
ap-proach´a·ble
ap-proached´
ap-proach´ing
ap-pro-ba´tion
ap-pro´pri-ate
ap-pro´pri-at·ed
ap-pro´pri-at·ly
ap-pro´pri-ate-
ness
ap-pro´pri-at-ing
ap-pro-pri-a´tion
ap-prov´al
ap-prove´
ap-proved
ap-prov´ing
ap-prov´ing·ly
ap-prox´i-mate
ap-prox´i-
mate·ly
ap-prox´i-mat´
ing
ap-prox-i-ma´
tion
ap-pur´te-nance
ap-pur´te-nant
a´pron
ap´ro-pos
apse
ap´ti-tude
apt´ly
apt´ness

aq´ua
aq´ua-cade
aq´ua-cul-ture
aq´ua-lung
aq-ua-ma-rine´
aq´ua-plane
a·quar´i·um
a·quat´ic
a·quat´i-cal·ly
aq´ue-duct
a´que-ous
aq´ui-fer
a-quiv´er
ar´a·ble
ar´bi-ter
ar´bi-trage
ar´bi-trar-i·ly
ar´bi-trar·y
ar´bi-trate
ar´bi-trat-ing
ar-bi-tra´tion
ar´bi-tra-tive
ar´bi-tra-tor
ar´bi-tress
ar´bor
ar-bo´re·al
ar´bour *(Br.)*
ar-cade´
ar-cane´
ar-chae-ol´o-gist
ar-chae-ol´o·gy
ar-cha´ic
ar-cha´i-cal·ly
ar-che-o-log´ic
ar-che-o-log´i-
cal
ar-che-ol´o-gist

ar-che-ol´o·gy
arch´er
arch´er·y
ar´che-type
ar´chi-tect
ar-chi-tec´tur·al
ar´chi-tec-ture
ar-chi´val
ar´chive
ar´chi-vist
arch´way
arc´ing
ar´dent
ar´dent·ly
ar´dor
ar´du-ous
ar´du-ous·ly
ar´e·a-way
a·re´na
ar´go·sy
ar´gu-a·ble
ar´gue
ar´gued
ar´gu-ing
ar´gu-ment
ar-gu-men-ta´
tion
ar-gu-men´ta-
tive
a´ri·a
ar´id
a·rid´i·ty
ar´id-ness
a·right´
a´ri-ose
a·rise´
a·ris´en

16

a·ris´ing
ar-is-toc´ra·cy
a·ris´to-crat
a·ris-to-crat´ic
a·rith´me-tic *(n.)*
ar-ith-met´ic
  (adj.)
ar-ith-met´i-cal
ar-ma´da
ar´ma-ment
ar´ma-ture
arm´band
arm´chair
armed
arm´ful
ar´mies
ar´mil-lar·y
ar´mi-stice
ar-moire´
ar´mor
ar´mored
ar-mo´ri·al
armor–plated
ar´mo·ry
ar´mour *(Br.)*
arm´pit
arm´rest
ar´my
a·ro´ma
ar-o-mat´ic
ar-o-mat´i-cal·ly
a·ro´ma-tize
a·rose´
a·round´
a·rous´al
a·rouse´
a·rous´ing

ar-raign´
ar-raign´ment
ar-range´
ar-range´a·ble
ar-range´ment
ar-rang´er
ar-rang´ing
ar-ray´
ar-rayed´
ar-ray´ing
ar-rear´
ar-rear´age
ar-rest´
ar-rest´ed
ar-rest´er
ar-rest´ing
ar-res´tive
ar-riv´al
ar-rive´
ar-riv´ing
ar´ro·gance
ar´ro-gant
ar´ro-gate
ar´ro-gat-ing
ar-ro-ga´tion
ar´se-nal
ar´se-nate
ar´se-nic *(n.)*
ar-sen´ic *(adj.)*
ar´son
ar´son-ist
art´ful
art´ful·ly
ar´ti-cle
ar-tic´u-late
ar-tic´u-lat·ed
ar-tic-u-la´tion

ar-tic´u-la-tor
ar´ti-fact
ar´ti-fice
ar-ti-fi´cial
ar-ti-fi-ci-al´i·ty
ar-ti-fi´cial·ly
ar´ti-san
art´ist
ar-tiste´
ar-tis´tic
ar-tis´ti-cal
ar-tis´ti-cal·ly
ar´tist·ry
art´less
art´work
art´y
as-cend´
as-cend´a·ble
as-cend´an·cy
as-cend´ant
as-cend´ing
as-cen´sion
as-cent´
as-cer-tain´
as-cer-tain´a·ble
as-cet´ic
as-cet´i-cism
as-crib´a·ble
as-cribe´
as-crip´tive
as-crip´tion
a·sex´u·al
a·shamed´
a·sham´ed·ly
ash´en
a·shore´
ash´tray

17

ash´y
a·side´
as´i-nine
a·skance´
a·skew´
a·sleep´
a-so´cial
as´pect
as´per-ate
as-per´i·ty
as-perse´
as-per´sion
as-phyx´i·a
as-phyx´i-ate
as´pic
as´pi-rant
as´pi-rate
as´pi-ra´tion
as´pi-ra-tor
as-pire´
as´pi-rin
as-pir´ing
as-pir´ing·ly
as-sail´
as-sail´a·ble
as-sail´ant
as-sas´sin
as-sas´si-nate
as-sas-si-na´tion
as-sas´si-na-tor
as-sault´
as-sault´er
as´say *(n.)*
as-say´ *(v.)*
as-say´er
as-sem´blage
as-sem´ble

as-sem´bling
as-sem´bly
as-sent´
as-sert´
as-ser´tion
as-ser´tive
as-sess´
as-sess´ment
as´ses´sor
as´set
as-sid´u-ous
as-sid´u-ous·ly
as-sign´
as-sign-a-bil´i·ty
as-sign´a·ble
as-sig-na´tion
as-sign·ee´
as-sign´er
as-sign´ment
as-sign´or
as-sim´i-late
as-sim´i-lat-ing
as-sim-i-la´tion
as-sim´i-la-tive
as-sim´i-la-tor
as-sist´
as-sist´ance
as-sist´ant
as-sist´ed
as-sist´er
as-sist´ing
as-so´ci-ate
as-so´ci-at-ing
as-so-ci-a´tion
as-sort´
as-sort´ed
as-sort´ment

as-suage´
as-suag´ing
as-sum´a·ble
as-sum´a·bly
as-sume´
as-sumed´
as-sum´er
as-sum´ing
as-sump´tion
as-sump´tive
as-sur´ance
as-sure´
as-sured´
as-sur´ed·ly
as-sur´ed-ness
as-sur´ing
as´ter-isk
a·stern´
as´ter-oid
a·stir´
as-ton´ish
as-ton´ished
as-ton´ish-ing
as-ton´ish-ing·ly
as-ton´ish-ment
as-tound´
as-tound´ed
as-tound´ing·ly
as´tral
a·stray´
a·stride´
as-trin´gen·cy
as-trin´gent
as´tro-dome
as´tro-labe
as-trol´o-ger
as-tro-log´i-cal·ly

18

as-trol´o·gy
as´tro-naut
as-tron´o-mer
as-tro-nom´ic
as-tro-nom´i-
　cal·ly
as-tron´o·my
as-tro-phys´i-
　cist
as-tro-phys´ics
as-tute´
as-tute´ly
as-tute´ness
a·sun´der
a·sy´lum
a·sym-met´ric
a·sym-met´ri-cal
a·sym´me-try
a·te-lier´
a´the-ism
a´the-ist
a·the-is´tic
a·the-is´ti-cal·ly
ath lete
ath-let´ic
ath-let´i-cal·ly
a·tin´gle
at´mo-sphere
at-mo-spher´ic
at´oll
at´om
a·tom´ic
at´om-iz·er
a·ton´al
a·ton-al-is´tic
a·to-nal´i·ty
a·tone´

a·tone´ment
a·ton´ing
a·top´
a-trem´ble
a´tri·um
a·tro´cious
a·tro´cious·ly
a·troc´i·ty
at-tach´
at-tach´a·ble
at-ta-ché´
at-tached´
at-tach´ment
at-tack´
at-tacked´
at-tack´er
at-tack´ing
at-tain´
at-tain-a·bil´i·ty
at-tain´a·ble
at-tain´ment
at-tempt´
at-tend´
at-tend´ance
at-tend´ant
at-tend´ing
at-ten´tion
at-ten´tive
at-ten´tive·ly
at-ten´u-ate
at-ten-u-a´tion
at-test´
at´tic
at-tire´
at´ti-tude
at-ti-tu´di-nize
at-tor´ney

at-tract´
at-trac´tion
at-tract´ive·ly
at-tract´ive-ness
at-trib´ut-a·ble
at´tri-bute *(n.)*
at-trib´ute *(v.)*
at-tri-bu´tion
at-trib´u-tive
at-tri´tion
at-tri´tus
at-tune´
a·typ´i-cal
au´burn
auc´tion
auc-tion-eer´
au-da´cious
au-dac´i·ty
au-di-bil´i·ty
au´di·ble
au´di·bly
au´di-ence
au´di·o
au-di-o–vis´u·al
au´dit
au-di´tion
au´di-tor
au-di-to´ri·um
au´di-to·ry
au´ger
aug-ment´ *(v.)*
aug´ment *(n.)*
aug-ment´a·ble
aug-men-ta´tion
aug-men´ta-tive
au´gu·ry
au-gust´

19

au´ra
au´re-ole
au´ri-cle
au-ric´u-lar
au-ro´ra
aus´cul-tate
aus-cul-ta´tion
aus-pi´cious
aus-pi´cious·ly
aus-tere´
aus-tere´ly
aus-ter´i·ty
au-then´tic
au-then´ti-cal·ly
au-then´ti-cate
au-then-ti-ca´tion
au-then-tic´i·ty
au´thor
au-thor-i-tar´i·an
au-thor´i-ta-tive
au-thor´i·ty
au-tho-ri-za´tion
au´tho-rize
au´tho-rized
au´tho-riz-ing
au´thor-ship
au´tism
au´to
au-to-bi-og´ra-phy
au-toc´ra·cy
au´to-crat
au-to-crat´ic
au-to-crat´i-cal·ly

au´to-graph
au-to-im-mune´
au´to-mate
au-to-mat´ic
au-to-mat´i-cal·ly
au-to-ma´tion
au-tom´a-ton
au-to-mo-bile´
au-to-mo´tive
au-ton´o-mist
au-ton´o-mous
au-ton´o·my
au´top·sy
au´tumn
au-tum´nal
aux-il´ia·ry
a·vail´
a·vail-a·bil´i·ty
a·vail´a·ble
a·vailed´
av´a-lanche
av´a-rice
av-a-ri´cious
a·venge´
a·venged´
a·veng´er
a·veng´ing
av´e-nue
a·ver´
av´er-age
a·verse´
a·ver´sion
a·vert´
a·vert´ed
a´vi-ar·y
a´vi-ate

a·vi-a´tion
a´vi-a-tor
a·vi-a´trix
av´id
a·vid´i·ty
av´id·ly
av-o-ca´tion
a·void´
a·void´a·ble
a·void´a·bly
a·void´ance
a·void´ed
a ´vow´
a·vow´al
a·vowed´
a·vow´ed·ly
a·vul´sion
a·vun´cu-lar
a´wait´
a·wake´
a·wak´en-ing
a·wak´ing
a·ward´
a·ward´ed
a·ware´
a·ware´ness
a·wash´
a·way´
awe
a·weigh´
awe´some
awe´stricken
awe´struck
aw´ful
aw´ful·ly
a·while´
a·whirl´

20

awk´ward
awk´ward·ly
awk´ward-ness
aw´ning
a·woke´
a·wry´
ax´i·om
ax-i-o-mat´ic
ax´is
ax´le
az´i-muth
az´ure
bab´ble
bab´bler
bab´bling
babe
ba´bied
ba´bies
ba´by
ba´by-ish
baby–sit
bac-ca-lau´re-
  ate
bac´cha-nal
bac-cha-na´lia
bac-cha-na´lian
bach´e-lor
back´ache
back´bend
back´bite
back´bit-ing
back´board
back´bone
back´break-ing
back´date
back´drop
backed

back´er
back´field
back´fire
back´flip
back´gam-mon
back´ground
back´hand·ed
back´ing
back´lash
back´list
back´log
back´pack
back–pedal
back´rest
back´slap-ping
back´slash
back´slid-ing
back´stage´
back´stop
back´stretch
back´stroke
back´swing
back´talk
back´track
back´up
back´ward
back´ward-ness
back-woods´
back-yard´
ba´con
bac-te´ri·a
bac-te´ri·al
bad´ly
bad´min-ton
bad–mouth
bad–tem-pered
baf´fle

baf´fling
bag´a-telle´
ba´gel
bag´ful
bag´gage
bagged
bag´ger
bag´ging
bag´gy
bag´pipe
ba-guette´
bail
bailed
bai´liff
bai´li-wick
bail´ment
bail´or
bail´out
bake
bak´er
bak´er·y
bak´ing
bal´ance
bal´anc·er
bal´anc-ing
bal´co-nies
bal´co·ny
bal´der-dash
bald´head·ed
bald´ness
bale´ful
bal´er
bal´ing
balk´i·er
balk´ing
balk´y
bal´lad

21

bal´lad·ry
bal´last
bal-le-ri´na
bal´let
bal-loon´
bal-loon´ist
bal´lot
ball´room
bal´ly-hoo
balm´i-ness
balm´y
ba-lo´ney
bal´us-ter
bal-us-trade´
bam-boo´
bam-boo´zle
ba´nal
ba-nal´i·ty
ban´dage
ban´dag-ing
ban-dan´na
band´box
band´ed
band´er
ban´dit
ban´dit·ry
band´stand
band´wag·on
ban´dy
ban´dy-ing
bandy–legged
ban´gle
ban´ish
ban´ish-ment
ban´is-ter
ban´jo
ban´jos

bank
bank´a·ble
bank´er
bank´ing
bank´rupt
bank´rupt·cy
ban´ner
ban´quet
ban´tam
ban´ter
ban´ter-ing·ly
bap´tism
bap´tis´mal
bap-tize´
bap-tized´
bap-tiz´ing
bar
bar-bar´i·an
bar-bar´ic
bar-bar´i-cal·ly
bar´ba-rism
bar´ba-rous
bar´be-cue
bar´bell
bar´ber
bar´ber-shop
bare
bare´back
bared
bare´faced
bare´foot
bare–handed
bare´head·ed
bare´leg-ged
bare´ly
bar´gain
bar´gain·er

barge
bar´keep
bark´er
bark´ing
bar´maid
bar´man
bar mitz´vah
bar´na-cle
barn´dance
barn´storm
barn´yard
ba-rom´e-ter
bar-o-met´ric
ba-roque´
bar´rack
bar-rage´
barred
bar´rel
bar´ren
bar´ren-ness
bar-rette´
bar´ri-cade
bar´ri-cad´ing
bar´ri·er
bar´ring
bar´ris-ter
bar´room
bar´tender
bar´ter
ba´sal
base´ball
base´board
base´less
base´ly
base´ment
base´ness
bash´ful

bash´ful·ly	bat´tle-ship	bear´ing
bash´ful-ness	bat´ty	bear´ish
bash´ing	bau´ble	bear´skin
ba´sic	bawd´i-ness	beast
ba´si-cal·ly	bawd´y	beast´li-ness
ba-sil´i·ca	bay´o-net	beast´ly
ba´sin	bay´ou	beat
ba´sin-like	ba-zaar´	beat´en
ba´sis	ba-zoo´ka	beat´er
bas´ket	beach´ball	be-at-i-fi-ca´tion
bas´ket-ball	beach´comb·er	be-at´i-fied
bas´ket-ful	beach´front	be-at´i·fy
bas´ket·ry	beach´head	beat´ing
bas´ket-work	beach´wear	be-at´i-tude
bas-si-net´	bea´con	beau´te-ous
bas´tion	bead´ed	beau-ti´cian
bath *(n.)*	bead´ing	beau´ties
bathe *(v.)*	bead´work	beau´ti-fi-ca´tion
bath´er	bead´y	beau´ti-fied
bath´house	beak	beau´ti-fi·er
bath´ing	beaked	beau´ti-ful·ly
bath´robe	beak´er	beau´ti-fy-ing
bath´room	beam	beau´ty
bath´tub	beamed	be-calm´
ba-ton´	beam´ing	be-came´
bat-tal´ion	bean	be-cause´
bat´ten	bean´bag	beck´on
bat´ter	bean´ie	beck´on-ing
bat´ter-ies	bean´pole	be-cloud´
bat´ter-ing	bean´stalk	be-come´
bat´ter·y	bear	be-com´ing
bat´ting	bear´able	be-daub´
bat´tle	bear´a·bly	be-daz´zle
bat´tle-field	beard	be-daz´zle-ment
bat´tle-ground	beard´ed	be-daz´zling
bat´tle-ment	beard´less	bed´bug
battle–scarred	bear´er	bed´clothes

bed´ded
bed´ding
be-dev´il
bed´fel-low
bed´jack·et
bed´lam
bed´post
be-drag´gle
bed´rid-den
bed´rock
bed´roll
bed´room
bed´sheet
bed´side
bed´sore
bed´spread
bed´spring
bed´stead
bed´time
beef
beef´i-ness
beef´steak
beef·y
bee´hive
bee´keep·er
bee´keep-ing
bee´line
beep
beep´er
bees´wax
be-fall´
be-fall´en
be-fell´
be-fit´
be-fog´
be-fogged´
be-fog´ging

be-fore´
be-fore´hand
be-fore´time
be-friend´
be-fud´dle
beg
be-gan´
beg´gar
beg´gar-li-ness
beg´gar·ly
beg´ging
be-gin´
be-gin´ner
be-gin´ning
be-grudge´
be-grudg´ing·ly
be-guile´ment
be-guil´er
be-guil´ing·ly
be-gun´
be-half´
be-hav´ior
be-hav´ior-al
be-hav´ior-al·ly
be-hav´ior-ism
be-head´
be-head´ed
be-held´
be-he´moth
be-hest´
be-hind´
be-hind´hand
be-hold´
be-hold´en
be-hold´er
be-hold´ing
be´ing

be-jew´el
be-jew´eled
be-la´bor
be-lat´ed
be-lat´ed·ly
be-lay´
belch
be-lea´guered
bel´fry
be-lie
belief´
be-li´er
be-liev-a·bil´i·ty
be-liev´a·ble
be-liev´a·bly
be-lieve´
be-lieved´
be-liev´er
be-liev´ing
be-lit´tle
be-lit´tle-ment
be-lit´tling
bel´li-cose
bel´li-cose·ly
bel´li-cose-ness
bel-li-cos´i·ty
bel-lig´er-ence
bel-lig´er-en·cy
bel-lig´er-ent
bel´low
bell–shaped
bell´tow·er
bell´weth·er
bel´ly
bel´ly-ache
bel´ly-but-ton
bel´ly-ful

be-long´
be-longed´
be-long´ing
be-long´ings
be-loved´
be-low´
belt
belt´ed
belt´ing
be-ly´ing
be-moan´
be-moaned´
be-moan´ing
be-muse´
be-mused´
be-mus´ed·ly
be-muse´ment
be-mus´ing
bend´a·ble
bend´ed
bend´er
bend´ing
be-neath´
ben-c-dic´tion
ben-e-dic´to·ry
ben´e-fac-tor
ben´e-fice
ben-e-fi´cial
ben-e-fi´cial·ly
ben-e-fi´cia-ries
ben-e-fi´cia·ry
ben´e-fit
ben´e-fit·ed
ben´e-fit-ing
be-nev´o-lence
be-nev´o-lent
be-nign´

be-nign´ly
be-numb´
be-queath´
be-quest´
be-rate´
be-rat´ed
be-rat´ing
be-reave´
be-reaved´
be-reave´ment
be-reav´ing
be-reft´
ber´ries
ber´ry
ber´ry-like
ber-serk´
berth
berth´ing
be-seech´
be-seeched´
be-seech´er
be-seech´ing·ly
be-set´
be-side´
be-smirch´
be-smirch´er
best–known
best–liked
be-stow´
be-stow´al
best–paid
be-stride´
best–selling
be-tide´
be-times´
be-tray´
be-tray´al

be-tray´er
be-troth´
be-troth´al
be-throthed´
bet´ter
bet´ter–off
bet´ter-ment
bet´ting
be-tween´
be-twixt´
bev´el
bev´eled
bev´el-ing
bev´er-age
bev´ies
bev´y
be-wail´
be-wail´ing
be-ware´
be-wil´der
be-wil´dered
be-wil´der-ing·ly
be-wil´der-ment
be-witch´
be-witch´ing·ly
be-yond´
bi-an´nu-al
bi-an´nu-al·ly
bi´as
bi´ased
bib-li-og´ra-phy
bib´li-o-phile
bi-cam´er·al
bi-cen-ten´a·ry
bi-cen-ten´ni·al
bick´er
bick´er-ing

25

bi´cy-cle
bi´cy-cler
bi´cy-clist
bid
bid´den
bid´der
bid´ding
bid´dy
bide
bid´ing
bi-di-rec´tion·al
bi-en´ni-al·ly
bi-fo´cals
bi´fur-cate
bi´fur-cat·ed
bi-fur-ca´tion
big´a-mist
big´a-mous
big´a·my
big´ger
big´heart·ed
big´heart-ed·ly
big´ heart-ed-
   ness
big´ness
big´ot
big´ot·ed
big´ot·ry
big´wig
bike
bik´er
bi-ki´ni
bi-lat´er·al
bi-lat´er-al·ly
bi-lin´e·ar
bi-lin´gual
bil´ious

bil´ious·ly
bil´ious-ness
bill´board
bil´liards
bill´ing
bil´lion
bil´lion-aire
bil´lionth
bil´low
bil´low·y
bi-month´ly
bi´na·ry
bind
bind´er
bind´er·y
bind´ing
bin-oc´u-lars
bi·o-de-grad´
   a·ble
bi·o-feed´back
bi·o-gen´e-sis
bi-o-ge-net´ic
bi-og´ra-pher
bi·o-graph´ic
bi·o-graph´i-cal
bi-og´ra-phy
bi-o-log´i-cal·ly
bi-ol´o-gist
bi-ol´o·gy
bi-on´ic
bi-on´i-cal·ly
bi´o-rhythm
bi´o-sphere
bi-par´ti-san
bird´bath
bird´cage
bird´house

bird´seed
bird's—eye
birth´day
birth´place
birth´rate
birth´right
birth´stone
bis´cuit
bi´sect´
bi-sec´tion
bish´op
bish´op-ric
bite
bit´er
bit´ing
bit´ten
bit´ter
bit´ter-ness
bit´ter-sweet
biv´ouac
biv´ouacked
biv´ouack-ing
bi-week´ly
bizarre´
blab
blab´ber
black´mail
black´out
black´smith
blam´a·ble
blam´a·bly
blame
blamed
blame´ful
blame´less·ly
blame´less-ness
blame´wor-thy

blam´ing
blanch
blanch´ing
bland
blan´dish-ment
bland´ly
bland´ness
blank
blan´ket
blank´ly
blank´ness
blar´ney
bla-sé´
blas´pheme
blas´phem·er
blas´phem-ing
b l a s ´ p h e -
   mous·ly
blas´phe·my
blast
blast´ed
blast´er
bla´tant
bla´tant·ly
blath´er
blath´er-ing
blaze
blazed
blaz´er
blaz´ing
bla´zon
bleak
bleak´ly
blear´i·ly
blear´i-ness
blear´y
blear´y–eyed

bleed
bleed´er
bleed´ing
blem´ish
blend
blend´er
blend´ing
bless
bless´ed·ly
bless´ing
blind´ing·ly
blind´ly
blind´ness
blink
blink´er
blink´ing
bliss
bliss´ful·ly
bliss´ful-ness
blis´ter
blis´ter-ing
blis´ter·y
bliz´zard
bloat
bloat´ed
bloat´er
block
block-ade´
block-ad´ed
block-ad´er
block-ad´ing
block´age
block´buster
block´head
blond, blonde
blood
blood´cur-dling

blood´hound
blood´i-est
blood´less
blood´let-ting
blood´shed
blood´stain
blood´suck·er
blood´thirst·y
blood´y
bloom
bloom´ers
bloom´ing
bloop´er
blos´som
blot
blotch
blotch´y
blot´ted
blot´ter
blot´ting
blouse
blow
blow–dry
blow–dryer
blow´er
blown
blow´out
blow´torch
bludg´eon
blue´berry
blue´bird
blue–black
blue–blooded
blue–collar
blue–eyed
blue´grass
blue–pencil

27

blue´print
bluff
bluff´ing
blun´der
blun´der·er
blun´der-ing·ly
blunt
blunt´ly
blunt´ness
blur
blurred
blur´ring
blur´ry
blurt
blurt´ed
blush
blushed
blush´er
blush´ing·ly
blus´ter
blus´ter-ing·ly
blus´ter-ous
blus´ter·y
board´er
board´ing-house
board´walk
boast
boast´er
boast´ful
boast´ing·ly
boat´house
boat´ing
bob´bin
bob´bing
bob´sled
bo-da´cious
bod´ice

bod´i·ly
bod´y
bod´y-build·er
bod´y-guard
body–search
bod´y-work
bog´gle
bo´gus
bo´gy
boil
boil´er
boil´ing
bois´ter-ous
bois´ter-ous·ly
bois´ter-ous-
    ness
bold
bold´face
bold–faced
bold´ly
bold´ness
bol´ster
bom-bard´
bom-bard´ment
bom-bas´tic
bom-bas´ti-cal·ly
bo´na fide
bo-nan´za
bond´age
bond´ed
bond´ing
bon´fire
bon´net
bon´ny
bo´nus
bon´y
book

book´bind-ing
book´case
book´end
book´ie
book´ing
book´ish-ness
book´keep·er
book´keep-ing
book´let
book´mak·er
book´mark
book´sell·er
book´sell-ing
book´shelf
book´store
book´worm
boor
boor´ish
boor´ish·ly
boor´ish-ness
boost
boost´er
boot
boot´black
boot´ed
boot´ie
boot´leg
boot´leg-ger
boot´leg-ging
boot´strap
boo´ty
booze
booz´er
booz´y
bop
bor´der
bor´dered

28

bor´der-line
bore´dom
bor´er
bor´ing
born
borne
bor´ough
bor´row
bor´row·er
bor´row-ing
boss´i-ness
boss´y
bo-tan´i-cal
bot´a-nist
bot´a·ny
both´er
both´er-some
bot´tle
bot´tle–fed
bot´tle-neck
bot´tler
bot´tling
bot´tom
bot´tom-less
bought
boul´der
bou´le-vard
bounce
bounc´er
bounc´ing
bounc´y
bound
bound´a-ries
bound´a·ry
bound´ed
bound´er
bound´less-ness

boun´te-ous·ly
boun´te-ous-
　ness
boun´ti-ful·ly
boun´ti-ful-ness
boun´ty
bou-quet´
bour´bon
bour´geois,
　bour´geoise
bour´geoi-sie´
bourne
bou-tique´
bou´ton-niere´
bow´er
bow´er·y
bow´ing
bow´leg-ged
bowl´er
bowl´ing
box´car
box´er
box´ing
box´y
boy´cott
boy´friend
boy´ish
boy´ish-ness
brace´let
brac´ing·ly
brac´ing-ness
brac´ing
brack´et
brack´ish
brag
brag-ga-do´ci·o
brag´gart

bragged
brag´ger
brag´ging
braid
braid´ing
brain
brain´child
brain–dead
brain´i·er
brain´i·ly
brain´i-ness
brain´less
brain´pow·er
brain´storm
brain´storm-ing
brain´teas·er
brain´wash
brain´wash-ing
brain´y
braise
braised
brais´ing
bram´ble
bram´bly
bran´died
bran´dish
brand–new
bran´dy
brash
brash´ly
brash´ness
bras-siere´
brass´i-ness
brass´y
brave
brave´heart·ed
brave´ly

brav´er·y	breath	bridge´head
brav´est	breath´a·ble	bridge´work
bra´vo	breathe	brief
bra-vu´ra	breath´er	brief´case
brawl	breath´ing	brief´ing
brawl´er	breath´less·ly	brief´ly
brawn	breath´less-ness	bright
brawn´i·er	breath´tak-ing·ly	bright´en
brawn´i-est	breed	bright´en·er
brawn´i-ness	breed´er	bright–eyed
brawn´y	breed´ing	bright´ly
bra´zen	breeze	bright´ness
bra´zen·ly	breeze´way	bril´liance
bra´zen-ness	breez´i·ly	bril´lian·cy
braz´er	breez´i-ness	bril´liant
bra´zier	breez´y	bril´liant·ly
braz´ing	breth´ren	bril´liant-ness
bread	brev´i·ty	brim
bread´bas-ket	brew	brim´ful
bread´board	brew´er	brim´less
bread´box	brew´er·y	brimmed
bread´crumb	brew´ing	brim´ming
bread´pan	bribe	bring
breadth	bribed	bring´ing
bread´win-ner	brib´er	brin´y
break	brib´er·y	brisk
break´a·ble	brib´ing	brisk´ly
break´age	bric–a–brac	brisk´ness
break´a-way	brick	bris´tle
break´down	brick´lay·er	bris´tling
break´er	brick´laying	bris´tly
break–e´ven	brick´work	brit´tle
break´fast	brick´yard	brit´tle-ness
break–in	brid´al	broad´cast
break´ing	bride´groom	broad´cast-ing
break´through	brides´maid	broad´en
break´up	bridge	broad´ly

30

broad–mind·ed
broad–spectrum
bro-cade´
bro-cad´ed
bro-chure´
broil
broil´er
broke
bro´ken
broken–down
bro´ken-heart·ed
bro´ker
bro´ker-age
broth´el
broth´er-hood
brother–in–law
broth´er-li-ness
broth´er·ly
brou´ha·ha
brow´beat
brow´beat·er
brow´beat-ing
brown–bag
brown´out
brown´stone
browse
brows´er
brows´ing
bruise
bruised
bruis´er
bruis´ing
brush
brushed
brush–off
brush´work
brusque

brusque´ly
brusque´ness
bru´tal
bru-tal´i·ty
bru´tal-ize
bru´tal·ly
brute
brut´ish·ly
brut´ish-ness
bub´ble
bub´ble-gum
bub´ble-top
bub´bli-ness
bub´bling
bub´bly
buc´ca-neer
buck´et
buck´le
buck´ler
buck´ling
buck´shot
buck´skin
buck´tooth
bu-col´ic
bu-col´i-cal·ly
bud´ding
bud´dy
bud´get
bud´get-ar·y
bud´get·ed
bud´get·er
bud´get-ing
buff´er
buf´fet *(strike)*
buf-fet´ *(food)*
buf-foon´
buf-foon´er·y

buf-foon´ish
bug´a-boo
bug–eyed
bug´gy
bu´gle
bu´gler
bu´gling
build
build´er
build´ing
build´up
built
built–in
built–up
bul´bous
bul´bous·ly
bulge
bulg´i-ness
bulg´ing
bulg´y
bulk´i·er
bulk´i-ness
bulk´y
bull´doze
bull´doz·er
bull´doz-ing
bul´le-tin
bul´let-proof
bull´fight
bull´fight·er
bull´fight-ing
bull´head·ed
bull´horn
bul´lied
bull´ish
bull´ish-ness
bull´pen

bull's–eye
bul´ly
bul´ly-ing
bum´ble
bum´bler
bum´bling
bum´mer
bump´er
bump´i·er
bump´i·ly
bump´i-ness
bump´kin
bump´tious
bump´y
bun´dle
bun´dling
bun´ga-low
bun´gee
bun´gle
bun´gled
bun´gler
bun´gling
bunk´house
bunt´ing *(cloth)*
buoy´an·cy
buoy´ant
bur´den
bur´dened
bur´den-some
bu´reau
bu-reau´ra·cy
bu´reau-crat
bu-reau-crat´ic
bur´geon
burg´er
bur´glar
bur´gla-ries

bur´glar-ize
bur´glar-proof
bur´gla·ry
bur´i·al
bur´ied
bur´ies
bur´lap
bur´lesque´
bur´li-ness
bur´ly
burn
burned
burn´er
burn´ish
burnt
bur´row
bur´row·er
burst
burst´ing
bur´y
bur´y-ing
bus´boy
bush
bushed
bush´el
bush´i·er
bush´i-ness
bush´y
bus´ied
bus´i·er
bus´i-est
bus´i·ly
bus´i-ness
bus´i-ness-like
bus´i-ness-man
bus´tle
bus´tled

bus´tler
bus´tling
bus´y
bus´y-bod·y
butch´er
butch´er·y
but´ler
butt
butte
but´ter *(spread)*
butt´er *(one who butts)*
but´ter-ball
but´ter-fat
but´ter-fin-gers
but´ter·y
but´ton
button–down
but´ton-hole
but´tress
bux´om
bux´om·ly
bux´om-ness
buy
buy´back
buy´er
buy´ing
buy´off
buy´out
buzz´er
buzz´ing
buzz´word
by
by–and–by
bye
by´gone
by´law

by–line
by´pass
by–product
by´stand·er
byte
by´way
by´word
ca-bal´
cab´a·la
cab-a-lis´tic
cab-a-ret´
cab´by
cab´driv·er
cab´in
cab´i-net
cab´i-net-mak·er
cab´i-net·ry
cab´i-net-work
ca´ble
ca´ble-gram
ca´ble vi-sion
ca´bling
ca-boose´
cab´stand
cache
cached
ca-chet´
cack´le
cack´ling
ca-coph´o-nous
ca-coph´o·ny
ca-dav´er
ca-dav´er-ous
cad´dy
ca´dence
ca´denced
ca-det´

cadge
cad´re
ca-fé´
caf-e-te´ri·a
caf´fein-at·ed
caf´feine
caf´tan
ca´gey
ca´gi·er
ca´gi·ly
cag´i-ness
ca-jole´
ca-jol´er·y
ca-jol´ing·ly
ca-lam´i-tous·ly
ca-lam´i·ty
cal´cu-la·ble
cal´cu-la-bly
cal´cu-late
cal´cu-lat·ed
cal´cu-lat-ing
cal´cu-lat-ing·ly
cal-cu-la´tion
cal´cu-la-tor
cal´cu·li
cal´cu-lous
cal´cu-lus
cal´en-dar
calf´skin
cal´i-ber
cal´i-brate
cal-i-bra´tion
cal´i-bra-tor
cal´i·co
cal´i-per
ca´liph
ca´liph-ate

cal-is-then´ics
calk
calk´ing
call
call´able
call´er
cal-lig´ra-pher
cal-lig´ra-phy
call´ing
cal-li´o·pe
cal´low
cal´low-ness
calm´ing·ly
calm´ly
calm´ness
ca-lor´ic
cal´o-rie
cal-o-rif´ic
ca-lum´ni-ate
ca-lum-ni-a´tion
ca-lum´ni-a-tor
cal´um-nies
cal´um·ny
ca-lyp´so
ca-ma-ra´de-rie
cam´bric
cam´cord·er
cam´er·a
cam´er-a-man
camera–ready
camera–shy
cam´i-sole
cam´ou-flage
cam-paign´
cam-paign´er
camp´er
camp´fire

camp´ground
camp´site
cam´pus
camp´y
ca-nal´
ca´na·pé
ca-nard´
can´cel
can´cel-a·ble
can´celed
can´cel·er
can´cel-ing
can-cel-la´tion
can´cer
can´cer-ous
can-de-la´bra
can-de-la´brum
can´did
can´di-da·cy
can´di-date
can´did·ly
can´did-ness
can´died
can´dies
can´dle
can´dle-light
can´dle-pow·er
can´dler
can´dle-stick
can´dor
can´dy
cane´brake
ca´nine
can´is-ter
can´ker
canned
can´ner

can´ner·y
can´ni-bal
can´ni-bal-ism
can-ni-bal-is´tic
can´ni-bal-ize
can´ni·ly
can´ni-ness
can´ning
can´non
can´non-ade´
can´non-ball
can´non-eer
can´not
can´ny
ca-noe´
ca-noe´ing
ca-noe´ist
ca-noes´
can´o·la
ca-non´i-cal
can-on-i-za´tion
can´on-ize
can´o-pies
can´o·py
can-tan´ker-ous
can-ta´ta
can-teen´
can´vas
can´vas-back
can´vass
can´vass·er
can´yon
ca-pa·bil´i-ties
ca-pa·bil´i·ty
ca´pa·ble
ca´pa·bly
ca-pa´cious

ca-pac´i-tate
ca-pac´i·ty
cap´ful
cap´i·ta
cap´i-tal
cap´i-tal-ism
cap´i-tal-ist
cap-i-tal-is´tic
cap´i-tal-ize
cap´i-tol
ca-pit´u-late
ca-pit-u-la´tion
cap-puc-ci´no
ca-price´
ca-pri´cious·ly
ca-pri´cious-
  ness
cap´size
cap´siz-ing
cap´su-lar
cap´sule
cap´tain
cap´tion
cap´tious
cap´tious·ly
cap´tious-ness
cap´ti-vate
cap´ti-vat-ing·ly
cap-ti-va´tion
cap´tive
cap-tiv´i·ty
cap´tor
cap´ture
cap´tur·er
cap´tur-ing
ca-rafe´
car´a-mel

car´a-mel-ize
car´at
car´a-van
car-a-van´sa·ry
car´barn
car-bo-hy´drate
car´bon
car-bon-a´tion
car´bun-cle
car´cass
card´board
card–carrying
card´case
car´di-nal
card´sharp
ca-reen´
ca-reer´
care´free
care´ful·ly
care´giv·er
care´less·ly
care´less-ness
ca-ress´
ca-ress´ing·ly
car´et
care´tak·er
care´worn
car´fare
car´go
car´i-ca-ture
car´i-ca-tur-ist
car´il-lon
car´nage
car´nal
car´nal·ly
car-na´tion
car´ni-val

car´ni-vore
car-niv´o-rous
car´ol
car´ol·er
car´om
ca-rous´al
ca-rouse´
car-ou-sel´
ca-rous´ing
ca-rous´ing·ly
car´pen-ter
car´pen-try
car´pet
car´pet-ing
carp´ing
car´pool
car´port
car´riage
car´ri·er
car-rou-sel´
car´ried
car´ry
car´ry-all
car´ry–on
car´sick
cart´age
car-tel´
car-tog´ra-pher
car-tog´ra-phy
car´ton
car-toon´
car-toon´ist
car´tridge
cart´wheel
carve
carv´er
carv´ing

cas-cade´
case´book
case´ment
cash–and–carry
cash-ier´
cash´mere
cas´ing
cas´ket
cas´se-role
cas-sette´
cas-ta-net´
cast´a-way
cas´ti-gate
cas-ti-ga´tion
cas-ti-ga´tor
cast´ing
ca´su-al
ca´su-al·ly
ca´su-al-ness
ca´su-al·ty
cat´a-comb
cat´a-log, cat´a-
   logue
cat´a-log·er,
   cat´a-logu·er
cat´a-log-ing,
   cat´a-logu-ing
cat´a-lyst
cat-a-lyt´ic
cat-a-ma-ran´
cat´a-pult
ca-tas´tro-phe
cat-a-stroph´ic
catch´all
catch´er
catch´i·er
catch´ing

catch´word
catch´y
cat-e-gor´i-cal
cat-e-gor´i-cal·ly
cat´e-go-rize
cat´e-go·ry
cat´e·nate
ca´ter
ca´ter·er
ca-the´dral
cath´ode
cat´nap
cat´nip
cat´sup
cat´ty
cau´cus
caul´dron
caulk´ing
caus´al
cau-sa´tion
caus´a-tive
cause
cause´way
caus´ing
caus´tic
caus´ti-cal·ly
cau´tion
cau´tion-ar·y
cau´tious·ly
cau´tious-ness
cav´al-cade´
cav´a-lier´
cav-a-lier´ly
cav´al·ry
ca´ve·at
cave–in
cave´man

cav´ern
cav´ern-ous
cav´il
cav´i·ty
cavort´
ca-vort´ing
cease´less
cease´less·ly
ceas´ing
cede
ced´ed
ced´ing
ceil´ing
ceil´inged
cel´e-brate
cel´e-brat·ed
cel-e-bra´tion
cal´e-bra-tive
cel´e-bra-tor
cel´e-bra-to·ry
ce-leb´ri·ty
ce-ler´i·ty
ce-les´tial
cel´i-ba·cy
cel´i-bate
cel´lar
cell´mate
cel´lo
cel´lo-phane
cel´lu-lar
cel´lu-lite
ce-ment´
cem´e-ter-ies
cem´e-ter·y
cen´sor
cen´sor-a·ble
cen-so´ri·al

cen-so´ri-ous·ly
cen´sor-ship
cen´sur-a·ble
cen´sure
cen´sured
cen´sur-ing
cen´sus
cen-te-nar´i·an
cen-ten´ni·al
cen´ter
cen´ter-fold
cen´ter-line
cen´ter-piece
cen´ti-grade
cen´ti-gram
cen´ti-me-ter
cen´tral
cen-tral-i-za´tion
cen´tral-ize
cen´tral·ly
cen´tre *(Br.)*
cen´tric
cen-trif´u-gal
cen´tri-fuge
cen´trist
cen´tu·ry
ce-ram´ic
ce´re·al
cer-e-mo´ni·al
cer-e-mo´ni-al·ly
cer´e-mo-nies
cer-e-mo´ni-ous
c e r - e - m o ´ n i -
ous·ly
cer´e-mo·ny
cer´tain
cer´tain·ly

36

cer´tain·ty
cer´ti-fi-a·ble
cer´ti-fi-a·bly
cer-tif´i-cate
cer-ti-fi-ca´tion
cer´ti-fied
cer´ti·fy
cer´ti-fy-ing
ces-sa´tion
cess´pool
cha-grin´
cha-grined´
chair
chair´lift
chair´per-son
chaise
chal-ced´o·ny
chal´dron
cha´let
chal´ice
chalk
chalk´y
chal´lenge
chal´leng·er
chal´leng-ing
cham´ber
cham´ber-maid
cham´ois
cham´o-mile
cham-pagne´
cham´pi·on
cham´pi-on-ship
chan´cel
chan´cel-lor
chanc´i-ness
chanc´y
chan´de-lier´

change´a·ble
change´a·bly
changed
change´less·ly
change´ling
chang´er
chang´ing
chan´nel
chan´neled
chan´nel-ing
chant
chant´er
cha´os
cha-ot´ic
cha-ot´i-cal·ly
chap´el
chap´er·on
chap´lain
chap´lain·cy
chap´ter
char´ac-ter
char-ac-ter-is´tic
char-ac-ter-i-
   za´tion
char´ac-ter-ize
cha-rade´
char´coal
charge´a·ble
charge´a·bly
charged
charg´er
charg´ing
cha-ris´ma
char´is-mat´ic
char´i-ta·ble
char´i-ta·ble-
   ness

char´i-ta·bly
char´i·ty
char´la-tan
charm
charmed
charm´er
charm´ing·ly
char´ter *(grant)*
chart´er   *(plan-
   ner)*
chartreuse´
chase
chased
chas´er
chas´ing
chasm
chas´sis
chaste
chaste´ly
chaste´ness
chas´ten
chas-tise´ment
chas-tis´er
chas´ti·ty
châ-teau´
cha-teaux´ *(pl.)*
chat´tel
chat´ter
chat´ter-box
chat´ter·er
chat´ti·ly
chat´ti-ness
chat´ting
chat´ty
chauf´feur
chau´vin-ism
chau´vin-ist

37

cheap
cheap´en
cheap´ened
cheap´ly
cheap´skate
cheat
cheat´er
check´book
checked
cheek´er
check´er-board
check´ered
check´ers
check´list
check–out
check´point
check´up
cheek´bone
cheek´y
cheer´ful
cheer´ful·ly
cheer´ful-ness
cheer´i·ly
cheer´i-ness
cheer´lead·er
cheer´less
cheer´y
chees´y
chem´i-cal
chem´i-cal·ly
che-mise´
chem´ist
chem´is-try
cher´ish
cher´ub
che-ru´bic
cher´u-bim *(pl.)*

chest
chest´ed
chest´ful
chest´i·ly
chest´nut
chev´ron
chew´a·ble
chew´ing
chew´y
chew´i-ness
chi-ca´ner·y
chi´cle
chide
chid´ing·ly
chief
chief´ly
chief´tain
chif-fon´
chif-fo-nade´
chi´gnon
child
child´bear-ing
child´birth
child´hood
child´ish·ly
child´ish-ness
child´like
chil´dren
chill´i-ness
chill´y
chime
chimed
chim´er
chi-me´ra
chi-mer´i-cal
chim´ing
chim´ney

chi´na-ware
chintz
chintz´y
chip´board
chip´per
chis´el
chis´el·er
chis´el-ing
chit´chat
chi-val´ric
chiv´al-rous·ly
chiv´al-rous-
 ness
chiv´al·ry
choc´o-late
choice
choir
choir´boy
choir´mas-ter
choke
choked
chok´er
chok´ing
chol´er
cho-les´ter·ol
cho´line
choose
choos´y
choos´ing
chop
chop´per
chop´pi-ness
chop´ping
chop´py
chop´stick
cho´ral
cho-rale´

38

cho´re-o-graph
cho-re-og´ra-
  pher
cho-re-og´ra-phy
cho´ris-ter
chor´tle
chor´tling
cho´rus
chose
cho´sen
chow´der
chris´ten
chris´ten-ing
chron´ic
chron´i-cal·ly
chron´i-cle
chron´i-cler
chron´i-cling
chron-o-log´ic
chron-o-log´i-cal
chro-nol´o·gy
chro-nom´e-ter
chub´by
chuck´le
chuck´led
chuckle-head
chuck´ling
chum´mi·ly
chum´mi-ness
chum´my
chunk´i·ly
chunk´i-ness
chunk´y
church
church´go·er
church´yard
churl

churl´ish
churl´ish·ly
churl´ish-ness
churn
churn´er
chutz´pa
ci-gar´
cig-a-rette´,
  cig-a-ret´
cinc´ture
cin´der
cin´e·ma
cin-e-ma-
  theque´
cin-e-mat´ic
ci´pher
cir´cle
cir´cled
cir´clet
cir´cling
cir´cuit·ry
cir-cu´i·ty
cir-cu´i-tous
cir´cu-lar
cir´cu-late
cir-cu-la´tion
cir´cu-la-tor
cir´cu-la-to·ry
cir-cum´fer-ence
cir-cum-fer-en´
  tial
cir-cum-lo-cu´
  tion
cir-cum-nav´i-
  gate
cir´cum-scribe
cir´cum-spect

cir´cum-stance
cir´cum-stan´tial
cir-cum-stan´ti-
  ate
cir´cum-vent
cir-cum-ven´tion
cir´cus
cis´tern
cit´a-del
ci-ta´tion
cit´ies
cit´i-fied
cit´i·fy
cit´ing
cit´i-zen
cit´i-zen·ry
cit´i-zen-ship
cit´y
cit´y-scape
city–state
cit´y-wide
civic–minded
civ´ics
civ´il
ci-vil´ian
ci-vil´i·ty
civ-i-li-za´tion
civ´i-lize
civ´i-lized
civ´i-liz-ing
civ´il·ly
claim
claim´ant
claim´er
clair-voy´ance
clair-voy´ant
clair-voy´ant·ly

clam´ber	clat´ter	clem´en·cy
clam´mi-ness	clat´tered	clem´ent
clam´my	clat´ter-ing	cler´gy
clam´or	clau-di-ca´tion	cler´gy-man
clam´or-ous	claus´al	cler´ic
clam´or-ous·ly	clause	cler´i-cal
clamp	claus-tro-pho´	clev´er
clan-des´tine	bi·a	clev´er·ly
clan-des´tine·ly	claus-tro-pho´	clev´er-ness
clang	bic	cli-che´
clang´or-ous	cla-vier´	cli-ched´
clan´nish	clay	click
clans´man	clean	click´er
clap	clean–cut	cli´ent
clapped	clean´er	cli´en-tele´
clap´per	clean–handed	cliff
clap´ping	clean´li-ness	cliff˝hang·er
clap´trap	clean´ly	cli-mac´tic
clar-i-fi-ca´tion	clean´ness	cli-mac´ti-cal·ly
clar´i-fied	cleanse	cli´mate
clar´i·fy	cleansed	cli-mat´ic
clar´i-fy-ing	cleans´er	cli´ma-tize
clar´i·on	clean–shaven	cli-ma-tol´o·gy
clar´i·ty	cleans´ing	cli´max
clasp	clean´up	climb
clasp´er	clear´ance	climb´a·ble
clas´sic	clear–cut	climbed
clas´si-cal·ly	clear–eyed	climb´er
clas´si-fi-a·ble	clear˝head·ed	climb´ing
clas-si-fi-ca´tion	clear´ing-house	clinch
clas´si-fied	clear´ly	clinch´er
clas´si-fi·er	clear–sight´ed	cling
clas´si·fy	cleav´age	cling´er
clas´si-fy-ing	cleave	cling´i-ness
class´mate	cleaved	cling´ing
class´room	cleav´er	cling´y
class´y	cleav´ing	clin´ic

clin´i-cal·ly
cli-ni´cian
clink
clink´er
clip
clip´board
clip–on
clipped
clip´per
clip´ping
clique
cli´quish
cloak
cloak–and–dag-
  ger
clob´ber
cloche
clock´mak·er
clock´mak-ing
clock´wise
clock´work
clod
clod´hopper
clod´dish
clois´ter
clois´tered
clois´tral
close
close–by
closed
closed–circuit
closed–door
close–fisted
close–fitting
close–knit
close´ly
close´mouthed

close´ness
close´out
clos´est
clos´et
clos´et-ful
close–up
clos´ing
clo´sure
cloth
clothe
clothes´horse
clothes´line
clothes´pin
cloth´ier
cloth´ing
clo´ture
cloud´burst
cloud´i-ness
cloud´less
cloud´y
clo´ver-leaf
clown
clown´ish
clown´ish·ly
cloy´ing·ly
club
clubbed
club´bi-ness
club´bing
club´by
club´house
clum´si·er
clum´si·ly
clum´si-ness
clum´sy
clunk
clunk´er

clunk´y
clus´ter
clutch
clut´ter
co-ag´u-lant
co-ag´u-late
co-ag-u-la´tion
co-a-lesce´
co-a-les´cence
co-a-les´cent
co-a-lesc´ing
co-a-li´tion
co-an´chor
coarse´ly
coars´en
coarse´ness
coast´al
coast´er
coast´line
coast–to–coast
coat
coat´ed
coat´ing
coat´rack
coat´room
coat´tail
co - au´t h o r ,
  co–au´thor
coax
co-ax´i-al
coax´ing
coax´ing·ly
cob´bler
cob´ble-stone
cob´web
cock´eyed
cock´i·ly

41

cock´i-ness
cock´tail
cock´y
co-coon´
cod´dle
code
cod´ed
co-de-fend´ant
co-de-pend´ence
co-de-pend´
  en·cy
co-de-pend´ent
codg´er
cod´i-cil
cod-i-fi-ca´tion
cod´i-fied
cod´i·fy
cod´ling
co´ed
co-ed-u-ca´
  tion·al
co´ef-fi´cient
co-erce´
co-erç´i·ble
co-erc´ing
co-er´cion
co-er´cive-ness
co-ex-ist´
co-ex-is´tence
cof´fee-cake
cof´fee-house
cof´fee-pot
cof´fer
cof´fin
co´gent
cog´i-tate
cog´i-tat-ing

cog-i-ta´tion
cog´i-ta-tor
cog-ni´tion
cog´ni-tive
co-hab´it
co-hab-i-ta´tion
co-here´
co-her´ence
co-her´ent·ly
co-he´sion
co-he´sive·ly
co-he´sive-ness
co´hort
co—host´
coin´age
co-in-cide´
co-in´ci-dence
co-in´ci-dent
co-in-ci-den´tal
co-in-ci-den´
  tal·ly
co-in-cid´ing
co-in-sur´ance
co-in-sure´
col´an-der
cold´–blood´ed
cold´heart´ed
cold´ly
cold´ness
col´ic
col´ick·y
col-i-se´um
col-lab´o-rate
col-lab´o-rat-ing
col-lab-o-ra´tion
col-lab´o-ra-tive
col-lab´o-ra-tor

col-lage´
col-lapse´
col-lapsed´
col-laps´i·ble
col-laps´ing
col´lar
col´lar-bone
col-late´
col-lat´er·al
col-lat´er-al-ize
col-lat´ing
col-la´tion
col-la´tor
col´league
col-lect´
col-lect´ed
col-lect´i·ble
col-lec´tion
col-lec´tive·ly
col-lec´tor
col´leen
col´lege
col-le´gi·al
col-le´gian
col-le´giate
col-lide´
col-lid´ing
col-li´sion
col-lo´qui-al
col-lo´qui-al-ism
col-lo´qui-al·ly
col´lo-quy
col-lude´
col-lu´sion
col-lu´sive
co-logne´
co´lon

42

col´o-nel
co-lo´ni·al
co-lo´ni-al-ism
col-o-ni-za´tion
col´o-nize
col-on-nade´
col´o-phon
col´or
col´or-ant
col-or-a´tion
col´or-bear·er
color–blind
color–code
col´ored
col´or-fast
col´or-ful
col´or-ist
col´or-ize
col-or-i-za´tion
col´or-less
co-los´sal
co-los´sus
col´our *(Br.)*
colt´ish
col´umn
co-lum´nar
col´um-nist
co´ma
co´ma-tose
com´bat *(n., v.)*
com-bat´ *(v.)*
com-bat´ant
com-bat´ing
com-bat´ive
comb´er
com-bin´a·ble
com-bi-na´tion

com–bine´ *(join)*
com´bine *(n.
　harvester)*
com-bin´ing
com´bo
com-bust´
com-bus´ti·ble
com-bus´tion
come´back
co-me´di·an
co-me´dic
com´e-dies
com´e·dy
come–hither
come´li-ness
come·ly
come–on
co-mes´ti·ble
com´et
come-up´pance
com´fit
com´fort
com´fort-a·ble
com´fort-a·bly
com´fort·er
com´fy
com´ic
com´i-cal·ly
com´ing
coming–out
com´ma
com-mand´
com´man-dant
com´man-deer´
com-mand´er
com-mand´ing
com-mand´ing·ly

com-mand´ment
com-man´do
com-man´dos
com-mem´o-rate
com-mem´o-rat-
　ing
com-mem-o-ra´
　tion
com-mem´o-ra-
　tive
com-mence´
c o m - m e n c e ´
　ment
com-menc´ing
com-mend´a·ble
com-mend´a·bly
c o m - m e n - d a ´
　tion
c o m - m e n ´ s u -
　rate
com´ment
com´men-tar·y
com´men-ta-tor
com´merce
com-mer´cial
c o m - m e r ´ c i a l -
　ism
com-mer-cial-i-
　za´tion
com-mer´cial-ize
com-mer´cial·ly
com-min´gle
com-min´gling
com-mis´er-ate
c o m - m i s - e r -
　a´tion
com´mis-sar·y

com-mis´sion
com-mis´sion-
  a·ble
com-mis´sioned
com-mis´sion·er
com-mit´ment
com-mit´ted
com-mit´tee
com-mit´ting
com-mo´di-ous
c o m - m´o ´ d i -
  ous·ly
com-mod´i-ties
com-mod´i·ty
com´mo-dore
com´mon
com-mon-al´i·ty
com´mon·er
com´mon·ly
com´mon-place
com´mon-weal
com´mon-wealth
com-mo´tion
com-mu´nal
com-mu´nal·ly
com-mu´nal-ize
com-mune´ (v.)
com´mune (n.)
c o m - m u ´ n i -
  ca·ble
com-mu´ni-cate
com-mu´ni-cat-
  ing
com-mu´ni-ca´
  tion
com-mu´ni-ca-
  tive

com-mu´ni-ca-
  tor
com-mu´nion
com´mu-nism
com´mu-nist
com´mu-nis´tic
com-mu´ni-ties
com-mu´ni·ty
com-mu-ta´tion
com-mute´
com-mut´er
com-mut´ing
com´pact (n.)
com-pact´ (adj.,
  v.)
com-pact´ed
com-pact´ly
com-pact´ness
com-pac´tor
com´pa-nies
com-pan´ion
c o m - p a n ´ i o n-
  ship
com´pa·ny
com´pa-ra·ble
com´pa-ra·bly
com-par´a-tive·ly
com-pare´
com-par´ing
com-par´i-son
com-part´ment
com-part-men´
  tal
com-part-men´
  tal-ize
com´pass
com´pass·es

com-pas´sion
com-pas´sion-
  ate
com-pat-i·bil´i·ty
com-pat´i·ble
com-pat´i·bly
com-pa´tri·ot
com-pel´
com-pelled´
com-pel´ling
com-pel´ling·ly
com-pen´di-ous
c o m - p e n ´ d i -
  ous·ly
com-pen´di·um
com´pen-sate
com´pen-sat-ing
com-pen-sa´tion
c o m - p e n - s a ´
  tion·al
c o m - p e n ´ s a -
  to·ry
com-pete´
com´pe-tence
com´pe-ten·cy
com´pe-tent
com´pe-tent·ly
com-pet´ing
com-pe-ti´tion
com-pet´i-tive
com-pet´i-tive·ly
com-pet´i-tive-
  ness
com-pet´i-tor
com-pi-la´tion
com-pile´
com-pil´er

44

com-pil´ing
com-pla´cence
com-pla´cen·cy
com-pla´cent·ly
com-plain´
com-plain´ant
com-plain´ing·ly
com-plaint´
com-plai´sance
com-plai´sant·ly
com-plect´ed
com´ple-ment
com-ple-men´
  ta·ry
com-plete
com-plet´ed
com-plete´ly
com-plete´ness
com-ple´tion
com´plex
com-plex´ion
com-plex´ioned
com-plex´i·ty
com-plex´ness
com-pli´a·ble
com-pli´ance
com-pli´ant
com´pli-cate
com´pli-cat·ed
com´pli-ca´tion
com-plic´i·ty
com-plied´
com´pli-ment
com-pli-men´
  ta·ry
com-ply´ing
com-po´nent

com-port´ment
com-pose´
com-posed´
com-pos´er
com-pos´ite
com-po-si´tion
com-pos´i-tor
com´post
com-po´sure
com´pote
com´pound *(n.,*
  adj.)
com-pound´ *(v.,*
  adj.)
com-pre-hend´
com-pre-hend´
  i·ble
com-pre-hen´
  si·ble
com-pre-hen´
  sion
com-pre-hen´
  sive
com´press *(n.)*
com-press´ *(v.)*
com-pressed´
com-press´i·ble
com-pres´sion
com-prise´
com-pris´ing
comp-trol´ler
com-pul´sion
com-pul´sive·ly
com-pul´sive-
  ness
com-pul´so·ry
com-punc´tion

com-punc´tious
com-pu-ta´tion
com-put´a·ble
com-pute´
com-put´er
com-put´er-ize
com-put-er-i-za´
  tion
com-put´ing
com´rade
com´rade·ly
com´rade-ship
con-cat´e-nate
con-cat-e-na´
  tion
con´cave
con´cave´ness
con-cav´i·ty
con-ceal´a·ble
con-ceal-a·bil´
  i·ty
con-ceal´ment
con-cede´
con-ced´er
con-ced´ing
con-ceit´
con-ceit´ed
con-ceiv-a·bil´
  i·ty
con-ceiv´a·ble
con-ceiv´a·bly
con-ceive´
con-ceiv´ing
con´cen-trate
con´cen-trat·ed
con´cen-trating
con´cen-tra´tion

45

con-cen´tric
con-cen´tri-cal·ly
con-cen-tric´i·ty
con´cept
con-cep´tu·al
con-cep´tu·al-ize
con-cep-tu·al-i-
　za´tion
con-cep´tu·al·ly
con-cern´
con-cerned´
con-cern´ing
con´cert (n.)
con-cert´ (v.)
con-cert´ed
con-cer´to
con-ces´sion
con-ces´sion-
　aire´
con-cierge´
con-cil´i-ate
con-cil´i-at-ing
con-cil-i-a´tion
con-cil´i-a-tor
con-cil´ia-to·ry
con-cise´ly
con-cise´ness
con´clave
con-clude´
con-clud´ing
con-clu´sion
con-clu´sive·ly
con-coct´
con-coc´tion
con-com´i-tance
con-com´i-tan·cy
con-com´i-tant

con´cord (n.)
con-cord´ (v.)
con-cor´dance
con-cor´dant
con´course
con´crete,
　con-crete´
con-crete´ly
con´cu-bine
con-cur´
con-curred´
con-cur´rence
con-cur´ren·cy
con-cur´rent·ly
con-cur´ring·ly
con-cus´sion
con-demn´
con-dem´na·ble
con-dem-na´tion
con-demned´
con-demn´er
con-demn´ing
con-dens´a·ble
con-den´sate
con-den-sa´tion
con-dense´
con-densed´
con-dens´er
con-dens´ing
con-de-scend´
con-de-scend´
　ence
con-de-scend´-
　ing·ly
con-de-scen´sion
con´di-ment
con-di´tion·al

con-di´tion-al·ly
con-di´tioned
con-di´tion·er
con-di´tion-ing
con-do´lence
con-dol´ing
con´dom
con-do-min´i·um
con-don´a·ble
con-done´
con-duce´
con-du´cive
con´duct (n.)
con-duct´ (v.)
con-duct´ed
con-duc´tion
con-duc-tiv´i·ty
con-duc´tor
con´duit
con-fab´u-late
con-fab-u-la´tion
con-fec´tion-ar·y
con-fec´tion·er
con-fec´tion-er·y
con-fed´er-a·cy
con-fed´er-ate
con-fed-er-a´tion
con-fer´
con´fer·ee´
con´fer-ence
con-ferred´
con-fer´ring
con-fess´
con-fessed´
con-fess´ed·ly
con-fes´sion
con-fes´sion·al

con-fes´sor
con´fi-dant
con-fide´
con-fid´ed
con´fi-dence
con´fi-dent
con-fi-den´tial
con-fi-den-ti-al´
 i·ty
con-fi-den´tial·ly
con´fi-dent·ly
con-fig-u-ra´tion
con-fig´ure
con-fin´a·ble
con-fine´ *(v.)*
con´fine *(n.)*
con-fined´
con-fine´a·ble
con-fine´ment
con-fin´er
con-fin´ing
con-firm´
con-firm´a·ble
con-firm-a·bil´
 i·ty
con-fir-ma´tion
con-fis´ca·ble
con´fis-cate
con-fis-ca´tion
con-fis´ca-to·ry
con-fla-gra´tion
con´flict *(n.)*
con-flict´ *(v.)*
con-flict´ing
con-flic´tive
con-flic´to·ry
con´flu-ence

con´flu´ent
con-form´
con-form´a·ble
con-form´ance
con-for-ma´tion
con-form´ist
con-form´i·ty
con-found´
con-found´ed
con-fra-ter´ni·ty
con-front´
con-fron-ta´
 tion·al
con-fus´a·ble
con-fus´a·bly
con-fuse´
con-fused´
con-fus´ing·ly
con-fu´sion
con-fu-ta´tion
con-fute´
con-geal´
con-geal´a·ble
con´ge-ner
con-ge-ner´ic
con-ge´nial
con-ge-ni-al´i·ty
con-gen´i-tal
con-gen´i-tal·ly
con-gest´
con-gest´ed
con-ges´tion
con-ges´tive
con-glom´er-ate
con-glom-er-a´
 tion
con-grat´u-late

con-grat-u-la´
 tion
con-grat´u-la-
 to·ry
con´gre-gate
con-gre-ga´
 tion·al
con´gress
con-gres´sion·al
con´gress-man
con´gress-
 wom·an
con-gru´ence
con-gru´en·cy
con-gru´ent·ly
con-gru´i·ty
con´gru-ous·ly
con´ic
con´i-cal
con-jec´tur-a·bly
con-jec´tur·al
con-jec´ture
con-join´
con´ju-gal
con´ju-gal·ly
con-junc´tion
con-junc´tive
con-junc´ture
con´jure,   con-
 jure´
con´jur·er
con-nect´
con-nect-a·bil´
 i·ty
con-nect´a·ble
con-nect´ed
con-nect´er

con-nect-i·bil´
  i·ty
con-nect´i·ble
con-nec´tion
con-nec´tive
con-nec-tiv´i·ty
con-nec´tor
con-nip´tion
con-niv´ance
con-nive´
con-niv´er·y
con´nois-seur´
con-no-ta´tion
con´no-ta-tive
con´no-ta-tive·ly
con-note´
con-not´ing
con-nu´bi·al
con´quer
con´quer-a·ble
con´quered
con´quer-ing
con´quer·or
con´quest
con-quis´ta-dor
con-san-guin´
  e·ous
con-san-guin´
  e·ous·ly
con-san-guin´
  i·ty
con´science
con-sci-en´tious
c o n - s c i - e n ´
  tious·ly
con-sci-en´tious-
  ness

con´scion-a·ble
con´scion-a·bly
con´scious·ly
con´scious-ness
con-scribe´
con´script (n.)
con-script´ (v.)
con-scrip´tion
con´se-crate
con´se-crat-ing
con-se-cra´tion
con´se-cra-tor
con-sec´u-tive·ly
con-sen´su-al·ly
con-sen´sus
con-sent´er
con-sen´tient·ly
con´se-quence
con´se-quent
con-se-quen´tial
c o n - s e - q u e n ´
  tial·ly
con´se-quent·ly
con-serv´an·cy
c o n - s e r - v a ´
  tion·al
con-serv´a-tism
c o n - s e r v ´ a -
  tive·ly
con-serv´a-tive-
  ness
con´ser-va-tor
con-serv´a-to·ry
con-serve´
con-serv´ing
con-sid´er
con-sid´er-a·ble

con-sid´er-a·bly
con-sid´er-ate·ly
con-sid-er-a´tion
con-sid´ered
con-sid´er-ing
con-sign´
con-sign´a·ble
con-sig-na´tion
con´sign·ee´
con-sign´ment
con-sign´or
con-sist´
con-sist´ence
con-sist´en·cy
con-sist´ent·ly
con-sis´to·ry
con-sol´a·ble
con-so-la´tion
con-sole´ (v.)
con´sole (n.)
con-sol´i-date
con-sol´i-dat-ing
con-sol-i-da´tion
con-sol´ing
con-sol´ing·ly
con´so-nance
con´so-nant
con-sort´ (v.)
con´sort (n.)
con-sor´ti·um
con-spic´u-ous
c o n - s p i c ´ u -
  ous·ly
con-spic´u-ous-
  ness
con-spir´a·cy
con-spir´a-tive

con-spir´a-tor
con-spir´a-to´ri-
  al·ly
con-spire´
con-spir´ing
con´sta·ble
con-stab´u-lar·y
con´stan·cy
con´stant
con´stant·ly
con-stel-la´tion
con´ster-nate
con-ster-na´tion
con´sti-pate
con´sti-pat·ed
con-sti-pa´tion
con-stit´u-en·cy
con-stit´u-ent
con´sti-tute
con-sti-tu´tion
con-sti-tu´tion·al
con -sti-tu´-tion-
  al·ly
con-strain´
con-strain´a·ble
con-strained´
con-strain´ing
con-straint´
con-strict´
con-stric´tion
con-stric´tive
con-stric´tor
con-strin´gen·cy
con-strin´gent
con-stru´al
con-struct´ *(v.)*
con´struct *(n.)*

con-struct´i·ble
con-struc´tion
con-struc´tive
con-struc´tive·ly
con-struc´tor
con-strue´
con-strued´
con-stru´ing
con´sul
con´sul·ar
con´sul-ate
con-sult´
con-sult´an·cy
con-sult´ant
con-sul-ta´tion
con-sult´ing
con-sul´tor
con-sum´a·ble
con-sume´
con-sumed´
con sum´er
con-sum´er-ism
con-sum´ing
con-sum´mate
  (adj.)
con´sum-mate
  (v., adj.)
c o n - s u m -
  ma´tion
con-sump´tion
con´tact
con-ta´gion
con-ta´gious
con-tain´
con-tain´a·ble
con-tained´
con-tain´er-ize

con-tain´ing
con-tain´ment
con-tam´i-na·ble
con-tam´i-nant
con-tam´i-nate
con-tam´i-nat·ed
con-tam´i-nat-
  ing
con-tam-i-na´
  tion
con-tam´i-na-tor
con-temn´
con-temn´er
con´tem-plate
con-tem-pla´tion
con-tem´pla-tive
con-tem-po-ra-
  ne´i·ty
con-tem-po-ra´
  ne-ous
con-tem-po-ra-
  ´ne-ous·ly
con-tem´po-rar·y
con-tem´po-rize
con-tempt´
con-tempt-i-bil´
  i·ty
con-tempt´i·ble
con-tempt´i·ble-
  ness
con-temp´tu-ous
c o n - t e m p´ tu-
  ous·ly
con-tend´
con-tend´er
con-tent´ *(adj.,*
  v., n.)

con´tent *(n.)*
con-tent´ed
con-tent´ed·ly
con-tent´ed-ness
con-ten´tion
con-ten´tious·ly
con-teņ´tious-
 ness
con-tent´ly
con-tent´ment
con´tents
con-ter´mi-nous
c o n - t e r´ m i -
 nous·ly
con´test *(n.)*
con-test´ *(v.)*
con-test´a·ble
con-test´a·bly
con-tes´tant
con´text
con-tex´tu·al
con-tex´tu-al·ly
con-ti-gu´i·ty
con-tig´u-ous
con-tig´u-ous·ly
con´ti-nence
con´ti-nent
con-ti-nen´tal
con-ti-nen´tal·ly
con-tin´gence
con-tin´gen·cy
con-tin´gent·ly
con-tin´u-a·ble
con-tin´u-al
con-tin´u-al·ly
con-tin´u-ance
con-tin-u-a´tion

con-tin´ue
con-tin´u-ing
con-ti-nu´i·ty
con-tin´u-ous·ly
con-tin´u·um
con-tort´
con-tort´ed
con-tor´tion
con-tor´tion-ist
con´tour
con´tra
con´tra-band
con´tra-cep´tion
con´tra-cep´tive
con´tract *(n., v.)*
con-tract´ *(v.)*
con-tract´ed
con-tract-i·bil´
 i·ty
con-tract´i·ble
con-trac´tion
con´trac-tor
con-trac´tu·al
con-trac´tu-al·ly
c o n - t r a - d i c t´
 a·ble
con-tra-dict´
con-tra-dic´tion
c o n - t r a - d i c´
 tive·ly
con-tra-dic´to·ry
con-tral´to
con-trap´tion
con´trar-i-ness
con´trar·i-wise
con´trar·y
con-trast´ *(v.)*

con´trast *(n.)*
con-trast´ing·ly
con-tra-vene´
con-tra-ven´tion
con´tre-temps
con-trib´ute
con-trib´ut-ing
con-tri-bu´tion
con-trib´u-tive
con-trib´u-tor
con-trib´u-to·ry
con-trite´
con-trite´ly
con-trite´ness
con-tri´tion
con-triv´ance
con-trive´
con-trived´
con-triv´er
con-triv´ing
con-trol´
con-trol´la·ble
con-trol´la·bly
con-trol-led´
con-trol´ler
con-trol´ling
con-tro-ver´sial
c o n - t r o - v e r´
 sial·ly
con´tro-ver·sy
con´tro-vert
con-tro-vert´i·ble
con-tro-vert´i·bly
con-tu-ma´cious
c o n - t u - m a´
 cious·ly
con-tu´ma·cy

con-tu-me´li-ous
con-tu-me´li-
  ous·ly
con-tu´me·ly
con-tu´sion
co-nun´drum
con-va-lesce´
con-va-les´cence
con-va-les´cent
con-va-lesc´ing
con-vect´
con-vec´tion
con-vene´
con-ve´nience
con-ve´nient
con-ve´nient·ly
con-ven´ing
con´vent
con-ven´tion
con-ven´tion·al
con-ven´tion-
  al·ly
con-ven-tion-
  cer´
con-verge´
con-ver´gence
con-ver´gent
con-verg´ing
con-ver´sance
con-ver´sant
con-ver-sa´tion
con-ver-sa´
  tion·al
con-ver-sa´tion-
  al-ist
con´verse
  (reversed)

con-verse´
  (speak)
con-verse´ly
con-vers´ing
con-ver´sion
con´vert *(n.)*
con-vert´ *(v.)*
con-vert´i·ble
con´vex
con-vey´
con-vey´a·ble
con-vey´ance
con-vey´ing
con-vey´or
con´vict *(n.)*
con-vict´ *(v.)*
con-vict´a·ble
con-vic´tion
con-vince´
con-vinc´i·ble
con-vinc´ing·ly
con-viv´i·al
con-viv-i-al´i·ty
con-viv´l-al·ly
con-vo-ca´tion
con-vo-ca´tion·al
con-voke´
con-vok´ing
con´vo-lute
con´vo-lut·ed
con-vo-lu´tion
con-vo-lu´tion·al
con´voy
con-vulse´
con-vul´sion
con-vul´sive
con-vul´sive·ly

cook´book
cook´er
cook´er·y
cook´ie
cook´ing
cook´off
cook´out
cook´stove
cool´ant
cool´er
cool´ness
coop´er-age
co-op´er-ate
co-op-er-a´tion
co-op´er-a-tive·ly
co-or´di-nate
co-or-di-na´tion
co-or´di-na-tor
cop´i·er
cop´ies
co´pi·lot
cop´ing
co´pi-ous
co´pi-ous·ly
co´pi-ous-ness
cop–out
copse
cop´ter
cop´u-late
cop-u-la´tion
cop´y
cop´y-cat
cop´y-ed-i-tor
cop´y-ing
cop´y-right
cop´y-right·ed

cor´dial	cor-rec´tion·al	cor´us-cate
cor-dial´i·ty	cor-rec´tive	cor-us-ca´tion
cor´dial·ly	cor-rect´ly	co´sign
cord´less	cor-rect´ness	co-sig´na-to·ry
cor´du-roy	cor´re-late	co´sign·er
co-re-la´tion	cor-rel´a-tive	cos-met´ic
co-re-spon´dent	cor-re-spond´	cos-met´i-cal·ly
cork´age	c o r - r e - s p o n´ dence	cos-me-tol´o·gy
cork´board		cos´mic
cork´screw	cor-re-spon´dent	cos´mi-cal·ly
cork´y	cor-re-spond´ing	cos-mo-log´i-cal
cor´ner	cor´ri-dor	cos-mol´o·gy
cor´nered	cor-ri-gi·bil´i·ty	cos´mo-naut
cor´ner-stone	cor´ri-gi·ble	cos-mo-pol´i-tan
cor-net´	cor-rob´o-rate	cos´mos
corn´fed	cor-rob-o-ra´tion	cost´li-ness
corn´field	cor-rob´o-ra-tive	cost´ly
cor´nice	cor-rob´o-ra-tor	cos´tume
corn´stalk	cor-rode´	cos´tum·er
cor-nu-co´pi·a	cor-rod´i·ble	co-ten´an·cy
corn´y	cor-rod´ing	co-ten´ant
cor´o-nar·y	cor-ro´sion	co´te-rie
cor-o-na´tion	cor-ro´sive	co-til´lion
cor´o-ner	cor-ro´sive-ness	cot´tage
cor-o-net´	cor´ru-gate	cot´ter
cor´po-rate	cor´ru-gat·cd	cot´ton
cor´po-rate·ly	cor-ru-ga´tion	cot´ton-seed
cor-po-ra´tion	cor-rupt´	cough
cor-po´re·al	cor-rupt´er	could
corps	cr-rupt´i·ble	coun´cil
corpse	cor-rup´tion	coun´sel
cor´pu-lence	cor-rup´tive	coun´sel-lor *(Br.)*
cor´pu-lent	cor-rupt´ly	coun´sel·or
cor-ral´	cor-rupt´ness	coun´te-nance
cor-rect´	cor-sage´	coun´ter *(contra)*
cor-rect´a·ble	cor´set	count´er *(ledge)*
cor-rec´tion	cor´tege	coun-ter-act´

coun´ter-bal-
 ance
coun´ter-claim
coun´ter-clock´-
 wise
coun´ter-cul-
 ture
coun´ter-feit·er
coun´ter-mand
coun´ter-mine
coun´ter-of-fer
coun´ter-part
coun´ter-point
coun-ter-pro-
 duc´tive
coun´ter-sign
coun´ter-suit
count´er-top
count´ess
coun´ties
count´less
coun´tries
coun´tri-fied
coun´try
coun´try-man
coun´try-side
coun´ty
cou´ple
cou´pler
cou´plet
cou´pling
cou´pon
cour´age
cou-ra´geous·ly
cou-ra´geous-
 ness
cou´ri·er

course
cours´ing
court
cour´te-ous
cour´te-ous·ly
cour´te-ous-ness
cour´te-san
cour´te·sy
court´house
cour´tier
court´li-ness
court´ly
court´room
court´ship
court´yard
cous´in
cov´en
cov´e-nant
cov´er
cov´er-age
cov´er all
cov´ered
cov´er-ing
cov´er-let
cov´ert
co´vert·ly
cov´er–up
cov´et
cov´e-tous·ly
cov´e-tous-ness
cov´ey
cow´ard
cow´ard-ice
cow´ard·ly
cow´er
cowl
cowl´ing

co–worker
coy
coy´ly
coy´ness
co´zi-est
co´zi·ly
co´zi-ness
co´zy
crab´bi-ness
crab´by
crack´down
cracked
crack´er
cracker–barrel
crack´ing
crack´le
crack´ling
crack´pot
crack–up
cra´dle
craft
craft´i·ly
craft´i-ness
crafts´man-ship
craft´y
crag´gi-ness
crag´gy
cram
crammed
cram´ming
cramp
cramped
crane
craned
cran´ing
crank
crank´case

crank´i-ness
crank´shaft
crank´y
cran´ny
crash´ing
crash–land
crass´ly
crass´ness
crater (chasm)
crat´ing
cra-vat´
crave
cra´ven
crav´ing
craw
craw´dad
craw´fish
crawl
crawl´ing
crawl´space
crawl´y
cray´fish
cray´on
craze
crazed
cra´zi·ly
cra´zi-ness
cra´zy
creak
creak´i-ness
creak´y
cream
cream´er
cream´er·y
cream´i-ness
cream´y
cre-ate´

cre-at´ing
cre-a´tion-ism
cre-a´tive
cre-a´tive·ly
cre-a-tiv´i·ty
cre-a´tor
crea´ture
cre´dence
cre-den´tial
cre-den´za
cred-i·bil´i·ty
cred´i·ble
cred´it
cred´it-a·ble
cred´i-tor
cre´do
cre-du´li·ty
cred´u-lous
cred´u-lous·ly
creed
creel
creek
creep
creep´er
creep´i-ness
creep´ing
creep´y
cre´mate
cre-ma´tion
cre-ma-to´ri·um
cre´o-sote
crêpe
cre-scen´do
cres´cent
crest
crest´ed
crest´fall·en

crest´ing
crev´ice
crev´iced
crew´el-work
crew´man
crib´bage
crib´bing
crick´et
crick´et·er
cried
cri´er
crime
crim´i-nal
crim-i-nal´i·ty
crim´i-nal·ly
crim-i-nol´o-gist
crim-i-nol´o·gy
crimp
crim´son
cringe
cringed
cring´ing
crin´kle
crin´kly
crin´o-line
crip´ple
crip´pled
crip´pler
crip´pling
cri´sis
crisp´er
crisp´i-ness
crisp´ly
crisp´ness
crisp´y
criss´cross
cri-te´ri·on

crit´ic
crit´i-cal
crit´i-cal·ly
crit´i-cism
crit´i-cize
crit´i-ciz-ing
cri-tique´
crit´ter
cro-chet´
cro-cheted´
cro-chet´er
cro-chet´ing
crock´er·y
crock´et
cro´cus
crois-sant´
cro´ny
cro´ny-ism
crook´ed *(v.)*
crooked *(adj.)*
croon´er
cross
cross´bar
cross´bow
cross´–coun´try
cross´cur-rent
cross´–ex-am´ine
cross´hatch
cross´ing
cross´–leg´ged
cross´ness
cross´o·ver
cross´patch
cross´–pur´pose
cross´–ref´er-
   ence
cross´walk

crotch´et
crow´bar
crowd´ed
crowned
crow's–nest
cru´cial
cru´ci·ble
cru´ci-fix
cru´ci·fy
crude
crude´ly
cru´el
cru´el·ly
cru´el·ty
cru´et
cruise
cruised
cruis´er
cruis´ing
crumb
crum´ble
crum´bling
crum´bly
crumb´y
crum´my
crum´ple
crum´pling
crunch
crunch´ing
cru-sade´
cru-sad´er
cru-sad´ing
crush
crush´a·ble
crus-ta´cean
crust´ed
crust´i·ly

crust´i-ness
crust´y
crutch
crux
cry´ba·by
cry´ing
cry-o-gen´ics
cry-on´ics
crypt
cryp´tic
cryp´to-gram
cryp-tog´ra-pher
cryp-tog´ra-phy
crys´tal
crys´tal-line
crys-tal-li-za´
   tion
crys´tal-lize
cub´by-hole
cube
cubed
cu´bic
cu´bi-cal *(adj.)*
cu´bi-cle *(n.)*
cub´ism
cub´ist
cud´dle
cud´dled
cud´dling
cud´dly
cud´gel
cui-sine´
cul´–de–sac
cul´i-nar·y
cul´mi-nate
cul-mi-na´tion
cu-lotte´

cul-pa·bil´i·ty
cul´pa·ble
cul´pa·bly
cul´prit
cult
cul´ti-vate
cul´ti-vat·ed
cul-ti-va´tion
cul´ti-va-tor
cul´tur·al
cul´ture
cul´tured
cul´vert
cum´ber-some
cu´mu-la-tive
cu´mu-la-tive·ly
cup´ful
cu-pid´i·ty
cu´po·la
cupped
cup´ping
cur´a·ble
cu´ra-tive
cu-ra´tor
curb´ing
curb´side
curb´stone
curd
cur´dle
cur´dling
cure–all
cur´few
cu´ri·o
cu-ri-os´i·ty
cu´ri-ous
cu´ri-ous·ly
curl´er

cur´li-cue
curl´i-ness
curl´ing
curl´y
cur-mud´geon
cur´ren·cy
cur´rent
cur´rent·ly
curse
cursed
curs´ing
cur´sive
cur´sive·ly
cur´sive-ness
cur´sor
cur´so·ry
curt
cur-tail´
cur-tail´ment
cur´tain
curt´ly
curt´ness
curt´sy, curt´sey
cur-va´ceous
cur´va-ture
curve
curved
curv´ing
cush´ion
cush´y
cuss´ed-ness
cus-to´di·al
cus-to´di·an
cus´to·dy
cus´tom
cus´tom-ar´i·ly
cus´tom-ar·y

cus´tom–built´
cus´tom·er
cus´tom-ize
cus´tom–made´
cut´a·way
cut´back
cut´down
cute
cute´ly
cute´ness
cute´sy
cu´ti-cle
cut´ie
cut´ler·y
cut´off
cut´–rate´
cut´ter
cut´throat
cut´ting
cut´up
cy-ber-net´ics
cy´ber-space
cy´cle
cy´clic, cy´cli-cal
cy´cling
cy´clist
cy´clone
cyl´in-der
cy-lin´dri-cal·ly
cym´bal
cyn´ic
cyn´i-cal·ly
cyn´i-cism
dab´ble
dab´bling
dad´dy
daf´fo-dil

daf´fy
dag´ger
dai´lies
dai´ly
dain´ti·ly
dain´ti-ness
dain´ty
dai´qui·ri
dair´ies
dair´y
dair´y-man
dai-shi´ki
dal´li-ance
dal´lied
dal´li·er
dal´ly
dal´ly-ing
dam´age
dam´age-a·ble
dam´ag-ing
dam´ask
dam-na´tion
damned
damn´ing
damp´en
damp´en·er
damp´er
damp´ish
damp´ness
dam´sel
dance´a·ble
danced
danc´er
danc´er-cise
danc´ing
dan´der
dan´di-fied

dan´di·fy
dan´druff
dan´dy
dan´ger
dan´ger-ous·ly
dan´gle
dan´gled
dan´gling
dank´ness
dap´per
dap´ple
dare´dev·il
dare´say
dar´ing
dar´ing·ly
dark´en
dark´ly
dark´ness
dark´room
dar´ling
darn
darned
darn´ing
dash´board
dashed
dash´er
da-shi´ki
dash´ing
das´tard·ly
da´ta
da´ta-base
date
date´book
dat´ed
date´line
dat´ing
da´tum

daub´er
daugh´ter
daugh´ter–in–la
  w
daunt
daunt´ing·ly
daunt´less·ly
dav´en-port
daw´dle
daw´dler
daw´dling
dawn
day´bed
day´break
day´dream
day´light
day´time
day–to–day
dazed
daz´ed·ly
daz´zle
daz´zling
daz´zling·ly
dea con
dea´con-ess
de-ac´ti-vate
de-ac-ti-va´tion
de-ac´ti-va-tor
dead´beat
dead´bolt
dead´en
dead´en-ing
dead´li·er
dead´line
dead´li-ness
dead´lock
dead´ly

dead´pan
deaf´en
deaf´en-ing
deaf´ness
deal´er
deal´er-ship
deal´ing
dealt
dear´ie
dear´ly
death´bed
death–dealing
death´less
death´ly
death´trap
de-ba´cle
de-bar´
de-bark´
de-bar-ka´tion
de-based´
de-bas´ing
de-bat´a·ble
de-bate´
de-bat´er
de-bat´ing
de-bauch´
de-bauched´
de-bauch´er
de-bauch´er·y
de-ben´ture
de-bil´i-tate
de-bil´i-tat·ed
de-bil-i-ta´tion
deb´it
deb´o-nair´
de-bone´
debt´or

de-bug´
de´but
deb´u-tante
dec´ade
dec´a-dence
dec´a-dent
de-caf´fein-ate
de´cal
de-cant´
de-cant´er
de-cap´i-tate
de-cap-i-ta´tion
de-cay´
de-cayed´
de-cay´ing
de-ceased´
de-ce´dent
de-ceit´
de-ceit´ful·ly
de-ceit´ful-ness
de-ceiv´a·ble
de-ceiv´a·bly
de-ceive´
de-ceiv´er
de-cel´er-ate
de-cel-er-a´tion
de´cen·cy
de´cent
de´cent·ly
de-cen-tral-i-za´
  tion
de-cen´tral-ize
de-cep´tion
de-cep´tive·ly
de-cer´ti·fy
dec´i-bel
de-cide´

de-cid´ed·ly
de-cid´ing
de-cid´u-ous
de-cid´u-ous·ly
dec´i-mal
dec´i-mate
dec-i-ma´tion
de-ci´pher
de-ci´pher-a·ble
de-ci´sion
de-ci´sive·ly
de-ci´sive-ness
deck´le
de-claim´
dec-la-ma´tion
de-clam´a-to·ry
dec-la-ra´tion
de-clare´
de-clas´si·fy
de-claw´
de-cline´
de-clined´
de-clin´ing
de-cliv´i·ty
de-code´
de-cod´er
de-cod´ing
dé-col-le-tage´
de-com-mis´sion
de-com-pose´
de-com-press´
de-com-pres´
  sion
de-con-tam´i-
  nate
de-cor´
dec´o-rate

dec-o-ra´tion
dec´o-ra-tive·ly
dec´o-ra-tor
dec´o-rous·ly
de-co´rum
dé-cou-page´
de´-coy
de´coyed
de´crease *(n.)*
de-crease´ *(v.)*
de-creas´ing·ly
de-cree´
de-creed´
de-cree´ing
de-crep´it
de-cried´
de-crim´i·nal-ize
de-cry´
ded´i-cate
ded´i-cat·ed
ded-i-ca´tion
ded´i-ca-to·ry
de-duce´
de-duced´
de-duc´i·ble
de-duc´i·bly
de-duc´ing
de-duct´
de-duct´i·ble
de-duc´tion
de-duc´tive
de-duc´tive·ly
deed
deem
de–em´pha-size
de–em´pha-sis
deep´en

deep–freeze
deep–fry
deep–rooted
deep–seated
deer´skin
de-face´
de-faced´
de-face´ment
de-fac´ing
de fac´to
def-a-ma´tion
de-fam´a-to·ry
de-fame´
de-fault´
de-fault´er
de-feat´ed
de-feat´ist
def´e-cate
def-e-ca´tion
de´fect *(n.)*
de-fect´ *(v.)*
de-fect´ed
de-fec´tion
de-fec´tive
de-fec´tor
de-fend´
de-fend´a·ble
de-fend´ant
de-fend´er
de-fense´
de-fense´less
de-fen´si·ble
de-fen´si·bly
de-fen´sive
de-fen´sive·ly
de-fer´
def´er-ence

def´er-ent
def-er-en´tial
def-er-en´tial·ly
de-fer´ment
de-ferred´
de-fi´ance
de-fi´ant·ly
de-fi´cien·cy
de-fi´cient
de-fi´cient·ly
def´i-cit
de-fied´
de-fi´er
de-file´
de-file´ment
de-fil´er
de-fil´ing
de-fin´a·ble
de-fin´a·bly
de-fine´
de fin´ing
def´i-nite
def´i-nite·ly
def-i-ni´tion
de-fin´i-tive
de-fin´i-tive·ly
de-flate´
de-fla´tion
de-fla´tion-ar·y
de-fla´tor
de-flect´
de-flec´tion
de-flec´tive
de-flec´tor
de-fog´ger
de-fo´li-ant
de-fo´li-ate

de-for-est-a´tion
de-form´
de-for-ma´tion
de-formed´
de-for´mi·ty
de-fraud´
de-fraud´ed
de-fray´
de-frayed´
de-fray´ing
de-frock´
de-frost´er
deft´ly
deft´ness
de-funct´
de-fuse´
de-fy´
de-fy´ing
de-gen´er-a·cy
de-gen´er-ate
de-gen-er-a´tion
de-gen´er-a-tive
de-glaze´
deg-ra-da´tion
de-grade´
de-grad´ed
de-grad´ing
de-grease´
de-gree´
de-hu´man-ize
de-hu-mid´i-fi·er
de-hy´drate
de-hy-dra´tion
de-ice´
de-ic´er
de-i-fi-ca´tion
de´i-fied

de´i·fy
deign
de´i-ties
de´i·ty
de-ject´
de-ject´ed
de-ject´ed·ly
de-jec´tion
de-lam´i-nate
de-lam-i-na´tion
de-lay´
de-layed´
de-lay´ing
de-lec´ta·ble
de-lec´ta·bly
del´e-gate
del-e-ga´tion
de-lete´
de-let´ed
del-e-te´ri-ous
de-le´tion
del´i
de-lib´er-ate·ly
de-lib-er-a´tion
de-lib´er-a-tive
del´i-ca-cies
del´i-ca·cy
del´i-cate
del´i-cate·ly
del´i-cate-ness
del-i-ca-tes´sen
de-li´cious
de-li´cious·ly
de-light´ed·ly
de-light´ful·ly
de-lim´it
de-lim´it·er

de-lin´e-ate
de-lin-e-a´tion
de-lin´e-a-tor
de-lin´quen·cy
de-lin´quent
de-lin´quent·ly
de-lir´i-ous
de-lir´i-ous·ly
de-lir´i·um
de-liv´er
de-liv´er-ance
de-liv´er·er
de-liv´er-ies
de-liv´er·y
de-louse´
de-lude´
de-lud´ed
de-lud´ing
del´uge
del´uged
de-lu´sion
de-lu´sion·al
de-luxe´
delved
delv´ing
de-mag´net-ize
dem´a-gog´ic
dem´a-gogue
de-mand´
de-mand´ed
de-mand´ing
de-mar-ca´tion
de-mean´
de-mean´or
de-ment´ed
de-men´tia
de-mer´it

de-mil´i-ta-rize
de-mise´
dem´i-tasse
de-mo´bi-lize
de-moc´ra·cy
dem´o-crat
dem´o-crat´ic
dem´o-crat´i-cal·ly
de-moc´ra-tize
de-mod´u-late
de-mod-u-la´tion
de-mod´u-la-tor
de´mo-graph´ics
de-mol´ish
dem-o-li´tion
de´mon
de-mon´ic
de-mon-ol´o·gy
de-mon´stra·ble
de-mon´stra·bly
dem´on-strate
dem´on-strat-ing
dem-on-stra´tion
de-mon´stra-tive
dem´on-stra-tor
de-mor´al-ize
de-mor´al-iz-ing
de-mote´
de-mot´ed
de-mo´tion
de-mur´ *(v.)*
de-mure´ *(adj.)*
de-mure´ly
de-mys´ti·fy
de-my-thol´o-gize

de-na´tured
de-ni´a·ble
de-ni´al
de-nied´
de-nies´
den´i-grate
den-i-gra´tion
den´i-gra-tor
den´im
den´i-zen
de-nom-i-na´tion
de-nom´i-na-tor
de-note´
de-no´tive
de-noue-ment´
de-nounced´
de-nounc´ing
dense´ly
den´si·ty
den´tal
den´tist
den´tis-try
den´ture
dc-nun´ci-ate
de-nun-ci-a´tion
de-ny´ing
de-o´dor-ant
de-o´dor-ize
de-o´dor-iz·er
de-part´ed
de-part´ment
de-part-men´tal-ize
de-par´ture
de-pend´
de-pend-a·bil´i·ty

de-pend´a·ble
de-pen´dence
de-pen´dent
de-pict´
de-pic´tion
de-pil´a-to·ry
de-ple´tion
de-plor´a·ble
de-plor´a·bly
de-plore´
de-plored´
de-plor´ing·ly
de-ploy´ment
de-po´lar-ize
de-port´
de-por-ta´tion
de-port´ed
de-port-ee´
de-port´ment
de-pose´
de-posed´
de-pos´ing
de-pos´it
de-pos´it·ed
dep-o-si´tion
de-pos´i-to·ry
de´pot
dep-ra-va´tion
de-praved´
de-prav´i·ty
dep´re-cate
dep´re-cat-ing
dep-re-ca´tion
de-pre´cia·ble
de-pre´ci-ate
de-pre-ci-a´tion
de-press´

de-pres´sant
de-pressed´
de-press´ing
de-pres´sion
dep-ri-va´tion
de-prive´
de-prived´
de-priv´ing
depth
dep-u-ta´tion
dep´u-ties
dep´u-tize
dep´u·ty
de-rail´ment
de-range´ment
de-rang´ing
der´by
der´e-lict
der-e-lic´tion
de-ride´
de-rid´ing
de-ri´sion
de-ri´sive
de-ri´sive·ly
de-ri´sive-ness
der-i-va´tion
de-riv´a-tive
de-rive´
de-rived´
de-riv´ing
der-ma-tol´o-gist
der-ma-tol´o·gy
der´o-gate
der-o-ga´tion
de-rog´a-tive
de-rog´a-tive·ly
de-rog´a-to·ry

der´rick
de-scend´ed
de-scend´ent
de-scend´er
de-scribe´
de-scribed´
de-scrip´tion
de-scrip´tive
de-scrip´tor
des-cry´
des-cry´ing
des´e-crate
des-e-cra´tion
des´e-cra-tor
des´ert *(waste-
land)*
de-sert´ *(fore-
sake)*
de-sert´er
de-ser´tion
de-served´
de-serv´ed·ly
de-serv´ing
de-sign´
des´ig-nate
des-ig-na´tion
des´ig-na-tor
de-sign´er
de-sign´ing
de-sir-a·bil´i·ty
de-sir´a·ble
de-sir´a·bly
de-sire´
de-sir´ous
de-sist´
desk´top
des´o-late

des-o-la´tion
de-spaired´
de-spair´ing
de-spair´ing·ly
des-per-a´do
des-per-a´does
des´per-ate
des´per-ate·ly
des´per-ate-ness
des-per-a´tion
de-spic´a·bly
de-spised´
de-spis´ing
de-spite´
de-spoil´er
de-spoil´ing
de-spond´
de-spon´dence
de-spon´den·cy
de-spon´dent
des´pot
des-pot´ic
des´po-tism
des-sert´
des-ti-na´tion
des´tined
des´ti-nies
des´ti·ny
des´ti-tute
des-ti-tu´tion
de-stroyed´
de-stroy´er
de-struct´
de-struc´tion
de-struc´tive·ly
de-struc´tive-
ness

des´ul-to·ry
de-tach´
de-tach´a·ble
de·tached´
de-tach´ment
de-tail´, de´tail
de-tailed´
de´tail-ing
de-tain´
de-tain´ment
de-tect´
de-tect´a·ble
de-tec´tion
de-tec´tive
de-tec´tor
dé-tente
de-ten´tion
de-ter´
de-te´ri-o-rate
de-te-ri-o-ra´tion
de-ter´ment
de-ter´min-a·ble
de-ter´mi-nant
de-ter-mi-na´tion
de-ter´mined
de-terred´
de-ter´rence
de-ter´rent
de-test´
de-test´a·ble
de-test´a·bly
det´o-nate
det-o-na´tion
det´o-na-tor
de´tour

de-tox-i-fi-ca´tion
de-tox´i·fy
de-tract´
de-trac´tion
de-trac´tor
det´ri-ment
det-ri-men´tal
deuce
deuc´ed
deuc´ed·ly
de-val´u-ate
de-val-u-a´tion
de-val´ue
dev´as-tate
dev´as-tat·ed
dev´as-tat-ing
dcv´as-tat-ing·ly
dev-as-ta´tion
de-vel´op
de-vel´oped
de-vel´op·er
de-vel´op-ing
de vel´op-mcnt
de-vel´op-men´tal
de´vi-ance
de´vi-ant
de´vi-ate
de-vi-a´tion
de-vice´
dev´il
dev´il-ish·ly
dev´il-ment
dev´il-try
de´vi-ous·ly
de´vi-ous-ness

de-vise´
de-vi-tal-i·za´tion
de-vi´tal-ize
de-void´
de-vote´
de-vot´ed
de-vot´ed·ly
de-vot´ed-ness
dev´o-tee´
de-vo´tion
de-vo´tion·al
de-vour´
de-vout´
de-vout´ly
de-vout´ness
dew´i-ness
dew´lap
dew´point
dew´y
dex-ter´i·ty
dex´ter-ous
dex´ter-ous·ly
dex´ter-ous-ness
dex´trous
di-a-bol´ic
di-a-bol´i-cal
di-a-bol´i-cal·ly
di´ag-nose
di-ag-no´sis
di´ag-nos-ti´cian
di´ag-nos-tics
di-ag´o-nal
di-ag´o-nal·ly
di´a-gram
di´a-gram-mat´ic
di´al

63

di´a-lect	di-e-ti´tian	di-gress´
di´aled	dif´fered	di-gres´sion
di´al·er	dif´fer-ence	di-gres´sive
di´al-ing	dif´fer-ent	di-lap´i-date
di´a-logue	dif-fer-en´tial	di-lap´i-dat·ed
di-am´e-ter	dif-fer-en´ti-ate	di-late´
di-a-met´ric	dif´fer-ent·ly	di-lat´ing
di-a-met´ri-cal·ly	dif´fi-cult	di-la´tion
di´a-per	dif´fi-cul-ties	di-lem´ma
di-aph´a-nous	dif´fi-cul·ty	dil-et-tante´
di´a-ries	dif´fi-dence	dil´i-gence
di´a-rist	dif´fi-dent	dil´i-gent
di´a·ry	dif´fi-dent·ly	dil´i-gent·ly
di-as´po·ra	dif-fract´	di-lute´
di´a-spore	dif-frac´tion	di-lut´ing
di´a-tribe	dif-fuse´	di-lu´tion
dic´ey	dif-fus´i·ble	di-men´sion
di-chot´o·my	dif-fu´sion	di-min´ish
dick´er	dif-fu´sive	dim-i-nu´tion
dick´ey	di´gest *(n.)*	dim´ly
dic´tate	di-gest´ *(v.)*	dimmed
dic´tat-ing	di-gest´i·ble	dim´mer
dic-ta´tion	di-ges´tion	dim´ming
dic´ta-tor	di-ges´tive	dim´ness
dic-ta-to´ri·al	dig´ger	dim´ple
dic´ta´tor-ship	dig´gings	dim´pling
dic´tion	dig´it	dim´wit
dic´tio-nar-ies	dig´i-tal	dined
dic´tio-nar·y	dig´it-al·ly	din´er
dic´tum	dig´i-tize	di-nette´
di-dac´tic	dig´ni-fied	din´gi-ness
di-dac´ti-cal·ly	dig´ni·fy	din´gy
die´sel	dig´ni-fy-ing	din´ing
di´et	dig´ni-tar-ies	din´ner
di´e-tar·y	dig´ni-tar·y	din´ner-time
di´et·er	dig´ni-ties	din´ner-ware
di-e-tet´ic	dig´ni·ty	di´no-saur

di´o-cese
di-o-ram´a
diph´thong
di-plo´ma
di-plo´ma·cy
dip´lo-mat
dip-lo-mat´ic
dip-lo-mat´i-
　cal·ly
dipped
dip´per
dip-so-ma´ni·a
dip-so-ma´ni·ac
dip´stick
di-rect´
di-rect´ed
di-rec´tion
di-rec´tive
di-rect´ly
di-rect´ness
di-rec´tor
di-rec´tor-ate
di-rec´to·ry
dire´ly
dirge
dir´i-gi·ble
dirt´i·er
dirt´i-ness
dirt´y
dis-a·bil´i·ty
dis-a´ble
dis-a´bled
dis-a´bling
dis-ad-van´taged
dis-a·gree´
dis-a·gree-a·bil´
　i·ty

dis-a·gree´a·ble
dis-a·gree´a·bly
dis-a·gree´ment
dis-ap-pear´
dis-ap-pear´ance
dis-ap-peared´
dis-ap-point´
dis-ap-point´ing
dis-ap-point´
　ment
dis-ap-pro-ba´
　tion
dis-ap-prov´al
dis´ap-prove´
dis´ap-prov´ing
dis´ap-prov´
　ing·ly
dis-arm´
dis-ar´ma-ment
dis-arm´ing
dis-arm´ing·ly
dis-ar-ray´
dis-as-so´ci-ate
di-sas´ter
di-sas´trous·ly
dis-a·vow´al
dis-a·vow´ed·ly
dis-band´
dis-bar´
dis-bar´ment
dis-be-lief´
dis-burse´
dis-burse´ment
dis-burs´ing
dis´card (n.)
dis-card´ (v.)
dis-cern´i·ble

dis-cern´i·bly
dis-cern´ing
dis-cern´ment
dis´charge (n.)
dis-charge´ (n.,
　v.)
dis-ci´ple
dis-ci-pli-nar´
　i·an
dis´ci-pli-nar·y
dis´ci-pline
dis-claim´er
dis-close´
dis-clo´sure
dis-col-or-a´tion
dis-com´fit
dis-com´fi-ture
dis-com´fort
dis-con-cert´
dis-con-cert´ed
dis-con-cert´ing
dis-con-nect´ed
dis-con-tent´
dis-con-tent´ed
dis-con-tent´
　ment
dis-con-tin-u-a´
　tion
dis-con-tin´ue
dis´cord
dis-cor´dance
dis-cor´dant·ly
dis´co-theque
dis´count
dis-cour´age
dis-cour´age-
　ment

65

dis-cour´ag-ing
dis´course *(n.)*
dis-course´ *(v.)*
dis-cour´te-
　ous·ly
dis-cour´te·sy
dis-cov´er
dis-cov´er·er
dis-cov´er-ies
dis-cov´er·y
dis-creet´ *(pru-
　dent)*
dis-creet´ly
dis-creet´ness
dis-crep´an·cy
dis-crete´ *(dis-
　tinct)*
dis-cre´tion
dis-cre´tion-ar·y
dis-crim´i-nate
dis-crim´i-nat-
　ing
dis-crim-i-na´
　tion
dis-cuss´
dis-cussed´
dis-cus´sion
dis-dain´ful·ly
dis-eased´
dis-em-bark´
dis-em-bar-ka´
　tion
dis-em-bod´y
dis-en-chant´
dis-en-chant´ing
dis-en-chant´
　ment

dis-en-fran´chise
dis-en-gage´
dis-en-gage´
　ment
dis-fig-u-ra´tion
dis-fig´ure
dis-fig´ur-ing
dis-gorge´
dis-grace´
dis-grace´ful·ly
dis-grun´tled
dis-guise´
dis-gust´ed
dis-gust´ed·ly
dis-gust´ing·ly
dis-ha·bille´
dis-har´mo·ny
dish´cloth
dis-heart´en
dis-heart´en-ing
dished
di-shev´eled
di-shev´el-ment
dish´mop
dis-hon´est
dis-hon´est·ly
dis-hon´es·ty
dis-hon´or
dis-hon´or-a·ble
dis-hon´or-a·bly
dish´pan
dish´wash·er
dish´wa·ter
dis-il-lu´sion
dis-in-fect´
dis-in-fec´tant
dis-in-gen´u-ous

dis-in´te-grate
dis-in-te-gra´
　tion
dis-in-ter´
dis-in´ter-est
dis-in´ter-est·ed
dis-join´
dis-joint´ed
disk
disk-ette´
dis-like´
dis´lo-cate
dis-lo-ca´tion
dis-lodge´
dis-loy´al
dis-loy´al·ly
dis-loy´al·ty
dis´mal
dis´mal·ly
dis-man´tle
dis-man´tling
dis-may´
dis-mem´ber-
　ment
dis-miss´
dis mis´sal
dis-miss´ive
dis-mount´
dis-o·be´di-ence
dis-o·be´di-ent·ly
dis-o·bey´
dis-o·beyed´
dis-or´der
dis-or´dered
dis-or´der·ly
dis-or-ga-ni-za´-
　tion

dis-or´ga-nize
dis-o´ri-ent
dis-o-ri-en-ta´tion
dis-own´
dis-par´age-ment
dis-par´ag-ing·ly
dis-par´i·ty
dis-patch´er
dis-pel´
dis-pelled´
dis-pens´a·ble
dis-pen´sa·ry
dis-pen-sa´tion
dis-pense´
dis-pens´er
dis-per´sal
dis-per´sant
dis-perse´
dis-per´sion
di-spir´it·ed
dis-place´
dis-placed´
dis-place´ment
dis-play´
dis-plea´sure
dis-pos´a·ble
dis-pos´al
dis-pose´
dis-posed
dis-po-si´tion
dis-pos-sessed´
dis-proof´
dis-pro-por´tion
dis-pro-por´tion-ate·ly

dis-prove´
dis-put´a·ble
dis-put´a·bly
dis-pu´tant
dis-pu-ta´tion
dis-pute´
dis-qual´i-fied
dis-qual´i·fy
dis-qui´et
dis-re-gard´
dis-rep´u-ta·ble
dis-re-pute´
dis-robe´
dis-rupt´
dis-rup´tion
dis-rup´tive
dis-sect´
dis-sect´ed
dis-sec´tion
dis-sem´blance
dis-sem´ble
dis-sem´i-nate
dis-sem-i-na´tion
dis-sen´sion
dis-sent´er
dis-sen´tious
dis-ser-ta´tion
dis´si-dence
dis´si-dent
dis´si-pate
dis´si-pat·ed
dis-si-pa´tion
dis-so´ci-ate
dis-so-ci-a´tion
dis´so-lute
dis´so-lute·ly

dis-solv´a·ble
dis-solve´
dis-solv´ing
dis´so-nance
dis´so-nant
dis-suade´
dis-sua´sion
dis-sua´sive
dis´taff
dis´tance
dis´tant·ly
dis-taste´ful
dis-tem´per
dis-tend´ed
dis-tend´er
dis-till´
dis´til-late
dis-til-la´tion
dis-till´er
dis-till´er·y
dis-till´ing
dis-tinct´
dis-tinc´tion
dis-tinc´tive·ly
dis-tinct´ly
dis-tinct´ness
dis-tin´guish
dis-tin´guish-a·ble
dis-tin´guished
dis-tort´ed
dis-tor´tion
dis-tract´
dis-tract´ed
dis-tract´ed·ly
dis-trac´tion
dis-traught´

dis-tressed´
dis-tress´ing
dis-tress´ing·ly
dis-trib´ute
dis-tri-bu´tion
dis-trib´u-tor
dis´trict
dis-trust´ful
dis-turb´
dis-tur´bance
dis-turbed´
dis-turb´er
dis-use´
ditch
dit´to
dit´ty
di´va
di-van´
dive
div´er
di-verge´
di-ver´gence
di-ver´gent
di-ver´gent·ly
di´vers　　*(dis-parate)*
di-verse´
di-ver´si-fied
di-ver´sion
di-ver´sion-ar·y
di-ver´si·ty
di-vert´
di-vert´ing
di-vest´
di-vest´i-ture
di-vide´
di-vid´ed

div´i-dend
di-vid´er
div-i-na´tion
di-vine´
di-vine´ly
div´ing
di-vin´i·ty
di-vis´i·ble
di-vi´sion
di-vi´sive
di-vi´sive·ly
di-vi´sive-ness
di-vorce´
div´ot
di-vulge´
di-vulg´ing
diz´zi·ly
diz´zi-ness
diz´zy
do´a·ble
doc´ile
doc´ile·ly
dock´et
dock´side
dock´yard
doc´tor
doc´tor·al
doc´tor-ate
doc´tri-naire´
doc´tri-nal
doc´trine
doc´u-dra·ma
doc´u-ment
doc´u-men´ta·ry
doc-u-men-ta´ tion
dod´der

dod´dered
dod´der-ing
dodge
dodg´er
dodg´ing
doe
do´er
doe´skin
does´n't
doff
dog´bite
dog´catch·er
dog–eared
dog´ged·ly
dog´ged-ness
dog´ger·el
dog´gy
dog´house
dog´leg
dog´ma
dog-mat´ic
dog´ma-tism
doi´lies
doi´ly
do´ing
dole´ful
dol´lar
dol´lop
dol´ ly
do´lo-rous·ly
do´lo-rous-ness
do-main´
domed
do-mes´tic
do-mes´ti-cate
do-mes´ti-cal·ly
do-mes-tic´i·ty

dom´i-cile
dom´i-nance
dom´i-nant
dom´i-nate
dom-i-na´tion
dom´i-neer´ing
do-min´ion
do-nate´
do-nat´ing
do-na´tion
done
don´ny-brook
do´nor
doo´dad
doo´dle
doo´dling
doom
doom´say·er
dooms´day
door´bell
door´frame
door´jamb
door´keep·er
door´mat
door´stop
door´way
doo´zie
dop´ey
dork´y
dor´man·cy
dor´mant
dor´mi-to-ries
dor´mi-to·ry
dos´age
dosed
dos´ing
dos´sier

dot´age
dote
dot´ed
dot´ing
dot´ish
dot´ted
dot´ty
dou´ble
dou´ble–deck´er
dou´ble-head´er
dou´bly
doubt´ful
doubt´ful·ly
doubt´less
dough´nut
dough´ti·ly
dough´ty
dough´y
dour´ly
doused
dous´ing
dove´tail
dow´a-ger
dowd´y
dow´el
dow´er
down´beat
down´cast
down´draft
down´er
down´fall
down´grade
down´heart·ed
down´hill´
down´pour
down´right
down´size

down´stairs´
down´time
down–to–earth
down´town´
down´trod´den
down´turn
down´ward
down´y
dow´ries
dow´ry
dowse
dows´er
dox-ol´o·gy
doze
doz´en
doz´er
doz´ing
drab´ness
draft´i-ness
draft´y
drag
dragged
drag´ging
drag´net
drag´on
drain´age
drain´er
dra´ma
dra-mat´ic
dra-mat´i-cal·ly
dram´a-tist
dram´a-tize
dram´shop
drap´er·y
drap´ing
dras´tic
dras´ti-cal·ly

69

draw´back	drink´a·ble	drug´store
draw´bridge	drink´er	drum´beat
draw´er	drink´ing	drummed
draw´ing	dripped	drum´mer
drawl	drip´ping	drum´ming
drawl´ing	drive	drum´stick
drawn	driv´el	drunk´ard
draw´string	driv´en	drunk´en
dray´age	driv´er	drunk´en-ness
dread´ful	drive´way	dry´er
dread´ful·ly	driv´ing	dry´goods
dread´ful-ness	driz´zle	dry´ing
dread´locks	driz´zling	dry´ly
dread´nought	driz´zly	dry´ness
dream´er	droll´er·y	du´al
dream´i·ly	drone	du-al´i·ty
dream´ing	dron´ing	du´al·ly
dreamt	drool	dub´bing
dream´y	droop´i-ness	du´bi-ous
drear´i·ly	droop´ing	duck´ling
drear´i-ness	droop´y	duck´y
drear´i-some	drop´let	dud´geon
drear´y	drop´out	du´el
dredge	dropped	du-et´
dredg´er	drop´per	duf´fer
dredg´ing	drop´ping	duf´fle
drench	dross	dug´out
dress´er	drowse	dul´cet
dress´ing	drows´i·ly	dull
dress´mak·er	drows´i-ness	dul´lard
dress´mak-ing	drows´y	du´ly
dress´y	drub´bing	dumb´bell
drib´bled	drudge	dumb´found
drift´er	drudg´er·y	dumb´ly
drift´ing	drug	dumb´struck
drift´wood	drugged	dum´found
dri´ly	drug´gist	dum·my

dump´ling
dump´y
dunce
dun´der-head
dun-ga-ree´
dun´geon
dun´nage
dunned
dun´ning
duped
dup´ing
du´plex
du´pli-cate
du-pli-ca´tion
du´pli-ca-tor
du-plic´i-tous
du-plic´i-ty
du-ra·bil´i·ty
du´ra·ble
du´ra·bly
du-ra´tion
dur´ing
dusk´i-ness
dusk´y
dust´bin
dust´cloth
dust´er
dust´i-ness
dust´pan
dust´y
du´ties
du´ti-ful
du´ti-ful·ly
du´ty
dwarf
dwarf´ish
dwell´er

dwell´ing
dwelt
dwin´dle
dwin´dling
dye
dyed
dye´ing
dye´stuff
dy´ing
dy-nam´ic
dy-nam´i-cal·ly
dy´na-mism
dy´na-mite
dy´na-mit·ed
dy´na-mit·er
dy´na·mo
dy-nas´tic
dy´nas·ty
each
ea´ger
ea´ger·ly
ea´ger-ness
ear
ear´ache
ear´drop
ear´drum
eared
ear´flap
ear´ful
ear´li·er
ear´li-est
ear´li-ness
ear´lobe
ear´ly
ear´mark
ear´muff
earn

earn´er
ear´nest
ear´nest·ly
ear´nest-ness
earn´ing
ear´piece
ear´phone
ear´plug
ear´ring
ear´shot
ear´split-ting
earth
earth´bound
earth´en
earth´en-ware
earth´i·er
earth´i-ness
earth´li-ness
earth´ling
earth´ly
earth´mov·er
earth´mov-ing
earth´quake
earth´rise
earth´shak-ing
earth´y
ease
eased
ea´sel
ease´ment
eas´i·er
eas´i-est
eas´i·ly
eas´i-ness
eas´ing
east
east´bound

east´er·ly
east´ern
east´ern·er
east´ern-most
east´ward
eas´y
eat
eat´en
eat´er
eat´er·y
eat´ing
eaves
eaves´drop
eaves´drop-per
eaves´drop-ing
ebb
ebbed
ebb´ing
ebb tide
eb´o·ny
e·bul´lience
e·bul´lien·cy
e·bul´lient
e·bul´lient·ly
ec-cen´tric
ec-cen-tric´i·ty
ec-cle-si-as´tic
ec-cle-si-as´ti-
　cal
ech´o
ech´oed
ech´oes
ech´o-ing
ech-o-lo-ca´tion
é´clair
e·clat´
ec-lec´tic

e·clipse´
e·clips´ing
ec-o-log´ic
ec-o-log´i-cal
e·col´o·gy
ec-o-nom´ic
ec-o-nom´i-cal
ec-o-nom´i-cal·ly
ec-o-nom´ics
e·con´o-mies
e·con´o-mist
e·con´o-mize
e·con´o-miz·er
e·con´o-miz-ing
e·con´o·my
ec´o-sphere
ec´o-sys-tem
ec´ru
ec´sta-sies
ec´sta·sy
ec-stat´ic
ec-stat´i-cal·ly
ec-u-men´i-cal
ec-u-men´i-cal·ly
ed´died
ed´dies
ed´dy
ed´dy-ing
e·de´ma
edge
edged
edge´less
edg´er
edge´ways
edge´wise
edg´i·ly
edg´i-ness

edg´ing
edg´y
ed´i·ble
e´dict
ed-i-fi-ca´tion
ed´i-fice
ed´i-fy-ing
ed´it
e·di´tion
ed´i-tor
ed-i-to´ri-al
ed-i-to´ri-al-ize
ed-i-to´ri-al·ly
ed´u-ca·ble
ed´u-cate
ed´u-cat·ed
ed´u-cat-ing
ed-u-ca´tion
ed-u-ca´tion·al
ed´u-ca-tor
e·duce´
e·duc´i·ble
e·duc´tion
e·duc´tive
e·duc´tor
e´duct
ee´rie
ee´ri·ly
ee´ri-ness
ef´fa·ble
ef-face´
ef-face´a·ble
ef-face´ment
ef-fac´ing
ef-fect´
ef-fec´tive
ef-fec´tive·ly

ef-fec´tive-ness
ef-fec´tor
ef-fects´
ef-fec´tu·al
ef-fec´tu-al·ly
ef-fem´i-na·cy
ef-fem´i-nate
ef-fem´i-nate·ly
ef´fer-ent
ef-fer-vesce´
ef-fer-ves´cence
ef-fer-ves´cent
ef-fer-vesc´ing
ef-fete´
ef-fete´ly
ef-fi-ca´cious
ef-fi-ca´cious·ly
ef´fi-ca·cy
ef-fi´cien·cy
ef-fi´cient
ef-fi´cient·ly
ef´fi·gy
ef´flu-ence
ef´flu-ent
ef-flu´vi·al
ef-flu´vi·um
ef´flux
ef´fort
ef´fort-less
ef´fort-less·ly
ef-fron´ter·y
ef-ful´gent
ef-fuse´
ef-fu´sion
ef-fu´sive
ef-fu´sive·ly
ef-fu´sive-ness

e·gal-i-tar´i·an
egg´beat·er
egg´cup
egg´head
egg´shaped
egg´shell
e´go
e´go-cen´tric
e´go-ism
e´go-ist
e´go-is´tic
e´go-is´ti-cal·ly
e·go-ma´ni·a
e·go-ma´ni·ac
e´go-tism
e´go-tist
e´go-tis´tic
e´go-tis´ti-cal
e´go-tis´ti-cal·ly
e-gre´gious
e·gre´gious·ly
e·gre´gious-ness
e´gress
cight
eight´ball
eigh-teen´
eigh-teenth´
eighth
eight´i-eth
eight´y
ei´ther
e·jac-u-la´tion
e·jac´u-la-to·ry
e·ject´
e·jec´tion
eke
eked

e·lab´o-rate
e·lab´o-rate·ly
e·lab´o-rat-ing
e·lab-o-ra´tion
e·lapse´
e·laps´ing
e·las´tic
e·las´ti-cal·ly
e·las-tic´i·ty
e·las´ti-cize
e·late´
e·lat´ed
e·la´tion
el´bow
el´der
el´der-ber·ry
el´der·ly
el´dest
e·lect´
e·lec-tee´
e·lec´tion
e·lec´tion-eer´
e·lec´tive
e·lec´tor
e·lec´tor·al
e·lec´tor-ate
e·lec´tric
e·lec´tri-cal
e·lec´tri-cal·ly
e·lec-tri´cian
e·lec-tric´i·ty
e·lec-tri-fi-ca´
  tion
e·lec´tri-fied
e·lec´tri·fy
e·lec´tro-cute
e·lec-tro-cu´tion

73

e·lec´trode
e·lec-trol´y-sis
e·lec´tro-lyte
e·lec´tron
e·lec-tron´ic
e·lec-tron´i-cal·ly
e·lec-tron´ics
e l - e e - m o s´ y -
  nar·y
el´e-gance
el´e-gant
el´e-gant·ly
el´e-gize
el´e·gy
el´e-ment
el-e-men´tal·ly
el-e-men´ta·ry
el´e-phan´tine
el´e-vate
el´e-vat·ed
el-e-va´tion
el´e-va-tor
e·lev´en
e·lev´enth
elf´in
elf´ish
e·lic´it
e·lic´i-tor
e·lide´
e·lid´i·ble
e·lid´ing
el-i-gi·bil´i·ty
el´i-gi·ble
el´i-gi·bly
e·lim´i-nate
e·lim-i-na´tion
e·lim´i-na-tor

e·lite´
e·lit´ism
e·lit´ist
e·lix´ir
el-lipse´
el-lip´tic
el-lip´ti-cal
el-o-cu´tion
el-o-cu´tion-ar·y
e·lon´gate
e·lon´gat·ed
e·lon-ga´tion
e·lope´
e·lope´ment
e·lop´ing
el´o-quence
el´o-quent·ly
else´where
e·lu´ci-date
e·lu-ci-da´tion
e·lude´
e·lud´er
e·lu´sive
e·lu´sive·ly
e·lu´so·ry
e·lu·vi·al
e·lu´vi-ate
e·lu-vi-a´tion
e·lu´vi·um
e·ma´ci-ate
e·ma´ci-at·ed
E´–mail
em´a-nate
em-a-na´tion
em´a-na-tive
em´a-na-tor
e·man´ci-pate

e·man´ci-pat·ed
e·man-ci-pa´tion
e·man´ci-pa-tor
e·mas´cu-late
e·mas-cu-la´tion
em-balm´
em-balm´er
em-bank´
em-bank´ment
em-bar´go
em-bar´goes
em-bark´
em-bar-ka´tion
em-bar´rass
em-bar´rassed
em-bar´rass·es
e m - b a r´ r a s s -
  ing·ly
e m - b a r´ r a s s -
  ment
em´bas-sies
em´bas·sy
em-bat´tle
em-bed´ded
em-bel´lish
e m - b e l´ l i s h -
  ment
em´ber
em-bez´zle
em-bez´zled
em-bez´zle-ment
em-bez´zler
em-bit´ter
em-blaze´
em-bla´zon
em´blem
em´blem-at´ic

em-bod´i-ment
em-bod´y
em-bold´en
em-boss´
em-bossed´
em-boss´ing
em-bow´el
em-brace´
em-brace´a·ble
em-brac´er
em-brac´ing
em-bra´sure
em-broi´der
em-broi´der·y
em-broil´
em´cee
e·mend´
e·mend´er
e·merge´
e·mer´gence
e·mer´gen-cies
e·mer´gen·cy
e·mer´gent
e·merg´ing
e·mer´i-tus
e·mersed´
e·mer´sion
em´er·y
em´i-grant
em´i-grate
em´i-grat-ing
em-i-gra´tion
e·mi-gre´
em´i-nence
em´i-nen·cy
em´i-nent
em´i-nent·ly

em´is-sar-ies
em´is-sar·y
e·mis´sion
e·mis´sive
e·mit´
e·mit´ted
e·mit´ter
e·mit´ting
e·mol´lience
e·mol´lient
e·mol´u-ment
e·mote´
e·mot´er
e·mot´ing
e·mo´tion
e·mo´tion·al
e·mo´tion-al·ly
e·mo´tive
em-pan´el
em-pan´el-ing
em-path´ic
em-path´i-cal·ly
em-pa-thet´i-
    cal·ly
em´pa-thize
em´pa-thy
em´per·or
em´pha-ses
em´pha-sis
em´pha-size
em´pha-siz-ing
em-phat´ic
em-phat´i-cal·ly
em´pire
em-pir´i-cal
em-pir´i-cism
em-place´ment

em-ploy´
em-ploy-a·bil´i·ty
em-ploy´a·ble
em-ploy·ee´
em-ploy´er
em-ploy´ment
em-po´ri·um
em-pow´er
em-pow´er-ment
em´press
emp´tied
emp´ti·er
emp´ties
emp´ti-ness
emp´ty
emp´ty-ing
em´u-late
em-u-la´tion
em´u-la-tor
e·mul-si-fi-
    ca´tion
e·mul´si-fied
e·mul´si-fi·er
e·mul´si·fy
e·mul´sion
en-a´ble
en-a´bler
en-a´bling
en-act´
en-ac´tor
en-am´el
en-am´eled
en-am´el-ware
en-am´or
en-am´ored
en-camp´
en-cap´su-late

75

en-case´
en-chant´
en-chant´er
en-chant´ing
en-chant´ing·ly
en-chant´ment
en-chant´ress
en-cir´cle
en-cir´cling
en´clave
en-close´
en-clo´sure
en-code´
en-co´mi·um
en-com´pass
en´core
en-coun´ter
en-cour´age
en-cour´age-
  ment
en-cour´ag-ing
en-croach´
en-crust´
en-crus-ta´tion
en-crypt´
en-cum´ber
en-cum´brance
en-cy-clo-pae´
  di·a *(Br.)*
en-cy-clo-pe´di·a
en-cy-clo-pe´dic
end
en-dan´gered
en-dan´ger-ment
en-dear´
en-dear´ing
en-dear´ment

en-deav´or
en-deav´our *(Br.)*
en-dem´ic
en-dem´i-cal·ly
end´ing
end´less·ly
end´most
en-dorse´
en-dors·ee´
en-dorse´ment
en-dors´er
en-dors´ing
en-dow´
en-dow´er
en-dow´ment
en-due´
en-dur´a·ble
en-dur´a·bly
en-dur´ance
en-dure´
en-dur´ing
end´ways
end´wise
en´e-mies
en´e·my
en-er-get´ic
en´er-gize
en´er-giz·er
en´er·gy
en´er-vate
en-er-va´tion
en-fee´ble
en-fee´bling
en-fold´
en-force´
en-force´a·ble
en-force´ment

en-forc´er
en-forc´ing
en-fran´chise
en-gage´
en-gaged´
en-gage´ment
en-gag´er
en-gag´ing
en-gag´ing·ly
en-gen´der
en´gine
en-gi-neer´ing
en-gorge´
en-grave´
en-grav´er
en-grav´ing
en-gross´
en-gross´ing
en-gulf˜
en-hance´
en-hance´ment
en-hanc´ing
e·nig´ma
e·nig-mat´ic
en-join´
en-join´der
en-joy´
en-joy´a·ble
en-joy´a·bly
en-joy´ment
en-large´
en-large-ment
en-light´en
en-light´en·er
en-light´en-ment
en-list´
en-list´ed

en-list´ment
en-liv´en
en-liv´en·er
en-liv´en-ing
en-mesh´
en´mi-ties
en´mi·ty
en-no´ble
en-no´bler
en-no´bling
en-nui´
e·nor´mi·ty
e·nor´mous·ly
e·nough´
en-rage´
en-rapt´
en-rap´ture
en-rich´
en-rich´ment
en-robe´
en-roll´
en-rolled´
en-roll·ee´
en-roll´ing
en-roll´ment
en-rol´ment
en-sem´ble
en-shrine´
en-shrine´ment
en-slave´
en-snare´
en-sue´
en-su´ing
en-tail´ment
en-tan´gle
en-tan´gle-ment
en-tan´gling

en-tente´
en´ter
en-ter´ic
en-ter-i´tis
en´ter-prise
en´ter-pris-ing
en´ter-pris-ing·ly
en-ter-tain´
en-ter-tain´er
en-ter-tain´ing
en-ter-tain´ment
en-thrall
en-thrall´ing·ly
en-throne´ment
en-thuse´
en-thu´si-asm
en-thu´si-ast
en-thu-si-as´tic
en-tice´ment
en-tic´ing
en-tic´ing·ly
en-tire´ly
en-tire´ty
en-ti´tle
en-ti´tle-ment
en´ti·ty
en-tomb´ment
en-to-mo-log´ic
en-to-mo-log´i-
   cal
en-to-mol´o-gist
en-to-mol´o·gy
en´tou-rage´
en´trance (n.)
en-trance´ (v.)
en-tranc´ing
en´trant

en-trap´ment
en´tre
en-treat´
en-treat´ies
en-treat´ing
en-treat´y
en´trée
en´tre-pre-neur´
en-tre-pre-neur´
   i·al
en´tries
en-trust´
en´try
en-twine´
e·nu´mer-ate
e·nu-mer-a´tion
e·nun´ci-ate
e·nun-ci-a´tion
en-ure´
en-vel´op
en´ve-lope
en-vel´oped
en-vel´op-ing
en-vel´op-ment
en´vi-a·ble
en´vi-a·bly
en´vied
en´vi·er
en´vi-ous
en´vi-ous·ly
en-vi´ron
en-vi´ron-ment
en-vi´ron-men´
   tal·ly
en-vi´ron-men´
   tal-ist
en-vi´rons

en-vis´age
en-vi´sion
en´voy
en´vy
e´on
e·phem´er·al
e·phem´er-al·ly
ep´ic
ep´i-cen´ter
ep´i-cure
ep´i-cu-re´an
ep´i-dem´ic
ep´i-gram
ep´i-logue
ep´i-sode
ep-i-sod´ic
e·pis´tle
ep´i-taph
ep´i-thet
e·pit´o·me
e·pit-o-mize
ep´och
ep´och·al
ep-ox´y
eq´ua·ble
eq´ua·bly
e´qual
e´qualed
e´qual-ing
e·qual´i·ty
e´qual-ize
e´qual-iz´er
e´qual·ly
e·qua-nim´i·ty
e·qua´tion
e·qua´tor
e·qua-to´ri·al

e·ques´tri·an
e´qui-dis´tant
e´quine
e·quip´ment
e·quipped´
e·quip´ping
eq´ui-ta·ble
eq´ui-ta·bly
eq´ui·ty
e·quiv´a-lence
e·quiv´a-len·cy
e·quiv´a-lent·ly
e·quiv´o-ca·cy
e·quiv´o-cal
e·quiv´o-cal·ly
e·quiv´o-cate
e·quiv´o-ca´tion
e·quiv´o-ca-tor
e·rad´i-cate
e·rad-i-ca´tion
e·rase´
e·rased
e·ras´er
e·ras´ing
e·ra´sure
e·rect´
e·rec´tion
er-go-nom´ic
er-go-nom´i-
  cal·ly
er-go-nom´ics
e·rode´
e·rod´i·ble
e·rog´e-nous
e·ro´sion
e·ro´sive
e·rot´ic

e·rot´i·ca
e·rot´i-cism
er´ran·cy
er´rand
er´rant
er´rant·ly
er-rat´ic
err´ing
err´ing·ly
er-ro´ne-ous
er-ro´ne-ous·ly
er´ror
er´satz
erst´while´
er´u-dite
er-u-di´tion
e·rupt´
e·rup´tion
e·rup´tive
es´ca-late
es´ca-la´tion
es´ca-la-tor
es´ca-pade
es-cape´
es-caped´
cs-cap·ee´
es-cap´ing
es-cap´ist
es-chew´
es´cort (n.)
es-cort´ (v.)
es´crow
es´o-ter´ic
es-o-ter´i-cal·ly
es-pe´cial
es-pe´cial·ly
es´pi-o-nage

es´pla-nade
es-pous´al
es-pouse´
es-pous´er
es-pous´ing
es´quire
es´say *(n.)*
es-say´ *(v.)*
es-say´er
es´say-ist
es´sence
es-sen´tial
es-sen´tial·ly
es-tab´lish
es-tab´lished
es-tab´lish-ment
es-tate´
es-teem´
es´ti-ma·ble
es´ti-mate
es-ti-ma´tion
es´ti-ma-tor
es-trange´
es-trange´ment
es-trang´ing
es´tu-ar·y
etch´ing
e·ter´nal·ly
e·ter´ni·ty
e·the´re·al
e·the´re-al·ly
eth´ic
eth´i-cal·ly
eth´ics
eth´nic
eth´ni-cal·ly
eth-nic´i·ty

eth´no-cen´tric
et´i-quette
e´tude
et-y-mol´o·gy
eu´lo·gy
eu´phe-mis´tic
eu´phe-mize
eu·pho´ri·a
eu·phor´ic
eu·tha-na´sia
e·vac´u-ate
e·vac-u-a´tion
e·vade´
e·vad´ing
e·val´u-ate
e·val-u-a´tion
e´van-gel´ic
e´van-gel´i-cal
e·van´ge-lism
e·van´ge-list
e·van´ge-lis´tic
e·vap´o-rate
e·vap´o-rat-ing
e·vap-o-ra´tion
e·vap´o-ra-tor
e·va´sion
e·va´sive
e·va´sive·ly
e·va´sive-ness
e´ven-hand·ed
e´ven-ing *(equat-
　ing)*
eve´ning *(night)*
e´ven·ly
e´ven-ness
e·vent´
e·vent´ful

e·ven´tu·al
e·ven´tu-al´i·ty
e·ven´tu-al·ly
e·ven´tu-ate
ev´er-green
ev-er-last´ing
ev-er-more´
e·vert´
ev´er·y-bod·y
ev´er·y-day
ev´er·y-one
ev´er·y-thing
ev´er·y-where
e·vic´tion
ev´i-dence
ev´i-denc-ing
ev´i-dent
ev´i-den´tial
ev-i-den´ti-a·ry
ev´i-dent·ly
ev´i-dent ness
e´vil
e´vil-do·er
e´vil·ly
e´vil–mind´ed
e·vince´
e·vinc´ing
e·vis´cer-ate
e·vis-cer-a´tion
ev´i-ta·ble
e·voke´
e·vok´ing
ev-o-lu´tion
ev-o-lu´tion-ar·y
ev-o-lu´tion-ist
e·volve´
e·volv´ing

e·vul´sion
ex-ac´er-bate
ex-ac´er-bat-ing
ex-act´
ex-act´ing
ex-ac´ti-tude
ex-act´ly
ex-act´ness
ex-ac´tor
ex-ag´ger-ate
ex-ag´ger-at·ed
ex-ag-ger-a´tion
ex-alt´
ex-al-ta´tion
ex-alt´ed
ex-alt´ed·ly
ex-am´
ex-am-i-na´tion
ex-am´ine
ex-am´in·er
ex-am´ple
ex-as´per-ate
ex-as´per-at-ing
ex-as-per-a´tion
ex´ca-vate
ex-ca-va´tion
ex´ca-va-tor
ex-ceed´
ex-ceed´ing·ly
ex-cel´
ex-celled´
ex´cel-lence
ex´cel-lent
ex-cel´ling
ex-cept´a·ble
ex-cept´ing
ex-cep´tion

ex-cep´tion-al
ex´cerpt *(n.)*
ex-cerpt´ *(v.)*
ex-cess´ *(n.)*
ex´cess *(adj.)*
ex-ces´sive·ly
ex-change´
ex-chang´ing
ex´che-quer
ex´cise *(n. tax)*
ex-cise´ *(v. cut out)*
ex-ci´sion
ex-cit´a·ble
ex-ci-ta´tion
ex-cite´
ex-cit´ed·ly
ex-cite´ment
ex-cit´ing
ex-claim´
ex-claim´er
ex-clam´a-to·ry
ex-clude´
ex-clud´ing
ex-clu´sion-ar·y
ex-clu´sive·ly
ex-clu-siv´i·ty
ex-com-mu´ni-cate
ex-com-mu-ni-ca´tion
ex-co´ri-ate
ex-co-ri-a´tion
ex´cre-ment
ex-crete´
ex-cru´ci-at-ing·ly

ex´cul-pate
ex-cul´pa-to·ry
ex-cur´sion
ex-cus´a·ble
ex-cus´a·bly
ex-cuse´
ex-cus´ing
ex´e-crate
ex-e-cra´tion
ex´e-cute
ex-e-cu´tion
ex-ec´u-tive
ex-ec´u-tor
ex-em´pla·ry
ex-em´pli·fy
ex-empt´
ex-emp´tion
ex´er-cise
ex´er-cis·er
ex-ert´
ex-er´tion
ex-ert´ive
ex-fo´li-ate
ex´hal´ant
ex-ha-la´tion
ex´hale
ex-haust´ed
ex-haust´i·ble
ex-haus´tion
ex-hib´it
ex-hi-bi´tion-ism
ex-hi-bi´tion-ist
ex-hib´i-tor
ex-hil´a-rate
ex-hil-a-ra´tion
ex-hort´
ex-hor-ta´tion

ex-hu-ma´tion
ex-hume´
ex´i-gen-cies
ex´i-gen·cy
ex-ig´u-ous
ex´ile
ex-ist´
ex-is´tence
ex-is´tent
ex-is-ten´tial
ex-is-ten´tial-
  ism
ex´o-dus
ex-on´er-ate
ex-on-er-a´tion
ex-or´bi-tance
ex-or´bi-tant
ex-or´bi-tant·ly
ex´or-cise
ex´or-cism
ex´or-cist
ex-ot´ic
ex-ot´i·ca
ex-pand´
ex-pand´a·ble
ex-pand´ed
ex-panse´
ex-pan´sion
ex-pan´sion-ar·y
ex-pan´sive·ly
ex-pa´tri-ate
ex-pa-tri-a´tion
ex-pect´an·cy
ex-pect´ant·ly
ex-pec-ta´tion
ex-pec´to-rant
ex-pec´to-rate

ex-pe´di-ence
ex-pe´di-en·cy
ex-pe´di-ent
ex-pe´di-ent·ly
ex´pe-dite
ex´pe-dit·er
ex´pe-dit-ing
ex-pe-di´tion
ex-pe-di´tion-
  ar·y
ex-pe-di´tious·ly
ex-pel´
ex-pelled´
ex-pel´ling
ex-pend´
ex-pend´a·ble
ex-pend´i-ture
ex-pense´
ex-pe´ri-ence
ex-pe´ri-enced
ex-pe´ri-enc-ing
ex-per´i-ment
ex-per´i-men´tal
ex-per´i-men´-
  tal·ly
ex-per-i-men-
  ta´tion
ex-pert´ *(adj.)*
ex´pert *(n., adj.)*
ex-per-tise´
ex´pert·ly
ex´pi-ate
ex-pi-ra´tion
ex-pire´
ex-pired´
ex-pir´ing
ex-plain´

ex-pla-na´tion
ex-plan´a-to·ry
ex´ple-tive
ex-plic´a·ble
ex´pli·ca·bly
ex´pli-cate
ex-pli-ca´tion
ex-plic´it
ex-plic´it·ly
ex-plode´
ex-plod´ing
ex-ploit´ *(v.)*
ex´ploit *(n.)*
ex-ploi-ta´tion
ex-ploit´er
ex-ploit´ive
ex-plo-ra´tion
ex-plor´a·tive
ex-plor´a-to·ry
ex-plore´
ex-plor´er
ex-plor´ing
ex-plo´sion
ex-plo´sive
ex-po´nent
ex-po-nen´tial
ex-po-nen´tial·ly
ex´port *(n., v.)*
ex-port´ *(v.)*
ex-port´er
ex-pose´
ex-po-sé´
ex-posed´
ex-pos´ing
ex-pos´tu-late
ex-po´sure
ex-press´

81

ex-press´ing
ex-pres´sion
ex-pres´sion-less
ex-pres´sive·ly
ex-press´ly
ex-press´way
ex-pro´pri-ate
ex-pro-pri-a´tion
ex-pul´sion
ex-punge´
ex´pur-gate
ex-pur-ga´tion
ex-quis´ite·ly
ex´tant
ex-tem-po-ra´ne-
 ous·ly
ex-tem´po-rize
ex-tend´
ex-tend´ed
ex-tend´er
ex-ten´si·ble
ex-ten´sion
ex-ten´sive·ly
ex-tent´
ex-ten´u-ate
ex-ten´u-at-ing
ex-ten-u-a´tion
ex-te´ri·or
ex-ter´mi-nate
ex-ter-mi-na´
 tion
ex-ter´mi-na-tor
ex-ter´nal
ex-ter´nal-ize
ex-ter´nal·ly
ex-tinct´
ex-tinc´tion

ex-tin´guish
ex-tin´guish·er
ex´tir-pate
ex-tol´
ex-tolled´
ex-tol´ling
ex-tort´
ex-tort´ed
ex-tor´tion
ex-tor´tion-ist
ex´tra
ex´tract (n.)
ex-tract´ (v.)
ex-trac´tion
ex´tra-cur-ric´u-
 lar
ex´tra-dite
ex-tra-di´tion
ex-tra-le´gal
ex´tra-mar´i-tal
ex-tra´ne-ous
ex-tra´ne-ous·ly
ex-traor´di-nar´
 i·ly
ex-traor´di-nar·y
ex-trap´o late
ex-trap-o-la´tion
ex-tra-sen´so·ry
e x - t r a - t e r -
 res´tri·al
ex-trav´a-gance
ex-trav´a-gant·ly
ex-trav-a-gan´za
ex-treme´ly
ex-trem´ist
ex-trem´i·ty
ex-tric´a·ble

ex´tri-cate
ex-tri-ca´tion
ex´tro-vert
ex-trude´
ex-trud´er
ex-trud´ing
ex-tru´sion
ex-tru´sive
ex-ude´
ex-ult´
ex-ul-ta´tion
ex-ur´ban-ite
ex-ur´bi·a
eye´ball
eye´brow
eye´ful
eye´glass
eye´ing
eye´lash
eye´let
eye´lid
eye´sight
eye´sore
fa´ble
fa´bled
fab´ric
fab´ri-cate
fab-ri-ca´tion
fab´u-list
fab´u-lous
fab´u-lous·ly
fa-çade´
face´less
face´lift
face´–off
fac´et
fac´et·ed

fa-ce´tious
fa-ce´tious·ly
fa´cial
fac´ile
fa-cil´i-tate
fa-cil´i-ties
fa-cil´i·ty
fac´ing
fac-sim´i·le
fact´find-ing
fac´tion
fac´tion·al
fac´tious
fac-ti´tious
fac´tor
fac´to-ries
fac´to·ry
fac-to´tum
fac´tu·al
fac´ul-ties
fac´ul·ty
fad´dish
fad´er
fail´ing
fail´ure
faint´ed
faint´heart·ed
faint´ly
fair´ground
fair´ies
fair´ly
fair–mind´ed
fair´ness
fair´way
fair´y
faith´ful·ly
faith´less

faith´less·ly
fake
fak´er
fak´er·y
fal´la-cies
fal-la´cious
fal´la·cy
fall´ing
fall´out
fal´low
false´hood
false´ly
fal-si-fi-ca´tion
fal´si-fied
fal´si·fy
fal´ter
fal´ter-ing
fame
famed
fa-mil´ial
fa-mil´iar
fa-mil-iar´i·ty
fa-mil-iar-i·za´
　tion
fa-mil´iar-ize
fa-mil´iar·ly
fam´i-lies
fam´i·ly
fam´ine
fam´ish
fam´ished
fa´mous
fa´mous·ly
fa-nat´ic
fa-nat´i-cal·ly
fa-nat´i-cism
fan´cied

fan´ci·er
fan´cies
fan´ci-ful
fan´cy
fan´fare
fan´fold
fang
fanged
fanned
fan´ning
fan´ta-size
fan-tas´tic
fan´ta·sy
far´ci-cal
fare-well´
far´fetched
farm´er
farm´hand
farm´house
farm´ing
farm´land
farm´yard
far´sight·ed
far´ther
far´thest
fas´ci·a
fas´ci-nate
fas´ci-nat·ed
fas´ci-nat·ing
fas-ci-na´tion
fash´ion
fash´ion-a·ble
fash´ion-a·bly
fast´ten
fas´ten·er
fas´ten-ing
fas-tid´i-ous

fas-tid´i-ous·ly
fast´ing
fa´tal-ist
fa-tal-is´tic
fa-tal´i·ty
fa´tal·ly
fate´ful
fa´ther
fa´ther-land
fa´ther-less
fa´ther·ly
fath´om
fath´om-a·ble
fath´om-less
fa-tigue´
fa-tigued´
fa-tigu´ing
fat´ten
fat´ty
fat´u-ous
fat´u-ous·ly
fau´cet
fault
fault´find-ing
fault´less·ly
fault´y
fau´na
fa´vor
fa´vor-a·ble
fa´vor-a·bly
fa´vor-ite
fa´vor-it-ism
fa´vour *(Br.)*
fawn´ing
fe´al·ty
fear´ful
fear´less·ly

fea´sance
fea-si·bil´i·ty
fea´si·ble
fea´si·bly
feast
feath´er
feath´er-bed-
　　ding
feath´ered
feath´er-weight
feath´er·y
fea´ture
fea´tured
feb´rile
feck´less
fed´er·al
fed´er-al-ist
fed-er-a´tion
fe-do´ra
fee´ble
fee´ble-ness
feed´back
feed´er
feed´ing
feel´er
feel´ing
feign
feigned
feign´ing
feint
feist´i-ness
feist´y
fe-lic-i-ta´tion
fe-lic´i-tous·ly
fe-lic´i·ty
fe´line
fel´low

fel´low-ship
fel´on
fe-lo´ni-ous
fel´o·ny
fe´male
fem´i-na·cy
fem-i-nin´i·ty
fem´i-nism
fem´i-nist
fem´i-nize
fenc´ing
fend´er
fe´ral
fer-ment´
fer-men-ta´tion
fe-ro´cious·ly
fe-roc´i·ty
fer´ried
fer´ries
fer´ry
fer´ry-boat
fer´ry-ing
fer´tile
fer-til´i·ty
fer-til-i·za´tion
fer´til-ize
fer´til-iz·er
fer´vent
fer´vent·ly
fer´vid
fer´vid·ly
fer´vor
fes´ter
fes´ti-val
fes´tive
fes-tiv´i·ty
fes-toon´

84

fe´tal	fifth	fi-nan´cial·ly
fetch´ing	fif´ti-eth	fin-an-cier´
fet´id	fif´ty	fi-nanc´ing
fet´ish	fight´er	find´er
fet´ter	fight´ing	find´ing
fet´tle	fig´ment	fine´ly
fe´tus	fig´ure	fine´ness
feud	fig´ured	fin´er·y
feu´dal	fig´ure-head	fi-nesse´
feu-dal-is´tic	fil´a-ment	fin´ger
fe´ver	filch´er	fin´gered
fe´ver-ish	fi-let´	fin´ger-ing
fe´ver-ish·ly	fil´i·al	fin´ger-ling
few´er	fil´i-bus-ter	fin´ger-nail
fi-as´co	fil´i-gree	fin´ger-print
fi´at	fill	fin´i·al
fib´bing	fill´er	fin´ick·y
fi´brous	fil´let	fin´ish
fick´le	fill´ing	fin´ished
fic´tion-al-ize	fil´ly	fin´ish·er
fic-ti´tious·ly	film´i·er	fi´nite
fid´dle	film´y	fin´nick·y
fid´dler	fil´ter	fire´arm
fid´dle-sticks	filth	fire´brand
fid´dling	filth´i·er	fire´crack·er
fi-del´i·ty	filth´i-ness	fire´fly
fid´get	filth-y	fire´man
fi-du´ci-ar·y	fil´trate	fire´place
fief´dom	fil-tra´tion	fire´proof
field´er	fi´nal	fire´works
field´stone	fi-nal´e	fir´ing
fiend´ish	fi´nal-ist	fir´ma-ment
fierce´ly	fi-nal´i·ty	firm´er
fi´er·y	fi´na-lize	firm´ly
fi-es´ta	fi-na-li-za´tion	fir´ry
fif-teen´	fi´nal·ly	first´born
fif-teenth´	fi-nance´	fis´cal·ly

85

fish´bowl
fish´er-man
fish´er·y
fish´hook
fish´ing
fish´mon-ger
fish´net
fish´y
fis´sion
fis´sion-a·ble
fis´sure
fist´fight
fist´ful
fit´ful·ly
fit´ness
fit´ted
fit´ting·ly
fix´ate
fix-a´tion
fixed
fix´ing
fix´ture
fiz´zle
fiz´zling
fizz´y
flab´ber-gast
flab´bi-ness
flab´by
flac´cid
flag´el-late
flagged
flag´ging
flag´on
fla´grant
fia´grant·ly
flake
flaked

flak´i·er
flak´i-ness
flak´ing
flak´y
flam-boy´ant
flam-boy´ant·ly
flame
flamed
flam´ing
flam´ma·ble
flange
flanged
flank
flan´nel
flap´jack
flap´pa·ble
flapped
flap´per
flap´ping
flare
flare´–up
flar´ing
flash
flash´back
flash´bulb
flash´ing
flash´light
flash´y
flat´car
flat–footed
flat´ly
flat´ten
flat´ter
flat´ter·er
flat´ter-ing
flat´ter·y
flat´top

flat´ware
flaunt´ing
fla´vor
fla´vor-ful
fla´vour *(Br.)*
flaw´less·ly
flea´bag
flea´bite
flea´–bit-ten
fledged
flee´ing
fleet´ing·ly
fleet´ness
flesh´y
flex-i·bil´i·ty
flex´i·ble
flex´i·bly
flex´time
flick´er·y
fli´er
flight´i-ness
flight´less
flight´y
flim´flam
flim´si-ness
flim´sy
flinch´ing
fling
flip´pant
flipped
flip´per
flip´ping
flirt
flir-ta´tion
flir-ta´tious·ly
flirt
flit´ting

fliv´ver
float´er
float´ing
flocked
flock´ing
flog´ging
flood´light
floor´board
floor´ing
floor´walk·er
flop´house
flop´py
flo´ra
flo´ral
flo-res´cence
flo-res´cent
flor´id
flo´rist
flo-ta´tion
flo-til´la
flot´sam
flounced
flounc´ing
flounc´y
flour´ish
flour´ished
flour´ish-ing
flour´y
flout
flout´ing
flow´ered
flow´er·et
flow´er-ing
flow´er-pot
flow´er·y
flow´ing
flown

fluc´tu-ate
fluc´tu-at-ing
fluc-tu-a´tion
flu´en·cy
flu´ent·ly
fluff´i·er
fluff´i-ness
fluff´y
flu´id
fluke
flum´mer·y
flunk´out
flu-o-res´cence
flu-o-res´cent
flu-o-resc´ing
flu-o-ri-da´tion
flu´o-ride
flur´ry
flus´ter
flut´ed
flut´ing
flut´ist
flut´tered
flut´ter-ing
flut´ter·y
fly´er
fly´ing
fly´wheel
foam´i·er
foam´ing
fo´cal
fo´cus
fo´cused
fo´cus-ing
fod´der
fog´bound
fog´gi-ness

fog´gy
fog´horn
fo´gy
foi´ble
foiled
foil´ing
foist´ed
fold´ed
fold´er
fold´ing
fold´out
fo´li-age
fo-li-a´tion
folk´lore
folk´lor·ic
folks·y
folk´way
fol´low
fol´lowed
fol´low·er
fol´low-ing
fol´low–through
fol´low–up
fo-ment´
fon´dled
fon´dler
fon´dling
fond´ly
fond´ness
food´stuff
fool´er·y
fool´har·dy
fool´ing
fool´ish·ly
fool´ish-ness
fool´proof
foot´age

foot´ed
foot´er
foot´fall
foot´hill
foot´hold
foot´ing
foot´light
foot´print
foot´step
fop´per·y
fop´pish
for´age
for´aged
for´ag·er
for´ag-ing
for´ay
for-bear´
for-bear´ance
for-bid´den
for-bid´ding
forced
force´ful
forc´i·bly
forc´ing
fore´arm
fore-bod´ing
fore´cast
fore´cast·er
fore-close´
fore-clo´sure
fore´fa-ther
fore´go
fore´go-ing
fore´gone´
fore´ground
fore´head
for´eign

for´eign·er
fore´knowl-edge
fore´most
fo-ren´sic
fore-or-dain´
fore´run-ner
fore-see´a·ble
fore-seen´
fore-shad´ow-ing
fore-short´en
fore´sight·ed
for´est
for-est-a´tion
for´est·ed
for´est·ry
fore-tell´
for-ev´er
fore-warn´
fore´word
for´feit
for´fei-ture
forg´er
for´ger·y
for-get´ful
for-get´ful-ness
for-get´ta·ble
for-get´ting
forg´ing
for-give´
for-giv´en
for-giv´ing
for-go´ing
for-got´ten
fork´ful
for-lorn´
for´mal
for-mal´i·ty

for´mal-ize
for´mal-wear
for´mat
for-ma´tion
form´a-tive·ly
for´mer
for´mer·ly
for´mi-da·ble
for´mi-da·bly
form´less
for´mu·la
for´mu-late
for-mu-la´tion
for´ni-cate
for-sake´
for-sak´en
for-sook´
for-swear´
forth´com-ing
forth´right
for´ti-eth
for-ti-fi-ca´tion
for´ti-fied
for´ti-fi·er
for´ti·fy
for´ti-tude
for´tress
for-tu´i-tous·ly
for-tu´i·ty
for´tu-nate·ly
for´tune
for´ty
fo´rum
for´ward
fos´sil
fos´sil-ize
fos´ter

foun-da´tion
found´er *(n.)*
foun´der *(v.)*
found´ling
found´ries
found´ry
foun´tain
foun´tain-head
four´flush·er
four´fold
four´some
four-teen´
four-teenth´
fourth
fowl´er
fox´i-ness
fox´y
foy´er
fra´cas
frac´tion
frac´tious·ly
frac´ture
frag´ile
fra-gil´i·ly
frag´ment
frag´men-tar·y
frag´ment·ed
fra´grance
fra´grant
fra´grant·ly
frail´ties
frail´ty
framed
fram´er
frame´work
fram´ing
fran´chise

fran´chis·er
fran´gi·ble
frank´ly
frank´ness
fran´tic
fran´ti-cal·ly
fran´tic·ly
fra-ter´nal-ism
fra-ter´nal·ly
fra-ter´ni·ty
frat´er-nize
frat´ri-ci-dal
frat´ri-cide
fraud´u-lent
fraud´u-lent·ly
fraught
frayed
fraz´zle
freak´ish
freak´y
freck´led
free´bie
free´dom
free´ly
fre´er
free´stand´ing
free´think·er
free-wheel´ing
free´will
freez´er
freez´ing
freight´er
fre-net´ic
fren´zied
fren´zy
fre´quen·cy
fre´quent

fre´quent·er
fre´quent·ly
fre´quent-ness
fres´co
fres´coes
fresh´en
fresh´ly
fresh´man
fret´ful
fret´ful-ness
fri-a·bil´i·ty
fri´a·ble
fri´ar
fri´ar·y
fric´tion
friend´less
friend´li·er
friend´li-ness
friend´ly
fright´en
fright´ened
fright´en-ing
fright´ful·ly
frig´id
fri-gid´i·ty
frill´i-ness
frill´y
fringed
frisk´i·er
frisk´i-ness
frisk´y
frit´ter
fri-vol´i·ty
friv´o-lous·ly
friz´zle
friz´zly
frol´ic

89

frol´icked
frol´ick-ing
frol´ic-some
front´age
fron´tal
fron-tier´
fron´tis-piece
frost´bite
frost´bit-ten
frost´ed
frost´i·ly
frost´ing
frost´y
froth´i·er
froth´i-ness
froth´y
frowned
frown´ing
frow´zy
fro´zen
fru´gal
fru-gal´i·ty
fruit´cake
fruit´ful
fruit´i-ness
fru-i´tion
fruit·y
frump´y
frus´trate
frus´trat·ed
frus´trat-ing
frus-tra´tion
fu´el
fu´gi-tive
fugue
ful´crum
ful-fill´ing

ful-fill´ment
ful´gent
full´ness
ful´ly
ful´mi-nate
ful-mi-na´tion
ful´some
fum´ble
fum´bling
fu´mi-gant
fu´mi-gate
fu´mi-gat-ing
fu-mi-ga´tion
fu´mi-ga-tor
fum´ing
func´tion
func´tion·al
func´tion-al·ly
func´tion-ar·y
fun-da-men´tal
f u n - d a - m e n ´
  tal·ly
fu´ner·al
fu´ner-ar·y
fu-ne´re·al
fun´gi-cide
fun´gus
fun´neled
fun´nel-ing
fun´ny
fu´ri-ous
fu´ri-ous·ly
fur´lough
fur´nace
fur´nish-ings
fur´ni-ture
fu´ror

fur´row
fur´ry
fur´ther-ance
fur´ther-more
fur´thest
fur´tive·ly
fu´ry
fu´se-lage
fu´sion
fuss´i-ness
fuss´y
fu´tile·ly
fu-til´i·ty
fu´ton
fu´ture
fu-tur-is´tic
fuzz´y
gab´ar-dine
gab´bing
gab´ble
gab´by
ga´bled
ga´bling
gad´a·bout
gad´fly
gad´gct
gad´get·ry
gaffe
gag
gagged
gag´ging
gag´gle
gai´e·ty
gai´ly
gain
gain´ful·ly
gait´ed

ga´la
ga-lac´tic
gal´ax·y
gal´lant
gal´lant·ly
gal´lant·ry
gal´le·on
gal-le-ri´a
gal´ler·y
gal´ley
gall´ing
gal´li-vant
gal´lon
gal´loped
gal´lop·er
gal´lop-ing
gal´lows
gall´stone
ga-loot´
ga-lore´
gal-va-ni-za´tion
gal´va-nize
gam´bler
gam´bling
gam´bol
gam´boled
gam´bol-ing
game´keep·er
game´ly
games´man-ship
gam´ey
gam´i·ly
gam´y
gan´der
gang´bust·ers
gan´gly
gang´ster

gang´way
ga-rage´
gar´bage
gar´ble
gar´bled
gar´den
gar´den·er
gar-gan´tu·an
gar´gled
gar´gling
gar´goyle
gar´ish·ly
gar´ish-ness
gar´land
gar´lic
gar´lick·y
gar´ment
gar´ner
gar´nish
gar´nish·ee´
gar´nish·er
gar´nish-ment
gar´ret
gar´ri-son
gar´ru-lous
gar´ter
gas´e-ous
gas-o-line´
gasp´ing
gas´tric
gate´house
gate´keep·er
gath´ered
gath´er-ing
gauche
gaud´i·ly
gaud´y

gauged
gaug´ing
gaunt
gaunt´let
gauze
gav´el·er
gazed
ga-zette´
gaz´et-teer´
gaz´ing
gear´box
gear´shift
gee´zer
gel´a-tin
gel´a-tine
ge-lat´i-nous
gel´id
gelled
gel´ling
gen·e-al´o·gy
gen´er·al
gen-er-al´i·ty
gen-er-al-i·za´
   tion
gen´er-al-ize
gen´er-al·ly
gen´er-ate
gen´er-at-ing
gen-er-a´tion
gen´er-a-tive
gen´er-a-tor
ge-ner´ic
ge-ner´i-cal·ly
gen-er-os´i·ty
gen´er-ous·ly
ge-net´ic
ge-net´i-cal·ly

91

ge´nial
ge-ni-al´i·ty
ge´nie
ge´nius
gen´o-cide
gen´re
gen-teel´ly
gen´tile
gen-til´i·ty
gen´tle
gen´tle-man
gen´tle-wom·an
gen´tlest
gent´ly
gen-tri-fi-ca´tion
gen´try
gen´u-flect
gen´u-ine·ly
ge´ode
ge-o-graph´ic
ge-o-graph´i-cal
ge-og´ra-phy
ge-o-log´ic
ge-o-log´i-cal
ge-ol´o-gist
ge-ol´o·gy
ge-o-met´ric
ge-o-met´ri-cal
ge-om´e-try
ge-o-po-lit´i-cal
ger-i-at´rics
ger-mane´
ger´mi-cide
ger´mi-nate
ges´ture
ges´tur·er
ges´tur-ing

get´a·way
get´ting
gey´ser
ghast´li-ness
ghast´ly
gher´kin
ghet´to
ghost´li-ness
ghost´ly
ghost´writ·er
ghoul´ish
gi´ant
gib´ber-ish
gibe
gid´di·ly
gid´di-ness
gid´dy
gift´ed
gig´a-byte
gi-gan´tic
gig´gle
gig´gling
gig´gly
gild´ing
gim´let
gim´mick·ry
gim´mick·y
gin´ger
gin´ger-bread
gin´ger·ly
gin´ger-snap
gird´er
gird´ing
gir´dle
girl´friend
gis´mo
give´a·way

giv´en
giv´er
giv´ing
gla´cial
gla´cier
glad´den
glade
glad´i-a-tor
glad´i-a-to´ri·al
glad´ly
glad´ness
glam´or-ize
glam´o-rous·ly
glam´our
glance
glanc´ing
glan´du-lar
glar´ing
glass´es
glass´mak-ing
glass´ware
glass´y
gleam´ing
glee´ful·ly
glib´ly
glid´er
glid´ing
glim´mer-ing
glimpse
glimps´ing
glis´ten
glitch
glit´ter
glit-te-ra´ti
glit´ter-ing
glit´ter·y
glitz´y

gloat´ing
glob´al-ism
glob-al-i-za´tion
glob´al·ly
glob´u-lar
glob´ule
gloom´i·ly
gloom´i-ness
gloom´y
glo-ri-fi-ca´tion
glo´ri-fied
glo´ri·fy
glo´ri-fy-ing
glo´ri-ous·ly
glo´ry
glos´sa·ry
glos´si-ness
gloss´y
gloved
glow´er-ing
glow´ing
glued
glum´ly
glut´ted
glut´ton-ous
glut´ton·y
gnarl
gnarled
gnarl´y
gnaw
gnaw´ing
gnome
gnos´tic
goad´ed
goal´keep·er
goal´tend·er
goal´tend-ing

gob´ble-dy-gook
gob´bler
gob´bling
gob´let
gob´lin
god´dess
god´fa-ther
god´less
god´like
god´li-ness
god´ly
god´moth·er
god´par-ent
god´send
gold´en
golf´er
gon´do·la
gon-do-lier´
gone
gon´er
good–by´
good-bye´
good´ies
good´ness
good´y
goo´ey
goof´i-ness
goof´y
gorge
gor´geous
gor´geous-ness
gor´mand-ize
gor´y
gos´pel
gos´sa-mer
gos´sip-ing
gos´sip-mon-ger

gos´sip·y
goth´ic
got´ten
gouge
goug´er
goug´ing
gour´mand
gour´man-dise´
gour´met
gout´y
gov´ern-a·ble
gov´ern-ance
gov´er-ness
gov´ern-ment
gov´er-nor
grab´ber
grab´bing
grab´by
grace´ful·ly
grace´ful-ness
grace´less
gra´cious·ly
gra´cious-ness
gra-da´tion
grad´ed
grad´er
gra´di-ent
grad´ing
grad´u-al·ly
grad´u-at·ed
grad´u-at-ing
grad-u-a´tion
graf-fi´ti
graf-fi´to
graft´ing
grain´i-ness
grain´y

gram-mar
gra´na·ry
grand-child
grand´chil-dren
grand´dad
grand-daugh-ter
gran-dee´
gran´deur
grand´fa-ther
g r a n - d i l ´ o -
  quence
gran-dil´o-quent
gran´di-ose
grand´ly
grand´ma
grand´moth·er
grand´neph·ew
grand´niece
grand´pa
grand´par-ent
grand´son
grand´stand
grang´er
gran´ny
grant´er
grant´or
gran´u-lar
gran-u-lar´i·ty
gran´u-lat·ed
gran´ule
grape´vine
graph´ic
graph´i-cal·ly
grap´ple
grasped
grasp´ing
grass´land

grass´y
grate´ful·ly
grate´ful-ness
grat´er
grat-i-fi-ca´tion
grat´i-fied
grat´i·fy
grat´i-fy-ing
grat´ing
gra´tis
grat´i-tude
gra-tu´i-ties
gra-tu´i-tous·ly
gra-tu´i·ty
grav´el
grav´el·ly
grave´ly
grav´en
grav´i-tate
grav´i-tat-ing
grav-i-ta´tion·al
grav´i·ty
gra-vure´
gra´vy
gray´beard
gray´ish
graz´er
graz´ing
grease´less
greas´y
great´ly
great´ness
greed´i·ly
greed´i-ness
greed´y
green´er·y
green´gro-cer

green´ish
greet´ing
gre-gar´i-ous
grid´dle
grid´lock
grief´strick·en
griev´ance
grieve
griev´er
griev´ing
griev´ous·ly
grim´ace
grime
grim´y
grind´er
grind´ing
grind´stone
gripe
grip´er
grip´ing
grippe
gris´ly
grist
gris´tle
grit´ty
griz´zled
groaned
groan´ing
gro´cer
gro´cer-ies
gro´cer·y
grog´gy
grooms´man
gros´grained
gross´ly
gross´ness
gro-tesque´ly

94

grouch´i-ness
grouch´y
ground´break·er
ground´break-
ing
ground´less
grounds´keep·er
ground´swell
group´ie
grov´el
grov´eled
grov´el·er
grov´el-ing
grow´er
grow´ing
grown
growth
grub´by
grudg´ing·ly
grue´some
grum´bler
grum´bling
grum´bly
grump´i·ly
grump´i-ness
grump´ish
grump´y
grun´gy
guar´an-tee´
guar´an-ties
guar´an-tor
guar´an·ty
guard´ed·ly
guard´i·an
guard´i-an-ship
guess´er
guess´ing

guess´ti-mate
guess´work
guest´house
guf-faw´
guid´ance
guide´book
guide´post
guile´ful
guile´less
guilt´i·ly
guilt´less
guilt´y
guise
gull´i·ble
gull´i·bly
gum´mi-ness
gum´my
gump´tion
gun´fight·er
gun´fire
gun´ner·y
gun´ny-sack
gun´shot
gur´gle
gur´gling
gush´er
gush´i-ness
gush´ing·ly
gush´y
gust´i·ly
gust·to
gust´y
gut´less
guts´y
gut´ted
gut´ter
gut´tur·al

guz´zle
guz´zling
gym-na´si·um
gym´nast
gym-nas´tics
gy-ne-col´o-gist
gy-ne-col´o·gy
gyp´sy
gy´rate
gy-ra´tion
gy´rat-ing
gy´ro-scope
gy -ro-scop´ic
ha-bil-i-ta´tion
hab´it
hab´i-tat
hab-i-ta´tion
ha-bit´u-al·ly
ha-bit´u-ate
ha-bit-u-a´tion
ha-bit´u·é
hack´er
hack´le
hack´neyed
hag´gard
hag´gle
hair´do
hair´line
hairs´breadth
hair´spring
hair´style
hair´y
half´heart·ed
half´way
hal-i-to´sis
hal-le-lu´jah
hal´lowed

95

hal-lu-ci-na´tion
hal-lu´ci-na-
  to·ry
ham´let
ham´per
hand´bas-ket
hand´ful
hand´i-cap
hand´i-capped
hand´i-cap-per
hand´i-craft
hand´i·ly
hand´i-ness
hand´ker-chief
han´dle
han´dler
han´dling
hand´rail
hand´shake
hand´some·ly
hand´stand
hand´wo´ven
hand´writ-ing
hand´y
hang´ing
hang´o·ver
hang´–up
han´ker-ing
han´ky
hap-haz´ard·ly
hap´less
hap´pen-ing
hap´pen-stance
hap´pi·ly
hap´pi-ness
hap´py
ha-rangue´

ha-rangu´ing
ha-rass´
ha-rassed´
ha-rass´ing
ha-rass´ment
har´bin-ger
hard´en
hard´ened
hard´en·er
hard´en-ing
hard´head·ed
har´di-ness
hard´ly
hard´ness
hard´ship
har´dy
harm´ful
harm´less·ly
harm´less-ness
har-mon´ic
har-mon´i·ca
har-mo´ni-ous·ly
har´mo-nize
har´mo-niz-ing
har´mo·ny
harp´si-chord
har´ri-dan
harsh´ly
harsh´ness
har´vest
har´vester
has´sle
has´sled
haste
has´ten
hast´i·ly
hast´y

hate´ful
hate´mon-ger
ha´tred
haugh´ti·ly
haugh´ti-ness
haugh´ty
haunt´ed
haunt´ing
hav´oc
hawk´er
hawk´ish
haw´ser
hay´mow
hay´ride
haz´ard
haz´ard-ous
ha´zel-nut
haz´ing
ha´zy
head´ache
head´ach·y
head´dress
head´er
head´hunt·er
head´ing
head´quar-ters
head´strong
head´wait´er
head´y
heal´er
heal´ing
health´ful
health´i·er
health´i-est
health´i-ness
health´y
hear´ing

heark´en
hear´say
hearse
heart´ache
heart´beat
heart´bro-ken
heart´burn
heart´en
heart´felt
heart´less
heart´sick
heart´warm-ing
heart´y
heat´ed
heat´ed·ly
heat´er
hea´then
heat´stroke
heav´en·ly
heaven–sent
heav´en-ward
heav´i·er
heav´i·ly
heav´y
heav´y-set
heck´le
heck´ler
heck´ling
hec´tic
hedg´er
hedg´ing
he´do-nism
he´do-nist
heed´ful
heed´less
heft´i·er
heft´i-est

heft´y
heif´er
height´en
hei´nous
heir´loom
heist
hel´i-cop-ter
he´li·um
he´lix
hel´lion
hell´ish
hel´lo´
hel´met·ed
helms´man
help´er
help´ful
help´ing
help´less·ly
help´less-ness
hem´i-sphere
hem´line
hem´lock
hence´forth´
hench´man
her´ald
he-ral´dic
her´ald·ry
her-ba´ceous
herb´al
her´bi-cide
her´biv-ore
here-af´ter
here´by
he-red´i-tar·y
he-red´i·ty
here´in-af´ter
here-of´

her´e·sy
her´e-tic
here´to-fore´
her´i-tage
her´mit-age
her´ni·a
her´ni-ate
he´ro
he´roes
he-ro´ic
he-ro´i-cal·ly
her´o-ism
her-self´
hes´i-tan·cy
hes´i-tant
hes´i-tant·ly
hes´i-tate
hes´i-tat-ing·ly
hes-i-ta´tion
het-er-o-sex´u·al
heu-ris´tic
heu-ris´ti-cal·ly
hex-a-dec´i-mal
hex´a-gon
hex-ag´o-nal
hi-a´tus
hi´ber-nate
hi´ber-nat-ing
hi-ber-na´tion
hic´cough
hic´cup
hid´den
hide´a-way
hide´bound
hid´e-ous·ly
hid´ing
hi´er-ar´chal

97

hi´er-ar-chy
hi´er-o-glyph´ic
high´born
high´bred
high´brow
high´lev´el
high´life
high´light
high´way
hik´er
hik´ing
hi-lar´i-ous·ly
hi-lar´i·ty
hill´i-ness
hill´side
hill´top
hill´y
him-self´
hind´most
hin´drance
hind´sight
hip´po-drome
hire´ling
hir´sute
his-to´ri·an
his-tor´ic
his-tor´i-cal·ly
his´to-ries
his´to·ry
his-tri-on´ics
hitch´hike
hitch´hik·er
hoa´gy
hoard´ing
hoarse·ly
hoarsc-ness
hoar´y

hoax
hob´ble
hob´by
hob´by-ist
hob´nob-bing
hock´ey
hodge´podge
hoist´ed
hold´ing
hold´out
hol´i-day
ho´li-ness
ho-lis´tic
ho-lis´ti-cal·ly
hol´low
hol´o-caust
hol´o-gram
hol´o-graph
ho-log´ra-phy
hol´ster
ho´ly
hom´age
home´bod·y
home´buy·er
home´com-ing
home´less
home´li-ness
home´ly
home´mak·er
ho´me·o-path´ic
home´sick-ness
home´stretch
home´ward
hom´ey-ness
hom´i-ci-dal
hom´i-cide
hom´i-lies

hom´i·ly
hom´i·ny
ho-mo-ge´ne·ous
ho-mog´e-nize
ho-mo-sex´u·al
hon´est·ly
hon´es·ty
hon´ey-moon
hon´or-a·ble
hon´or-a·bly
hon-o-rar´i·um
hon´or-ar·y
hon´our *(Br.)*
hood´ed
hood´lum
hood´wink
hoofed
hoof´er
hook´ed
hook´y
hoo´li-gan
hoop´la
hoo-ray´
hoose´gow
hoot´en-an·ny
hoot´er
hope´ful·ly
hope´less·ly
hope´less-ness
hop´per
hop´ping
ho-ri´zon
hor´i-zon´tal·ly
hor´mone
hor´o-scope
hor-ren´dous·ly
hor´ri·ble

hor´ri·bly
hor´rid
hor-rif´ic
hor-rif´i-cal·ly
hor´ri-fied
hor´ri·fy
hor´ror
hors d'oeuvre
horse´pow·er
hors´y
hor-ti-cul´tur·al
hor´ti-cul-ture
hor´ti-cul´tur-ist
ho´sier·y
hos´pice
hos-pit´a·ble
hos-pit´a·bly
hos´pi-tal
hos-pi-tal´i·ty
hos´pi-tal-ize
hos´tage
hos´tel
host´ess
hos´tile ly
hos-til´i·ty
hos´tler
hot´bed
ho-tel´
hot´head·ed
hot´house
hot´ly
hot´shot
hound
hour´glass
hour´ly
house´bro-ken
house´clean´ing

house´ful
house´keep·er
house´top
house´wares
house´warm-ing
house´work
hous´ing
hov´el
hov´er
hov´er-ing
how´dy
how-ev´er
howl´ing
hub´bub
hu´bris
huck´ster
hud´dle
huff´i-ness
huff´y
huge´ly
hug´ging
hulk´ing
hu´man
hu-mane´ly
hu-man-i-tar´
   i·an
hu-man´i·ty
hu´man-ize
hu´man·ly
hu´man-oid
hum´ble
hum´bling
hum´bly
hum´bug
hum´ding´er
hum´drum
hu´mid

hu-mid´i-fi·er
hu-mid´i·fy
hu-mid´i·ty
hu´mi-dor
hu-mil´i-ate
hu-mil´i-at-ing
hu-mil-i-a´tion
hu-mil´i·ty
hum´ming
hu´mor
hu´mor-ist
hu´mor-less
hu´mor-ous·ly
hu´mour *(Br.)*
hump´backed
hunch´back
hun´dred
hun´dred-fold
hun´dredth
hun´ger-ing
hun´gri·er
hun´gri·ly
hun´gry
hunt´er
hunt´ing
hur´dle
hurl´er
hurl´ing
hur-rah´
hur´ri-cane
hur´ried·ly
hur´ry
hurt´ful·ly
hurt´ful-ness
hurt´ing
hur´tle
hur´tling

99

hus´band
hus´band·ly
hus´band·ry
husk´i·ly
husk´i-ness
husk´y
hus´sy
hus´tler
hus´tling
hy´brid
hy´drant
hy´drate
hy-dra´tion
hy-drau´lic
hy-drau´li-cal·ly
hy-dro-e·lec´tric
hy´dro-foil
hy´dro-gen
hy´giene
hy´gien´ist
hymn
hym´nal
hype
hyp´er
hy´per-link
hy-per-sen´si-
  tive
hy´per-text
hy´phen
hy´phen-ate
hy´phen-at·ed
hy-phen-a´tion
hyp-no´sis
hyp-no-ther´a·py
hyp-not´ic
hyp´no-tism
hyp´no-tist

hyp´no-tize
h y - p o - c h o n´
  dri·ac
hy-poc´ri·sy
hyp-o-crit´i-cal
hy-poth´e-ses
hy-poth´e-sis
hy-poth´e-size
hy-po-thet´i-cal
hys-ter´i-cal·ly
hys-ter´ics
i-bu-pro´fen
ice´berg
ice´break·er
ice´mak·er
ic´i-cle
ic´i·ly
ic´ing
i´con
i-con´o-clast
ic´y
i·de´a
i·de´al
i·de´al-ism
i·de´al-ist
i·de´al-is´tic
i·de-al-is´ti-cal·ly
i·de´al·ly
i´de-ate
i·de-a´tion
i·den´ti-cal·ly
i·den´ti-fi-a·ble
i·den-ti-fi-ca´tion
i·den´ti-fied
i·den´ti-fies
i·den´ti·fy
i·den´ti·ty

i·de·o-log´ic
i·de·o-log´i-cal
i·de-ol´o·gy
id´i-o·cy
id´i·om
id´i-o-mat´ic
id-i-o-syn´cra·sy
id´i·ot
id-i-ot´ic
i´dled
i´dle-ness
i´dler
i´dling
i´dly
i´dol
i·dol´a-ter
i·dol´a-trous
i·dol´a-try
i´dol-ize
i´dyll
i·dyl´lic
if´fy
ig-nite´
lg-nit´ing
ig-ni´tion
ig-no´ble
ig-no´bly
i g - n o - m i n´ i -
  ous·ly
ig´no-rance
ig´no-rant
ig-nore´
ill´–ad-vised´
il-le´gal
il-le-gal´i·ty
il-le´gal·ly
il-leg´i·ble

il-le-git´i-ma·cy
il-le-git´i-mate
il-lic´it
il-lic´it·ly
il-lit´er-a·cy
il-lit´er-ate
ill´ness
il´log´i-cal
il-lu´mi-nate
il-lu-mi-na´ti
il-lu-mi-na´tion
il-lu´mi-nat-ing
il-lu-mi-na´tion
il-lu´sion-ar·y
il-lu´sion-ist
il-lu´sive·ly
il-lu´so·ry
il´lus-trate
il´lus-trat-ing
il-lus-tra´tion
il-lus´tra-tive
il´lus-tra-tor
il-lus´tri-ous·ly
im´age
im´ag-e·ry
im·ag´i-nar·y
im·ag´i-na´tion
im·ag´i-na-tive·ly
im·ag´ine
im·ag´ing
im·ag´in-ing
im-bal´ance
im´be-cile
im-be-cil´ic
im-bibe´
im-bib´er
im-bro´glio

im-bue´
im-bu´ing
im´i-tate
im-i-ta´tion
im´i-ta-tive
im-mac´u-late·ly
im-ma-te´ri·al
im-ma-ture´
lm-ma-tur´i·ty
im - mea´ sur -
    a·ble
im - mea´ sur -
    a·bly
im-me´di-a·cy
im-me´di-ate·ly
im-mense´ly
im-mersed´
im-mers´i·ble
im-mer´sion
im´mi-grant
im-mi-gra´tion
im´mi-nent
im-mo´bile
im-mo´bi-lize
im-mod´er-ate
im-mod´er-ate·ly
im-mod´est·ly
im-mod´es·ty
im-mo-la´tion
im-mor´al
im-mo-ral´i·ty
im-mor´al·ly
im-mor´tal
im-mor-tal´i·ty
im-mor´tal-ize
im-mov´a·ble
im-mune´

im - mu - ni - za´
    tion
im´mu-nize
im-mu-nol´o-gist
im-mu-nol´o·gy
im-mu´ta·ble
im´pact
im-pact´ed
im-pair´ment
im-pale´
im-part´
im-par´tial
im-par-ti·al´i·ty
im-par´tial·ly
im-pass´a·ble
im´passe
im-pas´sioned
im-pas´sive·ly
im-pa´tience
im-pa´tient·ly
im-peach´a·ble
iin-peach´ment
im-pec´ca·ble
im-pec´ca·bly
im-pe-cu´ni·ous
im-ped´ance
im-pede´
im-ped´i-ment
im-ped´ing
im-pel´
im-pend´ing
im-pen´e-tra·ble
im-pen´e-tra·bly
im-pen´i-tent
im-per´a-tive
im-per-cep´ti·ble
im-per-cep´ti·bly

im-per-cep´tive
im-per´fect
im-per-fec´tion
im-pe´ri-al-ist
im-pe´ri-al·ly
im-per´il
im-pe´ri-ous·ly
im-per´ish-a·ble
im-per´ma-nent
im-per´me-a·ble
im-per´son·al
im-per´son-ate
im-per-son-a´-
tion
im-per´son-a-tor
im-per´ti-nence
im-per´ti-nent
im-per´ti-nent·ly
im-per-turb´-
a·ble
im-per´vi-ous·ly
im-pet´u-ous·ly
im-pi´e·ty
im-pinge´
im´pi-ous·ly
imp´ish·ly
im-plac·a·bil´i·ty
im-plac´a·ble
im-plac´a·bly
im-plau´si·ble
im´ple-ment
im-ple-men´ta-
tion
im´pli-cate
im-pli-ca´tion
im-plic´it·ly
im-plic´i·ty

im-plied´
im-plore´
im-plor´ing
im-ply´
im-po-lite´
im-pon´der-a·ble
im-port´ *(v.)*
im´port *(n., v.)*
im-por´tance
im-por-ta´tion
im-port´er
im-por´tu-nate
im´por-tune´ly
im-pose´
im-pos´ing
im-po-si´tion
im-pos´si·ble
im-pos´si·bly
im´po-tence
im´po-ten·cy
im´po-tent
im-pound´ment
im-pov´er-ished
im-prac´ti-cal
im´pre-cate
im-pre-ca´tion
im-pre-cise´ly
im-pre-ci´sion
im-preg-na·bil´-
i·ty
im-preg´na·ble
im-preg´nate
im-preg-na´tion
im-pre-sar´i·o
im-press´ *(v.)*
im´press *(n.)*
im-pres´sion

im-pres´sion-
a·ble
im-pres´sion-ist
im-pres´sive·ly
im-pri-ma´tur
im-pri´mis
im´print *(n.)*
im-print´ *(v.)*
im-pris´on
im-pris´on-ment
im-prob´a·ble
im-prop´er·ly
im-pro-pri´e·ty
im-prove´ment
im-prov´i-dent·ly
im-prov´ing
im-prov·i-sa´tion
im´pro-vise
im-pru´dent·ly
im´pu-dent·ly
im-pugn´
im´pulse
im-pul´sive·ly
im-pu´ni·ty
im-pure´
im-pute´
in-a·bil´i·ty
in-ac-ces´si·ble
in-ac-ces´si·bly
in-ac´cu-ra·cy
in-ac´cu-rate·ly
in-ac´tion
in-ac´tive·ly
in-ad´e-qua·cy
in-ad´e-quate·ly
in-ad-mis´si·ble
in-ad-mis´si·bly

102

in-ad-ver´tent·ly
in-ad-vis´a·ble
in-a´lien-a·ble
in-ane´ly
in-an´i-mate·ly
in-an´i·ty
in-ap´pli-ca·ble
in-ap-pro´pri-ate
in-apt´ness
in-as-much´
in-at-ten´tive
in-au´di·ble
in-au´di·bly
in-au´gu-ral
in-au´gu-rate
in-au´gu-rat-ing
in-au-gu-ra´tion
in-aus-pi´
  cious·ly
in´breed-ing
in-cal´cu-la·ble
in-can-desce´
in-can-des´cence
in-can-des´cent
in-can-ta´tion
in-ca´pa·ble
in-ca-pac´i-tate
in-ca-pac-i-ta´
  tion
in-ca-pac´i·ty
in-car´cer-ate
in-car-cer-a´tion
in-car´nate
in-car-na´tion
in-cau´tious·ly
in-cen´di-ar·y
in´cense (n.)

in-cense´ (v.)
in-cen´tive
in-cep´tion
in-ces´sant·ly
in´cest
in-ces´tu-ous
in-ci-dent
in-ci-den´tal·ly
in-cin´er-ate
in-cin-er-a´tion
in-cin´er-a-tor
in-cip´i-ent
in-cise´
in-ci´sion
in-ci´sive
in-cite´
in-cit´er
in-cit´ing
in-clem´ent
in-cli-na´tion
in-cline´ (v., n.)
in´cline (n.)
in-clined´
in-clin´ing
in-clude´
in-clud´ed
in-clud´ing
in-clu´sion
in-clu´sive·ly
in-cog-ni´to
in-co-her´ence
in-co-her´ent·ly
in-com-bus´
  ti·ble
in´come
in-com-mo´di-
  ous

in-com-mu-ni-
  ca´do
in-com´pa-ra·ble
in-com´pa-ra·bly
in-com-pat´i·ble
in-com´pe-tence
in-com´pe-ten·cy
in-com´pe-
  tent·ly
in-com-plete´
in-com-pli´ant
in-com-pre-hen´
  si·ble
in-con-ceiv´a·ble
in-con-clu´sive
in-con´gru-ent·ly
in-con-gru´i·ty
in-con´gru-ous
in-con-se-quen´
  tial
in-con-sid´er-
  a·ble
in-con-sid´er-ate
in-con-sist´en·cy
in-con-sist´ent·ly
in-con-sol´a·ble
in-con-spic´u-
  ous
in-con-test´a·ble
in-con´ti-nence
in-con-trol´la·ble
in-con-tro-vert´
  i·ble
in-con-ve´nience
in-con-ven´
  ient·ly
in-cor´po-rate

in-cor´po-rat·ed
in-cor-po-ra´tion
in-cor-po´re·al
in-cor-rect´ly
in-cor´ri-gi·ble
in-cor-rupt´i·ble
in-crease´ *(v.)*
in´crease *(n.)*
in-creas´ing·ly
in-cred´i·ble
in-cred´i·bly
in-cre-du´li·ty
in-cred´u-lous·ly
in´cre-ment
in´cre-men´tal·ly
in-crim´i-nate
in-crim-i-na´tion
in-crus-ta´tion
in´cu-bate
in-cu-ba´tion
in´cu-bus
in-cul´cate
in-cul-ca´tion
in-cul´pate
in-cul-pa´tion
in-cul´pa-to·ry
in-cum´ben·cy
in-cum´bent·ly
in-cur´
in-cur´a·ble
in-cur´sion
in-debt´ed-ness
in-de´cen·cy
in-de´cent
in-de-ci´pher-
   a·ble
in-de-ci´sion

in-de-ci´sive·ly
in-dec´o-rous·ly
in-deed´
in-de-fen´si·ble
in-de-fin´a·ble
in-def´i-nite·ly
in-del´i·ble
in-del´i·bly
in-del´i-cate·ly
in-dem-ni-fi-ca´
   tion
in-dem´ni-fied
in-dem´ni-fies
in-dem´ni·fy
in-dem´ni·ty
in-dent´
in-den-ta´tion
in-dent´ed
in-den´ture
in-de-pen´dence
in-de-pen´
   dent·ly
in-de-scrib´a·ble
in-de-struc´ti·ble
in-de-ter´mi-
   na·cy
in-de-ter´mi-
   nate
in´dex·er
in´dex·es
in´di-cate
in-di-ca´tion
in-dic´a-tive
in-dic´a-to·ry
in-di´cia
in-dict´a·ble
in-dict´er

in-dif´fer-ence
in-dif´fer-ent·ly
in´di-gence
in-dig´e-nous
in´di-gent
in-di-gest´i·ble
in-di-ges´tion
in-dig´nant·ly
in-dig-na´tion
in-di-rect´ly
in-dis-cern´i·ble
in-dis-creet´
in´dis-crete´
in-dis-cre´tion
in-dis-crim´i-
   nate
in-dis-pens´a·ble
in-dis-posed´
in-dis-put´a·ble
in-dis-tinct´
in-dis-tin´guish-
   a·ble
in-dite´ment
in-di-vid´u·al
in-di-vid-u-al´
   i·ty
in-di-vid´u-al·ly
in-di-vis´i·ble
in-doc´tri-nate
in-doc-tri-na´
   tion
in´do-lence
in´do-lent·ly
in-dom´i-ta·ble
in´doors´
in-du´bi-ta·ble
in-du´bi-ta·bly

104

in-duce´ment
in-duc´ing
in-dulge´
in-dul´gent
in-dulg´ing
in-dus´tri-al-ist
in-dus-tri-al-i·za´tion
in-dus´tri-al-ize
in´dus-tries
in-dus´tri-ous·ly
in´dus-try
in-e´bri-ant
in-e´bri-ate
in-e·bri-a´tion
in-ed´i·ble
in-ef-fec´tive·ly
in-ef-fec´tu-al·ly
in-ef-fi´cient·ly
in-el´e-gant·ly
in-el´i-gi·ble
in-ept´
in-ep´ti-tude
in-e·qual´i·ty
in-eq´ui-ta·ble
in-eq´ui·ty
in-ert´
in-er´tia
in-es-cap´a·ble
in-es´ti-ma·ble
in-ev´i-ta·ble
in-ex-act´
in-ex-act´ly
in-ex-cus´a·ble
in-ex-haust´i·ble
in-ex´o-ra·ble
in-ex-pen´sive·ly

in-ex-pe´ri-enced
in-ex´pert·ly
in-ex´pert-ness
in-ex-plain´a·ble
in-ex-plic´a·ble
in-ex-tric´a·ble
in-ex-tric´a·bly
in-fal-li·bil´i·ty
in-fal´li·ble
in-fal´li·bly
in´fa-mous·ly
in´fa·my
in´fan·cy
in´fant
in´fan-tile
in´fan-try
in-fat´u-ate
in-fat´u-at·ed
in-fat-u-a´tion
in-fec´tion
in-fec´tious·ly
in-fer´
in´fer-ence
in-fe´ri·or
in-fe-ri-or´i·ty
in-fer´nal
in-fer´no
in-ferred´
in-fer´ring
in-fer-til´i·ty
in-fest´
in-fes-ta´tion
in´fi-del
in-fi-del´i·ty
in-fil´trate
in-fil-tra´tion

in´fi-nite·ly
in-fin-i-tes´i-mal
in-firm´
in-fir´ma·ry
in-fir´mi·ty
in-flame´
in-flam´ma·ble
in-flam-ma´tion
in-flam´ma-to·ry
in-flat´a·ble
in-flate´
in-flat´ed
in-flat´ing
in-fla´tion
in-fla´tion-ar·y
in-flec-tion
in-flex´i·ble
in-flict´
in´flu-ence
in´flu-en´tial
in-flu-en´za
in-fo-mer´cial
in-form´
in-for´mal
in-for-mal´i·ty
in-for´mant
in-for-ma´tion
in-form´a-tive
in-formed´
in-form´er
in-frac´tion
in´fra-struc-ture
in-fre´quent·ly
in-fringe´ment
in-fu´ri-ate
in-fu´ri-at-ing
in-fuse´

in-fu´sion
in-ge´nious
in-ge-nu´i·ty
in-gen´u-ous
in-gest´
in-grained´
in-gra´ti-ate
in-grat´i-tude
in-gre´di-ent
in-hab´i-tant
in-hab´it·ed
in-hal´ant
in-ha-la´tion
in-hale´
in-hal´er
in-hal´ing
in-her´ent
in-her´it
in-her´i-tance
in-hib´it
in-hib´it·ed
in-hib´it·er
in-hi-bi´tion
in-im´i-cal
in-im´i-ta·ble
in-iq´ui-tous
in-iq´ui·ty
in·i´tial-ize
in·i´tial·ly
in·i´ti-ate
in·i-ti-a´tion
in-ject´
in-jec´tion
in-ju-di´cious
in-junc´tion
in´jure
in´ju-ries

in-ju´ri-ous
in´ju·ry
in´kling
in´laid
in´lay
in-nate´ly
in´ner
in´ner-most
in´no-cence
in´no-cent·ly
in-noc´u-ous·ly
in´no-va´tion
in´no-va-tive
in-nu-en´do
in-nu-en´does
in-nu´mer-a·ble
in-or´di-nate·ly
in´put
in´quest
in-quire´
in-quir´er
in´quir-ies
in-quir´ing
in-quir´ing·ly
in´quir·y
in-qui-si´tion
in-quis´i-tive
in´road
in-sa´tia·ble
in-scrip´tion
in-scru´ta·ble
in´sect
in-sec´ti-cide
in-sert´ *(v.)*
in´sert *(n.)*
in-ser´tion
in-sid´i-ous

in´sight
in´sight-ful
in-sig´ni·a
in-sin´u-ate
in-sin-u-a´tion
in-sip´id
in-sist´
in-sis´tence
in-sis´tent·ly
in´so-lence
in´so-lent·ly
in-sol´u·ble
in-solv´a·ble
in-sol´ven·cy
in-sol´vent
in-som´ni·ac
in-spect´
in-spec´tion
in-spec´tor
in-spi-ra´tion·al
in-spire´
in-spir´ing
in-sta·bil´i·ty
in-stall´
in-stal-la´tion
in-stalled´
in-stall´ing
in-stall´ment
in´stance
in´stant
in - s t a n - t a´
   ne·ous
in´step
in´sti-gate
in´sti-ga-tor
in-stil´ *(Br.)*
in-still´

in-stil-la´tion
in´stinct *(n.)*
in-stinc´tive·ly
in-stinc´tu-al·ly
in´sti-tute
in-sti-tu´tion·al
in-struct´ed
in-struc´tion·al
in-struc´tor
in´stru-ment
in-stru-men´tal
in-sub-or´di-
   nate
in-sub-or-di-
   na´tion
in-suf´fer-a·ble
in´su-lar
in-su-lar´i·ty
in´su-late
in´su-la´tion
in´sult *(n.)*
in-sult´ *(v.)*
in-sult´ing·ly
in-sur´a·ble
in-sur´ance
in-sure´
in-sured´
in-sur´er
in-sur´gence
in-sur´gen·cy
in-sur´gent
in-sur-rec´tion
in-tact´
in´take
in´te-ger
in´te-gral
in´te-grate

in-te-gra´tion
in-teg´ri·ty
in´tel-lect
in-tel-lec´tu-al
in-tel´li-gence
in-tel´li-gent·ly
in-tel-li-gen´tsi·a
in-tend´ing
in-tense´
in-tense´ly
in-ten´si-fied
in-ten´si-fi·er
in-ten´si-fies
in-ten´si·fy
in-ten´si·ty
in-tent´
in-ten´tion·al
in-tent´ly
in-ter´
in-ter-act´
in ter ac´tion
in-ter-ac´tive
in-ter-cede´
in-ter-ced´ing
in-ter-cept´ *(v.)*
in-ter-cep´tion
in´ter-course
in-ter-de-nom-i-
   na´tion·al
in-ter-de-part-
   men´tal
in-ter-dict´
in-ter-dic´tion
in´ter-est·ed
in´ter-est-ing
in´ter-face
in´ter-faith

in-ter-fere´
in-ter-fer´ence
in-ter-fer´ing
in´ter·im
in-te´ri·or
in-ter-ject´
in-ter-jec´tion
in´ter-leaf
in-ter-leav´ing
in´ter-lop·er
in´ter-lude
in-ter-me´di-ate
in-ter´ment
in-ter´mi-na·ble
in-ter-mis´sion
in-ter-mit´tent·ly
in-ter-mix´
in´tern
in-ter´nal
in-ter´nal-ize
in-ter-na´tion·al
in-terned´
in-tern´ment
in-ter´nist
in-ter´po-late
in-ter´pret
in-ter-pre-ta´tion
in-ter´pret·er
in-ter´pre-tive
in-ter´ro-gate
in-ter-ro-ga´tion
in-ter-rog´a-tive
in-ter´ro-ga-tor
in-ter-rupt´ed
in-ter-rupt´ing
in-ter-rup´tion
in-ter-sec´tion

107

in´ter-state´	in-tro-spec´tion	in-vig´o-rate
in-ter-stel´lar	in-tro-spec´tive	in-vig´o-rat-ing
in´ter-val	in-tro-ver´sion	in-vin´ci-ble
in-ter-vene´	in´tro-vert	in-vi-ta´tion·al
in-ter-ven´tion	in-trude´	in-vite´
in´ter-view·er	in-trud´er	in-vit´ing
in-tes´tate	in-tru´sion	in-vo-ca´tion
in-tes´ti-nal	in-tru´sive	in´voice
in-tes´tine	in-tu-i´tion	invoke´
in´ti-ma·cy	in-tu´i-tive	in-vok´ing
in´ti-mate·ly	in´un-date	in-volved´
in-ti-ma´tion	in-un-da´tion	in-volve´ment
in-tim´i-date	in-ure´	in-volv´ing
in-tim-i-da´tion	in-vade´	in´ward·ly
in-tol´er-a·ble	in-vad´er	i´o-dine
in-tol´er-ance	in-vad´ing	i´on
in-tol´er-ant	in-val´id *(void)*	i·on-i·za´tion
in´to-nate	in´va-lid *(dis-*	i´on-ize
in-to-na´tion	*abled)*	i·on´o-sphere
in-tone´	in-va´sion	i·o´ta
in-tox´i-cant	in-va´sive	i·ras´ci·ble
in-tox´i-cate	in-vec´tive	i·rate´ly
in-tox´i-cat-ing	in-vent´	ir-i-des´cence
in-tox-i-ca´tion	in-ven´tion	ir-i-des´cent·ly
in-trac´ta·ble	in-ven´tive	irk´some
in-tran´si-gence	in-ven´tor	i´ron
in-tran´si-gent	in´ven-to-ries	i·ron´ic
in-tra-pre-neur´-	in´ven-to·ry	i·ron´i-cal·ly
i·al	in-verse´ly	i´ro·ny *(satire)*
in-trep´id	in-ver´sion	ir-ra´di-ant
in´tri-ca·cy	in-vest´	ir-ra´di-ate
in´tri-cate·ly	in-ves´ti-gate	ir-ra´tion·al
in-trigued´	in-ves-ti-ga´tion	ir´ri-ga·ble
in-tri´guing	in-ves´ti-ga-tor	ir´ri-gate
in-tro-duce´	in-vest´ment	ir-ri-ga´tion
in-tro-duc´tion	in-ves´tor	ir´ri-ta·ble
in-tro-duc´to·ry	in-vet´er-ate	ir´ri-tant

ir´ri-tate
ir´ri-tat-ing
ir´ri-ta´tion
is´land·er
is´let
i´so-late
i·so-la´ting
i·so-la´tion-ist
i·so-met´ric
i´so-ton´ic
is´sue
is´su-ing
isth´mus
i·tal´ic
i·tal´i-cize
itch´i-ness
itch´y
i´tem-i·za´tion
i´tem-ize
it´er-ate
it-er-a´tion
i·tin´er-ant
i·tin´er-ar·y
its *(possessive)*
it´s *(it is)*
it-self
i´vied
i´vo·ry
i´vy
jab
jabbed
jab´ber
jab´bing
jack´al
jack´et·ed
jack´pot
jad´ed

jag´ged
jail´bird
jail´break
jail´er
ja-la-pe´ño
ja-lop´y
jal´ou-sie
jam´ming
jan´gle
jan´gling
jan´gly
jan´i-tor
jan-i-to´ri·al
jar´gon
jar´ring
jaun´diced
jaunt
jaun´ti·ly
jaun´ti-ness
jaun´ty
jav´e-lin
jaw´bone
jawed
jazz´y
jeal´ous·ly
jeal´ou·sy
jeer´ing·ly
je-june´
jel´lied
jel´ly
jeop´ar-dize
jeop´ar·dy
jerk´y *(shaky)*
jer´ky *(meat)*
jer´sey
jest´er
jet´sam

jet´ti-son
jet´ty
jew´eled
jew´el·er
jew´el·ry
jif´fy
jig´ger
jig´gle
jilt´ed
jin´gle
jin´gling
jin´gly
jit´ney
jit´ter-bug
jit´ters
jit´ter·y
job´ber
job´less
jock´ey
joc´u-lar
joc-u-lar´i·ty
jog´ging
join´er
joint´ed
joint´er
joint´ly
joist
joked
jok´er
joke´ster
jok´ing·ly
jol´li·ty
jol´ly
josh´er
josh´ing·ly
jos´tle
jos´tled

jos´tling
jour´nal
jour´nal-ism
jour´nal-ist
jour´nal-ize
jour´ney
jo´vi·al·ly
joy´ful·ly
joy´ful-ness
joy´less
joy´ous·ly
joy´ride
ju´bi-lance
ju´bi-lant·ly
ju-bi-la´tion
judge´ship
judg´ing
judg´ment
judg-men´tal
ju´di-ca-to·ry
ju-di´cial·ly
ju-di´ciar·y
ju-di´cious·ly
jug´gler
jug´gling
jug´u-lar
juice
juic´er
juic´i-ness
juic´y
ju-li·enne´
jum´bled
jum´bling
jump´er
jump´i-ness
jump´ing
jump´y

junc´tion
junc´ture
jun´gle
jun´ior
jun´ket
junk´ie
ju´ried
ju´ries
ju-ris-dic´tion·al
ju-ris-pru´dence
ju´rist
ju´ror
ju´ry
jus´tice
jus´ti-fi-a·ble
jus-ti-fi-ca´tion
jus´ti-fied
jus´ti-fi·er
jus´ti·fy
jut´ting
ju´ve-nile
jux-ta-po-si´tion
ka-lei´do-scope
ka-lei´do-scop´ic
ka´pok
kar´ma
kay´ak
keen´ly
keen´mess
keep´er
keep´ing
keep´sake
ken´nel
ker´a-tin
ker´chief
kerned
ker´nel

ke´tone
ket´tle-drum
key´board
key´hole
key´note
khak´i
kick´back
kid´ded
kid´ding
kid´nap
kid´naped
kid´nap-er
kid´nap-ing
kid´napped
kid´nap-per
kid´nap-ping
kid´ney
kill´er
kill´ing
kill´joy
kiln
ki´lo
kil´o-cy-cle
kil´o-gram
ki-lom´e-ter
kil´o-watt
kil´o-watt–hour
kilt´ed
ki-mo´no
ki-mo´nos
kin´der-gar-ten
kind´heart-ed
kin´dle
kind´li-ness
kin´dling
kind´ly
kind´ness

kin´dred	knuckle	la´dle-ful
ki-net´ic	ko´sher	la´dy
kin´folk	kow´tow	la´dy-like
king´dom	kum´quat	la´ger
king´ly	ky´ack	lag´gard
king´pin	la´bel	lag´ging
kink´y	la´beled	la-goon´
kin´ship	la´bel-ing	la´ic
ki´osk	la´bor	lais´sez–faire
kis´met	lab´o-ra-to-ry	la´i-ty
kiss´a·ble	la´bored	lake´side
kitch´en-ette´	la´bor-er	lam-baste´
kit´ten	la-bo´ri-ous-ly	la-mé´
kit´ty	la´bour *(Br.)*	lame´ly
klep-to-ma´ni·a	lab´y-rinth	lame´ness
klep-to-ma´ni-ac	lab-y-rin´thi-an	la-ment´
knap´sack	lab-y-rin´thine	lam´en-ta-ble
knav´er·y	lac´er-ate	lam´en-ta-bly
knead	lac-er-a´tion	lam-en-ta´tion
knee´cap	lace´work	la-ment´ed
kneel´ing	lac´ing	lam´i-na
knick´knack	lack-a-dai´si-cal	lam´i-nal
knife	lack´ey	lam´i-nar
knight´hood	lack´ing	lam´i-nate
knit´ting	lack´lus-ter	lam-i-na´tion
knives	la-con´ic	lamp´black
knob	la-con´i-cal-ly	lamp´light
knob´by	lac´quer	lam-poon´
knock´out	lac´tate	lamp´post
knoll	lac-ta´tion	lanc´er
knot´hole	lac´tose	lan´dau
knot´ted	lac´y	land´ed
knot´ting	lad´der	land´fall
knot´ty	lad´en	land´hold-er
know´ing-ly	la´dies	land´ing
knowl´edge	lad´ing	land´la-dy
knowl´edge-a·ble	la´dle	land´locked

111

land´lord
land´mark
land´own-er
land´scape
land´slide
lan´guage
lan´guid-ly
lan´guish
lan´guish-ing
lan´guor
lan´guor-ous
lank´y
lan´tern
lan´yard
la-pel´
lapse
lar´ce-nist
lar´ce-nous
lar´ce-ny
large´ly
large´ness
larg´er
lar-gess´
larg´est
lar´i-at
lar´va
lar´vae
lar´val
lar-yn-gi´tis
lar´ynx
las-civ´i-ous
la´ser
lash´ing
las´sie
las´si-tude
las´so
last´ing

latch
late´ly
late´ness
la´tent
lat´er
lat´er-al
lat´er-al-ly
lat´est
la´tex
lath
lathe
lath´er
lath´er-ing
lath´ing
lat´i-ce
lat´i-tude
la-trine´
lat´ter
lat´tice-work
laud´a·ble
lau´da-to-ry
laugh´a·ble
laugh´ing
laugh´ter
launched
launch´er
laun´der
laun´dries
laun´dry
lau´rel
la´va
lav´a-to-ry
lav´en-der
lav´ish
law´–a·bid´ing
law´break-er
law´ful

law´giv-er
law´less
law´suit
law´yer
lax´a-tive
lax´i-ty
lay´er
lay-ette´
lay´man
la´zi-ly
la´zi-ness
la´zy
lead´er-ship
leaf´less
leaf´y
league
leak´y
lean´ing
lean´ness
lean´–to
leap´frog
leap´ing
learned *(detect-
ed)*
learn´ed *(smart)*
learn´er
learn´ing
leased
lease´hold
leas´ing
leath´er
leath´er·y
leav´en
leav´ing
lech´er-ous
lech´er·y
lec´tern

112

lec´ture
lee´tured
lec´tur-er
lec´tur-ing
ledg´er
leer´ing
leer´y
lee´way
left´o·ver
leg´a-cies
leg´a-cy
le´gal
le-gal´i-ty
le-gal-i·za´tion
le´gal-ize
le´gal-ly
leg´ate *(delegate)*
l e - g a t e ´
　(bequeath)
leg´a-tee´
le-ga´tion
leg´end-ar·y
leg´er-de-main´
lcg´gings
leg-i-bil´i-ty
leg´i-ble
le´gion
leg´is-late
leg-is-la´tion
leg´is-la-tive
leg´is-la-tor
leg´is-la-ture
le-git´i-ma-cy
le-git´i-mate
le-git´i-mize
lei´sure-ly
lem´on-ade´

lend´er
lend´ing
length´en
length´wise
length´y
le´nience
le´nien-cy
le´nient
len´til
le´o-nine
le´o-tard
lep´er
lep´re-chaun
lep´ro-sy
lep´rous
le´sion
les-see´
less´en
less´er
les´son
le´thal
le-thar´gic
le-thar´gi-cal-ly
leth´ar-gy
let´ter
let´ter-head
let´ter–per´fect
let´tuce
leu-ke´mi·a
lev´el
lev´eled
lev´el-er
lev´el-ing
lev´er-age
le-vi´a-than
lev´i-tate
lev´i-tat-ing

lev-i-ta´tion
lev´i-ty
lev´y
lewd´ness
lex-i-cog´ra-pher
lex-i-cog´ra-phy
lex´i-con
li-a-bil´i-ty
li´a·ble
li´ai-son
li´ar
li-ba´tion
li´bel
li´beled
li´bel-er
li´bel-ous
lib´er-al
lib´er-al-ism
lib´er-al-ize
lib´er-al-ly
lib´er-ate
lib-er-a´tion
lib´er-a-tor
lib-er-tar´i-an
lib´er-tine
lib´er-ty
li-bi´do
li-brar´i-an
li´brar·y
li-bret´tist
li-bret´to
li´cens-a·ble
li´cense
li´censed
li´cens-ee´
li´cens-er
li´cens-ing

113

li-cen´tious
lic´it
lien
lieu-ten´ant
life´boat
life´guard
life´less
life´like
life´time
lift´er
lig´a-ment
li-ga´tion
lig´a-ture
light´ed
light´ened
light´en-ing *(v.)*
light´er
light´heart-ed
light´house
light´ing
light´ning *(adj., n.)*
light´weight
like´li-hood
like´ly
lik´en
like-ness
like´wise
lik´ing
lim´ber
lim´bo
lime´light
lim´er-ick
lim´it
lim-i-ta´tion
lim´it-ed
lim´it-less

lim´ou-sine
lim´pid
limp´ly
lin´e·age
lin´e·ar
line´man
lin´en
lin´er
lin´ger
lin-ge-rie´
lin´guist
lin-guis´tic
lin-guis´ti-cal-ly
lin-guis´tics
lin´i-ment
lin´ing
link´age
link´ing
li-no´le-um
lin´seed
lin´tel
li´on-ess
li´on-heart-ed
li´on-ize
lip´stick
liq´ue-fied
li-queur´
liq´uid
liq´ui-date
liq´ui-da´tion
liq´ui-da-tor
li-quid´i-ty
li´quor
lis´some
lis´ten-er
list´er
list´less

lit´a-ny
li´ter
lit´er-a-cy
lit´er-al-ly
lit´er-ar·y
lit´er-ate
lit-e-ra´ti
lit´er-a-ture
lithe´some
lit´i-gant
lit´i-gate
lit-i-ga´tion
lit´i-ga-tor
li-ti´gious
lit´mus
li´tre *(Br.)*
lit´ter
lit´tle
li-tur´gi-cal
lit´ur-gy
liv´a·ble
live´li-hood
live´ly
liv´er-ied
liv´er·y
live´stock
liv´id
liv´ing
lla´ma
loaf´er
loam´y
loath *(adj.)*
loathe *(v.)*
loath´ing
loath´some
loaves
lob´bied

lob´by-ist
lo-bot´o-my
lo´cal
lo-cale´
lo-cal´i-ty
lo´cal-ize
lo´cal-ly
lo´cate
lo-ca´tion
lock´er
lock´et
lock´jaw
lock´smith
lo´co
lo-co-mo´tion
lo-co-mo´tive
lo´cust
lodg´er
lodg´ing
loft´y
log´a-rithm
log´book
log´ging
log´ic
log´i-cal-ly
lo-gis´tic
log´o-type
loin´cloth
loi´ter-er
loll´ing
lol´li-pop
lone´li-ness
lone´ly
lone´some
long´er
long´est
lon-gev´i-ty

long´ing
lon´gi-tude
lon-gi-tu´di-nal
look´ing
look´out
loop´hole
loose´–leaf
loose´ly
loos´en
loot´er
lop´sid-ed
lo-qua´cious
lo-quac´i-ty
lord´li-ness
lor-gnette´
los´er
los´ing
lo´tion
lot´ter·y
lo´tus
loud´ness
loud´speak-er
lounged
loung´er
loung´ing
louse
lous´y
lout´ish
lou´ver
lov´a·ble
love´li-er
love´li-ness
love´lorn
love´ly
lov´er
love´sick
low´brow

low´er-ing
low´land
low´li-ness
low´ly
loy´al
loy´al-ist
loy´al-ly
loy´al-ty
lu´bri-cant
lu´bri-cate
lu-bri-ca´tion
lu´cid
lu-cid´i-ty
luck´i-er
luck´i-est
luck´i-ly
luck´y
lu´cra-tive
lu´cre
lu´di-crous
lug´gage
lug´ging
lu-gu´bri-ous
luke´warm
lull´a-by
lum-ba´go
lum´ber-yard
lu´men
lu´mi-nar·y
lu-mi-nes´cence
lu-mi-nes´cent
lu´mi-nous
lum´mox
lump´i-er
lump´y
lu´na-cy
lu´nar

lunch´eon-ette´
lunch´room
lunged´
lung´ing
lurched
lurch´ing
lure
lu´rid-ly
lurk´er
lurk´ing
lus´cious
lus´ter
lust´ful
lust´i-er
lust´i-ly
lus´trous
lust´y
lux-u´ri-ance
lux-u´ri-ant
lux-u´ri-ate
lux-u´ri-at-ing
lux´u-ries
lux-u´ri-ous
lux´u-ry
ly-can´thro-py
ly´ing
lymph
lym-phat´ic
lynch´ing
lyr´ic
lyr´i-cal
ma-ca´bre
mac´er-ate
ma-chet´e
mach-i-na´tion
mach´i-na-tor
ma-chine´

ma-chin´er-y
ma-chin´ist
mac´ra-me´
mac´ro-cosm
mac´ro-scop´ic
mad´am
ma-dame´
mad´cap
mad´den-ing
ma-de-moi-selle´
mad´house
mad´ly
mad´man
mad´ness
ma-dras´
mad´ri-gal
mael´strom
mae´stro
mag´a-zine´
ma-gen´ta
mag´got
ma´gi
mag´ic
mag´i-cal
mag´i-cal-ly
ma-gi´cian
mag-is-te´ri-al
mag´is-trate
mag´ma
mag-na-nim´i-ty
mag-nan´i-mous
mag´nate
mag´net
mag-net´ic
mag´net-ism
mag´net-ize
mag-ne´to

mag-nif´i-cence
mag-nif´i-cent
mag´ni-fied
mag´ni-fi-er
mag´ni-fy
mag´ni-tude
ma-hog´a-ny
maid´en
mail´a·ble
mail´box
mail´er
main´land
main´ly
main´stay
main-tain´
main´te-nance
ma-jes´tic
ma-jes´ti-cal-ly
maj´es-ty
ma´jor
ma-ior-do´mo
ma-jor´i-ty
make´–be-lieve
mak´er
make´shift
mak´ing
mal´ad-just´ed
mal´a-dy
mal-aise´
mal´a-prop-ism
ma-lar´ia
ma-lar´i-al
mal´con-tent
mal-e-dic´tion
mal´e-fac´tor
ma-lev´o-lence
ma-lev´o-lent

116

mal-fea´sance
mal´formed´
mal´ice
ma-li´cious-ly
ma-lign´
ma-lig´nan-cy
ma-lig´nant
ma-lin´ger
ma-lin´ger-er
mal-le-a·bil´i-ty
mal´le·a-ble
mal´let
mal-nu-tri´tion
mal-o´dor-ous
mal´prac-tice
mal-treat´ment
malt
mam´mal
mam-ma´li-an
mam´ma-ry
mam´mon
mam´moth
man´age
man´age-a·ble
man´age-ment
man´ag-er
man´a-ge´ri-al
man´ag-ing
man´a-kin
man´date
man´da-to-ry
man´do-lin´
ma-neu´ver
ma-neu´ver-
　a·ble
man´ful-ly
man´gle

man´gler
man´gling
man´gy
man´han-dle
ma´nia
ma´ni-ac
ma-ni´a-cal
man´ic
man´i-cure
man´i-cur-ist
man´i-fest
man-i-fes-ta´tion
man-i-fes´to
man´i-fold
man´i-kin
ma-nil´la
ma-nip´u-late
ma-nip-u-la´tion
man´kind´
man´li-ness
man´ly
man´ne-quin
man´ner-ism
man´ner-ly
man´ni-kin
man´nish
man´or
ma-no´ri-al
man´pow-er
man´sard
man´ser-vant
man´sion
man´slaugh-ter
man´tel
man´tel-piece
man´tle
man´tra

man´u-al-ly
man-u-fac´ture
man-u-fac´tur-er
man-u-fac´tur-
　ing
ma-nure´
man´u-script
man-y
mar´a-thon
ma-raud´er
ma-raud´ing
mar´ble
mar´bled
mar´bling
mar´ga-rine
mar´gin-al
mar-i-jua´na
ma-rim´ba
ma-ri´na
mar´i-nade´
mar´i-nate
ma-rine´
mar´i-ner
mar´i-o-nette´
mar´i-tal-ly
mar´i-time
mark´er
mar´ket
mar´ket-a·ble
mar´ket-er
mar´ket-ing
mar´ket-place
marks´man-ship
mar´ma-lade
ma-roon´
mar-quee´
mar´riage

mar´ried
mar´row
mar´ry
mar´shal
mar´shaled
marsh
marsh´mal-low
marsh-y
mar-su´pi-al
mar´tial
mar´ti-net´
mar-ti´ni
mar´tyr
mar´tyr-dom
mar´vel
mar´vel-ous-ly
mas-car´a
mas´cot
mas´cu-line
mas-cu-lin´i-ty
ma´ser
mash´er
mas´och-ism
mas´och-ist
mas´och-is´tic
ma´son
ma-son´ic
ma´son-ry
mas´quer-ade´
mas´sa-cred
mas´sa-cring
mas-sage´
mas-seur´
mas-seuse´
mas´sive
mas´ter-ful
mas´ter-ful-ly

mas´ter-piece
mas´ter·y
mas´ti-cate
mas-ti-ca´tion
mas´to-don
mas´toid
mas-toid-i´tis
mat´a-dor
match´less
match´mak-er
match´mak-ing
ma-te´ri-al-ist
ma-te´ri-al-is´tic
ma-te´ri-al-ism
ma-te´ri-al-ly
ma-te-ri-el´
ma-ter´nal-ly
ma-ter´ni-ty
math-e-mat´i-cal
math-e-ma-ti´
   cian
math-e-mat´ics
mat´i-nee´
mat´ing
ma´tri-arch
ma´tri-ar´chal
ma´tri-ar-chy
ma´tri-cide
ma-tric´u-late
ma-tric-u-la´tion
mat´ri-mo´ni-al
mat´ri-mo-ny
ma´trix
ma´tron-ly
mat´ter
mat´ting
mat´tress

mat´u-rate
mat-u-ra´tion
ma-ture´
ma-tur´i-ty
maud´lin
maul´er
mau-so-le´um
mauve
mav´er-ick
mawk´ish
max´im
max´i-mize
max´i-mum
may´be
may´hem
may´on-naise
may´or
may´or-al-ty
may´pole
maze
ma-zur´ka
mead´ow
mea´gre *(Br.)*
meal´time
meal´y
mean
me-an´der
mean´ing
mean´ly
mean´ness
meant
mean´time
mean´while
mea´sles
mea´sly
mea´sur-a·ble
mea´sure

118

mea´sured
mea´sure-less
mea´sure-ment
mea´sur-er
me-chan´ic
me-chan´i-cal
me-chan´i-cal-ly
mech´a-nism
mech´a-nize
med´al
med´al-ist
me-dal´lion
med´dle
med´dler
med´dle-some
me´dia
me´di-an
me´di-ate
me-di-a´tion
me´di-a-tor
med´ic
med´i-cal
med´i-cal-ly
me-dic´a-ment
med´i-cate
med-i-ca´tion
me-dic´i-nal
med´i-cine
me-di-e´val
me´di-o´cre
me-di-oc´ri-ty
med´i-tate
med-i-ta´tion
med´i-ta-tive
med´i-tat-or
me´di-um
med´ley

me-du´sa
meek´ness
meer´schaum
meet´ing
meg´a-cy-cle
meg´a-phone
meg´a-ton
mel´an-choly
me-lange´
meld´er
me´lee
mel´io-rate
mel-io-ra´tion
mel´io-ra-tive
mel-lif´er-ous
mel-lif´lu-ence
mel-lif´lu-ent
mel-lif´lu-ous
mel´low-ness
me-lod´ic
me-lod´i-cal-ly
me-lo´di-ous
mel´o-dra-ma
mel´o-dra-mat´ic
mel´o-dy
mem´ber-ship
mem´brane
mem´bra-nous
me-men´to
me-men´tos
mem´oir
mem-o-ra-bil´ia
mem´o-ra-ble
mem-o-ran´da
mem-o-ran´dum
me-mo´ri-al
me-mo´ri-al-ize

mem´o-ries
mem-o-ri-za´tion
mem´o-rize
mem´o-riz-er
mem´o-riz-ing
mem´o-ry
men´ace
men´ac-ing
men´ac-ing-ly
me-nag´er-ie
men-da´cious
men-dac´i-ty
mend´er
men´di-cant
me´nial
men-in-gi´tis
men´o-pause
men´ses
men´stru-al
men´stru-ate
men-stru-a´tion
men´tal
men-tal´i-ty
men´tal-ly
men´thol
men´thyl
men´tion-a·ble
men´tor
men´u
mer´can-tile
mer´ce-nary
mer´chan-dise
mer´chan-dis-er
mer´chan-dis-
   ing
mer´chant
mer´ci-ful-ly

119

mer´ci-less

mer-cu´ri-al

mer´cy

mere´ly

m e - r e n ´ g u e
(dance)

mer´est

mer-e-tri´cious

mer-gan´ser

merge

mer´gence

merg´er

me-rid´i-an

me-ringue´ (top-
ping)

mer´it

mer-i-to´ri-ous

mer´maid

mer´man

mer´ri-ly

mer´ri-ment

mer´ri-ness

mer´ry

mer´ry-mak-ing

me´sa

mesh´work

mes´mer-ism

mes´mer-ize

mes´mer-iz-ing

mes-quite´

mes´sage

mes´sen-ger

mess´i-ness

mess´mate

mess´y

met´a-bol´ic

me-tab´o-lism

me-tab´o-lize

met´al

me-tal´lic

met´al-lur´gi-cal

met´al-lur-gist

met´al-lur-gy

met´al-work-ing

met·a-mor´phic

met·a-mor´pho-
sis

met´a-phor

met-a-phor´i-cal

meta-phys´i-cal

met´a-phys´ics

me´te-or

me-te-or´ic

me´te-or-ite

m e - t e - o - r o l ´o-
gist

me-te-o-rol´o-gy

me´ter

meth´a-done

meth´ane

meth´a-nol

meth´od

me-thod´i-cal-ly

meth-od-ol´o-gy

me-tic´u-lous

met´ric

met´ri-cal

met´ro-nome

me-trop´o-lis

met´ro-pol´i-tan

mez´za-nine´

mi´crobe

mi´cro-bi-ol´o-
gist

mi´cro-bi-ol´o-gy

mi ´cro-cosm

mi´cro-fiche

mi´cro-film

mi-crom´e-ter

mi´cron

m i - c r o - o r ´g a-
nism

mi´cro-phone

mi´cro-scope

mi´cro-scop´ic

mi´cro-wave

mid´dle

mid´dle–aged´

mid´dle-man

midg´et

mid´night

mid´riff

mid´stream´

mid´sum´mer

mid´way

mid´wife

mid´wife-ry

might´i-er

might´i-ly

might´i-ness

might´y

mi´graine

mi´grant

mi´grate

mi´grat-ing

mi-gra´tion

mi´gra-to-ry

mil´dew

mild´ly

mild´ness

mile´age

mile´post	min´gle	mis-cel-la´neous
mile´stone	min´gling	mis´cel-la-ny
mi-lieu´	min´i-a-ture	mis´chief–mak´er
mil´i-tan-cy	min´i-a-tur-ist	mis´chie-vous
mil´i-tant	min´i-cam	mis´ci-ble
mi -i-tar´ily	min´i-mal	mis´con-strue´
mil´i-ta-rism	min´i-mize	mis´cre-ance
mil´i-ta-ris´tic	min´i-miz-er	mis´cre-ant
mil´i-tary	min´i-mum	mis´de-mean´or
mi-li´tia	min´ing	mi´ser
milk´i-ness	min´is-ter	mis´er-a-ble
milk´y	min´is-te´ri-al	mis´er-a-bly
mil´le-nary	min´is-try	mi´ser-ly
mil´li-gram	min´now	mis´ery
mil´li-me-ter	mi´nor	mis-giv´ing
mil´li-ner	mi-nor´i-ty	mis-guid´ed
mil´li-ner·y	min´strel	mis´hap
mil´lion	min-u-et´	mis-no´mer
mi´lion-aire´	mi´nus	mi-sog´a-mist
mil´lionth	min´us-cule	mi-sog´a-my
mill´pond	min´ute *(time)*	mi-sog´y-nist
mill´stream	mi-nute´ *(tiny)*	mi-sog´y-ny
mim´e-o-graph	min´ute-man	mis´sal
mim´ic	mi-nu´tia	mis´sile
mim´icked	mi-nu´ti-ae	miss´ing
mim´ick-er	mir´a-cle	mis´sion
mim´ick-ing	mi-rac´u-lous	mis´sion-ar-ies
mim´ic-ry	mi-rage´	mis´sion-ary
min´a-ret´	mir´ror	mis´sive
mince´meat	mirth´ful	mis-tak´able
mind´ful	mirth´less	mis-take´
mind´less	mis´an-thrope	mis-tak´en
min´er	mis´an-throp´ic	mis-tak´ing
min´er-al	mis-be-got´ten	mis´ter
min´er-al-ize	mis-car´riage	mist´i-ness
min-er-al´o-gist	mis-car´ried	mis´tress
min-er-al´o-gy	mis-car´ry	mist´y

mi´ter
mit´i-gate
mit´ten
mix´er
mix´ture
mne-mon´ic
moan
mo´bile
mo-bil´i-ty
mo-bi-li-za´tion
mo´bi-lize
mock´er·y
mock´ing
mock´ing-ly
mo-dal´i-ty
mod´el
mod´eled
mod´el-ing
mo´dem
mod´er-ate-ly
mod´er-at-ing
mod-er-a´tion
mod´er-a-tor
mod´ern-ist
mo-der´ni-ty
m o d - e r n - i · z a´
  tion
mod´ern-ize
mod´est-ly
mod´es-ty
mod´i-cum
mod´i-fi´able
mod-i-fi-ca´tion
mod´i-fied
mod´i-fi-er
mod´i-fy-ing
mod´ish

mod´u-lar
mod´u-late
mod-u-la´tion
mod´u-la-tor
mod´ule
mod´u-lus
mo´gul
mo´hair
moi´e-ty
moi-ré´
moist´en
moist´ness
mois´ture
mo´lar
mo-las´ses
mold
mold´i-ness
mold´ing
mold´y
mo-lec´u-lar
mol´e-cule
mole´hill
mo-lest´
mo-les-ta´tion
mo-lest´er
mol´li-fied
mol´li-fy
mol´li-fy-ing
mol´lusk
mol´ten
mo´ment
mo´men-tar´i-ly
mo´men-tar·y
mo-men´tous
mo-men´tum
mon´arch
mon´ar-chist

mon´ar-chy
mon´as-tery
mo-nas´tic
mo-nas´ti-cism
mon-e-tar´i-ly
mon´e-tar·y
mon´ey
mon´eyed
mon´ger
mon´grel
mon´i-ker
mon´i-tor
monks´hood
mon´o-chro-mat´
  ic
mon´o-cle
mo-nog´a-mist
mo-nog´a-mous
mo-nog´a-my
mon´o-gram
mon´o-grammed
mon´o-lith
mon´o-lith´ic
mon´o-log
mon´o-logue
mon´o-ma´nia
mon´o-nu-cle-o´
  sis
mo-nop´o-lis´tic
mo-nop´o-lize
mo-nop´o-ly
mon´o-rail
mon´o-syl-lab´ic
mon´o-syl´la-ble
mon´o-the-ism
mon´o-the-is´tic
mon´o-tone

mo-not´o-nous
mo-not´o-ny
mon-sieur´
mon-soon´
mon´ster
mon-stros´i-ty
mon´strous
mon-tage´
month´ly
mon´u-ment
mon-u-men´tal
mood´i-ly
mood´i-ness
mood´y
moon´beam
moon´light
moon´lit
moon´shine
moon´struck
moor´age
moor´ing
mop´pet
mop´ping
mor´al
mo-rale´
mor´al-ism
mor´al-ist
mo-ral´i-ty
mor´al-ize
mor´al-ly
mo-rass´
mor-a-to´ri-um
mor´bid
mor-bid´i-ty
mor´bid-ly
morgue
mor´i-bund

morn´ing
mo´ron
mo-ron´ic
mo-rose´
mo-rose´ly
mor´phine
mor´sel
mor´tal
mor-tal´i-ty
mor´tal-ly
mor´tar
mor´tar-board
mort´gage
mort´ga-gee´
mort´gag-ing
mor-ti´cian
mor-ti-fi-ca´tion
mor´ti-fied
mor´ti-fy
mor´ti-fy-ing
mor´tise
mor´tu-ary
mo-sa´ic
mosque
mos-qui´to
mos-qui´to
moss´y
most´ly
mo-tel´
moth´er
moth´er-ly
mo-tif´
mo´tile
mo-til´i-ty
mo-tion
mo´tion-less
mo´ti-vate

mo´ti-vat-ing
mo-ti-va´tion
mo-tive
mot´ley
mo´tor-boat
mo´tor-cade
mo´tor-cy-cle
mo´tor-cy-clist
mo´tor-ist
mo´tor-ize
mot´tle
mot´tled
mot´tling
mot´to
mot´toes
mould *(Br.)*
moun´tain
moun´tain-eer´
moun´tain-ous
mount´ed
mount´ing
mourn´er
mourn´ful
mouse´trap
mous´tache
mous´y
mouth´ful
mouth´piece
mov´able
move´ment
mov´er
mov´ie
mov´ing
mowed
mow´er
mow´ing
mown

mu´ci-lage
muck
muck´rake
mud´di-ness
mud´dle
mud´dled
mud´dy
mud´guard
muf´fin
muf´fle
muf´fler
muf´ti
mug´ger
mug´gi-ness
mug´ging
mug´gy
mul´ber-ry
mulch´er
mul´ish
mul´ti-far´i-ous
mul´ti-lat´er-al
mul´ti-lay-er
mul´ti-lev´el
mul´ti-lin´gual
mul´ti-me´di·a
mul´ti-na´tion-al
mul´ti-ple
mul´ti-plex
mul-ti-pli-ca´-
  tion
mul-ti-plic´i-ty
mul´ti-plied
mul´ti-pli-er
mul´ti-ply-ing
mul´ti-tude
mul-ti-tu´di-
  nous

mum´ble
mum´bling
mun´dane´
mu-nic´i-pal
mu-nic-i-pal´i-ty
mu-nif´i-cence
mu-nif´i-cent
mu-ni´tion
mu´ral
mur´der-er
mur´der-ess
mur´der-ous
murk´i-er
murk´y
mur´mur
mur´mur-ing
mus´cle–bound
mus´cu-lar
mus-cu-lar´i-ty
mus´cu-la-ture
mu-se´um
mush´room
mush´y
mu´sic
mu´si-cal
mu´si-cale´
mu´si-cal-ly
mu-si´cian
mu-si-col´o-gy
mus´ing
mus´ket
mus´ket-ry
musk´y
mus´lin
mus´ter
must´i-ness
must´y

mu´tant
mu´tate
mu-ta´tion
mut´ed
mute´ly
mu´ti-late
mu-ti-la´tion
mu´ti-la-tor
mu´ti-neer´
mut´ing
mu´ti-nied
mu´ti-nous
mu´tiny
mut´ter
mut´ter-ing
mu´tu-al
mu´tu-al-ly
muz´zle
muz´zling
my-o´pia
my-op´ic
myr´i-ad
myrrh
my-self´
mys´ter-ies
mys-te´ri-ous
mys-te´ri-ous-ly
mys´tery
mys´tic
mys´ti-cal
mys´ti-cism
mys´ti-fied
mys´ti-fy
mys´ti-fy-ing
mys-tique´
myth´ic
myth´i-cal

myth-o-log´i-cal
my-thol´o-gy
nabbed
nab´bing
na´bob
na´dir
nag´ging
na´iad
nail´er
na-ive´
na-ive-té´
na´ked
na´ked-ness
name´less
name´ly
nam´er
name´sake
nam´ing
na´per·y
naph´tha
nap´kin
nap´ping
nar´cis-sism
nar´cis-sist
nar´co-lep-sy
nar-co-lep´tic
nar-co´sis
nar-cot´ic
nar´rate
nar-ra´tion
nar´ra-tive
nar´ra-tor
nar´row
nar´row-ness
na´sal
nas´cent
nas´ti-ness

nas´ty
na´tal
na´tion
na´tion-al
na´tion-al-ism
na´tion-al-ist
na´tion-al-is´tic
na-tion-al´i-ty
na´tion-al-ize
na´tion-al-ly
na´tion-wide´
na´tive
na-tiv´i-ty
nat´ti-ly
nat´ty
nat´u-ral
nat´u-ral-ist
nat´u-ral-is´tic
nat-u-ral-i·za´
  tion
nat´u·ral·ize
nat´u-ral-ly
na´ture
naught
naugh´ti-ness
naugh´ty
nau´sea
nau´se-ate
nau´se-at-ed
nau´seous
nau´ti-cal
na´val *(marine)*
na´vel *(mark)*
nav´i-ga-ble
nav´i-gate
nav-i-ga´tion
nav´i-ga-tor

na´vy
near´by´
near´est
near´ly
near´ness
near´sight-ed
neat´ly
neat´ness
neb´u-la
neb´u-lae
neb´u-lous
nec´es-sar´i-ly
nec´es-sar·y
ne-ces´si-tate
ne-ces´si-ties
ne-ces´si-ty
neck´lace
neck´tie
nec´ro-man-cer
nec´ro-man-cy
nec´tar
need´ful
need´i-er
need´i-est
nee´dle
need´less
need´less-ly
nee´dle-work
need´y
ne'er--do--well
ne-far´i-ous
ne-gate´
ne-ga´tion
neg´a-tive
neg´a-tive-ly
neg-a-tiv´i-ty
ne-glect

ne-glect´ful
neg-li-gee´
neg´li-gence
neg´li-gent
neg´li-gi-ble
ne-go´tia-ble
ne-go´ti-ate
ne-go-ti-a´tion
ne-go´ti-a-tor
neigh´bor
neigh´bor-hood
neigh´bor-li-ness
neigh´bor-ly
neigh´bour (Br.)
nei´ther
nem´e-sis
ne´on
ne´o-phyte
neph´ew
nep´o-tism
nerve
ner´vous
ner´vous-ly
ner´vous-ness
nes´tle
nes´tling (snug-
   gle)
nest´ling (bird)
neth´er-most
net´ting
net´tle
net´tled
net´work
neu-ral´gia
neu-ri´tis
neu-rol´o-gist
neu-rol´o-gy

neu-ro´ses
neu-ro´sis
neu-rot´ic
neu´tral
neu-tral´i-ty
neu´tral-ize
neu-tri´no
neu´tron
nev´er
new´el
new´ness
news´y
ni´a-cin
nib´ble
nice´ly
nic´est
ni´ce-ty
niche
nick´el
nick´name
nic´o-tine
niece
nif´ty
nig´gle
nig´gling
night´ly
night´mare
night´time
ni´hi-lism
ni´hi-list
ni´hi-lis´tic
nim´ble
nim´bly
nim´bus
nin´com-poop
nine´fold
nine´teen´

nine´teenth´
nine´ti-eth
nine´ty
nin´ny
ninth
nip´per
nip´ping
nip´ple
nip´py
ni´trate
ni´tride
ni´trite
ni´tro-gen
ni´trous
no-bil´i-ty
no´ble
no´ble-man
no´ble-wom-an
no´bly
no´body
noc-tur´nal
noc´turne
nod´ding
nod´u-lar
nod´ule
noise´less
noise´less-ly
nois´i-ly
nois´i-ness
nois´ing
noi´some
nois´y
no´mad
no-mad´ic
no´men-cla-ture
nom´i-nal
nom´i-nal-ly

nom´i-nate
nom´i-nat-ed
nom-i-na´tion
nom´i-na-tive
nom´i-nee´
non·a-ge-nar´i-
  an
non-ag-gres´sion
non´cha-lance´
non´cha-lant´
non´cha-lant-ly
non-com-bat´ant
n o n - c o m - m i s´
  sioned
non-com-mit´tal
non-con-duc´tor
non-con-form´ist
non–con-form´i-
  ty
non´de-script
non-en´ti-ty
non-ex-is´tent
non´fic´tion
non-par´ti-san
non´pay´ment
non-plussed´
non-pro-duc´tive
non-prof´it
non-pro-li-fer-a´
  tion
non-sec-tar´i-an
non´sense
non-sen´si-cal
non se´qui-tur
non´stop´
noo´dle
noon´time

nor´mal
nor-mal´i-ty
nor´mal-ize
nor´mal-ly
nor´ma-tive
north´east´
north-east´er-ly
north-east´ern
north´er-ly
north´ern
north´ern-er
north´ern-most
north´ward
north´west´
north´west´er-ly
north-west´ern
nose´bleed
nose´–dive
nos-tal´gia
nos-tal´gic
nos´tril
nos´y
no´ta-ble
no´ta-bly
no´ta-ries
no´ta-rize
no´ta-ry
no-ta´tion
notched
notch´er
note´book
not´ed
note´pa-per
note´wor-thy
noth´ing
no´tice-able
no´tice-ably

no´tic-ing
no´ti-fi-ca´tion
no´ti-fied
no´ti-fi-er
no´ti-fy
no´ti-fy-ing
not´ing
no-to-ri´e-ty
no-to´ri-ous
no-to´ri-ous-ly
not-with-stand´
  ing
nou´gat
nour´ish
nour´ish-ing
nour´ish-ment
nov´el
nov-el-ette´
nov´el-ist
nov´el-ize
no-vel´la
nov´el-ties
nov´el-ty
no-ve´na
nov´ice
no-vi´tiate
no´where
nox´ious
noz´zle
nu´ance
nu´bile
nu´cle-ar
nu´clei
nu-cle´ic
nu´cle-us
nude´ness
nudged

127

nudg´er	nu-tri´tion-al	ob-jec´tive
nudg´ing	nu-tri´tion-ist	ob-jec´tive-ly
nud´ism	nu-tri´tious	ob-jec´tive-ness
nud´ist	nu´tri-tive	ob-jec-tiv´i-ty
nu´di-ty	nut´ti-er	ob´late
nug´get	nut´ti-ness	ob´li-gate
nui´sance	nut´ty	ob´li-gat-ing
nul-li-fi-ca´tion	nuz´zle	ob-li-ga´tion
nul´li-fied	ny´lon	ob´li-ga-tor
nul´li-fi-er	nymph	o·blig´a-to-ry
nul´li-fy	oak´en	o·blige´
nul´li-fy-ing	oar´lock	o·blig´er
num´ber	oars´man	o·blig´ing
num´bered	oa´ses	o·blig´ing-ly
num´ber-er	oa´sis	o·blique´
num´ber-less	oat´meal	o·blique´ly
numb´ing	ob´du-ra-cy	ob-lit´er-ate
numb´ly	ob´du-rate	ob-lit-er-a´tion
numb´ness	o·be´di-ence	ob-liv´i-on
nu´mer-al	o·be´di-ent	ob-liv´i-ous
nu-mer´i-cal	o·be´di-ent-ly	ob´long
nu-mer´i-cal-ly	o·bei´sance	ob-nox´ious
nu-mer-ol´o-gy	o·bei´sant	o´boe
nu´mer-ous	ob´e-lisk	o´bo-ist
nu-mis-mat´ics	o·bese´	ob-scene´
nu-mis´ma-tist	o·be´si-ty	ob-scene´ly
num´skull	o·bey´	ob-scen´i-ty
nun´nery	o·bey´ing	ob-scure´
nup´tial	ob-fus´cate	ob-scure´ness
nurse´maid	ob-fus-ca´tion	ob-scur´ing
nur´sery	o·bit´u-ar-ies	ob-scu´ri-ty
nurs´ing	o·bit´u-ary	ob-se´qui-ous
nur´ture	ob´ject *(n.)*	ob-se´qui-ous-ness
nur´tur-ing	ob-ject´ *(v.)*	
nu´tri-ent	ob-ject´ing	ob-serv´able
nu´tri-ment	ob-jec´tion	ob-serv´ance
nu-tri´tion	ob-jec´tion-able	ob-serv´ant

128

ob-ser-va´tion	oc-ca´sion	od´ic
ob-serv´a-to-ry	oc-ca´sion-al	o´di-ous
ob-serve´	oc-ca´sion-al-ly	od´ist
ob-serv´er	oc´ci-den´tal	o´di-um
ob-serv´ing	oc-clu´sion	odom´e-ter
ob-sess´	oc-cult´	o´dor
ob-ses´sion	oc-cul-ta´tion	o´dor-ant
ob-ses´sive	oc-cult´ism	o·dor-if´er-ous
ob-so-les´cence	oc´cupan-cy	o´dor-less
ob-so-les´cent	oc´cu-pant	o´dor-ous
ob-so-lete´	oc-cu-pa´tion	o´dour *(Br.)*
ob´sta-cle	oc-cu-pa´tion-al	of´fal
ob-stet´rics	oc´cu-pied	off´beat
ob´sti-na-cy	oc´cu-pi-er	off´–cen´ter
ob´sti-nance	oc´cu-py	off´–col´or
ob´sti-nate	oc´cu-py-ing	of-fend´
ob´sti-nate-ly	oc-cur´	of-fend´er
ob-strep´er-ous	oc-curred´	of-fend´ing
ob-struct´	oc-cur´rence	of-fense´
ob-struct´er	oc-cur´rent	of-fen´sive
ob-struc´tion	oc-cur´ring	of-fen´sive-ness
ob-struc´tion-ist	o´cean	of´fer
ob-struc´tive	o·ce-an´ic	of´fer-ing
ob-tain´able	o·cean-og´ra-phy	of-fer-to´ri-al
ob-trude´	oc´ta-gon	of´fer-to-ry
ob-trud´er	oc-tag´o-nal	of´fice
ob-trud´ing	oc´tal	of´fice-hold-er
ob-tru´sion	oc´tane	of´fi-cer
ob-tru´sive	oc´tave	of-fi´cial
ob-tru´sive-ly	oc-tet´	of-fi´cial-ly
ob-tuse´	Oc-to´ber	of-fi´ci-ate
ob´vi-ate	oc-to-ge-nar´i·an	of-fi´cious
ob´vi-at-ing	oc´u-list	of-fi´cious-ly
ob-vi-a´tion	odd´i-ty	off´shoot
ob´vi-ous	odd´ly	off´spring
ob´vi-ous-ly	odd´ment	of´ten
ob´vi-ous-ness	odd´ness	of´ten-times

o´gle
o´gling
o´gre
oil´cloth
oil´er
oil´i-ness
oil´stone
oil´y
oint´ment
o·kay´
old´en
old–fash´ioned
old´–line´
old´ster
old´–time´
old–tim´er
o´leo
o´le-o-mar´ga-
  rine
ol-fac´tive
ol-fac´to-ry
ol´i-gar-chy
o·meg´a
o´men
om´i-nous
om´i-nous-ly
o·mis´sion
o·mit´
o·mit´ted
o·mit´ting
om´ni-bus
om-nip´o-tence
om-nip´o-tent
om-ni-pres´ent
om-niv´o-rous
oncc–o´ver
on´com-ing

one´ness
one´–piece´
on´er-ous
one-self´
one´–sid´ed
one´time
one´–way´
on´ion-skin
on´look-er
on´ly
o n - o - m a t - o -
  poe´ia
on´rush
on´set
on´slaught
on´to
o´nus
on´ward
on´yx
oozed
ooz´ing
o·pac´i-ty
o´pal
o·pal-esce´
o·pal-es´cence
o·pal-es´cent
o·paque´
o·paque´ly
o·paqu´er
o·paqu´ing
o´pen
o´pen–air´
o´pen–door´
o´pen-er
o´pen–faced
o´pen-hand´ed
o´pen-ing

o´pen-ly
o´pen–mind´ed
o´pen-ness
o´pen-work
op´er-a-ble
op´er-ate
op-er-a´tion
op-er-a´tion-al
op´er-a-tive
op´er-a-tor
op-er-et´ta
oph-thal-mol´o-
  gist
oph-thal-mol´o-
  gy
o´pi-ate
opin´ion
opin´ion-at-ed
o´pi-um
op-po´nent
op´por-tune´
op´por-tune´ly
o p - p o r - t u n e ´
  ness
op-por-tun´ism
op-por-tun´ist
op-por-tu´ni-ty
op-pos´a·ble
op-pose´
op-pos´ing
op´po-site
op-po-si´tion
op-press´
op-pres´sion
op-pres´sive
op-pres´sor
op-pro´bri-ate

op-pro´bri-ous
op-pro´bri-um
op´tic
op´ti-cal
op-ti´cian
op´tics
op´ti-mal
op´ti-mism
op´ti-mist
op´ti-mis´tic
op-ti-mis´ti-cal-
  ly
op´ti-mum
op´tion
op´tion-al
op-tom´e-trist
op-tom´e-try
op´u-lence
op´u-len-cy
op´u-lent
o´pus
or´a-cle
o´ral
o´ral-ly
o·rate´
o·ra´tion
or´a-tor
or-a-tor´i-cal
or-a-tor´i-cal-ly
or-a-to´rio
or´a-to-ry
or´bit
or´bit-al
or´bit-ed
or´bit-er
or´bit-ing
or´chard

or´ches-tra
or-ches´tral
or´ches-trate
or-ches-tra´tion
or-dain´
or´deal
or´der
or´dered
or´der-li-ness
or´der-ly
or´di-nal
or´di-nance
or-di-nar´i-ly
or´di-nary
or´di-nate
or-di-na´tion
ord´nance
or´gan
or´gan-dy
or-gan´ic
or-gan´i-cal-ly
or´ga-nism
or´gan-ist
or´ga-niz´a·ble
or-ga-ni-za´tion
or´ga-nize
or´ga-niz-er
or´ga-niz-ing
or´gy
o´ri-ent
o´ri-en´tal
o´ri-en-tate
o·ri-en-ta´tion
or´i-fice
or´i-gin
o·rig´i-nal
o·rig-i-nal´i-ty

o·rig´i-nal-ly
o·rig´i-nate
o·rig´i-nat-ing
o·rig-i-na´tion
o·rig´i-na-tor
or´na-ment
or´na-men´tal
or-na-men-ta´-
  tion
or´nate´
or-nate´ness
or´nery
or-ni-thol´o-gist
or-ni-thol´o-gy
or´ni-thop-ter
or´phan
or´phan-age
or-tho-don´tia
or´tho-don´tics
or´tho-don´tist
or´tho-dox
or´tho-dox·y
or´tho-pae´dic
or´tho-pae´dist
os´cil-late
os-cil-la´tion
os-cil´lo-scope
os-si-fi-ca´tion
os´si-fied
os´si-fy
os-ten´si-ble
os-ten´si-bly
os-ten-ta´tion
os-ten-ta´tious
os-ten-ta´tious-
  ly
os´teo-my-e-li´tis

os´te-o-path	out´pour-ing	o·ver-rate´
os´te-o-path´ic	out´put	o·ver-rule´
os-te-op´a-thy	out´rage	o·ver-see´
os´tra-cism	out-ra´geous	o´ver-seer
os´tra-cize	out-ra´geous-ly	o·ver-shad´ow
os´tra-ciz-ing	out´reach	o´ver-sight´
oth´er	out´right	o·ver-slept´
oth´er-wise	out´set	o·vert´
ought	out-side´	o·ver-tak´en
ounce	out-sid´er	o·ver-throw´
our-selves´	out´skirts	o´ver-time
oust´er	out´spo´ken	o·vert´ly
out´break	out-stand´ing	o´ver-tone
out´burst	out-stretched´	o´ver-ture
out´cast	out´ward-ly	o´ver-weight
out´class´	out´wit´	o·ver-whelm´ing
out´come	o´va	o·ver-worked´
out´crop-ping	o´val	o´ver-wrought´
out´cry	o·va´tion	o´vu-late
out-do´	ov´en	o·vu-la´tion
out-doors´	o·ver-bear´ing	o´vule
out´er-most	o·ver-came´	ow´ing
out´fit	o´ver-cast	own´er
out´fit-ter	o´ver-coat	own´er-ship
out´go´ing	o·ver-come´	ox´en
out´grew´	o´ver-draft	ox´i-da´tion
out´grow´	o´ver-drive´	ox´ide
out´growth	o·ver-es´ti-mate	ox´i-dize
out-ing	o´ver-flow	ox´y-gen
out-land´ish	o´ver-hang´	ox´y-gen-ate
out´law	o´ver-head	ox-y-gen-a´tion
out´let	o´ver-joyed	o´zone
out´line	o´ver-lap´	paced
out´look	o·ver-lap´ping	pace´mak-er
out´mod´ed	o´ver-look´	pac´er
out–of–date	o´ver-ly	pa-cif´ic
out´post	o·ver-night´	pac-i-fi-ca´tion

pac´i-fied
pac´i-fi-er
pac´i-fism
pac´i-fist
pac´i-fy
pac´i-fy-ing
pac´ing
pack´age
pack´ag-er
pack´ag-ing
pack´er
pack´et
pack´ing
pack´ing-house
pad´ding
pad´dle
pad´dler
pad´dling
pad´lock
pa´gan
pa´gan-ism
pag´eant
pag´eant-ry
paged
pag´er
pag´i-nate
pag-i-na´tion
pag´ing
pa-go´da
pail´ful
pain´ful
pain´ful´ly
pain´less
pain´less-ly
pains´tak-ing
pains´tak-ing-ly
paint´brush

paint´er
paint´ing
pa-ja´ma
pal´ace
pal´at-able
pal´ate
pa-la´tial
pal´ette
pal´i-mo-ny
pal´in-drome
pal-i-sade´
pall´bear-er
pal´li-ate
pal´li·a-tive
pal´lid
pal´lor
palm´ist
palm´is-try
pal-pa-bil´i-ty
pal´pa-ble
pal´pa-bly
pal´pate
pal-pa´tion
pal´pi tate
pal´pi-tat-ing
pa´pi-ta´tion
pal´sied
pal´sy
pal´tri-ness
pal´try
pam´per
pamph´let
pam´phle-teer
pan-a-ce´a
pan-chro-mat´ic
pan-de-mo´ni-
    um

pan´el
pan´eled
pan´el-ing
pan´el-ist
pan´ic
pan´icked
pan´ick-ing
pan´icky
pan´ic–strick-en
pan´o-ply
pan-o-ram´a
pan´o-ram´ic
pant´ing
pan´to-mime
pan´to-mimist
pan´tries
pan´try
pa´pa-cy
pa´pal
pa´per-back
pa´per-board
pa´per-hang-er
pa´per-weight
par´a-ble
par´a-chute
pa-rade´
pa-rad´er
pa-rad´ing
par´a-digm
par´a-dise
par´a-dox
par´a-gon
par´a-graph
par´al-lax
par´al-lel
par´al-leled
par´a-lyse *(Br.)*

pa-ral´y-sis
par´a-lyt´ic
par´a-lyze
par´a-lyz-ing
par´a-mount
par´a·mour
par-a-noi´a
par´a-noid
par´a-ple´gic
par´a-site
par´a-sit´ic
par´a-sol
par´cel
par´celed
par´cel-ing
parch´ment
par´don
par´don-able
par´don-er
pared
par´ent-age
pa-ren´tal
pa-ren´the-ses
pa-ren´the-sis
pa-ren´the-size
par´en-thet´ic
par´en-thet´i-cal
par´ing
par´ish
pa-rish´ion-er
par´i-ty
par´lance
par´lay *(bet)*
par´ley *(talk)*
par´lia-ment
par-lia-men´ta-
  ry

par´lor
pa-ro´chial
par´o-dy
par´o-dy-ing
pa-role´
pa-roled´
pa-rol-ee´
pa-rol´ing
par-quet´
par´ried
par´ry
par´ry-ing
parse
par-si-mo´nious
par´si-mo-ny
pars´ing
par´son
par´son-age
par-take´
par-tak´en
par-tak´er
part´ed
par´tial
par-ti·al´i-ty
par´tial-ly
par-tic´i-pant
par-tic´i-pate
par-tic-i-pa´tion
par-tic´u-lar
par-tic´u-lar-ly
par´ties
part´ing
par´ti-san
par-ti´tion
par-ti´tion-er
par-ti´tion-ing
part´ly

part´ner
part´ner-ship
par-took´
part´–time´
par´ty
pass´able
pass´ably
pas´sage
pas´sage-way
pass´book
pas-sé´
pas´sen-ger
pass´er
pass´er-by
pass´ing
pas´sion
pas´sion-ate
pas´sion-ate-ly
pas´sive
pas´sive-ly
pas´sive-ness
pas´siv-ism
pas´siv-ist
pass´port
pass´word
paste´board
past´ed
pas-tel´
past´er
pas-teur-i·za´
  tion
pas´teur-ize
pas´time
past´ing
pas´tor
pas´to-ral
pas-to-rale´

pas´try	pa-trol´ler	peace´mak-er
pas´ture	pa-trol´ling	peace´time
patch´er	pa´tron	peach´y
patch´i-ness	pa´tron-age	peaked *(crested)*
patch´ing	pa´tron-ize	peak´ed *(sickly)*
patch´work	pa´tron-iz-ing	peas´ant
patch´y	pat´ter	peas´ant-ry
pat´ent	pat´tern	peb´ble
pat´ent-able	pat´terned	peb´bled
pat´ent-ly	pat´tern-mak-er	peb´bling
pa-ter´nal	pat´ting	peb´bly
pa-ter´nal-ism	pat´ty	pec´cant
pa-ter´nal-is´tic	pau´ci-ty	peck´ing
pa-ter´nal-ly	paunch´i-ness	pec´u-late
pa-ter´ni-ty	paunch´y	pec´u-lat-ing
pa-thet´ic	pau´per	pec-u-la´tion
pa-thet´i-cal-ly	pau´per-ism	pe-cu´liar
pa-thol´o-gist	paus´ing	pe-cu-li·ar´i-ty
pa-thol´o-gy	pave´ment	pe-cu´ni·ar·y
pa´thos	pav´er	ped´a-gog´ic
path´way	pa-vil´ion	ped´a-gogue
pa´tience	pav´ing	ped´a-gogy
pa´tient	pawn´bro-ker	ped´al
pa´tient-ly	pawn´shop	ped´aled
pat´io	pay´able	pe-dan´tic
pa-tis´se-rie	pay´day	ped´ant-ry
pa´tois	pay-ee´	ped´dle
pa´tri-arch	pay´er	ped´dler
pa´tri-ar´chal	pay´ing	ped´dling
pa´tri-archy	pay´ment	ped´es-tal
pa-tri´cian	pay-o´la	pe-des´tri-an
pa´tri-ot	pay´roll	pe-di-a-tri´cian
pa´tri-ot´ic	peace´able	pe-di-at´rics
pa´tri-ot´i-cal-ly	peace´ably	ped´i-gree
pa´tri-ot-ism	peace´ful	peel´er
pa-trol´	peace´ful-ly	peel´ing
pa-trolled´	peace´ful-ness	peep´er

peep´hole
peer´age
peer´less
pee´vish
pee´vish-ness
peign-oir´
pel-la´gra
pel´let
pel´vic
pel´vis
pe´nal
pe´nal-ize
pe´nal-iz-ing
pen´al-ties
pen´al-ty
pen´ance
pench´ant
pen´cil
pen´ciled
pen´cil-ing
pend´ing
pen´du-lous
pen´du-lum
pen´e-tra-ble
pen´e-trate
pen´e-trat-ing
pen-e-tra´tion
pen-i-cil´lin
pe-nin´su-la
pe-nin´su-lar
pen´i-tence
pen´i-tent
pen-i-ten´tia-ry
pen´i-tent-ly
pen´man-ship
pen´nant
pen´nies

pen´ni-less
pen´ning
pen´ny
pe-nol´o-gist
pe-nol´o-gy
pen´sion
pen´sion-er
pen´sive
pen´sive-ly
pen´ta-gon
pent´house
pent´–up´
pe´on
peo´ple
pep´per·y
pep´py
pep´sin
pep´tic
per-cale´
per-ceiv´a·ble
per-ceiv´a·bly
per-ceive´
per-cent´
per-cent´age
per-cent´ile
pcr-cep´ti-ble
per-cep´ti-bly
per-cep´tion
per-cep´tive
per´co-late
per-co-la´tion
per´co-la-tor
per-cus´sion
per-cus´sive
pe-remp´tive
pe-remp´to-ri-ly
pe-remp´to-ry

pe-ren´nial
per´fect *(adj.)*
per-fect´ *(v.)*
per-fect´er
per-fec´tion
per´fect-ly
per-fec´tor
per-fid´i-ous
per-fid´i-ous-ly
per-fid´i-ous-
  ness
per´fi-dy
per´fo-rate
per´fo-rat-ed
per-fo-ra´tion
per´fo-ra-tor
per-form´
per-form´ance
per-form´er
per´fume
per-fum´er
per-fum´er·y
per-func´to-ry
per-haps´
per´il
per´il-ous
per´il-ous-ly
pe-rim´e-ter
pe´ri-od
pe-ri-od´ic
pe-ri-od´i-cal
pe-ri-od´i-cal-ly
per·i-pa-tet´ic
pe-riph´er-al
pe-riph´er-al-ly
pe-riph´er·y
per´i-phrase

per´i-scope
per´ish
per´ish-a·ble
per´jure
per´jur-er
per´jur-ing
per-ju´ri-ous
per´jur·y
perk´i-ness
perk´y
per´ma-nence
per´ma-nen-cy
per´ma-nent
per´ma-nent-ly
per´me-a·ble
per´me-ate
per-mis´si-ble
per-mis´sion
per-mis´sive
per-mit´ (v., n.)
per´mit (n.)
per-mit´ted
per-mit´ting
per-mu-ta´tion
per-ni´cious
per-ox´ide
per-pen-dic´u-
lar
per´pe-trate
per´pe-tra-tor
per-pet´u-al
per-pet´u-ate
per-pe-tu´it·y
per-plex´
per-plexed´
per-plex´ing
per´qui-site

per´se-cute
per-se-cu´tion
per´se-cu-tor
per-se-ver´ance
per´se-vere´
per´se-ver´ing
per´si-flage
per-sist´
per-sist´ence
per-sist´ent
per-sist´ent-ly
per-snick´e-ty
per´son
per´son-al
per´son-al´i-ty
per´son-al-ize
per´son-al-ly
per-son-i-fi-ca´
tion
per-son´i-fy
per-son´i-fy-ing
per´son-nel´
per-spec´tive
per opi-ca´cious
per-spi-cac´i-ty
per-spi-cu´ity
per-spic´u-ous
per-spi-ra´tion
per-spire´
per-spir´ing
per-suad´a·ble
per-suade´
per-suad´er
per-suad´ing
per-sua´si·ble
per-sua´sion
per-sua´sive

per-sua´sive-ly
per-tain´
per´ti-nence
per´ti-nent
per-turb´
per-turb´a·ble
pe-rus´al
pe-ruse´
pe-rus´er
pe-rus´ing
per-vade´
per-vad´ing
per-va´sive
per-va´sive-ly
per-verse´
per-verse´ly
per-verse´ness
per-ver´sion
per-ver´sity
per-vert´ (v.)
per´vert (n.)
per-vert´ed
per´vi-ous
pes´ky
pes´si-mism
pes´si-mist
pes-si-mis´tic
pes-si-mis´ti-
cal-ly
pes´ter
pes´tered
pes´ti-lence
pes´tle
pe-tite´
pe-ti´tion
pe-ti´tion-er
pet´ri-fied

137

pet´ri-fy
pet´ti-ly
pet´ti-ness
pet´ty
pet´u-lance
pet´u-lant
pew´ter
pha´lanx
phal´lic
phal´lus
phan´tasm
phan´tom
phar´aoh
phar´ma-ceu´ti-
  cal
phar´ma-cist
phar-ma-col´o-
  gy
p h a r - m a - c o -
  pe´ia
phar´ma-cy
phase
phas´er
phi´al
phi-lan´der
phi-lan´der-er
phil´an-throp´ic
phi-lan´thro-pist
phi-lan´thro-py
phil´a-tel´ic
phil-lat´e-list
phil´har-mon´ic
phi-los´o-pher
phil´o-soph´i-cal
phi-los´o-phize
phi-los´o-phy
phil´ter

phle-bi´tis
phlegm
pho´bia
pho´bic
pho-net´ic
pho-net´i-cal-ly
phon´ic
pho´no-graph
pho´ny
phos´phate
phos´phor
phos-pho-resce´
p h o s - p h o - r e s ´
  cent
pho´to
pho´to-gen´ic
pho´to-graph
pho-tog´ra-pher
pho´to-graph´ic
pho-tog´ra-phy
pho´ton
pho´to-stat
pho-to-syn´the-
  sis
phras´al
phrase
phras´ing
phre-nol´o-gist
phre-nol´o-gy
phy´lum
phys´i-cal
phys´i-cal-ly
phy-si´cian
phys´i-cist
phys´ics
phy-sique´
pi-an´ist

pi-a´no *(softly)*
pi-an´o *(instru-*
  ment)
pi-an´o-forte
pic´a-resque´
pic´co-lo
pic´co-lo-ist
pick´ax
pick´er
pick´et
pick´et-er
pick´et-ing
pick´ing
pick´le
pick´led
pick´ling
pick´pock-et
pic´nic
pic´nicked
pic´nick-er
pic´nick-ing
pic-to´ri-al
pic´ture
pic-tur-esque´
pic´tur-ing
pieced
piece´meal
piece´work
piec´ing
pie´crust
pierced
pierc´er
pierc´ing
pi´e·tism
pi´e-ty
pif´fle
pi´geon

pi´geon-hole
pi´geon–toed
pig´head-ed
pig´ment
pig-men-ta´tion
pig´pen
pig´skin
pik´er
pi-las´ter
pil´fer
pil´fer-age
pil´grim-age
pil´ing
pil´lage
pil´lag-er
pil´low
pil´low-case
pil´low-slip
pi´lot
pim´ple
pim´pled
pim´ply
pin´a-fore
pince´–nez´
pin´cers
pinch´–hit
pin´hole
pin´na-cle
pin´ning
pin´point
pin´up
pin´y
pi´o-neer´
pi´o-neered´
pi´ous
pi´ous-ly
pipe´line

pip´er
pip´ing
pi´quan-cy
pi´quant
pique
piqued
pi´ra-cy
pi´rate
pir´ou-ette´
pir´ou-ett´ed
pir´ou-ett´ing
pis´ca-to´ri-al
pis´ca-to-ry
pis´tol
pis´ton
pitch´er
pitch´ing
pit´e-ous
pit´e-ous-ly
pit´fall
pith´i-ness
pith´y
pit´i-a·ble
pit´ied
pit´i-er
pit´ies
pit´i-ful
pit´i-ful-ly
pit´i-less
pit´tance
pit´ted
pit´ter–pat´ter
pit´ting
pit´y
pit´y-ing
piv´ot
piv´ot-al

piv´ot-er
pix´ie
pix´y
piz-ze-ri´a
plac´a-ble
plac´ard
pla´cate
pla´cat-er
pla´cat-ing
pla-ce´bo
place´–kick
place´ment
plac´er
plac´id
plac´id-ly
plac´ing
pla´gia-rist
pla´gia-rize
pla´gia-riz-ing
pla´gia-ry
plague
plagu´ed
plagu´ing
plaid
plain´ly
plain´ness
plain´tiff
plain´tive
plain´tive-ly
plait
plan´et
plan-e-tar´i-um
plan´e-tar·y
plank´ing
plank´ton
planned
plan´ner

plan´ning
plan´tain
plan-ta´tion
plant´er
plant´ing
plaque
plas´ma
plas´ter
plas´tered
plas´ter-er
plas´ter-ing
plas´tic
pla-teau´
plat´ed
plate´ful
plat´en
plat´form
plat´ing
plat´i-num
plat´i-tude
pla-ton´ic
pla-toon´
plat´ter
plau´dit
plau´si·ble
plau´sive
play´bill
play´boy
play´er
play´ful
play´ful-ly
play´ful-ness
play´go-er
play´ground
play´house
play´ing card
play´mate

play´–off (n.)
play´thing
plaz´a
plea
plead´er
plead´ing
plead´ing-ly
pleas´ant
pleas´ant-ly
pleas´ant-ness
pleas´ant-ry
pleas´ing
plea´sur-a·ble
plea´sure
pleat
pleat´ed
ple-be´ian
pleb´i-scite
plec´trum
pledged
pledg´er
pledg´ing
ple´na-ry
plen´te-ous
plen´ti-ful
plen´ti-ful-ly
plen´ty
pleu´ri-sy
pli´a·ble
pli´an-cy
pli´ant
plied
pli´ers
plight
plod´ded
plod´der
plod´ding

plot´ter
plot´ting
plow
plow´er
plow´–hand
plow´ing
plow´share
pluck´i-er
pluck´y
plu´mage
plumb
plumb´er
plumb´ing
plum´met
plump´er
plump´ness
plun´der
plun´der-er
plun´der-ous
plung´er
plung´ing
plu´ral
plu-ral´i-ty
plu-toc´ra-cy
ply´ing
pneu-mat´ic
pneu-mo´nia
poach´er
pock´et
pock´et-book
pock´et-ful
po-di´a-trist
po-di´a-try
po´di-um
po´em
po´e-sy
po´et

140

po-et´ic
po-et´i-cal
po´et-ry
po-grom´
poi´gnan-cy
poi´gnant
point´ed
point´ed-ly
point´er
poin´til-lism
point´less
poised
pois´ing
poi´son
poi´son-er
poi´son-ous
pok´er
pok´ing
pok´y
po´lar
po-lar´i-ty
po-lar-i·za´tion
po´lar-ize
po´lar-iz-er
po´lar-iz-ing
po-lice´
po-lic´ing
pol´i-cy
pol´ish
pol´ish-er
po-lite´
po-lite´ly
po-lite´ness
pol´i-tic
po-lit´i-cal
po-lit´i-cal-ly
pol-i-ti´cian

po-lit´i-cize
pol´ka
pol´len
pol´len-ize
pol´li-nate
pol´li-nat-ing
po´li-na´tion
poll´ster
pol-lu´tant
pol-lute´
pol-lut´er
pol-lut´ing
pol-lu´tion
pol´o-naise´
poly-chro-mat´ic
pol´y-chrome
pol´y-es-ter
poly-eth´yl-ene
po-lyg´a-mist
po-lyg´a-mous
po-lyg´a-my
pol´y-graph
pol´y-mer
pol´y-no´mi-al
pol´yp
pol´y-syl-lab´ic
pol´y-the-ism
pol´y-the-ist
pol´y-the-is´tic
poly-vi´nyl
pom´mel
pom´meled
pom´pa-dour
pom-pos´i-ty
pomp´ous
pon´cho
pon´der

pon´der-a·ble
pon´der-ous
po´nies
pon´tiff
pon-tif´i-cate
pon-tif´i-ca-tor
pon-toon´
po´ny
poo´dle
poor´ly
pop´gun
pop´lar
pop´lin
pop´over
pop´pies
pop´ping
pop´py
pop´py-cock
pop´u-lace
pop´u-lar
pop-u-lar´i-ty
pop-u-lar-i·za´tion
pop´u-lar-ize
pop´u-lar-ly
pop´u-late
pop-u-la´tion
pop´u-lous
por´ce-lain
por-nog´ra-pher
por-no-graph´ic
por-nog´ra-phy
po-ros´i-ty
po´rous
por´ridge
por´ta-ble
por´tal

141

por-tend´
por´ter
port-fo´lio
port´hole
por´ti-co
por´ti-coes
por´tion
port´li-ness
port´ly
por´trait
por´trai-ture
por-tray´
posed
pos´er
pos´ing
po-si´tion
po-si´tion-er
pos´i-tive
pos´i-tive-ly
pos´i-tiv-ism
pos´i-tiv-is´tic
pos´i-tron
pos´se
pos-sess´
pos-sessed´
pos-sess´es
pos-ses´sion
pos-ses´sive
pos-ses´sive-ly
pos-ses´sor
pos-si-bil´i-ty
pos´si-ble
pos´si-bly
post´age
post´al
post´card
post´date´

post´er
pos-te´ri-or
pos-ter´i-ty
post´hu-mous
post´hu-mous-ly
post -hyp-not´ic
post´mark
post´mas-ter
post´mis-tress
post´–mor´tem
post´paid´
post-pone´
post-pone´ment
post´script
pos´tu-late
pos´tu-lat-ing
pos´ture
pos´tur-ing
po´ta-ble
pot´bel-lied
pot´bel-ly
pot´boil-er
po´ten-cy
po´tent
po-ten´tial
po-ten-ti-al´i-ty
po-ten´tial-ly
po´tent-ly
pot´hole
po´tion
pot´luck´
pot-pour-ri´
pot´shot
pot´ted
pot´ter
pot´ter·y
poul´tice

poul´try
pounc´ing
pound´age
pound´er
pound´–fool´ish
poured
pour´er
pour´ing
pout´er
pout´ing
pout´ing-ly
pout´y
pov´er-ty
p o v´ e r -
ty–strick´en
pow´der
pow´dered
pow´der·y
pow´er
pow´ered
pow´er-ful
pow´er-ful-ly
pow´er-house
pow´er-less
pow´wow
prac´ti-cal
prac-ti-cal´i-ty
prac´ti-cal-ly
prac´tice
prac´ticed
prac´tic-er
prac´tic-ing
prac-ti´tion-er
prag-mat´ic
prag-mat´i-cal-ly
prag´ma-tism
prag´ma-tist

prai´rie
praise´wor-thy
prais´ing
pranced
pranc´er
pranc´ing
prank´ster
prat´tle
prat´tler
prayed
prayer *(plea)*
pray´er *(asker)*
prayer´ful
preached
preach´er
preach´ing
preach´ment
preach´y
pre´am-ble
pre´ar-range´
pre-car´i-ous
pre-cau´tion
pre-cau´tion-ar·y
pre-cau´tious
pre-cede´
prec´e-dence
prec´e-dent
pre-ced´ing
pre´cept
pre-ces´sion
pre´cinct
pre´cious
prec´i-pice
pre-cip´i-tate
pre-cip´i-tate-ly
pre-cip-i-ta´tion
pre-cip´i-tous

pre-cip´i-tous-ly
pre-cise´
pre-cise´ly
pre-cise´ness
pre-ci´sion
pre-clude´
pre-clud´ing
pre-clu´sion
pre-co´cious
pre-coc´i-ty
pre´con-ceive´
pre-con-cep´tion
pre-cur´sor
pre-cur´so-ry
pred´a-tor
pred´a-to-ry
pred´e-ces-sor
pre-des-ti-na´
  tion
pre-des´tine
pre-de-ter´mine
pre-dic´a-ment
pre-dict´
pre-dict´a·ble
pre-dic´tion
pre-dic´tor
pred´i-lec´tion
pre´dis-pose´
pre-dis-pos´ing
pre-dis-po-si´
  tion
pre-dom´i-nant
pre-dom´i-nate
pre-em´i-nence
pre-em´i-nent
pre-em´i-nent-ly
pre-empt´

pre-emp´tion
pre-emp´tive
pre-emp´to-ry
preened
pre-fab´ri-cate
pref´ace
pref´ac-ing
pref´a-to-ry
pre-fer´
pref´er-a·ble
pref´er-a·bly
pref´er-ence
pref´er-en´tial
pre-ferred´
pre-fer´ring
pre´fix
preg´na-ble
preg´nan-cy
preg´nant
pre-hen´sile
pre-his tor´ic
prej´u-dice
prej-u-di´cial
prel´ate
pre-lim´i-nar·y
prel´ude
pre-ma-ture´
pre-ma-ture´ly
pre-med´i-tate
pre-med-i-ta´
  tion
pre-med´i-ta-tive
pre-med´i-ta-tor
pre-mier´
pre-miere´
prem´ise
pre´mi-um

pre-mo-ni´tion
pre-oc-cu-pa´tion
pre-oc´cu-pied
pre-oc´cu-py
pre-or-dain´
pre-paid´
prep-a-ra´tion
pre-par´a-tive
pre-par´a-to-ry
pre-pare´
pre-pared´
pre-par´ed-ness
pre-par´er
pre-pay´ment
pre-pon´der-ance
pre-pos´ter-ous
pre-pos´ter-ous-ly
pre-req´ui-site
pre-rog´a-tive
pre´school´
pre´scient
pre-scribe´
pre-scrip´tion
pres´ence
pres´ent *(adj., n.)*
pre-sent´ *(v.)*
pre-sent´able
pre-sen-ta´tion
pre-sent´er
pres´ent-ly
pres-er-va´tion
pre-serv´a-tive
pre-serve´
pre-serv´er

pre-side´
pres´i-den-cy
pres´i-dent
pres´i-den´tial
pre-sid´er
pre-sid´ing
press´er
press´ing
press´man
pres´sure
pres´sur-ize
pres-ti-dig-i-ta´tion
pres-tige´
pres-tig´i-ous
pre-sum´a-ble
pre-sum´a-bly
pre-sume´
pre-sumed´
pre-sum´er
pre-sump´tion
pre-sump´tive
pre-sump´tu-ous
pre-sup-pose´
pre-tend´
pre-tend´ed
pre-tend´er
pre´tense
pre-ten´tious
pre´text
pret´ti-ly
pret´ti-ness
pret´ty
pret´zel
pre-vail´
pre-vail´ing

prev´a-lence
prev´a-lent
pre-var´i-cate
pre-vent´
pre-vent´a·ble
pre-vent´a·tive
pre-ven´tion
pre-ven´tive
pre´view
pre´vi-ous
pre´vi-ous-ly
price´less
pric´ing
prick´le
prick´ly
priest´hood
priest´ly
prig´gish
pri´ma-cy
pri´mal
pri-mar´i-ly
pri´mar·y
pri-me´val
prim´i-tive
prim´ness
pri-mor´di-al
prince-ly
prin´cess
prin´ci-pal
prin-ci-pal´i-ty
prin´ci-pal-ly
prin´ci-ple
print´er
print´ing
pri´or
pri-or´i·tize
pri-or´i-ty

prism
pris´on-er
pris´sy
pris´tine
pri´va-cy
pri´vate
pri´vate-ly
pri-va´tion
pri´vat-ize
priv´i-lege
priv´i-leged
prob-a-bil´i-ty
prob´a·ble
prob´a·bly
pro´bate
pro-ba´tion
pro-ba´tion-al
pro-ba´tion-ar·y
prob´ing
prob´lem
prob´lem-at´ic
prob´lem-at´i-cal
pro-ce´dur-al
pro-ce´dure
pro-ceed´
pro-ceed´ing
proc´ess
proc´ess-ing
pro-ces´sion
pro-ces´sion-al
pro-claim´
proc-la-ma´tion
pro-cliv´i-ty
pro-cras´ti-nate
proc-tol´o-gy
proc´tor
pro-cure´

pro-cured´
pro-cure´ment
pro-cur´er
pro-cur´ing
prod´ding
prod´i-gal
pro-di´gious
prod´i-gy
pro-duce´ *(v.)*
prod´uce *(n.)*
pro-duc´ing
prod´uct
pro-duc´tion
pro-duc´tive
pro-duc-tiv´i-ty
pro-fane´
pro-fane´ly
pro-fan´er
pro-fan´ing
pro-fan´i-ty
pro-fess´
pro-fessed´
pro-fes´sion
pro-fes´sion-al
pro-fes´sion-al-ly
pro-fes´sor
pro´fes-so´ri-al
prof´fer
pro-fi´cien-cy
pro-fi´cient
pro´file
prof´it
prof´it-able
prof´it-ably
prof´it-less
prof´li-ga-cy
prof´li-gate

pro-found´
pro-found´ly
pro-fuse´
pro-fuse´ly
pro-fu´sion
prog´e-ny
prog-no´sis
prog-nos´ti-cate
prog-nos´ti-ca-
  tor
pro´gram
pro´gramed
pro´gram-er
pro´gram-ing
pro´grammed
pro´gram-mer
pro´gram-ming
prog´ress *(n.)*
pro-gress´ *(v.)*
pro-gres´sion
pro-gres´sive
pro-gres´sive-ly
pro-hib´it
pro-hi-bi´tion
pro-hi-bi´tion-ist
pro-hib´i-tive
proj´ect *(n.)*
pro-ject´ *(v.)*
pro-ject´ed
pro-jec´tile
pro-jec´tion
pro-lif´er-ate
pro-lif´ic
pro´log
pro´logue
pro-long´
pro-longed´

prom´e-nade´
prom´i-nence
prom´i-nent
prom´i-nent-ly
prom-is-cu´i-ty
pro-mis´cu-ous
prom´ise
prom´is-er
prom´is-ing
prom´is-so-ry
prom´on-to-ry
pro-mote´
pro-mot´er
pro-mot´ing
pro-mo´tion
pro-mo´tion-al
prompt
prompt´er
prompt´ly
prompt´ness
prom´ul-gate
prom-ul-ga´tion
pro´noun
pro-nounce´
pro-nounce´able
pro-nounced´
p r o - n o u n c e ´
　ment
pro-nounc´ing
p r o - n u n - c i · a ´
　tion
proof´read-er
prop-a-gan´da
prop´a-gate
prop´a-ga´tion
prop´a-ga-tive
pro-pelled´

pro-pel´ler
pro-pel´ling
pro-pen´si-ty
prop´er
prop´er-ly
prop´er-ties
prop´er-ty
proph´e-cies
proph´e-cy *(n.)*
proph´e-sied
proph´e-si-er
proph´e-sy *(v.)*
proph´et
pro-phet´ic
pro-phet´i-cal
pro´phy-lac´tic
pro-pi´ti-ate
pro-pi´tious
pro-po´nent
pro-por´tion
pro-por´tion-al
pro-por´tion-ate
pro-por´tioned
pro-pos´al
pro-pose´
pro-pos´er
pro-pos´ing
prop-o-si´tion
pro-pri´e-tar·y
pro-pri´e-tor
pro-pri´e-ty
pro-pul´sion
pro-ra´ta
pro-rate´
pro-sa´ic
pro-scribe´
prose

pros´e-cute
pros-e-cu´tion
pros´e-cu-tor
pros´e-cu-to-ry
pros´e-lyte
pros´e-ly-tize
pros´pect
pro-spec´tive
pro-spec´tive-ly
pro-spec´tus
pros´per
pros-per´i-ty
pros´per-ous
pros´per-ous-ly
pros´the-sis
pros-thet´ic
pros´trate
pros´trat-ing
pros-tra´tion
pro-tect´
pro-tect´ing
pro-tect´ing-ly
pro-tec´tion
pro-tec´tive
pro-tec´tive-ly
pro-tec´tor
pro´té-gé´
pro´té-gée´
pro´tein
pro´test *(n.)*
pro-test´ *(v.)*
prot-es-ta´tion
pro-test´er
pro-test´ing
pro´to-col
pro´ton
pro-tract´ed

146

pro-trude´
pro-tru´sion
proud´ly
prov´a·ble
proved
prov´en
prov´en-der
prov´erb
pro-ver´bi·al
pro-vide´
pro-vid´ed
prov´i-dence
prov´i-dent
prov´i-den´tial
pro-vid´er
pro-vid´ing
pro-vin´cial
prov´ing
pro-vi´sion
prov-o-ca´tion
pro-voke´
pro-vok´ing
prow´ess
prowl´er
prox´ies
prox´y
prude
pru´dence
pru´dent
prud´er·y
prud´ish
prun´er
prun´ing
pru´ri-ence
pru´ri-ent
pried
pry´ing

psalm´ist
psal´ter
pseu´do
pso-ri´a-sis
pso-ro´sis
psy´che
psy-chi-at´ric
psy-chi´a-trist
psy-chi´a-try
psy´chic
psy-cho-anal´y-
  sis
psy-cho-an´a-lyze
psy´cho-log´i-cal
psy-chol´o-gist
psy-chol´o-gy
psy´cho-path´ic
psy-cho´sis
psy-chot´ic
pto-maine´
pu´ber-ty
pu-bes´cence
pu-bes´cent
pub´lic
pub-li-ca´tion
pub´li-cist
pub-lic´i-ty
pub´li-cize
pub´lic-ly
pub´lic–spir´it-ed
pub´lish
pub´lish-er
puck´er
puck´ered
puck´ish
pud´dle
pud´dling

pudg´i-ness
pudg´y
puff´i-ness
puff´y
pu´gi-lism
pu´gi-list
pug-na´cious
pug-na´cious-ly
pul´chri-tude
pul´ley
pull´ing
pul´mo-nary
pulp´i-ness
pul´pit
pulp
pulp´y
pul-sa´tion
pu´ver-i-za´tion
pul´ver-ize
pum´mel
punc´tu-al
punc-tu-al´i-ty
punc´tu-ate
punc-tu-a´tion
punc´ture
punc´tured
punc´tur-ing
pun´dit
pun´gen-cy
pun´gent
pu´ni-ness
pun´ish
pun´ish-a·ble
pun´ish-ment
pu´ni-tive
punned
pun´ning

147

pun´ster
pu´ny
pu´pil
pup´pet
pup´pe-teer´
pup´py
pur´chase
pur´chased
pur´chas-er
pur´chas-ing
pure´ly
pur´ga-to-ry
purge
purg´er
purg´ing
pu-ri-fi-ca´tion
pu´ri-fi-er
pu´ri-fy
pur´ist
pu-ri-tan´i-cal
pu´ri-ty
pur-loin´
pur-port´
pur´pose
pur´pose-ful
pur´pose-ly
pur-su´ant
pur-sue´
pur-sued´
pur-su´er
pur-su´ing
pur-suit´
push´er
push´ing
push´over
pu´sil-lan´i-
  mous

puz´zle
puz´zle-ment
puz´zler
puz´zling
pyr´a-mid
quack´ery
quack´ish
quack´ish-ly
quack´ish-ness
quad
quad´ded
quad´ran-gle
quad-ran´gu-lar
quad´rant
quad-ra-phon´ic
q u a d - r a -
  phon´ics
qua-draph´o-ny
qua-drat´ic
qua-dren´ni-al
qua-dren´ni-um
quad´ric
quad-ri-cen-ten´
  ni-al
quad´ri-ceps
quad´ri-cip´i-tal
quad´ri-lat´er-al
quad´ri-lat´er-al-
  ly
quad´ri-lin´gual
qua-drille´
qua-dril´lion
qua-dril´lionth
quad-ri-phon´ic
quad-ri-phon´ics
quad´ru-ped
quad´ru-pe-dal

quad-ru´ple
quad-ru´ply
quad-rup´let
quad´ru-plex
qua-dru´pli-cate
quad-ru´pling
quads
quaff
quaffed
quag´gy
quag´mire
quag´mir-y
qua´hog
quail
quaint
quaint´ly
quaint´ness
quake
quaked
quake´proof
quak´i-ly
quak´i-ness
quak´ing
quak´ing-ly
quak´y
qua´le
qual-i-fi-ca´tion
qual´i-fi-ca-to-ry
qual´i-fied
qual´i-fied-ly
qual´i-fied-ness
qual´i-fi-er
qual´i-fy
qual´i-fy-ing
qual´i-fy-ing-ly
qual´i-ta-tive
qual´i-ta-tive-ly

qual´i-ty
qualm
qualm´ish
qualm´ish-ly
qualm´ish-ness
quan´da-ry
quan´tic
quan´ti-fi-a-ble
quan´ti-fi-a-bly
quan-ti-fi-ca´
  tion
quan´ti-fi-er
quan´ti-fy
quan´tile
quan-tim´e-ter
quan´ti-tate
quan´ti-ta-tive
quan´ti-ta-tive-ly
quan´ti-ty
quan-ti-za´tion
quan´tum
quar´an-tin-a-
  ble
quar´an-tine
quar´an-tin-er
quark
quar´rel
quar´reled
quar´rel-ing
quar´rel-ing-ly
quar´rel-some
quar´rel-some-ly
quar´ri-er
quar´ry
quart
quar´tan
quar´ter

quar´ter-age
quar´ter-back
quar´ter-deck
quar´tered
quar-ter-fi´nal
quar´ter–hour´
quar´ter-ing
quar´ter-ly
quar´ter-mas-ter
quar´tern
quar´ter-staff
quar-tet´
quar´tic
quar´tile
quar´to
quar´tos
quarts
quartz
quartz-if´er-ous
quartz´ite
quartz-it´ic
quartz´ose
qua´sar
quash
qua´si
qua-si-crys´tal
qua-si–ju-di´cial
qua-si-par´ti-cle
quas´sia
qua´train
qua´tre
qua´ver
qua´vered
qua´ver-er
qua´ver-ing
qua´ver-ing-ly
qua´ver-y

quay
quay´age
quea´si-ly
quea´si-ness
quea´sy
queen´dom
queen´hood
queen´like
queen´li-ness
queen´ly
queen´–size
queer´ly
queer´ness
quell
quelled
quell´er
quench
quench´a-ble
quenched
quench´er
quench´less
que-nelle´
que´ried
que´rist
quer´u-lous
quer´u-lous-ly
quer´u-lous-
  ness
que´ri-er
que´ry
que´ry-ing
que´ry-ing-ly
que-sa-dil´la
quest
quest´er
quest´ing-ly
ques´tion

ques´tion-a-ble
ques´tion-a-bly
ques´tion-ar-y
ques´tion-er
ques´tion-ing
ques´tion-ing-ly
ques´tion-less
ques´tion-less-ly
ques´tion-naire´
quet-zal´
queue
queu´ing
quib´ble
quib´bled
quib´bler
quib´bling
quiche
quick
quick´en
quick´en-er
quick´en-ing
quick´–freeze´
quick´ie
quick´lime
quick´ly
quick´ness
quick´sand
quick´sand-y
quick´–set´ting
quick´sil-ver
quick´sil-ver-y
quick´step
quick´–tem´
   pered
quick´–wit´ted
quick´–wit´ted-ly
quid

quid´di-ty
quid´nunc
qui-es´cence
qui-es´cen-cy
qui-es´cent
qui-es´cent-ly
qui´et
qui´et-ism
qui´et-ist
qui-et-is´tic
qui´et-ly
qui´et-ness
qui´e-tude
qui-e´tus
quill
quilt
quilt´ed
quilt´ing
quince
qui-nel´la
qui´nine
qui-nin´ic
quin´sy
quin´tain
quin´tal
quin´tant
quin-tes´sence
quin-tes-sen´tial
quin-tes-sen´
   tial-ly
quin-tet´
quint-tile
quin-til´lion
quin-til´lionth
quin-tu´ple
quin-tup´let
quip

quipped
quip´ping
quip´ster
quirk
quirk´i-ly
quirk´i-ness
quirk´y
quirt
quit
quit´claim
quite
quit´tance
quits
quit´ted
quit´ter
quit´ting
quit´tor
quiv´er
quiv´ered
quiv´er-er
quiv´er-ing
quiv´er-ing-ly
quiv´er-y
quix-ot´ic
quix-ot´i-cal-ly
quix´o-tism
quiz
quiz´mas-ter
quizzed
quiz´zi-cal
quiz-zi-cal´i-ty
quiz´zi-cal-ly
quiz´zing
quoin
quoit
quon´dam
quo´rum

quo´ta
quot-a-bil´i-ty
quot´a-ble
quot´a-bly
quo-ta´tion
quote
quot´ed
quot´er
quoth
quo-tid´i-an
quo´tient
quot´ing
rab´bet
rab´bet-ed
rab´bi
rab´bin-ate
rab-bin´ic
rab-bin´i-cal
rab´bin-ism
rab´bit
rab´bit-ry
rab´ble
rab´ble-ment
rab´bler
rab´ble–rous-er
rab´ble–rous-ing
rab´id
ra-bid´i-ty
rab´id-ly
rab´id-ness
ra´bies
rac-coon´
race
race´course
race´horse
rac´er
race´track

race´way
ra´cial
ra´cial-ism
ra´cial-ly
rac´i-ly
rac´ing
rac´ism
rac´ist
rack
rack´er
rack´et
rack´e-teer´
rack´ety
rack´ing-ly
rack´–rent
rac´i-ly
rac´i-ness
ra´con
rac´on-teur
rac´quet
rac´y
rad
ra´dar
ra´dar-scope
ra´di-al
ra´di-al-ly
ra´di-an
ra´di-ance
ra´di-an-cy
ra´di-ant
ra´di-ant-ly
ra´di-ate
ra-di-a´tion
ra-di-a´tion-al
ra´di-a-tive
ra´di-a-tor
rad´i-cal

rad´i-cal-ism
rad-i-cal-i-za´
　tion
rad´i-cal-ize
rad´i-cal-ly
ra´di·i
ra´di·o
ra-di·o-ac´tive
ra-di·o-ac´tive-ly
ra´di·o-ac-tiv´i-ty
ra´di·o-broad-
　cast
ra-di·o-car´bon
ra´di·o-cast
ra´dio-gram
ra´dio-graph
ra-di·og´ra-pher
ra-di·o-graph´ic
ra-di·o-graph´i-
　cal-ly
ra di og´ra-phy
ra´di·o-i´so-tope
ra-di·o-lo-ca´tion
ra-di·o-log´i-cal
ra-di-ol´o-gist
ra-di-ol´o-gy
ra-di·o-lu´cent
ra-di-om´e-ter
ra-di-o·paque´
ra´di·o-phone
ra-di·o-scop´ic
ra-di·o-scop´i-cal
ra-di-os´co-py
ra-di·o-ther´a-
　pist
ra-di·o-ther´a-py
ra´di-um

151

ra´di-us
ra´don
raf´fia
raff´ish
raff´ish-ly
raff´ish-ness
raf´fle
raf´fled
raf´fling
raft
raf´ter *(timber)*
raft´er *(boatman)*
rafts´man
rag
rag´a-muf-fin
rag´ged
rag´ged-ly
rag´ged-ness
rag´ged-y
rag´ing
rag´gle–tag´gle
rag´man
ra-gout´
rag´pick-er
rag´time
raid
raid´er
rail
rail´er
rail´head
rail´ing
rail´lery
rail´road
rail´road-ing
rail´–split-ter
rail´way
rai´ment

rain´bow
rain´coat
rain´drop
rain´fall
rain´i-er
rain´mak-er
rain´mak-ing
rain´proof
rain´squall
rain´storm
rain´wa´ter
rain´wear
rain´y
raise
raised
rais´er
rai´sin
rais´ing
rai-son´
rake
raked
rake´–off
rak´er
rak´ing
rak´ish
rak´ish-ly
rak´ish-ness
ral´lied
ral´ly
ram
ram´ble
ram´bler
ram´bling
ram´bling-ly
ram´bling-ness
ram-bunc´tious
ram´e-kin

ra´men
ram-i-fi-ca´tion
ram´i-fied
ram´i-form
ram´i-fy
ram´i-fy-ing
ram´jet
rammed
ram´ming
ramp
ram´page
ram-pa´geous
ram-pa´geous-ly
ram´pag-er
ram´pag-ing
ramp´an-cy
ram´pant
ram´pant-ly
ram´part
ram´rod
ram´shack-le
ranch
ranch´er
ran-che´ro
ranch´man
ran´cid
ran-cid´i-ty
ran´cid-ly
ran´cid-ness
ran´cor
ran´cor-ous
ran´cor-ous-ly
ran´cor-ous-
   ness
rand´i-ness
ran´dom
ran´dom-ize

ran´dom-ly
ran´dom-ness
rand´y
range
ranged
rang´er
rang´i-ness
rang´ing
rang´y
rank
rank´er
rank´ing
rank´ish
ran´kle
ran´kled
ran´kling
ran´kling-ly
rank´ly
rank´ness
ran´sack
ran´som
ran´som-er
rant
rant´er
rant´ing
rant´ing-ly
ra-pa´cious
ra-pa´cious-ly
ra-pa´cious-ness
ra-pac´i-ty
rape
rap´id
rap´id–fire
ra-pid´i-ty
rap´id-ly
ra´pier
rap´ine

rap´ist
rapped
rap-pel´
rap´per
rap´ping
rap-port´
r a p - p r o c h e -
    ment´
rap-scal´lion
rapt
rapt´ly
rapt´ness
rap-to´ri-al
rap´ture
rap´tur-ous
rap´tur-ous-ly
rap´tur-ous-ness
rare
rare´bit
rar´e-fied
rar´e-fy
rare´ly
rare´ness
rar´ing
rar´i-ty
ras´cal
ras-cal´i-ty
ras´cal-ly
rash
rash´er
rash´like
rash´ly
rash´ness
rasp
rasp´ber-ry
rasp´er
rasp´i-ness

rasp´ing
rasp´ing-ly
rasp´ing-ness
rasp´ish
rasp´y
ras´ter
rat´a-ble
rat´a-bly
ra-ta-touille´
ratch´et
rate
rat´er
rath´er
raths´kel-ler
rat-i-fi-ca´tion
rat´i-fied
rat´i-fy
rat´i-fy-ing
rat´ing
ra´tio
ra´tion
ra´tio-nal
ra´tion-al-ly
ra´tion-al-ness
ra´tio-nale´
ra´tio-nal-ism
ra´tio-nal-ist
ra-tio-nal-is´tic
ra-tio-nal´i·ty
r a - t i o - n a l -
    i·za´tion
ra´tio-nal-ize
ra´tio-nal-ly
rat´ite
rat´line
rat-tan´
rat´tle

153

rat´tler
rat´tle-trap
rat´tling
rat´tly
rat´ty
rau´cous
rau´cous-ly
rau´cous-ness
raunch
raun´chi-ly
raun´chi-ness
raun´chy
rav´age
rav´age-ment
rav´ag-er
rav´ag-ing
rave
rav´el
rav´eled
rav´el-er
rav´el-ing
rav´en-ous
rav´en-ous-ly
rav´en-ous-ness
ra-vine´
rav´ing
rav´ing-ly
rav-i-o´li
rav´ish
rav´ish-er
rav´ish-ing
rav´ish-ing-ly
raw´boned´
raw´hide
raw´ly
raw´ness
ray

ray´on
raze
ra´zor
ra´zor-back
raz´zle–daz-zle
reach´a-ble
reach´er
re-act´
re-ac´tance
re-ac´tant
re-ac´tion
re-ac´tion-al
re-ac´tion-ar-y
re-ac´ti-vate
re-ac-ti-va´tion
re-ac´tive
re-ac´tive-ly
re-ac´tive-ness
re-ac´tor
read
read-a-bil´i-ty
read´a-ble
read´a-ble-ness
read´a-bly
re-ad-dress´
read´er
read´er-ship
read´i-ly
read´i-ness
read´ing
re-ad-just´
re-ad-just´a-ble
re-ad-just´er
re-ad-just´ment
read´–on´ly
read´out
read´y

read´y–made
read´y–mix
read´y–to–wear´
re-af-firm´
re-a´gent
re´al-ism
re´al-ist
re´al-is´tic
re-al-is´ti-cal-ly
re-al´i-ty
re-al-iza´tion
re´al-ize
re´al–life
re´al-ly
realm
re´al-ness
re-al´po-li-tik
re´al-tor
re´al-ty
ream´er
re-an´i-mate
re-an-i-ma´tion
reap
reap´er
re-ap-pear´
re-ap-pear´ance
re-ap-point´
re-ap-por´tion
re-ap-por´tion-
    ment
rear
rear´–end´
re-arm´
re-ar´ma-ment
rear´most
re-ar-range´
re-ar-rang´ing

rear´ward
rea´son
rea´son-a-ble
rea´son-a-ble-
   ness
rea´son-a-bly
rea´son-er
rea´son-ing
re-as-sem´ble
re-as-sert´
re-as-sume´
re-as-sur´ance
re-as-sure´
re-as-sur´ing
re-as-sur´ing-ly
re-awak´en
re´bar
re´bate
re´bat-er
reb´el *(n., adj.)*
re-bel´ *(v.)*
re-belled´
re-bel´ling
re-bel´lion
re-bel´lious
re-bel´lious-ly
re-bel´lious-ness
re´birth´
re´born´
re-bound´
re-broad´cast
re-buff´
re-build´
re-built´
re-buke´
re-buk´ing
re´bus

re-but´
re-but´ta-ble
re-but´tal
re-but´ted
re-but´ter
re-but´ting
re-cal´ci-tran-cy
re-cal´ci-trance
re-cal´ci-trant
re-call´ *(v., n.)*
re´call *(n.)*
re-call´a-ble
re-cant´
re´cap
re-cap-i-tal-i-
   za´tion
re-cap´i-tal-ize
re-ca-pit´u-late
re-ca-pit-u-la´
   tion
re-ca-pit´u-la-
   tive
re-ca-pit´u-la-to-
   ry
re-cap´pa-ble
re´capped´
re´cap´ping
re-cap´ture
re-cast´
re-cede´
re-ced´ed
re-ced´er
re-ced´ing
re-ceipt´
re-ceiv´a-ble
re-ceive´
re-ceived´

re-ceiv´er
re-ceiv´er-ship
re-ceiv´ing
re´cent
re´cent-ly
re´cent-ness
re-cep´ta-cle
re-cep´tion
re-cep´tion-ist
re-cep´tive
re-cep´tive-ly
re-cep´tive-ness
re-cep-tiv´i-ty
re-cep´tor
re´cess
re´cess´er
re-ces´sion
re-ces´sion-al
re-ces´sion-ar-y
re-ces´sive
re-ces´sive-ly
re-ces´sive-ness
re-charge´
re-charge´a-ble
re-cid´i-vism
re-cid´i-vist
re-cid-i-vis´tic
re-cid´i-vous
rec´i-pe
re-cip´i-ence
re-cip´i-ent
re-cip´ro-cal
re-cip-ro-cal´i-ty
re-cip´ro-cal-ly
re-cip´ro-cate
re-cip-ro-ca´tion
re-cip´ro-ca-tive

re-cip´ro-ca-tor
re-cip´ro-ca-to-
 ry
rec-i-proc´i-ty
re-ci´sion
re-cit´a-ble
re-cit´al
rec-i-ta´tion
rec´i-ta-tive´
re-cite´
re-cit´er
re-cit´ing
reck´less
reck´less-ly
reck´less-ness
reck´on
reck´on-a-ble
reck´on-er
reck´on-ing
re-claim
re-claim´able
rec-la-ma´tion
re-clas-si-fi-ca´
 tion
re-clas´si-fy
re-clin´able
re-cline´
re-clin´er
re-clin´ing
re-clos´a-ble
rec´luse
re-clu´sive
rec-og-ni´tion
re-cog´ni-tive
re-cog´ni-to·ry
rec´og-niz-a-ble
rec´og-niz-a-bly

re-cog´ni-zance
rec´og-nize
rec´og-niz-er
re-coil´ *(react)*
re—coil´ *(to wind)*
re-coil´ing-ly
re-coil´less
r e c - o l - l e c t ´
 (recall)
r e – c o l - l e c t ´
 (amass)
rec-ol-lect´ed
rec-ol-lect´ed-ly
rec-ol-lec´tion
re´com-bine´
re-com-mence´
rec-om-mend´
rec-om-mend´a-
 ble
rec-om-men-da´-
 tion
rec-om-mend´er
re-com-mit´
re-com-mit´tal
re-com-mit´ment
r e c ´ o m - p e n -
 sa·ble
rec´om-pense
rec´om-pens-er
rec´om-pens-ing
re-con´
re-con´cen-trate
r e c - o n - c i l - a -
 bil´i-ty
rec´on-cil-a-ble
rec´on-cil-a-ble-
 ness

rec´on-cil-a-bly
rec´on-cile
rec´on-cile-ment
rec´on-cil-er
r e c - o n - c i l - i - a ´
 tion
rec´on-cil´ia-to-
 ry
rec´on-cil-ing
rec´on-dite
rec´on-dite-ly
rec´on-dite-ness
re-con-di´tion
r e - c o n ´ n a i s -
 sance
re-con-noi´ter
re-con-sid´er
re-con-sid´er-a´-
 tion
re-con´sti-tute
r e - c o n ´ s t i - t u t -
 a·ble
r e - c o n ´ s t i - t u t -
 i·ble
r e - c o n - s t i - t u ´
 tion
re-con-struct´
re-con-struct´er
re-con-struct´i-
 ble
re-con-struc´tion
r e - c o n - s t r u c ´
 tion-al
re-con-struc´tor
re-cord´ *(v.)*
rec´ord *(n., adj.)*
re-cord´able

re-cord´er
rec´ord–hold-er
re-cord´ing
re-count´
re-coup´
re-coup´a-ble
re-coup´ment
re´course
re-cov´er
re-cov´er-a·ble
re-cov´ery
rec´re-ance
rec´re-an·cy
rec´re-ant
rec´re-ant-ly
rec´re-ate *(play)*
re–cre-ate´ *(do over)*
rec-re-a´tion
rec-re-a´tion-al
re–cre-a´tive
rec´re-a-tive
re-crim´i-nate
re-crim´i-nat-ing
re-crim´i-na´tion
re-crim´i-na-tive
re-crim´i-na-tor
re-crim´i-na-to-ry
re-cru-desce´
re-cru-des´cence
re-cru-des´cent
re-cruit´
re-cruit´a-ble
re-cruit´er
re-cruit´ment
rec´tal-ly

rec´tan-gle
rec-tan´gu-lar
rec-tan-gu-lar´i-ty
rec´ti-fi-a·ble
rec-ti-fi-ca´tion
rec´ti-fied
rec´ti-fi-er
rec´ti-fy
rec´ti-tude
rec´to
rec´tor
rec´tor-ate
rec-to´ri-al
rec´to-ry
re-cum´bence
re-cum´ben-cy
re-cum´bent
re-cum´bent-ly
re-cu´per-ate
re-cu-per-a´tion
re-cu´per-a-tive
re-cur´
rc-curred´
re-cur´rence
re-cur´rent
re-cur´rent-ly
re-cur´ring
re-cuse´
re-cy´cla·ble
re-cy´cle
re-dact´
re-dac´tion
re-dac´tor
red´–blood´ed
red´cap
red´den

red´dish
red´dish-ness
re-dec´o-rate
re-dec-o-ra´tion
re-deem´
re-deem´a-ble
re-deem´er
re-demp´ti-ble
re-demp´tion
re-demp´tion-al
re-demp´tive
re-demp´tor
re-demp´to-ry
re-de-ploy´
re-de-ploy´ment
red´–faced
red´–hand´ed
red´head
red´head-ed
red´–hot´
re-di-rect´
re-dis-cov´er
re-dis-cov´er·y
re-dis-trib´ute
re-dis-tri-bu´tion
re-dis´trict
red´–let´ter
red´ness
re-do´
red´o-lence
red´o-len-cy
red´o-lent
red´o-lent-ly
re-dou´ble
re-dou´bling
re-doubt´
re-doubt´a-ble

157

re-draw´
re-dress´
re-dress´able
re-dress´er
re-duce´
re-duc´er
re-duc-i-bil´i-ty
re-duc´i-ble
re-duc´i-bly
re-duc´ing
re-duc´tion
re-duc´tion-al
re-duc´tion-ist
re-duc-tion-is´tic
re-duc´tive
re-duc´tive-ly
re-dun´dan-cy
re-dun´dant
re-dun´dant-ly
re-du´pli-cate
re-du-pli-ca´tion
re-du´pli-ca-tive
reed´i-ness
reed´ing
re-ed´u-cate
re-ed´u-ca-tive
reed´y
reef
reek
reel´a-ble
re-elect´
re-elec´tion
reel´er
reel´-to–reel´
re-em-bark´
re-en-act´
re-en-force´

re-en-force´ment
re-en-gage´
re´en-list´
re-en´ter
re-en´trant
re-en´try
re-es-tab´lish
re-es-tab´lish-
    ment
re-ex-am-i-na´
    tion
re-ex-am´ine
re-fas´ten
re-fer´
ref´er-ee´
ref´er-ence
ref-er-en´dum
ref-er´ent
ref-er-en´tial
re-fer´ral
re-ferred´
re-fer´ring
re´fill *(n.)*
re-fill *(v.)*
re-fill´a-ble
re-fi-nance´
re-fine´
re-fined´
re-fine-ment
re-fin´er
re-fin´ery
re-fin´ing
re-fin´ish
re-fit´
re-flect´
re-flec´tance
re-flect´i·ble

re-flec´tion
re-flec´tion-al
re-flec´tive
re-flec´tive-ly
re-flec´tive-ness
re-flec-tiv´i-ty
re-flec´tor
re´flex
re-flex´ive
re-flex´ive·ly
re-flex´ive-ness
re-flex-iv´i·ty
re-flex-ol´o-gist
re-flex-ol´o-gy
ref´lu-ent
re´flux
re-for-est-a´tion
re-form´ *(amend)*
re–form *(remold)*
re-form´a-ble
ref-or-ma´tion
    (improvement)
re–for-ma´tion
    (new mold)
re-for´ma-to-ry
re-formed´
re-form´er
re-form´ism
re-form´ist
re-for´mu-late
rc-for-mu-la´tion
re-fract´
re-frac´tion
re-frac´tion-al
re-frac´tive
re-frac´tive·ly
re-frac´tor

re-frac´to-ry
re-frain´
re-fran-gi-bil´i-ty
re-fran´gi-ble
re-fresh´
re-fresh´ing
re-fresh´ing-ly
re-fresh´ment
re-frig´er-ant
re-frig´er-ate
re-frig´er-at-ing
re-frig-er-a´tion
re-frig´er-a-tor
re-fu´el
ref´uge
ref´u-gee
re-ful´gence
re-ful´gen-cy
re-ful´gent
re-ful´gent-ly
re´fund *(n.)*
re-fund´ *(v.)*
re-fund´a-ble
re-fur´bish
re-fur´bish-ment
re-fur´nish
re-fus´a-ble
re-fus´al
re-fuse´ *(decline)*
ref´use *(trash)*
re–fuse´ *(join)*
re-fus´ing
re-fut´able
re-fut´ably
re-fute´
re-fut´er
re-fut´ing

re-gain´
re-gain´a-ble
re´gal
re-gale´
re-gale´ment
re-ga´lia
re-gal´ing
re´gal-ly
re´gal-ness
re-gard´
re-gard´ful
re-gard´ful-ly
re-gard´ing
re-gard´less
re-gard´less-ly
re´gen-cy
re-gen´er-a-ble
re-gen´er-a-cy
re-gen´er-ate
re-gen-er-a´tion
re-gen´er-a tive
re-gen´er-a-tive-
   ly
re-gen´er-a-tor
re´gent
reg´gae
re-gime´
reg´i-men
reg´i-ment
reg´i-men´tal
reg´i-men´tal-ly
reg-i-men´ta-ry
r e g - i - m e n - t a´
   tion
re´gion
re´gion-al
re´gion-al-ism

re-gion-al-is´tic
re´gion-al-ize
re´gion-al-ly
reg´is-ter
reg´is-tered
reg´is-tra-ble
reg´is-trant
reg´is-trar
reg´is-trate
reg-is-tra´tion
reg´is-try
re-gress´
re-gres´sion
re-gres´sive
re-gres´sive-ly
re-gres´sor
re-gret´
re-gret´ful
re-gret´ful-ly
re-gret´ful-ness
re-gret´ta-ble
re-gret´ta-ble-
   ness
re-gret´ta-bly
re-gret´ted
re-gret´ter
re-gret´ting
re-group´
reg´u-lar
reg-u-lar´i-ty
reg-u-lar-i-za´
   tion
reg´u-lar-ize
reg´u-lar-ly
reg´u-lat-able
reg´u-late
reg-u-la´tion

159

reg´u-la-tive
reg´u-la-tive-ly
reg´u-la-tor
reg´u-la-to-ry
re-gur´gi-tate
re-gur-gi-ta´tion
re´hab
re-ha-bil´i-tant
re-ha-bil´i-tate
re-ha-bi´i-ta´tion
re-ha-bil´i-ta-tive
re-ha-bil´i-ta-tor
re´hash´
re-hear´
re-hear´ing
re-hears´a·ble
re-hears´al
re-hearse´
re-hears´er
re-hears´ing
re-heat´
re-house´
re-hy´drate
re-hy-dra´tion
re-i-fi-ca´tion
re´i-fy
reign
re-im-burs´able
re-im-burse´
re-im-burse´ment
re-im-port´
re-im-por-ta´tion
re-in-car´nate
re-in-car-na´tion
re-in-force´

re-in-forced´
re-in-force´ment
reins
re-in-sert´
re-in-stall´
re-in-stal-la´tion
re-in-state´
re-in-state´ment
re-in-sur´ance
re-in-sure´
re-in´te-grate
re-in-te-gra´tion
re-in-vent´
re-in-vest´
re-in-vig´o-rate
re-is´su-a-ble
re-is´sue
re-it´er-a-ble
re-it´er-ate
re-it-er-a´tion
re-it´er-a-tive
re-it´er-a-tive-ly
re-ject´ (v.)
re´ject (n.)
re-ject´able
re-ject´er
re-jec´tion
re-jec´tive
re-jec´tor
re-joice´
re-joic´ing
re-joic´ing-ly
re-join´
re-join´der
re-ju´ve-nate
re-ju-ve-na´tion
re-ju´ve-na-tive

re-ju´ve-na-tor
re-ju-ve-nes´cence
re-kin´dle
re-lapse´
re-lapsed´
re-laps´ing
re-lat´a-ble
re-late´
re-lat´ed
re-lat´ed-ness
re-lat´er
re-lat´ing
re-la´tion
re-la´tion-al
re-la´tion-ship
rel´a-tive
rel´a-tive-ly
rel´a-tive-ness
rel´a-tiv-ism
rel´a-tiv-ist
rel-a-tiv-is´tic
rel-a-tiv´i-ty
re-la´tor
re-lax´
re-lax´ant
re-lax-a´tion
re-laxed´
re´lay (send on)
re-lay´ (place again)
re´layed
re-lease´ (liberate)
re´–lease´ (rent anew)
re-leased´

re-leas´er
re-leas´ing
rel´e-gate
rel´e-gat-ed
rel-e-ga´tion
re-lent´
re-lent´ing
re-lent´ing-ly
re-lent´less
re-lent´less-ly
re-lent´less-ness
rel´e-vance
rel´e-van·cy
rel´e-vant
rel´e-vant·ly
re-li-a-bil´i·ty
re-li´a-ble
re-li´a-ble-ness
re-li´a-bly
re-li´ance
re-li´ant
re-li´ant·ly
rel´ic
re-lied´
re-lief´
re-liev´a·ble
re-lieve´
re-lieved´
re-liev´er
re-liev´ing
re-li´gion
re-li´gion-ism
re-li´gion-ist
re-li-gi-ose´
re-li-gi-os´i-ty
re-li´gious
re-li´gious-ly

re-li´gious-ness
re-lin´quish
re-lin´quish-er
re-lin´quish-
    ment
rel´ish-ing
re-live´
re-load´
re-lo´cat-a·ble
re-lo´cate
re-lo-ca´tion
re-lu´cent
re-luc´tance
re-luc´tant
re-luc´tant·ly
rel-uc-tiv´i·ty
re-lume´
re-ly´
re-ly´ing
re-made´
re-main´
re-main´der
re-main´ing
re-make´
re-mand´
re-mand´ment
re-mark´
re-mark´a·ble
re-mark´a·ble-
    ness
re-mark´a·bly
re-mar´riage
re-mar´ry
re´match
re-me´di-a-ble
re-me´di-a-ble-
    ness

re-me´di-a-bly
re-me´di-al
re-me´di-al-ly
re-me-di-a´tion
rem´e-died
rem´e-dies
rem´e-dy
re-mem´ber
re-mem´ber-
    a·ble
re-mem´brance
re-mem´branc-er
re-mind´
re-mind´er
rem-i-nisce´
rem-i-nis´cence
rem-i-nis´cent
rem-i-nis´cent-ly
rem-i-nis´cer
rem-i-nis´cing
re-miss´
re-miss-i-bil´i-ty
re-miss´i-ble
re-miss´i-ble-
    ness
re-mis´sion
re-mis´sive
re-mit´
re-mit´ta-ble
re-mit´tal
re-mit´tance
re-mit´ted
re-mit´tence
re-mit´ten-cy
re-mit´tent
re-mit´tent-ly
re-mit´ter

re-mit´ting
re-mix´
rem´nant
re-mod´el
re-mod´eled .
re-mon-e-ti-za´
tion
re-mon´e-tize
re-mon´strance
re-mon´strant
re-mon´strate
re-mon´strat-
ing-ly
re-mon-stra´tion
re-mon´stra-tive
re-mon´stra-
tive-ly
re-mon´stra-tor
re-morse´
re-morse´ful
re-morse´ful-ly
re-morse´ful-
ness
re-morse´less
re-morse´less-ly
re-morse´less-
ness
re-mote´
re-mote´ly
re-mote´ness
re-mot´est
ré-mou-lade´
re-mount´
re-mov´a-ble
re-mov´a-ble-
ness
re-mov´a-bly

re-mov´al
re-move´
re-moved´
re-mov´ed-ly
re-mov´ed-ness
re-mov´er
re-mov´ing
re-mu´da
re-mu-ner-a-bil´
i-ty
re-mu´ner-a-ble
re-mu´ner-a-bly
re-mu´ner-ate
re-mu-ner-a´tion
re-mu´ner-a-tive
re-mu´ner-a-
tive-ly
re-mu´ner-a-
tive-ness
re-mu´ner-a-tor
ren´ais-sance´
re-name´
rend
ren´der
ren´der-a·ble
ren´dez-vous
ren-di´tion
ren´e-gade
re-nege´
re-neg´er
re-neg´ing
re-ne-go´ti-ate
re-ne-go-ti-
a´tion
re-new´
re-new-a-bil´i·ty
re-new´a·ble

re-new´al
re-newed´
ren´net
ren´nin
re-nom´i-nate
re-nom-i-na´tion
re-nounce´
re-nounce´a·ble
re-nounce´ment
re-nounc´ing
ren´o-vat-a·ble
ren´o-vate
ren´o-vat-ing
ren-o-va´tion
ren´o-va-tor
re-nown´
re-nowned´
rent´a·ble
rent´–a–car
rent´al
rent´er
rent´–free´
rent´ing
re-nun-ci-a´tion
re-nun´ci-a-tive
re-nun´ci-a-to·ry
re-oc´cu-py
re-o´pen
re-or-ga-ni-za´
tion
re-or´ga-nize
re-pack´age
re-paid´
re-paint´
re-pair´
re-pair-a-bil´i·ty
re-pair´a·ble

162

re-pair´er
re-pair´man
rep´a-ra·ble
rep´a-ra·bly
rep-a-ra´tion
re-par´a-tive
re-par´a-to·ry
re-par-ti´tion
re-past´
re-pa´tri-ate
re-pa-tri-a´tion
re-pay´
re-pay´a·ble
re-pay´ing
re-pay´ment
re-peal´
re-peal´a·ble
re-peal´er
re-peat´
re-peat-a-bil´i·ty
re-peat´a·ble
re-peat´ed
re-peat´ed-ly
re-peat´er
re-pel´
re-pelled´
re-pel´lence
re-pel´len·cy
re-pel´lent
re-pel´lent·ly
re-pel´ling
re-pent´
re-pent´ance
re-pent´ant
re-pent´ant-ly
re-pent´ing-ly
re-peo´ple

re-per-cus´sion
re-per-cus´sive
rep´er-toire
rep-er-to´ri-al
rep´er-to-ry
rep-e-ti´tion
rep´e-ti´tious
rep-e-ti´tious-ly
rep´e-ti´tious-
    ness
re-pet´i-tive
re-pet´i-tive-ly
re-pet´i-tive-ness
re-phrase´
re-place´
re-place´able
re-place´ment
re-plac´ing
re-plant´
re´play (n.)
re play´ (v.)
re-plen´ish
re-plen´ish-er
re-plen´ish-ment
re-plete´
re-plete´ness
re-ple´tion
rep´li-ca
rep´li-cate
rep-li-ca´tion
rep´li-ca-tive
re-plied´
re-ply´
re-ply´ing
re´po
re-port´
re-port´a·ble

re-port´age
re-port´ed·ly
re-port´er
rep-or-to´ri-al
rep-or-to´ri-al-ly
re-pose´
re-pos´er
re-pose´ful
re-pose´ful-ly
re-pose´ful-ness
re-pos´ing
re-pos´it·
re-po-si´tion
re-pos´i-to·ry
re-pos-sess´
re-pos-sess´a·ble
re-pos-ses´sion
rep-re-hend´
rep-re-hend´er
rep-re-hen-si-
    bil´i·ty
rep-re-hen´si·ble
rep-re-hen´
    si·ble-ness
rep-re-hen´si·bly
rep-re-hen´sion
rep-re-sent´
rep-re-sent´a·ble
rep-re-sen-
    ta´tion
rep-re-sen-
    ta´tion-al
rep-re-sent´a-
    tive
rep-re-sent´a-
    tive-ly
rep-re-sent´er

re-press´
re-pressed´
re-press´er
re-press´i·ble
re-pres´sion
re-pres´sive
re-pres´sive-ly
re-pres´sive-ness
re-pres´sor
re-prieve´
rep´ri-mand
rep´ri-mand-er
rep´ri-mand-ing-ly
re-print´ *(v.)*
re´print *(n.)*
re-pri´sal
re-prise´
re-proach´
re-proach´a·ble
re-proach´a·ble-ness
re-proach´a·bly
re-proach´ful
re-proach´ful-ly
re-proach´ful-ness
re-proach´ing
re-proach´ing-ly
rep´ro-bate
rep-ro-ba´tion
re´pro-duce´
re´pro-duc´er
re-pro-duc´i·ble
re-pro-duc-i-bil´i·ty
re´pro-duc´ing

re-pro-duc´tion
re-pro-duc´tive
re-pro-duc´tive-ly
re-pro-duc´tive-ness
re-proof´
re-prov´a·ble
re-prov´a·ble-ness
re-prov´al
re-prove´
re-prov´ing
re-prov´ing-ly
rep´tile
rep-til´i·an
re-pub´lic
re-pub´li-can
re-pub´li-can-ism
re-pub-li-can-i-za´tion
re-pub´li-can-ize
re-pub-li-ca´tion
re-pub´lish
re-pu´di-ate
re-pu-di-a´tion
re-pu´di·a-tive
re-pu´di·a-tor
re-pu´di·a-to·ry
re-pugn´
re-pug´nance
re-pug´nan-cy
re-pug´nant
re-pug´nant-ly
re-pulse´
re-puls´ing

re-pul´sion
re-pul´sive
re-pul´sive-ly
re-pul´sive-ness
re-pur´chase
rep-u-ta-bil´i·ty
rep´u-ta·ble
rep´u-ta·ble-ness
rep´u-ta·bly
rep-u-ta´tion
re-pute´
re-put´ed
re-put´ed-ly
re-put´ing
re-quest´
re-quest´er
req´ui-em
re-quir´a·ble
re-quire´
re-quire´ment
re-quir´er
re-quir´ing
req´ui-site
req´ui-site-ly
req´ui-site-ness
req-ui-si´tion
req-ui-si´tion-ar·y
req-ui-si´tion-er
re-quit´a·ble
re-quit´al
re-quite´
re-quit´ed
re-quite´ment
re-quit´ing
re-read´

re´–re-cord´
re-re-lease´
re-run´
re-sal´a·ble
re´sale
re-scale´
re-sched´ule
re-scind´
re-scind´a·ble
re-scind´ment
re-scis´si-ble
re-scis´sion
re-scis´so·ry
re´script
res´cu-a·ble
res´cue
rea´cued
res´cu-er
res´cu-ing
re-search´
re-search´a·ble
re-search´er
re-search´ist
re-seat´
re-sect´
re-sect-a-bil´i·ty
re-sect´a·ble
re-sec´tion
re-sell´
re-sem´blance
re-sem´blant
re-sem´ble
re-sem´bler
re-sem´bling
re-sem´bling-ly
re-sent´
re-sent´ful

re-sent´ful-ly
re-sent´ful-ness
re-sent´ing-ly
re-sent´ment
re-serv´a·ble
res-er-va´tion
re-serve´
re-served
re-serv´ed-ly
re-serv´ed-ness
re-serv´ist
res´er-voir
re-set´
re-set´ting
re-set´tle-ment
re-ship´
re-ship´ment
re-side´
res´i-dence
res´i-den-cy
res´i-dent
res´i-den´tial
res-i-den´ti-ar·y
re-sid´ing
re-sid´u-al
re-sid´u-al-ly
re-sid´u-ar·y
res´i-due
re-sid´u-um
re-sign´
res-ig-na´tion
re-signed´
re-sign´ed-ly
re-sign´ed-ness
re-sil´ience
re-sil´ien-cy
re-sil´ient

re-sil´ient-ly
res´in
res´in-ous
re-sist´
re-sist´ance
re-sist´ant
re-sist´ant-ly
re-sist´er
re-sist-i·bil´i·ty
re-sist´i·ble
re-sist´i-ble-ness
re-sist´i·bly
re-sist´ing-ly
re-sis´tive
re-sis´tive-ly
re-sis´tive-ness
re-sis-tiv´i·ty
re-sis´tor
re-sold´
re-sole´
re-sol-u-bil´i·ty
re-sol´u·ble
re-sol´u·ble-ness
res´o-lute
res´o-lute-ly
res´o-lute-ness
res-o-lu´tion
re-solv´a·ble
re-solve´
re-solved´
re-solv´ed-ly
re-solv´ed-ness
re-solv´er
re-solv´ing
res´o-nance
res´o-nant
res´o-nant-ly

res´o-nate
res-o-na´tion
res´o-na-tor
re-sorb´
re-sorb´ent
re-sorp´tive
re-sort´
re-sound´
re-sound´ed
re-sound´ing
re-sound´ing-ly
re´source
re-source´ful
re-source´ful-ly
re-source´ful-
  ness
re-spect´
re-spect-
  a·bil´i·ty
re-spect´a·ble
re-spect´a·ble-
  ness
re-spect´a·bly
re-spect´er
re-spect´ful
re-spect´ful-ly
re-spect´ful-ness
re-spect´ing
re-spec´tive
re-spec´tive-ness
re-spell´
res´pi-ra·ble
res-pi-ra´tion
res-pi-ra´tion-al
res´pi-ra-tor
res´pi-ra-to·ry
re-spire´

re-spir´ing
res´pite
re-splen´dence
re-splen´den·cy
re-splen´dent
re-splen´dent-ly
re-spond´
re-spon´dence
re-spon´den-cy
re-spon´dent
re-spond´er
re-sponse´
re-spon-si-bil´
  i·ty
re-spon´si·ble
re-spon´si-ble-
  ness
re-spon´si·bly
re-spon´sive
re-spon´sive·ly
re-spon´sive-
  ness
re-spon-siv´i·ty
re-spon´sor
re-spon´so·ry
re´state´
res´tau-rant
res´tau-ra-teur´
rest´ful
rest´ful-ly
rest´ful-ness
rest´ing
res´ti-tute
res-ti-tu´tion
res´tive
res´tive-ly
res´tive-ness

rest´less
rest´less-ly
rest´less-ness
re´stock´
re-stor´a·ble
re-stor´a·ble-
  ness
re-stor´al
res-to-ra´tion
re-stor´a·tive
re-store´
re-stor´er
re-stor´ing
re-strain´
re-strain´a·ble
re-strained´
re-straint´
re-strict´
re-strict´ed
re-stric´tion
re-stric´tive
re-stric´tive-ly
re-stric´tive-ness
re-strike´
re-struc´ture
re-sult´
re-sult´ant
re-sum´a·ble
re-sume´ *(go on)*
ré´su-mé´ *(sum-
  mary)*
re-sum´ing
re-sump´tion
re-sur´face
re-surge´
re-sur´gence
re-sur´gent

res-ur-rect´
res-ur-rec´tion
res-ur-rec´tion-
   al
res-ur-rec´tion-
   ist
res-ur-rec´tor
re-sus´ci-ta·ble
re-sus´ci-tate
re-sus-ci-ta´tion
re-sus´ci-ta-tive
re-sus´ci-ta-tor
re´tail
re´tail-er
re-tain´
re-tain´a·ble
re-tain´er
re-tain´ing
re-take´
re-tal´i-ate
re-tal-i-a´tion
re-tal´i-a-tive
re-tal´i-a-tor
re-tal´i·a-to·ry
re-tard´
re-tard´ant
re-tar-da´tion
re-tard´ed
retch
re-tell´
re-ten´tion
re-ten´tive
re-ten´tive-ly
re-ten´tive-ness
re-ten-tiv´i-ty
re-ten´tor
re-think´

ret´i-cence
ret´i-cen-cy
ret´i-cent
ret´i-cent-ly
ret´i-na
ret´i-nal
ret-i-ni´tis
ret´i-nue
re-tire´
re-tired´
re-tir´ee´
re-tire´ment
re-tir´ing
re-tir´ing-ly
re-told´
re-tool´
re-tort´
re-touch´
re-trace´
re-trace´a·ble
re-trac´ing
re-tract´
re-tract-a·bil´i-ty
re-tract´a·ble
re-trac´tile
re-trac´tion
re-trac´tive
re-trac´tive-ly
re-trac´tive-ness
re-trac´tor
re´tread´
re-treat´
re-trench´
re-trench´ment
ret-ri-bu´tion
re-trib´u-tive
re-trib´u-tive-ly

re-trib´u-to-ry
re-triev-a-bil´i-ty
re-triev´a·ble
re-triev´al
re-trieve´
re-triev´er
re-triev´ing
ret-ro-ac´tive
ret-ro-ac´tive-ly
ret-ro-ac-tiv´i-ty
ret´ro-fit
ret´ro-grade
ret´ro-gress
ret-ro-gres´sion
ret-ro-gres´sive
ret-ro-gres´sive-
   ly
ret´ro-rock-et
ret´ro-spect
ret-ro-spec´tion
ret-ro-spec´tive
ret-ro-spec´tive-
   ly
re-turn´
re-turn´a·ble
re-turn´ee´
re-un´ion
re-u-nit´a·ble
re-u·nite´
re-u·nit´ing
re-used´
re-val´u-ate
re-val-u-a´tion
re-val´ue
re-vamp´
re-vamp´er
re-vamp´ment

167

re-veal´
re-veal´a·ble
re-veal´ing
re-veal´ing-ly
re-veal´ment
re-veg´e-tate
re-veg-e-ta´tion
rev´eil-le
·rev´el
rev-e-la´tion
rev-e-la´tion-al
re-vel´a-to-ry
rev´eled
rev´el-er
rev´el-ing
rev´el-ment
rev´el-ry
re-venge´
re-venge´ful
re-venge´ful-ly
re-venge´ful-
ness
re-veng´er
re-veng´ing
re-veng´ing-ly
rev´e-nue
re-ver´ber-ant
re-ver´ber-ant-ly
re-ver´ber-ate
re-ver-ber-a´tion
re-ver´ber-a-tive
re-ver´ber-a-tor
re-ver´ber-a-to-
ry
re-vere´
rev´er-ence
rev´er-end

rev´er-ent
rev´er-en´tial
rev´er-ent-ly
rev´er-ie
re-ver´ing
re-ver´sal
re-verse´
re-verse´ly
re-vers´er
re-vers-i·bil´i·ty
re-vers´i·ble
re-vers´i·ble-
ness
re-vers´i·bly
re-vers´ing
re-ver´sion
re-ver´sion-al
re-ver´sion-ar·y
re-vert´
re-vert´er
re-vert-i-bil´i-ty
re-vert´i·ble
re-vert´ment
re-view´
re-view´a·ble
re-view´er
re-vile´
re-vile´ment
re-vil´er
re-vil´ing
re-vil´ing-ly
re-vin´di-cate
re-vis´a-ble
re-vis´al
re-vise´
re-vised´
re-vis´er

re-vi´sion
re-vi´sion-al
re-vi´sion-ar-y
re-vi´sion-ism
re-vi´sion-ist
re-vis´it
re-vis-i-ta´tion
re-vis´er
re-vi´so-ry
re-vi-tal-i-za´tion
re-vi´tal-ize
re-viv-a·bil´i-ty
re-viv´a·ble
re-viv´a·bly
re-viv´al
re-viv´al-ism
re-viv´al-ist
re-viv-al-is´tic
re-vive´
re-viv´i-fy
re-viv´ing
rev-o-ca-bil´i-ty
rev´o-ca·ble
rev´o-ca·ble-ness
rev´o-ca·bly
rev-o-ca´tion
rev´o-ca-tive
rev´o-ca-to·ry
re-voice´
re-vok´a·ble
re-voke´
re-vok´er
re-vok´ing
re-volt´
re-volt´ing
re-volt´ing-ly
rev-o-lu´tion

rev´o-lu´tion-ar·y
rev-o-lu´tion-ist
rev-o-lu´tion-ize
re-volv´a·ble
re-volv´a·bly
re-volve´
re-volv´er
re-volv´ing
re-volv´ing–door´
re-vue´
re-vul´sion
re-vul´sion-ar-y
re-vul´sive
re-ward´
re-ward´a·ble
re-ward´ing
re-ward´ing-ly
re-wind´
re-wind´er
re-wir´a·ble
re-wire´
re-word´
re-write´ *(v.)*
re´write *(n.)*
re-zone´
rhap-sod´ic
rhap-sod´i-cal
rhap-sod´i-cal-ly
rhap´so-dize
rhap´so-diz-ing
rhap´so-dy
rhe´o-stat
rhet´o-ric
rhe-tor´i-cal
rhe-tor´i-cal-ly
rhe-tor´i-cal-
  ness

rhet-o-ri´cian
rheu-mat´ic
rheu´ma-tism
rhine´stone
rhi-ni´tis
rhi´no
rhi-noc´er-os
rhi-nol´o-gist
rhi-nol´o-gy
rhi´no-plas-ty
rhom´boid
rhom´bus
rhu´barb
rhyme
rhyme´ster
rhym´ing
rhythm
rhyth´mic
rhyth´mi-cal
rhyth´mi-cal-ly
rhyth´mics
rhyth´mist
rib´ald
rib´ald-ly
rib´al-dry
rib´and
ribbed
rib´bing
rib´bon
rib´boned
rib´bon-y
ri-bo-fla´vin
ri-bo-nu´cle-ase
ri´bo-nu-cle´ic
ri´bo-some
ric´er
rich´en

rich´es
rich´ly
rich´ness
rick
rick´et-i-ness
rick´ets
rick-ett´si-al
rick´et·y
rick´ey
ric´o-chet
ric´o-cheted
ri-cot´ta
rid´dance
rid´den
rid´der
rid´ding
rid´dle
rid´dled
ride´a·ble
rid´er
rid´er-less
rid´er-ship
ridge
ridge´pole
ridg´ing
ridg´y
rid´i-cule
ri-dic´u-lous
ri-dic´u-lous-ly
ri-dic´u-lous-
  ness
rid´ing
rife´ly
rife´ness
riff
rif´fle
rif´fling

riff´raff
ri´fle
ri´fle-man
ri´fle-ry
ri´fling
rig-a-to´ni
rigged
rig´ger
rig´ging
right´–an´gled
righ´teous
righ´teous-ly
righ´teous-ness
right´ful
right´ful-ly
right´ful-ness
right´–hand-ed
right´–hand-ed-
  ly
right´–hand-ed-
  ness
right´–hand-er
right´ist
right´ly
right´–mind-ed
right´ness
right´–of–way
right´–think´ing
right´–to–die´
right´–to–life´
right´–to–work´
right´ward
rig´id
ri-gid´i-ty
rig´id-ly
rig´id-ness
rig´ma-role

rig´or
rig´or-ism
rig´or-ist
rig-or-is´tic
rig´or-ous
rig´or-ous-ly
rig´or-ous-ness
rig´our *(Br.)*
rime
rim´fire
rim´less
rimmed
rim´ming
rim´y
rind
ring
ringed
ring´er
ring´ing
ring´ing-ly
ring´lead-er
ring´let
ring´mas-ter
ring´–necked
ring´side
ring´–tailed
ring´toss
rink´y–dink
rins´a·ble
rinse
rinsed
rins´er
rins´ing
ri´ot
ri´ot-er
ri´ot-ous
ri´ot-ous-ly

ri´ot-ous-ness
ripe´ly
rip´en
ripe´ness
rip´off
ripped
rip´per
rip´ping
rip´ple
rip´pled
rip´plet
rip´pling
rip´pling-ly
rip´ply
rip´–roar-ing
rip´saw
rip´snort´er
rise
ris´en
ris´er
ris´i·ble
ris´ing
risk
risk´i-ly
risk´i-ness
risk´less
risk´y
ri-sot´to
ris-qué´
rite
rit´u-al
rit´u-al-ism
rit´u-al-ist
rit´u-al-is´tic
rit´u-al-is´ti-cal-
  ly
rit´u-al-ize

170

rit-u-al-i-za´tion
rit´u-al-ly
ritz´i-ness
ritz´y
ri´val
ri´valed
ri´valing
ri´val-ly
ri´val-rous
ri´val-ry
rive
riv´en
riv´er
riv´er-bank
riv´er-bed
riv´er-boat
riv´er-side
riv´et
riv´et-er
riv´et-ing
riv´u-let
road´bed
road´block
road´house
road´ie
road´run-ner
road´side
road´ster
road´way
road´work
roam´er
roar´ing
roar´ing-ly
roast´a·ble
roast´ed
roast´er
rob

robbed
rob´ber
rob´ber·y
rob´bing
robe
rob´in
rob´ing
ro´bot
ro-bot´ics
ro´bot-ize
ro-bust´
ro-bus´tious
ro-bus´tious-ly
ro-bust´ly
ro-bust´ness
rock´-bot´tom
rock´er
rock´et
rock´e-teer´
rock´et-er
rock´et-ry
rock´ing
rock´ing-ly
rock y
ro-co´co
ro´dent
ro´de·o
roe
roent´gen
roent-gen-og´ra-
    phy
roent-gen-ol´o·gy
rogue
rogu´er·y
rogu´ish
rogu´ish-ly
rogu´ish-ness

roil
rois´ter
rois´ter-er
rois´ter-ous
rois´ter-ous-ly
role´–play-ing
roll´a-way
roll´back
rolled
roll´er
rol´lick
rol´lick-ing
rol´lick-ing-ly
rol´lick-some
roll´ing
roll´mops
roll´–on
ro´ly–po´ly
ro-maine´
ro-mance´
ro-manc´er
ro-manc´ing
ro-man´tic
ro-man´ti-cal-ly
ro-man´ti-cism
ro-man´ti-cist
ro-man-ti-ci-za´-
    tion
ro-man´ti-cize
romp´er
romp´ing-ly
romp´ish
ron´do
roof´er
roof´ing
roof´less
roof´line

171

roof´top
rook´er·y
rook´ie
room´er
room-ette´
room´ful
room´ie
room´i-ly
room´i-ness
room´mate
room´y
roost´er
root´age
root´ed
root´ed-ness
root´er
root´less
root´less-ness
root´let
root´stock
root´y
rope
roped
rope´dance
rope´danc-er
rope´danc-ing
rope´mak-er
rope´mak-ing
rop´er
rop´i-ness
rop´y
ro´sa-ry
rose´bud
rose´bush
rose´-col-ored
rose´mar·y
ro-se´o-la

ro-sette´
rose´wood
ros´in
ros´i-ness
ros´ter
ros´trum
ros´y
ro´ta-ry
ro´tat-a·ble
ro´tate
ro-ta´tion
ro-ta´tion-al
ro´ta-tive
ro´ta-tive-ly
ro´ta-tor
rote
ro-tis´ser-ie
ro´to-gra-vure´
ro´to-till-er
rot´ten-ly
rot´ten-ness
rot´ter
rot´ting
ro-tund´
ro-tun´da
ro-tun´di-ty
ro-tund´ly
ro-tund´ness
rou·é´
rouge
rouged
rough
rough´age
rough´-and-read´y
rough´-and-tum´ble

rough´en
rough´en-er
rough´er
rough´house
rough´ish
rough´ly
rough´neck
rough´ness
rough´shod
roug´ing
rou-lade´
rou-lette´
round´a·bout
round´ed
round´ed-ly
round´ed-ness
round´er
round´house
round´ish
round´ly
round´ness
round´-shoul-dered
round´up (n.)
rouse
roused
rous´er
rous´ing
roust´a·bout
rout
route
rout´ed
rout´er
rou-tine´
rou-tine´ly
rou-tine´ness
rou-tin´ize

172

rout´ing
roux
rove
rov´er
rov´ing
row´boat
row´dies
row´di-ly
row´di-ness
row´dy
row´dy-ish
row´dy-ism
row´er
roy´al
roy´al-ist
roy´al-ly
roy´al-ty
rubbed
rub´ber
rub´ber-ize
rub´ber-neck
rub´ber-y
rub´bing
rub´bish
rub´bish-y
rub´ble
rub´bly
rub´down
rube
ru-be´o-la
ru´bric
ru´bri-cal
ru´bri-cate
ru´bri-ca´tion
ru´bri-ca-tor
ru´by
ruck´sack

ruck´us
rud´der
rud´di-ness
rud´dy
rude
rude´ly
rude´ness
rud´est
ru´di-ment
ru-di-men-ta´ri-
　ly
ru-di-men´ta-ri-
　ness
ru-di-men´ta-ry
rue´ful
rue´ful-ly
rue´ful-ness
ru-fes´cence
ru-fes´cent
ruff
ruffed
ruf´fi-an
ruf´fi-an-ly
ruf´fi-an-ism
ruf´fle
ruf´fled
ruf´fler
ruf´fling
rug
rug´ged
rug´ged-ly
rug´ged-ness
ru´in
ru´in-a·ble
ru´in-ate
ru-in-a´tion
ru´ined

ru´in-ing
ru´in-ous
ru´in-ous-ly
ru´in-ous-ness
rul´a·ble
rule
ruled
rul´er
rul´er-ship
rul´ing
rum
ru-ma´ki
rum´ble
rum´bler
rum´bling
rum´bling-ly
rum´bly
ru´mi-nant
ru´mi-nate
ru-mi-na´tion
ru´mi-na-tive
ru´mi-na-tive-ly
ru´mi-na-tor
rum´mage
rum´mag-er
rum´mag-ing
rum´my
ru´mor
ru´mor-mon-ger
rump
rump´er
rum´ple
rum´pled
rum´pling
rum´ply
rum´pus
rum´run-ner

173

run´a·bout
run´a·round
run´a·way
run´dle
run´–down´
rung
run´–in
run´ner
run´ner–up´
run´ning
run´ny
run´off
run´–of–the–mill´
runt
run´–through
runt´ish
runt´y
run´way
rup´tur-a·ble
rup´ture
rup´tured
rup´tur-ing
ru´ral
ru´ral-ism
ru´ral-ist
ru´ral-ite
ru-ral-i-za´tion
ru´ral-ize
ru´ral-ly
ru´ral-ness
rush´ing
rus´set
rust
rus´tic
rus´ti-cal-ly
rus´ti-cate
rus-ti-ca´tion

rus´ti-ca-tor
rus-tic´i·ty
rust´i-ness
rus´tle
rus´tler
rust-tling
rust´proof
rust´y
ru´ta-ba´ga
ruth´ful
ruth´ful-ly
ruth´ful-ness
ruth´less
ruth´less-ly
ruth´less-ness
rut´ted
rut´tish
rut´tish-ly
rut´tish-ness
rut´ty
sab-bat´i-cal
sa´ber
sa´ber–rat-tling
sa´ber-tooth
sa´ber–toothed
sa´ble
sa·bot´
sab´o-tage
sab´o-teur´
sac´cha-rate
sac´cha-ride
s a c ´ c h a - r i n
 (sweetener)
s a c ´ c h a - r i n e
 (sweet)
sa-chet´
sack´cloth

sack´ful
sack´ing
sac´ra-ment
sac-ra-men´tal
sac-ra-men´tal-
 ism
sac-ra-men´tal-
 ist
sac-ra-men´tal-
 ly
sa´cred
sa´cred-ly
sa´cred-ness
sac´ri-fice
sac´ri-fice-a·ble
sac´ri-fi´cial
sac´ri-fic-ing
sac´ri-lege
sac´ri-le´gious
sac´ri-le´gious-ly
sac´ri-le´gious-
 ness
sac´ris-ty
sac´ro-il´i·ac
sac´ro-sanct
sac´ro-sanc´ti·ty
s a c ´ r o - s a n c t -
 ness
sad
sad´den
sad´den-ing
sad´der
sad´dle
sad´dle-bag
sad´dler
sad´dler·y
sad´dle-sore

sad´dle-tree	saint´ed	sal´sa
sa´dism	saint´hood	sal´si-fy
sa´dist	saint´li-ness	salt´box
sa-dis´tic	saint´ly	salt´cel-lar
sa-dis´ti-cal-ly	sa´ke (wine)	salt´ed
sad´ly	sa-laam´	salt´er
sad´ness	sal-a·bil´i-ty	salt´i-er
sa-fa´ri	sal´a·ble	salt´i-ly
safe–con´duct	sal´a·bly	sal-tim-boc´ca
safe´crack-er	sa-la´cious	sal-tine´
safe´–de-pos-it	sa-la´cious-ly	salt´i-ness
safe´guard	sa-la´cious-ness	salt´ish
safe´keep-ing	sa-lac´i-ty	salt´ish-ness
safe´ly	sal´ad	salt´less
saf´est	sal´a-man-der	salt´ness
safe´ty	sa-la´mi	salt´shak-er
saf´fron	sal´a-ried	salt´wa-ter
sa´ga	sal´a-ry	salt´y
sa-ga´cious	sales´clerk	sa-lu´bri-ous
sa-ga´cious-ly	sales´peo-ple	sa-lu´bri-ous-ly
sa-ga´cious-ness	sales´per son	sa-lu´bri-ous-
sa-gac´i-ty	sa´lience	ness
sage´ly	sa´li-ent	sa-lu´bri-ty
sage´ness	sal-i-na´tion	sal-u-tar´i·ly
sagged	sa´line	sal´u-tar-i-ness
sag´ger	sa-lin´i-ty	sal´u-tar·y
sag´ging	sa-li´va	sal-u-ta´tion
sag´gy	sal´i-var·y	sal-u-ta´tion-al
sail´boat	sal´i-vate	sa-lu´ta-to·ry
sail´cloth	sal-i-va´tion	sa-lute´
sailed	sal´lied	sa-lut´ing
sail´er	sal´low	sal´va·ble
sail´fish	sal´ly	sal´vage
sail´ing	sal´ly-ing	sal´vage-a·ble
sail´or	sal-mo-nel´la	sal´vag-er
sail´or-ing	sa-lon´	sal-va´tion
sail´plane	sa-loon´	sal-va´tion-al

175

salve	san´dal-wood	sap´id
salved	sand´bag	sa-pid´i-ty
sal´ver	sand´bank	sap´id-ness
sal´vo	sand´blast	sap´i-ence
same´ness	sand´box	sa´pi-ens
sam´o-var	sand´er	sap´i-ent
sam´pan	sand´i-er	sap´i-ent-ly
sam´ple	sand´i-ness	sap´ling
sam´pler	sand´lot	sa´por
sam´pling	sand´man	sap´o-rif´ic
sa´mu-rai	sand´pa-per	sap´per
san´a-tive	sand´stone	sap´phire
san-a-to´ri-um	sand´storm	sap´ping
san´a-to·ry	sand´wich	sap´py
sanc´ti-fi-a-ble	sand´y	sap-sa´go
sanc-ti-fi-ca´tion	sane	sap´suck-er
sanc´ti-fied	san-er	sar´casm
sanc´ti-fi-er	sane´ly	sar-cas´tic
sanc´ti-fy	sane´ness	sar-cas´ti-cal-ly
sanc´ti-fy-ing	san´for-ize	sar-co´ma
sanc-ti-mo´ni-ous	san-grí´a	sar-coph´a-gi
sanc-ti-mo´ni-ous-ly	san´guine	sar-coph´a-gus
sanc-ti-mo´ni-ous-ness	san´guine-ly	sar-dine´
sanc´ti-mo-ny	san´guine-ness	sar-don´ic
sanc´tion	san-guin´e-ous	sar-don´i-cal-ly
sanc´tion-a·ble	san-guin´e-ous-ness	sar-don´i-cism
sanc´tion-er	san-i-tar´i-an	sa´ri
sanc´ti-ty	san´i-tar-i-ly	sa-rong´
sanc´tu-ar·y	san´i-tar-i-ness	sar-sa-pa-ril´la
sanc´tum	san´i-tar´i·um	sar-to´ri-al
sanc´tus	san´i-tar·y	sar-to´ri-al-ly
sand	san-i-ta´tion	sash
san´dal	san-i-ti-za´tion	sa-shay´
san´daled	san´i-tize	sa-shi´mi
	san´i-tiz-er	sas´sa-fras
	san´i-ty	sas´sy
		sa-tan´ic

sa-tan´i-cal
sa-tan´i-cal-ly
satch´el
sat´ed
sa-teen´
sat´el-lite
sa-tia-bil´i·ty
sa´tia-ble
sa´tia-bly
sa´ti-ate
sa-ti-a´tion
sa-ti´e·ty
sat´in
sat´in·y
sat´ire
sa-tir´ic
sa-tir´i-cal
sa-tir´i-cal-ly
sat´i-rist
sat´i-riz-a·ble
sat-i-ri-za´tion
sat´i-rize
sat´i-riz-er
sat´i-riz ing
sat-is-fac´tion
sat-is-fac´to-ri-ly
sat-is-fac´to-ri-
   ness
sat´is-fac´to-ry
sat´is-fied
sat´is-fi-er
sat´is-fy
sat´is-fy-ing
sat´is-fy-ing-ly
sa-to´ri
sa´trap
sa´tra-py

sat´u-ra·ble
sat´u-rant
sat´u-rate
sat´u-rat-ed
sat´u-rat-er
sat´u-rat-ing
sat-u-ra´tion
sat´u-ra-tor
sat-ur-na´lia
sa´tyr
sauced
sauce´pan
sau´cer
sau´ci-ly
sau´ci-ness
sau´cy
sau´er-bra-ten
sau´er-kraut
sau´na
saun´ter
saun´ter-ing
sau´sage
sau-té´
sau-téed´
sau-té´ing
sau-terne´
sav´able
sav´age
sav´age-ly
sav´age-ness
sav´age-ry
sa-van´na
sa-vant´
saved
sav´er
sav´ing
sav´ior

sa´vor
sa´vor-ous
sa´vory
sa´vour *(Br.)*
sav´vi-ness
sav´vy
saw´buck
saw´dust
sawed´–off´
saw´horse
saw´mill
saw´tooth
saw´–toothed
saw´yer
sax´o-phone
sax´o-phon-ist
say´a-ble
say´ing
say´–so
scab´bard
scabbed
scab´bi-ly
scab´bi-ness
scab´bing
sca´bi-ous
scab´ble
scab´bler
scab´by
sca´bies
scab´rous-ly
scaf´fold
scaf´fold-ing
scag
scal´a-ble
scal´a-wag
scald´ed
scald´er

177

scale	scarce´ness	scheme
scaled	scar´city	schem´er
scale´down	scare´crow	schem´ing
scal´er	scared	schem´ing-ly
scal´ing	scarf	schism
scal´lion	scar´i-ly	schiz´oid
scal´lop	scar´ing	schiz-o-phre´ni-
scal´loped	scar´let	a
sca-lop-pi´ni	scarred	schiz-o-phren´ic
scalp	scar´ring	schlep
scal´pel	scary	schlock
scalp´er	scathe	schmaltz
scal´y	scath´ing	schmaltz´y
scam	scat´ter	schmear
scamp	scat´ter-brain	schmooze
scam´per	scat´tered	schmuck
scam´pi	scat´ter-er	schnook
scamp´ish	scat´ter-ing	schol´ar
scan´dal	scat´ter-shot	schol´ar-li-ness
scan´dal-ize	scav´enge	schol´ar-ly
scan´dal-monger	scav´eng-er	schol´ar-ship
scan´dal-ous	scav´eng-ing	scho-las´tic
scan´dal-ous-ly	sce-nar´io	scho-las´ti-cal-ly
scan´dal-ous-	scene	school´book
ness	sce´ner·y	school´boy
scanned	sce´nic	school´child
scan´ner	sce´ni-cal	school´girl
scan´ning	scent´ed	school´house
scant´i-ly	scep´ter	school´ing
scant´i-ness	scep´tic	school´marm
scant´ling	scep´ti-cal	school´mas-ter
scant´ly	scep´ti-cism	school´mate
scant´ness	sched´ule	school´room
scant´y	sched´uled	school´teach-er
scape´goat	sched´ul-ing	school´work
scarce	sche-mat´ic	school´yard
scarce´ly	sche-mat´i-cal-ly	schoo´ner

schuss
sci-at´ic
sci-at´i-ca
sci´ence
sci-en-tif´ic
sci-en-tif´i-cal-ly
sci´en-tism
sci´en-tist
scim´i-tar
scin-til´la
scin´til-late
scin´til-lat-ing
scin-til-la´tion
scin´til-la-tor
sci´on
scis´sors
scle-ro´sis
scoff´er
scoff´ing-ly
scoff´law
scold´er
scold´ing
scold´ing-ly
sco-li-o´sis
sconce
scone
scoop´er
scoop´ful
scoot´er
scope
scorch´er
scorch´ing
score´board
score´card
scored
score´keep-er
scor´ing

scorn´er
scorn´ful
scorn´ful-ly
scorn´ful-ness
scor´pi-on
scot´–free´
scoun´drel
scour
scourge
scourg´er
scourg´ing
scour´ings
scout
scout´ing
scowl´er
scowl´ing-ly
scrab´ble
scrab´bler
scrab´bling
scrab´bly
scrag´gi-ly
scrag´gi-ness
scrag´gly
scrag´gy
scram´ble
scram´bler
scram´bling
scrap´book
scrape
scraped
scrap´er
scrap´ing
scrapped
scrap´per
scrap´pi-ly
scrap´pi-ness
scrap´ping

scrap´ple
scrap´py
scratch´board
scratch´er
scratch´i-ly
scratch´i-ness
scratch´proof
scratch´y
scrawl´er
scrawl´y
scrawn´i-ness
scrawn´y
screak
screak´y
scream
scream´er
scream´ing
screech
screech´y
screed
screen´a-ble
screen´er
screen´ing
screen´play
screen´writ-er
screw´ball
screw´driv-er
screw´up
screw´y
scrib´ble
scrib´bler
scrib´bling
scribe
scrib´er
scrim´mage
scrim´mag-er
scrimp

179

scrimp´i-ly
scrimp´i-ness
scrimp´y
scrim´shaw
scrip
script
script´er
scrip´tur-al
scrip´tur-al-ly
scrip´ture
script´writ-er
script´writ-ing
scriv´en-er
scrof´u-lous
scrof´u-lous-ly
scrof´u-lous-
    ness
scroll
scroll´work
scro´tum
scrounge
scroung´er
scroung´ing
scrub´ba·ble
scrub´ber
scrub´bi-ness
scrub´bing
scrub´by
scruff´y
scrump´tious
scrump´tious-ly
scrump´tious-
    ness
scrunch
scru´ple
scru-pu-los´i·ty
scru´pu-lous

scru´pu-lous-ly
scru´pu-lous-
    ness
scru-ta-bil´i·ty
scru´ta·ble
scru-ti-ni-
    za´tion
scru´ti-nize
scru´ti-niz-er
scru´ti-niz-ing-ly
scru´ti-ny
scu´ba–dive
scud´ded
scuff
scuf´fle
scuf´fling
scuf´fling-ly
scull
scul´ler·y
sculpt
sculp´tor
sculp´tur-al
sculp´tur-al-ly
sculp´ture
sculp´tured
scum
scum´ble
scum´bled
scum´my
scurf
scurf´y
scur-ril´i-ty
scur´ril-ous
scur´ril-ous-ly
scur´ril-ous-
    ness
scur´ried

scur´ry
scur´ry-ing
scur´vy
scut
scutch´eon
scut´tle
scut´tle-butt
scut´tling
scuzz´y
scythe
scyth´ing
sea´bed
sea´bird
sea´borne
sea´coast
sea´far-er
sea´far-ing
sea´floor
sea´food
sea´go-ing
seal´able
seal´ant
sealed´–beam´
seal´er
sea´lift
scal´ing
seal´skin
sea´man
sea´man-like
sea´man-ship
sea´men
seam´i-ness
seam´less
seam´less-ly
seam´less-ness
seam´ster
seam´stress

180

seam´y
sé´ance
sea´plane
sea´port
search´a-ble
search´er
search´ing
search´ing-ly
search´light
sea´scape
sea´shell
sea´shore
sea´sick
sea´sick-ness
sea´side
sea´son
sea´son-a-ble
sea´son-a-bly
sea´son-al
sea´son-al-ly
sea´son-ing
seat´ed
seat´er
seat´ing
seat´mate
seat´–of–the–pan
  ts´
sea´wall
sea´ward
sea´way
sea´weed
sea´wor-thi-ness
sea´wor-thy
se-ba´ceous
se´bum
se´cant
se-cede´

se-ced´ed
se-ced´er
se-ced´ing
se-ces´sion
se-ces´sion-al
se-ces´sion-ism
se-ces´sion-ist
se-clude´
se-clud´ed
se-clud´ed-ness
se-clud´ing
se-clu´sion
se-clu´sive
se-clu´sive-ly
se-clu´sive-ness
sec´ond
sec´ond-ar-i-ly
sec´ond-ar-i-
  ness
sec´ond-ar-y
sec´ond–er
sec´ond–guess´
sec´ond-hand´
sec´ond-ly
sec´ond–rate´
se´cre-cy
se´cret
sec´re-tar´i-al
sec-re-tar´i-at
sec´re-tary
se-crete´
se-cret´ed
se-cre´tion
se-cre´tion-ar-y
se´cre-tive
se´cre-tive-ly
se´cre-tive-ness

se´cret-ly
se´cret-ness
sect
sec-tar´i-an
sec-tar´i-an-ism
sec´tion-al
sec´tion-al-ism
sec´tion-al-ist
sec´tion-al-ly
sec-tion-al-i-za´
  tion
sec´tion-al-ize
sec´tor
sec-to´ri-al
sec´u-lar
sec´u-lar-ism
sec´u-lar-ist
sec-u-lar´i-ty
sec-u-lar-i·za´
  tion
sec´u-lar-ize
sec´u-lar-ly
se-cur´a·ble
se-cure´
se-cure´ly
se-cure´ness
se-cur´ity
se-dan´
se-date´
se-date´ly
se-date´ness
se-da´tion
sed´a-tive
sed´en-tar´i-ly
sed´en-tar´i-ness
sed´en-tar·y
sed´i-ment

sed-i-men´tal
sed´i-men-tar´i-
ly
sed´i-men-ta-ry
sed-i-men-ta´
tion
sed-i-men-tol´o-
gy
sed-i-men-to-
log´ic
sed-i-men-to-
log´i-cal
sed-i-men-tol´o-
gist
se-di´tion
se-di´tious
se-di´tious-ly
se-di´tious-ness
se-duce´
se-duc´er
se-duc´i-ble
se-duc´ing
se-duc´tion
se-duc´tive
se-duc´tive-ly
se-duc´tive-ness
se-duc´tress
se-du´li-ty
sed´u-lous
sed´u-lous-ly
sed´u-lous-ness
seed´bed
seed´cake
seed´case
seed´er
seed´i-ness
seed´ing

seed´less
seed´ling
seed´pod
seed´y
see´ing
seek´er
seem´ing
seem´ing-ly
seem´li-ness
seem´ly
seep´age
seer´suck-er
see´saw
seethe
seethed
seeth´ing
seeth´ing-ly
see´–through
seg´ment
seg-men´tal
seg-men´tal-ly
seg´men-tar-y
seg-men-ta´tion
seg´re-ga·ble
seg´re-gate
seg´re-gat-ed
seg-re-ga´tion
seg-re-ga´tion-
ist
se´gue
sei-gneur´
seine
seis´mic
seis´mi-cal-ly
seis-mic´i-ty
seis´mism
seis´mo-gram

seis´mo-graph
seis-mog´ra-pher
seis-mo-graph´ic
seis-mog´ra-phy
seis-mo-log´ic
seis-mo-log´i-cal
seis-mol´o-gist
seis-mol´o-gy
seis-mom´e-ter
seis-mom´et-ry
seiz´a·ble
seize
seiz´er
seiz´ing
sei´zure
sel´dom
se-lect´
se-lec´tion
se-lec´tive
se-lec´tive-ly
se-lec´tive-ness
se-lec-tiv´i-ty
se-lect´man
se-lec´tor
self´-a-base´
ment
self–ab-sorbed´
self´–ab-sorp´
tion
self–act´ing
self–ap-point´ed
self–as-sur´ance
self–as-sured´
self–cen´tered
self´–cen´tered-
ness

182

self´–com-posed´
self´–con-fessed´
self–con´fi-dence
self–con´fi-dent
self–con´fi-dent-ly
self–con-grat´u·la-to·ry
self–con´scious
self–con´scious-ly
self–con´scious-ness
self–con-tained´
self–con-tra-dic´ting
self–con-tra-dic´tion
self–con-tra-dic´tor-y
self–con-trol´
self–con-trol´led
self–de-ceit´
self–de-cep´tion
self–de-fense´
self–de-lud´ed
self–de-lu´sion
self–de-ni´al
self–de-ny´ing
self´–de-struct´
self´–de-struc´tion
self´–de-struc´tive
self–de-ter-mi-na´tion
self–de-vo´tion

self–dis´ci-pline
self–dis´ci-plined
self´–doubt´
self´–doubt´ing
self´–ef-face´ment
self´–ef-fac´ing
self´–em-ployed´
self–es-teem´
self–ev´i-dent
self–ev´i-dent·ly
self´–ex-plan´a-to·ry
self´–ex-pres´sion
self–ful-fill´ing
self–ful-fill´ment
self–gov´erned
self–gov´ern-ing
self–gov´ern-ment
self´–grat-i·fi-ca´tion
self–help´
self´–hyp-no´sis
self´–im´age
self–im-por´-tance
self–im-por´tant
self–im-por´tant·ly
self–im-posed´
self´–im-prove´ment
self´–in-crim-in-a´tion
self´–in-duced´

self´–in-dul´gence
self´–in-dul´gent
self–in´ter-est
self´ish
self´ish-ly
self´ish-ness
self–know´ledge
self´less
self´less-ly
self´less-ness
self´–lim´it-ing
self–liq´ui-dat-ing
self´–load´er
self´–load´ing
self´–love´
self´–made´
self´–mail´er
self´–per-pet´u·at-ing
self–pit´y
self–por´trait
self–pos-sessed´
self–pres-er-va´tion
self´–pro-pelled´
self´–pro-pul´sion
self–pro-tec´tion
self–re-gard´
self–reg´ulating
self–re-li´ance
self–re-li´ant
self–re-spect´
self–re-spect´ing
self´–re-straint´

self–right´eous
self–right´eous·ly
self–right´eous-
  ness
self–sac´ri-fice
self–sac´ri-fic-
  ing
self´same
self–sat´is-fied
self´–serv´ing
self´–start-er
self´–start-ing
self–suf-fi´cien-
  cy
self–suf-fi´cient
self–sup-port´ing
self´–taught´
self´–will´
self´–wind´ing
self´–worth´
sell´a·ble
sell´er
sell´ing
sell´–off
sell´out
selt´zer
sel´vage
selves
se-man´tic
se-man´ti-cal´ly
se-man´tics
sem´a-phore
sem-a-phor´ic
sem´blance
se-mes´ter
sem-i-ab´stract
sem-i-an´nu-al

sem-i-an´nu-al-
  ly
sem-i-ar´id
sem-i-au-to-
  mat´ic
sem-i-au-ton´o-
  mous
sem´i-cir-cle
sem-i-cir´cu-lar
sem-i-clas´si-cal
sem´i-co-lon
sem´i-con-duc-
  tor
sem-i-con´scious
sem-i-con´-
  scious-ness
sem-i-dark´ness
sem´i-de-tached´
sem´i-fi-nal
sem-i-fi´nal-ist
sem-i-for´mal
sem´i-gloss
sem-i-lit´er-a-cy
sem-i-lit´er-ate
sem´i-month´ly
sem´i-nal
sem´i-nal-ly
sem´i-nar
sem-i-nar´i-an
sem´i-nary
sem-i-of-fi´cial
sem-i-per´me-
  a·ble
sem´i-pre´cious
sem-i-pri´vate
sem-i-pro-fes´-
  sion-al

sem-i-pro-fes´-
  sion-al-ly
sem-i-pub´lic
sem-i-skilled´
sem-i-soft´
sem-i-sol´id
sem-i-sweet´
sem-i-week´ly
sem-i-year´ly
sem-o-li´na
sen´ate
sen´a-tor
sen-a-to´ri-al
send´a-ble
send´er
send´ing
send´–off
se´nile
se-nil´i-ty
sen´ior
se-nior´i-ty
sen´na
se-ñor´
se-ño´ra
se-ño-ri´ta
sen´sate
sen-sa´tion
sen-sa´tion-al
sen-sa´tion-al-
  ism
sen-sa´tion-al-
  ist
sen-sa-tion-al-
  is´tic
sen-sa´tion-al-
  ize
sen-sa´tion-al-ly

sensed
sense´less
sense´less-ly
sense´less-ness
sen-si-bil´i-ty
sen´si-ble
sen´si-ble-ness
sen´si-bly
sens´ing
sen´si-tive
sen´si-tive-ly
sen´si-tive-ness
sen-si-tiv´i·ty
sen-si-ti·za´tion
sen´si-tize
sen´si-tiz-er
sen´sor
sen-so´ri-al
sen´so-ry
sen´su-al
sen´su-al-ism
sen´su-al-ist
sen-su-al-is´tic
o c n - s u - a l - i -
 za´tion
sen´su-al-ize
sen-su-al´i-ty
sen´su-al-ly
sen´su-ous
sen´su-ous-ly
sen´su-ous-ness
sen´tence
sen-ten´tial
sen-ten´tial-ly
sen´tience
sen´tient
sen´tient-ly

sen´ti-ment
sen-ti-men´tal
sen-ti-men´tal-
 ism
sen-ti-men´tal-
 ist
sen-ti-men-tal´i-
 ty
sen-ti-men-tal-i-
 za´tion
sen-ti-men´tal-
 ize
sen-ti-men´tal-ly
sen´ti-nel
sen´try
sep-a-ra-bil´i-ty
sep´a-ra·ble
sep´a-ra·bly
sep´a-rate
sep´a-rate-ly
sep´a-rate-ness
sep-a-ra´tion
sep´a-rat-ism
sep a-rat-ist
sep´a-ra-tive
sep´a-ra-tor
se´pia
sep´sis
sep-ten´ni-al
sep-ten´ni-al-ly
sep-tet´
sep´tic
sep-ti-ce´mia
sep-tic´i-ty
sep-til´lion
sep´tu´age-nar´i-
 an

sep´tu-ple
sep´ul-cher
se-pul´chral
se-pul´chral-ly
se-qua´cious
se-qua´cious-ly
se-quac´i-ty
se´quel
se´quence
se´quenc-er
se´quenc-ing
se´quent
se-quen´tial
se-quen-ti-al´i-ty
se-quen´tial-ly
se-ques´ter
se-ques´tered
se´quin
se´quined
se-quoi´a
se-ra´glio
se-ra´pe
ser´a-phim
ser´e-nade´
ser´e-nad´er
ser´e-nad´ing
ser-en-dip´i-tous
s e r - e n - d i p´ i -
 tous-ly
ser-en-dip´i-ty
se-rene´
se-rene´ly
se-rene´ness
se-ren´i-ty
serf´dom
serge
ser´geant

se´ri-al
se´ri-al-ism
se´ri-al-ist
se´ri-al-ize
se´ri-al-ly
se´ri-ate
se´ri-ate-ly
se´ries
ser´if
se-ri-o-com´ic
se´ri-ous
se´ri-ous-ly
s e ´ r i -
 ous–mind´ed
se´ri-ous–mind´
 ed-ly
se´ri-ous–mind´
 ed-ness
se´ri-ous-ness
ser´mon
ser-mon´ic
ser-mon´i-cal
ser´mon-ize
ser´mon-less
se´rous-ness
ser´pent
ser´pen-tine
ser´rate
ser´rat-ed
ser-ra´tion
ser´ried
ser´ried-ly
se´rum
serv´a-ble
ser´vant
served
serv ´er

serv´ice
serv-ice-a-bil´i-
 ty
serv´ice-a·ble
serv´ice-a·ble-
 ness
serv´ice-a·bly
ser-vi-ette´
ser´vile
ser´vile-ly
ser´vile-ness
ser-vil´i-ty
serv´ing
ser´vi-tor
ser´vi-tude
ses´a-me
ses´qui-cen-ten´
 ni-al
ses´sion
ses´tet
set´back
set´off
set´screw
set-tee´
set´ter
set´ting
set´tle
set´tle-a-ble
set´tle-ment
set´tler
set´tling
set´–to
set´up
sev´en
sev´en-fold
sev´en-teen´
sev´en-teenth´

sev´enth
sev´en-ti-eth
sev´en-ty
sev´en-ty–six´
sev´er
sev-er-a-bil´i-ty
sev´er-a·ble
sev´er-al
sev´er-al-ly
sev´er-al-ty
sev´er-ance
se-vere´
sev´ered
se-vere´ly
se-vere´ness
se-ver´i-ty
sew´a-ble
sew´age
sew´er
sew´er-age
sew´ing
sex-a-ge-nar´i-
 an
sex-ag´e-nary
sex´i-ly
sex´i-ness
sex´ism
sex´ist
sex´less
sex-ol´o-gist
sex-ol´o-gy
sex´tant
sex-tet´
sex-til´lion
sex´ton
sex-tup´let
sex´u-al

186

sex-u-al´i-ty
sex´u-al-ly
sex´y
shab´bi-ly
shab´bi-ness
shab´by
shack´le
shack´led
shack´ling
shade
shad´ed
shad´i-er
shad´i-ly
shad´i-ness
shad´ing
shad´ow
shad´ow-box
shad´ow-i-ness
shad´ow-ing
shad´ow·y
shad´y
shaft
shag´gi-ly
shag´gi-ness
shag´gy
shak´a·ble
shake´down
shak´en
shak´er
shake´–up
shak´i-ly
shak´ing
shak´y
shal-lot´
shal´low-ly
shal´low-ness
sha´man

sham´ble
shame
shamed
shame´faced
shame´ful
shame´ful-ly
shame´ful-ness
shame´less
shame´less-ly
shame´less-ness
sham´ing
shammed
sham´mer
sham´ming
sham-poo´
sham-pooed´
sham´rock
shan´dy
shan´dy-gaff
shank
shan´ty
shan´ty-town
shap´a-ble
shape
shaped
shape´less
shape´less-ly
shape´less-ness
shape´li-ness
shape´ly
shap´er
shape´–up
shap´ing
shar´able
shard
share
share´crop-per

share´hold-er
shar´er
share´ware
shar´ing
shark´skin
sharp´–eared´
sharp´–edged´
sharp´en
sharp´en-er
sharp´en-ing
sharp´er
sharp´–eyed´
sharp´ly
sharp´ness
sharp´shoot-er
sharp´shoot-ing
sharp´–sight-ed
sharp´–tongued
sharp´–wit´ted
shat´ter
shat´tered
shat´ter-er
shat´ter-proof
shaved
shave´ling
shave´tail
shav´en
shav´er
shav´ing
shawl
sheaf
shear
shear´er
shear´ing
sheath
sheathe
sheathed

sheath´ing
sheave
shed´der
she´–dev-il
shed´ding
sheen
sheep´cote
sheep dog
sheep´fold
sheep´herd-er
sheep´ish
sheep´ish-ly
sheep´ish-ness
sheep´shank
sheep´shear-ing
sheep´skin
sheep´walk
sheer
sheer´ness
sheet´ing
sheik´dom
shelf
shel-lac´
shel-lacked´
she´lack´ing
shelled
shell´er
shell´fish
shell´–shocked
shel´ter
shel´tered
shel´ter-ing
shel´ter-less
shelves
shelv´ing
she-nan´i-gan
shep´herd

shep´herd-ess
sher´bet
sher´iff
sher´ry
shi-at´su
shib´bo-leth
shield
shift´er
shift´i-er
shift´i-ly
shift´i-ness
shift´ing
shift´less
shift´less-ly
shift´less-ness
shift´y
shil´ling
shil´ly–shal-ly
shim´mer
shim´mer-ing-ly
shim´mery
shim´ming
shim´my
shin´bone
shin´dig
shine
shin´er
shin´gle
shin´gled
shin´i-er
shin´i-ly
shin´ing
shin´i-ness
shin´ing
shin´ny
shin´plas-ter
shin´y

ship´board
ship´build-er
ship´build-ing
ship´fit-ter
ship´load
ship´mate
ship´ment
ship´own-er
shipped
ship´per
ship´ping
ship´shape
ship´wreck
ship´wright
ship´yard
shire
shirk´er
shirr
shirred
shirr´ing
shirt´ing
shirt´mak-er
shirt´mak-ing
shirt´sleeve
shirt´tail
shirt´waist
shiv´ery
shoal
shoat
shock
shock´a-ble
shock´er
shock´ing
shock´ing-ly
shock´proof
shock´–re-sist´-
   ant

188

shod´di-ly
shod´di-ness
shod´dy
shoe´horn
shoe´ing
shoe´lace
shoe´mak-er
shoe pol´ish
shoe´shine
shoe´string
sho´gun
shoo´–in
shoot´er
shoot´ing
shoot´out
shop´keep-er
shop´keep-ing
shop´lift
shop´lift-er
shopped
shop´per
shop´ping
shop´talk
shop´worn
shore´line
shor´ing
short´age
short´bread
short´cake
short´change
short´com-ing
short´cut
short´en
short´en-er
short´en-ing
short´fall
short´haired

short´hand´ed
short´–haul
short´–lived´
short´ly
short´ness
short´–range´
short´sight-ed
short´sight-ed-ly
short´sight-ed-
  ness
short´stop
s h o r t´ – t e m´
  pered
short´wave´
short´–wind´ed
short´y
shot´gun
should
shoul´der
shoul´dered
shout´ed
shout´er
shove
shoved
shov´el
shov´eled
shov´el-er
shov´el-ful
shov´el-ing
shov´er
shov´ing
show´boat
show´case
show´down
showed
show´er
show´i-ness

show´ing
show´man
show´man-ship
shown
show´–off
show´room
show´–stop-per
show´y
shrap´nel
shred´der
shred´ding
shrew
shrewd´ly
shrewd´ness
shrew´ish
shrieked
shriek´ing
shrill
shril´ly
shrill´ness
shril´ly
shrimp´er
shrine
shrined
shrin´er
shrink´a·ble
shrink´age
shrink´–wrap
shrive
shriv´el
shriv´eled
shriv´el-ing
shroud´ed
shrub´ber-y
shrub´by
shrug
shrugged

shrug´ging
shrunk´en
shtick
shuck´ing
shud´der
shuf´fle
shuf´fle-board
shuf´fled
shut´fling
shunned
shun´ning
shun´pike
shunt´ing
shut´down *(n.)*
shut´eye
shut´–in
shut´off
shut´out
shut´ter
shut´ting
shut´tle
shut´tle-cock
shy´ly
shy´ness
shy´ster
sib´ling
sick´bed
sick´en
sick´en-ing
sick´en-ing-ly
sick´ie
sick´le
sick´led
sick´li-er
sick´li-ness
sick´ly
sick´ness

sick´room
side´bar
side´board
side´burns
side´car
sid´ed
side´kick
side´line
si-de´re-al
side´sad-dle
side´show
side´split-ter
side´split-ting
side´swipe
side´track
side´walk
side´wall
side´ways
side´wind-er
si´dle
si´dled
si´dling
siege
si-es´ta
sieve
sift´er
sift´ings
sigh´ing
sight´ed
sight´er
sight´less
sight´less-ly
sight´less-ness
sight´ly
sight´–read
sight´–read-er
sight´see

sight´see-ing
sight´seer
sig´ma
sig´moid
sign
sig´nal
sig´naled
sig´nal-ing
sig-nal-i-za´tion
sig´nal-ize
sig´nal-ly
sig´nal-man
sig´na-to-ry
sig´na-ture
sign´board
sig´net
sig-nif´i-cance
sig-nif´i-cant
sig-nif´i-cant-ly
sig-ni-fi-ca´tion
sig-nif´i-ca-tive
sig-nif´i-ca-tive-
    ness
sig´ni-fi-a·ble
sig´ni-fied
sig´ni-fier
sig´ni-fy
sig´ni-fy-ing
sign´post
si´lence
si´lenc-er
si´lenc-ing
si´lent
si´lent-ly
sil-hou-ette´
sil-hou-et´ted
sil´i-con

190

silk´en
silk´i-er
silk´i-ly
silk´i-ness
silk´screen
silk´worm
silk´y
sil´li-ly
sil´li-ness
sil´ly
si´lo
si´los
silt´y
sil´van
sil´ver
sil´ver–plat´ed
sil´ver-smith
sil´ver–tongued´
sil´ver-ware
sil´very
sim´i-lar
sim-i-lar´i-ty
sim´i-lar-ly
sim´i-le
si-mil´i-tude
sim´mer
sim-pat´i-co
sim´per
sim´pered
sim´per-er
sim´per-ing
sim´per-ing-ly
sim´ple
sim´ple–mind´ed
sim´ple–mind´
  ed-ness
sim´ple-ness

sim´pler
sim´plest
sim´ple-ton
sim´plex
sim-plic´i-ty
sim-pli-fi-ca´tion
sim´pli-fied
sim´pli-fi-er
sim´pli-fy
sim´pli-fy-ing
sim-plis´tic
sim-plis´ti-cal-ly
sim´ply
sim´u-late
sim´u-lat-ing
sim-u-la´tion
sim´u-la-tive
sim´u-la-tor
si´mul-cast
si-mul-ta-ne´i-ty
si-mul-ta´ne-ous
si-mul-ta´ne-
  ous-ly
si-mul-ta´ne-
  ous-ness
since
sin-cere´
sin-cere´ly
sin-cere´ness
sin-cer´est
sin-cer´i-ty
sin´e-cure
sin´e-cur-ist
sin´ew
sin´ew-y
sin´ful
sin´ful-ly

sin´ful-ness
sing´a·ble
singe
singed
singe´ing
sing´er
sing´ing
sin´gle
sin´gle–act´ing
sin´gle–ac´tion
sin´gle–breast´ed
sin´gle–dig´it
sin´gle–hand´ed
sin´gle–hand´ed-
  ly
sin´gle–knit
sin´gle–mind´ed
sin´gle–mind´ed-
  ness
sin´gle-ness
sin´gle–phase
sin´gle–space´
sin´gling
sin´gly
sing´song
sin´gu-lar
sin-gu-lar´i-ty
sin´gu-lar-ize
sin´gu-lar-ly
sin´is-ter
sin´is-ter-ly
sin´is-ter-ness
sin´is-tral
sin´is-tral-ly
sink´a·ble
sink´age
sink´er

sink´hole
sink´ing
sin´less
sinned
sin´ner
sin´ning
sin´u-ate
sin´u-ate-ly
sin-u-a´tion
sin-u-os´i-ty
sin´u-ous
sin´u-ous-ly
sin´u-ous-ness
si´nus
si-nus-i´tis
si´phon
sipped
sip´per
sip´ping
sired
si´ren
sir´ing
sir´loin
sis´si-ness
sis´sy
sis´sy-ish
sis´ter
sis´ter-hood
sis´ter–in–law
sis´ter-li-ness
sis´ter-ly
si-tar´
si-tar´ist
sit´com
sit´–in
sit´ter
sit´ting

sit´u-ate
sit´u-at-ed
sit-u-a´tion
sit-u-a´tion-al
sit-u-a´tion-al-ly
sit´–up
six´fold
six´–foot´
six´–pack
six´pence
six´–shoot-er
six´teen´
six´teenth´
sixth
six´ti-eth
six´ty
six´ty–nine´
siz´a-ble
siz´a-ble-ness
siz´a-bly
sized
siz´ing
siz´zle
siz´zled
siz´zling
siz´zling-ly
skate´board
skat´ed
skat´er
skat´ing
ske-dad´dle
skeet
skein
skel´e-tal
skel´e-tal-ly
skel´e-ton
skel´e-ton-ize

skep´tic
skep´ti-cal
skep´ti-cal-ly
skep´ti-cism
sketch
sketch´book
sketched
sketch´i-est
sketch´i-ly
sketch´i-ness
sketch´y
skew´er
skew´ness
skid´ded
skid´der
skid´ding
skid´dy
skid´proof
skied
skies
skiff
ski´ing
skilled
skil´let
skill´ful
skill´ful-ly
skill´ful-ness
skim
skimmed
skim´mer
skim´ming
skimp´i-est
skimp´i-ly
skimp´i-ness
skimp´ing
skimp´ing-ly
skimp´y

skin–deep´	sky´dive	slap´dash
skin´–dive	sky´div-er	slap´hap-py
skin´flint	sky´div-ing	slap´jack
skin´ful	sky´–high	slapped
skin´head	sky´hook	slap´ping
skin´less	sky´jack	slap´stick
skinned	sky´lark	slash´er
skin´ner	sky´light	slash´ing
skin´ni-est	sky´line	slat´–back
skin´ni-ness	sky´rock-et	slate
skin´ning	sky´scrap-er	slat´ed
skin´ny	sky´writ-ing	slat´ing
skin´ny–dip	slack´en	slat´ted
skin´tight´	slack´ened	slat´tern
skip´pa-ble	slack´er	slat´tern-li-ness
skip´per	slack´ness	slat´tern-ly
skip´ping	slacks	slat´ting
skip´ping-ly	slag´gy	slat´y
skir´mish	slain	slaugh´ter
skir´mish-er	slake	slaugh´ter-er
skirt´ing	slaked	slaugh´ter-house
skit´ter	slak´ing	
skit´ter-y	sla´lom	slaugh´ter-ous
skit´tish	slam´–bang´	slave
skit´tish-ly	slammed	slav´ery
skit´tish-ness	slam´mer	slav´ish
skit´tles	slam´ming	slav´ish-ly
skive	slan´der	slav´ish-ness
skiv´er	slan´der-er	slay´er
skoal	slan´der-ing-ly	slay´ing
skul´dug´ger-y	slan´der-ous	sleaze
skulk´er	slan´der-ous-ly	slea´zi-er
skulk´ing	slang´i-ness	slea´zi-ly
skull´cap	slang´y	slea´zi-ness
sky´–blue´	slant´ing	slea´zy
sky´box	slant´ing-ly	sled´der
sky´cap	slant´wise	sled´ding

sledge
sledge´ham-mer
sleek´ly
sleek´ness
sleep
sleep´er
sleep´i-ly
sleep´i-ness
sleep´ing
sleep´less
sleep´less-ly
sleep´less-ness
sleep´walk-er
sleep´walk-ing
sleep´wear
sleep´y
sleep´y-head
sleet
sleet´y
sleeve´less
sleigh´ing
sleight
slen´der
slen´der-ize
slen´der-ness
slept
sleuth
slew
slice´a·ble
sliced
slic´er
slic´ing
slick
slick´er
slick´ly
slick´ness
slid´a·ble

slide
slid´er
slid´ing
slight
slight´ing
slight´ing-ly
slight´ly
slight´ness
slime
slim´i-er
slim´i-ly
slim´i-ness
slim´ly
slim´ness
slim´y
sling´–back
sling´er
sling´shot
slink´i-ly
slink´i-ness
slink´ing
slink´y
slip´case
slip´cov-er
slip´knot
slip´–on
slip´page
slipped
slip´per
slip´per-i-ness
slip´pery
slip´ping
slip´shod
slip´stream
slip´–up
slip´way
slith´er

slith´er·y
slit´ting
sliv´er
sliv´o-vitz
slob´ber
slob´ber-ing
sloe´berry
sloe´–eyed
slo´gan
slo-gan-eer´
slog´ging
sloped
slop´ing
slopped
slop´pi-ly
slop´pi-ness
slop´ping
slop´py
sloshed
slosh´y
slot
sloth
sloth´ful
sloth´ful-ly
sloth´ful-ness
slot´ted
slouch
slouch´i-ly
slouch´i-ness
slouch´ing
slouch´y
slough
slough´y
slov´en
slov´en-li-ness
slov´en-ly
slow´down

194

slow´–foot´ed
slow´–foot´ed-ness
slow´ly
slow´ness
slow´poke
slow´–release
slow´–wit´ted
slow´–wit´ted-ly
slow´–wit´ted-ness
sludge
sludg´er
sludg´y
slug´fest
slug´gard
slug´gard-li-ness
slug´gard-ly
slug´ger
slug´gish
slug´gish-ly
slug´gish-ness
sluice´way
sluic´ing
slum´ber
slum´ber-ous
slum´ber-ous-ly
slum´ber-ous-ness
slum´lord
slum´ming
slum´my
slump
slurp
slurred
slur´ring
slur´ry

slush´i-ness
slush´y
slut´tish
slut´tish-ly
slut´tish-ness
sly´ly
sly´ness
smack´er
smack´ing
smack´ing-ly
small´–claims´
small´ish
small´–mind´ed
small´–mind´ed-ly
small´–mind´ed-ness
small´ness
small´pox
small´–time´
smarm´i-ness
smarm´y
smart´en
smart´ly
smart´ness
smart´y
smart´y–pants
smashed
smash´er
smash´ing
smash´ing-ly
smash´up
smat´ter-ing
smear
smeared
smear´i-ness
smear´y

smell´er
smell´i-ness
smell´ing
smell´y
smelt´er
smid´gen
smiled
smil´ing
smil´ing-ly
smirk´er
smirk´ing
smirk´ing-ly
smith-er-eens´
smith´y
smit´ten
smock
smock´ing
smog´gy
smok´able
smoke´house
smoke´less
smok´er
smoke´stack
smok´i-er
smok´ing
smok´i-ness
smok´y
smol´der
smol´dered
smol´der-ing
smooch
smooth´bore
smooth´en
smooth´ie
smooth´ly
smooth´ness
smor´gas-bord

smoth´er
smoth´ered
smoth´er-y
smudge
smudg´er
smudg´i-ly
smudg´i-ness
smudg´ing
smudg´y
smug
smug´gle
smug´gler
smug´ly
smug´ness
smut
smut´ti-ly
smut´ti-ness
smut´ty
sna´fu´
snag
snagged
snag´ging
snag´gle-tooth
snag´gle-toothed
snail´like
snake´bite
snake´skin
snak´i-ly
snak´i-ness
snak´y
snap´per
snap´pi-ly
snap´pi-ness
snap´pish
snap´pish-ly
snap´pish-ness
snap´py

snap´shot
snared
snar´ing
snarled
snarl´ing
snarl´ing-ly
snarl´ish
snatch´er
snatch´y
snaz´zy
sneaked
sneak´er
sneak´i-ly
sneak´i-ness
sneak´ing
sneak´y
sneer´ing
sneer´ing-ly
sneezed
sneeze´guard
sneez´er
sneez´ing
snick´er
snick´er-ing
snide´ness
sniff´er
sniff´ing
snif´fle
snif´fler
snif´fly
snif´ter
snig´ger
snipe
snip´er
snip´ing
snipped
snip´pet

snip´pi-er
snip´pi-ly
snip´pi-ness
snip´ping
snip´py
snit
snitch
sniv´el
sniv´el-er
sniv´el-ing
snob´ber-y
snob´bish
snob´by
snook´er
snoop´er
snoop´y
snoot´i-ly
snoot´i-ness
snoot´y
snooze
snored
snor´er
snor´ing
snor´kel-er
snort´er
snort´ing
snout
snow´ball
snow´bank
snow´bird
snow´–blind
snow´bound
snow´drift
snow´fall
snow´flake
snow´i-er
snow´i-ly

snow´i-ness
snow´man
snow´mo-bile
snow´pea
snow´plow
snow´shoe
snow´slide
snow´storm
snow´suit
snow´tire
snow´y
snub
snubbed
snub´ber
snub´bing
snub´–nosed
snuff´box
snuff´er
snuf´fle
snuf´fled
snuf´fler
snuf´fly
snug´ger-y
snug´gle
snug´gled
snug´gling
snug´ly
snug´ness
soak´ing
soap´box
soap´i-er
soap´i-ly
soap´i-ness
soap op´era
soap´stone
soap´suds
soap´y

soar´ing
soar´ing-ly
so´a-ve
sob´bing
so´ber
so´ber-ly
so´ber–mind´ed
so´ber-ness
so´ber-sides
so-bri´e-ty
so´bri-quet
so´–called´
soc´cer
so-cia-bil´i-ty
so´cia-ble
so´cia-ble-ness
so´cia-bly
so´cial
so´cial-ism
so´cial-ist
so-cial-is´tic
so´cial-ite
so-ci-al´i-ty
so-cial-i-za´tion
so´cial-ize
so´cial-iz-er
so´cial-ly
so´cial–mind´ed
so´cial-ness
so-ci´e-tal
so-ci´e-tal-ly
so-ci´e-ty
so-ci-o-ec-o-
  nom´ic
so-ci-o-ec-o-
  nom´i-cal-ly
so´ci-o-log´ic

so-ci-o-log´i-cal
so-ci-o-log´i-cal-
  ly
so´ci-ol´o-gist
so-ci-ol´o-gy
so´ci-o-path
so-ci-o-path´ic
sock´et
so´da
sod´bust-er
sod´den
sod´den-ly
sod´den-ness
sod´ding
so´di-um
sod´om-ite
sod´omy
so´fa
sof´fit
soft´–boiled´
soft´bound
soft´–core
soft´–cov-er
soft´en
soft´en-er
soft´en-ing
soft´head
soft´head´ed
soft´head´ed-
  ness
soft´heart-ed
soft´heart-ed-ly
soft´heart-ed-
  ness
soft´ly
soft´ness
soft´–shell

soft´–shoe
soft´–soap
soft´–spo´ken
soft´ware
soft´y
sog´gi-ly
sog´gi-ness
sog´gy
soil´age
soiled
soil´ure
soi-rée´
so´journ
so´journ-er
sol´ace
sol´aced
sol´ac-er
sol´ac-ing
so´lar
so-lar´i-um
so-lar-iza´tion
so´lar-ize
sol´der
sol´der-a-ble
sol´dered
sol´der-er
sol´dier
sol´dier-li-ness
sol´dier-ly
sold´–out´
sol´e-cism
sol´e-cist
sol´e-cis´tic
soled
sole´ly
sol´emn
so-lem´ni-fy

so-lem´ni-ty
sol-em-ni-za´-
  tion
sol´em-nize
sol´emn-ly
sol´emn-ness
so´le-noid
sole´plate
so-lic´it
so-lic-i-ta´tion
so-lic´i-tor
so-lic´i-tous
so-lic´i-tous-ly
so-lic´i-tous-
  ness
so-lic´i-tude
sol´id
so´i-dar´i-ty
so-lid-i-fi-ca´tion
so-lid´i-fied
so-lid´i-fi-er
so-lid´i-fy
so-lid´i-ty
sol´id–look-ing
sol´id-ly
sol´id-ness
sol´id–state´
so-lil´o-quist
so-lil´o-quize
so-lil´o-quy
sol´ip-sism
sol´ip-sist
sol-ip-sis´tic
sol´i-taire
sol´i-tar-i-ly
sol´i-tar-i-ness
sol´i-tar-y

sol´i-tude
sol-i-tu-di-nar´i-
  an
so´lo
so´lo-ist
sol´stice
sol-sti´tial
sol-u-bil´i-ty
sol´u-ble
sol´u-ble-ness
sol´u-bly
sol´ute
so-lu´tion
solv-a-bil´i-ty
solv´a·ble
solve
solved
sol´ven-cy
sol´vent
solv´ing
so-mat´ic
so-mat´i-cal-ly
so´ma-to-gen´ic
so-ma-tol´o-gy
som´ber-ly
som´ber-ness
som-bre´ro
some´body
some´day
some´how
some´one
some´place
som´er-sault
some´thing
some´time
some´times
some´way

198

some´what
some´where
som-me-lier´
som-nam´bu-
   lant
som-nam´bu-
   late
som-nam-bu-
   la´tion
som-nam´bu-
   lism
som-nam´bu-list
som-nam´bu-lis´
   tic
som-ni-fa´cient
som-nif´er-ous
som-nif´ic
som-nil´o-quist
som-nil´o-quy
som´no-lence
som´no-lent
som´no-lent-ly
so´nance
so´nant
so´nar
so-na´ta
song´bird
song´book
song´fest
song´ster
song´stress
song´writ-er
son´ic
son´-in-law
son´net
son´ne-teer´
son´ny

son´o-gram
so-nom´e-ter
so-nor´i-ty
so-no´rous
so-no´rous-ly
so-no´rous-ness
soon´er
soon´est
soothe
soothed
sooth´er
sooth´ing
sooth´ing-ly
sooth´say
sooth´say-er
sooth´say-ing
soot´i-ly
soot´i-ness
soot´y
soph´ism
soph´ist
soph´is-ter
so-phis´tic
so-phis´ti-cal-ly
so-phis´ti-cate
so-phis´ti-cat-ed
so-phis-ti-
   ca´tion
soph´is-try
soph´o-more
soph-o-mor´ic
soph-o-mor´i-
   cal-ly
so´por
sop-o-rif´er-ous
sop-o-rif´ic
sop´ping

sop´py
so-pra´no
sorb-a·bil´i-ty
sorb´a·ble
sor´be-fa´cient
sor´bet
sor´cer-er
sor´cer-ess
sor´cer-ous
sor´cery
sor´did
sor´did-ly
sor´did-ness
sore´head
sore´head-ed-
   ness
sore´ly
sore´ness
sor´ghum
so-ror´i-ty
sorp´tion
sorp´tive
sor´rel
sor´ri-ly
sor´ri-ness
sor´row-ful
sor´row-ful-ly
sor´row-ful-ness
sor´ry
sort
sort´a-ble
sort´ed
sor´ter
sor´tie
sort´ing
sot´ted
sot´tish

199

sot´tish-ly
sot´tish-ness
souf-flé´
sought´–af-ter
soul´ful
soul´ful-ly
soul´ful-ness
soul´less
soul´less-ly
soul´less-ness
soul´–search-ing
sound´a·ble
sound´a-like
sound´board
sound´er
sound´ing
sound´less
sound´less-ly
sound´less-ness
sound´ly
sound´ness
sound´proof
sound´proof-ing
sound´track
soup-çon´
soup´i-er
soup´spoon
soup´y
sour´ball
source´book
source´ful
source´ful-ness
source language
source´less
sour´dough
sour´ish
sour´ly

sour´ness
sour´puss
sou´sa-phone
souse
soused
south´bound
south-east´
south-east´er
south-east´er-ly
south-east´ern
south´er-ly
south´ern
south´ern-er
south´ern-ly
south´ern-most
south´land
south´ward
south-west´
south-west´er
south-west´er-ly
south-west´ern
sou-ve-nir´
souv-la´ki
sov´er-eign
sov´er-eign-ty
so´vi-et
soy´a
soy´bean
space´–age
space´borne
space´craft
spaced´–out
space´flight
space´less
space´man
space´port
space´ship

space´shot
space´suit
space´walk
spac´ey
spa´cial
spac´ing
spa´cious
spa´cious-ly
spa´cious-ness
spack´le
spade
spad´ed
spade´ful
spade´work
spad´er
spad´ing
spa-ghet´ti
span
span´dex
span´gle
span´gled
span´gly
span´iel
spank´er
spank´ing
spanned
span´ner
span´ning
spare´a-ble
spared
spare´ly
spare´ness
spare´rib
spar´ing
spar´ing-ly
spar´ing-ness
spark´i-ly

spar´kle
spar´kler
spark´let
spark´like
spar´kling
spar´kling-ly
spar´kly
spark´y
sparred
spar´ring
spar´row
sparse´ly
sparse´ness
spar´si-ty
spasm
spas-mod´ic
spas-mod´i-cal
spas´tic
spas´ti-cal-ly
spate
spa´tial
spa-ti-al´i-ty
spat´ter
spat´ter-ing
spat´ting
spat´u-la
spat´u-late
spawn
spawned
spawn´er
speak´able
speak´easy
speak´er
speak´er-phone
speak´ing
spear´fish
spear´head

spear´mint
spec
spe´cial-ism
spe´cial-ist
spe-ci-al´i-ty
spe-cial-i·za´tion
spe´cial-ize
spe´cial-ly
spe´cial-ty
spe´cie (money)
spe´cies (class)
spec´i-fi-a·ble
spe-cif´ic
spe-cif´i-cal-ly
spec-i-fi-ca´tion
spec-i-fic´i-ty
spec´i-fied
spec´i-fi-er
spec´i-fy
spec´i-fy-ing
spec´i-men
spe´cious
spe´cious-ly
spe´cious-ness
speck´le
speck´led
speck´ling
specs
spec´ta-cle
spec´ta-cled
spec-tac´u-lar
spec-tac´u-lar-ly
spec´tate
spec´ta-tor
spec´ter
spec´tral
spec-tral´i-ty

spec´tral-ly
spec´tral-ness
spec´tro-gram
spec´tro-graph
s p e c - t r o -
graph´ic
spec-trol´o-gy
spec´tro-scope
spec-tro-scop´ic
spec´trum
spec´u-late
spec´u-lat-ing
spec-u-la´tion
spec´u-la-tive
spec´u-la-tive-ly
spec´u-la-tive-ly
spec´u-la-tor
speech´i-fi-er
speech´i-fy
speech´less
speech´less-ly
speech´less-ness
speed´boat
speed´boat-ing
speed´er
speed´i-ly
speed´i-ness
speed´ing
speed-om´e-ter
speed´–read
speed´ster
speed´–up
speed´way
speed´writ-ing
speed´y
spe´le-ol´o-gist
spe-le-o-log´i-cal

spe-le-ol´o-gist
spe-le-ol´o-gy
spell´bind-er
spell´bind-ing-ly
spell´bound
spell´er
spell´ing
spe-lunk´er
spe-lunk´ing
spend´a-ble
spend´er
spend´ing
spend´thrift
spent
sperm
sphere
spher´i-cal
spher´i-cal-ly
sphe´roid
sphinx
spiced
spic´i-ly
spic´i-ness
spic´ing
spic´y
spi´der
spi´dery
spiel´er
spiff´i-ly
spiff´i-ness
spiff´y
spig´ot
spiked
spik´i-ly
spik´i-ness
spik´ing
spik´y

spill´a-ble
spill´age
spilled
spill´er
spill´ing
spill´–o-ver
spill´proof
spill´way
spin
spin´ach
spi´nal
spin´dle
spin´dling
spin´dly
spin´–dry´
spine´less
spine´less-ly
spine´less-ness
spin´et
spin´ner
spin´ning
spin´–off
spin´ster
spin´ster-ish
spin´y
spi´ral
spi´raled
spi´ral-ing
spi´ral-ly
spire
spir´it
spir´it-ed
spir´it-ed-ly
spir´it-ed-ness
spir´it-ism
spir´it-less
spir´it-less-ly

spi-ri-to´so
spir´i-tu-al
spir´i-tu-al-ism
spir´i-tu-al-ist
spir-i-tu-al-is´tic
spir-i-tu-al´i-ty
spir´i-tu-al-ize
spir´i-tu-al-ly
spit´ball
spite´ful
spite´ful-ly
spite´ful-ness
spit´ing
spit´ting
spit´tle
splash´down
splash guard
splash´i-ly
splash´i-ness
splash´ing
splash´y
splat´ter
splay
splen´dent-ly
splen´did
splen´did-ly
splen´did-ness
splen-dif´er-ous
splen-dif´er-ous-
ly
splen-dif´er-ous-
ness
splen´dor
splen´dor-ous
splen´drous
spliced
splic´er

splic´ing
splint
splin´ter
splin´tered
split´–lev´el
split´ting
split´–up
splotch´y
splurge
splurged
spoil´age
spoiled
spoil´er
spoil´ing
spoil´sport
spoke
spo´ken
spokes´per-son
sponge
sponged
spong´er
spon´gi-ness
spong´ing
spong´y
spon´sor
spon´sor-ship
spon-ta-ne´i-ty
spon-ta´ne-ous
spon-ta´ne-ous-
   ly
spon-ta´ne-ous-
   ness
spook´i-ness
spook´ish
spook´y
spool´er
spoon´–feed

spoon´ful
spoon´y
spo-rad´ic
spo-rad´i-cal-ly
sport´fish-ing
sport´i-ly
sport´i-ness
sport´ing
sport´ing-ly
spor´tive
spor´tive-ly
spor´tive-ness
sports´cast-er
sports´cast-ing
sports´man
sports´man-like
sports´man-ship
sports´wear
sports´woman
sports´writ-er
sports´writ-ing
sport´y
spot´less
spot´less-ly
spot´less-ness
spot´light
spot´ted
spot´ter
spot´ti-er
spot´ti-ness
spot´ting
spot´ty
spot´–weld
spous´al
spouse
spout´er
sprained

sprang
sprawl´er
sprawl´ing
sprayed
spray´er
spread´er
spread´ing
spright´ful
spright´ful-ly
spright´li-ness
spright´ly
spring´board
spring´er
spring´i-ly
spring´i-ness
spring´ing
spring´–load´ed
spring´time
spring´y
sprin´kle
sprin´kler
sprin´kling
sprint´er
spritz´er
sprock´et
spruced
spruc´ing
spruce´ly
spry´ly
spry´ness
spu-mo´ni
spunk
spunk´i-ly
spunk´i-ness
spunk´y
spu´ri-ous
spu´ri-ous-ness

spurn´ing	squawk´y	sta-bil´i-ty
spurred	squeak´er	sta-bi-li-za´tion
spur´ring	squeak´i-ly	sta´bi-lize
spurt´ed	squeak´i-ness	sta´bi-liz-er
sput´ter	squeak´ing	sta´ble
sput´ter-ing	squeak´y	sta´bled
spy´ing	squeak´y–clean´	sta´ble-ness
squab´ble	squeal´er	sta´bly
squab´bled	squeal´ing	sta´bling
squab´bler	squea´mish	stack´a-ble
squab´bling	squeam´ish-ly	stacked
squad´ron	squeam´ish-ness	stack´er
squal´id	squee´gee	sta´di-um
squal´id-ly	squeez´a-ble	staffed
squal´id-ness	squeez´a-bly	staff´er
squall	squeeze´box	stage´coach
squal´or	squeezed	stage´hand
squan´der	squeez´er	stag´er
squan´dered	squeez´ing	stage´struck
squan´der-er	squelch	stage´y
squan´der-ing	squelched	stag´ger
square	squelch´er	stag´ger-ing
squared	squig´gle	stag´i-ness
square´ly	squig´gly	stag´ing
squar´ing	squint´ed	stag´nance
squar´ish	squint´er	stag´nant
squash´i-ness	squint´ing	stag´nant-ly
squash´ing	squint´y	stag´nate
squash´y	squirm	stag´nat-ing
squat´ly	squirm´er	stag-na´tion
squat´ness	squirm´ing	stag´y
squat´ted	squirm´y	stain´a-ble
squat´ter	squirt´ed	stain´er
squat´ting	squirt´ing	stain´ing
squat´ty	squish´y	stain´less
squawked	stabbed	stair´case
squawk´er	stab´bing	stair´way

204

stair´well
stake´out
stak´ing
stalac´tite
stalag´mite
stale´mate
stale´ness
stalked
stalk´er
stalk´ing
stal´wart
stam´i-na
stam´mer
stam´mer-er
stam´mer-ing
stamped
stam-pede´
stamp´er
stance
stand´a-lone
stan´dard–bear-
 er
stan-dard-i-za´
 tion
stan´dard-ize
stand´ing
stand´off ish
stand´out
sta´ple
sta´pled
sta´pler
sta´pling
star´board
starch´i-ness
starch´y
star´–crossed
star´dom

stared
star´er
star´gaze
star´gaz-er
star´gaz-ing
star´ing
stark´ly
stark´ness
star´less
star´let
star´light
starred
star´ri-ness
star´ring
star´ry
star´ry–eyed
star´–shaped
star´ship
star´–stud-ded
start´er
star´tle
star´tling
star´tling-ly
start´–up
star-va´tion
starve
starved
starve´ling
starv´er
starv´ing
stat´ed
state´hood
state´li-ness
state´ly
state´ment
state´room
states´man

states´man-like
state´wide
stat´ic
sta´tion
sta´tion-ary
sta´tio-ner
sta´tio-nery
sta´tion-mas-ter
sta-tis´tic
sta-tis´ti-cal
sta-tis´ti-cal-ly
stat-is-ti´cian
sta-tis´tics
stat´u-ary
stat´ue
stat-u-esque´
stat´u-ette´
stat´ure
sta´tus
stat´ute
stat´u-to-ry
staunch´ly
staunch´ness
stay´ing
stead´fast
stead´fast-ly
stead´fast-ness
stead´i-ly
stead´i-ness
stead´y
stealth´ful
stealth´ful-ly
stealth´i-ly
stealth´i-ness
stealth´y
steam´bath
steam´boat

steam´er
steam´i-ness
steam´roll-er
steam´ship
steam´y
steel´i-ness
steel´work-er
steel´y
steep´en
steep´er
stee´ple
stee´ple-chase
stee´pled
stee´ple-jack
stee´ple-less
steep´ly
steep´ness
steer´age
steer´ing
stein
stel´lar
stemmed
stem´ming
stem´ware
sten´cil
sten´ciled
sten´cil-ing
sten´o
ste-nog´ra-pher
sten´o-graph´ic
sten-to´ri-an
step´broth-er
step´child
step´daugh-ter
step´fa-ther
step´lad-der
step´moth-er

step´par-ent
stepped´-up´
step´per
step´ping
step´sis-ter
ster-e-o-phon´ic
ster´e-o-type
ster-e-o-typ´i-cal
ster´ile
ster´ile-ness
ste-ril´i-ty
ster-i-li-za´tion
ster´i-lize
ster´i-liz-er
stern´ly
stern´most
stern´ness
ster´oid
steth´o-scope
ste´ve-dore
stew´ard
stew´ard-ess
stew´ard-ship
stick´ball
stick´er
stick´i-er
stick´i-ness
stick´ing
stick´-in-the-m
    ud
stick´ler
stick´pin
stick´y
stiff´en
stiff´en-er
stiff´en-ing
stiff´ly

stiff´-necked´
stiff´ness
sti´fle
sti´fling
sti´fling-ly
stig´ma
stig´ma-tize
sti-let´to
still´born
still´ness
stilt´ed
stim´u-lant
stim´u-late
stim-u-la´tion
stim´u-la-tor
stim´u-li
stim´u-lus
sting´er
stin´gi-er
stin´gi-ly
stin´gi-ness
sting´ing
stin´gy
stink´er
stink´ing
stink´y
stint´ing
sti´pend
stip´ple
stip´pled
stip´pling
stip´u-la-ble
stip´u-late
stip´u-lat-ing
stip-u-la´tion
stip´u-la-tor
stip´u-la-to-ry

stir´–fry
stirred
stir´ring
stitch´er
stitch´ing
stock-ade´
stock´bro-ker
stock´hold-er
stock´ing
stock´pile
stock´room
stock´y
stodg´i-ness
stodg´y
sto´gie
sto´gy
sto´ic
sto´i-cal
sto´i-cism
stoke
stoked
stok´er
stok´ing
stole
sto´len
stol´id
stol´id-ly
stom´ach
stom´ach-ache
stone´–broke
stone china
stone crush´er
stone´cut-ter
stone´–deaf
ston´i-ly
ston´i-ness
ston´ing

ston´y
stop´gap
stop´light
stop´–off
stop´o-ver
stopped
stop´per
stop´ping
stop´watch
stor´age
stored
store´front
store´house
store´keep-er
store´room
sto´ried
stor´ing
storm´i-ly
storm´i-ness
storm´proof
storm´y
sto´ry-board
sto´ry-book
sto´ry-tell-er
stout´–heart´ed
stout´–heart´ed-
    ly
stout´–heart´ed-
    ness
stout´ish
stout´ly
stout´ness
stove´pipe
stow´age
strad´dle
strad´dler
strad´dling

strag´gle
strag´gler
strag´gling
strag´gly
straight´–ahead
straight´away
straight´en-er
straight´–faced
straight-for´ward
straight´ness
straight´–out´
strained
strain´er
strait´jacket
strait´–laced
strange´ly
strange´ness
strang´er
stran´gle
stran´gler
stran´gling
stran´gu-late
stran-gu-la´tion
strap´less
strapped
strap´ping
stra´ta
stra-te´gic
stra-te´gi-cal
stra-te´gi-cal-ly
strat´e-gist
strat´e-gy
strat-i-fi-ca´tion
strat´i-fied
strat´i-form
strat´i-fy
strat´i-fy-ing

207

strat´o-sphere
straw´ber-ry
stray´er
stray´ing
streak´i-ness
streak´y
stream
stream´bed
stream´er
stream´ing
stream´let
stream´lined
street´car
street´light
street´–smart
strength´en
strength´en-er
strength´en-ing
stren´u-ous
stren´u-ous-ly
stren´u-ous-
  ness
stressed´–out´
stress´ful
stress´ful-ly
stress´less
stretch´a-ble
stretch´er
stretch´er–bear-
  er
stretch´i-ness
strewn
stri´ate
stri´at´ed
stri-a´tion
strick´en
strict´ly

strict´ness
stric´ture
stride
stri´dence
stri´den-cy
stri´dent
stri´dent-ly
strid´er
strid´ing
strike´break-er
strike´break-ing
strike´out
strik´er
strik´ing
strik´ing-ly
strin´gen-cy
strin´gent
strin´gent-ly
string´er
string´i-ness
string´ing
string´y
striped
strip´er
strip´ing
strip´ling
stripped
stripped´–down´
strip´per
strip´ping
strive
striv´en
striv´ing
stroke
stroked
strok´er
strok´ing

stroll´er
strong
strong´box
strong´hold
strong´–mind´ed
strong´–willed´
struc´tur-al
struc´tur-al-ize
struc´tur-al-ly
struc´ture
strug´gle
strug´gled
strug´gler
strug´gling
strum´mer
strum´ming
strum´pet
strung´–out´
strut´ted
strut´ter
strut´ting
stub´ble
stub´born-ly
stub´born-ness
stuc´co
stuck´–up
stu´dent
stud´ied
stu´dio
stu´di-ous
stu´di-ous-ly
stu´di-ous-ness
stud´y
stud´y-ing
stuffed
stuff´i-ly
stuff´i-ness

208

stuff´ing
stuff´y
stul´ti-fied
stul´ti-fy
stul´ti-fy-ing
stum´ble
stum´bler
stum´bling
stunned
stun´ning
stun´ning-ly
stunt´ed
stu´pe-fied
stu´pe-fy
stu´pe-fy-ing
stu-pen´dous
stu-pen´dous-ly
stu´pid
stu-pid´i-ty
stu´pid-ly
stu´pid-ness
stu´por
stur´di-ness
stur´dy
stur´geon
stut´ter
stut´ter-er
stut´ter-ing
style
styled
style´less
styl´ing
styl´ish
styl´ish-ly
styl´ish-ness
styl´ist
styl´ize

sty´lus
sty´mie
sty´mied
suave´ly
suave´ness
suav´i-ty
sub´com-mit-tee
sub-con´scious
sub-con´scious-
    ly
sub-con´scious-
    ness
sub-con´tract
sub´con-trac-tor
sub´cul-ture
sub´di-vide
sub´di-vid-er
sub´di-vid-ing
sub´di-vi-sion
sub-due´
sub-dued´
sub-du´er
sub-du´ing
sub´ject *(n., adj.)*
sub-ject´ *(v.)*
sub-jec´tion
sub-jec´tive
sub-jec´tive-ly
sub-jec´tive-ness
sub-jec-tiv´i-ty
sub´ju-gate
sub´ju-gat-ing
sub-ju-ga´tion
sub´lease´
sub-let´
sub´let´ting
sub-lime´

sub-lime´ly
sub-lim´in-al
sub-lim´in-al-ly
sub´ma-rine
sub-ma-rin´er
sub-merge´
sub-merged´
sub-merse´
sub-mersed´
sub-mers´i-ble
sub-mer´sion
sub-min´i-a-ture
sub-mis´sion
sub-mis´sive
sub-mis´sive-ly
sub-mis´sive-
    ness
sub-mit´ted
sub-mit´ter
sub-mit´ting
sub-or´di-nate
sub-or´di-nate-ly
sub-or-di-
    na´tion
sub-poe´na
sub-poe´naed
sub´rou-tine
sub-scribe´
sub-scrib´er
sub-scrib´ing
sub-script
sub´sec´tion
sub´se-quent
sub´se-quent-ly
sub-ser´vi-ence
sub-ser´vi-ent
sub-ser´vi-ent-ly

sub-side´
sub-sid´ence
sub-sid´i-ar-y
sub-sid´ing
sub´si-dize
sub´si-dy
sub-sist´
sub-sist´ence
sub-sist´ent
sub´stance
sub-stand´ard
sub-stan´tial
sub-stan´tial-ly
sub-stan´ti-ate
sub-stan-ti-a´tion
sub´stan-tive
sub´sta-tion
sub´sti-tute
sub´sti-tut-ed
sub´sti-tut-ing
sub-sti-tu´tion
sub´strate
sub´ter-fuge
sub-ter-ra´ne-an
sub-ter-ra´ne-ous
sub´ti-tle
sub´tle
sub´tle-ness
sub´tle-ty
sub´tly
sub´to-tal
sub-tract´
sub-trac´tion
sub-trac´tive
sub-trop´ics

sub´urb
sub-ur´ban
sub-ur´ban-ite
sub-ur´bi-a
sub-ver´sive
sub-vert´
sub´way
sub–ze´ro
suc-cess´ful
suc-cess´ful-ly
suc-ces´sion
suc-ces´sive-ly
suc-ces´sor
suc-cinct´
suc-cinct´ly
suc-cinct´ness
suc´cor
suc´co-ry
suc´cu-lence
suc´cu-lent
suc-cumb´
suck´er
suck´le
suck´ling
suc´tion
sud´den-ly
sud´den-ness
suds-y
sued
suede
su´et
suf´fer
suf´fer-ance
suf´fer-er
suf´fer-ing
suf-fice´
suf-ficed´

suf-fi´cien-cy
suf-fi´cient
suf-fi´cient-ly
suf-fic´ing
suf´fix
suf´fo-cate
suf´fo-cat-ing
suf-fo-ca´tion
suf´frage
suf´frag-ette´
suf´frag-ist
suf-fuse´
suf-fus´ing
suf-fu´sion
suf-fu´sive
sug´ar-free
sug´ar-i-ness
sug´ar-less
sug´ar-plum
sug´ar-y
sug-gest´
sug-gest´i-ble
sug-gest´i-bly
sug-ges´tion
sug-ges´tive
sug-ges´tive-ly
su´i-ci´dal
su´i-cide
suit´a-ble
suit´a-bly
suit´case
suite
suit´ing
suit´or
sul´fate
sul´fide
sul´fite

sul´fur
sul-fu´ric
sul´fu-rous
sulk´i-ly
sulk´i-ness
sulk´y
sul´len-ly
sul´len-ness
sul´lied
sul´ly
sul´tri-er
sul´tri-ness
sul´try
sum´mable
sum-mar´i-ly
sum´ma-rize
sum´ma-ry
sum-ma´tion
sum´mer
sum´mer-house
sum´mer-sault
sum´mer-time
sum´mery
sum´ming-up
sum´mit
sum´mon
sum´moned
sum´mon-er
sum´mon-ing
sum´mons
sump´tu-ous
sump´tu-ous-ly
sump´tu-ous-
　ness
sun´beam
sun´burn
sun´burned

sun´dae
sun´der
sun´di-al
sun´down
sun´dried
sun´dry
sun´glass-es
sunk´en
sun´lamp
sun´light
sun´lit
sun´ni-er
sun´ning
sun´ny
sun´rise
sun´room
sun´screen
sun´set
sun´shine
sun´stroke
sun´tan
su´per
su-per-a·bun´
　dance
su-per-a·bun´
　dant
su-perb´
su-perb´ly
su-per-cil´i-ous
su´per-com-put-
　er
su-per-con-duc´
　tor
su-per-e-go
su-per-fi´cial
su-per-fi-ci-al´i-
　ty

su-per-fi´cial-ly
su-per´flu-ous
su-per´flu-ous-ly
su´per-he-ro
su´per-high-way
su-per-hu´man
su-per-hu´man-
　ly
su´per-im-pose´
su-per-in-tend´
su-per-in-tend´
　ent
su-pe´ri-or
su-pe-ri-or´i-ty
su-per´la-tive
su-per´la-tive-ly
su´per-mar-ket
su-per-nat´u-ral
su-per-no´va
su´per-nu´mer-
　ar·y
su-per-sede´
su´per-sed´ing
su-per-son´ic
su´per-star
su-per-sti´tion
su-per-sti´tious
su-per-sti´tious-
　ly
su´per-struc-
　ture
su´per-vise
su´per-vis-ing
su´per-vi´sion
su´per-vi-sor
su´per-vi´so-ry
sup´per

sup´per-time
sup-plant´
sup-plant´er
sup´ple
sup´ple-ment
sup-ple-men´tal
sup-ple-men´tal-
  ly
sup´ple-men´
  tar·y
sup´ple-ness
sup´pli-cant
sup´pli-cate
sup´pli-cat-ing
sup-pli-ca´tion
sup-plied´
sup-pli´er
sup-ply´
sup-ply´ing
sup-port´a-ble
sup-port´er
sup-port´ing
sup-port´ive
sup-pos´a-bly
sup-pose´
sup-posed´
sup-pos-ed´ly
sup-pos´ing
sup-po-si´tion
sup-pos´i-to-ry
sup-press´
sup-pres´sant
sup-pres´sion
sup-pres´sor
su-prem´a-cy
su-preme´
su-preme´ly

sur-cease´
sur´charge
sure´fire´
sure ´foot-ed
sure´ly
sur´e-ty
sur´face
sur´faced
sur´fac-er
sur´fac-ing
surf´board
sur´feit
surf´er
surf´ing
surge
sur´geon
sur´gery
sur´gi-cal
sur´gi-cal-ly
surg´ing
sur´li-ness
sur´ly
sur-mise´
sur-mis´ing
sur-mount´
sur-mount´a-ble
sur-mount´ed
sur´name
sur-pass´
sur-pass´ing
sur´plice
sur´plus
sur-pris´able
sur-prise´
sur-prised´
sur-pris´ing
sur-pris´ing-ly

sur-re´al
sur-re´al-ist
sur-ren´der
sur-ren´der-er
sur-rep-ti´tious
sur-rep-ti´tious-
  ly
sur´rey
sur´ro-gate
sur-round´ed
sur-round´ing
sur´tax
sur-veil´lance
sur-vey´ (v.)
sur´vey (n.)
sur-vey´ing
sur-vey´or
sur-viv´a-ble
sur-viv´al
sur-viv´al-ist
sur-vive´
sur-vi´vor
sus-cep-ti-bil´i-
  ty
sus-cep´ti-ble
sus-cep´tive
sus´pect (n.)
sus-pect´ (v.)
sus-pend´ed
sus-pend´er
sus-pend´i-ble
sus-pense´
sus-pense´ful
sus-pen´sion
sus-pi´cion
sus-pi´cious
sus-pi´cious-ly

sus-tain´
sus-tain´a-ble
sus-tained´
sus-tain´ing
sus´te-nance
su´ture
su´tur-ing
svelte
swabbed
swab´ber
swab´bing
swad´dle
swad´dled
swad´dling
swag´ger
swag´ger-ing
swag´ger-ing-ly
swal´low
swal´low-er
swamp
swamp´i-ness
swamp´land
swamp´y
swank´i-ness
swank´y
swarmed
swarm´ing
swarth´i-ness
swarth´y
swash´buck-ler
swash´buck-ling
swathe
swat´ter
sway´back
sway´backed
sway´ing
swear´ing

sweat´band
sweat´i-ness
sweat´pants
sweat´shirt
sweat´shop
sweat´y
sweep´er
sweep´ing
sweep´stakes
sweet´–and–sour

sweet´bread
sweet´en
sweet´en-er
sweet´en-ing
sweet´heart
sweet´ie
sweet´ish
sweet´ly
sweet´meats
sweet´ness
sweet´shop
swelled
swell´ing
swel´ter
swel´ter-ing
swept´back
swerved
swerv´ing
swift´ly
swift´–foot´ed
swift´ness
swim´mer
swim´ming
swin´dle
swin´dler
swin´dling

swing´er
swing´ing
swiped
swip´ing
swirl´ing
swirl´y
switch´board
switch´er
switch´man
switch´yard
swiv´el
swiv´eled
swiv´el-ing
swiz´zle
swol´len
swoon´ing
sword´fish
sword´play
swords´man
syc´o-phant
sy-co´sis
syl-lab´ic
syl-lab-i-ca´tion
syl-lab´i-ty
syl´la-ble
syl´la-bub
sylph´like
syl´van
sym-bi´o-sis
sym-bi-ot´ic
sym´bol
sym-bol´ic
sym-bol´i-cal-ly
sym´bol-ism
sym´bol-ize
sym-met´ri-cal
sym´me-try

213

sym-pa-thet´ic
sym´pa-thize
sym´pa-thiz-er
sym´pa-thiz-ing
sym´pa-thy
sym-phon´ic
sym-phon´i-cal-
  ly
sym´pho-ny
sym-po´si-um
symp´tom
symp-to-mat´ic
syn´a-gogue
syn´chro-nize
syn´chro-niz-ing
syn´co-pate
syn´co-pat-ed
syn´co-pat-ing
syn-co-pa´tion
syn´di-cate
syn´di-cat-ing
syn-di-ca´tion
syn´di-ca-tor
syn´drome
syn´er-gy
syn´od
syn´o-nym
syn-on´y-mous
syn-on´y-mous-
  ly
syn-op´sis
syn´tax
syn´the-sis
syn´the-size
syn´the-siz-er
syn´the-siz-ing
syn-thet´ic

syn-thet´i-cal-ly
sy´phon
sy-ringe´
syr´up
syr´up-y
sys´tem
sys-tem-at´ic
sys-tem-at´i-cal-
  ly
sys´tem-a-tize
sys-tem´ic
sys-tol´ic
tabbed
tab´bing
tab´by
tab´er-na-cle
ta´ble
tab´leau
tab´leaux
ta´ble-cloth
ta´ble-ful
ta´ble–hop
ta´ble-land
tab´let
ta´ble-top
ta´ble-ware
ta´bling
tab´loid
ta-boo´
tab´u-lar
tab´u-late
tab´u-lat-ing
tab-u-la´tion
ta-chom´e-ter
tac´it
tac´it-ly
tac´i-turn

tac-i-tur´ni-ty
tac´i-turn-ly
tack´i-ness
tack´le
tack´ler
tack´less
tack´ling
tack´y
tact´ful
tact´ful-ly
tact´ful-ness
tac´tic
tac´ti-cal
tac´ti-cal-ly
tac-ti´cian
tac´tics
tac´tile
tac-til´i-ty
tact´less
tact´less-ly
tad´pole
taf´fe-ta
taf´fy
tag´a-long
tagged
tag´ging
tail´board
tailed
tail´gate
tail´ing
tail´less
tail´light
tai´lor
tai´lored
tai´lor-ing
tai´lor–made´
tail´pipe

tail´spin
tail´wind
taint
take´a-way
tak´en
take´out
take´o-ver
tak´er
tak´ing
talc
tal´cum
tale´bear-er
tal´ent-ed
tale´tell-er
tale´tell-ing
tal´is-man
talk´a-thon
talk´a-tive
talk´a-tive-ly
talk´a-tive-ness
talk´er
talk´i-ness
talk´ing–to
tal´lied
tall´ness
tal´low
tal´ly
ta´lus
tam´able
tam´bou-rine´
tam´a-ble
tame´a-ble
tamed
tame´ly
tame´ness
tam´er
tam´ing

tamp
tam´per
tan´dem
tan´ge-lo
tan´gent
tan-gen´tial
tan-gen´tial-ly
tan´ger-ine´
tan-gi-bil´i-ty
tan´gi-ble
tan´gi-ble-ness
tan´gi-bly
tang´i-ness
tan´gle
tan´gled
tan´gle-ment
tan´gler
tan´gling
tan´gly
tan´go
tan´goed
tang´y
tan´kard
tank´er
tank´ful
tanned
tan´ner
tan´nery
tan´nic
tan´nin
tan´ning
tan´nish
tan´ta-lize
tan´ta-liz-er
tan´ta-liz-ing-ly
tant´amount
tan´trum

taped
tape´line
ta´per
tap´er
ta´per-ing
ta´per-ing-ly
tap´es-tried
tap´es-try
tape´worm
tap-i-o´ca
tapped
tap´per
tap´ping
tap´room
tap´root
tar-an-tel´la
ta-ran´tu-la
tar´di-ly
tar´di-ness
tar´dy
tar´get
tar´get-a-ble
tar´iff
tar-na´tion
tar´nish
tar´nish-able
ta´rot
tar´pa-per
tar-pau´lin
tar´pon
tar´ra-gon
tarred
tar´ried
tar´ring
tar´ry
tar´ry-ing
tar´sus

tar´tan
tar´tar
tart´ish
tart´ly
tart´ness
tart´y
task´mas-ter
tas´sel
tas´seled
tas´sel-ing
taste
taste´ful
taste´ful-ly
taste´ful-ness
taste´less
taste´less-ly
taste´less-ness
taste´mak-er
tast´er
tast´i-ness
tast´ing
tast´y
tat´ter
tat´tered
tat´ter-sall
tat´ting
tat´tle
tat´tler
tat´tle-tale
tat-too´
tat-too´er
taught
taunt´er
taunt´ing
taunt´ing-ly
taupe
taut´en

taut´ly
taut´ness
tau-to-log´ic
tau-to-log´i-cal
tau-to-log´i-cal-
  ly
tau-tol´o-gy
tav´ern
ta-ver´na
taw´dri-ly
taw´dri-ness
taw´dry
tawn´i-er
taw´ni-ness
tawn´y
tax-a-bil´i-ty
tax´a-ble
tax´a-ble-ness
tax-a´tion
tax´–ex-empt´
tax´–free
tax´i
tax´i-cab
tax´i-der-mist
tax´i-der-my
tax´ied
tax´ing
tax´pay-er
tax´pay-ing
tea´cake
teach´a-ble
teach´a-bly
teach´er
teach´–in
teach´ing
tea´cup
tea´cup-ful

tea´house
tea´ket-tle
team´mate
team´ster
team´work
tea´pot
tear´a-ble
tear´a-way
tear´drop
tear´ful
tear´ful-ly
tear´ful-ness
tear´i-ly
tear´i-ness
tear´ing
tear´ing-ly
tear´jerk-er
tear´less
tea´room
tear´–stained
tear´y
teas´a-ble
teased
teas´er
teas´ing
teas´ing-ly
tea´spoon
tea´spoon-ful
tea´time
tech
tech´ie
tech´ni-cal
tech-ni-cal´i-ty
tech´ni-cal-ly
tech-ni´cian
tech´nics
tech-nique´

tech´no-crat
tech-nol´o-gy
tech´y
tec-ton´ic
tec-ton´i-cal-ly
tec-ton´ics
ted´dy
te´di-ous
te´di-ous-ly
te´di-ous-ness
te´di-um
teem´ing
teen´age
teen´–ag´er
teen´sy
teen´y-bop-per
tee´ny–wee´ny
tee´ter-board
teethe
teethed
teeth´ing
tee-to´tal
tee´to-tal-er
teg´u-ment
teg-u-men´tal
tel´e-cast
tel´e-cast-er
t e l - e - c o m -
   mu´ni-cate
tel-e-com-mu-
   ni-ca´tions
tel´e-com-mut-
   ing
t e l´e-con-fer-
   ence
tel´e-gram
tel´e-graph

te-leg´ra-pher
tel-e-graph´ic
te-leg´ra-phy
tel-e-ki-ne´sis
tel-e-ki-net´ic
tel´e-mar-ket-er
tel´e-mar-ket-ing
te-lem´e-try
tel-e-path´ic
tel-e-path´i-cal-
   ly
te-lep´a-thy
tel´e-phone
tel-e-phon´ic
tel´e-pho´to
tel´e-port
tel-e-por-ta´tion
tel´e-scope
tel´e-scop´ic
tel´e-scop´i-cal-
   ly
tel´e-thon
tel´e-vise
tel´e-vi-sion
tel´ex
tell´a-ble
tell´er
tell´ing
tell´ing-ly
tell´tale
te-mer´i-ty
tem´peh
tem´per
tem´per-a
tem´per-a-ment
t e m´p e r - a -
   men´tal

tem´per-ance
tem´per-ate
tem´per-ate-ly
tem´per-ate-ness
tem´per-a-ture
tem´pered
tem´per-er
tem´pest
tem-pes´tu-ous
tem-pes´tu-ous-
   ly
tem-pes´tu-ous-
   ness
tem´plar
tem´plate
tem´ple
tem´plet
tem´po
tem´po-ral
tem´po-ral-ly
tem-po-rar´i-ly
t e m´p o - r a r - i -
   ness
tem´po-rar-y
tem´po-rize
tempt´a-ble
temp-ta´tion
tempt´er
tempt´ing
tempt´ing-ly
tempt´ing-ness
tempt´ress
tem-pu´ra
ten´a-ble
ten´a-ble-ness
ten´a-bly
te-na´cious

te-na´cious-ly
te-na´cious-ness
te-nac´i-ty
ten´an-cy
ten´ant
tend´en-cy
ten-den´tious
ten-den´tious-ly
ten-den´tious-
  ness
tend´er
ten´der
ten-der-a-bil´i-ty
ten´der-a-ble
ten´der-foot
ten´der-heart-ed
ten´der-ize
ten´der-iz-er
ten´der-loin
ten´der-ly
ten´der-ness
ten-di-ni´tis
ten´don
ten´dril
ten´e-ment
ten´et
ten´fold
ten´nis
ten´on
ten´or
ten´pins
tense
tense´ly
tense´ness
ten´si-ble
ten´sile
ten´sile-ly

ten´sile-ness
ten´sion
ten´sion-less
ten´sor
ten´–speed
ten´–spot
ten´ta-cle
ten´ta-cled
tent´age
ten´ta-tive
ten´ta-tive-ly
ten´ta-tive-ness
tent´ed
tent´er
ten´ter-hook
tent´mak-er
ten´u-ous
ten´u-ous-ly
ten´u-ous-ness
ten´ure
tep´id
tep´id-ly
tep´id-ness
te-qui´la
ter-i-ya´ki
term´er
ter´mi-na-ble
ter´mi-na-bly
ter´mi-nal
ter´mi-nal-ly
ter´mi-nate
ter-mi-na´tion
ter´mi-na-tive
ter´mi-na-tive-ly
ter´mi-na-tor
ter-mi-nol´o-gy
ter´mi-nus

ter´mite
ter´ra
ter´race
ter´ra–cot´ta
ter-rain´
ter´ra-pin
ter-raz´zo
ter´ri-ble
ter´ri-ble-ness
ter´ri-bly
ter´ri-er
ter-rif´ic
ter-rif´i-cal-ly
ter´ri-fied
ter´ri-fy
ter´ri-fy-ing-ly
ter-rine´
ter-ri-to´ri-al
ter-ri-to´ri-al-ize
ter-ri-to´ri-al-ly
ter´ri-to-ry
ter´ror
ter´ror-ism
ter´ror-ist
ter´ror-ize
ter´ror-iz-cr
ter´ry-cloth
terse´ly
terse´ness
ter´ti-ar-y
test´a-ble
tes´ta-ment
tes´tate
test´–drive
test´er
tes´ti-fi-er
tes´ti-fy

tes´ti-ly
tes-ti-mo´ni-al
tes´ti-mo-ny
tes´ti-ness
tes-tos´ter-one
test´–tube
tes´ty
tet´a-nus
tet´a-ny
tête–à–tête
teth´er
teth´ered
te´trarch
text´book
tex´tile
tex´tu-al
tex´ture
thank´ful
thank´ful-ly
thank´ful-ness
thank´less
thanks´giv´ing
thank´–you
that
thatch
thatch´er
the´a-ter
the´a-ter-go-er
the´ater–in–the–r
  ound´
the´a-tre *(Br.)*
the-at´ri-cal
the-at-ri-cal´i-ty
the-at´ri-cal-ly
the-at´rics
their
the-mat´ic

the-mat´i-cal-ly
theme
them-selves´
thence´forth
the-oc´ra-cy
the-o-crat´ic
the-o-crat´i-cal
the-o-lo´gian
the-o-log´i-cal
the-ol´o-gize
the-ol´o-giz-er
the-ol´o-gy
the´o-rem
the-o-ret´i-cal
the-o-ret´ics
the´o-rist
the´o-rize
the´o-ry
the-os´o-phy
ther´a-peu´tic
ther´a-peu´ti-
  cal-ly
ther´a-pist
ther´a-py
there´abouts
there´af´ter
there´by´
there´fore´
there-in´
there-of´
there-to´
there´upon´
there-with´
ther´mal
ther´mo-cou-ple
t h e r - m o - d y -
  nam´ics

ther-mog´ra-phy
ther-mom´e-ter
ther´mo-nu´cle-
  ar
ther´mo-stat
ther´mo-stat´ic
the-sau´rus
the´sis
thi-am´ine
thick´en
thick´en-ing
thick´et
thick´–head-ed
thick´ish
thick´ness
thick´set´
thick´–skinned´
thief
thieve
thiev´ery
thieves
thiev´ing
thiev´ish
thiev´ish-ly
thiev´ish-ness
thigh´bone
thim´ble
thim´ble-ful
think´a-ble
think´a-bly
think´er
think´ing
thin´ly
thin´ner
thin´ness
thin´–skinned´
third´–class

third´–degree´
third´ly
third´–rate´
thirst´i-ly
thirst´i-ness
thirst´y
thir´teen´
thir´teenth´
thir´ti-eth
thir´ty
this´tle
thith´er
thong
tho´rax
thorn´bush
thorn´i-ly
thorn´i-ness
thorn´less
thorn´like
thorn´y
thor´ough
thor´ough-bred
thor´ough-fare
thor´ough-go-ing
thor´ough-ly
thor´ough-ness
thought´ful
thought´ful-ly
thought´ful-ness
thought´less
thought´less-ly
thought´less-
  ness
thought´–out´
thou´sand
thou´sandth
thrash´er

thrash´ing
thread´bare
thread´er
thread´worm
threat´en
threat´en-ing
threat´en-ing-ly
three´–cor´nered
three´–di-men´-
  sion-al
three´fold
three´–leg´ged
three´pence
three´pen-ny
three´–phase
three´–piece´
three´–ply´
three´–quar´ter
three´–ring
three´some
three´–speed
three´–wheel´er
thresh´er
thresh´ing
thresh´old
threw
thrice
thrift´i-er
thrift´i-ly
thrift´i-ness
thrift´shop
thrift´y
thrill´er
thrill´ing
thrill´ing-ly
thrive
thriv´ing

throat´i-ly
throat´i-ness
throat´y
throb´bing
throb´bing-ly
throe
throm-bo´sis
throne
throng
throt´tle
throt´tled
through-out´
throw´a-way
throw´back
thrust´er
thrust´ing
thru´way
thug´ger-y
thug´gish
thumb´hole
thumb´nail
thumb´print
thumb´screw
thumbs´–down
thumbs´–up
thumb´tack
thump´er
thump´ing
thun´der
thun´der-a-tion
thun´der-bolt
thun´der-clap
thun´der-cloud
thun´der-head
thun´der-ing
thun´der-ing-ly
thun´der-ous

thun´der-ous-ly
thun´der-show-
  er
thun´der-storm
thun´der-struck
thus´ly
thwart
thyme
thy´roid
thy-roid-ec´to-
  my
ti-ar´a
tick´er
tick´et
tick´et-er
tick´ing
tick´le
tick´ler
tick´lish
tick´lish-ly
tick´lish-ness
tid´al
tid´bit
tide´land
tide´wa-ter
ti´di-ly
ti´di-ness
ti´dings
ti´dy
tie´back
tie´break-er
tie´–dye
tie´–dye-ing
tie´pin
tiered
tight´en
tight´en-er

tight´en-ing
tight´–fist´ed
tight´–fist´ed-
  ness
tight´–knit´
tight´–lipped
tight´ly
tight´ness
tight´rope
tight´wad
ti´gress
tiled
til´ing
till´age
till´er
tilt´a-ble
tilt´er
tim´ber
tim´bered
tim´ber-land
tim´ber-line
tim´bre
time´card
time´–con-sum´
  ing
time´–hon´ored
time´keep-er
time´less
time´less-ly
time´less-ness
time´li-er
time´li-ness
time´ly
time´–out
time´piece
tim´er
time´sav-ing

time´–share
time´ta-ble
time´–test-ed
time´worn
tim´id
ti-mid´i-ty
tim´id-ly
tim´id-ness
tim´ing
tim´o-rous
tim´o-rous-ly
tim´o-rous-ness
tinc´ture
tin´der-box
tin´foil
tinge´ing
tin´gle
tin´gled
tin´gler
tin´gly
tin´gling
ti´ni-er
ti´ni-ness
tin´ker
tin´ker-er
tin´ner
tin´ni-er
tin´ni-ly
tin´ni-ness
tin´ny
tin´sel
tin´seled
tin´sel-ly
tin´smith
tint´er
tin´type
tin´work

ti´ny	toad´ish	to´ken-ism
tip´off	toad´stool	tol´er-a-ble
tip´per	toad´y	tol´er-a-ble-ness
tip´ping	to´–and–fro´	tol´er-a-bly
tip´ple	toast´er	tol´er-ance
tip´si-ly	toast´mas-ter	tol´er-ant
tip´si-ness	toast´mis-tress	tol´er-ant-ly
tip´ster	toast´i-ness	tol´er-ate
tip´sy	toast´y	tol-er-a´tion
tip´toe	to-bac´co	toll´booth
tip´–top	to-bac´co-nist	toll´–free´
ti´rade	to-bog´gan-er	toll´gate
tired	to-bog´gan-ing	toll´house
tired´ly	to-bog´gan-ist	to-ma-til´lo
tire´less	to-day´	to-ma´to
tire´less-ly	tod´dle	tom´boy
tire´less-ness	tod´dler	tomb´stone
tire´some	tod´dy	tom´cat
tire´some-ly	to–do´	tom-fool´er-y
tir´ing	toe´hold	to-mor´row
tis´sue	toe´nail	ton´al
ti´tan	toe´–to–toe´	to-nal´i-ty
ti-tan´ic	tof´fee	tone´–deaf
ti-ta´ni-um	to´fu	tone´less
tithe	to´ga	ton´er
tith´er	to´gaed	tongs
tith´ing	to-geth´er	tongue
tit´il-late	to-geth´er-ness	tongue´–tied
tit´il-lat-ing	tog´ger-y	ton´ic
tit-il-la´tion	tog´gle	to-night
tit´il-la-tive	toil´er	ton´nage
ti´tle	toi´let	ton-neau´
ti´tled	toi´let-ry	ton´sil
ti´tle-hold-er	toi-lette´	ton-sil-lec´to-my
tit´ter	toil´some	ton-sil-li´tis
tit´ter-ing	toil´some-ly	ton-so´ri-al
tit´u-lar	to´ken	ton´y

tool´box
tool´mak-er
tool´mak-ing
tool´room
tool´shed
tooth´ache
tooth´brush
tooth´less
tooth´paste
tooth´some
tooth´y
top´coat
top´flight´
top´–heavy
top´ic
top´i-cal-ly
top´less
top´most
top´–notch´
to-pog´ra-pher
top-o-graph´ic
to-pog´ra-phy
top´per
top´ping
top´ple
top´pling
top´–se´cret
top´soil
torch´bear-er
torch´light
tor-ment´ (v.)
tor´ment (n.)
tor-ment´ing-ly
tor-men´tor
tor-na´do
tor-na´does
tor-pe´do

tor-pe´does
tor´pid
tor-pid´i-ty
tor´pid-ly
tor´por
tor´por-if´ic
torque
tor´rent
tor-ren´tial
tor´rid
tor´sion
tor´sion-al
tor´so
tor´toise
tor´toise-shell
tor´tu-ous
tor´ture
tor´tur-er
tor´tur-ous-ly
toss´ing
toss´pot
to´tal
to´taled
to´tal-ing
to´tal-ism
to-tal´i-tar´i-an
to-tal´i-ty
to´tal-ize
to´tal-ly
to´tem
tot´ing
tot´ter
tot´ter-ing
touch´a-ble
touch´down
tou-ché´
touched

touch´i-ness
touch´ing
touch´stone
touch´–type
touch´–typ´ist
touch´–up
touch´y
tough´en
tough´en-er
tough´ie
tough´ly
tough´–mind´ed
tough´ness
tou-pee´
tour´ism
tour´ist
tour´ist-y
tour´na-ment
tour´ney
tour´ni-quet
tou´sle
tou´sled
tow´a-ble
tow´age
to´ward
tow´el
tow-el-ette´
tow´el-ing
tow´er
tow´er-ing
tow´line
town´ house
towns´folk
town´ship
towns´peo-ple
tow´rope
tox´ic

tox´i-cant
tox-ic´i-ty
tox-i-col´o-gist
tox-i-col´o-gy
tox´in
trace´a-ble
trace´a-bly
trac´er
tra´chea
tra´che-al
trac´ing
track´a-ble
track´er
track´ing
track´less
tract
trac-ta-bil´i-ty
trac´ta-ble
trac´ta-ble-ness
trac´ta-bly
trac´tion
trac´tor
trade´mark
trade´–off
trad´er
trad´ing
tra-di´tion
tra-di´tion-al
tra-di´tion-al-ist
tra-di´tion-al-ly
tra-duce´
tra-duce´ment
tra-duc´er
tra-duc´ing-ly
traf´fic
traf´ficked
traf´fick-er

traf´fick-ing
tra-ge´di-an
trag´e-dy
trag´ic
trag´i-cal-ly
trag-i-com´e-dy
trail´blaz-er
trail´er
train´a-ble
train-ee´
train´er
train´ing
train´load
trai´tor
trai´tor-ous
trai´tor-ous-ly
trai´tor-ous-ness
tra-jec´to-ry
tramp´er
tram´ple
tram´pler
tram´pling
tram´po-line´
tram´way
tran´quil
tran´quil-ize
tran´quil-iz-er
tran-quil´li-ty
tran´quil-ly
tran´quil-ness
trans-act´
trans-ac´tion
tran-scend´
tran-scen´den-cy
tran-scen´dent
tran-scen-den´
   tal

trans-con-ti-
   nen´tal
tran-scribe´
tran-scrib´er
tran´script
tran-scrip´tion
trans´fer *(n., v.)*
trans-fer´ *(v.)*
trans-fer´a-ble
trans-fer´al
trans-fer´ence
trans-ferred´
trans-fer´ring
trans-fig-u-ra´
   tion
trans-fig´ure
trans-fix´
trans-form´
trans-for-ma´
   tion
trans-form´er
trans-fuse´
trans-fu´sion
trans-gress´
trans-gres´sion
trans-gres´sor
tran´sience
tran´sien-cy
tran´sient
tran´sient-ly
tran-sis´tor
tran-sis´tor-ize
tran´sit
tran-si´tion
tran-si´tion-al
tran-si´tion-al-ly
tran´si-to-ry

trans-lat´a-ble
trans-late´
trans-la´tion
trans-la´tion-al
trans-la´tive
trans-la´tor
t r a n s - l i t - e r -
a´tion
trans-lu´cence
trans-lu´cen-cy
trans-lu´cent
trans-lu´cent-ly
trans-mi´grate
t r a n a - m i - g r a´
tion
trans-mis´si-ble
trans-mis´sion
trans-mit´
trans-mit´ta·ble
trans-mit´tal
trans-mit´ter
trans-mog´ri-fy
trans-oce-an´ic
tran´som
trans-par´en-cy
trans-par´ent
trans-par´ent-ly
tran-spire´
trans-plant´
trans-plant´er
tran-spon´der
trans-port´ *(v.)*
trans´port *(n.)*
trans-port´a-ble
trans-por-ta´tion
trans-pose´
trans-po-si´tion

trans-ship´ment
tran-sub-stan´ti-
ate
trans-verse´
tra-peze´
trap´per
trap´pings
trash´i-ness
trash´man
trash´y
trat-to-ri´a
trau´ma
trau-mat´ic
trau-mat´i-cal-ly
trau´ma-tism
trau´ma-tize
travail´
trav´el
trav´eled
trav´el-er
trav´el-ing
trav´el-ogue
tra-vers´able
trav´erse
tra-verse´
trav´es-ty
trawl´er
treach´er-ous
treach´er-ous-ly
treach´ery
trea´cle
tread´ing
trea´dle
tread´mill
trea´son
trea´son-a-ble
trea´son-ous

trea´son-ous-ly
trea´sure
trea´sur-er
trea´sur·y
treat´a-ble
trea´ties
trea´tise
treat´ment
trea´ty
tre´ble
tree´less
tree´lined
tree´top
trek´king
trel´lis
trel´lis-work
trem´ble
trem´bler
trem´bling
trem´bling-ly
trem´bly
tre-men´dous
tre-men´dous-ly
trem´e-tol
trem´or
trem´u-lous
trem´u-lous-ly
t r e m´u - l o u s -
ness
tren´chant
trench´er-man
trend´i-ness
trend´set-ter
trend´y
tres´pass-er
tressed
tres´tle

tri´ad
tri´al
tri´an-gle
tri-an´gu-lar
tri-an´gu-late
tri-an-gu-la´tion
tri-ath´lon
trib´al
trib´al-ism
trib´al-ly
tribes´man
tri-bu´nal
trib´u-tar-y
trib´ute
trich-i-no´sis
tri´chro-mat´ic
tri-chro´ma-tism
tri´–cit´y
trick´er-y
trick´i-ly
trick´i-ness
trick´le
trick´ster
trick´y
tri´cy-cle
tried´–and–true´
tri-en´nial
tri-en´nial-ly
tri´fle
tri´fler
tri´fling
tri´fling-ly
tri-fo´cal
trig´ger
trig-o-nom´e-try
tri-lat´er-al
tri-lat´er-al-ly

tri-lin´gual
tri-lin´gual-ly
tril´lion
tril´lionth
tril´o-gy
tri-mes´ter
trim´ly
trim´mer
trim´ming
trin´ket
tri´o
tri´ple
tri´ple–deck´er
tri´ple–space
trip´let
trip´li-cate
tri´pod
trip´ping-ly
trip´tych
trip´wire
tri-sect´
tri-sec´tion
tris-kai-dek-a-
　pho´bi-a
tris-kai-dek-a-
　pho´bic
tri´state
trite´ly
trite´ness
tri´umph
tri-um´phal
tri-um´phant
tri-um´phant-ly
tri-um´vi-rate
triv´et
triv´ia
triv´i-al

triv-i-al´i-ty
triv´i-al-ize
triv´i-al-ly
tri-week´ly
tro´che
trod´den
trog´lo-dyte
troi´ka
troll´er
trol´ley
trol´lop
trom-bone´
trom-bon´ist
tromp
troop´er
troop´ship
tro´phy
trop´ic
trop´i-cal
trop´i-cal-ly
trot´ter
trot´ting
trou´ba-dour
trou´ble
trou´bled
trou´ble-mak-er
trou´ble-mak-ing
trou´ble-shoot
trou´ble-shoot-er
trou´ble-some
trough
trounce
troupe
troup´er
trou´sers
trous´seau
trow´el

trow´eled

tru´an-cy

tru´ant-ly

truck´driv-er

truck´er

truck´le

truck´ling

truck´load

truc´u-lence

truc´u-lent

trudge

trudg´ing

true´heart´ed

true´–life´

truf´fle

tru´ism

tru´ly

trumped´–up´

trum´pery

trum´pet

trum´pet-er

trun´cate

trun´cat-ed

trun-ca´tion

trun´cheon

trun´dle

trunk´ful

truss´ing

trust´bust-er

trust´ee´

trust-ee´ship

trust´ful

trust´ful-ness

trust´i-ness

trust´ing

trust´wor-thi-
    ness

trust´wor-thy

trust´y

truth´ful-ly

truth´ful-ness

try´ing

try´ing-ly

tryst

tsu-nam´i

tub´by

tube´less

tu´ber

tu´ber-ous

tub´ing

tu´bu-lar

tuft´ed

tuft´ing

tug´–of–war´

tu-i´tion

tu´lip

tum´ble-down

tum´bler

tum´bling

tum´my

tu´mor

tu´mour *(Br.)*

tu´mult

tu-mul´tu-ous

tu-mul´tu-ous-ly

tun´dra

tune´ful

tune´less

tun´er

tune´–up

tu´nic

tun´ing

tun´nel

tun´neled

tun´nel-er

tun´nel-ing

tur´ban

tur´bine

tur´bo-charg-er

tur´bot

tur´bu-lence

tur´bu-lent

tu-reen´

tur´gid

tur-gid´i-ty

tur´gid-ly

tur´gid-ness

tur´key

tur´mer-ic

tur´moil

turn´a-bout

turn´a-round

turn´coat

turn´ing

tur´nip

turn´off

turn´on

turn´pike

turn´stile

turn´ta-ble

tur´pen-tine

tur´pi-tude

tur´quoise

tur´ret

tur´ret-ed

tur´tle

tus´sle

tu´te-lage

tu´tor

tu´tored

tu-to´ri-al

tux-e´do
twad´dle
twang´y
tweez´ers
twelfth
twelve
twen´ti-eth
twen´ty
twice´–told´
twi´light
twine
twinge
twin´ing
twin´kle
twin´kling
twist´a-ble
twist´er
twitch´er
twitch´ing
twitch´y
twit´ter-ing
twit´ter-y
two´–faced
two´fer
two´–fist´ed
two´–seat´er
two´–sid´ed
two´some
two´–step
two´–tone
ty-coon´
ty´ing
tyke
tym´pan
tym´pa-nist
type´cast
type´set

type´writ-er
type´writ-ten
ty´phoid
ty-phoon´
ty´phus
typ´i-cal-ly
typ-i-fi-ca´tion
typ´i-fy
typ´ist
ty´po
ty-pog´ra-pher
ty-po-graph´ic
ty-po-graph´i-cal
ty-pog´ra-phy
ty-pol´o-gist
ty-pol´o-gy
ty-ran´ni-cal
tyr´an-nize
tyr´an-nous
tyr´an-nous-ly
tyr´an-ny
ty´rant
ty´ro
ubiq´ui-tous
ubiq´ui-tous-ly
ubiq´ui-tous-
  ness
ubi´qui-ty
ud´der
ug´li-ness
ug´ly
uku-le´le
ul´cer
ul´cer-ate
ul-cer-a´tion
ul´cer-a-tive
ul´cer-ous

ul-te´ri-or
ul´ti-ma
ul´ti-ma-cy
ul´ti-mate
ul´ti-mate-ly
ul-ti-ma´tum
ul´tra
ul-tra-clean´
ul-tra-con-serv´
  a-tive
ul-tra-fine´
ul-tra-light´
ul´tra-ma-rine´
ul-tra-mod´ern
ul-tra-pure´
ul-tra-pu´ri-ty
ul-tra-son´ic
ul-tra-son´i-cal-
  ly
ul-tra-son´ics
ul-tra-sound´
ul-tra-vi´o-let
um´ber
um-bil´i-cal
um-bil´i-cal-ly
um´brage
um-bra´geous
um-bra´geous-ly
um´laut
um´pire
un-abat´ed
un-a´ble
un-abridged´
un-ac-cept´a·ble
un-ac-cent´ed
un-ac-com´pa-
  nied

un-ac-count´-
  a·ble
un-ac-count´a-
  bly
u n - a c - c u s ´
  tomed
un-ac-quaint´ed
un-adorned´
un-adul´ter-at-
  ed
un-ad-vised´
un-ad-vis´ed-ly
un-af-fect´ed
un-af-fect´ed-ly
un-afraid´
un-aid´ed
un-al´ter-a-ble
un-al´ter-a·bly
un-al´tered
un-am-bi´tious
un-am-biv´a-lent
una-nim´i-ty
u-nan´i-mous
u-nan´i-mous-ly
un-an-nounced´
u n - a n ´ s w e r -
  a·ble
u n - a n ´ s w e r -
  a·bly
un-ap-peal´a·ble
un-ap-peal´a·bly
un-ap-proach´
  a·ble
un-ap-proach´
  a·ble-ness
un-ap-proach´
  a·bly

un-ap-pro´pri-
  at-ed
un-apt´
un-apt´ly
un-apt´ness
un-arm´
un-armed´
un-a-shamed´
un-a-sham´ed-ly
un-asked´
un-as-sail´a·ble
un-as-sail´a·bly
un-as-sist´ed
un-as-sum´ing
un-at-tached´
un-at-tain´able
un-at-tend´ed
un-at-trac´tive
un-au´tho-rized
un-a-vail´ing
un-a-vail´ing-ly
un-avoid´a·ble
un-avoid´a·bly
un-a-ware´
un-a-ware´ly
un-a-ware´ness
un-a-wares´
un-bal´ance
un-bal´anced
un-barred´
un-bear´a·ble
un-bear´a·ble-
  ness
un-bear´a·bly
un-beat´a·ble
un-beat´a·bly
un-beat´en

un-be-com´ing
un-be-com´ing-
  ly
un-be-got´ten
un-be-known´
un-be-lief´
un-be-liev´a·ble
un-be-liev´a·bly
un-be-liev´er
un-be-liev´ing
un-bend´
un-bend´a·ble
un-bend´ing
un-bend´ing-ly
un-bent´
un-bi´ased
un-bi´ased-ly
un-bid´den
un-bind´
un-blam´able
un-bleached´
un-blem´ished
un-blink´ing
un-blink´ing-ly
un-block´
un-blush´ing
un-blush´ing-ly
un-bolt´
un-bolt´ed
un-born´
un-bos´om
un-bound´
un-bound´ed
un-bound´ed-ly
un-bowed´
un-brace´
un-braid´

un-brand´ed
un-break´able
un-bri´dle
un-bri´dled
un-bro´ken
un-bro´ken-ly
un-bro´ken-ness
un-buck´le
un-budge´a·ble
un-budge´a·bly
un-bun´dle
un-bun´dled
un-bur´den
un-but´ton
un-but´toned
un-cage´
un-caged´
un-called–for
un-can´ni-ly
un-can´ni-ness
un-can´ny
un-cap´
un-cared´–for
un-ceas´ing
un-ceas´ing-ly
un-cer-e-mo´ni-
  ous
un-cer-e-mo´ni-
  ous-ly
un-cer´tain
un-cer´tain-ly
un-cer´tain-ness
un-cer´tain-ty
un-chain´
un-chained´
un-chal´lenged
un-change´able

un-changed´
un-charged´
un-char´i-ta·ble
un-char´i-ta·bly
un-chart´ed
un-char´tered
un-chaste´
un-checked´
un-chris´tian
un-chris´tian-ly
un´ci-al
un´ci-form
u n - c i r´ c u m -
  cised
un-civ´il
un-civ´il-ized
un-civ´il-ly
un-civ´il-ness
un-clad´
un-clasp´
un-clasped´
un-clas´si-fied
un´cle
un-clean´
un-clean´li-ness
un-clean´ly
un-clean´ness
un-cloak´
un-clog´
un-closed´
un-clothe´
un-cloud´ed
un-coil´
u n - c o m´ f o r t -
  a·ble
u n - c o m´ f o r t -
  a·bly

un-com-mit´ted
un-com´mon
un-com´mon-ly
u n - c o m´ m o n -
  ness
un-com-mu´ni-
  ca-tive
u n - c o m -
  plain´ing
u n - c o m´ p r o -
  mis-ing
u n - c o m´ p r o -
  mis-ing-ly
un-con-cern´
un-con-cerned´
un-con-cern´ed-
  ly
un-con-di´tion-
  al
un-con-di´tion-
  al-ly
un-con-di´tioned
u n - c o n - f o r m -
  a·bil´i-ty
u n - c o n -
  form´a·ble
u n - c o n -
  form´a·bly
un-con-form´i-ty
un-con-nec´ted
un-con-nect´ed-
  ly
un-con´quered
un-con´scion-
  a·ble
un-con´scion-a-
  bly

un-con´scious
un-con´scious-ly
un-con´scious-
　ness
un-con-sti-tu´
　tion-al
un-con-sti-tu-
　tion-al´i-ty
un-con-sti-tu´
　tion-al-ly
un-con-trol´
　la·ble
un-con-trolled´
un-con-struct´ed
un-con-ven´tion-
　al
un-con-ven´tion-
　al-ist
un-con-ven´tion-
　al-ly
un-cork´
un-cor-rupt´ed
un-count´ed
un-cou´ple
un-couth´
un-couth´ly
un-couth´ness
un-cov´er
un-cov´ered
un-crit´i-cal
un-crit´i-cal-ly
un-cross´
unc´tion
unc´tu-ous
unc´tu-ous-ly
un-cul´ti-vat-ed
un-cul´tured

un-cured´
un-curl´
un-cut´
un-damped´
un-daunt´ed
un-daunt´ed-ly
un-de-ceiv´a·ble
un-de-ceive´
un-de-ceiv´er
un-de-cid´ed
un-de-cid´ed-y
un-de-feat´ed
un-de-filed´
un-de-fined´
un-dem-o-crat´ic
un-de-mon´stra-
　ble
un-de-mon´stra-
　tive
un-de-mon´stra-
　tive-ly
un-de-ni´a·ble
un-de-ni´a·bly
un´der
un-der-a-chieve´
un-der-a-chieve´
　ment
un-der-a-chiev´
　er
un-der-act´
un-der-ac´tive
un-der-age´
un´der-age
un´der-arm
un´der-bel-ly
un-der-bid´
un´der-bid-der

un´der-bite
un´der-bod-y
un´der-brush
un-der-cap-i-tal-
　i-za´tion
un-der-cap´i-tal-
　ize
un´der-car-riage
un-der-charge´
un´der-class
un-der-class´
　man
un´der-clothes
un´der-cloth´ing
un´der-coat
un´der-coat-ing
u n - d e r -
　com´pen-sate
un-der-cov´er
un´der-croft
un´der-cur-rent
un´der-cut
un-der-de-vel´op
un-der-de-vel´
　oped
un-der-de-vel´
　op-ment
un´der-dog
un´der-done
un-der-em´pha-
　size
u n - d e r - e m -
　ployed´
un-der-em-ploy´
　ment
u n - d e r - e s´t i-
　mate

un-der-es-ti-ma´-
tion
un-der-ex-pose´
un-der-ex-po´
sure
un-der-feed´
un´der-foot´
un´der-fur
un´der-gar-ment
un-der-gird´
un´der-glaze
un-der-go´
un´der-gone´
un´der-grad
un-der-grad´u-ate
un´der-ground
un´der-growth
un´der-hand
un´der-hand-ed
un´der-hand-ed-
ly
un´der-hand-ed-
ness
un-der-in-sure´
un-der-in-sured´
un-der-lay´
un-der-lie´
un´der-line
un´der-lin-er
un´der-ling
un´der-ly-ing
un-der-mine´
un´der-most
un-der-neath´
un-der-nour´
ished

un-der nour´ish-
ment
un´der-paid´
un´der-pants
un´der-pass
un-der-pay´
un-der-pay´
ment
un-der-pin´
un´der-pin-ning
un-der-price´
un´der-priv´i-
leged
un-der-rate´
un-der-run´
un´der-score
un´der-sea
un-der-seas´
un´der-sec´re-
tary
un-der-sell´
un´der-shirt
un-der-shoot´
un´der-side
un´der-sign
un´der-signed
un´der-size
un´der-sized
un´der-skirt
un-der-staffed´
un-der-stand´
un-der-stand´-
a·ble
un-der-stand´-
a·bly
un-der-stand´
ing

un-der-stand´
ing-ly
un-der-state´
un-der-stat´ed
un´der-state-
ment
un-der-stood´
un-der-strength´
un´der-study
un´der-sur-face
un´der-take
un´der-tak-er
un´der-tak´ing
un´der-the–coun
´ter
un´der-the–ta
´ble
un´der-things
un´der-tone
un-der-took´
un´der-tow
un´der-trick
un-der-val-u-a´
tion
un-der-val´ue
un´der-wa´ter
un´der-way
un´der-wear
un´der-weight
un´der-world
un-der-work´
un´der-write
un´der-writ-er
un´der-writ´ten
un-de-served´
un-de-sign´ing
un-de-sir´a·ble

un-de-sir´a·bly
un-de-vel´oped
un´dies
un-di-rect´ed
un-dis´ci-plined
un-dis-cov´ered
un-dis-mayed´
un-dis-posed´
un-dis-put´ed
u n - d i s - t i n ´
   guished
un-dis-turbed´
un-di-ver´si-fied
un-di-vid´ed
un-do´
un-dock´
un-do´ing
un-done´
un-doubt´ed
un-doubt´ed-ly
un-dress´
un-dressed´
un-due´
un´du-lant
un´du-late
un´du-lat-ed
un´du-la´tion
un´du-la-tor
un´du-la-to-ry
un-du´ly
un-dy´ing
un-earned´
un-earth´
un-earth´li-ness
un-earth´ly
un-eas´i-ly
un-eas´i-ness

un-eas´y
un-ed´u-cat-ed
u n - e m - p l o y ´
   a·ble
un-em-ployed´
u n ´ e m - p l o y ´
   ment
un-end´ing
un-en-dur´a·ble
un-e´qual
un-e´qual-ly
un-e´qual-ness
un-e´qualed
un-e-quiv´o-cal
un-e-quiv´o-cal-
   ly
un-err´ing
un-err´ing-ly
un-es-sen´tial
un-es-sen´tial-ly
un-e´ven
un-e´ven-ly
un-e´ven-ness
un-e-vent´ful
un-e-vent´ful-ly
un-ex-cep´tion-
   a·ble
un-ex-cep´tion-
   a·bly
un-ex-cep´tion-
   al
un-ex-pect´ed
un-ex-pect´ed-ly
u n - e x - p e c t ´ e d -
   ness
un-ex-plained´
un-ex-plored´

un-ex-pres´sive
un-ex´pur-gat-
   ed
un-fail´ing
un-fail´ing-ly
un-fair´
un-fair´ly
un-fair´ness
un-faith´ful
un-faith´ful-ly
un-faith´ful-ness
un-fa-mil´iar
un-fa-mil-i-ar´i-
   ty
un-fa-mil´iar-ly
un-fas´ten
un-fath´om-a·ble
un-fa´vor-a·ble
un-fa´vor-a·bly
un-feel´ing
un-feel´ing-ly
un-feel´ing-ness
un-feigned´
un-feign´ed-ly
un-fet´ter
un-fet´tered
un-fin´ished
un-fit´
un-fit´ting
un-flag´ging
un-flap-pa-bil´i-
   ty
un-flap´pa-ble
un-flap´pa-bly
un-fledged´
un-flinch´ing
un-flinch´ing-ly

un-fo´cused
un-fold´
un-fore-seen´
un-for-get´ta-ble
un-for-get´ta-bly
un-for-giv´a·ble
un-for-giv´ing
un-formed´
un-for´tu-nate
un-for´tu-nate-ly
un-found´ed
un-found´ed-ly
un-freeze´
un-friend´ly
un-frock´
un-fruit´ful
un-fruit´ful-ly
un´ful-filled´
un-fund´ed
un-furl´
un-fur´nished
un-gain´li-ness
un-gain´ly
un-gen´er-ous
un-gen´er-ous-ly
un-gird´
un-girt´
un-glue´
un-glued´
un-god´li-ness
un-god´ly
un-gov-ern-a·bil´
  i-ty
un-gov´ern-a·ble
un-gov´ern-
  a·ble-ness
un-gov´ern-a·bly

un-gra´cious
un-gra´cious-ly
un-gra´cious-
  ness
un-gram-mat´i-
  cal
un-grate´ful
un-grate´ful-ly
un-grate´ful-
  ness
un-ground´ed
un-grudg´ing
un-grudg´ing-ly
un-guard´ed
un-guard´ed-ly
un´guent
un´gu-late
un-ham´pered
un-hand´
un-hand´y
un-hap´pi-ly
un-hap´pi-ness
un-hap´py
un-harmed´
un-har´ness
un-health´ful
un-health´i-ly
un-health´y
un-heard´
un-heard´-of
un-hes´i-tat-ing
un-hes´i-tat-ing-
  ly
un-heed´ed
un-heed´ing
un-hes´i-tat-ing-
  ly

un-hinge´
un-ho´ly
un-hook´
unhoped´-for
un-horse´
un-hur´ried
un-hur´ried-ly
un-hurt´
u´ni-corn
u´ni-cy-cle
un-iden´ti-fied
u´ni-fi-a-ble
u-ni-fi-ca´tion
u´ni-fied
u´ni-form
uni-form´i-ty
u´ni-form-ly
u´ni-form-ness
u´ni-fy
u´ni-fy-ing
u-ni-lat´er-al
u-ni-lat´er-al-ly
un-imag´i-na-
  tive
un-im-paired´
un-im-peach-a-
  bil´i-ty
un-im-peach´
  a·ble
un-im-peach´
  a·bly
un-im-por´tance
un-im-por´tant
un-im-proved´
un-in-cor´po-
  rat-ed
un-in-formed´

un-in-hab´it-ed
un-in-hib´it-ed
un-in-i´ti-at-ed
un-in´jured
un-in-spired´
un-in-tel´li-gent
un-in-tel´li-gent-
ly
un-in-tel-li-gi-
bil´i-ty
un-in-tel´li-gi-
bly
un-in-ten´tion-al
un-in-ten´tion-
al-ly
un-in´ter-est-ed
un-in-ter-rupt´
ed
un-in-vit´ed
un´ion
un´ion-ist
un-ion-i-za´tion
un´ion-ize
u-ni-po´lar
u-nique´
u-nique´ly
u-nique´ness
u´ni-sex
u´ni-son
u´nit
u´ni-tary
u-nite´
u-nit´ed
u-nit´ing
u´nit-ize
u´nit-iz-er
u´ni-ty

u-ni-ver´sal
u-ni-ver´sal-ism
uni-ver-sal´i-ty
u-ni-ver-sal-i-
za´tion
u-ni-ver´sal-ize
u-ni-ver´sal-ly
u´ni-verse
u-ni-ver´si-ty
un-just´
un-jus´ti-fi-able
un-just´ly
un-just´ness
un-kempt´
un-kempt´ly
un-kind´
un-kind´li-ness
un-kind´ly
un-kind´ness
un-know´a·ble
un-know´ing
un-know´ing-ly
un-known´
un-lace´
un-law´ful
un-law´ful-ly
un-law´ful-ness
un-lead´ed
un-learn´
un-learned´
un-learn´ed-ly
un-leash´
un-leav´ened
un-less´
un-let´tered
un-li´censed
un-like´

un-like´li-hood
un-like´ly
un-lim´ber
un-lim´it-ed
un-link´
un-liq´ui-dat-ed
un-list´ed
un-live´
un-load´
un-lock´
un-looked´–for
un-loose´
un-loos´en
un-luck´i-ly
un-luck´i-ness
un-luck´y
un-made´
un-make´
un-man´
un-man´age-
a·ble
un-man´li-ness
un-man´ly
un-manned´
un-man´nered
un-man´nered-ly
un-man´ner-ly
un-mar´ried
un-mask´
un-masked´
un-mean´ing
un-mean´ing-ly
un-meas´ur-
a·ble
un-meas´ur-
a·bly
un-meas´ured

un-meas´ured-ly
un-mel´lowed
un-mend´a·ble
un-men´tion-
　a·ble
un-mer´ci-ful
un-mer´ci-ful-ly
un-mer´ci-ful-
　ness
un-mind´ful
un-mind´ful-ly
un-mind´ful-
　ness
un-mis-tak´a·ble
un-mit´i-gat-ed
un-mit´i-gat-ed-
　ly
un-mixed´
un-moor´
un-mort´gaged
un-moved´
un-mov´ing
un-muz´zle
un-named´
un-nat´u-ral
un-nat´u-ral-ly
un-nat´u-ral-
　ness
un-nec-es-sar´i-
　ly
un-nec´es-sar-y
un-nerve´
un-no´ticed
un-num´bered
un-ob-served´
un-ob-tru´sive
un-oc´cu-pied

un-of-fi´cial
un-o´pened
un-or´ga-nized
un-or´tho-dox
un-pack´
un-paged´
un-paid´
un-pal-at-a-bil´i-
　ty
un-pal´at-a·ble
un-pal´at-a·bly
un-par´al-leled
un-par´don-
　a·ble
un-par-lia-men´
　ta-ry
un-per´fo-rat-ed
un-per-turbed´
un-pile´
un-pin´
un-pleas´ant
un-pleas´ant-ly
un-pleas´ant-
　ness
un-plug´
un-plumbed´
un-pop´u-lar
un-pop-u-lar´i-
　ty
un-pop´u-lar-ly
un-prac´ti-cal
un-prac-ti-cal´i-
　ty
un-prac´ti-cal-ly
un-prac´ticed
un-prec´e-dent-
　ed

un-pre-dict-
　a·bil´i-ty
un-pre-dict´a·ble
un-pre-dict´
　a·ble-ness
un-pre-dict´a·bly
un-prej´u-diced
un-pre-med´i-
　tat-ed
un-pre-pared´
un-pre-ten´tious
un-prin´ci-pled
un-print´a·ble
un-print´a·bly
un-proc´essed
un-pro-duc´tive
un-pro-fes´sion-
　al
un-pro-fes´sion-
　al-ly
un-prof-it-a·bil´
　i-ty
un-prof´it-a·ble
un-prof´it-a·ble-
　ness
un-prof´it-a·bly
un-prom´is-ing
un-prom´is-ing-
　ly
un-pro-pi´tious
un-pro-tect´ed
un-pro-voked´
un-pub´lished
un-pun´ished
un-qual´i-fi-a·ble
un-qual´i-fied
un-quench´able

un-ques´tion-
  a·ble
un-ques´tion-
  a·bly
un-ques´tioned
un-quote´
un-rav´el
un-rav´el-er
un-read´
un-read-a·bil´i-
  ty
un-read´a·ble
un-read´a·ble-
  ness
un-read´a·bly
un-read´y
un-re´al
un-re-al´i-ty
un-re´al-iz-a·ble
un-re´al-ized
un re´al ly
un-rea´son
un-rea´son-a·ble
un-rea´son-
  a·ble-ness
un-rea´son-a·bly
un-rea´son-ing
un-rec´og-niz-
  able
un-re-con-
  struct´ed
un-reel´
un-re-flect´ing
un-re-flec´tive
un-re-flec´tive-ly
un-re-gen´er-a-
  cy

un-re-gen´er-ate
un-re-gen´er-
  ate-ly
un-re-lent´ing
un-re-lent´ing-ly
un-re-li´able
un-re-li´gious
un-re-mit´ting
un-re-mit´ting-ly
un-re-quit´ed
un-re-serve´
un-re-served´
un-re-serv´ed-ly
un-rest´
un-re-strained´
un-re-straint´
un-re-strict´ed
un-righ´teous
un-righ´teous-ly
un-righ´teous-
  ness
un-ripe´
un-ripe´ly
un-ripe´ness
un-ri´valed
un-roll´
un-root´
un-ruf´fled
un-ru´li-ness
un-ru´ly
un-sad´dle
un-safe´
un-said´
un-sal´able
un-san´i-tar·y
un-sat-is-fac´to-
  ri-ly

un-sat-is-fac´to-
  ry
un-sat´is-fied
un-sa´vor-i-ly
un-sa´vor-i-ness
un-sa´vor·y
un-scathed´
un-schol´ar-ly
un-schooled´
un-sci-en-tif´ic
un-sci-en-tif´i-
  cal-ly
un-scram´ble
un-screw´
un-script´ed
un-scru´pu-lous
un-scru´pu-
  lous-ly
un-scru´pu-
  lous-ness
un-seal´
un-sealed´
un-sea´son-a·ble
un-sea´son-
  a·ble-ness
un-sea´son-a·bly
un-sea´soned
un-seat´
un-seem´li-ness
un-seem´ly
un-seen´
un-self´ish
un-self´ish-ly
un-self´ish-ness
un-set´tle
un-set´tled
un-shack´le

237

un-shak´a·ble
un-shak´en
un-shaped´
un-shap´en
un-shav´en
un-sheathe´
un-shell´
un-shod´
un-sight´ly
un-signed´
un-skilled´
un-skill´ful
un-skill´ful-ly
un-snap´
un-snarl´
un-so´cia-ble
un-so´cia-ble-
   ness
un-so´cia-bly
un-so-lic´it-ed
un-so-lic´i-tous
un-so-phis´ti-
   cat-ed
un-so-phis´ti-
   cat-ed-ly
un-so-phis-ti-
   ca´tion
un-sound´
un-sound´ly
un-sound´ness
un-spar´ing
un-spar´ing-ly
un-speak´a·ble
un-speak´a·bly
un-spe´cial-ized
un-spec´u-la-
   tive

un-spoiled´
un-spo´ken
un-spot´ted
un-sta´ble
un-sta´ble-ness
un-sta´bly
un-stained´
un-stead´i-ly
un-stead´i-ness
un-stead´y
un-stick´
un-stop´
un-stop´pa-ble
un-stop´pa-bly
un-strap´
un-stressed´
un-string´
un-struc´tured
un-strung´
un-stuck´
un-stud´ied
un-sub-stan´tial
un-sub-stan-ti-
   al´i-ty
un-sub-stan´
   tial-ly
un-suc-cess´ful
un-suit´a·ble
un-suit´ed
un-sul´lied
un-sung´
un-sup-port´ed
un-sur-passed´
un-sus-pect´ed
un-sym-pa-
   thet´ic
un-taint´ed

un-tam´a·ble
un-tamed´
un-tan´gle
un-tar´nished
un-taught´
un-teach´
un-ten-a·bil´i-ty
un-ten´a·ble
un-ten´a·ble-
   ness
un-think´
un-think´a·ble
un-think´a·bly
un-think´ing
un-think´ing-ly
un-ti´di-ly
un-ti´di-ness
un-ti´dy
un-tie´
un-til´
un-time´li-ness
un-time´ly
un-tir´ing
un-ti´tled
un´to
un-told´
un-touch-a·bil´i-
   ty
un-touch´a·ble
un-touched´
un-to´ward
un-trained´
un-tram´meled
un´trans-lat´
   a·ble
un-trav´eled
un-tra-vers´a·ble

un-tried´
un-trou´bled
un-true´
tin-truth´
un-truth´ful
un-truth´ful-ly
un-tu´tored
un-used´
un-u´su-al
un-u´su-al-ly
un-ut´ter-a·ble
un-ut´ter-a·bly
un-var´nished
un-var´y-ing
un-veil´
un-veil´ing
un-ven´ti-lat-ed
un-ver´i-fied
un-vir´tu-ous-ly
un-voiced´
un-want´ed
un-war´i-ly
un-war´i-ness
un-war´rant-ed
un-war´y
un-washed´
un-wa´ver-ing
un-wel´come
un-well´
un-wept´
un-whole´some
un-whole´some-
  ly
un-whole´some-
  ness
un-wield´i-ness
un-wield´y

un-will´ing
un-will´ing-ly
un-will´ing-ness
un-wind´
un-wise´
un-wise´ly
un-wished´–for
un-wit´ting
un-work´able
un-world´ly
un-wor´thi-ly
un-wor´thi-ness
un-wor´thy
un-wrap´
un-writ´ten
un-yield´ing
un-yoke´
un-zip´
up´–and–com´in
  g
up´–and–down´
up´beat
up´braid´
up´bring-ing
up´com-ing
up´date
up´draft
up´end´
up´–front´
up´grade
up-heav´al
up-held´
up-hill´
up-hold´
up-hold´er
up-hol´ster
up-hol´ster-er

up-hol´ster·y
up´lift (n.)
up´lift´ (v.)
up´load
up´most   ·
up-on´
up´per
up´per-class´
  man
up´per-cut
up´per-most
up´pish
up´pish-ly
up´pish-ness
up´pi-ty
up-raise´
up-rear´
up´right
up´right-ly
up´right-ness
up´ris-ing
up´roar
up-roar´i-ous
up-roar´i-ous-ly
up´root
up´set (n.)
up-set´ (v., adj.)
up´shot
up´stage´
up´stairs´
up-stand´ing
up´start
up´stream´
up´stroke
up-surge´
up´swept
up´thrust

up´tight´
up´–to–date´
up´town´
ura´ni-um
ur´ban
ur-bane´
ur-bane´ly
ur-bane´ness
ur´ban-ize
ur´chin
urge
ur´gen-cy
ur´gent-ly
urg´ing
u´ri-nary
u·rol´o-gist
u·rol´o-gy
us´a·ble
us´a·bly
us´age
use´a·ble
used
use´ful
use´ful-ly
use´ful-ness
use´less
use´less-ness
us´er
us´er–friend´ly
ush´er
u´su-al-ly
u-surp´
u-sur-pa´tion
u-surp´er
u´su-ry
uten´sil
u´ter-ine

u´tile
u-til-i-tar´i-an
u-til-i-tar´i-an-
    ism
u-til´i-ty
u´ti-liz-a-ble
u´ti-li-za´tion
u´ti-lize
ut´most
u·to´pi-an
ut´ter-a-ble
ut´ter-ance
ut´ter-er
ut´ter-most
va´can-cy
va´cant
va´cant-ly
va´cant-ness
va´cate
va´cat-ing
va-ca´tion-er
va-ca´tion-land
vac´ci-nate
vac-ci-na´tion
vac-cine´
vac´il-lant
vac´il-late
vac´il-lat-ing
vac-il-la´tion
vac´il-la-tor
vac´il-la-to-ry
va-cu´i-ty
vac´u-ous
vac´u-ous-ly
vac´u-um
vac´uum–packed
vag´a-bond

va´gary
va´gran-cy
va´grant
va´grant-ly
vague
vague´ly
vague-ness
vain-glo´ri-ous
vain-glo´ri-ous-
    ly
vain´glo-ry
vain´ly
vain´ness
val´ance
val-e-dic´tion
val-e-dic-to´ri-an
val´e-dic´to-ry
va´lence
val´en-tine
val´et
val´iance
val´iant
val´iant-ly
val´id
val´i-date
val-i-da´tion
va-lid´i-ty
val´id-ly
val´id-ness
va-lise´
val´ley
val´or
val´or-ous
val´or-ous-ly
val´our *(Br.)*
val´u-a·ble
val´u-a·bly

val´u-ate
val-u-a´tion
val´u-a-tor
val´ue
val´ue–add´ed
val´ued
val´ue-less
val´u-ing
valve
val´vu-lar
val´vu-late
val´vule
val-vu-li´tis
va-moose´
vamp´er
vam´pire
vam-pir´ic
vam´pir-ish
vam´pir-ism
vamp´ish
van´dal
van´dal-ism
van-dal-is´tic
van´dal-ize
van-dyke´
vane
van´guard
va-nil´la
va-nil´lin
van´ish-er
van´ish-ing
van´i-ty
van´quish
van´quish-a·ble
van´quish-er
van´quish-ment
van´tage

vap´id
va-pid´i-ty
vap´id-ly
vap´id-ness
va´por
va-por-es´cence
va´por-if´ic
va´por-ish
va´por-iz-a·ble
va-por-i·za´tion
va´por-ize
va´por-iz-er
va´por-ous
va´por-ous-ly
var-i-a·bil´i-ty
var´i-a·ble
var´i-a·ble-ness
var´i-a·ble–rate´
var´i-a·bly
var´i-ance
var´i-ant
var-i-a´tion
var´i-col-ored
var´i-cose
var-i-cos´i-ty
var´ied
var´ied-ness
var´i-e-gate
var´i-e-gat-ed
var-i-e-ga´tion
var´i-e-ga-tor
va-ri´e-tal
va-ri´e-ty
var´i-ous
var´i-ous-ly
var´nish
var´nish-er

var´si-ty
var´y
var´y-ing-ly
vas´cu-lar
vase
va-sec´to-my
vast´ly
vast´ness
vaude´ville
vaude-vil´lian
vault´ing
vaunt
vaunt´ing
vaunt´ing-ly
vec´tor
veer
veer´ing
ve´gan
veg´e-ta-ble
veg-e-tar´i-an
veg-e-tar´i-an-
ism
veg´e-tate
veg-e-ta´tion
veg´e-ta-tive
veg´e-ta-tive-ly
veg´gie
ve´he-mence
ve´he-ment
ve´he-ment-ly
ve´hi-cle
ve-hic´u-lar
veiled
veil´ing
veined
veldt
vel´lum

ve-loc´i-ty
ve-lour´
ve-lou-té´
vel´vet
vel´vet·y
ve´nal
ve-nal´i-ty
ve´nal-ly
vend´er
ven-det´ta
vend´i·ble
vend´i·bly
ven´dor
ve-neer´
ve-neer´ing
ven´er-a·ble
ven´er-a·ble-
 ness
ven´er-a·bly
ven´er-ate
ven-er-a´tion
ven´er-a-tor
ven´geance
venge´ful
venge´ful-ly
venge´ful-ness
ve´ni-al
ve-ni-al´i-ty
ve´ni-al-ly
ven´i-son
ven´om
ven´om-ous
ven´om-ous-ly
ve´nous
ve´nous-ly
ven´ti-late
ven-ti-la´tion

ven´ti-la-tor
ven-tril´o-quism
ven-tril´o-quist
ven´ture
ven´tur-er
ven´ture-some
ven´tur-ing
ven´tur-ous
ven´tur-ous-ly
ven´ue
ve-ra´cious
ve-ra´cious-ly
ve-ra´cious-ness
ve-rac´i-ty
ve-ran´da
ver´bal *(adj.)*
verb´al *(n.)*
ver´bal-ist
ver-bal-i-za´tion
ver´bal-ize
ver´bal-iz-er
ver´bal-ly
ver-ba´tim
ver´bi-age
verb´i-fy
ver-bose´
ver-bose´ly
ver-bose´ness
ver-bos´i-ty
ver´dan-cy
ver´dant
ver´dant-ly
ver´dict
verge
verg´ing
ver´i-fi-a·ble
ver-i-fi-ca´tion

ver´i-fied
ver´i-fy
ver-i-si-mil´i-
 tude
ver´i-ta-ble
ver´i-ta-bly
ver´i-ty
ver-mi-cel´li
ver-mil´ion
ver´min
ver-mouth´
ver-nac´u-lar
ver-nac´u-lar-
 ism
ver-nac´u-lar-ly
ver´nal
ver´nal-ly
ver´sant
ver´sa-tile
ver´sa-tile-ly
ver-sa-til´i-ty
versed
ver-si-fi-ca´tion
ver´si-fied
ver´si-fi-er
ver´si-fy
ver´sion
ver´so
ver´sus
ver´te-bra
ver´te-brae
ver´te-bral
ver´te-brate
ver´ti-cal
ver´ti-cal-ly
ver´ti-go
verve

ver´y
ves´per
ves´sel
vest´ed
ves´tige
ves-tig´ial
ves-tig´ial-ly
vest´ing
ves´ti-ture
vest´ment
vest´–pock-et
ves´try
ves´try-man
vet´er-an
vet-er-i-nar´i-an
vet´er-i-nar·y
ve´to
ve´toed
ve´to-er
ve´toes
ve´to-ing
vex-a´tion
vex-a´tious
vex-a´tious-ly
vex´ed
vex´ed-ly
vi-a·bil´i-ty
vi´a-ble
vi´a-duct
vi´al
vi´and
vi´bran-cy
vi´brant
vi´brant-ly
vi´bra-phone
vi´bra-phon-ist
vi´brate

vi´brat-ing
vi-bra´tion
vi-bra´tion-al
vi-bra´to
vi´bra-tor
vi´bra-to-ry
vic´ar
vic´ar-age
vi-car´i-ous
vi-car´i-ous-ly
vi-car´i-ous-ness
vice–con´sul
vice–pres´i-dent
vice´roy
vi-chys-soise´
vi-cin´i-ty
vi´cious
vi´cious-ly
vi´cious-ness
vi-cis´si-tude
vi-cis-si-tu´di-
  nar-y
vi-cis-si-tu´di-
  nous
vic´tim
vic-tim-i-za´tion
vic´tim-ize
vic´tim-iz-er
vic-to´ri-ous
vic´to-ry
vict´ual
vict´ualed
vict´ual-er
vid´e-o-cas-sette
vid´e-o-con-fer-
  ence
vid´e-o-disc

vid´e-o-re-cord-
  er
vid´e-o-tape
vid´e-o-tap-er
view´a·ble
view´er
view´er-ship
view´find-er
view´ing
view´point
view´y
vig´il
vig´i-lance
vig´i-lant
vig´i-lant-ly
vig-i-lan´te
vig-i-lan´tism
vi-gnette´
vig´or
vig´or-ous
vig´or-ous-ness
vig´our *(Br.)*
vile
vile´ly
vile´ness
vil-i-fi-ca´tion
vil´i-fi-er
vil´i-fy
vil´i-fy-ing
vil´la
vil´lage
vil´lag-er
vil´lain
vil´lain-ess
vil´lain-ous
vil´lain-y
vin-ai-grette´

243

vin-ci-bil´i-ty
vin´ci-ble
vin´di-ca-ble
vin´di-cate
vin-di-ca´tion
vin´di-ca-tive
vin´di-ca-tor
vin-dic´tive
vin-dic´tive-ly
vin-dic´tive-ness
vin´e-gar
vin´e-gar-y
vin´er·y
vine´yard
vin´tage
vint´ner
vi´nyl
vi-o´la
vi-o-la-bil´i-ty
vi´ol-a·ble
vi´ol-a·ble-ness
vi´ol-a·bly
vi´o-late
vi-o-la´tion
vi´o-la-tor
vi´o-lence
vi´o-lent-ly
vi´o-let
vi-o-lin´
vi-o-lin´ist
vi´per
vi´per-ish
vi´per-ous
vi´per-ous-ly
vi´ral
vir´gin
vir´gin-al

vir-gin´i-ty
vir´ile
vi-ril´i-ty
vi-rol´o-gist
vi-rol´o-gy
vir´tu-al
vir-tu-al´i-ty
vir´tu-al-ly
vir´tue
vir´tue-less
vir-tu-os´i-ty
vir-tu-o´so
vir´tu-ous-ly
vir´tu-ous-ness
vir´u-lence
vir´u-lent-ly
vi´rus
vis´age
vis´cose
vis-cos´i-ty
vis´cous
vis´cous-ly
vis´cous-ness
vis-i·bil´i-ty
vis´i·ble
vis´i·ble-ness
vis´i·bly
vi´sion
vi´sion-al
vi´sion-ar-i-ness
vi´sion-ar·y
vi´sioned
vi´sion-less
vis´it
vis´i-tant
vis-it-a´tion
vis´i-tor

vi´sor
vis´ta
vi´su-al
vis´u-al-ist
vis-u-al´i-ty
vis´u-al-iz-a·ble
vis-u-al-i-za´tion
vis´u-al-ize
vis´u-al-iz-er
vis´u-al-ly
vi´tal
vi-tal´i-ty
vi-tal-i-za´tion
vi´tal-ize
vi´tal-ly
vi´tal-ness
vi´ta-min
vi-ta-min´ic
vi´ti-ate
vi´ti-at-ed
vi-ti-a´tion
vi´ti-a-tor
vit´re-ous
vit´re-ous-ly
vit´re-ous-ness
vi-tres´cence
vi-tres´cent
vit´ric
vit´ri-fi-a·ble
vit-ri-fi-ca´tion
vit´ri-fy
vit´ri-ol
vit´ri-ol´ic
vi-tu´per-ate
vi-tu-per-a´tion
vi-tu´per-a-tive
vi-tu´per-a-tor

vi-va´cious
vi-va´cious-ly
vi-va´cious-ness
vi-vac´i-ty
viv´id
viv´id-ly
viv´id-ness
viv-i-fi-ca´tion
viv´i-fied
viv´i-fy
viv´i-sect
viv-i-sec´tion
viv-i-sec´tion-al
viv-i-sec´tion-ist
vix´en
vix´en-ish
vix´en-ly
vi-zier´
vo-cab´u-lar·y
vo´cal
vo´cal-ist
vo-cal-i-za´tion
vo´cal-ize
vo´cal-iz-er
vo´cal-ly
vo-ca´tion
vo-ca´tion-al
vo-ca´tion-al-ism
vo-ca´tion-al-ist
vo-ca´tion-al-ly
voc´a-tive
voc´a-tive-ly
vo-cif´er-ant
vo-cif´er-ate
vo-cif-er-a´tion
vo-cif´er-a-tor
vo-cif´er-ous

vo-cif´er-ous-ly
vo-cif´er-ous-
  ness
vod´ka
vogue
vogu´ish
vogu´ish-ness
voice
voiced
voic´ed-ness
voice´ful
voice´ful-ness
voice´less
voice´less-ly
voice´–o-ver
voice´print
voic´ing
void´a·ble
void´ance
void´ed
void´ness
vol´a-tile
vol´a-tile-ness
vo-a-til´i-ty
vol´a-til-iz-a·ble
vo-a-til-i-za´tion
vol-can´ic
vol-can´i-cal-ly
vol-ca´no
vol-ca´noes
vol-can-ol´o-gist
vol-can-ol´o-gy
vo-li´tion
vo-li´tion-al
vo-li´tion-al-ly
vo-li´tion-ar·y
vol´i-tive

vol´ley
vol´ley-ball
volt´age
vo´u-bil´i-ty
vol´u-ble
vol´u-ble-ness
vol´u-bly
vol´ume
vo-lu-mi-nos´i-ty
vo-lu´mi-nous
vo-lu´mi-nous-ly
vo-lu´mi-nous-
  ness
vol´un-tar´i-ly
vol´un-ta-rism
vol´un-tar-y
vol-un-tar´i-ly
vol-un-teer´
vol´un-teered
vo-lup´tu-ar·y
vo-lup´tu-ous
vo-lup´tu-ous-ly
vo-lup´tu ous
  ness
vom´it
voo´doo
vo-ra´cious-ly
vo-ra´cious-ness
vo-rac´i-ty
vor´tex
vor´ti-ces
vot´a-ble
vote
vot´er
vot´ing
vo´tive
vouch´er

vouch-safe´
vow
vow´el
voy´age
voy´ag-er
voy´a-geur´
vo-yeur´
vo-yeur´ism
voy-eur-is´tic
voy-eur-is´ti-cal-
  ly
vul-can-i·za´tion
vul´can-ize
vul´can-iz-er
vul´gar
vul-gar´i-an
vul´gar-ism
vu´gar´i-ty
vul´gar-ly
vul´gar-ness
vul-ner-a·bil´i-ty
vul´ner-a·ble
vul´ner-a·ble-
  ness
vul´ner-a·bly
vul´ture
vul´tur-ous
vy´ing
wack´i-ly
wack´i-ness
wack´o
wack´y
wad´ding
wad´dle
wad´dled
wad´dler
wad´dling

wad´dling-ly
wad´dly
wade
wad´er
wad´ing
wa´fer
waf´fle
waf´fler
waf´fling
waf´fly
waft
waft´er
wage´less
wa´ger
wag´es
wag´ger-y
wag´gish
wag´gish-ness
wag´gle
wag´gling
wag´gly
wag´ing
wag´on
wag´on-er
wag´on-load
wail´ing
wain´scot-ing
waist´band
waist´coat
waist´ed
waist´line
wait´er
wait´ing
wait´list
wait´per-son
wait´ress
waive

waiv´er
wake´ful
wake´ful-ness
wak´en
wak´en-er
wak´en-ing
wake´–up
walk´a·ble
walk´a-bout
walk´a-thon
walk´a-way
walk´er
walk´ie–talk´ie
walk´–in
walk´ing
walk´–on
walk´way
wall´board
wall´cov-er-ing
walled
wal´let
wall´flow-er
wal´lop
wal´lop-er
wal´lop-ing
wal´low
wall´paper
wall´–to–wall´
wal´nut
wal´rus
waltz´er
wan´der
wan´der-er
wan´der-ing
wan´der-ing-ly
wan´der-lust
wan´gle

wan´gled
wan´gler
wan´gling
wan´ing
wan´ly
wan´na-be
wan´ness
want´ing
wan´ton
wan´ton-ly
wan´ton-ness
war´ble
war´bled
war´bler
war´bling
war´den
ward´er
ward´robe
ward´room
ware´house
war´fare
war´–horse
war´i-ly
war´i-ness
war´like
war´lord
warm´–blood´ed
warmed´–o´ver
warm´er
warm´heart-ed
warm´heart-ed-
  ly
warm´heart-ed-
  ness
warm´ish
warm´ly
war´mon-ger

warm´ness
warm´up
warn´er
warn´ing
warn´ing-ly
warp´age
war´path
warp´ing
war´rant
war´rant-a-ble
war´rant-ee´
war´rant-er
war´ran-tor´
war´ran-ty
war´ri-or
war´time
war´y
wash´a-ble
wash´–and–wear

wash´ba-sin
wash´board
wash´bowl
wash´cloth
wash´day
washed´–out´
washed´–up´
wash´er
wash´er-wom-an
wash´ing
wash´room
wash´stand
wash´tub
wash´up
wash´y
wasp´i-ly
wasp´i-ness

wasp´ish
wasp´ish-ly
wasp´ish-ness
wasp´y
was´sail
was´sail-er
wast´age
waste´bas-ket
wast´ed
waste´ful
waste´ful-ly
waste´ful-ness
waste´land
wast´er
wast´ing
was´trel
watch´band
watch cap
watch´case
watch´dog
watch´er
watch´ful
watch´ful-ly
watch´ful-ness
watch´mak-er
watch´mak-ing
watch´tow-er
watch´word
wa´ter-bed
wa´ter-borne
wa´ter bug
wa´ter-col-or
wa´ter-course
wa´ter-craft
wa´tered
wa´ter-er
wa´ter-fall

wa´ter-fowl
wa´ter-front
wa´ter-i-ness
wa´ter-less
wa´ter-less-ly
wa´ter-less-ness
wa´ter-line
wa´ter-locked
wa´ter-logged
wa´ter-mark
wa´ter-mel-on
wa´ter-pick
wa´ter-pow-er
wa´ter-proof
wa´ter-proof-ing
wa´ter–re-pel-
  lent
wa´ter–ski
wa´ter-sport
wa´ter-spout
wa´ter-tight
wa´ter-way
wa´ter-wheel
wa´ter-works
wa´ter-y
watt´age
wave´length
wav´er (hailer)
wa´ver (vacillate)
wa´ver-er
wa´ver-ing
wav´i-ness
wav´ing
wav´y
wax´en
wax´i-ness
wax´ing

wax´works
wax´y
way´bill
way´far-er
way´far-ing
way´laid
way´lay
way´lay-er
way´–out´
way´ward
way´ward-ness
wa-zir´
weak´en
weak´ened
weak´en-er
weak´ling
weak´–kneed´
weak´ly
weak´–mind´ed
weak´–mind´ed-
  ly
weak´ness
wealth´i-er
wealth´i-ness
wealth´y
wean´ling
weap´on
weap´on-ry
wear-a·bil´i-ty
wear´a·ble
wear´er
wea´ri-ful
wea´ri-ful-ly
wea´ri-ful-ness
wea´ri-less
wea´ri-less-ly
wea´ri-ly

wea´ri-ness
wear´ing
wea´ri-some
wea´ry
wea´ry-ing
wea´seled
wea´sel-ly
weath´er
weath´er–beat-
  en
weath´er-cock
weath´ered
weath´er-ing
weath´er-ize
weath´er-proof
weath´er-strip-
  ping
weave
weav´er
weav´ing
web
webbed
web´bing
web´site
wed´ded
wed´ding
wedged
wedge–shaped
wedg´ing
wedg´y
wed´lock
weed´er
weed´i-ness
weed´kill-er
weed´y
week´day
week´end-er

week´ly	well´–ground´ed	what´not
week´night	well´–han´dled	what-so-ev´er
weep´er	well´–heeled´	whee´dle
weep´i-ness	well´–in-formed´	whee´dled
weep´ing	w e l l ´ – i n t e n ´	whee´dler
weep´y	tioned	wheel´bar-row
wee´vil	well´–known´	wheel´base
weigh	well´–made´	wheel´chair
weight	well´–man´nered	wheel´er–deal´er
weight´ed	well´–mean´ing	wheel´house
weight´i-ly	well´–off´	wheel´wright
weight´i-ness	well´–read´	wheeze
weight´less	well´–round´ed	wheez´y
weight´less-ness	well´spring	when-ev´er
weight´lift-er	well´–thought´–o	when´so-ev´er
weight´lift-ing	f	where´a-bouts
weight´y	well´–timed´	where´as´
weird´ly	well´–to–do´	where´by´
weird´ness	well´–trained´	where´fore´
wel´come	well´–wish-er	where´of´
wel´com-er	well´–worn´	where´so-ev´er
weld´a-ble	wend´ing	where´up-on´
weld´er	west´er	wher-ev´er
wel´fare	west´er-ly	where´with-al
well´–ad-vised´	west´ern	wheth´er
well´–ap-point´-	west´ern-er	whet´stone
ed	west´ern-ism	which-ev´er
well–bal´anced	west´ern-most	whim´per
well–be-haved´	west´ward	whim´pered
well´–be´ing	weth´er	whim´per-ing
well´–belov´ed	wet´land	whim´si-cal
well´born	wet´ness	whim´si-cal-ly
well´bred´	wet´ting	whim´sy
well´–defined´	whacked	whined
well´–fed´	whal´er	whin´ing
well´–found´ed	whal´ing	whin´nied
well´–groomed´	what-ev´er	whin´ny

249

whip´cord
whip´lash
whip´ping
whip´poor-will
whip´saw
whirl´pool
whirl´wind
whirl´y-bird
whir´ring
whisk´er
whisk´ered
whisk´er·y
whis´key
whis´ky
whis´per
whis´pered
whis´per-er
whis´per-ing
whis´per·y
whis´tle
whis´tle–blow-er
whis´tle–blow-ing
whis´tler
whis´tling
white´cap
white´–hot´
whit´en-ing
white´–tie
white´wall
white´wash
whith´er
whit´ish
whit´tle
whit´tled
whit´tler
whit´tling

who-ev´er
whole´–grain
whole´heart-ed-ly
whole´ness
whole´sale
whole´sal-er
whole´some
whole´some-ly
whole´some-ness
whol´ly
whom-so-ev´er
whoop´ee
whop´per
whorl
who-so-ev´er
wick´ed
wick´ed-ly
wick´ed-ness
wick´er
wick´er-work
wick´et
wick´ing
wide´–an´gle
wide´–awake´
wide´bod·y
wide´–eyed
wide´ly
wid´en
wide´–o´pen
wide´–rang´ing
wide´–screen´
wide´spread´
wid´get
wid´ow
wid´ow-er

width
wield
wield´er
wield´y
wie´ner-wurst
wife´less
wife´li-ness
wife´ly
wig´gle
wig´gler
wig´gling
wig´gly
wig´let
wild´–and–wool´ly
wild´cat
wil´der-ness
wild´fire
wild´life
wild´ly
wild´ness
willed
will´ful
will´ful-ly
will´ful-ness
will´ing
will´ing-ly
will´ing-ness
will´–o´–the–wisp
wil´low-y
will´pow-er
wil´y
wimp´y
win
wince
winch
winc´ing

wind´age	winged	wish´ful-ly
wind´bag	wing´less	wish´ful-ness
wind´blown	wing´span	wish´y–wash·y
wind´–borne	wing´spread	wisp´i-ness
wind´break-er	wing´tip	wisp´y
wind´burn	wink´er	wist´ful
wind´ed	wink´ing	wist´ful-ly
wind´fall	win´na-ble	wist´ful-ness
wind´i-er	win´ner	witch´craft
wind´i-ness	win´ning	witch´y
wind´ing	win´ning-ly	with-al´
wind´ing-ness	win´nings	with-draw´
wind´jam-mer	win´now-er	with-draw´al
wind´lass	win´some-ly	with-drawn´
wind´less	win´some-ness	with-drew´
wind´mill	win´ter-green	with´er
win´dow	win´ter-ish	with´ered
win´dow-less	win´ter-ize	with´er-ing
win´dow-pane	win´ter-time	with´er-ing-ly
win´dow–shop	win´try	with-held´
win´dow–shop-er	wipe´out	with-hold´
win´dow–shop-	wip´er	with-hold´er
ping	wip´ing	with-hold´ing
win´dow-sill	wired	with-in´
wind´pipe	wire´less	with-out´
wind´proof	wir´er	with-stand´
wind´shield	wire´tap	with-stand´ing
wind´storm	wire´tap-per	wit´less
wind´surf-er	wir´ing	wit´less-ly
wind´surf-ing	wir´y	wit´less-ness
wind´–swept	wis´dom	wit´ness
wind´ward	wise´a-cre	wit´ness–box
wind´y	wise´crack	wit´ness-er
wine´glass	wise´ly	wit´ted
wine´mak-ing	wis´est	wit´ti-cism
win´er-y	wish´bone	wit´ti-ly
wine´tast-ing	wish´ful	wit´ti-ness

251

wit´ting
wit´ting-ly
wit´ty
wiz´ard
wiz´ard-ry
wiz´ened
wob´ble
wob´bler
wob´bli-ness
wob´bly
woe´be-gone
woe´ful
woe´ful-ly
woe´ful-ness
wom´an-hood
wom´an-ish
wom´an-ize
wom´an-iz-er
wom´an-kind
wom´an-ly
wom´en
wom´en-folk
won´der
won´dered
won´der-er
won´der-ful
won´der-ful-ly
won´der-ful-ness
won´der-land
won´der-ment
won´der–work-er
won´drous
won´drous-ly
won´drous-ness
wont *(habit)*
won't *(will not)*
wood´block

wood´carv-ing
wood´craft
wood´cut
wood´cut-ter
wood´ed
wood´en
wood´en-ly
wood´en-ness
wood´grain
wood´i-er
wood´i-ness
wood´land
wood´pile
wood´shed
woods´y
wood´wind
wood´work
wood´work-er
wood´work-ing
wood´y
woo´er
wool´en
wool´li-ness
wool´ly
wooz´i-ly
wooz´i-ness
wooz´y
word
word´i-ly
word´i-ness
word´ing
word´less
word´less-ly
word´play
word´y
work
work´a·ble

work´a-day
work-a-hol´ic
work´bas-ket
work´bench
work´book
work´day
worked
worked´–up´
work´er
work´flow
work´horse
work´ing
work´man-ship
work´place
work´room
work´shop
work´ta-ble
work´week
world´beat-er
world´–class´
world´li-ness
world´ly–mind´e
  d
world´ly–wise
world´–shak-ing
world´–wea-ry
world´wide´
worm´–eat-en
worm´y
worn´–out´
wor´ried
wor´ried-ly
wor´ri-some
wor´ri-some-ly
wor´ry
wor´ry-ing
worse

wors´en	wretch	xen´o-phile
wor´ship	wretch´ed	xen-o-phil´i-a
wor´shiped	wretch´ed-ly	X–ray
wor´ship-er	wretch´ed-ness	xy´lo-graph
wor´ship-ful	wrig´gle	xy-log´ra-pher
wor´ship-ing	wrig´gler	xy-lo-graph´ic
worst´–case´	wrig´gly	xy-lo-graph´i-cal
worth	wring´er	xy-log´ra-phy
wor´thi-ly	wring´ing	xy´lo-phone
wor´thi-ness	wrin´kle	xy´lo-phon-ist
worth´less	wrin´kled	yacht
worth´less-ly	wrin´kling	yacht´ing
worth´less-ness	wrin´kly	yachts´man
worth´while´	wrist´band	yam´mer
wor´thy	wrist´watch	yam´mer-er
would´–be	write´–in	yam´mer-ing-ly
wound´ed	writ´er	yap´per
wo´ven	writhe	yap´ping
wraith´like	writhed	yap´ping-ly
wran´gle	writh´er	yard´age
wran´gler	writh´ing	yard´stick
wran´gling	writh´ing-ly	yawn´er
wrap´a-round	writ´ing	yawn´ing
wrap´per	writ´ten	year´book
wrap´ping	wrong´do-er	year´–end´
wrap´–up	wrong´do-ing	year´ling
wrath´ful	wrong´ful	year´long
wrath´ful-ly	wrong´ful-ly	year´ly
wrath´ful-ness	wrong´ful-ness	yearn´ing
wreck´age	wrong´head´ed	yearn´ing-ly
wreck´er	wrong´ly	year´–round´
wreck´ing	wrong´ness	yeast´i-ness
wrench	wroth	yeast·y
wrest	wrought	yel´low
wres´tle	wrought´–up´	yel´low-ish
wres´tler	wry´ly	yel´low·y
wres´tling	wry´ness	yelp´er

yeo´man	yum´my	zing´er
yes´–man	yup´pie	zing´y
yes´ter-day	za´ni-ly	zin´ni-a
yes´ter-year	za´ni-ness	zip´per
yield´a-ble	za´ny	zip´py
yield´er	zeal´ot	zith´er
yield´ing	zeal´ot-ry	zo´di-ac
yo´del	zeal´ous	zo-di´a-cal
yo´del-er	zeal´ous-ly	zom´bie
yo´del-ing	zeal´ous-ness	zon´al
yo´ga	ze´bra	zon´al-ly
yo´gi	ze´nith	zo´na-ry
yo´gurt	zeph´yr	zoned
yo´kel	ze´ro	zon´ing
yon´der	ze´roes	zo-o-graph´ic
young´ish	ze´ros	zo-o-graph´i-cal
young´ster	zest´ful	zo-og´ra-phy
your-self´	zest´ful-ly	zoo´keep-er
youth´ful	zest´ful-ness	zo-o-log´i-cal
youth´ful-ly	zest´y	zo-o-log´i-cal-ly
youth´ful-ness	zig´zag	zo-ol´o-gist
yuck´y	zig´zag-ging	zo-ol´o-gy
yule		